The Handbook of
MENTORING
at WORK

This book is dedicated to our models of mentoring:

*To our parents—who planted the seeds of wisdom, gave
us the gift of guidance, and nourished us with their love;*

To our families—for their unwavering support, love, and patience; and

*To the beautiful memory of Ellen Fagenson-Eland, a
mentor who transformed hearts as well as minds.*

The Handbook of
MENTORING at WORK

Theory, Research, and Practice

Editors

Belle Rose Ragins Kathy E. Kram

University of Wisconsin-Milwaukee   *Boston University*

SAGE Publications
Los Angeles • London • New Delhi • Singapore

For information:

Sage Publications, Inc.
2455 Teller Road
Thousand Oaks, California 91320
E-mail: order@sagepub.com

Sage Publications India Pvt. Ltd.
B 1/I 1 Mohan Cooperative Industrial Area
Mathura Road, New Delhi 110 044
India

Sage Publications Ltd.
1 Oliver's Yard
55 City Road
London EC1Y 1SP
United Kingdom

Sage Publications Asia-Pacific Pte. Ltd.
33 Pekin Street #02–0
Far East Square
Singapore 048763

Printed in the United States of America

Library of Congress Cataloging-in-Publication Data

The handbook of mentoring at work: Theory, research, and practice/[edited by] Belle Rose Ragins, Kathy E. Kram.
   p. cm.
Includes bibliographical references and index.
ISBN 978-1-4129-1669-1 (cloth)
   1. Mentoring in business. 2. Mentoring in the professions. 3. Interpersonal relations.
4. Organizational behavior. I. Ragins, Belle Rose II. Kram, Kathy E., 1950-

HF5385.H26 2008
658.3'124—dc22   2007016878

This book is printed on acid-free paper.

07   08   09   10   11   10 9 8 7 6 5 4 3 2 1

Acquisitions Editor:	Al Bruckner
Editorial Assistant:	MaryAnn Vail
Production Editor:	Diane S. Foster
Copy Editor:	Carla Freeman
Typesetter:	C&M Digitals (P) Ltd.
Proofreader:	Anne Rogers
Indexer:	Molly Hall
Cover Designer:	Candice Harman

Contents

Preface

Cultivating the Garden of Mentoring

A little over 20 years ago, the first seeds of mentoring research were planted in a foundational book: *Mentoring at Work* (Kram, 1985). More than 20 years of research and exploration in the field of mentoring have now passed, and it is time for us to step back and assess where we have been, where we are, and where we need to go in the field. It is time for us to take a "bird's-eye view" of the landscape of mentoring, to plant new seeds, break new theoretical ground, and design sound bridges between the practice and study of mentoring and other developmental relationships. *The Handbook of Mentoring at Work* was designed to meet these goals by chronicling the current state of the field and by cultivating new directions for theory, research, and practice in the field of mentoring.

As we pondered how best to approach this task, we realized that the field of mentoring may be likened to a garden. Some parts of the garden have been carefully cultivated by mentoring scholars and have blossomed and matured over the past 20 years, while other parts hold great promise but have been relatively neglected. (One could even argue that parts of the mentoring garden have been overwatered and overfertilized!). We soon came to recognize that for our mentoring garden to flourish, we need a soil that is theoretically rich with the cross-fertilization of ideas from related disciplines; new tools that reflect seismic changes in technology, organizational structures, and career paths; and, most important, a vision for the future that unveils a landscape rich with opportunities for research grounded in theory but driven by practice.

Toward that end, we invited a stellar group of scholars and practitioners to become "landscape designers" in the garden of mentoring. Our garden offers three paths. First, to understand the current state of the field, we invited mentoring scholars, who represent virtually every key contributor in the field, to offer their unique insights to this volume. We asked these scholars to chronicle the current state of research in their areas and to offer fresh new visions for future research that cultivates and grows the field of mentoring.

Second, we sought to enrich and broaden the theoretical soil of mentoring by inviting leading scholars in related fields to apply their theoretical lenses to the discourse on mentoring. These scholars planted fresh new seeds that enrich the garden of mentoring and extend the horizons of mentoring to incorporate new theoretical perspectives.

Third, to craft vital new bridges between the study and practice of mentoring, we asked leading practitioners in the field to share their best practices and their innovative new approaches in the practice of mentoring. Because mentoring research needs to both inform and be informed by practice, we asked these contributors to identify research that needs to be done to address the changing practice of mentoring. Their chapters offer the critical perspective that growth in the garden of mentoring requires not only the careful cultivation of both practice and research but also the complementary cross-fertilization of needs, knowledge, and practice that yields important new hybrids of developmental relationships.

Combined, the three paths cultivated in this volume offer rich insight into where we have been, provocative new ideas for where we can go, and practical perspectives on the best way to get there. We hope this volume offers the reader a vision of a richly landscaped garden of mentoring: a garden in which mentoring research, theory, and practice can flourish.

—Belle and Kathy

Acknowledgments

This book represents the collective efforts of so many remarkable individuals. First, we are grateful to an extraordinary doctoral student, Amy Klemm Verbos, who took on the massive role of coordinating this book project. She is competence personified, and we are grateful for her dedication, creativity, foresight, and patience in working with the contributors to ensure the smooth and timely flow of submissions, revisions, and finalized chapters. We would also like to thank Robin Baker for her insightful and effective editorial work. Special thanks go to the Lubar School of Business at the University of Wisconsin–Milwaukee, to the Boston University School of Management, and to Sage Publications for providing funding support for this project. Last, but certainly not least, we would like to thank the contributors to this volume for their collective wisdom, experience, and insight. We asked our contributors to give their very best to this venture, and their response was nothing less than amazing.

PART I

Introduction

1

The Roots and Meaning of Mentoring

Belle Rose Ragins

Kathy E. Kram

You must do the things you think you cannot do.

—Eleanor Roosevelt

We don't accomplish anything in this world alone . . . and whatever happens is the result of the whole tapestry of one's life and all the weavings of individual threads from one to another that creates something.

—Justice Sandra Day O'Connor

When asked to contemplate relationships that have made a difference in our lives—relationships that have given us the courage to do the things we think we cannot do, relationships that have guided our professional development or even changed the course of our lives—many of us think of mentoring relationships. At its best, mentoring can be a life-altering relationship that inspires mutual growth, learning, and development. Its effects can be remarkable, profound, and enduring; mentoring relationships have the capacity to transform individuals, groups, organizations, and communities.

While our interest in mentoring is relatively young, mentoring is an ancient archetype originating in Greek mythology. A figure in Homer's *Odyssey,* Mentor was a wise and faithful advisor entrusted to protect Odysseus's son, Telemachus, while Odysseus sailed against Troy. It is interesting to note that the original mentoring archetype embodied both male and female attributes. Mentor was a man, but Athena, the female goddess of wisdom, assumed his form in order to guide, teach, and protect young Telemachus. This archetype offers provocative insights into the meaning of mentoring as a relationship that transcends time, gender, and culture. Moreover, while the roots of mentoring can be traced to mythology, mentoring is no myth; it is a very real relationship that has been an integral part of social life and the world of work for thousands of years.

Intrigued by this enduring and timeless relationship, Daniel Levinson (1978) explored the impact of mentoring on men's development in his seminal book *The Seasons of a Man's Life.* Shortly thereafter, Kathy Kram (1985) published *Mentoring at Work,* which offered a theoretical foundation for understanding developmental relationships at work for both men and women. This book captured and defined the construct of mentoring, planted a theoretical foundation for the field, and ignited a program of research that moved the concept of *mentoring* from an abstract academic construct to a household word.

Scholars then spent the next 20 years grappling with the myths and meaning of mentoring. The result is a literal explosion of research that crosses disciplines, professions, and continents (see reviews by Allen, Eby, Poteet, Lentz, & Lima, 2004; Clutterbuck & Ragins, 2002; Noe, Greenberger, & Wang, 2002; Ragins, 1999; Wanberg, Welsh, & Hezlett, 2003). Interest in mentoring continues to gain momentum, and this groundswell of attention can be traced to the practical application of mentoring in organizational settings, as well as to the general appeal of mentoring as a personal, tangible, and transformational relationship. However, even as mentoring is accessible when framed within our own experience, scholars continue to struggle with understanding the complexity of this pivotal, life-altering relationship. In a nutshell, we know it works; we are still grappling with why, when, and how.

After 20 years of research, it is time for us to step back and assess where we have been, where we are, and where we need to go in the field of mentoring. So much has changed since *Mentoring at Work* was published over 20 years ago. In the 1980s, organizations were stable and hierarchical; workforces were homogeneous and primarily male; employees looked forward to their "30-year gold watches"; and "web" referred to spiders rather than the Internet. Seismic changes in technology, globalization, organizational structures, career paths, and diversity require a critical analysis and reassessment of the field. In addition to these massive structural changes, new hybrid forms of mentoring were being offered by organizations without guidance or connection to empirical research. Clearly, the time is right for a volume that allows us to reflect on our past and plan our future. Accordingly, the purpose of the *Handbook of Mentoring at Work* is to consolidate what we have learned, bring new theoretical lenses to the discourse on mentoring, and forge important new bridges between the research and practice of mentoring.

In this introductory chapter, we first give the reader a brief overview of the roots and evolution of mentoring relationships. Next, we offer an introduction to the new perspectives on mentoring that will be addressed in this book. Following this, we provide the reader with the purpose, vision, and objectives of the handbook. We conclude with an overview of how the volume is organized.

Understanding the Lay of the Land: The Roots and Evolution of Mentoring

Early Perspectives of Mentoring

Traditionally, *mentoring* has been defined as a relationship between an older, more experienced mentor and a younger, less experienced protégé for the purpose of helping and developing the protégé's career (Kram, 1985; Levinson, 1978; see also reviews by Noe et al., 2002; Ragins, 1999; Wanberg et al., 2003). The mentor may or may not be employed in the same organization as the protégé or be in the protégé's chain of command or profession.

Although the definition of mentoring has been refined over the years, a core feature that defines mentoring relationships and distinguishes it from other types of personal relationships is that mentoring is a developmental relationship that is embedded within the career context. While learning, growth, and development may occur in many different types of work and close personal relationships, mentoring relationships are unique in that the primary focus of the relationship is on career development and growth. Let us now turn to a brief overview of the types of behaviors or functions offered in mentoring relationships.

Mentoring Functions

Mentors are generally viewed as providing two types of functions to their protégés (Kram, 1985). First, mentors may offer *career functions*. Career functions involve a range of behaviors that help protégés "learn the ropes" and prepare them for hierarchical advancement within their organizations. These behaviors include coaching protégés, sponsoring their advancement, increasing their positive exposure and visibility, and offering them protection and challenging assignments. Second, mentors may provide *psychosocial functions*. Psychosocial functions build on trust, intimacy, and interpersonal bonds in the relationship and include behaviors that enhance the protégé's professional and personal growth, identity, self-worth, and self-efficacy. They include mentoring behaviors such as offering acceptance and confirmation and providing counseling, friendship, and role-modeling.

As research in the field has progressed, four key insights about mentoring functions have emerged. First, career and psychosocial functions have different roots and outcomes. In her early work, Kram (1985) observed that career functions depend on the mentor's position and influence in the organization, while psychosocial functions rely on the quality of emotional bonds and psychological attachments in the relationship. Subsequent research has indeed found that career and psychosocial functions constitute two relatively independent dimensions of mentoring behaviors (Noe, 1988; Ragins & McFarlin, 1990), although some studies have found that role-modeling may represent a third dimension of mentoring (Scandura, 1992; Scandura & Ragins, 1993). Mentoring scholars have also discovered that different mentoring functions predict different protégé outcomes: Career functions are a stronger predictor of protégés' compensation and advancement, while psychosocial functions have a stronger relationship with protégés' satisfaction with the relationship (Allen et al., 2004; Wanberg et al., 2003). However, both career and psychosocial functions predict protégés' job and career satisfaction (Allen et al., 2004).

Second, there is significant variation in the range and degree of mentoring functions within and across relationships. Like other relationships, no two mentoring relationships are alike. Some relationships provide either career or psychosocial functions, while other relationships offer a broad range of behaviors that incorporate both types of mentoring functions (Noe, 1988; Ragins & McFarlin, 1990; Scandura, 1992). In addition, mentoring relationships vary in the degree to which a given mentoring function is provided. For example, mentors may offer high, medium, or low levels of a specific function in a given relationship. The range and degree of functions provided by a mentor may be driven by the needs of the protégé, the mentor's ability to meet those needs (i.e., their interpersonal skills, resources, and power), the mentor's needs, the "chemistry" in the relationship, and the organizational context (Kram, 1985; Ragins, 1997). Finally, because mentoring relationships may represent a "fit" between the needs of the protégé and the mentor's ability and interest in meeting those needs, the same mentor may offer different functions and degrees of functions to different protégés.

Third, mentoring functions may vary across the phases of the relationship (Kram, 1983, 1985). Mentoring relationships are not static, but evolve through phases that reflect different functions, experiences, and patterns of interactions. Kram's (1983) study of 18 mentoring relationships revealed that functions vary across four distinct phases in the relationship: initiation, cultivation, separation, and redefinition. Some career functions may be offered in the *initiation phase,* but career and psychosocial functions usually peak during the *cultivation phase.* The cultivation phase is marked by strengthened interpersonal bonds and a shift from a one-way, helping relationship to a relationship entailing more mutual exchange and reciprocity (Kram, 1985). The cultivation phase ends when changes in individual needs or the organizational environment disrupt the equilibrium of the relationship. The relationship may shift into this *separation phase* because of psychological or physical reasons. For example, the protégé may psychologically outgrow the relationship, or the relationship may terminate because one or both members physically leave the organization. Although mentoring relationships may terminate for functional or dysfunctional psychological reasons, existing research indicates that most relationships terminate because of physical separation (Ragins & Scandura, 1997). Some mentoring relationships disband at the separation phase, but relationships that offer strong psychosocial functions may continue to a *redefinition phase.* In this phase, the relationship becomes redefined as a peer relationship or friendship. Career functions are less evident in this phase, but friendship, some counseling, and occasional coaching may continue in the redefinition phase.

The final insight about mentoring functions is that individuals may provide these functions without necessarily being mentors. There are a number of examples that illustrate this point. A manager may offer career functions to his or her employee without either individual viewing the relationship as a mentoring relationship. Similarly, psychosocial functions of friendship and counseling often occur in many work relationships that are not perceived as mentoring relationships by either member of the relationship. Individuals may serve as role models without being mentors. The distinction between mentoring behaviors and mentoring relationships is important from both a methodological and practical perspective (see Dougherty & Dreher, Chapter 3, this volume; Ragins, 1999). As we will see later in this volume, the idea of *mentoring episodes,* which are short-term developmental interactions, offers a useful lens for distinguishing between mentoring behaviors and mentoring relationships (see Fletcher & Ragins, Chapter 15, this volume).

Now that we have reviewed some of the complexities involved with understanding the behaviors in mentoring relationships, let us turn to a brief review of the outcomes of these relationships.

Outcomes for Protégés

Most mentoring research has focused on career outcomes for protégés and has found a positive relationship between the presence of a mentor and career outcomes (see qualitative reviews by Noe et al., 2002; Ragins, 1999; Wanberg et al., 2003). Concurring with qualitative reviews, a meta-analysis conducted by Allen and her colleagues (Allen et al., 2004) found that mentored individuals receive more promotions and earn higher salaries than their nonmentored counterparts. In addition to these instrumental outcomes, protégés report more career satisfaction, career commitment, and job satisfaction and greater expectations for advancement than those without mentors.

While these results have led mentoring scholars to conclude that mentoring relationships offer a significant career advantage for protégés, recent critiques point out that because most mentoring research is cross-sectional, we are unable to draw clear causal links between mentoring and protégé career outcomes (see Wanberg et al., 2003). The relationship between the presence of a mentor and protégé career outcomes may be a function of the "rising-star effect" (Ragins, 1999; Ragins & Cotton, 1993). This refers to the potential scenario in which high-performing, "rising-star" employees may be more likely than other employees to enter mentoring relationships. This selection artifact obscures whether the outcomes associated with mentoring are due to the relationship, the protégé's independent abilities, or some combination of these two factors. A recent longitudinal test of the rising-star effect revealed that rising stars are more likely than other employees to obtain mentors (Singh, Tharenou, & Ragins, 2007). These results complement other research that has found that mentors select protégés on the basis of their competency and potential (Allen, Poteet, & Burroughs, 1997; Olian, Carroll, & Giannantonio, 1993). However, while rising stars are more likely to obtain mentors, Singh and her colleagues (Singh et al., 2007) found that they also experience a sharp increase in salary, career satisfaction, and advancement expectations after entering the mentoring relationship. These results suggest that the significant relationship typically found between mentoring and protégé outcomes may be due to both preexisting protégé attributes as well as the independent effects of mentoring relationships. In addition, the organization may also play a significant role in protégé outcomes. Although there has been a lack of research on this topic, high-performing protégés may seek organizations that offer developmental cultures and stretch assignments that support their career trajectories. This represents a provocative area for new research.

Outcomes for Mentors

Although quite a bit of research has explored the effects of mentoring on protégé outcomes, relatively little attention has been paid to the benefits received by mentors (see Allen, Chapter 5, this volume). The research that has been done indicates that mentors report that their relationships offer them benefits such as improved job performance, career success and revitalization, recognition by others, a loyal base of support from their protégés, and a sense of personal fulfillment and satisfaction (Allen, Poteet, & Burroughs, 1997; Kram, 1985; Mullen & Noe, 1999; Ragins & Scandura, 1999). Other cross-sectional research has found that these benefits are associated with increased job satisfaction and organizational commitment (Eby, Durley, Carr, & Ragins, 2006) and that mentors report greater career success and have faster promotion rates than nonmentors (Bozionelos, 2004). This research offers needed insight into the potential benefits and outcomes associated with being a mentor.

However, similar to the rising-star effect, the outcomes associated with being a mentor may be a function of preexisting differences between individuals who choose to be mentors and those who choose not to enter such relationships. In particular, individuals who choose to become mentors may be high-performing "established stars" who already experience high levels of career success, as well as positive job and career attitudes. In addition, high-performing mentors may be drawn to organizations that offer climates and assignments that lead to positive career outcomes. A positive relationship between mentoring and these outcomes could therefore reflect existing differences in characteristics of those who choose to be mentors, rather than the effects of the relationship. Future research could use longitudinal designs to untangle this potential selection artifact.

In sum, a review of the evolution of mentoring illustrates that we have focused much of our attention on a relatively narrow aspect of mentoring relationships. Using the "garden metaphor," we have thoroughly cultivated one aspect of the garden of mentoring but have neglected other areas of the garden. As described in a recent critique of the field (Ragins & Verbos, 2007), historically, we have viewed mentoring as a one-sided, hierarchical relationship in which mentors provide career outcomes to their protégés. Relatively little attention has been placed on the mentor's side of the relationship; in fact, we are not even clear on the functions or behaviors that protégés provide in the relationship. In addition, we have used a narrow lens to assess the effectiveness of the mentoring relationship. Historically, most research has focused on instrumental outcomes relating to career advancement and work attitudes but has not examined relational outcomes that are central to effective relationships, learning, and growth. In essence, the relationship has become valued for "what it can do" rather than for "what it can be" (Ragins & Verbos, 2007). Finally, while we have focused on mentoring behaviors and protégé outcomes, we have not explored the dynamic and interactive processes underlying mentoring relationships.

Increasingly, mentoring scholars have recognized and begun to address these limitations. Let us now turn to a brief overview of some of the exciting new developments in the garden of mentoring.

New Growth in the Garden: Emerging Perspectives on the Meaning of Mentoring

The chapters in this handbook illustrate exciting new perspectives that explore, examine, and uncover the meaning of mentoring. For example, mentoring scholars now recognize that mentoring relationships exist on a continuum of quality that reflects a full range of positive and negative experiences, processes, and outcomes (see Eby, Chapter 13; Fletcher & Ragins, Chapter 15). We are now examining both sides of the relationship (see Allen, Chapter 5) and are taking a broader perspective that incorporates the affective, cognitive, and behavioral aspects of the relationship (see Dougherty & Dreher, Chapter 3; Fletcher & Ragins, Chapter 15). Increasingly, we recognize the significance of learning in mentoring relationships (see Lankau & Scandura, Chapter 4) and the role mentoring plays in career learning cycles (see Hall & Chandler, Chapter 19). We now strive to understand how individual attributes, such as personality (see Turban & Lee, Chapter 2), developmental stage (see McGowan, Stone, & Kegan, Chapter 16), and emotional intelligence (see Cherniss, Chapter 17) affect and are affected by mentoring relationships. We recognize the significance of mentoring as an important form of socialization (see Chao, Chapter 7) that changes mentors and protégés in physiological, mental, emotional, and perhaps even spiritual ways (see Boyatzis, Chapter 18). Finally, mentoring scholars are discovering the importance of context, and they are offering critical new insight into the effects of diversity (see Blake-Beard, Murrell, & Thomas, Chapter 9; Giscombe, Chapter 22; McKeen & Bujaki, Chapter 8), work-life balance (see Greenhaus & Singh, Chapter 21), technology (see Ensher & Murphy, Chapter 12), and global perspectives (see Clutterbuck, Chapter 26) on mentoring relationships.

In addition to new insight into the antecedents, processes, outcomes, and context of mentoring relationships, we witness the emergence of new perspectives on the very form of the relationship. We now recognize that mentoring relationships exist within the context of developmental networks (Higgins & Kram, 2001) and that these constellations of relationships have important ramifications for the types of functions and processes offered in a given relationship (see Chao, Chapter 7; Higgins, Chandler, & Kram, Chapter 14). In addition to contextualizing mentoring, we are delving into differences inherent in peer mentoring relationships (see McManus & Russell, Chapter 11), and we are trying to uncover the complexities underlying the leadership-mentoring interface (see Godshalk & Sosik, Chapter 6; McCauley & Guthrie, Chapter 23). Formal mentoring has become a core area of investigation for mentoring research, and mentoring scholars and practitioners struggle in their quest to understand the unique offerings of formal relationships and the conditions under which they thrive (see Baugh & Fagenson-Eland, Chapter 10; Blake-Beard, O'Neill, & McGowan, Chapter 25; P-Sontag, Vappie, & Wanberg, Chapter 24). Finally, with communication becoming increasingly electronic, virtual or e-mentoring (see Ensher & Murphy, Chapter 12) has become a new area of research that illuminates the full range of mentoring relationships.

These emerging perspectives offer exciting and needed insight into the new meaning of mentoring. While mentoring relationships are as old as the hills, the terrain in which they reside has certainly changed since Odysseus set sail for Troy thousands of years ago. A contextualized perspective on mentoring allows us to grasp the subtle and stark changes in the evolution of mentoring relationships. As described in the next section, this handbook was designed to showcase, chronicle, and extend these new perspectives so that scholars and practitioners alike can understand the roots, evolution, and meaning of mentoring.

Why the Time Is Right for This Handbook

There are three compelling reasons why the time is right for the *Handbook of Mentoring at Work.*

We Need to Chronicle the Current State of the Field and Chart New Directions for Future Research

Mentoring researchers have studied a wide array of mentoring topics over the past 20 years. For example, they have examined the predictors, processes, and outcomes of mentoring from both protégés' and mentors' perspectives. They have examined the role and influence of personality, race, gender, and other forms of diversity on mentoring relationships. They have explored how learning emerges as a function and process of the relationship, why and how mentoring relationships become dysfunctional, and how mentoring maps onto leadership and socialization processes in organizations. New research examines the differences between formal and informal mentoring, the role of peers in developmental relationships, and the benefits and drawbacks of virtual or electronic mentoring relationships.

With over 20 years of research behind us, it is clear that the time is right for a book that chronicles the current state of knowledge in the field of mentoring. In particular, there is a need for a comprehensive volume that offers an in-depth assessment of what is known in the topic areas of mentoring, what needs to be explored in these areas, and the best way to approach and conduct this research.

We Need to Extend the Theoretical Horizons of Mentoring

Most research conducted over the past 20 years is based on Kram's (1985) early theoretical work. Although this work continues to offer a solid theoretical foundation for mentoring scholarship, significant changes have occurred over time that necessitate the extension, broadening, and development of new theoretical perspectives on mentoring relationships. To start, societal and organizational changes have radically transformed the constructed meaning and contextualized experience of careers. We witness new technology, organizational transformations, and strategic redirections that have massively altered employee-employer relationships. These factors have also had a profound effect on the meaning of work and careers, as well as the form, function, and context of work relationships in organizational life. Changing workforce demographics, increased diversity, and shifting work-life balance demands have forever altered employees' needs, expectations, and work relationships. Since mentoring relationships are embedded within these contexts, an accurate vision of the meaning of mentoring requires the development and use of new theoretical lenses.

Fortunately, the past 20 years have given us new theoretical paradigms from related fields and disciplines that offer great promise for the field of mentoring. Theoretical advancements in related disciplines of adult development, networks, communication, careers, work-life balance, and psychology (clinical, social, cognitive, and vocational) offer important new insight into the meaning of mentoring. The field of mentoring needs fresh new theoretical directions to guide our growing garden of research, and these new perspectives offer an abundant cross-fertilization of ideas that can deepen, broaden, and enrich our garden.

In sum, we need a volume that integrates and incorporates new theoretical perspectives in order to offer new frameworks, models, and theories of mentoring that are aligned within the changing landscape of careers and organizations.

We Need to Build Bridges Between the Research and Practice of Mentoring

Mentoring research needs to both inform and be informed by mentoring practice. However, there is a serious gap in the bridge between research and practice; even as mentoring scholars analyze the determinants of effective mentoring relationships, mentoring practitioners are often unaware of the results of this research. Given the sustained surge of interest in formal mentoring programs and the use of mentoring in diversity, leadership development, and international programs, the bridge between research and practice has become absolutely critical. Yet practitioners often develop these programs without the benefit or guidance of empirical research.

On the other side of the synergy bridge, mentoring theorists and scholars need to be connected to practice in order to provide relevant research on new and emerging forms of developmental relationships. For example, traditional forms of mentoring relationships have been joined, or even replaced by, nontraditional relationships involving group mentoring, peer mentoring, and formally assigned relationships. These relationships are designed to achieve ambitious short- and long-term objectives, but practitioners need a better understanding of their unique processes and outcomes. Mentoring scholars can offer these needed insights by conducting empirical research and building new theoretical models that explain the underlying processes that distinguish different types of developmental relationships.

In short, the field needs a volume that bridges research and practice (a) by offering a forum for discussing current issues and challenges in the practice of mentoring and (b) by identifying the research and theory that need to be developed to address the changing practice of mentoring.

The Handbook of Mentoring at Work was explicitly designed to address these pressing needs.

The Handbook's Vision, Mission, and Structure

The Vision and Mission of the Handbook

The Handbook of Mentoring at Work brings together a select group of scholars and practitioners for the purpose of developing the definitive reference book on mentoring relationships. Our vision is to offer a comprehensive volume that defines the current state of the field, offers fresh new theoretical perspectives, identifies the key debates and issues facing mentoring scholars and practitioners, and provides a theory-driven road map that guides future research and practice in the field of mentoring.

With this ambitious vision in mind, this handbook was designed to achieve the following four objectives:

1. To bring together leading scholars for the dual purpose of chronicling the current state of research in the field of mentoring and identifying important new areas of research

2. To stimulate new theoretical perspectives on mentoring by integrating and applying related theoretical perspectives and disciplines to the mentoring arena

3. To encourage a mutual synergy between research and practice by providing a forum for the discussion of current issues and challenges in the practice of mentoring

4. To examine the above objectives within the broader perspective of changes in technology, organizational structure, and diversity—factors that have radically altered the general landscape of careers in organizations

The Structure of the Handbook

Based on these objectives, the handbook is divided into three sections: research, theory, and practice. To provide coherence across chapters, contributors were asked to address a specific set of objectives for their sections. As described below, the set of objectives varies for each of the three sections of the handbook.

Mentoring Research: Past, Present, and Future

The handbook's research section brings together preeminent scholars in the field of mentoring for the dual purpose of chronicling the current state of research in the field of mentoring and identifying important new areas of scholarship. This section offers an in-depth and cutting-edge review of core topics in mentoring research, such as diversity in mentoring relationships, learning processes in mentoring relationships, formal mentoring, peer mentoring, socialization and mentoring, leadership and mentoring, dysfunctional mentoring, personality and mentoring, and electronic mentoring.

As experts in their respective topic areas, we asked the contributors of this section to address three specific objectives in their chapters. First, they were asked to provide the reader with a comprehensive review and assessment of the research in their areas. Second, they were asked to identify research gaps, research opportunities, and agendas for future research. Third, they were asked to provide a road map that gives the reader specific guidance on the best methods, approaches, and theories to use in conducting research in their areas of mentoring.

This section therefore offers readers a comprehensive and up-to-date assessment of what is known in a given content area of mentoring, what needs to be explored, and the best way to approach future research in the area.

Mentoring Theory: Applying New Lenses and Perspectives

The goal of the theory section is to integrate and apply related theoretical perspectives and disciplines in order to extend the theoretical horizon of the field. To achieve this objective, we invited a group of stellar scholars from related disciplines to apply their theoretical lenses to the field of mentoring. The chapters in this section draw on a diverse and rich literature of related theories, such as network theory, adult development theory, relational cultural theory, communication theory, personal change theory, work-family theory, and theories of emotional intelligence. Given this broad base, the theoretical advances made in this section extend far beyond mentoring in the workplace. The theoretical foundation developed in these chapters explains generic processes of mentoring relationships that occur across a range of settings, populations, and environments.

The authors in this section were asked to address three objectives that would extend the theoretical horizons of mentoring. First, they were asked to set a foundation for their chapters by introducing the reader to the specific theoretical lenses that they apply to the field of mentoring. Second, they were asked to explain why and how their theoretical lenses could be used for developing and enriching mentoring theory. Next, they were asked to present new theoretical models or frameworks, along with specific research propositions that can be tested in future research. Last, they were asked to identify methodological challenges that may be encountered in empirically testing the new theory, as well as recommendations for meeting these challenges.

By applying and integrating theories from related fields to mentoring, this section offers mentoring scholars important new theoretical perspectives that explain how, why, and under what conditions mentoring relationships are effective within and outside the workplace.

Mentoring in Practice: Programs and Innovations

The practice section of the handbook builds a bridge between the practice and study of mentoring. We invited an internationally acclaimed group of practitioners to share best practices, challenges, dilemmas, and solutions for creating effective mentoring relationships in organizations. This section includes chapters that address not only formal mentoring programs but also mentoring practices related to leadership development, diversity programs, and international populations and perspectives.

To build the bridge between the study and practice of mentoring, the authors in this section were asked to first provide descriptions of their mentoring programs, practices, or applications. Next, they were asked to discuss the challenges, problems, and constraints they face as well as opportunities and solutions they have discovered in their mentoring applications. The authors examine the contextual factors that have affected their practice (e.g., technology, globalization, diversity, changing nature of organizations, and careers) and the lessons they have learned from their experiences. Third, the authors were asked to specify the types of research and theory that have been useful to their practice and the types of research that would be beneficial to their practice. The authors offer insights into relationships that need to be clarified and outcomes that need to be studied, and they give specific suggestions for research that would have a significant impact on the practice of mentoring.

This section offers a practical perspective for mentoring scholars and practitioners. It offers practitioners' insights into effective practices, as well as the challenges and solutions involved in fostering effective mentoring in organizations. It offers scholars' critical insights "from the trenches" on the types of research that can make a difference in organizational practice. Together, this section offers a critical bridge between the research and practice of mentoring.

The handbook concludes with our summary chapter, which builds upon the collective wisdom developed in this volume to offer the reader an integrated array of insights into the meaning of mentoring and the individual and contextual factors that shape a wide range of developmental relationships. In sum, we hope that this volume will offer scholars and practitioners a comprehensive collection of ideas, inspirations, and insights that can be used to enrich, enliven, and grow the garden of mentoring.

References

Allen, T. D., Eby, L. T., Poteet, M. L., Lentz, E., & Lima, L. (2004). Career benefits associated with mentoring for protégés: A meta-analysis. *Journal of Applied Psychology, 89,* 127–136.

Allen, T. D., Poteet, M. L., & Burroughs, S. M. (1997). The mentor's perspective: A qualitative inquiry and future research agenda. *Journal of Vocational Behavior, 51,* 70–89.

Bozionelos, N. (2004). Mentoring provided: Relation to mentor's career success, personality, and mentoring received. *Journal of Vocational Behavior, 64,* 24–46.

Clutterbuck, D., & Ragins, B. R. (2002). *Mentoring and diversity: An international perspective.* Oxford, UK: Butterworth-Heinemann.

Eby, L. T., Durley, J. R., Carr, S. E., & Ragins, B. R. (2006). The relationship between short-term mentoring benefits and long-term mentoring outcomes. *Journal of Vocational Behavior, 69,* 424–444.

Higgins, M. C., & Kram, K. E. (2001). Reconceptualizing mentoring at work: A developmental network perspective. *Academy of Management Review, 26,* 264–288.

Kram, K. E. (1983). Phases of the mentor relationship. *Academy of Management Journal, 26,* 608–625.

Kram, K. E. (1985). *Mentoring at work.* Glenview, IL: Scott, Foresman.

Levinson, D. J. (with Darrow, C. N., Klein, E. B., Levinson, M. H., & McKee, B.). (1978). *The seasons of a man's life.* New York: Knopf.

Mullen, E. J., & Noe, R. A. (1999). The mentoring information exchange: When do mentors seek information from their protégés? *Journal of Organizational Behavior, 20,* 233–243.

Noe, R. A. (1988). An investigation of the determinants of successful assigned mentoring relationships. *Personnel Psychology, 41,* 457–479.

Noe, R. A., Greenberger, D. B., & Wang, S. (2002). Mentoring: What we know and where we might go. *Research in Personnel and Human Resources Management, 21,* 129–173.

Olian, J. D., Carroll, S. J., & Giannantonio, C. M. (1993). Mentor reactions to protégés: An experiment with managers. *Journal of Vocational Behavior, 43,* 266–278.

Ragins, B. R. (1997). Diversified mentoring relationships in organizations: A power perspective. *Academy of Management Review, 22,* 482–521.

Ragins, B. R. (1999). Gender and mentoring relationships: A review and research agenda for the next decade. In G. Powell (Ed.), *Handbook of gender and work* (pp. 347–370). Thousand Oaks, CA: Sage.

Ragins, B. R., & Cotton, J. L. (1993). Gender and willingness to mentor in organizations. *Journal of Management, 19,* 97–111.

Ragins, B. R., & McFarlin, D. (1990). Perception of mentor roles in cross-gender mentoring relationships. *Journal of Vocational Behavior, 37,* 321–339.

Ragins, B. R., & Scandura, T. A. (1997). The way we were: Gender and the termination of mentoring relationships. *Journal of Applied Psychology, 82,* 945–953.

Ragins, B. R., & Scandura, T. A. (1999). Burden or blessing? Expected costs and benefits of being a mentor. *Journal of Organizational Behavior, 20,* 493–509.

Ragins, B. R., & Verbos, A. K. (2007). Positive relationships in action: Relational mentoring and mentoring schemas in the workplace. In J. Dutton & B. R. Ragins (Eds.), *Exploring positive relationships at work: Building a theoretical and research foundation* (pp. 91–116). Mahwah, NJ: Lawrence Erlbaum.

Scandura, T. A. (1992). Mentorship and career mobility: An empirical investigation. *Journal of Organizational Behavior, 13,* 169–174.

Scandura, T. A., & Ragins, B. R. (1993). The effects of gender and role orientation on mentorship in male-dominated occupations. *Journal of Vocational Behavior, 43,* 251–265.

Singh, R., Tharenou, P., & Ragins, B. R. (2007). *Examining the rising star effect: A longitudinal study of protégé career competencies and the development of mentoring relationships.* Unpublished manuscript.

Wanberg, C. R., Welsh, E. T., & Hezlett, S. A. (2003). Mentoring research: A review and dynamic process model. *Research in Personnel and Human Resources Management, 22,* 39–124.

PART II

Mentoring Research

Past, Present, and Future

Section Purpose and Structure

This section brings together the leading scholars in the field of mentoring for the dual purpose of chronicling the current state of our research and for identifying new agendas for future research within each of the major content areas of mentoring. Given that they are experts in their respective topic areas, we asked our contributors to focus on three objectives in their chapters. First, they were asked to provide the reader with a comprehensive review and assessment of the literature in their areas. Second, we asked our authors to identify research gaps, research opportunities, and agendas for future research. Some chapters offer the reader new models, frameworks, and research propositions that can serve as a foundation for future research. Finally, in response to our request for recommendations on how to move scholarship forward, the reader is given a road map that offers specific guidance on the best methods, approaches, and theories to use in conducting research in the major content areas of mentoring.

Overview of Chapters

This section begins with Dan Turban and Felissa Lee's comprehensive chapter on personality and mentoring relationships. Their chapter offers a detailed and thoughtful analysis of how personality characteristics affect the development, functioning, and effectiveness of formal and informal mentoring relationships across time and phases of the relationship. The authors examine the effects of mentor and protégé personality profiles and offer a rich research agenda that explores how personality profiles may combine to influence the development, quality, and outcomes of mentoring relationships.

Next, Tom Dougherty and George Dreher review the career outcomes associated with mentoring and offer an insightful critique of the definitional, conceptual, and methodological issues facing research in this area. They present an incisive analysis of the conceptual and methodological challenges faced by mentoring scholars and then offer concrete recommendations for how to meet and overcome these challenges. Their chapter concludes with a framework that specifies potential mediators and moderators in the relationship between mentoring and career outcomes.

The chapter by Melenie Lankau and Terri Scandura examines an important new area of scholarship: the relationship between mentoring and personal learning in organizations. Their chapter first provides a detailed review of the empirical research on learning in mentoring relationships and offers a needed typology of the learning outcomes associated with mentoring relationships. They then offer a detailed map for future research by presenting an innovative needs-based process model of the antecedents, moderators, and outcomes of personal learning in developmental relationships.

Next, Tammy Allen offers critical and needed insights into the mentor's side of the relationship. She provides a thorough review and critical analysis of the work that has been done, and needs to be done, in this area of scholarship. Her chapter offers a model of mentoring processes that concisely and poignantly illustrates how mentors' dispositions, motives, and characteristics affect the mentoring relationship. The chapter concludes with a detailed agenda for future research in this understudied area of research.

Veronica Godshalk and John Sosik tackle the complex relationship between mentoring and leadership. They incorporate theoretical perspectives from the leadership literature to offer a thoughtful analysis of the theoretical similarities and empirical distinctions between mentoring and leadership. Viewing mentoring and leadership as overlapping relationships that exist on a continuum, they offer detailed research propositions that examine how the form, type, focus, and context of the relationship influence the processes and outcomes of mentoring and leadership relationships. This is followed by a research agenda that identifies methodological constraints and tools for conducting future research in this area.

Georgia Chao presents a rich analysis of the relationship between mentoring and organizational socialization. After offering a review and critique of the literature, she broadens our understanding of this relationship by offering an innovative developmental network perspective that explains how multiple mentors influence the socialization process. Based on the idea that different mentors address different socialization needs of protégés, her chapter offers a conceptual matrix that details the effects of developers and types of mentoring functions on organizational socialization.

Carol McKeen and Merridee Bujaki offer a keen critique of the research on gender and mentoring in organizations. They use a multilevel conceptual process model as an organizing framework for reviewing research in this area and identify critical challenges and methodological issues faced by scholars who study the effects of gender on mentoring relationships. After offering a detailed review of the literature, they provide a comprehensive list of research questions that can guide future scholars in this area.

In their chapter, Stacy Blake-Beard, Audrey Murrell, and David Thomas offer an incisive critique of the intersection of race and mentoring in organizations. They explore the literature on mentoring with an eye toward examining some of the broader issues involved with faulty and incomplete conceptualizations of race in organizational research. They examine how race influences access, interactions, and outcomes of mentoring and offer a process model that examines the role of racial identity perspectives, work group composition, organizational culture, and relationship characteristics on the dynamics of cross-race mentoring relationships.

Gayle Baugh and Ellen Fagenson-Eland provide a timely and needed review of the empirical research on formal mentoring relationships. They examine the distinctive benefits offered by formal relationships and the conditions under which benefits from formal relationships can be optimized. They review research that examines and compares formal and informal relationships and research that examines characteristics of formal programs that are associated with effective relationships and outcomes. Their chapter then offers mentoring scholars a blueprint for future research and develops a framework that shows how mentor and protégé characteristics, structural features of the program, the matching process, training, and organizational support combine to affect the processes, outcomes, and effectiveness of formal mentoring relationships.

In their chapter, Stacy McManus and Joyce Russell offer an insightful and comprehensive examination of peer mentoring relationships within the context of developmental networks. They review the research on peer mentoring and use this as a springboard for developing a typology of peer relationships that both defines the construct and distinguishes it from other types of mentoring relationships. They offer theory-based propositions for future research that examine relational and learning processes in peer relationships, the effects of type of peer relationship on outcomes, and the conditions that foster effective peer mentoring relationships.

Ellen Ensher and Susan Murphy examine a rapidly growing, yet under-researched area of mentoring known as "electronic" or "virtual" mentoring. They identify a continuum of e-mentoring relationships and review research findings that highlight the advantages and disadvantages of these relationships. They then integrate research on mentoring, e-leadership, computer-mediated communication, and social networking theory and use these perspectives to develop a comprehensive conceptual model of e-mentoring that can be applied to both formal and informal relationships. Their chapter offers research propositions and concrete directions for future research in this emerging and provocative area of scholarship.

The final chapter in this section covers the "dark side" of mentoring. Lillian Eby provides a comprehensive assessment of the relational problems that may be encountered in mentoring relationships. Relational problems are first defined and conceptualized as occurring on a continuum of severity, marked by unique characteristics. Eby then offers a comprehensive review of the literature on relational problems in organizational mentoring, student-faculty mentoring, and clinical supervisory relationships. She then applies an established theory of close relationships to the mentoring arena in order to offer a conceptual model that explains how positive and negative aspects of mentoring relationships combine to influence relationship satisfaction, commitment, and stability.

Together, these chapters give the reader a comprehensive, cutting-edge assessment of the current state of knowledge in the field of mentoring and plant the seeds for continued growth in the garden of mentoring. These mentoring scholars have clarified what aspects of the garden require attention and offer the tools—theoretical frameworks, research propositions, and methodologies—to cultivate our understanding of mentoring in all of its forms.

2

The Role of Personality in Mentoring Relationships

Formation, Dynamics, and Outcomes

Daniel B. Turban

Felissa K. Lee

During the past two decades, considerable research has examined the impact of mentoring relationships at work (see Noe, Greenberger, & Wang, 2002; Wanberg, Welsh, & Hezlett, 2003, for recent reviews). A traditional mentoring relationship[1] is an intense interpersonal exchange between a senior, experienced, and knowledgeable employee (i.e., the mentor) who provides advice, counsel, feedback, and support related to career and personal development for a less experienced employee (the protégé) (Kram, 1985; Noe et al., 2002). A recent meta-analysis confirmed earlier qualitative reviews by finding that mentoring relationships are related to both objective and subjective measures of career success (Allen, Eby, Poteet, Lentz, & Lima, 2004). More specifically, mentored versus nonmentored individuals reported higher compensation, more promotions, and greater career satisfaction, career commitment, and job satisfaction (Allen et al., 2004). Although such evidence indicates mentoring relationships are beneficial for protégés, little research has investigated processes through which mentoring influences career success, and thus we know little about *how* mentors or protégés can influence the value of mentoring relationships (Day & Allen, 2004). We believe that individual differences, in particular personality characteristics, influence the effectiveness of mentoring relationships, and thus we discuss the role of personality in mentoring relationships.

Somewhat surprisingly, given the resurgence of personality research in the behavioral management literature, there has been relatively little systematic research investigating the role of personality characteristics in mentoring relationships. For example, Wanberg et al. (2003) noted that it is striking that mentoring research has not examined current models of personality such as the five-factor model of personality (although see Bozionelos, 2004, and Waters, 2004, published after that review). In their review of the mentoring literature, Noe et al. (2002) discussed the individual differences of gender, race, age, and nationality with little mention of personality. These reviews reflect the fact that much mentoring research examining individual differences has examined male-female differences and the effects of cross-gender and cross-race dyads on mentoring outcomes. We agree, however, with Wanberg et al. (2003), who noted that research into the role of protégé and mentor personality characteristics in mentoring relationships should be a research priority.

Better understanding of how protégé and mentor personality characteristics influence mentoring relationship success can help organizations better utilize formal mentoring relationships. Many organizations have attempted to harness the potential benefits of mentoring relationships by introducing formal mentoring programs in which members of the mentoring dyad are "assigned" to one another. Interestingly, however, evidence indicates that the protégés in these formal programs typically do not receive the same benefits as employees who become involved in naturally occurring, informal mentoring relationships (Chao, Walz, & Gardner, 1992; Ragins & Cotton, 1999). One explanation relating to why formal relationships are not as beneficial as informal relationships is that some of the beneficial aspects of social attraction may be absent in formally assigned mentoring pairs, suggesting that we need to understand more about what individual differences promote success in mentoring relationships so as to be able to provide a model for more effectively matching employees in formal mentoring programs.

In addition, there is now a stream of research developing on the negative dynamics occurring in some mentoring relationships (see Eby, Chapter 13, this volume). Not all mentoring relationships are beneficial for protégés and mentors, and some relationships can actually be harmful (Eby & Allen, 2002; Eby, Butts, Lockwood, & Simon, 2004; Eby & McManus, 2004; Eby, McManus, Simon, & Russell, 2000; Ragins, Cotton, & Miller, 2000; Scandura, 1998). Eby and McManus (2004) suggested there is a continuum of dysfunctional relationships ranging from marginally effective, which provide some benefits to protégés and/or mentors, to highly dysfunctional, which can involve harassment, exploitation, and sabotage. Although little is known about whether or how individual differences of protégés or mentors influence the quality (or lack of quality) of mentoring relationships, it seems likely that mentor and protégé characteristics may influence the benefits (and costs) of a mentoring relationship for both protégés and mentors.

Therefore, the purpose of this chapter is to review the limited research investigating the role of personality in mentoring relationships and to discuss various research priorities we believe will advance the understanding of mentoring relationships. First, we outline key findings from the mentoring literature that serve as a foundation for our review. Second, we provide a brief description of the current state of personality research in organizations. Third, we review existing research on personality and mentoring. Finally, we outline ideas for future research that could advance the study of personality and mentoring. Let us now turn to a description of relevant mentoring research.

Mentoring Relationships and Mentoring Assistance

In her seminal work, Kram (1985) noted that mentors develop their protégés by supporting their tangible career needs and by enhancing their interpersonal skills and inner growth development. More specifically, Kram proposed that mentors provide two distinct, but related, sets of mentoring behaviors to protégés: career and psychosocial functions. *Career functions* enhance the likelihood of the junior colleague becoming successful and include activities such as sponsorship, exposure and visibility, coaching, protection, and challenging work assignments. *Psychosocial functions* enhance the junior colleague's sense of competence and professional identity and include activities such as role-modeling, acceptance and confirmation, counseling, and friendship. In general, much of the mentoring research has adopted this framework, although there is some evidence suggesting that role-modeling is not a subdimension of psychosocial mentoring, but rather a third distinctive function (Scandura, 1992).

As noted by Kram (1985), involvement in a mentoring relationship can provide mentors with benefits as well as costs (see Allen, Chapter 5, this volume, for a review of research from the mentor's perspective). The potential benefits for mentors include learning, increased job performance, a supportive network, and personal satisfaction and gratification (Allen & Eby, 2003; Allen, Poteet, & Burroughs, 1997; Ragins & Scandura, 1999). The potential costs include time and energy drain, as well as the possibility that a poor protégé can reflect poorly on the mentor (Ragins & Cotton, 1993; Ragins & Scandura, 1999). Mentoring relationships can also be costly to protégés, in particular if they become too reliant upon and associated with one mentor who provides inaccurate information or "falls out of favor" in the organization, with subsequent negative ramifications for the protégé (Kram, 1985). Thus, scholars have suggested that protégés should attempt to develop a "constellation" of mentoring relationships (Higgins, 2000; Higgins, Chandler, & Kram, Chapter 14, this volume; Higgins & Kram, 2001; Higgins & Thomas, 2001; Kram, 1985).

Kram (1983, 1985) proposed that mentoring relationships consist of four phases: initiation, cultivation, separation, and redefinition. The *initiation phase* lasts 6 to 12 months and involves setting expectations about the relationship. The *cultivation phase* typically lasts 2 to 5 years, and during this phase, protégés typically receive a wide range of career and psychosocial functions, which we call "mentoring assistance." During the *separation phase,* the junior colleague seeks more autonomy, and during the *redefinition phase,* the dyad members begin to see each other as peers. We believe personality characteristics of both the protégé and the mentor influence the relationship at each phase, as will be discussed in detail below. First, however, we discuss the studies we found that investigated the role of personality in organizations.

Personality Research in Organizations

Although there are various definitions of the concept, in general, *personality* is defined as the relatively stable dispositions (traits) of individuals that contribute to consistency in their thoughts, behaviors, and emotions (Funder, 2001; Leary, 1999). As such, personality is thought to be relatively stable throughout a person's lifetime, in particular during the adult years (Caspi, Roberts, & Shiner, 2005; Costa & McCrae, 1997). Interestingly, recent evidence suggests that approximately 50% of the variance in personality traits is heritable and thus a result of genetics (for a discussion of such research, see Caspi et al., 2005; Pervin, 2003; Rowe, 1999). We should note, however, that the extent to which personality is relatively malleable or fixed is a debatable issue (Pervin, 2003). Nonetheless, personality researchers who adopt a trait approach, which is the most common approach in organizational research and defines traits as relatively stable individual differences, are interested in how traits lead to consistent patterns of thoughts, feelings, and behavior (Costa & McCrae, 1997).

Personality researchers typically distinguish a *trait,* which is relatively stable, from a *state,* which is more transient and malleable (Leary, 1999). The distinction between states and traits is not always clear, however, as some individual differences have been measured both as traits and as domain-specific states. For example, goal orientation has been conceptualized as both a trait and a domain-specific state (see Elliot, 2005, for a review of this literature). Similarly, self-esteem has been conceptualized as a global trait (Rosenberg, 1965) and as a domain-specific variable (i.e., organizational-based self-esteem; Pierce, Gardner, Cummings, & Dunham, 1989). Nonetheless, if traits, as presumed, are relatively stable characteristics, then it seems more likely that personality will influence mentoring relationships than that mentoring relationships will influence personality. For example, Asendorpf and Wilpers (1998) reported that personality influences social relationships but such relationships do not influence personality. As noted, however, some individual differences are more domain-specific and thus may influence and be influenced by mentoring relationships. Ultimately, as we discuss below, longitudinal research is needed to investigate whether the relationship between mentoring and personality is bidirectional.

Although relatively few studies have examined the role of personality in mentoring relationships, research on personality in organizations has enjoyed increasing popularity in recent years. In particular, the five-factor model (FFM) has been credited with helping to revive workplace personality research since the 1980s and has been accepted by many scholars as a comprehensive framework for organizing a wide range of personality traits (Digman, 1996; Goldberg, 1993; McCrae & Costa, 1996). The FFM includes conscientiousness, extraversion, openness to experience, agreeableness, and neuroticism. *Conscientiousness* includes qualities such as dependability, achievement striving, and planfulness. *Extraversion* encompasses sociability, assertiveness, ambition, positive emotionality, energy, and adventurousness. *Openness to experience* refers to creativity, open-mindedness, unconventionality, and artistic sensitivity. *Agreeableness* is associated with being cooperative, trusting, compliant, flexible, courteous, and empathic. *Neuroticism,* which is also labeled by its opposite pole, *emotional stability,* includes proneness to negative feelings, such as anxiety, hostility, depression, personal insecurity, and low self-esteem. Recent meta-analyses have suggested that conscientiousness and neuroticism are related to motivation and performance (Barrick, Mount, & Judge, 2001; Judge & Illies, 2002). The other factors have been found to be related to work outcomes in specific contexts but are less consistent in predicting outcomes.

Although there is relatively widespread acceptance of the FFM, some have criticized it. One such criticism is that the five dimensions are too broad and heterogeneous to effectively predict certain work-related behaviors (Hough, 1998; Kanfer & Heggestad, 1997). For example, some researchers argue that achievement orientation and dependability—the two main factors within conscientiousness—relate differentially to certain outcomes (Hough, 1998). Similarly, neuroticism incorporates several narrower dispositions (i.e., tendency toward depression, anxiety, hostility) that relate to outcomes in different ways, potentially obscuring significant effects when combined into one broader trait. Critics of the FFM have also argued that a number of important traits do not fit within the framework of the five factors. For example, self-monitoring (Snyder, 1987), a personality variable discussed later in this chapter, is related to a variety of workplace outcomes but cannot be easily categorized within the FFM. Both of these criticisms of the FFM have relevance for the study of personality in mentoring relationships.

Therefore, we suggest that research on personality and mentoring will best be advanced though use of the broad traits within the FFM and the use of additional, more narrowly defined traits that have been shown to have relevance in organizational settings. Further, use of facet scales of the FFM (i.e., subcomponents of the five global traits) may also be appropriate in some cases, helping to pinpoint the source of personality effects (Barrick et al., 2001). We introduce these personality concepts in the section on future research, but, first, we review the existing research on personality and mentoring.

Individual Differences and Mentoring Relationships: What We Know

Table 2.1 provides an overview of studies that have examined relationships of individual differences—other than demographics—with mentoring outcomes. Before examining such studies, we want to highlight a couple of caveats to keep in mind when interpreting them. First, not all of the individual differences studied are personality characteristics as defined earlier (i.e., stable dispositions). We included these characteristics, however, because they seem closely related to personality concepts (e.g., need for achievement) and are thus important to include in our review. Second, all of the studies used a cross-sectional design, and thus the causal direction of effects is uncertain. Although it seems unlikely that a mentoring relationship would impact a fairly stable disposition, mentoring relationships may influence more malleable individual characteristics. As can be seen in the table, relatively little research has examined the role of personality, and, in particular, very little research has examined mentor personality characteristics. In the following section, we review studies that have measured personality, as well as other studies that provide insight into personality characteristics of mentors or protégés that may influence a mentoring relationship. We organize this literature in terms of (a) a comparison of mentored and nonmentored individuals, (b) personality characteristics related to protégés or mentors attempting to initiate mentoring relationships, (c) protégé and mentor personality characteristics related to perceptions of the relationship, and (d) characteristics of protégés or mentors that were attractive to a mentoring relationship partner.

Comparison of Mentored and Nonmentored Individuals

There is some evidence that individuals who are, or have been, protégés differ in terms of personality characteristics from individuals who have not been protégés. However, these studies are somewhat limited because it is not clear how the relationship developed (i.e., whether the protégé initiated the relationship, whether the mentor sought out the protégé, or both). For example, protégés who initiate mentoring relationships may have different personality characteristics than protégés who are selected by mentors, although research is needed to investigate this proposition. Nonetheless, some evidence indicates that in comparison to nonprotégés, protégés have a higher need for power and for achievement and possess more stereotypically masculine traits and more stereotypically feminine traits (Fagenson, 1989, 1992). In other words, protégés possess greater amounts of both sets of traits than do nonprotégés. Interestingly, a follow-up study using a subset of the data from Fagenson (1992) found that protégés with a high need for achievement, a need for dominance, and high self-esteem were more likely to be involved with *multiple* mentoring relationships (Fagenson-Eland & Baugh, 2001). As noted by Fagenson (1992), such results suggest that becoming a protégé is not a random process and that personality characteristics may differentiate those who become protégés from those who do not.

Initiation of Mentoring

Protégé Characteristics and Initiation of Mentoring

Although the implicit assumption of much of the mentoring research has been that protégés are chosen by mentors, evidence suggests that protégés' personality characteristics influence the extent to which they attempt to initiate mentoring relationships with others. For instance, Turban and Dougherty (1994) found that individuals with an internal locus of control, higher emotional stability, and high self-monitoring pattern initiated, and received, more mentoring (Turban & Dougherty, 1994). In a study conducted in Hong Kong, Aryee, Lo, and Kang (1999) found that extraversion, self-monitoring, and Type A behavior were related to initiation of mentoring but that work locus of control was not related. Although not a measure of actual initiation of mentoring, this area is also informed by a study indicating that undergraduate students reported they were more ready to be protégés when they had better interpersonal skills (Rice & Brown, 1990). Taken in sum,

Table 2.1 Personality and Mentoring Outcomes

Author	Study Characteristics	Personality Measures	Dependent Variables	Key Result(s)
Protégé Characteristics				
Aryee, Lo, & Kang (1999)	Field study conducted in Hong Kong with 184 Chinese graduate employees	Type A personality Extraversion Self-monitoring Work locus of control	Initiation of mentoring Mentoring received	Initiation of mentoring correlated with Type A personality, extraversion, and work locus of control. In regression analyses, only extraversion and Type A behavior related to initiation. Mentoring received correlated with extraversion and Type A behavior; only extraversion was significant in regression analyses.
Bozionelos (2004)	Field study with 176 white-collar workers who were administrators in 3 universities in the northwest of England	Agreeableness Conscientiousness Extraversion Neuroticism Openness to experience	Mentoring received	Mentoring received was correlated positively with extraversion and openness to experience and negatively with conscientiousness.
Day & Allen (2004)	Field study with 125 employees of a municipality	Career motivation Career self-efficacy	Protégé status (whether the person ever had a mentor) Career and psychosocial mentoring	Protégé status positively related to career motivation but not to self-efficacy. Career mentoring positively correlated with both career motivation and self-efficacy. Psychosocial mentoring positively correlated with career motivation.

(Continued)

Table 2.1 (Continued)

Author	Study Characteristics	Personality Measures	Dependent Variables	Key Result(s)
Fagenson (1989)	Field study with 246 employees of a large company in the health care industry	Masculinity and femininity	Protégé status	Protégés, in comparison with nonprotégés, had higher scores on both masculinity and femininity.
Fagenson (1992)	Field study of 100 employees in 2 small high-technology service companies	Need for achievement Need for affiliation Need for autonomy Need for power	Protégé status	Protégés reported higher need for achievement and need for power. Protégé status was not related to need for affiliation or need for autonomy.
Fagenson-Eland & Baugh (2001)	A subset of data from Fagenson (1992), analyzing the 46 individuals who reported one or more mentoring relationships	Need for achievement Need for dominance Self-esteem	Number of mentoring relationships	Protégés with only one mentoring relationship had lower need for achievement, need for dominance, and self-esteem than protégés with more than one mentoring relationship.
Godshalk & Sosik (2003)	Data collected from 217 adult MBA students who were full-time employees and their mentors	Learning goal orientation (completed by both protégé and mentor)	Career mentoring Psychosocial mentoring	Both career and psychosocial mentoring were correlated with both protégé and mentor learning goal orientation. In addition, they examined congruence of protégé and mentor learning goal orientation and found that psychosocial mentoring was highest when both the protégé and the mentor had high learning goal orientations.

Author	Study Characteristics	Personality Measures	Dependent Variables	Key Result(s)
				Career mentoring was also higher when both the mentor and protégé had high learning goal orientation in contrast to when they both had low learning goal orientation.
Scandura & Ragins (1993)	Field study of 800 accountants who received a mailed survey	Spence Personal Attributes Questionnaire used to measure masculinity (high masculinity and low femininity), femininity (high femininity and low masculinity), and androgyny (when high on both masculinity and femininity).	Whether in a mentoring relationship Career, psychosocial, and role-modeling mentoring	Respondents with mentoring relationships were more likely to have androgynous or masculine gender role orientations. Respondents who were androgynous reported more mentoring functions (career development and psychosocial support) than feminine or masculine respondents.
Turban & Dougherty (1994)	Field study of 147 managers and professionals in various occupations	Negative affectivity Self-esteem Self-monitoring Work locus of control	Initiation of mentoring Career and psychosocial mentoring received by protégé	Initiation of mentoring correlated with an internal locus of control, self-esteem, self-monitoring, and low negative affectivity. Career and psychosocial mentoring correlated with an internal locus of control and high self-esteem.

(Continued)

Table 2.1 (Continued)

Author	Study Characteristics	Personality Measures	Dependent Variables	Key Result(s)
Waters (2004)	Field study of 166 mentor and protégé dyads—protégés were administrative and IT staff at a university	Agreeableness Conscientiousness Emotional stability Extraversion Openness to experience	Protégé-mentor agreement of psychosocial support in the relationship	Protégé-mentor agreement was correlated with mentor and protégé agreeableness, openness, extraversion, and conscientiousness.
Mentor Characteristics				
Allen (2003)	Field study of 391 individuals employed in various occupations	Prosocial personality: other-oriented empathy and helpfulness	Experience as mentor Willingness to mentor Career and psychosocial mentoring provided (as reported by the mentor)	Experience as a mentor was correlated with both other-oriented empathy and helpfulness, but only helpfulness was significant in the regression analyses. Willingness to mentor was related (both with correlations and in regression analyses) to empathy and helpfulness. Career mentoring positively related (correlation and regressions) to helpfulness. Psychosocial mentoring was correlated with empathy and helpfulness, but only empathy was significant in the regression analyses.
Allen, Poteet, Russell, & Dobbins (1997)	Field study of 607 first-line supervisors employed by a state government	Locus of control Upward striving	Willingness to mentor	Willingness to mentor was related to an internal locus of control and to upward striving.

Author	Study Characteristics	Personality Measures	Dependent Variables	Key Result(s)
Bozionelos (2004)	Field study with 176 white-collar workers who were administrators in 3 universities in the northwest of England	Agreeableness Conscientiousness Extraversion Neuroticism Openness to experience	Mentoring provided (self-report)	Mentoring provided was correlated positively with openness to experience and negatively with agreeableness. In regression analyses, only openness was significant.
Mullen (1998)	Field study of 160 mentors from 17 organizations	Organizational-based self-esteem (OBSE)	Career and psychosocial mentoring provided (as indicated by the mentor)	Mentors with higher OBSE reported providing more mentoring to protégés.
Waters (2004)	Field study of 166 mentor and protégé dyads—protégés were administrative and IT staff at a university	Agreeableness Conscientiousness Emotional Stability Extraversion Openness to Experience	Protégé-mentor agreement of psychosocial support in the relationship	Protégé-mentor agreement was correlated with mentor and protégé agreeableness, openness, extraversion, and conscientiousness.

NOTE. Although we use the term *personality measures*, some of the individual differences measures were not personality measures (e.g., needs). We included studies, however, that measured relatively stable individual differences. Further, although we use the term *dependent variables*, we are not implying that the authors of the study necessarily conceptualized these variables as a dependent variable. For example, authors may conceptualize protégé status as influencing individual differences, such as self-efficacy.

such research suggests that individuals who are more comfortable in social situations are more likely to attempt to form mentoring relationships with others than are individuals who feel less comfortable and/or skilled.

Mentor Characteristics and Willingness to Mentor

Some evidence suggests that individuals who have been in mentoring relationships, either as protégés or as mentors, are more willing to serve as mentors than are individuals who have never been in mentoring relationships (Allen, Russell, & Maetzke, 1997; Ragins & Scandura, 1999). More specifically, individuals who have never been in mentoring relationships report greater costs and fewer benefits of such relationships than do individuals who have experience as mentors or protégés (Ragins & Scandura, 1999). Little is known, however, about how mentors initiate relationships with protégés, although some evidence suggests that personality does play a role (Allen, 2003; Allen, Poteet, Russell, & Dobbins, 1997). For example, in a field study with 607 first-line supervisors, locus of control and upward striving were related to intention to mentor others (Allen, Poteet, Russell et al., 1997). Further, Allen (2003) found that both helpfulness and other-oriented empathy were related to willingness to mentor others.

Although not directly related to personality, in a qualitative study, mentors reported engaging in mentoring relationships to help others or for the personal satisfaction of mentoring another person (Allen, Poteet, & Burroughs, 1997). A subsequent study of 391 individuals found that mentors provided more career-related mentoring when they had higher self-enhancement motives and "benefit-other" motives, and more psychosocial mentoring when they had higher benefit-other motives and intrinsic satisfaction motives (Allen, 2003). Such results indicate that mentor motives influence the mentoring provided to protégés (Allen, 2003). Further, such results suggest that mentors may have different reasons (motives) for developing relationships with protégés (see also Allen, Chapter 5, this volume).

Perceptions of the Relationship: Protégé and Mentor Characteristics and Mentoring Received

A few studies have investigated protégé personality characteristics related to protégé perceptions of mentoring received, although in general, the authors typically did not specify whether or how the personality characteristics influenced the process of mentoring. For example, Day and Allen (2004) reported that career motivation was related to both psychosocial and career mentoring received; career self-efficacy was related to career mentoring and marginally related to psychosocial mentoring. They theorized that mentoring may influence motivation and self-efficacy, although since they used a cross-sectional design, they noted that the causal flow could go in the other direction. More broadly, evidence indicates that mentors may provide more mentoring to protégés who are seen as more competent (Mullen, 1998; Mullen & Noe, 1999). Bozionelos (2004) examined the role of the Big Five characteristics in mentoring received and mentoring provided. Individuals' reports of mentoring received were correlated positively with their extraversion and openness to experience and, interestingly, were correlated negatively with conscientiousness. Study participants also reported the amount of mentoring provided to a subordinate in their organization. Results indicated that self-reported mentoring provided was correlated positively with openness to experience and negatively with agreeableness. Thus, individuals reported *receiving* more mentoring when they were more extraverted, open to experience, and low in conscientiousness; and individuals reported *providing* more mentoring when they were high in openness to experience and low in agreeableness.

In one of the few studies to measure personality characteristics from both the mentor and protégé perspectives, Godshalk and Sosik (2003) investigated the dispositional trait of *learning goal orientation,* defined as the extent to which the individual focuses on learning and developing competency, which, in turn, leads to pursuing challenging tasks. Results indicated that both mentor and protégé learning goal orientation were correlated with psychosocial and career mentoring as reported by the protégé. Furthermore, protégés reported receiving the most psychosocial mentoring when both the protégé and the mentor were high in learning goal orientation. Such results suggest that protégés may have more beneficial relationships when both parties are focused on learning and developing competencies. Although the authors measured what they called "dispositional learning goal orientation," goal orientation is also domain-specific and malleable (see Elliot, 2005, for a review) and thus may have been influenced by the mentoring relationship, suggesting the need for longitudinal research designs.

Characteristics Attractive to Mentoring Partners

Protégé Characteristics Sought by Mentors

Given the potential costs of being a mentor (i.e., more trouble than it's worth, reflects poorly on the mentor, an energy drain; see Ragins & Scandura, 1999), one might expect mentors to seek out protégés from whom they will obtain more rewards than costs. For example, in an early experimental study, individuals reported greater willingness to mentor protégés with higher versus lower work performance (Olian, Carroll, & Giannantonio, 1993). Similarly, Allen (2003) found that individuals indicated they were more likely to mentor protégés who were high in ability and high in willingness to learn than to mentor individuals who were low in these attributes. To the extent that personality is related to work performance and to willingness to learn, such results suggest that personality characteristics may be related to attractiveness of an individual as a protégé. More broadly, a qualitative study reported that mentors selected protégés who were motivated and competent, had a strong learning orientation, and possessed personality indicators of being people oriented, honest, confident, and dependable (Allen, Poteet, & Burroughs, 1997). To summarize, such results suggest that protégé personality characteristics that indicate ability, competence, and willingness to learn are seen as attractive to mentors (see Allen, Chapter 5, this volume, for a review of research investigating what mentors desire in protégés). Clearly, however, research is needed to investigate personality characteristics that influence attractiveness of an individual as a protégé.

Mentor Characteristics Sought by Protégés

Most studies investigating mentoring relationships have obtained measures from proteges, with fewer collecting measures from mentors. Thus, less is known about mentor characteristics than about protégé characteristics. Nonetheless, a series of three experimental studies found that the manipulated interpersonal competence of a potential mentor was related to protégé attraction to the potential mentor (Olian, Carroll, Giannantonio, & Feren, 1988). Although they did not investigate the mechanisms leading to this relationship, Olian et al. (1998) suggested that potential mentors with greater interpersonal competence (a) are seen as better able to provide the psychosocial benefits of mentoring and, (b) because they are better liked and respected, may be better able to promote the career of the protégé (i.e., provide career-related mentoring) than are mentors with less interpersonal competence. Such results suggest that protégés may be attracted to mentors with greater emotional intelligence (see Cherniss, Chapter 17, this volume).

Summary

Although few studies have investigated the role of personality in mentoring relationships, a few tentative conclusions can be drawn from the literature, although given the lack of longitudinal studies, we must be careful in describing the causal directions of such studies. Nonetheless, evidence suggests that protégé personality characteristics influence the extent to which the protégé will attempt to initiate mentoring relationships with others. Specifically, protégés with more confidence (e.g., higher self-esteem, higher perceived interpersonal skills) and who are higher self-monitors are more likely to initiate relationships (Aryee et al., 1999; Fagenson, 1992; Turban & Dougherty, 1994). Evidence is mixed, however, concerning whether an internal locus of control is related to initiation of relationships. Such evidence suggests that individuals who are more comfortable in social interactions are more likely to be in mentoring relationships. Furthermore, protégés tend to have a higher need for achievement and dominance than do nonprotégés (Fagenson, 1992). Finally, although there is limited empirical evidence, given the potential costs of mentoring relationships, individuals may be more likely to provide mentoring to protégés who possess personality characteristics that indicate ability, competence, and a willingness to learn (Allen, Poteet, & Burroughs, 1997; Olian et al., 1993).

Although fewer studies have investigated mentor characteristics than protégé personality characteristics, evidence suggests that individuals who have a prosocial personality—including other-oriented empathy and helpfulness—are more likely to get involved in mentoring relationships (Allen, 2003). Interestingly, upward striving is related to willingness to mentor others (Allen, Poteet, Russell, et al., 1997), and, given evidence that individual reports of mentoring provided are related to career success measures (Bozionelos, 2004), serving as a mentor may be a valuable career strategy, although more, preferably longitudinal, research is needed. Finally, Bozionelos (2004) found that mentor reports of mentoring were related positively to openness to experience, but surprisingly, negatively to agreeableness, which was opposite of what had been hypothesized. In summary, based on the limited evidence, it seems that individuals who have greater confidence (Mullen, 1998) and care about others (Allen, 2003) are likely to provide more mentoring.

As is evident by this brief review, some evidence suggests that personality characteristics of both mentors and protégés are related to involvement in and the quality of mentoring relationships, although much remains to be learned. Thus, in an attempt to stimulate further research, we discuss the phases of mentoring and provide a broad overview of how personality may influence mentoring relationships at each of the phases. We then focus on specific personality characteristics that we expect will have an impact on mentoring relationships.

Future Research: A Research Agenda for Personality and Mentoring Relationships

As noted earlier, Kram (1983, 1985) proposed that mentoring relationships go through four phases of development: initiation, cultivation, separation, and redefinition. For the purposes of examining the effects of personality characteristics on mentoring relationships, we combine the separation and redefinition phases. The separation and redefinition phases encompass the dissolution and reconfiguration of the relationship such that the causes of the separation can influence how the individuals (i.e., protégés and mentors) redefine the relationship. Since we expect that personality influences the separation and redefinition phases similarly, in our discussion, we describe the role of personality in the *dissolution* (encompassing separation and redefinition) of the mentoring relationship. Thus, we suggest researchers examine the potential effects of protégé and mentor personality characteristics—and their interactive effects—on the initiation of mentoring relationships, the cultivation, and the dissolution (encompassing separation and redefinition) of such relationships.

Personality may influence mentoring relationships, and perceptions of mentoring relationships, in several ways. An individual's (i.e., a protégé's or a mentor's) personality characteristics may influence the relationship, how that individual perceives the relationship, and how the other dyadic partner perceives the relationship. In addition, protégé and mentor personality characteristics may interact with one another such that dyadic members are attracted to (and more effective with) similar others or to others who have complementary personality characteristics. In general, much of the research investigating personality has examined the role of personality on an individual's (typically a protégé's) perceptions of the relationship, usually with a cross-sectional design. Although such research is useful, it is also limited due to same-source method variance concerns. Thus, to more fully understand how personality influences mentoring relationships, we urge researchers to investigate the effects of personality characteristics on the dyadic partner's perceptions of the relationship and to investigate the interactive effects of personality on mentoring relationships.

We next provide an overview of how protégé and mentor personality characteristics may influence mentoring relationships at various phases of development (see Table 2.2). After this broad overview, we provide examples of how specific personality characteristics may influence mentoring relationships at the various phases.

Table 2.2 Conceptual Bases for Relationship of Personality with Mentoring Relationships

Initiation of Mentoring

- **Overview:** Mentoring relationships begin when either the mentor or the protégé, or both, attempt to form a relationship. Thus, personality characteristics that influence a person's willingness to get involved in (or attempt to initiate) a mentoring relationship are important to examine. In addition, personality characteristics that influence the extent to which a person is perceived as a desirable partner will influence the initiation of the mentoring relationship.
- **Protégé:** Protégés that have personality characteristics indicative of proactive behaviors are more likely to attempt to initiate mentoring relationships. Furthermore, protégés with personality characteristics indicative of a positive interpersonal orientation (e.g., agreeableness, extraversion, emotional stability) are more likely to attempt to initiate mentoring relationships and are more likely to be sought out by mentors. Individuals who are seen as more competent with greater willingness to learn will be more sought by mentors than individuals who are seen as less competent and less willing to learn.
- **Mentor:** Individuals are more likely to mentor others and to be sought out as a mentor when they have personality characteristics indicative of a strong interpersonal orientation.

Cultivation of Mentoring

- **Overview:** Personality characteristics, of both mentors and protégés, that create a safe and supportive climate for learning from one another will result in more positive mentoring relationships.
- **Protégé:** Personality characteristics that reflect interpersonal comfort with others and that encourage others to be comfortable with the protégé will influence the cultivation of the mentoring relationship. Further, protégés who have a strong desire to learn and who seek advice and guidance from their mentor will have a more positive relationship.
- **Mentor:** Mentors with personality characteristics that create a supportive and nurturing environment will have protégés that report more positive mentoring relationships. In addition, mentors who are more sensitive and understanding of the protégé's perspective may provide the protégé with a more positive relationship.

Dissolution and Redefinition of Mentoring

- **Overview:** In general, for a relationship to be redefined successfully, both the protégé and the mentor must have similar viewpoints on how and when the relationship should evolve. Further, each individual must accurately perceive the specific needs and expectations of the other party while renegotiating their respective roles.
- **Protégé:** Protégés with personality characteristics that are sensitive to others and confident in their ability to function autonomously are more likely to have a positive redefinition of the mentoring relationship.
- **Mentor:** Similarly, mentors with personality characteristics that make them sensitive to others and who are supportive of their protégé's increasing need for autonomy are more likely to have a positive redefinition of the mentoring relationship. Mentors with personality characteristics that allow (encourage) the relationship to evolve to a peer relationship will experience more positive redefinition of the mentoring relationship.

The Role of Personality in Mentoring Phases

Overview

During the *initiation stage* of an informal mentoring relationship, typically one of the two parties (i.e., the potential protégé or mentor) initiates contact with the other person in an effort to generate a mentoring relationship. Since a mentoring relationship can be seen as a social exchange relationship (Ensher, Thomas, & Murphy, 2001), we expect that both parties will consider the benefits and costs of getting involved in such a relationship. The perceived benefits for both protégés and mentors include the potential for learning from and/or enhancing the development of the other person, having one's prestige and/or career success enhanced through association with the person, experiencing general interpersonal enjoyment of working with the other person, and fulfilling emotional needs through the other person (e.g., desire to be taken care of, desire to feel important). For both parties, there are also potential costs: Mentoring relationships can take considerable time; there is the possibility of affiliating with someone who subsequently performs poorly or is seen in a bad light politically; and a failed relationship may negatively impact how the participants are seen by others. Based on past evidence (Aryee et al., 1999; Turban & Dougherty, 1994), we expect that personality characteristics influence the extent to which an individual will initiate and/or get involved in a mentoring relationship, although longitudinal research investigating such relationships would be useful. Furthermore, as discussed below, we expect that individuals with certain personality characteristics are more likely to be seen as desirable partners, and thus an individual's personality characteristics influence perceptions of costs and benefits of a mentoring relationship with that person. We expect that individuals are more likely to initiate mentoring relationships with prospective partners who are seen as having personality characteristics that will result in more positive relationships.

For those mentoring relationships that make it past the initiation stage, the *cultivation stage* is when the parties develop more familiarity with one another and the mentoring functions are in evidence. Mentoring relationships are most effective when both individuals in the relationship feel comfortable opening up to the other person and sharing aspects of themselves. In particular, protégés will benefit most from these relationships when problems and questions may be shared freely with mentors who, in turn, provide reliable advice and guidance on those issues. Similarly, the protégé will benefit most from a mentoring relationship in which the mentor has the skills and interest to provide effective coaching—both career and psychosocial. We expect that individuals' personality characteristics will influence their interpersonal comfort in relationships and will also influence the degree of comfort felt by their dyad partners. Further, there may be interactive effects of protégé and mentor personality characteristics that result in greater interpersonal ease and, thus, sharing of problems and advice in the relationship. Thus, to summarize, we expect personality characteristics to influence protégés' willingness to seek guidance and mentors' willingness to provide guidance. Similarly, protégés may be more willing to seek advice from mentors with certain personality characteristics, and mentors may be more likely to provide coaching to protégés with certain personality characteristics. Finally, ease of interaction between the mentor and protégé may be related to the combined effects of their personality types.

During the *dissolution phase*, the protégé typically becomes more independent, and eventually the roles are renegotiated such that the protégé and mentor are essentially peers. In terms of interpersonal processes, this shift requires that both parties be accepting of the change and be willing to discuss the change in roles and/or associated feelings. These interpersonal processes are of particular importance for informal relationships and may be less relevant in formal relationships in which the time line is shorter and externally defined. We expect that personality characteristics of mentors and protégés may influence how their relationships are redefined. For example, personality characteristics may influence the extent to which a protégé and mentor are willing to allow the relationship to evolve into a peer relationship and friendship. Similarly, personality characteristics may influence *when* individuals will want to redefine the relationship. Problems in the relationship may arise if the protégé and mentor have different personality characteristics such that one party is not ready for the relationship to shift and becomes resentful of the other's attempts to redefine roles, resulting in negative feelings.

Having highlighted some key issues that may arise during a mentoring relationship, we now turn to a discussion of the personality characteristics that should have a bearing on these issues. Our suggestions for future research are not intended to represent an exhaustive list, but rather are intended to provide initial guidance in this exciting area of mentoring scholarship. To begin, we provide an extended description of how agreeableness may influence different phases of the mentoring relationship. We subsequently discuss other personality characteristics that we expect to impact mentoring relationships but, given space constraints, provide a less extended discussion of these traits. Although individuals have profiles of traits, we first discuss the possible influence of each trait on mentoring relationships individually, since there is little research examining personality profiles. We then discuss possible effects of personality profiles on mentoring relationships.

Agreeableness and Associated Traits

As a broad trait, *agreeableness* refers to the degree to which an individual is trusting, cares about others, is easy to get along with, and is pleasant to have around (Graziano & Eisenberg, 1997). As is evident from this definition, this characteristic is fundamentally interpersonal in nature. A moderately high amount of agreeableness tends to mean positive interactions for those with the trait. However, as is true for each of the Big Five traits, being extremely high or extremely low on a trait may create difficulties for the person. Those who are very high on agreeableness tend to be fairly compliant, are concerned about others liking them, attempt to avoid conflict, and are concerned about sparing others' feelings. Those who are quite low on agreeableness may be seen as prone to conflict, self-serving, suspicious of others, and relatively unconcerned with others' feelings. A recent review found that low agreeableness predicted negative relationship outcomes for romantic relationships (Ozer & Benet-Martinez, 2006). More broadly, since agreeableness is fundamentally about one's behavior in social relationships, it should have relevance for all phases of the mentoring relationship.

In the initiation phase, individuals who are more agreeable should receive more interest from others (i.e., potential protégés or potential mentors), as they would be seen as more enjoyable to spend time with and, in general, may be expected to care more about the well-being of others. Further, the higher individuals are on agreeableness, the more likely they should be to respond to others' attempts to initiate relationships, either because they care about helping others (say, in the case of a potential mentor) or because they do not want to create conflict with other persons by denying them their requests (such as in the case of a potential protégé). Thus, individuals higher on agreeableness would be more sought out for a mentoring relationship and would be more willing to get involved in a relationship if sought out by others.

In the cultivation phase of mentoring, higher agreeableness should make it more likely that participants in the mentoring relationship will interact positively and resolve differences of opinion fairly smoothly. By contrast, if just one individual in the relationship is low on agreeableness, there may be problematic interactions and possible dissolution of the relationship due to conflict, resentment, or general lack of enjoyment. It also may be that being extremely high on agreeableness would place constraints on the effectiveness of the relationship if the highly agreeable person (perhaps in particular a mentor) is reluctant to express concerns and provide feedback to the other individual. Similarly, high agreeableness may lead individuals to maintain relationships longer than is productive. This dynamic could be especially strong if the highly agreeable individual is the protégé, who typically has less power in the relationship.

The dissolution phase may be affected by agreeableness in one of a few ways. For instance, those who are moderately high on agreeableness, being pleasant to interact with at other stages of a mentoring relationship, are likely to be mindful of addressing the needs of their mentoring partners in the dissolution phase. However, as noted earlier, extremely high agreeableness may make an individual stick with the relationship longer than that person wants to—meaning that the dissolution phase comes later in time—or agree to having greater contact than the individual wants after formal roles have changed. By contrast, an individual who is extremely low on agreeableness may experience the dissolution phase of a mentoring relationship rather quickly or experience a greater number of "dissolutions" than one might expect given the individual's apparent technical skill and level of ambition.

While agreeableness is a useful trait to examine at the global level, there are several narrower traits that may be considered facets of agreeableness and may be useful for exploring more specific phenomena. For example, *reciprocation wariness* is a personality variable that measures the extent to which a person fears being exploited in relationships. Considerable evidence indicates that reciprocation wariness influences involvement and behaviors in social exchange relationships (Cotterell, Eisenberger, & Speicher, 1992; Eisenberger, Cotterell, & Marvel, 1987; Lynch, Eisenberger, & Armeli, 1999; Perugini, Gallucci, Presaghi, & Ercolani, 2003). We expect that individuals high in reciprocation wariness are less likely to attempt to initiate mentoring relationships with others and are less willing to mentor others than are individuals with lower reciprocation wariness.

In the initiation stage of mentoring relationships, reciprocation wariness may function as a moderator of other characteristics that would normally prompt initiation of a mentoring relationship. For instance, a senior employee may be "high energy" and sociable, and even want to see junior employees succeed. However, concern on the part of the more senior employee about what will be expected of him or her in the long run may cause this (wary) person to hold back from making connections with others in a mentoring context, either informally or in terms of willingness to participate in a formal mentoring program. A potential protégé may be achievement oriented and self-confident yet never approach senior employees for informal guidance out of a fear of being exploited. In that participation in informal mentoring relationships has been linked with a variety of long-term success outcomes, such reluctance to initiate contact with others may have a negative impact on long-term career success.

Perspective taking (Davis, 1980, 1983), which also may be considered an aspect of agreeableness, is a cognitive variable that involves attempting to consider issues from others' viewpoints. Being high on perspective taking should facilitate mentors' attempts to help protégés learn, such as by parsing tasks in a manner that is helpful for a beginner, giving feedback in ways that are helpful, and perceiving and building upon individual differences in how different protégés are motivated. When protégés have high perspective taking, they may be better able to attract and maintain relationships with mentors, understanding how to provide added value for mentors.

Empathic concern (Davis, 1980, 1983), which is also within the scope of agreeableness, deals primarily with emotional experience in having concern for others' feelings and difficulties. This characteristic should be particularly relevant to explaining the willingness of senior employees to engage in mentoring relationships (Allen, 2003), particularly with those junior employees who are not "stars" in terms of performance. Further, mentors who have greater empathy may be more understanding about personal problems and be more willing (and better able) to provide the psychosocial mentoring functions. However, developing a reputation of being empathetic may also become problematic for these mentors if people lower in competence tend to seek them out for guidance and mentoring.

In sum, we expect that the global trait of agreeableness, and the narrower traits of reciprocation wariness, empathy, and perspective taking, impact the formation, cultivation, and dissolution of mentoring relationships. Indirect support for such expectations is provided by Allen (2003), who found that empathy and helpfulness (components of a prosocial personality) were related to willingness to mentor others. We encourage additional research examining agreeableness and some of its components across the various phases of mentoring relationships.

Emotional stability is a trait that includes the tendency to be relatively calm, free from troubling emotions, and self-assured. Being low on emotional stability (i.e., high on neuroticism) suggests that the person tends to experience a range of negative emotions, such as sadness, anger, and anxiety, and to struggle with feelings of insecurity and self-consciousness (Costa & McCrae, 1992; Goldberg, 1993). Evidence from romantic relationships indicates that being low on emotional stability (high neuroticism) predicts negative relationship outcomes such as conflict and dissatisfaction (Ozer & Benet-Martinez, 2006). We expect that being low on emotional stability is likely to impede progress at all stages of the mentoring relationship and to be part of a pattern of "dysfunctional mentoring" (Eby & McManus, 2004). However, we expect emotional stability to have different implications for protégés than for mentors in the relationship.

For protégés, being insecure and anxious is likely to be negatively related to attempts to initiate contact with a potential mentor, because these people may assume that they do not have much to offer a senior employee or may be too nervous to approach the potential mentor (see Turban & Dougherty, 1994). In addition, a junior employee who is low on emotional stability may project a poor professional image, thereby making it less likely that the junior employee will be approached by a potential mentor. Alternatively, the junior employee may be perceived as a liability because of behaviors that are an outgrowth of low emotional stability, perhaps handling conflicts poorly, experiencing frequent stress-related illness, or downplaying abilities and successes.

Throughout the cultivation stage of mentoring, a protégé who lacks self-confidence and routinely avoids challenges because of negative feelings may project an image of someone who is not successful, making it hard for the mentor to show ongoing confidence in the protégé's abilities. Alternatively, if protégés low on emotional stability are quite vocal about their feelings, the mentor might feel drained by the need to provide ongoing counseling and support (psychosocial mentoring). A protégé who is low on emotional stability may also have more difficulty than others becoming independent and renegotiating the boundaries of the mentoring relationship when it is time to modify roles.

When a senior employee (potential mentor) is low in emotional stability, that person may be avoided by potential protégés who perceive the senior person to be a potential liability. Further, mentors who are low in emotional stability may have difficulty cultivating relationships on a long-term basis and may develop a reputation as being "difficult" among other employees. If a mentor is very sensitive to perceived slights and is also prone to retribution, the relationship may become very unpleasant for the protégé and perhaps become entirely counterproductive. Similarly, mentors low in emotional stability may experience difficulty with the changes brought about by dissolution of the relationship. To summarize, although little research has investigated the role of emotional stability in mentoring relationships, we believe it may be an important personality characteristic to investigate, in particular for dysfunctional relationships.

Extraversion includes the tendency to be sociable, have high energy, experience positive emotions and, like agreeableness, is a trait that is central to interpersonal processes (Watson & Clark, 1997). Although few studies have investigated whether personality predicts the popularity and status of adults, some evidence indicates that extraversion is related to those social factors (Ozer & Benet-Martinez, 2006). Thus, extraversion may influence the desirability of another person as a mentoring partner. In addition, we expect that extraversion should predict individuals having the interest and energy to participate in informal mentoring relationships. In particular, people who are higher on extraversion should be more likely to initiate mentoring relationships, perceiving that the activity will be an enjoyable (interactive) experience. Further, they should be more likely to feel they will have energy to devote to such relationships, which will be adopted in addition to other required work activities. The tendency to experience positive emotions should enhance the development of the relationship during the cultivation stage, in that people who experience and display positive emotions should be more attractive to others than those who do not. It is unclear whether extraversion of either the protégé or mentor will influence the redefinition of the relationship, however.

Conscientiousness involves being achievement oriented, detail oriented, and organized and is likely to influence mentoring relationships because it is related to and signals competence, which both protégés and mentors tend to appreciate (Olian et al., 1993, 1988). In terms of initiation, those who engage in more conscientious behavior should be more attractive potential partners because they are seen as competent. Further, during the cultivation phase, both mentors and protégés who are conscientious are more likely to earn the trust of their mentoring partners because they can be counted on to produce quality work and follow through on commitments.

Those who are high on *openness to experience* are creative, intellectual, open-minded, and appreciate many forms of art (Costa & McCrae, 1992). Research evidence reveals a positive relationship between openness to experience and successful training outcomes in the workplace (Barrick et al., 2001; Salgado, 1997), suggesting that those who are high on this dimension enjoy learning new things and so are motivated to participate fully in training opportunities (Barrick & Mount, 1991). In that mentoring relationships involve opportunities to learn from another person (particularly in the case of a protégé) and necessitate some understanding and acceptance of work styles and interests different from one's own (particularly in the case of a mentor), those who are higher on openness to experience should be more interested in initiating mentoring relationships. Further, it is possible that those who are very low on openness to experience are perceived as difficult to work with during the cultivation stage of a mentoring relationship.

A *learning goal orientation* (mastery goal orientation), although not part of the FFM, can be seen as a trait that is related to, but narrower than, openness to experience. Achievement goal theory/goal orientation theory addresses the process by which goals are pursued (Dweck & Leggett, 1988; Elliot & Church, 1997; VandeWalle, 1997). Those with a strong learning goal orientation are highly interested in mastering new skills and are typically willing to risk failure in order to achieve that end. This trait should facilitate initiation of mentoring, in that (like openness to experience) both the potential protégé and mentor will view the prospect of learning from a new person as a rewarding experience. Further, those with a higher learning orientation should enjoy the process of learning to work with a new person, appreciate the new skills they are learning, and enjoy the process involved, even if these activities do not transfer immediately into tangible career gains. This enjoyment should promote a sense of reward and facilitate a continued cultivation process. In support of such logic, Godshalk and Sosik (2003) found that both protégé and mentor learning goal orientations were related to protégé reports of psychosocial and career mentoring received.

Further, when both the protégé and mentor are highly learning oriented, perceived similarity should be increased, in that both people value learning and can tolerate the failure that often occurs as part of this process. Although they did not investigate perceived similarity, Godshalk and Sosik (2003) found that career and psychosocial mentoring were highest when both the protégé and mentor were high in learning goal orientation. Such evidence suggests that learning orientation may be an important personality characteristic in mentoring relationships, or at least the cultivation of such relationships; thus, we encourage further research investigating the role of goal orientation in mentoring relationships. Based on recent conceptualizations of the goal orientation construct, we encourage researchers to examine the measures by Elliot and McGregor (2001), who propose that the learning goal orientation has an approach and avoidance dimension similar to how performance goals are conceptualized (VandeWalle, 1997).

Our intent in discussing the role of certain personality characteristics in mentoring relationships is to provide examples of how personality may impact such relationships (see Table 2.3). Although we have discussed predominantly direct effects of personality on mentoring relationship outcomes, we encourage researchers to investigate interactive effects of personality (i.e., personality profiles) and also to investigate similarity/complementarity of mentor and protégé personality characteristics. For example, recent evidence indicates that conscientiousness is related to helping behaviors only when the person has a positive interpersonal orientation, as evidenced by high agreeableness, extraversion, and emotional stability (King, George, & Hebl, 2005). Extending such results to mentoring relationships, perhaps highly conscientious individuals will mentor others only when they also are high in agreeableness, extraversion, and emotional stability. In addition, research is needed to investigate how patterns of mentor and protégé personality characteristics influence outcomes. For example, although we speculated that extraversion is important in initiating and cultivating mentor relationships, perhaps only one individual needs to be extraverted in order to provide the initial momentum for two individuals to begin interacting. Further, perhaps a detail-oriented, conscientious person might complement a creative, open-to-experience individual in terms of generating work products and providing learning opportunities for both parties. We urge researchers to examine the effects of both similarity and complementarity of mentor and protégé personality characteristics. We now turn to a discussion of how future research on these topics might be conducted.

Suggestions for Design of Future Research (Or, How Do We Get There From Here?)

As noted in a previous section, we believe it is important to select personality characteristics that parallel the dependent variables in terms of specificity. In addition, future research will benefit from longitudinal designs and examining moderators of the effects of personality on outcomes.

In terms of methodology, use of longitudinal designs may allow for more detailed assessment of the role of personality in mentoring relationship dynamics. We expect that personality (i.e., relatively stable traits) will influence behaviors at various stages of the mentoring relationship (see Table 2.3). However, mentoring relationships may also have an impact on more malleable individual differences,

Table 2.3 Examples of Potentially Important Personality Variables at Different Phases of the Mentoring Relationship

Phase	Protégé Personality Characteristics	Mentor Personality Characteristics
Initiation	Agreeableness Reciprocation Wariness Conscientiousness Emotional Stability Extraversion Self-Monitoring	Agreeableness Reciprocation Wariness Emotional Stability Extraversion
Cultivation	Agreeableness Perspective-Taking Conscientiousness Emotional Stability Extraversion Openness to Experience Learning Goal Orientation	Agreeableness Perspective-Taking Empathic Concern Conscientiousness Emotional Stability Extraversion Openness to Experience Learning Goal Orientation
Dissolution/Redefinition	Agreeableness Emotional Stability	Agreeableness Emotional Stability

NOTE. The table suggests possible main effects of personality variables at various mentoring relationship phases. As described more fully in the text, however, it seems very likely that personality profiles of both protégés and mentors may influence the development of their relationships. For example (and there are many other possible examples), conscientiousness and agreeableness may interact such that mentor conscientiousness is related positively to protégé perceptions of mentoring functions received when agreeableness is high but is negatively related when agreeableness is low (see King et al., 2005). In addition, mentor and protégé characteristics may interact with one another to influence mentoring relationships. For example, an introverted protégé may be able to form a relationship with an extraverted mentor (in particular, if the introverted protégé is highly conscientious).

such as career self-efficacy or motivation. Tracking a cohort of business school graduates over a period of years may allow for assessment of the type and range of informal mentoring relationships that are developed and how individual differences influence and are influenced by mentoring relationships. In addition, the use of a longitudinal design may be especially useful in the context of a formal mentoring program, in which a wider range of personality traits and degrees of dyad similarity may be present.

We also encourage researchers to collect data from both members of relationships (i.e., protégés and mentors). Collecting data from both parties of the dyad will allow for investigation of actual similarity effects as well as minimize or perhaps reduce concerns with monosource method variance. For example, actual deep-level similarity (e.g., Harrison, Price, & Bell, 1998) in underlying qualities such as personality traits and values may influence perceived similarity reported by mentoring partners, which is related to positive mentoring outcomes (Ensher & Murphy, 1997; Turban, Dougherty, & Lee, 2002). In addition, actual similarity in personality traits may facilitate relationship dynamics, especially for traits that are most directly related to goal choice, work style, and overall values (such as learning goal orientation). However, Glomb and Welsh (2005) suggested that complementarity of individuals may result from both similarity and dissimilarity in traits (e.g., similarity in affiliation and differences in dominance). They found that subordinates were most satisfied with their supervisors when supervisors were high in control (dominance) and subordinates were low to moderate (i.e., when they were dissimilar). In addition, dyads in which both members have similar and low levels of certain traits, such as emotional stability and learning goal orientation, may not have effective relationships. Thus, researchers should consider the profile of personality traits of dyad members and the traits on which they may be similar and dissimilar. In any case, to investigate such issues, we encourage researchers to assess both mentor and protégé personality characteristics. In addition, measurement of personality via secondary sources (such as peer ratings) may add credibility to such personality assessment.

We also recommend that researchers consider potential moderators of the personality-outcome links in mentoring relationships. For instance, *time spent* in a mentoring relationship may influence the importance of personality similarity between mentor and protégé (Turban et al., 2002) or the impact of individual personality characteristics on outcomes. In addition, the relationship between personality characteristics and outcomes may be moderated by *other personality characteristics or interpersonal processes*. For instance, a recent study found that the relationship between conscientiousness and performance is moderated by social skills, such that conscientiousness is more strongly related to job performance when social skills are high and is unrelated or negatively related to job performance when social skills are low (Witt & Ferris, 2003). Such results suggest that social skills influence behavioral manifestations of conscientiousness. In a similar way, perhaps the (hypothesized) positive relationship between agreeableness and mentoring cultivation processes is augmented by the presence of high extraversion. That is, a disagreeable person may be all the more difficult to tolerate if that person is also extraverted, as their disagreeableness may be expressed quite freely. Finally, *context* is likely to be an important moderator of personality-outcome relationships. For example, extraversion may be less important for the initiation of formal versus informal mentoring relationships. Further, although speculative, it may be that mentor personality characteristics have less influence on protégé initiation of mentoring relationships for the protégé with a larger or more diverse constellation of mentoring relationships (Higgins & Kram, 2001). For example, a protégé who has a supportive network of mentoring relationships may be more likely to attempt to initiate a mentor relationship with an emotionally unstable and disagreeable mentor who can provide career opportunities than would a protégé who does not have a supportive network.

Conclusion

In conclusion, we have attempted to provide a review of the current state of personality research in the mentoring literature and to provide some direction in terms of how to proceed in this line of research. Although limited research on personality and mentoring processes has been conducted to date, there are indications that this is a promising arena of future study. In particular, advances in the use of personality concepts to understand other aspects of work behavior may be applied to understanding mentoring dynamics and outcomes more thoroughly. We hope that we have provided some helpful ideas for mentoring scholars to consider as they develop future studies.

Note

1. As noted by Wanberg, Welsh, and Hezlett (2003), however, although mentoring is the most intense and powerful one-on-one developmental relationship, there are various other types of developmental relationships at work. People seek out and receive career-related support not only from mentors but also from other people, such as peers, subordinates, and supervisors (Higgins & Kram, 2001; Kram & Isabella, 1985). However, the focus of this chapter is on the traditional mentoring relationship, and so we use the term *mentoring* throughout the chapter.

References

Allen, T. D. (2003). Mentoring others: A dispositional and motivational approach. *Journal of Vocational Behavior, 62,* 134–154.

Allen, T. D., & Eby, L. T. (2003). Relationship effectiveness for mentors: Factors associated with learning and quality. *Journal of Management, 29,* 469–486.

Allen, T. D., Eby, L. T., Poteet, M. L., Lentz, E., & Lima, L. (2004). Career benefits associated with mentoring for protégés: A meta-analysis. *Journal of Applied Psychology, 89,* 127–136.

Allen, T. D., Poteet, M. L., & Burroughs, S. M. (1997). The mentor's perspective: A qualitative inquiry and future research agenda. *Journal of Vocational Behavior, 51,* 70–89.

Allen, T. D., Poteet, M. L., Russell, J., & Dobbins, G. H. (1997). A field study of factors related to supervisors' willingness to mentor others. *Journal of Vocational Behavior, 50,* 1–22.

Allen, T. D., Russell, J. E. A., & Maetzke, S. B. (1997). Formal peer mentoring: Factors related to protégés' satisfaction and willingness to mentor others. *Group & Organization Management, 22,* 488–507.

Aryee, S., Lo, S., & Kang, I. L. (1999). Antecedents of early career stage mentoring among Chinese employees. *Journal of Organizational Behavior, 20,* 563–576.

Asendorpf, J. B., & Wilpers, S. (1998). Personality effects on social relationships. *Journal of Personality and Social Psychology, 74,* 1531–1544.

Barrick, M. R., & Mount, M. K. (1991). The big five personality dimensions and job performance: A meta-analysis. *Personnel Psychology, 44,* 1–26.

Barrick, M. R., Mount, M. K., & Judge, T. A. (2001). Personality and performance at the beginning of the new millennium: What do we know and where do we go next? *International Journal of Selection & Assessment, 9,* 9–30.

Bozionelos, N. (2004). Mentoring provided: Relation to mentor's career success, personality, and mentoring received. *Journal of Vocational Behavior, 64,* 24–46.

Caspi, A., Roberts, B. W., & Shiner, R. L. (2005). Personality development: Stability and change. *Annual Review of Psychology, 56,* 453–484.

Chao, G. T., Walz, P. M., & Gardner, P. D. (1992). Formal and informal mentorships: A comparison of mentoring functions and contrast with nonmentored counterparts. *Personnel Psychology, 45,* 619–636.

Costa, P. T., Jr., & McCrae, R. R. (1992). *Professional manual for the NEO PI-R and NEO-FFI.* Odessa, FL: Psychological Assessment Resources.

Costa, P. T., Jr., & McCrae, R. R. (1997). Longitudinal stability of adult personality. In R. Hogan, J. Johnson, & S. Briggs (Eds.), *Handbook of personality psychology* (pp. 269–290). San Diego, CA: Academic Press.

Cotterell, N., Eisenberger, R., & Speicher, H. (1992). Inhibiting effects of reciprocation wariness on interpersonal relationships. *Journal of Personality & Social Psychology, 67,* 658–668.

Davis, M. H. (1980). A multidimensional approach to individual differences in empathy. *JSAS Catalog of Selected Documents in Psychology, 10,* 85.

Davis, M. H. (1983). Measuring individual differences in empathy: Evidence for a multi-dimensional approach. *Journal of Personality and Social Psychology, 44,* 113–126.

Day, R., & Allen, T. D. (2004). The relationship between career motivation and self-efficacy with protégé career success. *Journal of Vocational Behavior, 64,* 72–91.

Digman, J. M. (1996). The curious history of the five-factor model. In J. S. Wiggins (Ed.), *The five-factor model of personality: Theoretical perspectives* (pp. 1–20). New York: Guilford Press.

Dweck, C. S., & Leggett, E. L. (1988). A social-cognitive approach to motivation and person-ality. *Psychological Review, 95,* 256–273.

Eby, L. T., & Allen, T. D. (2002). Further investigation of protégés' negative mentoring expe-riences. *Group & Organization Management, 27,* 456–479.

Eby, L. T., Butts, M., Lockwood, A., & Simon, S. A. (2004). Protégés' negative mentoring experi-ences: Construct development and nomological validation. *Personnel Psychology, 57,* 411–447.

Eby, L. T., & McManus, S. E. (2004). The protégé's role in negative mentoring experiences. *Journal of Vocational Behavior, 65,* 255–275.

Eby, L. T., McManus, S. E., Simon, S. A., & Russell, J. E. A. (2000). The protégé's perspective regarding negative mentoring experiences: The development of a taxonomy. *Journal of Vocational Behavior, 57,* 1–21.

Eisenberger, R., Cotterell, N., & Marvel, J. (1987). Reciprocation ideology. *Journal of Personality and Social Psychology, 53,* 743–750.

Elliot, A. J. (2005). A conceptual history of the achievement goal construct. In A. J. Elliot & C. S. Dweck (Eds.), *Handbook of competence and motivation* (pp. 52–72). New York: Guilford Press.

Elliot, A. J., & Church, M. A. (1997). A hierarchical model of approach and avoidance achievement motivation. *Journal of Personality and Social Psychology, 72,* 218–232.

Elliot, A. J., & McGregor, H. A. (2001). A 2 × 2 achievement goal framework. *Journal of Personality and Social Psychology, 80,* 501–519.

Ensher, E. A., & Murphy, S. E. (1997). Effects of race, gender, perceived similarity, and con-tact on mentor relationships. *Journal of Vocational Behavior, 50,* 460–481.

Ensher, E. A., Thomas, C., & Murphy, S. E. (2001). Comparison of traditional, step-ahead, and peer mentoring on protégés' support, satisfaction, and perceptions of career suc-cess: A social exchange perspective. *Journal of Business and Psychology, 15,* 419–438.

Fagenson, E. A. (1989). The mentor advantage: Perceived career/job experiences of protégés vs. nonprotégés. *Journal of Organizational Behavior, 10,* 309–320.

Fagenson, E. A. (1992). Mentoring: Who needs it? A comparison of proteges' and non pro-teges' needs for power, achievement, affiliation, and autonomy. *Journal of Vocational Behavior, 41,* 48–60.

Fagenson-Eland, E. A., & Baugh, S. G. (2001). Personality predictors of protégé mentoring history. *Journal of Applied Social Psychology, 31,* 2502–2517.

Funder, D. C. (2001). Personality. *Annual Review of Psychology, 52,* 197–221.

Glomb, T. M., & Welsh, E. T. (2005). Can opposites attract? Personality heterogeneity in supervisor-subordinate dyads as a predictor of subordinate outcomes. *Journal of Applied Psychology, 90,* 749–757.

Godshalk, V. M., & Sosik, J. J. (2003). Aiming for career success: The role of learning goal orientation in mentoring relationships. *Journal of Vocational Behavior, 63,* 417–437.

Goldberg, L. R. (1993). The structure of phenotypic personality traits. *American Psychologist, 48,* 26–34.

Graziano, W. G., & Eisenberg, N. (1997). Agreeableness: A dimension of personality. In R. Hogan, J. Johnson, & S. Briggs (Eds.), *Handbook of personality psychology* (pp. 767–793). San Diego, CA: Academic Press.

Harrison, D. A., Price, K. H., & Bell, M. P. (1998). Beyond relational demography: Time and the effects of surface- and deep-level diversity on work group cohesion. *Academy of Management Journal, 41,* 96–107.

Higgins, M. C. (2000). The more the merrier? Multiple developmental relationships and work satisfaction. *Journal of Management 19,* 277–296.

Higgins, M. C., & Kram, K. E. (2001). Reconceptualizing mentoring at work: A developmental network perspective. *Academy of Management Review, 26,* 264–288.

Higgins, M. C., & Thomas, D. A. (2001). Constellations and careers: Toward understanding the effects of multiple developmental relationships. *Journal of Organizational Behavior, 22,* 223–247.

Hough, L. M. (1998). Personality at work: Issues and evidence. In M. D. Hakel (Ed.), *Beyond multiple choice: Evaluating alternatives to traditional testing for selection* (pp. 131–166). Mahwah, NJ: Lawrence Erlbaum.

Judge, T. A., & Illies, R. (2002). Relationship of personality to performance motivation: A meta-analytic review. *Journal of Applied Psychology, 87,* 797–807.

Kanfer, R., & Heggestad, E. D. (1997). Motivational traits and skills: A person-centered approach to work motivation. *Research in Organizational Behavior, 19,* 1–56.

King, E. B., George, J. M., & Hebl, M. R. (2005). Linking personality to helping behaviors at work: An interactional perspective. *Journal of Personality, 73,* 585–607.

Kram, K. E. (1983). Phases of the mentor relationship. *Academy of Management Journal, 26,* 608–625.

Kram, K. E. (1985). *Mentoring at work.* Boston: Scott, Foresman.

Kram, K. E., & Isabella, L. (1985). Mentoring alternatives: The role of peer relationships in interpersonal development. *Academy of Management Journal, 28,* 110–132.

Leary, M. R. (1999). The scientific study of personality. In V. J. Derlega, B. A. Winstead, & W. H. Jones (Eds.), *Personality: Contemporary theory and research* (pp. 3–26). Chicago: Nelson-Hall.

Lynch, P. D., Eisenberger, R., & Armeli, S. (1999). Perceived organizational support: Inferior versus superior performance by wary employees. *Journal of Applied Psychology, 84,* 467–483.

McCrae, R. R., & Costa, P. T., Jr. (1996). Toward a new generation of personality theories: Theoretical contexts for the five-factor model. In J. S. Wiggins (Ed.), *The five-factor model of personality: Theoretical perspectives* (pp. 1–20). New York: Guilford Press.

Mullen, E. J. (1998). Vocational and psychosocial mentoring functions: Identifying mentors who serve both. *Human Resource Development Quarterly, 9,* 319–339.

Mullen, E. J., & Noe, R. A. (1999). The mentoring information exchange: When do mentors seek information from their protégés? *Journal of Organizational Behavior, 20,* 233–242.

Noe, R., & Greenberger, D. B., & Wang, S. (2002). Mentoring: What we know and where we might go. *Research in Personnel and Human Resources Management, 21,* 129–173.

Olian, J., Carroll, S., & Giannantonio, C. M. (1993). Mentor reactions to protégés: An experiment with managers. *Journal of Vocational Behavior, 43,* 266–278.

Olian, J., Carroll, S., Giannantonio, C. M., & Feren, D. (1988). What do proteges look for in a mentor? Results of three experimental studies. *Journal of Vocational Behavior, 33,* 15–37.

Ozer, D. J., & Benet-Martinez, V. (2006). Personality and the prediction of consequential outcomes. *Annual Review of Psychology, 57,* 401–421.

Perugini, M., Gallucci, M., Presaghi, F., & Ercolani, A.P. (2003). The personal norm of reciprocity. *European Journal of Personality, 17,* 251–283.

Pervin, L. A. (2003). *The science of personality* (2nd ed.). New York: Oxford Press.

Pierce, J. L., Gardner, D. G., Cummings, L. L., & Dunham, R. B. (1989). Organization-based self-esteem: Construct definition, measurement, and validation. *Academy of Management Journal, 32,* 622–648.

Ragins, B. R., & Cotton, J. L. (1993). Gender and willingness to mentor in organizations. *Journal of Management, 19,* 97–111.

Ragins, B. R., & Cotton, J. L. (1999). Mentor functions and outcomes: A comparison of men and women in formal and informal mentoring relationships. *Journal of Applied Psychology, 84,* 529–550.

Ragins, B. R., Cotton, J. L., & Miller, J. S. (2000). Marginal mentoring: The effects of type of mentor, quality of relationship, and program design on work and career attitudes. *Academy of Management Journal, 43,* 1177–1194.

Ragins, B. R., & Scandura, T. A. (1999). Burden or blessing? Expected costs and benefits of being a mentor. *Journal of Organizational Behavior, 20,* 493–509.

Rice, M. B., & Brown, R. D. (1990). Developmental factors associated with self-perceptions of mentoring competence and mentoring needs. *Journal of College Student Development, 31,* 293–299.

Rosenberg, M. (1965). *Society and the adolescent self-image.* Princeton, NJ: Princeton University Press.

Rowe, D. C. (1999). Heredity. In V. J. Derlega, B. A. Winstead, & W. H. Jones (Eds.), *Personality: Contemporary theory and research* (pp. 66–100). Chicago: Nelson-Hall.

Salgado, J. F. (1997). The five-factor model of personality and job performance in the European community. *Journal of Applied Psychology, 82,* 30–43.

Scandura, T. A. (1992). Mentorship and career mobility: An empirical investigation. *Journal of Organizational Behavior, 13,* 169–174.

Scandura, T. A. (1998). Dysfunctional mentoring relationships and outcomes. *Journal of Management, 24,* 449–467.

Scandura, T. A., & Ragins, B. R. (1993). The effects of sex and gender role orientation on mentorship in male-dominated occupations. *Journal of Vocational Behavior, 43,* 251–265.

Snyder, M. (1987). *Public appearance/private realities.* New York: Freeman.

Turban, D. B., & Dougherty, T. W. (1994). Role of protégé personality in receipt of mentoring and career success. *Academy of Management Journal, 37,* 688–702.

Turban, D. B., Dougherty, T. W., & Lee, F. K. (2002). Gender, race, and perceived similarity effects in developmental relationships: The moderating role of relationship development. *Journal of Vocational Behavior, 61,* 240–262.

VandeWalle, D. (1997). Development and validation of a work domain goal orientation instrument. *Educational & Psychological Measurement, 57,* 995–1015.

Wanberg, C. R., Welsh, E. T., & Hezlett, S. A. (2003). Mentoring research: A review and dynamic process model. *Research in Personnel and Human Resource Management, 22,* 39–124.

Waters, L. (2004). Protégé-mentor agreement about the provision of psychosocial support: The mentoring relationship, personality, and workload. *Journal of Vocational Behavior, 65,* 519–532.

Watson, D., & Clark, L. A. (1997). Extraversion and its positive emotional core. In R. Hogan, J. Johnson, & S. Briggs (Eds.), *Handbook of personality psychology* (pp. 767–793). San Diego, CA: Academic Press.

Witt, L. A., & Ferris, G. R. (2003). Social skill as a moderator of the conscientiousness-performance relationship: Convergent results across four studies. *Journal of Applied Psychology, 88,* 809–820.

3

Mentoring and Career Outcomes

Conceptual and Methodological Issues in an Emerging Literature

Thomas W. Dougherty

George F. Dreher

O ver the approximately 20-year span of research on mentoring in the workplace, one of the key research questions pertains to the value of mentors and mentoring for the career success of protégés. Researchers in the early 1990s began to publish work that investigated (along with other issues) whether mentoring received by protégés was related to their objective career progress as measured by variables such as promotion rates and compensation (e.g., Dreher & Ash, 1990; Scandura, 1992; Turban & Dougherty, 1994; Whitely, Dougherty, & Dreher, 1991). Scholars soon acknowledged that the construct of career success includes more than objective outcomes, and they began to include subjective outcomes of mentoring, including perceived career success, career expectations, organizational justice, job involvement, job satisfaction, organizational commitment, intention to stay, job burnout, and organizational power, among other outcomes (Fagan & Walter, 1982; Fagenson, 1988; Koberg, Boss, & Goodman, 1998). In this chapter, we provide an overview of a variety of issues regarding the relationships of mentoring to the receipt of protégé career outcomes. First, we

AUTHORS' NOTE: We thank Jamie Cheung and James Wilbanks for their assistance in preparing this chapter.

provide an overview of empirical research on this topic, including key characteristics of past studies. Next, we discuss definitional issues in mentoring research and implications for future studies, followed by some additional conceptual issues related to broadening the criteria used in studies of mentoring and career outcomes. We then highlight some research design issues that are particularly relevant for the study of mentoring and protégé career outcomes, including internal validity, method variance, and external validity issues. Finally, we turn to discussion of the need for a better understanding of intermediate linkages—or specific paths—by which mentors can influence the career trajectories of protégés, followed by some concluding comments. We now turn to an overview of key findings of the studies that constitute this literature.

Mentoring and Career Outcomes: Where We Have Been

Empirical Research Results on Mentoring and Career Outcomes

Within the past 5 years, three major mentoring reviews relevant to this chapter have been published. These include two recent monographs on mentoring by Noe, Greenberger, and Wang (2002) and Wanberg, Welsh, and Hezlett (2003) and a meta-analysis focused specifically on research examining mentoring's career benefits for protégés by Allen, Eby, Poteet, Lentz, and Lima (2004). We now provide an overview of findings and conclusions relevant to the focus of this chapter.

Noe et al. (2002) delineated both the proximal (more immediate) and distal (longer-term) outcomes of mentoring for protégés. They categorized *proximal outcomes* as including the various mentoring functions received by protégés, including psychosocial, career-related, and role-modeling functions. They suggested a number of *distal outcomes* for protégés, such as promotions, compensation, work alienation, job involvement, and perceived career success. Noe et al. discussed a variety of issues and suggested new directions in the study of mentoring. They reported that their reading of the literature led them to conclude that mentored individuals (versus nonmentored) report more career and job satisfaction, promotions, higher incomes, and lower turnover intentions and work alienation. However, their monograph did not systematically or in a detailed fashion review the literature focusing on mentoring and protégé career outcomes.

Wanberg and colleagues (2003) provided a lengthy and comprehensive review of the workplace mentoring literature, with a special review and discussion of formal mentoring. Their review included a table summarizing key characteristics of studies of both protégé and mentor outcomes. These characteristics included focus, methodology, type of mentoring examined, source of data, and sample size—reporting that most studies used cross-sectional surveys, relied upon self-reports, and focused on protégé (versus mentor) outcomes. Sample sizes ranged from 22 to 3,321, with most sample sizes over 100. Wanberg et al. noted that it was difficult to code studies on the formal/informal dimension, in that many authors did not explicitly make this distinction. They did not indicate any explicit criteria for inclusion of studies generating their summary statistics on these studies examining outcomes. Moreover, they did not identify the individual studies included in these summary statistics or provide a review of these studies, pointing out the difficulty of such a narrative review. They did summarize the results of the (early version of the) Allen et al. (2004) meta-analysis in reporting an overall synthesis of protégé outcome results across studies. In addition, Wanberg et al. (2003) cited some research issues and priorities, including differentiating formal from informal mentoring, using control variables and longitudinal studies to confirm the "incremental" value of mentoring beyond protégé characteristics, examining the mechanisms through which mentoring leads to career success (offering a detailed model for formal mentoring in their monograph), examining work performance-related outcomes, and examining multiple mentors and negative mentoring experiences. We take up a number of these issues in the present chapter.

In regard to the meta-analytic review by Allen et al. (2004), they provided some explicit criteria for inclusion of studies in their analysis and a systematic review and synthesis of research on protégé outcomes from workplace mentoring. Therefore, it makes sense in the present chapter to focus attention on their findings about mentoring and protégé outcomes as a springboard for our discussion of conceptual and methodological issues. We also provide a study-by-study overview of research characteristics and results of their 43 studies, displayed in Table 3.1. We chose to add 4 more recently published studies of mentoring and protégé outcomes to Table 3.1 (Gonzalez-Figueroa & Young, 2005; Kirchmeyer, 2005; Payne & Huffman, 2005; Scandura & Williams, 2004), which fit the Allen et al. (2004) criteria for inclusion in analyses.

Allen et al. (2004) included both objective (e.g., compensation) and subjective (e.g., career satisfaction) outcomes and studies examining both "amount of mentoring provided" and studies configured as comparisons of "mentored versus nonmentored" individuals. For inclusion in the meta-analysis, a study had to have reported the sample size, been conducted in an organizational setting, collected separate measures of major mentoring functions (e.g., career, psychosocial), and reported a relationship(s) between mentoring and an outcome variable using a correlation or comparable index. In these studies, Allen and colleagues observed that the primary indicators of *objective career success* were total annual compensation, salary growth (e.g., percentage change over some time period), and self-reported promotions. The primary indicants of *subjective career success* were career satisfaction, advancement expectations, career commitment, job satisfaction, and intention to stay with one's organization.

Allen and colleagues' (2004) results indicated, first, that individuals who have been mentored receive greater career outcomes than those who have not, including both objective and subjective outcomes (with the exception of intention to stay). Second, results indicated that career-related mentoring was positively related to career outcomes, including compensation, salary growth, promotions, career satisfaction, job satisfaction, and satisfaction with the mentor. Third, the analyses indicated that psychosocial mentoring was also related to career outcomes (as hypothesized).

(Text continues on page 73)

Table 3.1 Characteristics of (Expanded Set of) Studies Included in Allen et al. (2004) Meta-Analysis

Author/ Journal/Year	Sample Characteristics	Measure of Mentoring Functions	Definition of Mentoring?	Data Source	Outcomes	Moderators/ Mediators	Methodology	Key Findings
Aryee & Chay *British Journal of Management* (1994)	164 professional and managerial employees in public and private sector organizations in Singapore	Ragins & McFarlin's 15 items for career functions	Yes	Protégé self-report	Career satisfaction, organizational commitment, career commitment, & job involvement	N/A	Cross-sectional survey	Mentored individuals were significantly higher on all outcomes versus nonmentored
Aryee, Wyatt, & Stone *Journal of Management Studies* (1996)	432 professional and managerial midcareer employees in local and multinational organizations in Hong Kong	Dreher & Ash's four items for career functions	Yes	Protégé self-report	Career satisfaction, number of promotions, & salary	Ingratiation as independent variable and moderator	Cross-sectional survey	Mentoring and ingratiation was unrelated to annual salary. Mentoring was related to number of promotions and career satisfaction, but ingratiation and their interaction terms were not.
Barker, Monks, & Buckley *British Accounting Review* (1999)	287 professional employees in two of the Big Five accountancy firms in Ireland	Scandura & Viator's 15 items for career development, social support, & role-modeling functions	Yes	Protégé self-report	Turnover intentions	Gender as moderator	Cross-sectional survey	U-shaped relationship between protégé grade and mentoring. Male mentors provided a stronger role-modeling function to male protégés but not between female mentors and protégés. Career development and social support were related to turnover intentions.

Author/ Journal/Year	Sample Characteristics	Measure of Mentoring Functions	Definition of Mentoring?	Data Source	Outcomes	Moderators/ Mediators	Methodology	Key Findings
Baugh, Lankau, & Scandura *Journal of Vocational Behavior* (1996)	176 female and 99 male managers and executives in the United States	Respondents reported whether they had mentors or not	Yes	Protégé self-report	Organizational commitment, job satisfaction, career expectation, role conflict, role ambiguity, & perceived employment alternatives	Gender as moderator	Cross-sectional survey	Male nonprotégés showed lower organizational commitment, job satisfaction, and career expectations and increased role ambiguity relative to male protégés and female protégés and nonprotégés. Female nonprotégés reported lower career expectations and lower perceived employment alternatives than female protégés and male protégés and nonprotégés.
Chao, Walz, & Gardner *Personnel Psychology* (1992)	212 informal protégés, 53 formal protégés, & 284 nonmentored professional and managerial employees	Noe's 21 items for psychosocial and career-related functions	Yes	Protégé self-report	Job satisfaction, organizational socialization, & salary	N/A	Cross-sectional survey	Informal protégés reported more career-related support. Mentored protégés reported higher level of job satisfaction, organizational socialization, & salary than nonmentored individuals. Formal and informal protégés did not report different outcomes. Career-related mentoring had stronger effect on the outcomes than psychosocial mentoring.

(Continued)

Table 3.1 (Continued)

Author/ Journal/Year	Sample Characteristics	Measure of Mentoring Functions	Definition of Mentoring?	Data Source	Outcomes	Moderators/ Mediators	Methodology	Key Findings
Colarelli & Bishop *Group & Organization Studies* (1990)	426 professional and managerial employees	Respondents reported whether they had mentors or not	Yes	Protégé self-report	Career commitment	N/A	Cross-sectional survey	Mentoring was positively related to career commitment.
Corzine, Buntzman, & Busch *Journal of Social Behavior and Personality* (1994)	208 bank officers	Respondents reported whether they had mentors or not	Yes	Protégé self-report	Job satisfaction, salary, & career plateau	Gender & downsizing as moderators	Cross-sectional survey	Mentored individuals reported higher level of job satisfaction and were less likely to perceive reaching a career plateau. However, salary was not related to mentoring. No interaction effects were found between gender and mentoring, and downsizing and mentoring.
Cox & Nkomo *Work & Occupations* (1991)	729 MBA alumni	Respondents rated the extent to which their career had been aided by a mentor(s)	Yes	Protégé self-report	Job involvement, career satisfaction, & hierarchical level	Gender & race as moderators	Cross-sectional survey	Black MBAs had less access to mentors. No significant differences between males and females on levels of mentoring received. No interaction effects found between gender and race on mentoring received.

Author/ Journal/Year	Sample Characteristics	Measure of Mentoring Functions	Definition of Mentoring?	Data Source	Outcomes	Moderators/ Mediators	Methodology	Key Findings
Day & Allen Journal of Vocational Behavior (2004)	125 supervisory, administrative, managerial, & professional employees in a municipality	Noe's 21 items for psychosocial and career-related functions	Yes	Protégé self-report	Subjective career success, performance effectiveness, salary, & promotion	Career motivation & career self-efficacy as mediators	Cross-sectional survey	Mentored individuals reported higher levels of career motivation but not career self-efficacy. Psychosocial and career mentoring were related to career motivation. Career mentoring was related to career self-efficacy. but psychosocial mentoring was not. Career motivation fully mediated the relationship between career mentoring and performance effectiveness.
Dreher & Chargois Journal of Vocational Behavior (1998)	127 African American managerial and professional employees	Respondents reported whether they had mentors or not	Yes	Protégé self-report	Total annual compensation	N/A	Cross-sectional survey	Individuals with White male mentors reported higher levels of compensation.
Dreher & Cox Journal of Applied Psychology (1996)	1,018 MBA alumni	Respondents reported whether they had mentors or not	Yes	Protégé self-report	Total annual compensation	Gender & race as moderators	Cross-sectional survey	Blacks and Hispanics were less likely than Whites to have White male mentors. Men were more likely than women to have White male mentors. Protégés with White male mentors reported higher compensation than protégés with other types of mentors.

(Continued)

Table 3.1 (Continued)

Author/ Journal/Year	Sample Characteristics	Measure of Mentoring Functions	Definition of Mentoring?	Data Source	Outcomes	Moderators/ Mediators	Methodology	Key Findings
Ensher & Murphy *Journal of Vocational Behavior* (1997)	104 interns (high school seniors)	Noe's 22 items for career-related and psychosocial functions	Yes	Protégé self-report	Satisfaction with mentor and likelihood of continuing relationship	Gender & race as moderators	Cross-sectional survey	Protégés assigned to same-race mentors reported more instrumental support. Perceived similarity was related to protégés' liking and satisfaction and contact frequency with mentors but not to racial similarity. Liking, perceived similarity, and mentoring were related to protégés' satisfaction with mentors. Career mentoring and liking were related to likelihood of continuing relationship.
Ensher, Thomas, & Murphy *Journal of Business and Psychology* (2001)	142 hourly, nonmanagerial, & managerial employees	Scandura & Katerberg's 18 items for vocational from multiple organizations	Yes support, role-modeling, & psychosocial support	Protégé self-report	Job satisfaction & perceived career success	N/A	Cross-sectional survey	Role-modeling, reciprocity, and vocational support were related to protégés' satisfaction with mentors. Traditional mentors were reported to provide more vocational support, role-modeling, and

Author/Journal/Year	Sample Characteristics	Measure of Mentoring Functions	Definition of Mentoring?	Data Source	Outcomes	Moderators/Mediators	Methodology	Key Findings
								mentoring satisfaction than peer mentors. Vocational support was related to job satisfaction and perceived career success. Protégés with traditional mentors reported higher levels of job satisfaction than protégés with nontraditional mentors.
Fagenson *Journal of Organizational Behavior* (1989)	246 employees in health care industry	Two items measuring mentors' helpfulness and organizational influence	Yes	Protégé self-report	Career mobility/ opportunity, recognition, satisfaction, security, & promotion	Protégé's gender & organizational level as moderators	Cross-sectional survey	Mentored individuals reported higher levels of all outcome variables except security.
Finkelstein, Allen, & Rhoton *Group & Organization Management* (2003)	88 professional employees in a university	Scandura's 15 items for career development, social support, and role-modeling	Yes	Protégé self-report	Mentorship quality, & mutual learning	Mentors' age as a moderator	Cross-sectional survey	Older protégés reported receiving less career mentoring but higher quality mentoring and more mutual learning. Older mentors were perceived to provide the

(Continued)

Table 3.1 (Continued)

Author/ Journal/Year	Sample Characteristics	Measure of Mentoring Functions	Definition of Mentoring?	Data Source	Outcomes	Moderators/ Mediators	Methodology	Key Findings
								least mentoring. Protégés perceived similar-aged and younger mentors to be less competent in mentoring.
Gaskill & Sibley Clothing and Textiles Research Journal (1990)	205 female executives in middle- and upper-level retail positions	Respondents indicated the extent to which their mentors fulfilled Kram's (1985) five career and four psychological functions	Yes	Protégé self-report	Job satisfaction, job motivation, & promotion	N/A	Cross-sectional survey	Mentored mid-level executives reported more promotions than nonmentored executives. Upper-level mentored executives perceived higher levels of job motivation than nonmentored executives. Mentored executives placed more importance on mentoring relationships as a means of career advancement than did nonmentored executives.
Godshalk & Sosik Group & Organization Management (2000)	199 mentoring dyads— corporate employees in multiple firms	Noe's 20 items for career-related and psychosocial functions	Yes	Protégé self-report & mentor self-report	Quality of mentoring relationship (i.e., mentoring functions and mentoring effectiveness)	N/A	Cross-sectional survey	Protégés reported lowest quality of mentoring relationships with mentors who overestimated their transformational leadership behavior. Highest quality of

Author/ Journal/Year	Sample Characteristics	Measure of Mentoring Functions	Definition of Mentoring?	Data Source	Outcomes	Moderators/ Mediators	Methodology	Key Findings
								mentoring found in dyads in which mentors and protégés both underestimated mentor's transformational leadership behavior.
Gonzalez-Figueroa & Young *Cultural Diversity and Ethnic Minority Psychology* (2005)	103 Latina women with professional roles in the areas of business, academia, policy, and politics	Noe's 29 item measure of mentoring functions related to career functions	Yes	Protégé self-report	Professional success	Willingness to be mentored and strength of ethnic identity as moderators of mentoring received	Cross-sectional survey	Ethnic minority females preferred to be mentored by someone of similar ethnicity.
Higgins & Thomas *Journal of Organizational Behavior* (2001)	130 attorneys	12 items were developed for career-related and psychosocial functions	Yes	Protégé self-report & secondary data	Work satisfaction, intentions to remain, organizational retention, & promotion to partner	N/A	Longitudinal study	Developmental relationship quality with primary developers was positively related to work satisfaction and intention to remain. Developmental relationship with the constellation of developers was positively related to organizational retention. The hierarchical status of the constellation was positively related to promotion.

(Continued)

Table 3.1 (Continued)

Author/ Journal/Year	Sample Characteristics	Measure of Mentoring Functions	Definition of Mentoring?	Data Source	Outcomes	Moderators/ Mediators	Methodology	Key Findings
Johnson, Lall, Holmes, Huwe, & Nordlund Military Medicine (2001)	576 midshipmen	15 items developed for career-related and psychosocial functions	Yes	Protégé self-report	Assessment of mentor relationship	N/A	Cross-sectional survey	Psychosocial functions were more strongly related to quality of mentor relationship than were career functions.
Kirchmeyer Journal of Management (1998)	292 midcareer managers	Respondents indicated whether they had a mentor and the extent to which their peer network support and supervisor support was helpful to their careers	Yes	Protégé self-report	Career progression (i.e., income & organizational levels) & perceived career success	Gender as moderator	Cross-sectional survey	Having a mentor or peer network support had stronger effects on men's career progression. Having supervisor support had stronger effect on women's income. Having superior support had positive effect on both men's and women's perceived career success.
Kirchmeyer Journal of Applied Psychology (2002)	292 midcareer managers at Time 1 and 207 at Time 2	Respondents indicated whether they had a mentor or had been a mentor	Yes	Self-report as both mentor and protégé	Masculinity & femininity at Time 2	Gender & career/life experience as moderators	Longitudinal study	Having been a mentor was related to increases in masculinity for both genders and stability of masculinity for women. Having a mentor was related to increases in masculinity for men only. The stability of masculinity for mentored managers was lower than nonmentored managers.

Author/Journal/Year	Sample Characteristics	Measure of Mentoring Functions	Definition of Mentoring?	Data Source	Outcomes	Moderators/Mediators	Methodology	Key Findings
Kirchmeyer Human Relations (2005)	143 American academics who earned doctoral degrees in accounting between 1984 and 1987	Respondents reported whether they had mentors or not, and, if yes, how many	Yes	Protégé self-report and secondary data	Salary and rank	Publications as mediator of mentoring's influence on rank and salary	Longitudinal study	Mentoring in academia benefits both career advancement and performance. Higher-ranking mentors influenced protégés' salary even after controlling for publications.
Koberg, Boss, Chappell, & Ringer Group & Organization Management (1994)	635 technical, professional, and managerial hospital employees	Noe's 7 items for career functions	Yes	Protégé self-report	Job satisfaction & work alienation	N/A	Cross-sectional survey	Mentoring was higher for men than for women. Organizational variables accounted for more variance in mentoring than individual variables. Mentoring was related to higher job satisfaction and lower work alienation.
Koberg, Boss, & Goodman Journal of Vocational Behavior (1998)	387 technical, professional, and managerial hospital employees	Noe's 14-item for psychosocial functions	Yes	Protégé self-report	Self-esteem at work, job involvement, & intention to quit	Gender & race as moderators	Cross-sectional survey	Mentoring was higher for Whites than for Hispanics or African Americans, but no difference was found between men and women. Protégés in same-sex and same-race dyads reported more mentoring.

(Continued)

Table 3.1 (Continued)

Author/ Journal/Year	Sample Characteristics	Measure of Mentoring Functions	Definition of Mentoring?	Data Source	Outcomes	Moderators/ Mediators	Methodology	Key Findings
								Mentoring was positively related to job involvement and self-esteem, and negatively related to intention to quit.
Mobley, Jarat, Marsh, & Lim *Sex Roles* (1994)	1,132 lawyers	Respondents indicated whether they had a mentor or not	Yes	Protégé self-report	Job satisfaction & dissatisfaction with case responsibilities	N/A	Cross-sectional survey	Mentoring was positively related to job satisfaction and negatively related to dissatisfaction with case responsibilities. No gender difference was found for mentoring.
Murphy & Ensher *Journal of Career Development* (2001)	158 employees in a media organization and a school district	Scandura & Katerberg's 18 items for vocational support, role-modeling, & psychosocial support	Yes	Protégé self-report	Perceived career success and job satisfaction	Mentoring as moderator	Cross-sectional survey	Only vocational support was related to job satisfaction and perceived career success. Protégés with more vocational support and engaged in self-management reported greater job satisfaction. Protégés with more psychosocial support and engaged in self-management reported greater job and career satisfaction. Role-modeling and employing self-management were related to career satisfaction.

Author/ Journal/Year	Sample Characteristics	Measure of Mentoring Functions	Definition of Mentoring?	Data Source	Outcomes	Moderators/ Mediators	Methodology	Key Findings
Noe Personnel Psychology (1988)	139 educators and 43 mentors	32 items developed to assess career and psychosocial functions	Yes	Protégé and mentor self-report	Career and psychosocial functions	N/A	Cross-sectional survey	Women received more psychosocial benefits than men. Protégé characteristics, gender, effective utilization of the mentor and amount of time spent interacting with the mentor did not have an effect on career mentoring. Protégé gender explained significantly more variance in psychosocial mentoring than other predictor variables.
Orpen Journal of Social Psychology (1995)	97 newcomers in Britain	15 items from Noe & Burke for career and psychosocial functions	No	Protégé self-report	Number of promotions, salary growth	N/A	Cross-sectional survey	Career mentoring was related to the number of promotions and salary growth. But psychosocial mentoring was not related to career success.
Payne & Huffman Academy of Management Journal (2005)	1,334 U.S. Army officers	Respondents reported whether they had mentors or not, and, if	Yes	Protégé self-report	Organizational commitment & turnover	Supervisory vs. nonsupervisory conditions of mentoring as	Longitudinal study	Protégés had higher levels of both affective commitment and continuance commitment than nonmentored

(Continued)

Table 3.1 (Continued)

Author/ Journal/Year	Sample Characteristics	Measure of Mentoring Functions	Definition of Mentoring?	Data Source	Outcomes	Moderators/ Mediators	Methodology	Key Findings
		yes, whether they were supervisory or nonsupervisory				moderator, and affective commitment as mediator between mentoring and turnover		employees 1 year later. Protégés with supervisory mentors reported higher affective commitment than protégés with nonsupervisory mentors. Affective commitment partially mediates the relationship between mentoring and turnover.
Prevosto Military Medicine (2001)	100 army nurses	Dreher & Ash's mentoring scale	Yes	Protégé self-report	Job satisfaction & intention to stay	N/A	Cross-sectional survey	Mentored nurses reported more job satisfaction and higher intention to stay than nonmentored nurses.
Ragins & Cotton Journal of Applied Psychology (1999)	352 females and 257 males from national sample of journalists, social workers, & engineers	Ragins & McFarlin's 33 items for career and psychosocial functions	Yes	Protégé self-report	Mentor satisfaction, promotion rate, and current annual compensation	Gender & mentorship types as moderators	Cross-sectional survey	Protégés with informal mentoring reported higher levels of satisfaction with mentors and more compensation than protégés with formal mentoring. Having a history of male mentors was related to more compensation. Protégés in cross-gender dyads reported less career mentoring in formal mentoring. Female protégés may have the least to gain from formal mentoring.

Author/ Journal/Year	Sample Characteristics	Measure of Mentoring Functions	Definition of Mentoring?	Data Source	Outcomes	Moderators/ Mediators	Methodology	Key Findings
Ragins, Cotton, & Miller Academy of Management Journal (2000)	1,162 social workers, engineers, & journalists	Respondents indicated the type of mentoring program they were in	Yes	Protégé self-report	Career commitment, job satisfaction, organizational commitment, organization-based self-esteem, promotion opportunities, intention to quit, & procedural justice	Mentorship types as moderator	Cross-sectional survey	Satisfaction with mentoring relationships had a stronger link to protégés' job and career attitudes than the presence of a mentor. Mentoring program design did not have a positive effect on protégés' attitudes. Protégés in same-department dyads reported lower satisfaction. Women with formal mentors were less satisfied than men and reported less career commitment than men and nonmentored protégés.
Riley & Wrench Journal of Applied Social Psychology (1985)	171 female lawyers	29 items were developed to assess 4 facets of career support	Yes	Protégé self-report	Perceived career success & career satisfaction	N/A	Cross-sectional survey	Protégés in traditional mentoring perceived higher levels of career success and satisfaction than group-mentored protégés and nonmentored protégés.

(Continued)

Table 3.1 (Continued)

Author/ Journal/Year	Sample Characteristics	Measure of Mentoring Functions	Definition of Mentoring?	Data Source	Outcomes	Moderators/ Mediators	Methodology	Key Findings
Scandura & Schriesheim Academy of Management Journal (1994)	244 protégés (middle-level managers) & 191 mentors	Clawson's six items for supervisor career mentoring	Yes	Protégé and mentor self-report & personnel records	Promotion rate, salary growth, & supervisory ratings of performance	N/A	Cross-sectional survey	Mentoring augmented the effects of leader-member exchange (LMX) on salary growth and promotion rate. LMX augmented the effects of mentoring on performance but not salary growth and promotion rate.
Scandura & Williams Journal of Vocational Behavior (2004)	275 full-time employed MBAs	Scandura's seven items for measuring career mentoring	Yes	Protégé self-report	Job satisfaction, organizational commitment, & career expectations	Attributed charisma and individualized consideration as mediators	Cross-sectional survey	Supervisory career mentoring (SCM) was related to job satisfaction, organizational commitment, and career expectations beyond transformational leadership.
Seibert Journal of Vocational Behavior (1999)	109 newly hired engineers	Noe's 21 items for psychosocial and career-related functions, and interaction frequency	Yes	Protégé self-report	Job satisfaction, organizational commitment, work role stress, & self-esteem at work	N/A	Longitudinal study	Mentored engineers reported higher levels of job satisfaction than nonmentored engineers, but not organizational commitment, work role stress, & self-esteem at work.

Author/ Journal/Year	Sample Characteristics	Measure of Mentoring Functions	Definition of Mentoring?	Data Source	Outcomes	Moderators/ Mediators	Methodology	Key Findings
Seibert, Kraimer, & Liden *Academy of Management Journal* (2001)	448 managerial and professional employees	Dreher & Ash's eight items for career sponsorship	N/A (focus not mentoring)	Respondent self-report	Current salary, number of promotions, & career satisfaction	Network benefits as mediators	Cross-sectional survey	Access to information and career sponsorship mediated the relationship between career network contacts and career outcomes.
Sosik & Godshalk *Group & Organization Management* (2004)	217 mentoring dyads— corporate employees in multiple firms	Noe's 17 items for career-related and psychosocial functions	Yes	Protégé self-report & mentor self-report	Job satisfaction, career satisfaction, desired aspirations, & enacted aspirations	N/A	Cross-sectional survey	Protégés in overestimator dyads reported the least psychosocial support and career satisfaction. Protégés in underestimator dyads reported the most mentoring and favorable outcomes. Protégés in in-agreement/good dyads reported receiving more psychosocial support than those in in-agreement/poor dyads and overestimator dyads.
Sosik & Godshalk *Journal of Organizational Behavior* (2000)	204 mentor-protégé dyads— corporate employees in multiple firms	Noe's 20 items for career-related and psychosocial functions	Yes	Protégé self-report & mentor self-report	Job-related stress	Mentoring as moderator	Cross-sectional survey	Mentor's leadership style was related to mentoring received. Mentoring received was negatively related to job stress. Having male mentors was related to higher levels of job stress.

(Continued)

Table 3.1 (Continued)

Author/ Journal/Year	Sample Characteristics	Measure of Mentoring Functions	Definition of Mentoring?	Data Source	Outcomes	Moderators/ Mediators	Methodology	Key Findings
Tharenou *Australian Journal of Management* (2005)	3,220 lower- and middle-level managers from public and private sectors in Australia	Ragins & McFarlin's 21 items for career and psychosocial functions	Yes	Protégé self-report	Salary, number of promotions, & managerial level	Gender as moderator	Longitudinal study	Career support increased women's career advancement more than it did men's. Psychological support reduced women's advancement more than for men.
Turban & Dougherty *Academy of Management Journal* (1994)	147 managerial and professional employees	Dreher & Ash's 18 items for career and psychosocial functions	Yes	Protégé self-report	Salary, number of promotions, & perceived career success	N/A	Cross-sectional survey	Internal locus of control, high self-monitoring, and high emotional stability increased initiation of mentoring which mediated the relationships between personality traits and mentoring received. Mentoring received was positively related to career outcomes.
Wallace *Journal of Vocational Behavior* (2001)	231 female lawyers in Canada	Respondents reported whether they had mentors or not	Yes	Protégé self-report	Income, perceived promotional opportunities, procedural justice, social integration, career satisfaction,	Gender as moderator	Cross-sectional survey	Women with female mentors reported higher levels of subjective career outcomes. Women with male mentors reported higher earnings. Being mentored was positively related to all career outcomes except for

Author/ Journal/Year	Sample Characteristics	Measure of Mentoring Functions	Definition of Mentoring?	Data Source	Outcomes	Moderators/ Mediators	Methodology	Key Findings
					intention to stay, fulfillment of career expectation, & work-nonwork stress			intention to stay and work-nonwork stress.
Waters, McCabe, Kiellerup, & Kiellerup Journal of Business and Psychology (2002)	77 protégé and 68 mentors in a new business start-up program in Australia	Waters, McCabe, Kiellerup, & Kiellerup's eight-item "mentoring in new business" scale	Yes	Protégé self-report & mentor self-report	Profit, perceived success, & self-esteem	N/A	Cross-sectional survey	Perceived success and protégés' self-esteem were predicted by frequency of contacts with mentors and mentoring functions.
Wayne, Liden, Kraimer, & Graf Journal of Organizational Behavior (1999)	245 supervisor-subordinate dyads—exempt employees of large corporation	7-item supervisor career mentoring scale adopted from Noe and Whitely et al.	Yes	Protégé self-report & mentor self-report	Salary progression, promotability, & career satisfaction	N/A	Cross-sectional survey	Supervisor's mentoring was related only to higher level of promotability.

(Continued)

Table 3.1 (Continued)

Author/ Journal/Year	Sample Characteristics	Measure of Mentoring Functions	Definition of Mentoring?	Data Source	Outcomes	Moderators/ Mediators	Methodology	Key Findings
Whitely & Coetsier *Organization Studies* (1993)	148 early career managerial and professional employees in Belgium	Whitely, Dougherty, & Dreher's 10 items for career-related functions	Yes	Protégé self-report	Number of promotions, total compensation, general work satisfaction, & career satisfaction	N/A	Cross-sectional survey	Career mentoring was related to the number of promotions, general work satisfaction, and career satisfaction, but not to total compensation.
Whitely, Dougherty, & Dreher *Academy of Management Journal* (1991)	404 early career managerial and professional employees	Whitely, Dougherty, & Dreher's 10 items for career-related functions	Yes	Protégé self-report	Number of promotions & total compensation	Socioeconomic status as moderator	Cross-sectional survey	Career mentoring was related to the number of promotion- and total compensation. Career mentoring had a greater relationship with promotion for people from higher socioeconomic backgrounds.

Allen and colleagues (2004) had predicted that objective career outcomes would have a stronger relationship with career mentoring than with psychosocial mentoring. The results indicated mixed support. Compensation and promotions were slightly more strongly related to career than to psychosocial mentoring, although the removal of one large sample study indicated a much larger difference in the expected direction. Finally, the authors predicted that subjective career outcomes would be more strongly related to psychosocial mentoring than to career mentoring. However, the results provided little evidence that subjective career outcomes are more strongly linked to psychosocial versus career mentoring. In contrast, results indicated that psychosocial mentoring does appear to be related more strongly to satisfaction with mentoring than does career mentoring.

In summary, Allen and colleagues (2004) provided evidence, based on over 40 empirical studies, that mentoring is associated with protégés' receipt of both objective and subjective outcomes, although the effect sizes for objective outcomes tend to be small. The most consistent benefits of mentoring appear to be the relationships with affective reactions at work and positive feelings about one's career. It also appears that the type of mentoring (e.g., career versus psychosocial) may be important for outcomes, in that there is some evidence that objective outcomes are more strongly linked to career than to psychosocial mentoring. Allen et al. also made the interesting observation that effect sizes for objective indicants of career success were stronger when comparing "mentored versus nonmentored" individuals, as opposed to studies of the connection between mentoring functions provided and objective outcomes. They pointed out that, first, degree of mentoring provided may not be as important as the presence of a mentor and, second, current operationalizations of mentoring functions do not capture all aspects of mentoring that are related to career success. In this vein, some qualitative research has identified a variety of mentoring behaviors that may be important, such as provision of networking opportunities and breadth of skill development, which are not adequately captured by mentoring scales in common use (Eby & McManus, 2002). Finally, Allen et al. (2004) suggested that career mentoring is just as important for positive job and career attitudes as is psychosocial mentoring.

Mentoring and Career Outcomes: Characteristics of Studies and Implications

Considering the 47 studies of mentoring and protégé outcomes shown in Table 3.1, we offer some summary observations about this literature. First, the overwhelming majority of these studies used samples of managerial and professional employees. The sample sizes ranged from 77 to 3,220, with the median at slightly over 200, including a few studies collecting data from mentor-protégé dyads. Virtually every study collected self-report data from protégés, with a few also collecting data from mentors. Almost all of the studies provided some kind of definition of a mentor to respondents. In addition, about 75% of the studies measured mentoring functions received using a multi-item scale. Almost all of the studies were cross-sectional studies (i.e., all data were collected on the same survey at one time). However, there were six longitudinal studies. There were also several studies that examined moderator variables, especially gender and race.

We find it interesting that researchers have used such a wide variety of scales to measure mentoring functions. It appears that for more than one third of the studies, a unique scale was developed; there were 15 studies reporting scales with only one or two uses among all the studies in the meta-analysis. The most popular scale was that of Noe (1988), used in 12 of the studies, which measures career and psychosocial functions. Scales by Dreher and Ash (1990) and Ragins and McFarlin (1990) were cited in 4 and 3 (respectively) of the studies. Researchers would benefit from some systematic analysis of the equivalence and relative strengths and weaknesses of mentoring scales in use. As noted by Allen et al. (2004), these scales tend to provide a variety of kinds of instructions to participants. Finally, many studies did not specify or limit protégé self-reports of mentoring as to informal or formal mentoring relationships. A handful of studies did explicitly investigate formal mentoring relationships, and as Allen et al. observed, these formal and informal mentorships may not provide the same benefits.

Thus, Allen and colleagues' (2004) meta-analysis of studies of mentoring and career outcomes synthesized results typified by cross-sectional data collection from a few hundred managerial-professional protégés, who self-reported informal and/or formal mentoring received and their attainment of both objective and subjective career outcomes. We refer to these study characteristics (and Table 3.1) in subsequent parts of this chapter. We next turn to a more substantive exploration of a variety of conceptual matters.

Conceptual Issues in Mentoring Research

Where We Have Been in Defining Mentoring

The Concept of Mentoring and Mentoring Functions

Kram (1985) is the most often cited source for a definition of mentoring in the workplace. The traditional mentor is considered to be a senior individual who provides guidance and assistance to a more junior individual (the protégé). Kram's analysis of qualitative data led to two broad categories of mentoring functions provided to a protégé: career and psychosocial functions. *Career mentoring functions* involve specific mentor behaviors supportive of the protégé's career progress, which directly enhance the likelihood of the protégé becoming successful in his or her career. Whereas career functions directly help the protégé succeed in his or her career, *psychosocial functions* are more personal aspects of a relationship that tend to enhance a protégé's sense of professional competence and identity.

The vast majority of mentoring research in work organizations has adopted the Kram framework, although there is some evidence suggesting that role-modeling may be a third distinct function (Scandura, 1992). We also note that Kram did not use the term *mentor* in conducting her research, out of concern that the word had too many nuanced connotations. Instead, she chose to ask about "developmental relationships." We believe that attention to definitional issues is important for making future progress in understanding mentoring and career outcomes. We now turn to this issue.

Examining Alternative Definitions of Mentoring

To provide a discussion of how researchers have defined informal mentoring, we go beyond the studies in Table 3.1, drawing upon some recent work by Dougherty, Turban, and Haggard (2005). They performed an assessment of the variety of definitions and approaches to defining mentoring in empirical articles on informal workplace mentoring. In this effort, they examined articles appearing during the period from 1990 to 2005 in the five journals in which the majority of workplace mentoring studies have appeared. Their assessment was restricted to studies including the protégé (i.e., not exclusively studying mentors). The studies investigated a variety of aspects of mentoring in addition to protégé career outcomes, but we believe that this assessment of how scholars define mentoring is relevant for this chapter's consideration of conceptual and methodological issues.

Dougherty and colleagues' (2005) assessment revealed much variability as to the definition of mentoring used in research. For example, although many studies provided detailed definitions to respondents, several researchers chose to simply ask, "Do you currently have a mentor?" Some investigators also administered a mentoring functions scale to protégés, to establish the amount of mentoring provided, thus assuming that individuals who provide mentoring functions are in fact "mentors," which may or may not be the case. In the studies collecting data from protégés that did include a definition of a mentor (73%), there was appreciable variety in the definitions used. Not surprisingly, in these studies, the percentage of individuals who identified themselves as having a mentor ranged from 23% to 81%—a likely result of differing mentoring definitions and/or sample characteristics.

The variety of definitions of mentoring included several features that are especially notable. In regard to a focus on a specific mentor, the majority of definitions asked whether the respondent had "a mentor," thus implying one specific person. However, some definitions indicated that only one person should be considered, while others asked about mentoring received over the career history, especially those studies using mentoring functions scales. As to hierarchy, some definitions merely indicated that a mentor has "more" or "advanced" experience, implying some hierarchical difference, while other definitions specified that the mentor is at a higher level, although using varied terms such as *influential, higher-ranking, senior,* and *position of power.* These terms do not all clearly identify just where in the hierarchy the mentor is located. In addition, a handful of the studies included peers as a source of mentoring. Similarly, in several studies, definitions specifically included supervisors, whereas a few specifically excluded supervisors as mentors. About half of the studies assessed did not mention the supervisor at all.

Mentoring definitions have also provided differing levels of detail in describing mentoring functions received by protégés, with many including examples of both psychosocial and career functions, while others included only one. Interestingly, more of these definitions specified career functions than psychosocial functions. A well-exercised phrase was that a mentor is a person "committed to providing upward mobility to your career." Other definitions implied career support without spelling it out. As to intimacy of the relationship, some (only a few) defined mentoring relationships as being "close" or "intense." Finally, most mentoring definitions in research have either explicitly stated that the mentor is internal or at least implied it, using a phrase such as "in your work environment."

About a fourth of the studies measured mentoring functions using scales, without an explicit definition of a mentor. These researchers avoided the variety of connotations associated with the word *mentor*. However, the degree to which these scales ask about a particular mentor versus "mentoring functions received" raises the issue of whether the construct being measured is a mentoring relationship or, alternatively, mentoring functions received from any number of sources.

There may be notable implications of the variety of definitions used in research on mentoring and outcomes. Wanberg and colleagues (2003) pointed out that although there is a lack of definitional consistency, there is consistency in the general concept of mentoring, at least for traditional mentoring relationships. Nevertheless, scholars need to carefully consider the definition(s) of mentoring they present to research participants and consider the implications. We cite a few key issues and examples.

Defining the Mentoring Construct: Problems and Issues

The most obvious definitional problems for interpreting the literature stem from use of a vague definition of *mentoring* in some studies ("Do you have a mentor?") and in some cases no definition at all. With no definition, participants can decide who does or does not meet the test of mentorship. For studies using vague definitions, interpreting the results in comparison to other mentoring studies poses a challenge for the researcher. That is, reviews of the literature and meta-analyses of mentoring research are limited by this conceptual diversity, creating error variance restricting our ability to effectively assess mentoring relationships and summarize research findings.

In addition, there is a potential problem of vagueness even with studies that measure specific mentoring functions received by protégés. For example, consider studies that present a multi-item mentoring scale to participants, asking them to report their receipt of (mostly "secondary") mentoring assistance from multiple mentors over their careers (e.g., Turban & Dougherty, 1994; Whitely et al., 1991). Of course, the accuracy of participants' memories over time may be suspect. And as we discuss in more detail later in this chapter, such studies may be at least partly measuring a kind of generalized career affect. Some individuals might even indicate significant mentoring received (e.g., on scales), while not being able to name any one individual they ever considered to be a mentor to them.

Similarly, there may also be problems with the use of clearly defined but highly descriptive definitions of mentoring, such that the definitions of mentoring include, or strongly imply, the benefits received by protégés. Consider studies that include in the definition of a mentor that this person has "helped you by supporting your career" (Aryee, Lo, & Kang, 1999, p. 568) or definitions specifying that the person "is committed to providing upward mobility and support to your career" (Baugh, Lankau, & Scandura, 1996, p. 313). These descriptive definitions make sense for studies addressing topics such as willingness to mentor others. But they may be problematic for studies investigating mentoring and career outcomes received, in that the very definition of mentoring includes the provision of these outcomes. We acknowledge that one could also argue that this "common method variance" problem derives from how we measure the outcome variables. Regardless, overlapping content in the predictor and the criterion variables could artificially inflate correlations.

In contrast, some researchers have used highly precise and/or narrow definitions of mentoring, such as specifically excluding supervisors in definitions of mentoring. Even with diverse definitions across studies, precise (versus vague) definitions make it possible to better understand differing research results across studies.

It is likely that one agreed-upon, uniform definition of mentoring would be difficult, since mentoring falls along a range of quality. But whether studies include or do not include specification of the scope of mentoring is likely to have implications for their results. We cite a few examples. First, studies that define mentoring as career mentoring only (versus psychosocial) may be more likely to find relationships of mentoring with protégé career progress and less likely to find relationships of mentoring with work attitudes (although Allen et al.'s (2004) meta-analysis results did not support this prediction). Second, studies with mentoring definitions allowing for or specifying direct supervisory mentoring may find differences compared with nonsupervisory mentoring, such as protégés' receipt of less sponsorship and exposure/visibility, because of a direct supervisor's limited power compared with a top executive. However, supervisors might be able to provide more of some career functions, such as coaching and challenging work. A few studies have found differences in mentoring from supervisors versus others, although not necessarily along the lines suggested here (Burke, McKenna, & McKeen, 1991; Ragins & McFarlin, 1990; Tepper, 1995). A third example is that studies with definitions allowing for outside-the-organization ("external") mentoring might find less career mentoring and less enhancement of protégés' career progress. Each of these sources of speculation could be empirically tested if there were enough studies using various definitions and boundary conditions for what is considered to be mentoring. Our purpose here is to underscore the potential importance of alternative definitions of mentoring for our interpretation of the mentoring literature and comparisons among studies.

Defining Mentoring: Where We Should Be Going

The issues discussed above also lead to recommendations to researchers studying workplace mentoring. Instead of providing only a vague definition of a mentor or asking research participants to report on narrowly defined relationships—thereby limiting the definition of mentoring a priori—researchers should gather data on the full range of relationships and then collect additional, more detailed information describing the relationships. Researchers, for example, might ask about a general developmental relationship and then gather more specific information about the nature of this relationship (e.g., Is this person your supervisor, higher in the hierarchy? Is it formal or informal, internal or external? Would the person see himself/herself as a mentor?). Using this approach (see Ragins, 1999) would allow researchers to capture the full range of mentoring relationships and provide a more precise analysis. This approach would be consistent with Kram's (1985) original assertion that traditional mentoring is only one part of a person's relationship constellation including peers, family, subordinates, supervisors, and others. The approach is also consistent with Higgins and Kram's (2001) recent reconceptualization of mentoring as a developmental network.

Conceptual Issues: The Criterion Problem

As shown in our previous discussion of the mentoring literature, researchers have considered a variety of dependent variables in their studies of the benefits associated with the establishment of mentoring relationships. These are often categorized as being either objective or subjective in nature. Common criterion variables of the objective variety typically include measures of protégé compensation levels, salary growth, and promotion rates. Subjective measures typically include a focus on career and job satisfaction along with protégé satisfaction with the mentoring relationship. A few studies have also addressed protégé career commitment and intention to stay with a current employer. And actual turnover has been considered as a direct outcome of mentoring (Payne & Huffman, 2005).

While prior research has covered a relatively wide range of outcome variables, we first note that other interesting potential consequences would be worthy candidates for future studies. For example, on the benefits side, we would suggest moving beyond the organizational context and considering the effects of mentoring relationships on extraorganizational functioning and satisfaction. Here, a focus on life satisfaction, the ability to balance the competing demands of a career and a family (see Greenhaus & Singh, Chapter 21, this volume), and the ability to manage the stressful nature of very competitive labor markets could lead to some interesting findings. We also note recent calls for extending mentoring criteria to capture relational elements of mentoring as part of one's set of "positive relationships" and the experience of growth, learning, and development (Fletcher & Ragins, Chapter 15, this volume; Ragins & Verbos, 2007). The consideration of negative and unintended effects of mentoring also offers new insight. In this vein, we applaud some recent research on the potential negative effects of mentoring, including exploitation and sexual harassment of protégés (Eby, Chapter 13, this volume; Eby & McManus, 2002; Eby, McManus, Simon, & Russell, 2000). It also would be useful to study the consequences for the protégé of being associated with a mentor experiencing varying degrees of career failure (e.g., being found in violation of accounting rules, being discredited for initiating a failed strategic initiative, etc.).

Next, we point out that the mentoring literature has traditionally focused on outcomes at the individual level of analysis. Mentoring might be considered at the group level also, and there is a clear need to consider mentoring from the perspective of employing organizations. What is intriguing here is the possibility that in some situations, what is good for the individual protégé or mentor may not be good for the organization. We offer two examples. First, consider the mentor who helps the protégé by providing information about extraorganizational job opportunities. By helping a protégé learn about a profession and the opportunities that reside outside the employing organization, high-quality mentoring may encourage voluntary turnover. Of course, this outcome may be "bad" for one organization and "good" for another organization, and it might ultimately result in a better person-organization fit. Thus, the relationship between organizational mentoring programs and turnover rates may be rather complex.

Also, we know virtually nothing about the ability of mentors to accurately identify high-potential job candidates. Conventional wisdom would suggest that the establishment of a "mentoring/development-oriented culture" in an organization would lead to improved talent pool management. An organization with a strong developmental culture consciously uses work experiences and work relationships to develop employees, has intense involvement by senior management, includes a strong succession planning process, and empowers employees to be self-directed, among other characteristics (see Hall & Mirvis, 1996). But if accelerated developmental experiences are not being offered to the right individuals, talent pool management and the building of bench strength may be compromised. Systematically studying the linkages between mentoring-oriented organizational culture and indices of quality talent pool management could prove useful.

While the issues just discussed are important, we believe the most crucial issues related to the criterion problem are represented by the distinction between distal (long-term) and proximal (immediate) outcomes of mentoring relationships—a set of processes that are proposed to mediate the relationships between mentoring and outcomes represented in the literature. We turn our attention to this topic in the final section of this chapter.

Research Design Issues: Internal Validity and Method Variance Problems

Problems Presented by Cross-Sectional Field Studies of Mentoring

As we discussed earlier in the chapter, the vast majority of studies of mentoring and career outcomes are conducted as cross-sectional field studies. In this section, we discuss a variety of design issues relevant to these kinds of studies.

Internal Validity: Direction of Causality

One key research issue in these studies of mentoring outcomes relates to what could be placed under the category of *internal validity*. As Wanberg et al. (2003) pointed out, researchers have sometimes used causal language in reference to cross-sectional mentoring findings, such as referring to mentoring as a significant determinant of career success. There are several internal validity problems stemming from the use of cross-sectional designs. One internal validity problem pertains to *direction of causality*. Mentoring researchers, while testing associations only among variables, tend to interpret their findings as support for the notion that receipt of mentoring leads to one's career success, including outcomes such as promotions, compensation, and career satisfaction. However, as has been noted in reviews of the mentoring literature (e.g., Noe et al., 2002) we must acknowledge the possibility that these associations among variables reflect a reverse direction of causality—effects of protégé career success on receipt of mentoring. In this vein, Noe et al. cited the study by Dreher and Ash (1990), in which protégés with self-reported formal or informal mentoring relationships received more promotions than those who did not specify mentoring relationships, regardless of protégé gender. A reciprocal relationship could explain these results, such that early career success leads to being chosen for mentoring by senior managers or being selected for a mentoring program, thus enhancing protégé career success. In support of this line of thinking, some research demonstrates that mentors tend to choose protégés who are judged to be the highest performers (Olian, Carroll, & Giannantonio, 1993) and protégés who have high ability and motivation, as opposed to protégés who are most in need of assistance (Allen, Poteet, & Russell, 2000).

Clearly, longitudinal research is of great value in clarifying these causal directions. As we reported earlier (see Table 3.1), we identified only six studies of mentoring and protégé outcomes that were not strictly cross-sectional, with mentoring and outcome data collected at more than one time. Interestingly, these studies have typically been supportive of the researchers' hypothesized direction of causality. As examples, studies have found that mentoring (or developmental relationships) measured at one point in time was related to subsequent organizational commitment and organizational citizenship (Donaldson, Ensher, & Grant-Vallone, 2000) and to professionals' promotion to partner 7 years later (Higgins & Thomas, 2001). But as Allen et al. (2004) pointed out, we currently have little guidance as to the appropriate time lag for capturing the receipt of mentoring outcomes.

Internal Validity: Alternative or "Third-Variable" Explanations

A related internal validity issue for mentoring research pertains to ruling out alternative explanations for relationships of mentoring to career outcomes by taking other variables into account. Sometimes this is referred to as the problem of "third-variable explanations" for relationships between two variables. We cannot expect highly controlled experiments with random assignment to be feasible in the study of informal mentoring. But there clearly is a need for research demonstrating the extent to which mentoring is the unique driver of positive outcomes (Wanberg et al., 2003). We note that some studies have used quite extensive sets of control variables in cross-sectional studies of mentoring and outcomes, including human capital variables (e.g., education), job and organizational variables, motivational variables (e.g., hours worked per week), and demographic variables (see Dreher & Ash, 1990; Turban & Dougherty, 1994; Whitely et al., 1991). The extensive use of control variables requires larger samples but allows for examining the incremental value of mentoring for career success. It also allows for ruling out a considerable number of potential third-variable explanations for relationships of mentoring with career outcomes.

Nevertheless, we note that Wanberg et al. (2003) drew special attention to the need for mentoring studies to control for key individual characteristics of protégés, especially protégé ability and motivation, in examining the association of mentoring with protégés' career success. Few studies have controlled for these kinds of factors. Some studies have controlled for some aspects of ability, such as GPAs, test scores, and graduates' scholastic rankings. Similarly, some studies have examined "proxies" for motivation, such as work centrality and hours worked per week. But it appears that studies have not controlled for both protégé ability and motivation. One exception is a study of faculty advisors' career mentoring of doctoral students and linkages to students' career success (Green & Bauer, 1995). The researchers controlled for ability using GRE scores, and for motivation using a measure of doctoral-student commitment. When these factors were controlled, the relationship of mentoring to career success (publications) was no longer significant.

Self-Reports and Method Variance Inflation of Relationships

In addition to internal validity issues, a second key research design issue in cross-sectional mentoring studies stems from the predominant use of self-reports, usually from protégés, as the single source of data in studies of mentoring and career outcomes. Because all data comes from the same source, we should expect some inflation of observed relationships, resulting from several kinds of common methods bias. We draw from excellent treatments of this issue by Podsakoff, MacKenzie, Lee, and Podsakoff (2003) and Podsakoff and Organ (1986) in emphasizing some key sources of common methods bias we believe to be particularly relevant for mentoring research.

First, in self-reports, people may try to maintain consistency between their cognitions (e.g., receipt of mentoring functions) and their attitudes (e.g., perceived career success, career satisfaction). This desire of respondents to maintain consistency and appear to be rational in their responses is known as the *consistency motif.* A second, related source of common method bias is referred to as *illusory correlations and implicit theories,* meaning that respondents hold assumptions about how constructs or events are related. Thus, in the case of mentoring research, the relationships of mentoring with outcomes may reflect the true covariation of mentoring received with outcomes but also the implicit theories of respondents about the relationship between these events. For example, some respondents who feel that their careers have not been successful may also believe that (therefore) a lack of mentoring support is a major cause of this failure. The use of self-report data on mentoring and career outcomes in a cross-sectional survey provides ample opportunity for implicit theories to affect the research results. We recall that mentoring tends to be more strongly related to subjective indicators of career success (e.g., career satisfaction) than it is to indicators of objective career success (Allen et al., 2004). We suggest that one reason for these differential findings may be the various types of method variance inflation of relationships among subjective perceptions, especially when collected on one survey at the same time. Again, separation of the measurement of variables theorized to be causes from those seen as effects could be helpful.

A third source of method bias relevant for mentoring research is *social desirability*, which refers to the tendency for respondents to respond in a way that presents themselves in a favorable light (Crowne & Marlowe, 1964). Thus, mentoring research participants who report attaining much success may feel a kind of internal pressure to also report, as a socially desirable response, that they have been helped along the way by powerful mentors—which may not be a true reflection of the way they really perceive career events.

A final source of common method bias we discuss here is *positive and negative affectivity* of respondents (see Podsakoff et al., 2003). As a relatively stable personal characteristic, some people tend to view themselves and the world around them in negative terms (negative affectivity), while others tend to regularly take a positive view. These individual dispositions may influence observed relationships between variables in self-report, cross-sectional studies. An example in a mentoring context is that respondents with high negative affectivity may be more likely to report that no mentors have helped their careers and also that they dislike their jobs (Wanberg et al., 2003). A solution is to control for negative affectivity in multivariate analysis. We should acknowledge here that it may also be true that protégés with high negative affectivity are, in fact, less likely to have mentors. It is also possible that a more transient mood state of respondents at the time of completing a survey could result in artifactual relationships among measured variables. Again, for a recent discussion of these and other sources of common method bias, see Podsakoff et al. (2003). We have emphasized some sources of method variance bias that are particularly relevant for cross-sectional mentoring research.

External Validity and the Influence of Key Moderator Variables

External Validity

As traditionally presented by authors such as Campbell and Stanley (1966), issues of external validity have to do with interactions between treatments (in this case the establishment of mentoring relationships) and (a) persons, (b) settings, and (c) times. While we will stay within this framework when commenting on external validity within the context of the mentoring literature, we note that a variety of variables (at the level of the developmental treatment itself) may moderate relationships between mentoring and outcome variables—and to some extent, these variables have already been addressed in the previous discussion of measurement issues and the nature of the mentoring construct. For instance, the duration and comprehensiveness of mentoring relationships would seem to have a lot to do with whether or not "having" a mentor would lead to positive career outcomes. Likewise, the payoff associated with developing a mentoring relationship would seem to be highly dependent on a wide variety of mentor (and protégé) attributes.

For example, high-quality mentoring relationships would seem to depend on whether the mentor possesses accurate and meaningful information about the protégé's organizational culture and strategic type and about the protégé's chosen career path. Also, whether or not the mentor is a skillful trainer would seem central to understanding the possible returns associated with mentoring. Here, we are thinking of behaviors such as listening, coaching, and communication skills. To date, as illustrated in Table 3.1, very little empirical research has addressed these possible moderators of mentoring/career-outcome relationships.

One topic that does relate directly to the nature of the mentoring construct itself is the whole issue of the distinction between informal and formal mentoring. Informal and formal relationships may differ on multiple dimensions (Ragins & Cotton, 1999). The most obvious dimension is the way the mentoring relationship is formed, with the former resulting from naturally occurring exchanges at work or in other social and community settings and the latter resulting from some type of matching process initiated within a company-sponsored mentoring program. While little research has systematically addressed the formal/informal distinction, the few studies that have suggest that the two may not be equally beneficial (Allen et al., 2004; Chao, Waltz, & Gardner, 1992; Ragins & Cotton, 1999). Additional research on this particular topic is clearly needed, including the increasing use of "e-mentoring," which is often a component of formal programs (see Ensher & Murphy, Chapter 12, this volume).

Interaction of Selection and Treatment (Mentoring)

From the Campbell and Stanley (1966) perspective, the issue here is whether any observed correlational or cause-effect relationships can be generalized beyond the group or groups used in the initial research. That is, do the results from any particular study generalize to various racial, sex, social, geographical, age, or personality groups? A review of Table 3.1 reveals that very little is currently known about this class of moderator variables. The most commonly considered moderators are gender and race, with gender being considered in some form in 13 of 47 studies and race being considered in 4 instances. Other moderators such as mentor age, protégé and mentor race, protégé influence tactics, and protégé socioeconomic origins have received some, but less, attention. What is most striking is that 81% of the studies represented in the Allen et al. (2004) review were conducted using U.S.-based samples. Samples from Belgium, Great Britain, Canada, Hong Kong, Ireland, and Singapore were singularly represented in the review, and two studies focused on survey respondents from Australia. Geographical location may be relevant because cultural-value differences are observed across geographical regions and these differences may moderate mentoring/outcome relationships. Cultural differences may also be related to the definition of mentor. In a recent study, Ramaswami, Huang, and Dreher (2005) observed that power distance moderated the relationship between mentoring and organizational level, such that among Taiwanese managers and professionals (who are reasonably high on power distance), the positive return associated with mentoring was strongest among high power distance protégés. Programmatic research is needed to better understand whether the association between mentoring and career outcomes—most often studied within the context of U.S. culture—will generalize to national cultures that differ from the United States on an assortment of value and managerial-style dimensions.

Interaction of Setting and Treatment

Again, from the Campbell and Stanley (1966) perspective, this class of interactions asks whether relationships observed in one setting will generalize to other settings. *Settings* in this case typically refers to organizational, industrial, or occupational settings. Many of the studies displayed in Table 3.1 were based on managerial/professional samples (often drawn from North American alumni associations). This type of sampling provides for some degree of heterogeneity across employing industries and occupations for protégés but tends to ignore large segments of the workforce, such as clerical workers or service workers. We also know of no studies that have explicitly hypothesized and systematically studied the moderating effects of industry or occupation. We also note that there have been attempts to focus on more homogeneous samples. For example, Mobley, Jaret, Marsh, and Lim (1994) and Riley and Wrench (1985) studied mentoring-outcome relationships among U.S.-based lawyers; Prevosto (2001) studied U.S. Army reserve nurses; and Kirchmeyer (2005) studied U.S. professors. While this work is useful from the external validity perspective, it does not provide for a theory-based framework for understanding how the strength of mentoring-outcome relationships may be sensitive to the types of firms, occupations, and industries within which protégés pursue their careers. Here again, research designs, and also new theoretical typologies, are needed. We summarize the set of conceptual and methodological issues discussed in this chapter in Table 3.2.

Specifying Mediating Processes and Moderator Effects

Mentoring's Influence on Protégé Career Trajectories: Five Paths

In the previous section on research design issues, we mentioned the difficulty of interpreting direction of causality in cross-sectional research on mentoring and protégé outcomes. Causal inferences about the positive effects of mentoring would be more defensible if the mechanisms through which mentoring is proposed to affect career outcomes were to become the focus of empirical investigations. That is, while the suggested studies may still be dominated by cross-sectional field studies, it would be more persuasive to argue for the positive effects of mentoring if a new class of criterion variables were shown to be correlated with mentoring experiences. Ramaswami and Dreher (in press) have proposed frameworks for understanding the intermediate linkages between mentoring experiences and career outcomes (for both the protégé and the mentor). They show five paths through which mentoring relationships can influence the career trajectory of a protégé.

Table 3.2   Summary of Key Conceptual and Methodological Issues in Studies of Mentoring and Protégé Career Outcomes

Definitional Variability	No definitions of mentor and mentoring
	Vague definitions of mentor and mentoring
	Narrow/exclusive definitions of mentor and mentoring
Criterion Limitations	Need to focus more attention on:
	• Extraorganizational functioning and satisfaction
	• Positive relationships at work
	• Negative/unintentional effects of mentoring
	• The organizational perspective
	• Effective talent pool management
Internal Validity Problems	Ambiguous direction of causality
	Alternative/third-variable explanation of relationships
Method Variance Inflation	Consistency motif
	Illusory correlations and implicit theories
	Social desirability effects
	Positive/negative affectivity
External Validity Constraints	Interaction of selection and treatment (mentoring)
	Interaction of setting and treatment

Each path provides insight into what needs to be included in this new class of criterion variables. In what follows, we summarize the central tenets of the Ramaswami and Dreher protégé model and comment on some key moderator variables that have not received sufficient research attention.

Human Capital Path

Here, a variety of mentoring functions (i.e., providing challenging assignments, coaching, and role-modeling) could serve to enhance the capability of the protégé. The human capital path addresses the acquisition of job-related knowledge, skills, and abilities (KSAs) that ultimately should enhance the protégé's performance on the job. This, in turn, would be expected to contribute to an assortment of career-oriented benefits (e.g., increased salary and hierarchical advancement). What are needed are research designs that allow for the simultaneous examination of the structural paths making the connections between the various mentoring functions, protégé KSA acquisition, job performance, and career attainment and success. Even if these designs were not longitudinal, they would contribute to the literature. We know of no studies that have simultaneously examined the entirety of the human capital path. In fact, we know of only one study that has examined a component of this path. Ostroff and Kozlowski (1993) found that newly hired employees with mentors had more knowledge about the technical and organizational attributes of their business units than workers without mentors.

Movement Capital Path

A second way a mentor can enhance the career success of a protégé is to provide the protégé with information about the range of intra- and interorganizational opportunities that may exist in a labor market. The distinction between human capital and movement capital is subtle. While movement capital can be represented by increased knowledge (in this case, knowledge about labor market attributes), this knowledge has little to do with direct forms of performance enhancement. Movement capital helps the protégé to become more aware of available opportunity in the labor market. The link to career outcomes comes through a better match between capability and position requirements. Improvements in human capital prove useful because job performance is improved, even when holding position requirements constant. Past studies have shown that labor market mobility is related to career attainment, at least for male managers and professionals (Brett & Stroh, 1997; Dreher & Cox, 2000; Lam & Dreher, 2004). Although a few studies have addressed components of this path by considering the relationships between mentoring and organizational commitment, turnover, and perceived job opportunities (e.g., Barker, Monks, & Buckley, 1999; Mobley et al., 1994; Payne & Huffman, 2005; Prevosto, 2001), none has considered the entirety of the path. To do so would require looking at mentoring and mobility from a career perspective, not from the perspective of a particular job or organization.

Social Capital Path

At the heart of the social capital path is the increased degree of exposure and visibility for the protégé that is purported to be associated with establishing a relationship with a mentor. The *human capital path* involves changes in the protégé's capacity to perform work assignments; the *movement capital path* involves changes in the protégé's knowledge about labor market opportunity; and the *social capital path* involves changes in relationships that make powerful decision makers more knowledgeable about the protégé's potential. Hard work, talent, and perseverance would seem to be necessary attributes for success for individuals pursuing hierarchical career advancement. However, talent and hard work alone would not seem to be sufficient for career progress. Powerful decision makers must become aware of talented individuals before they can act to utilize this talent. Kram's (1985) mentoring functions of *sponsorship, exposure and visibility,* and *protection* seem well suited to help protégés make connections and become part of the professional networks of high-level decision makers. Note, the key theme here is not that mentors change the capability levels of their protégés; it is that mentors make senior-level decision makers aware of protégé attributes. There would seem to be a variety of ways mentors can help protégés in this way. One is by carefully placing the protégé in situations that will bring the protégé and senior-level managers and executives into direct contact. Of course, this must be orchestrated such that the protégé is prepared and ready to behave in ways that will impress the more-senior manager—that is, the protégé should not be placed in situations that provide a reasonable likelihood of failure.

Other ways to help the protégé could take the form of explicit sponsorship. Here, the mentor could work behind the scenes (note that in this situation, the protégé may not have direct knowledge of the mentor's behavior) in promoting the protégé's interests. Nominating a protégé for a key promotion or work assignment or building the case for a protégé during a meeting of a talent pool committee represent examples of behind-the-scene mentor behavior that could alter the career trajectory of the protégé. Again, in this case, the actual behavior or capability level of the protégé is not affected in any direct way.

The preferred way to examine processes associated with the acquisition of social capital would be for researchers to directly gather information about mentor behavior. This is the preferred way because protégés are often not good sources for this type of information. While protégés can describe a wide range of mentor behaviors, they are not always able to observe or be informed of what the mentor does on their behalf when interacting with senior managers. Therefore, ways of measuring mentor behavior that go beyond using protégé ratings and descriptions of mentor behavior should be used and then combined with data about protégé career success. We are not aware of any empirical research that has addressed this class of questions in this particular way.

Another way to address the social capital path is to explicitly examine the role of sponsorship and related mentor functions in fully estimated social capital/career success models. The best example of this approach is the study by Seibert, Kraimer, and Liden (2001). These researchers proposed a model of social capital effects on career success and then empirically tested it using a sample of business and engineering alumni. They used eight career sponsorship items from Dreher and Ash's (1990) global mentoring scale. Interestingly, their results showed that the structural properties of social networks and the nature of the resources embedded in these networks were antecedent to the role of career sponsorship in explaining career success. That is, career sponsorship partially mediated the relationships between network properties and three measures of career success. We would encourage future researchers to consider in more detail the linkages between the functions of mentoring and the properties of protégés' social networks. These studies also should take into account the notion of a developmental network (Higgins & Kram, 2001). The establishment of networks of diverse developers and mentors would likely have a more powerful effect on the properties of protégés' social networks than would the establishment of a single or primary mentoring relationship.

Path-Goal Clarity

In addition to helping protégés develop job-related capability, organizational knowledge, and social networks, mentors may influence protégés' sense of self-efficacy and other motivational states that could enhance career success. A study by Day and Allen (2004) is an excellent example of research that has considered the effects of career self-efficacy and career motivation on the relationships between mentoring functions and subjective and objective career outcomes. Additional research designs that consider the relationships between the various functions of mentoring and motivational states, such as self-efficacy, expectancy, and instrumentality perceptions, would enhance our understanding of this important mediating process. While the human capital path focuses on the development of enhanced capability, this path focuses on the motivation to aggressively pursue career objectives.

Values Clarity Path

By focusing on acceptance and confirmation, counseling, and friendship, mentoring relationships can provide the protégé with the opportunity to reflect on and make career and life choices within the context of guidance and feedback from a more experienced individual. According to Schulz (1995), protégés can use their mentors to test ideas about what constitutes realistic career goals and to think through whether a current employing organization can support these goals. In addition, discussions with mentors can prove useful when protégés attempt to clarify the centrality of work and career relative to other personal and family-oriented life goals. To the degree to which goal and value clarification contributes to making sound personal and career-oriented decisions, mentoring activities related to this path should contribute to life and career satisfaction. While some research has addressed criterion variables of the career satisfaction and career commitment variety (e.g., Aryee, Wyatt, & Stone, 1996; Collarelli & Bishop, 1990; Ragins, Cotton, & Miller, 2000), we know of no studies that have explicitly addressed the linkages between mentoring, value clarification and change, life planning, and life and career satisfaction.

Moderator Variables

Ramaswami and Dreher's model (in press) also proposes that key moderator variables must be taken into account if one is to understand which (if any) causal path is activated and whether or not a mentoring relationship is of sufficient quality to trigger proposed cognitive, affective, or behavior responses. They speculate that mentoring quality can be defined in terms of mentor attributes. Here, the focus is on aspects such as (a) mentor knowledge about organizational politics and culture, (b) mentor knowledge about protégés' chosen career paths, (c) mentor skill as a trainer and developer, (d) mentor motivation and opportunity to provide developmental assistance, and (e) mentor power and hierarchical position. We concur with their assessment and would like to add another likely key condition of mentoring quality. Here, high-quality mentoring is likely to be a function of the mentor's ability to accurately perceive what a protégé most needs and then being able to deliver protégé-specific developmental solutions. While this discussion suggests that these variables would be examined by introducing appropriate cross-product terms when conducting data analyses, in reality, this class of variables represents yet another way of defining the mentoring construct.

We encourage researchers to devise ways of combining these dimensions of mentor attributes into overall measures of mentoring quality and then using these measures as the independent variables of interest. That is, low scores would represent no or very-low-quality mentoring, and high scores would represent mentoring relationships of the highest quality. The use of measures of mentoring quality (versus presence or absence of a mentor) should produce mentoring-career outcome effect sizes much larger than those reported in the literature to date.

Concluding Comments

In this chapter, our goal was to discuss "where we have been" in the study of mentoring and protégé career outcomes and to explore a variety of ideas about directions for future research. We first provided an overview of the results of research on mentoring and protégé subjective and objective career success, and a summary of key characteristics of these studies. There are some clear boundary conditions of this literature, in terms of samples, contexts, and variables studied. We next addressed conceptual issues, beginning with a survey of the wide variety of definitions of *mentor* and *mentoring* in the research literature, agreeing with other recent recommendations for an approach to defining mentoring that allows for capturing a broad range of developmental relationships, while also specifying the particular types of relationships being studied. We also emphasized the need to consider an expanded set of outcomes for protégés, especially extraorganizational functioning, and outcomes of mentoring for organizations. We then reviewed key methodological constraints in the literature, relating to internal validity, methods bias, and external validity, and underscored needed improvements in the methodologies of future studies. Finally, we emphasized that this literature is notably deficient in conceptualizing and investigating *intermediate linkages* in the relationship of mentoring with protégé career success, providing a number of ideas about the avenues by which a mentor can influence a protégé's career trajectory. Throughout the chapter, we have attempted to stimulate the reader's thinking about where we have been, where we need to go, and how we might get there in studying mentoring and its vital role for protégés' subjective and objective career success.

References

Allen, T. D., Eby, L. T., Poteet, M. L., Lentz, E., & Lima, L. (2004). Career benefits associated with mentoring for protégés: A meta-analysis. *Journal of Applied Psychology, 89,* 127–136.

Allen, T. D., Poteet, M. L., & Russell, J. E. A. (2000). Protégé selection by mentors: What makes the difference? *Journal of Organizational Behavior, 21,* 271–282.

Aryee, S., & Chay, Y. W. (1994). An examination of the impact of career-oriented mentoring on work commitment attitudes and career satisfaction among professional and managerial employees. *British Journal of Management, 5,* 241–249.

Aryee, S., Lo, S., & Kang, I. L. (1999). Antecedents of early career stage mentoring among Chinese employees. *Journal of Organizational Behavior, 20,* 563–576.

Aryee, S., Wyatt, T., & Stone, R. (1996). Early career outcomes of graduate employees: The effect of mentoring and ingratiation. *Journal of Management Studies, 33,* 95–118.

Barker, P., Monks, K., & Buckley, F. (1999). The role of mentoring in the career progression of chartered accountants. *British Accounting Review, 31,* 297–312.

Baugh, S. G., Lankau, M. J., & Scandura, T. A. (1996). An investigation of the effects of protégé gender on responses to mentoring. *Journal of Vocational Behavior, 49,* 309–323.

Brett, J. M., & Stroh, L. K. (1997). Jumping ship: Who benefits from an external labor market career strategy? *Journal of Applied Psychology, 82,* 331–341.

Burke, R. J., McKenna, C. S., & McKeen, C. A. (1991). How do mentorships differ from typical supervisory relationships? *Psychological Reports, 68,* 459–466.

Campbell, D. T., & Stanley, J. C. (1966). *Experimental and quasi-experimental designs for research.* Boston: Houghton-Mifflin.

Chao, G. T., Walz, P. M., & Gardner, P. D. (1992). Formal and informal mentorships: A comparison of mentoring functions and contrast with nonmentored counterparts. *Personnel Psychology, 45,* 619–636.

Colarelli, S. M., & Bishop, R. C. (1990). Career commitment: Functions, correlates, and management. *Group & Organization Studies, 15,* 158–176.

Corzine, J. B., Buntzman, G. F., & Busch, E. T. (1994). Mentoring, downsizing, gender, and career outcomes. *Journal of Social Behavior and Personality, 9,* 517–528.

Cox, T. H., & Nkomo, S. M. (1991). A race and gender-group analysis of the early career experience of MBAs. *Work and Occupations, 18,* 431–446.

Crowne, D., & Marlowe, D. (1964). *The approval motive: Studies in evaluative dependence.* New York: John Wiley & Sons.

Day, R., & Allen, T. D. (2004). The relationship between career motivation and self-efficacy with protégé career success. *Journal of Vocational Behavior, 64,* 72–91.

Donaldson, S. I., Ensher, E. A., & Grant-Vallone, E. J. (2000). Longitudinal examination of mentoring relationships on organizational commitment and citizenship behavior. *Journal of Career Development, 26,* 233–249.

Dougherty, T. W., Turban, D. B., & Haggard, D. L. (2005). *Definitional issues and implications in the study of naturally-occurring workplace mentoring.* Unpublished manuscript.

Dreher, G. F., & Ash, R. A. (1990). A comparative study of mentoring among men and women in managerial, professional, and technical positions. *Journal of Applied Psychology, 75,* 539–546.

Dreher, G. F., & Chargois, J. A. (1998). Gender, mentoring experiences, and salary attainment among graduates of a historically Black university. *Journal of Vocational Behavior, 53,* 401–416.

Dreher, G. F., & Cox, Jr., T. H. (1996). Race, gender and opportunity: A study of compensation attainment and the establishment of mentoring relationships. *Journal of Applied Psychology, 81,* 297–308.

Dreher, G. F., & Cox, Jr., T. H. (2000). Labor market mobility and cash compensation: The moderating effects of race and gender. *Academy of Management Journal, 43,* 890–900.

Eby, L. T., & McManus, S. E. (2002, April). Protégés' most positive mentoring experience. In R. Day & T. D. Allen (Cochairs), *Underlying processes responsible for beneficial mentorships: Implications of emerging research.* Annual Meeting of the Society for Industrial and Organizational Psychology, Toronto, Canada.

Eby, L. T., McManus, S. E., Simon, S. A., & Russell, J. E. A. (2000). The protégé's perspective regarding negative mentoring experiences: The development of a taxonomy. *Journal of Vocational Behavior, 57,* 1–21.

Ensher, E. A., & Murphy, S. E. (1997). Effects of race, gender, perceived similarity, and contact on mentor relationships. *Journal of Vocational Behavior, 50,* 460–481.

Ensher, E. A., Thomas, C., & Murphy, S. E. (2001). Comparison of traditional, step-ahead, and peer mentoring on protégés' support, satisfaction, and perceptions of career success: A social exchange perspective. *Journal of Business and Psychology, 15,* 415–438.

Fagan, M. M., & Walter, G. (1982). Mentoring among teachers. *Journal of Educational Research, 76*(2), 115.

Fagenson, E. A. (1988). The power of a mentor: Protégés' and non-protégés' perceptions of their own power in organizations. *Group & Organization Studies, 13,* 182–194.

Fagenson, E. A. (1989). The mentor advantage: Perceived career/job experiences of protégés versus non-protégés. *Journal of Organizational Behavior, 10,* 309–320.

Finkelstein, L. M., Allen, T. D., & Rhoton, L. (2003). An examination of the role of age in mentoring relationships. *Group & Organization Management, 28,* 249–281.

Gaskill, L. R., & Sibley, L. R. (1990). Mentoring relationships for women in retailing: Prevalence, perceived importance, and characteristics. *Clothing and Textiles Research Journal, 9*(1), 1–10.

Godshalk, V. M., & Sosik, J. J. (2000). Does mentor-protégé agreement on mentor leadership behavior influence the quality of a mentoring relationship? *Group & Organization Management, 25,* 291–317.

Gonzalez-Figueroa, E., & Young, A. M. (2005). Ethnic identity and mentoring among Latinas in professional roles. *Cultural Diversity and Ethnic Minority Psychology, 11,* 213–226.

Green, S. G., & Bauer, T. N. (1995). Supervisory mentoring by advisors: Relationships with doctoral student potential, productivity, and commitment. *Personnel Psychology, 48,* 537–561.

Hall, D. T., & Mirvis, P. H. (1996). The new protean career: Psychological success and the path with a heart. In D. T. Hall & Associates (Eds.), *The career is dead—Long live the career: A relational approach to careers* (pp. 15–45). San Francisco: Jossey-Bass.

Higgins, M. C., & Kram, K. E. (2001). Reconceptualizing mentoring at work: A developmental network perspective. *Academy of Management Review, 26,* 264–288.

Higgins, M. C., & Thomas, D. A. (2001). Constellations and careers: Toward understanding the effects of multiple developmental relationships. *Journal of Organizational Behavior, 22,* 223–247.

Johnson, W. B., Lall, R., Holmes, E. K., Huwe, J. M., & Nordlund, M. D. (2001). Mentoring experiences among navy midshipmen. *Military Medicine, 166,* 27–31.

Kirchmeyer, C. (1998). Determinants of managerial career success: Evidence and explanation of male/female differences. *Journal of Management, 24,* 673–692.

Kirchmeyer, C. (2002). Change and stability in managers' gender roles. *Journal of Applied Psychology, 87,* 929–939.

Kirchmeyer, C. (2005). The effects of mentoring on academic careers over time: Testing performance and political perspectives. *Human Relations, 58,* 637–660.

Koberg, C. S., Boss, R. W., Chappell, D., & Ringer, R. C. (1994). Correlates and consequences of protégé mentoring in a large hospital. *Group & Organization Management, 19,* 219–239.

Koberg, C. S., Boss, R. W., & Goodman, E. (1998). Factors and outcomes associated with mentoring among health-care professionals. *Journal of Vocational Behavior, 53,* 58–72.

Kram, K. E. (1985). *Mentoring at work: Developmental relationships in organizational life.* Glenview, IL: Scott, Foresman.

Lam, S. K., & Dreher, G. F. (2004). Gender, extra-firm mobility, and compensation attainment in the United States and Hong Kong. *Journal of Organizational Behavior, 25,* 791–805.

Mobley, G. M., Jaret, C., Marsh, K., & Lim, Y. Y. (1994). Mentoring, job satisfaction, gender, and the legal profession. *Sex Roles, 31,* 79–98.

Murphy, S. E., & Ensher, E. A. (2001). The role of mentoring support and self-management strategies on reported career outcomes. *Journal of Career Development, 27,* 229–246.

Noe, R. A. (1988). An investigation of the determinants of successful assigned mentoring relationships. *Personnel Psychology, 41,* 457–479.

Noe, R. A., Greenberger, D. B., & Wang, S. (2002). Mentoring: What we know and where we might go. *Research in Personnel and Human Resources Management, 21,* 129–173.

Olian, J., Carroll, S., Giannantonio, C. M. (1993). Mentor reactions to protégés: An experiment with managers. *Journal of Vocational Behavior, 43,* 266–278.

Orpen, C. (1995). The effects of mentoring on employees' career success. *Journal of Social Psychology, 135,* 667–668.

Ostroff, C., & Kozlowski, S. W. (1993). The role of mentoring in the information gathering processes of newcomers during early organizational socialization. *Journal of Vocational Behavior, 42,* 170–183.

Payne, S. C., & Huffman, A. H. (2005). A longitudinal examination of the influence of mentoring on organizational commitment and turnover. *Academy of Management Journal, 48,* 158–168.

Podsakoff, P. M., MacKenzie, S. B., Lee, J. Y., & Podsakoff, N. P. (2003). Common method biases in behavioral research: A critical review of the literature and recommended remedies. *Journal of Applied Psychology, 88,* 879–903.

Podsakoff, P. M., & Organ, D. W. (1986). Self-reports in organizational research: Problems and prospects. *Journal of Management, 12,* 69–82.

Prevosto, P. (2001). The effect of mentored relationships on satisfaction and intent to stay of company-grade U.S. Army reserve nurses. *Military Medicine, 166,* 21–26.

Ragins, B. R. (1999). Where do we go from here and how do we get there? Methodological issues in conducting research on diversity and mentoring relationships. In A. Murrell, F. J. Crosby, & R. Ely (Eds.), *Mentoring dilemmas: Developmental relationships within multicultural organizations* (pp. 227–247). Mahwah, NJ: Lawrence Erlbaum.

Ragins, B. R., & Cotton, J. L. (1999). Mentor functions and outcomes: A comparison of men and women in formal and informal mentoring relationships. *Journal of Applied Psychology, 84,* 529–550.

Ragins, B. R., Cotton, J. L., & Miller, J. S. (2000). Marginal mentoring: The effects of type of mentor, quality of relationship, and program design on work and career attitudes. *Academy of Management Journal, 43,* 1177–1194.

Ragins, B. R., & McFarlin, D. B. (1990). Perceptions of mentor roles in cross-gender mentor relationships. *Journal of Vocational Behavior, 37,* 321–340.

Ragins, B. R., & Verbos, A. K. (2007). Positive relationships in action: Relational mentoring and mentoring schemas in the workplace. In J. E. Dutton & B. R. Ragins (Eds.), *Exploring positive relationships at work: Building a theoretical and research foundation* (pp. 91–116). Mahwah, NJ: Lawrence Erlbaum.

Ramaswami, A., & Dreher, G. F. (2007). The benefits associated with workplace mentoring relationships. In T. D. Allen & L. T. Eby (Eds.), *Blackwell handbook of mentoring: A multiple perspectives approach* (pp. 211–231). Malden, MA: Blackwell.

Ramaswami, A., Huang, J., & Dreher, G. F. (2005, June). *Career attainment among Taiwanese professionals: The role of mentoring and cultural values.* Paper presented at the 8th Conference on International Human Resource Management, Cairns, Australia.

Riley, S., & Wrench, D. (1985). Mentoring among women lawyers. *Journal of Applied Social Psychology, 15,* 374–386.

Scandura, T. A. (1992). Mentorship and career mobility: An empirical investigation. *Journal of Organizational Behavior, 13,* 169–174.

Scandura, T. A., & Schriesheim, C. A. (1994). Leader-member exchange and supervisor career mentoring as complementary constructs in leadership research. *Academy of Management Journal, 37,* 1588–1602.

Scandura, T. A., & Williams, E. A. (2004). Mentoring and transformational leadership: The role of supervisory career mentoring. *Journal of Vocational Behavior, 65,* 448–468.

Schulz, S. F. (1995). The benefits of mentoring. In M. W. Galbraith & N. H. Cohen (Eds.), *Mentoring: New strategies and challenges* (Vol. 66, pp. 57–68). San Francisco: Jossey-Bass.

Seibert, S. (1999). The effectiveness of facilitated mentoring: A longitudinal quasi-experiment. *Journal of Vocational Behavior, 54,* 483–502.

Seibert, S. E., Kraimer, M. L., & Liden, R. C. (2001). A social capital theory of career success. *Academy of Management Journal, 44,* 219–237.

Sosik, J. J., & Godshalk, V. M. (2000). Leadership style, mentoring functions received, and job-related stress: A conceptual model and preliminary study. *Journal of Organizational Behavior, 21,* 365–390.

Sosik, J. J., & Godshalk, V. M. (2004). Self-other rating agreement in mentoring: Meeting protégé expectations for development and career advancement. *Group & Organization Management, 29,* 442–469.

Tepper, B. J. (1995). Upward maintenance tactics in supervisory mentoring and nonmentoring relationships. *Academy of Management Journal, 38,* 1191–1205.

Tharenou, P. (2005). Does mentor support increase women's career advancement more than men's? The differential effects of career and psychosocial support. *Australian Journal of Management, 30,* 77–110.

Turban, D. B., & Dougherty, T. W. (1994). Role of protégé personality in receipt of mentoring and career success. *Academy of Management Journal, 37,* 688–702.

Wallace, J. E. (2001). The benefits of mentoring for female lawyers. *Journal of Vocational Behavior, 58,* 366–391.

Wanberg, C. R., Welsh, E. T., & Hezlett, S. A. (2003). Mentoring research: A review and dynamic process model. *Research in Personnel and Human Resources Management, 22,* 39–124.

Waters, L., McCabe, M., Kiellerup, D., & Kiellerup, S. (2002). The role of formal mentoring on business success and self-esteem in participants of a new business start-up program. *Journal of Business and Psychology, 17,* 107–121.

Wayne, S. J., Liden, R. C., Kraimer, M. L., & Graf, I. K. (1999). The role of human capital, motivation, and supervisor sponsorship in predicting career success. *Journal of Organizational Behavior, 20,* 577–595.

Whitely, W. T., & Coetsier, P. (1993). The relationship of career mentoring to early career outcomes. *Organization Studies, 14,* 419–441.

Whitely, W., Dougherty, T. W., & Dreher, G. F. (1991). Relationship of career mentoring and socioeconomic origin to managers' and professionals' early career progress. *Academy of Management Journal, 34,* 331–351.

4

Mentoring as a Forum for Personal Learning in Organizations

Melenie J. Lankau

Terri A. Scandura

T he reality of today's organizations involves unprecedented change in the way employees experience work. Advancements in technology and education, increases in competition and diversity of the workforce, downsizing, restructuring, mergers, and acquisitions are requiring organizations to rely more on human capital to adapt to these changes in the workplace. This has increased demands on individuals for self-development, flexibility, and change. The ability to learn, unlearn, and relearn are now indispensable (Arthur & Rousseau, 1996; Hall, 1996). Learning from training programs and books will not be sufficient to keep pace with required competencies for success in today's fast-paced work environment. Individuals often must look to others to learn new skills and keep up with the demands of their jobs and professions. Mentoring relationships can serve as a forum for such personal learning in organizations.

Somewhat surprisingly, the link between mentoring and learning is relatively new in the mentoring literature. The field apparently assumed that individuals learn from mentoring and has focused more on outcomes such as job attitudes and career progress. The purpose of this chapter is to review the emerging research on mentoring and learning and develop a typology of personal learning in developmental relationships to guide future research. We also propose that future research on personal learning adopt a needs-based contextual approach to obtain a more fine-grained understanding of the types of developmental relationships best suited to specific learning needs demanded by different situations. We offer a process model of antecedents, moderators, and outcomes of personal learning derived from developmental relationships to highlight variables for mentoring researchers to consider in future studies. To illustrate the needs-based contextual approach, we present research questions for mentoring and personal learning for three important organizational challenges: (a) building a learning organization, (b) developing future leaders, and (c) strengthening diversity competencies among employees.

Defining Personal Learning

Research interests on individual learning in the management literature have generally focused on how employees acquire technical job knowledge and declarative and procedural information about their organizations. However, complex changes in the nature of work over the past two decades have resulted in the need for employees to develop the capacity for continuous learning (Mirvis & Hall, 1996). It is no longer sufficient to examine employee learning as it relates to a particular job or role within a specific context.

In the adult learning literature, significant learning involves personal development and change in behavior, attitudes, or even the dispositions of the learner (Rogers, 1983). Personal development is characterized by transformations in how we see ourselves in relation to others and includes sophisticated interpersonal skills (Merriam & Heuer, 1996). Such development is an essential element of learning how to learn, which results in employability and job security for employees and competitive advantage for organizations (Ellinger, 2004; Hall, 2002).

To further clarify the distinctions among the types of learning employees are experiencing in the workplace, we introduce a 2 × 2 typology in Figure 4.1 based on Hall's (2002) dimensions of career effectiveness. In Hall's model, four types of career effectiveness were delineated based on a task focus versus self- and personal development focus in conjunction with short-term versus long-term time orientation. A focus on task challenges in the short term was associated with career effectiveness in job performance. A task challenge focus over the long term was associated with adaptability. Personal development in the short term was associated with career effectiveness (in the form of job attitudes), and a focus on personal development in the long term was associated with career identity. Hall (2002) utilized these dimensions to describe different career effectiveness outcomes.

We apply the same two dimensions of task/personal focus and short-term/long-term time orientation to differentiate four types of learning outcomes in mentoring relationships. In addition, we associate a short-term time orientation with context-specific learning, which refers to the type of learning that is tied to a specific job or role in an organization. In contrast, a long-term time orientation is characterized as context-free because the learning can be generalized or utilized across organizational boundaries. A learning focus on how to perform tasks associated with a role in a specific organizational context (short-term orientation) results in organizational socialization as a learning outcome. *Socialization* is broadly defined

	Short-Term Context-Specific	**Long-Term Context-Free**
Task/Role Learning	Organizational Socialization	Professional Socialization
Personal Learning	Personal Skill Development and Relational Job Learning	Personal Identity Growth and Personal Adaptability

Figure 4.1   A Typology of Learning Outcomes

as information acquisition about various aspects of organizational life, such as performance standards, important people in the organization, organization goals and values, and jargon (Bauer, Morrison, & Callister, 1998; Chao, O'Leary-Kelly, Wolf, Klein, & Gardner, 1994). A learning focus on tasks associated with a role that applies to various organizational contexts over time represents *professional socialization* (see Chao, Chapter 7, this volume). This is learning about the broader set of expectations, skills, behaviors, and performance demands associated with a particular profession.

Personal development in the short term, meaning that the personal learning is gained in a specific organizational context, is referred to as *personal skill development* and *relational job learning*. Personal skill development is acquisition of new skills and abilities that enable better working relationships within an organization. Relational job learning is increased understanding about the interdependence of one's job with others' roles in the organization. This form of personal learning was identified by Lankau and Scandura (2002) and will be covered in more detail in the literature review that follows.

A personal learning focus that transcends a particular organizational context and is developed and applied over time is associated with personal identity growth and personal adaptability (Hall, 2002). *Personal identity growth* is learning about one's strengths and deficiencies and involves not only knowing about oneself but also how to learn about oneself. *Personal adaptability* is the capacity to change and involves learning how to develop a diverse set of role behaviors to respond effectively to constantly changing environmental conditions. Hall (2002) identified identity and adaptability as metacompetencies required for continuous learning. We refer to this type of personal learning as *personal growth*.

Mentoring relationships represent an important forum to facilitate all forms of learning we have identified in this typology. Mentors have been examined as socialization agents and a source of information in the socialization process (Allen, McManus, & Russell, 1999; Ostroff & Kozlowski, 1993). A research review of mentoring and socialization is covered in detail by Chao, in Chapter 7 of this handbook. The major distinction between socialization (organizational and professional) and personal learning is the emphasis on individual development. The objective of socialization is "know how," whereas the objective behind personal learning is the ability to "learn how" (Hall, 2002). The purpose of this chapter is to focus on how mentoring contributes to personal learning. *Personal learning* can be defined as the acquisition of knowledge, skills, or competencies that contribute to an individual's personal development (Kram, 1996). We will address the learning associated with the two lower cells in Figure 4.1, since they are related to personal learning and growth. Next, we will present a summary of what we currently know about the link between mentoring and personal learning.

Personal Learning in Mentoring Relationships: A Research Update

Kram's (1985) seminal work based on qualitative interviews with 18 mentor-protégé dyads was the first to characterize the mentoring process and provide insight into how mentoring relationships facilitate personal learning. Kram identified two broad functions of mentoring relationships: career and psychosocial functions. *Career functions* include sponsorship, exposure and visibility, coaching, protection, and challenging work assignments. Kram stated that the first four of these provide opportunities for protégé advancement, but the challenging assignments are what enable the protégé to gain the skills necessary to take advantage of opportunities. Further, she suggested that mentors play a critical role in the learning process by designing assignments and providing ongoing support and critical feedback on performance.

Kram (1985) observed that *psychosocial functions* shape the quality of the interpersonal relationship and include activities such as role-modeling, acceptance and confirmation, counseling, and friendship. Through these activities, protégés increase their sense of competence, effectiveness, and self-worth. The concerns that are addressed by the psychosocial functions extend beyond organizational advancement to include "the individual's relationship with self and with significant others both within and outside the organization" (Kram, 1985, p. 32). Kram specifically stated that through a conscious modeling process, the protégé learns approaches, attitudes, and values held by his or her mentor. This learning then shapes the protégé's own style, values, and professional identity. Kram even noted that the role-modeling process can result in mentors rediscovering valued parts of themselves; in essence, mentors also learn from these relationships. Kram also explained how the mentor's acceptance and confirmation in the relationship can support learning by enabling the protégé to experiment with new behaviors. Rather than focus on conformity, protégés feel secure to explore self-differentiation in their roles in the organizational world. In addition,

Kram highlighted how counseling behaviors, serving as a sounding board, sharing personal experiences, and helping resolve problems through feedback, enable the protégé to cope with personal problems more effectively.

Kram's (1985) work showed that the type of learning that can result from mentoring is not restricted to technical expertise, but can be much more comprehensive and include development in professional and personal ways. However, very little research attention was devoted to personal learning as a process or outcome in the mentoring literature. Instead, the majority of early research on mentoring focused on mentoring functions and career outcomes. Yet mentoring functions implicitly represent the learning process, with the mentor serving as a teacher and guide and the protégé serving as the learner. Hence, research has examined relationships between mentoring functions, job attitudes, and job performance without explicit understanding of "what" is learned or "how" mentors and protégés engage in learning, resulting in a "black-box" approach that focused on inputs and outcomes more than processes.

While the mentoring literature has flourished over the past 20 years, only a small number of articles (less than 15) have included a specific focus on personal learning or personal growth. These articles can be organized into two distinct categories. The first category includes literature suggesting how mentoring can be utilized to help employees adapt to change and also how changing organizational conditions affect mentoring. These articles are mostly exploratory or prescriptive and will be briefly summarized, since learning was not directly measured. The second category of work includes four studies that have directly examined the link between mentoring and personal learning. A complete listing of the articles on mentoring and personal learning and their main contributions are provided in Table 4.1.

Organizational Change, Mentoring, and Learning

Several articles have suggested that mentoring may help employees learn to cope with stressful change situations in organizations. Kram and Hall (1989) conducted an exploratory investigation of managers and engineers of a company being downsized, and Scandura and Siegel (1995) studied developmental relationships in the merger of two accounting firms. Both studies concluded that mentoring could improve adjustment to organizational change by helping employees learn skills associated with adaptability, flexibility, and coping with uncertainty.

Several articles have emphasized how environmental and organizational changes drastically alter mentoring relationships. Both Kram and Hall (1996) and Clawson (1996) discuss how learning in mentoring relationships will be more reciprocal, such that protégés may be coaching mentors on new technologies, how to cope with rapid change, the perspectives of a younger generation, and how to appropriately mentor individuals of a gender or race different from the mentor's.

Kram (1996) introduced the notion that mentoring relationships that have the capacity to produce personal learning (i.e., new competencies and an enhanced sense of identity) are markedly different from traditional mentoring relationships. She explained that traditional models of career development view growth as a process of individuation. In this framework, individuals move from a stage of dependency on others to one of independence. Based on relational models of

Table 4.1 Summary of Literature on Mentoring and Personal Learning

I. Organizational Change, Mentoring, and Personal Learning Articles

Author(s)	Article Focus on Personal Learning	General Comments and Contributions of Article
Kram & Hall (1989)	Learning to cope with major organizational change is suggested as an outcome of mentoring.	• Survey of 161 managers and engineers of a manufacturing company being reorganized and downsized. • Perceptions of stressful or poor working conditions positively associated with interest in building mentoring alliances.
Scandura & Siegel (1995)	Learning is addressed as a process in which employees learn to adjust to change.	• Study of 34 developmental relationships in two international public accounting firms that had recently merged. • Employees reported increased stress and uncertainty as a result of the merger and valued psychosocial support more than career support from mentors during this time. • Conceptual model offered whereby changes in organizational context increase learning requirements. Mentoring is posited as a means to reduce stress and frustration, lower absenteeism and turnover, and improve employee adjustment. • An organizational culture characterized by a more open and structured communication process is offered as moderating the relationship between mentoring and outcomes during stressful times.
Kram & Hall (1996)	The focus on learning is on how mentors can become colearners by gaining work meaning and experiencing career growth.	• Book chapter describing how environmental conditions alter the nature of mentoring relationships. • Mentors have opportunities to learn from protégés. • Different forms of relationships (e.g., peers, work teams, and mentoring circles) can foster task and personal learning.
Clawson (1996)	The focus on learning is a discussion of how the content of what is learned in mentoring relationships will change due to the "Information Age" and emphasis that learning will be reciprocal in work-based relationships.	• Prescriptive article that proposes that nature of mentoring relationships will change due to shifts in business characterized by new "Information Age." • Mentors and protégés will develop greater respect for and tolerance of people from different cultures and learn how to develop and maintain balance between work and family.

Author(s)	Article Focus on Personal Learning	General Comments and Contributions of Article
Kram (1996)	Personal learning is referred to as an enhanced sense of identity and development of new competencies.	• Book chapter that suggests that mentoring relationships characterized by interdependence, mutuality, and reciprocity have the capacity to produce personal learning. • To foster personal learning, individuals need specific skills such as self-reflection, self-disclosure, active listening, empathy, and feedback.
Eby (1997)	Learning is referred to as job-related skill development and career-related skill development.	• Article offers a comprehensive typology of alternative forms of mentoring and posits which forms may contribute to job-related skill development and which forms may contribute to career-related skill development. • Discusses how forms of mentoring could be useful for specific learning needs required in situations of domestic relocation, international relocation, and surviving downsizing.
Higgins & Kram (2001)	Personal learning is referred to as an umbrella term that includes the learning outcomes of increased clarity of professional identity; increased clarity of personal values, strengths, and weaknesses; and increased awareness of developmental needs.	• Authors propose a typology of developmental networks based on two dimensions drawn from social network theory and methods: (1) diversity of individual's developmental networks and (2) strength of relationships within the networks. • Two networks are proposed to affect personal learning as an outcome. Entrepreneurial networks are likely to foster highest level of personal learning, while opportunistic networks are posited to be detrimental to personal learning.
De Janasz, Sullivan, & Whiting (2003)	Learning is referred to as a process of "knowing why" (people's beliefs and identities), "knowing how" (knowledge and skills), and "knowing whom" (networks or relationships).	• Authors provide recommendations on how executives can build and utilize a network of mentors to develop important competencies for career success and satisfaction. • Authors propose that executives will need a diverse network of multiple mentors to assist them in continuous learning and development of new expertise.
Hamilton & Scandura (2003)	Learning is referred to as a process and outcome that can be enhanced by the use of e-mentoring.	• Prescriptive article that differentiates e-mentoring as a form of mentoring and explains ways in which e-mentoring can enhance learning. • E-mentoring is proposed to enable more honest feedback and openness in sharing information than face-to-face communication.

(Continued)

Table 4.1 (Continued)

Author(s)	Article Focus on Personal Learning	General Comments and Contributions of Article
		• E-mentoring can facilitate the management of a network of mentors or help a team leader support the learning among team members. • E-mentoring can be used to more effectively share information on interpersonal and organizational aspects of job.

II. Empirical Studies of Personal Learning

Author(s)	Article Focus on Personal Learning	General Comments and Contributions of Article
Dymock (1999)	Learning is exemplified as broader understanding of company's operations and policies, information on how to deal with practical management issues, and personal development in terms of improved self-confidence and organizational skills.	• Interviews of six pairs of mentors and protégés involved in a formal program in an Australian company. • Author found that mentors and protégés reported learning. • Conclusion was that mentoring relationships can contribute to the development of a learning organization through facilitating the sharing of organizational knowledge and by encouraging professional and personal growth.
Lankau & Scandura (2002)	Personal learning is identified as consisting of relational job learning and personal skill development.	• A 12-item measure of personal learning was created, with 6 items assessing relational job learning and 6 items assessing personal skill development. • In a sample of hospital employees, the authors investigated the relationships between mentoring functions and personal learning dimensions and whether personal learning mediated the relationship between mentoring functions and job attitudes of job satisfaction, role ambiguity, intention to leave, and actual turnover.

Author(s)	Article Focus on Personal Learning	General Comments and Contributions of Article
Allen & Eby (2003)	Learning is addressed as an indicator of relationship effectiveness for mentors.	• Authors suggest that mentors can gain information and knowledge about technology and other levels of organization, as well as grow personally through mentoring others. • Mentorship type (formal vs. informal), gender similarity, perceived similarity, and mentorship duration were hypothesized to affect mentors' reports of relationship quality and learning. • Learning was higher when mentors perceived higher similarity with protégés. Relationship between perceived similarity and learning was stronger for shorter relationships. In formal programs, duration was significantly related to learning. • General five-item learning measure created.
Hirschfeld, Thomas, & Lankau (2006)	Motivational orientations are examined as predictors of extent of personal learning experienced by mentors and protégés.	• Data collected from 61 mentor-protégé dyads in formal program. • Lankau & Scandura's (2002) personal learning measure was used. • Achievement and avoidance orientations of mentors and protégés were examined. • Results indicated that protégés' orientations affected personal learning, not mentors' motivational orientations.

growth and development (Fletcher, 1996; Jordan, Kaplan, Miller, Stiver, & Surrey, 1991), Kram argued that mentoring relationships characterized by interdependence, mutuality, and reciprocity provide mentors and protégés with an opportunity to gain new understanding of their identities, values, and self-worth (see Chapter 15, by Fletcher & Ragins, this volume).

Several articles have proposed that a single, traditional mentoring relationship can no longer meet the learning needs of employees facing diverse and dynamic organizational contexts and careers. Eby (1997) pointed out that in the context of organizational transitions, individuals need to develop a diversified set of skills that will enable them to be marketable inside (i.e., job-related skills) and outside (i.e., career-related skills) their organizations. She offered a comprehensive typology of alternative forms of mentoring, which included intrateam mentoring, interteam mentoring, coworker mentoring, manager-subordinate mentoring, hierarchical mentoring, external collegial peer mentoring, internal and external sponsor-protégé mentoring, and group professional association mentoring. De Janasz, Sullivan, and Whiting (2003) suggested that executives need multiple mentors to address three critical career competencies: knowing why (people's beliefs and identities), knowing how (knowledge and skills), and knowing whom (networks or relationships). Individuals may need a diverse network of mentors inside the organization, members of professional organizations, executive coaches, friends, and coworkers to assist them in continuous learning and development of new expertise. Hamilton and Scandura (2003) discussed a newly emerging form of mentoring, "e-mentoring," and how this can address some of the barriers to traditional face-to-face mentoring that are emerging from the changing work context (see also Chapter 12, by Ensher & Murphy, this volume). The authors explained how e-mentoring may enhance task and personal learning in several ways. First, electronic communication may enable more honest feedback and openness in sharing information than face-to-face communication. Second, it can facilitate the management of a network of mentors or help a team leader support the learning among team members. Another benefit is that mentors and protégés can utilize computer technology to more effectively share information on the interpersonal and organizational aspects of their jobs, thereby enhancing the learning process in the relationship.

Higgins and Kram (2001) proposed that specific types of developmental networks would affect the extent of personal learning experienced by protégés. They defined *personal learning* as an umbrella term for the outcomes of increased clarity of professional identity; increased clarity of personal values, strengths, and weaknesses; and increased awareness of developmental needs. The authors suggested that individuals with entrepreneurial developmental networks (high range, strong ties) are more likely to experience the highest level of personal learning. Strong-tie relationships are more likely to be associated with higher levels of psychosocial support and characterized by mutual trust, interdependence, and reciprocity. These characteristics are more likely to facilitate learning. In addition, the high level of network diversity of an entrepreneurial network results in a broader range of knowledge that can be obtained about different industries, job, organizations, and markets, which increases opportunities for learning. Interestingly, the authors posited that opportunistic networks (high range, weak ties) may be detrimental to personal learning, since weak ties do not enable developers to evaluate protégés' strengths and weaknesses or become familiar with their developmental needs.

Summary

The literature reviewed above demonstrates that mentoring relationships, in various forms and networks, are critical for individuals to establish and maintain competence in their jobs and successfully manage their careers in a dynamic and complex environment. While these articles identify some general themes about the content of learning, they do not directly examine the process or outcome of personal learning. In the next section, we review the handful of empirical studies that more specifically address "what" personal learning is and the variables that may be antecedents and consequences to this process.

Empirical Investigations of Personal Learning

To date, only four studies have investigated personal learning as an outcome in the form of short-term, context-specific personal learning. Dymock (1999) interviewed six pairs of mentors and mentees involved in a formally structured mentoring program in an Australian company. One of the objectives of the program was to encourage the development of a learning organization culture by allowing people to gain from one another by sharing experience, skills, and knowledge. The researcher was interested in examining whether the program had met that objective. While the interview data provided evidence of task learning (e.g., understanding of the company's operations and policies), the study also found that mentors and protégés reported personal development in terms of improved self-confidence, improved listening skills, and a better understanding of relationships in organizations. Dymock concluded that mentoring relationships can encourage the professional and personal growth of employees.

The seminal empirical investigation on personal learning was conducted by Lankau and Scandura (2002) in a health care setting. A series of studies, including qualitative interviews, content adequacy tests, and field surveys (cross-sectional and longitudinal), resulted in a measure of personal learning that captured the short-term, context-specific aspects of personal skill development and relational job learning (defined above). The researchers then investigated the relationship between protégé status and mentoring functions and the two types of personal learning with a sample of 440 hospital employees. They examined whether personal learning served as a mediating mechanism to explain relationships between mentoring functions and role ambiguity, job satisfaction, turnover intentions, and actual turnover. The results of the study indicated that individuals with mentors reported significantly greater relational job learning (but not personal skill development) compared with respondents without mentors. The career function of mentoring was positively related to relational job learning, and role-modeling was positively related to personal skill development. Individuals who experienced higher levels of both types of personal learning also reported less role ambiguity and higher job satisfaction. Relational job learning was negatively related to intentions to leave, and personal skill development was significantly associated with actual turnover such that employees who reported less personal skill development were more likely to leave the organization. The authors also found support for the role of personal learning as a mediator. Relational job learning fully mediated the relationship between career support and role ambiguity and between career support and job satisfaction. Personal skill development fully mediated the relationship between role-modeling and job satisfaction. The study demonstrated the link between mentoring functions, personal learning, and attitudes and turnover and underscored the importance of personal learning.

Allen and Eby (2003) examined learning from the mentor's perspective. They investigated the effects of mentorship type (formal versus informal), gender similarity, perceived similarity, and mentorship duration on mentors' reports of relationship quality and relationship learning. A five-item measure of relationship learning was created for the purpose of the study and was broader in nature than personal learning, as defined in this chapter, but it did capture elements of personal learning such as gaining new perspective, reciprocal learning, and professional development. The results of the study showed that mentors reported higher levels of learning when perceived to be similar to their protégés.

The final study examined motivational orientations of mentors and protégés as predictors of the personal learning experienced by mentors and protégés in formally assigned relationships. Hirschfeld, Thomas, and Lankau (2006) utilized data collected from 61 mentor-protégé dyads to explore the relationships between achievement and avoidance orientations, mentoring functions, and the extent of personal learning reported by both mentors and protégés. *Achievement orientation* was defined as a propensity to approach the attainment of exceptional competence, and *avoidance orientation* was defined as a propensity to avoid the demonstration of insufficient competence. The results indicated that protégés' levels of achievement orientation were positively related to the personal learning of both parties, while protégés' levels of avoidance orientation were negatively related to the personal learning of their mentors. In addition, the highest level of protégé learning occurred within dyads where both the mentor and protégé were congruent on high achievement orientation. The study provided evidence for personal learning benefits for mentors and suggested that protégés' motivational orientations were critical for both mentor and protégé personal learning.

Summary

The few empirical studies conducted on personal learning provide preliminary evidence that mentoring relationships can contribute to short-term, context-specific personal learning for both protégés and mentors. We now have a measure of personal learning that captures relational job learning and personal skill development, and initial evidence that personal learning matters for employees and organizations. We also know that mentor and protégé characteristics, such as perceived similarity and motivational orientation, affect the extent of personal learning experienced from the relationship. However, there is a notable absence of empirical research on personal learning outcomes of personal identity growth and personal adaptability (long-term, context-free). This absence may be attributable to the difficulty of collecting longitudinal career data on individuals as well as the fact that personal growth and development have only recently emerged as outcomes of interest to mentoring and career researchers. There is much we don't know about the process of facilitating personal learning in mentoring relationships, the content of personal learning, and the consequences associated with personal learning and personal growth. To provide a framework to guide future research on mentoring and personal learning, we introduce a broad model of antecedents, moderators, and outcomes in the next section.

A Process Model for Examining Personal Learning

We believe that an important step for future research on mentoring and personal learning is to adopt a contingency approach. The leadership literature has long recognized that a leader's effectiveness depends on characteristics of the leader, characteristics of the followers, and situational demands. Similarly, the effectiveness of mentoring will depend on the unique learning needs of the protégé, which are determined by the demands of the organization and the ability of and opportunity for a mentor to meet those needs. Until recently, we have largely ignored the learning context of the relationship. We believe that context is an important consideration in determining the type of developmental relationship that may be best suited for meeting the protégé's personal learning needs.

In Figure 4.2, we propose a process model whereby the learning context influences the type of developmental relationships that form, which then affects the type of development most likely to occur in those relationships. In addition, we suggest that characteristics of the developer and learner affect the extent of development functions offered in the relationship. The development functions represent the learning process, and it is through this process that short-term, context-specific personal learning occurs. We also posit that certain developer and learner characteristics may have a direct effect on the level of personal learning experienced. We suggest that personal growth results from personal learning and that the extent to which this transition occurs depends on development functions that enable individuals to process the short-term, context-specific learning to more long-lasting personal growth. In the model, we also identify different individual outcomes for personal learning and personal growth. Next, we provide explanations of the variables in the model and suggest potential research areas for future study.

Learning Context

A needs-driven approach to mentoring recognizes the fact that employees in the workplace are required to engage in continuous learning to keep pace with changes taking place inside and outside the organization. For example, individuals experiencing downsizing, mergers, or switching careers likely have unique learning demands that stem from the situation. Research that takes a needs-driven approach and contingency perspective would focus on identifying the content of those personal learning demands (e.g., what new interpersonal skills have to be developed and

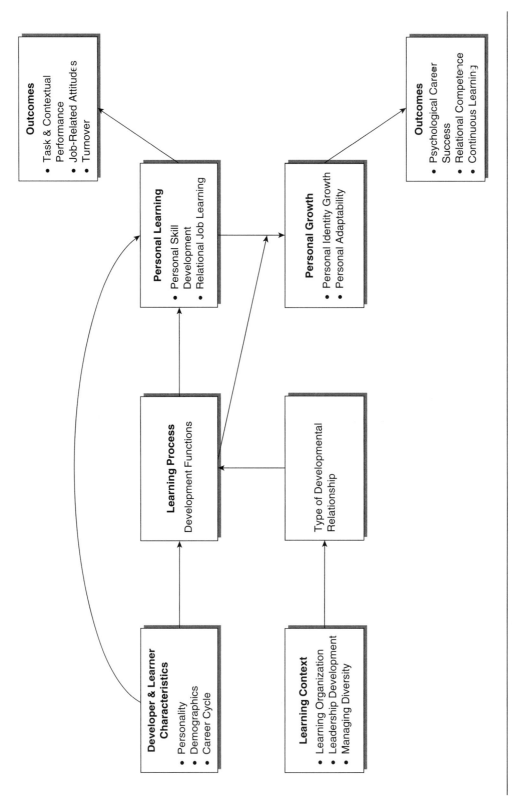

Figure 4.2 A Process Model for Studying Personal Learning

what identity and behavioral changes have to occur) and explore how configurations of mentoring relationships can contribute to that learning.

Recently, Mezias and Scandura (2005) introduced the concept of a needs-driven approach to mentoring in the context of international work assignments. They consider the unique learning needs of employees by identifying specific socialization and development challenges during three stages of expatriate assignments: predeparture, on-site, and repatriation. They propose that the most effective type of mentoring relationship for an individual will depend on the adjustment and development needs associated with each stage of the assignment. Four types of relationships (informal hierarchical, formal hierarchical, informal peer, and formal peer) are offered in the framework, and the importance of multiple relationships is also emphasized.

We propose that researchers follow in the footsteps of Mezias and Scandura (2005) by anchoring investigations of mentoring and personal learning in a specific learning context. We highlight three organizational challenges that require individuals to engage in personal learning: (a) building a learning organization, (b) participating in leadership development for managers, and (c) effectively managing diversity. While numerous situations necessitate employee development (e.g., team-based work or role changes), we chose these particular examples because of their current relevance in organizations and preliminary evidence that mentoring relationships may play an important role in these situations.

While there may be some overlap in the development needs of employees across the three learning contexts, some skills are unique to each situation. For example, employees in a learning organization have to be able to share information and communicate with one another, to reflect on actions and outcomes, to try new and different methods, and to disseminate new knowledge (Nonaka & Takeuchi, 1995). Managers participating in leadership development programs are preparing themselves to effectively engage in leadership roles and processes (Day, 2000; McCauley & Douglas, 1998). Unique learning needs in this context are intrapersonal competence (e.g., self-awareness, self-regulation, and self-motivation) and interpersonal competence (e.g., social awareness and social skills) (Day, 2000). Finally, working effectively with individuals from diverse backgrounds requires development of specific skills and attitudes, such as empathy, cross-cultural communication skills, and openness to diversity (Ragins, 1997; Scandura & Lankau, 1996). Because unique learning demands are associated with each learning context, we posit that the context is an important determinant of the type of developmental relationships that will be most effective.

Type of Developmental Relationships

The notion of a single, traditional, within-organization, hierarchical mentor being able to meet all of a protégé's developmental needs is no longer realistic in today's environment. Researchers now realize that individuals may be involved in a variety of developmental relationships and that the constellation of relationships will change over time as the protégé's learning needs change (Higgins & Kram, 2001). Types of developmental relationship have been differentiated by how they are initiated, hierarchical distance, organizational status, and primary communication method. Relationships can be labeled as informal or formal depending on whether they were initiated spontaneously between the participants or whether an organization (e.g., the employer, a professional association, or a mentoring network) facilitated the arrangement of the relationship. Relationships have also been differentiated by whether the mentor is on the same hierarchical level as the protégé (peer mentoring), one level higher (step-ahead or supervisory mentoring), or two or more levels higher (hierarchical mentoring). Types of mentoring relationships have also been differentiated by whether the mentor is employed in the same organization as the protégé (intraorganizational) or employed by a different organization (extraorganizational). Due to the increasing use of technology, developmental relationships have also recently been differentiated by primary communication method, such as face-to-face mentoring relationships or electronically mediated.

By considering the learning context, it is possible to posit the types of developmental relationships that may be best suited for meeting the protégé's learning needs. For the example of building a learning organization, a major challenge is internal transfer of employees' skills and knowledge of best practices. Successful internal transfer of knowledge is influenced by employees' *social capital*, which has been defined as "the sum of actual and potential resources that are embedded within, available through, and derived from the network of relationships possessed by an individual or social unit" (Nahapiet & Ghoshal, 1998, p. 243). Social capital facilitates knowledge creation and sharing, as it offers valuable knowledge networks and fuels collaboration (Kessels & Poell, 2004). Social capital is characterized by three components: (a) structural, the pattern of relationships found within organizations and the extent to which people are linked together; (b) relational, the quality of the interpersonal connections that organizational actors have with one another; and (c) cognitive, aspects of social capital that provide common representations, understanding, interpretation, and meaning among network members.

Mentoring may facilitate the development of social capital (Thomas & Lankau, 2003). Hierarchical mentoring relationships may have more impact than other types of developmental relationships on the development of structural and cognitive aspects of social capital. With regard to structural capital, hierarchical mentors may be in a better position (i.e., status and authority) to provide protégés with opportunities to work on assignments with people from different departments and hierarchical levels. These new ties (i.e., relationships) may provide access to resources and nonredundant information that enable protégés to share these resources with others in their social networks, thereby enhancing organizational learning. In addition, relationships with high-level senior managers may help protégés acquire shared mental representations and interpretations of organizational issues, thus contributing to the cognitive dimension of social capital (Day, 2000; Swap, Leonard, Shields, & Abrams, 2001).

Peer developmental relationships, however, may have the most influence on developing relational social capital. Relationships characterized by mutual trust and reciprocal social support provide a safe, nonthreatening environment for individuals to strengthen their communication skills, problem-solving skills, and creativity in developing relationships with others (see Chapter 11, this volume, on peer mentoring, by McManus & Russell). Discussions about personal experiences, work challenges, career aspirations, and understanding of the formal and informal systems and processes within the organization contribute to tacit knowledge becoming crystallized and integrated into organizational knowledge (Singh, Bains, & Vinnicombe, 2002). This knowledge then becomes part of the cultural network of the organization and can be accessible to members to assist them in establishing and maintaining productive work relationships, thereby facilitating the development of the relational social capital needed for a learning organization.

For the learning context of leadership development, there are several types of developmental relationships that we predict would play an important and specific role in the process. Feldman and Lankau (2005) discussed the practice of executive coaching and noted its increasing prevalence due to increasing demands for leadership development caused by changes in leadership competencies needed for organizations and the gap in managerial ranks as "baby boomers" retire. They define *executive coaching* as a short- to medium-term developmental relationship between an executive and a consultant for the purpose of improving an executive's work effectiveness. They differentiate executive coaching from a traditional mentoring relationship by explaining that coaches are from outside the organization and the relationships are shorter in duration (typically 6–18 months) and formally contracted rather than informally developed. This type of developmental relationship is particularly useful for leadership development because the executive coach represents an unbiased individual whose sole focus is to assist the participant in recognizing his or her strengths and weaknesses with regard to leadership competencies, to serve as a sounding board for ideas for skill development, and to offer support while the participant engages in developmental activities to improve effectiveness.

For the leadership development process to be successful, a supervisory mentoring relationship may be more critical than other intraorganizational developmental relationships. First, the supervisor represents an important source of information for 360-degree feedback on performance in key leadership behaviors. Second, and more important, participants in a leadership development program will need their supervisors' instrumental and social support for the developmental activities that are established as a result of 360-degree feedback and executive coaching (Maurer, Pierce, & Shore, 2002). From the training literature, we know that the supervisor represents a factor in the work environment that influences whether training affects performance on the job (Becker & Klimoski, 1989). Since a supervisor has such a direct influence on an employee's experience at work, a supervisory mentoring relationship can help create the psychological safety needed for intentional behavioral change (see Chapter 18, by Boyatzis, this volume). The extent to which supervisory mentors help their protégés process the lessons learned from developmental activities, share observations of participants' progress, and reinforce and support behavioral changes the participants want to make may largely determine whether participants improve their leadership skills.

The learning demands for organizations faced with the challenges and opportunities of a diverse workforce involve employees' abilities and skills to communicate and collaborate with people from various demographic and social groups. Thomas and Ely (1996) described an emerging organizational approach to diversity called the "learning-and-effectiveness paradigm," in which equal opportunity is promoted, cultural differences among people are recognized and valued, and experiences that bring new perspectives and knowledge are internalized so that employees can learn and grow from them. It seems reasonable to assert that diversified mentoring relationships (those in which mentors and protégés differ on the basis of group membership, such as race, ethnicity, gender, class, religion, etc.) (Ragins, 1997) and diversified developmental networks in organizations can provide a forum for discussion about identity group differences and implications for the way work gets done, and a way to promote the skills needed for the learning-and-effectiveness paradigm. While training seminars can provide awareness and information about diversity, relational learning experiences such as being specifically mentored to improve one's ability to manage diversity or being involved in a diversified mentoring relationship provide meaningful opportunities to develop and practice diversity-related intrapersonal and interpersonal skills.

The reality, however, is that informal mentoring relationships tend to form on the basis of demographic similarity between the mentor and protégé. Several studies have shown that protégés in diversified relationships (e.g., cross-gender and cross-race) do not experience the same levels of vocational and psychosocial support that protégés in homogeneous relationships report (see Chapter 8, by McKeen & Bujaki, and Chapter 9, by Blake-Beard, Murrell, & Thomas, this volume). For this particular learning context, formal peer or hierarchical mentoring relationships that are intentionally diverse for the specific purpose of enhancing knowledge of and comfort with diverse others may be more effective in meeting these learning needs. A formal mentoring assignment with an explicit focus on diversity skills legitimizes the discussion of how diversity affects relationships and the performance of work in the organization and demonstrates commitment to a learning-and-effectiveness approach to managing diversity. E-mentoring relationships may also be beneficial for this learning context, as researchers have suggested that participants in diversified mentoring relationships may communicate more openly and honestly in computer-mediated communication than in face-to-face relationships (see Chapter 12, by Ensher & Murphy, this volume; Hamilton & Scandura, 2003).

Development Functions

Development functions represent the behaviors that facilitate learning. The mentoring literature has utilized the functions of vocational support, psychosocial support, and, in some cases, role-modeling as a separate function to capture the learning process from the protégé's perspective. Protégés are asked to describe the extent to which mentors provide challenging assignments, coach them, offer social support, and so on. We believe the current measures of mentoring functions are too broad in nature and do not tap into specific types of behaviors that are oriented toward the learning process for both participants in a developmental relationship. In the process model, rather than refer to specific individuals, we use the terms *developer* and *learner* to represent participants' roles in the developmental relationship, as these roles can switch back and forth in any given relationship due to mutuality and reciprocity in the learning process.

Research is needed on the behaviors that developers and learners engage in to facilitate and process their learning for specific learning contexts. In the context of a learning organization, recent qualitative research has suggested that through specific coaching behaviors, managers can facilitate the individual learning needed to create a learning organization. These behaviors include encouraging employees to step out of their own mental frames and into another person's mental frame, exposing employees to different people and business segments within the organization, and sharing different viewpoints with employees so that they could envision different possibilities (Ellinger & Bostrom, 1999).

Feldman and Lankau (2005) discussed four major activities that occur in coaching relationships: data gathering, delivery of feedback, planning and monitoring of developmental activities to meet established developmental objectives, and assessment of the impact of coaching. The authors highlighted the need for research to outline more specific behaviors that are associated with positive coaching. For example, what behaviors help establish trust and empathy in the relationship? What behaviors increase the learner's ownership of the process? What behaviors increase commitment to developmental plans? In Chapter 23 in this handbook, McCauley and Guthrie provide some initial insight into this area by sharing examples of different learning relationship programs. The authors identify several behaviors that facilitate learning about leadership: collaborating with participants to assess and understand learning goals, challenging participants' perceptions of current constraints and helping them explore new possibilities, ensuring accountability, and serving as empathetic companions.

We also know very little about the developmental functions that enable employees to develop their diversity competence. How do you teach someone to be more tolerant to differences and more open to diversity? Can developers' role-modeling of the desired positive attitudes about diversity have an effect on learners' attitudes and subsequent behaviors? Thomas and Ely (1996) identified several characteristics of organizational cultures that support a learning-and-effectiveness approach to diversity: (a) a culture that creates expectations of high standards of performance from everyone, (b) a culture that stimulates personal development, (c) a culture that encourages openness, and (d) a culture that makes workers feel valued. Managers play an important role in establishing and maintaining employees' perceptions of culture. An interesting topic for research would be to explore the behaviors that managers and other developers engage in to create this culture, where employees can openly explore diversity issues that arise in relationships and diversity-related challenges in the organization.

Another starting point for research on development functions for diversity competence is the framework provided by Scandura and Lankau (1996) on developing diverse leaders. They identified several relationship processes that support the development of respect, trust, and mutual obligation in diverse leader-member relationships. Developers and learners have to manage conflict that may emerge due to diversity; they have to effectively communicate about diversity issues; and they have to demonstrate respect for other groups. These behaviors foster trust and positive interactions that facilitate learning and understanding diversity.

While we call for research that identifies specific developmental behaviors for specific learning contexts, we also posit that there may be fundamental behaviors that generalize across different learning contexts and facilitate personal learning. Reflection is an important activity in the learning process. *Reflection* has been defined as an intentional cognitive process in which a person attempts to increase his or her awareness of personal experiences and ability to learn from others (Hall, 2002). Reflection can be prompted in the workplace by feedback, interactions with others, performance demands, solitude, and debriefing at the conclusion of work assignments (Seibert, 1999). Developers and learners can increase personal learning by encouraging and supporting reflection.

Several mentoring researchers have argued that relational mentoring behaviors in developmental relationships will result in personal learning for mentors and protégés. *Relational mentoring* describes high-quality relationships characterized by interdependence, mutuality, and reciprocity (see Chapter 15, by Fletcher & Ragins, this volume; Kram, 1996). Actions that enhance these characteristics in mentoring relationships include active listening; demonstrating empathy; self-disclosure; collaboration; guiding, teaching, and explaining; willingness to switch roles from expert to learner; giving and receiving feedback; thanking others for assistance; and offering to help others (see Chapter 14, by Higgins, Chandler, & Kram, this volume; Kram, 1996). These behaviors are suggested for both the developer and learner.

Developer and Learner Characteristics

In the process model, we propose that characteristics of the developer and learner will influence the range and quality of development functions that are experienced in the relationship. While mentoring research has been conducted on characteristics of mentors and protégés, very little work has focused on identifying characteristics that may facilitate the extent of personal learning that can be derived from developmental relationships. We have included personality, demographics, and stage of career cycle as important antecedents that influence the learning process. This is not intended to be an exhaustive list, but a starting point for future research.

Research is just emerging on personality characteristics in developmental relationships that may contribute to personal learning. Earlier, we reviewed the study by Hirschfeld et al. (2006) that examined the motivational orientations of mentors and protégés as dispositional predictors of personal learning. This study showed how the effect of protégés' achievement and avoidance orientations worked partially through the mentoring functions but also had direct effects on both mentors' and protégés' reports of personal learning. Research has also investigated the dispositional trait of *learning goal orientation* (i.e., an individual's striving to increase his or her level of competence in a given activity) on traditional mentoring functions and career-related outcomes (not personal learning). Godshalk and Sosik (2003) found that protégés who were similar to their mentors in terms of high learning goal orientation reported the highest levels of psychosocial support and career development. These same protégés also reported higher levels of career aspirations and career satisfaction than those protégés and mentors who had low levels of learning goal orientation. Learning goal orientation of developers and learners may be an important personality characteristic to consider in future research on mentoring and personal learning. Ragins and Verbos (2007) suggested that high-quality relational mentoring is associated with a learning goal orientation rather than a performance orientation and goes beyond organizational needs of development to include broader developmental needs of the individuals.

Hall and Kahn (2002) proposed that individuals are more likely to engage in successful developmental relationships when they have the desire or willingness to learn from relationships. They state that willingness for some individuals is dispositional and can stem from affiliative needs or learning style. Another motivational characteristic of learners that may impact the quality of the developmental relationship is self-efficacy for development. Maurer, Weiss, and Barbeite (2003) proposed that individuals' beliefs about their capacity to improve skills shape their attitudes toward development and their intentions to participate in development activities and ultimately predict participation in activities. While their research did not focus on mentoring relationships as development activities, it seems that self-efficacy for development may influence the extent to which learners actively engage in the relational development process.

Other personality characteristics that seem relevant for influencing the quality of developmental relationships and personal learning include openness to experience, self-monitoring, and proactive personality. Individuals who score high on openness to experience are commonly described as imaginative, insightful, curious, inventive, creative, and original (James & Mazerolle, 2002). Hence, developers and learners who are high on openness to experience may be more creative in their approach and more likely to process learning from developmental activities than are individuals low on openness to experience. Self-monitoring represents individual differences in sensitivity to situational cues and adapting behavior to be consistent with those cues (Snyder, 1974). Mullen and Noe (1999) found that mentors high on self-monitoring were more likely to seek information from their protégés. Developers and learners who are high on self-monitoring may be more likely to respond to cues in the relationship and seek feedback to maintain high-quality developmental exchanges. Individuals with proactive personalities tend to be more active in influencing their environment and creating change (Crant, 1995). It has been suggested that individuals with proactive personalities may be attracted to mentoring relationships because they tend to engage in career management activities and be more active in obtaining support (Allen & O'Brien, 2006). Developers and learners with proactive personalities may take a more active role in planning, participating, and evaluating developmental activities in the relationship.

Developers' and learners' demographic characteristics are also posited to influence the learning process. In Chapter 14 in this handbook, Higgins, Chandler, and Kram suggest that demographic characteristics may be related to whether the learner actively participates in relational engagement behaviors. They propose socioeconomic status, gender, age, and international background as individual factors that influence whether someone is passive or active in initiating developmental relationships and engaging in development-seeking behaviors. More specifically, they suggest that men compared with women and international compared with

U.S. domestic employees may exhibit higher engagement behaviors. Employees with higher socioeconomic status (SES) compared with those with lower SES, and younger individuals compared with older individuals may be more passive in their engagement behaviors. However, other researchers have identified age as an important demographic variable that may be negatively related to individuals' preparedness for development (Maurer et al., 2003).

We also propose that the stages developers and learners have reached in their career cycles may affect the extent of development functions that can be provided in the relationship. Hall (2002) argued that each career stage is associated with task needs and socioemotional needs and that the goals in each stage are for individuals to experience psychological success with their work and expand their identities (i.e., personal growth). He argued that individuals in their early and late career stages may be more open to learning. Kegan's (1994) model of adult development explains why individuals later in their careers may make effective developers. His model explains that development occurs as a result of the person encountering new situations that contain increasingly greater complexity. As the person increases his or her capacity to deal with this complexity, the individual moves from being very dependent and self-focused to being autonomous and interdependent and able to comprehend a very complex system of relationships in which he or she operates. Kegan's model implies that experiences may be an important determinant of whether a developer can help a learner progress along this continuum.

In Chapter 19 of this handbook, Hall and Chandler discuss how careers in today's environment can be conceptualized as a series of learning cycles. These cycles may last from 3 to 5 years and consist of successive stages of exploration of new areas of work, trial activity, becoming established, mastery and high performance, and renewed exploration. The authors also propose that certain types of developmental assistance may be more helpful for the goals of each stage, and they emphasize the importance of understanding where a protégé is in the career learning cycle to understand how developers can best meet their needs. We reinforce this notion by also underscoring the need to identify where developers are in the career learning cycle. Developers in the mastery and high-performance stages may be the most effective in the developmental function of coaching for performance on tasks. If developers have moved into the first stage of a new learning cycle (e.g., recently promoted), they may have to spend time on their own learning efforts and have less resources to devote to a developmental relationship. Previous research has not taken the mentor's stage in the career cycle into consideration, and this may affect the quality of the developmental experience.

In the process model, we propose that developer and learner characteristics affect personal learning through the learning process, but we also suggest that these characteristics may have direct effects on personal learning. Our proposition for this direct effect is based on the findings from the study conducted by Hirschfeld et al. (2006), reviewed above. Even in developmental relationships in which the extent and quality of developmental behaviors is not high, individuals may still experience personal learning as a result of their own proactive efforts to reflect on what is happening and not happening in the relationship or to supplement their experience with participation in other development activities (e.g., reading books, taking online assessments, etc.). It may be that certain dispositional traits are more highly related to personal development and not much direct developmental assistance is required. We do not offer any specific recommendations on which characteristics may have stronger direct effects on personal learning, but suggest that researchers consider direct as well as indirect effects when examining individual characteristics, development functions, and personal learning.

Personal Learning and Personal Growth

We propose that personal learning in the form of personal skill development and relational job learning is a proximal learning outcome from the developmental process. With a needs-driven approach, the developmental functions serve the purpose of addressing learners' developmental needs for a specific context. Lankau and Scandura's (2002) measure of personal skill development, however, is quite broad, tapping into general communication and problem-solving skills. Additional research is needed on the measure, with a focus on identifying particular learning outcomes for specific learning contexts. For example, cross-departmental communication, networking skills, collaboration, and knowledge transfer may represent examples of specific skills that are enhanced from developmental relationships that form in the context of a learning organization (Singh et al., 2002). For the context of leadership development, improved self-awareness and self-management skills are relevant learning outcomes (Day, 2000). Finally, diversified mentoring relationships may result in specific learning outcomes, such as knowledge about minority group members that dispels stereotypes; increased understanding about the unique career needs of minorities and barriers to advancement; and the development of empathy and communication to bridge cultural, ethnic, and gender gaps (Ragins, 1997).

Personal growth represents a long-term and context-free learning outcome and is represented by personal identity growth and personal adaptability (Hall, 2002). In the process model, personal growth is positioned as a consequence of personal learning. The adult learning literature suggests that learning is embedded in an individual's daily work and is highly contextual (Yang, 2004). This learning at the social, interpersonal plane is then transformed into an intrapersonal plane, where individuals process the new knowledge and determine whether to modify their identities (Granott, 1998; Hall, 2002). We posit that individuals experience learning that is anchored in specific experiences and this personal learning has the potential to change how individuals perceive themselves in a broader context.

While individuals may be capable of engaging in this reflection and growth on their own, we propose that the extent to which personal learning translates into personal growth is influenced by the quality of the developmental learning process. Hall (2002) stated that identity growth involves understanding how to learn more about oneself and that identity development is a relational process. Fletcher (1996) characterized the process of adult growth as a process of understanding oneself as increasingly connected to others and moving through increasingly complex states of interdependence. This process requires new experiences, self-awareness, feedback, empathy and social support, and real-time reflection.

Developmental relationships characterized by high-quality learning processes are likely to facilitate this growth process.

Research on personal learning is in its infancy, and much less is known about personal growth. Longitudinal designs may be needed to capture how personal learning is transformed into personal growth. Research questions that warrant attention include the following: What kinds of developmental relationships have the most impact on personal growth? What developmental behaviors contribute to identity growth and adaptability? Is development in certain skills (e.g., leadership, emotional intelligence) more likely to result in personal growth?

Individual Outcomes

We propose different individual outcomes for personal learning and personal growth. Because personal learning is anchored in a specific organizational context, we posit that the most proximal impact of this type of learning will be on individual experiences and reactions to the organization. We suggest that personal learning will have a positive effect on task and contextual performance and job-related attitudes and a negative effect on turnover. Lankau and Scandura (2002) found that higher levels of personal learning among protégés were associated with less role ambiguity, greater job satisfaction, less intention to leave an organization, and less actual turnover. Since personal learning involves increased skill development and a better understanding of a person's job and role in the context of the organization, it should result in better task performance and contextual performance.

The individual outcomes proposed for personal growth are psychological career success, relational competence, and continuous learning. Hall (2002) identified *psychological career success* and *continuous learning* as outcomes of personal identity growth and personal adaptability. He defined psychological career success as a sense of competent identity and increased career involvement stemming from meeting challenging goals in work and the increased self-esteem due to goal attainment. He also proposed that personal identity growth and personal adaptability are competencies that enable an individual to continuously learn. In Chapter 15 of this handbook, Fletcher and Ragins suggest that one outcome from growth-fostering interactions is *relational competence*. They define this as the ability to operate effectively in a context of connection and interdependence and suggest that this relational competence transcends the organization, into personal relationships involving family, friends, and developers outside the organization.

With the exception of the Lankau and Scandura (2002) study, these outcomes have not been empirically explored, and research is needed to determine whether personal learning and personal growth are related to these outcomes and others. We chose to focus on individual outcomes to make the discussion of the process model more manageable. Future research could examine whether personal learning influences group-level outcomes, such as communication, coordination, cohesiveness, and team performance. It would also be interesting to explore organizational outcomes of personal learning and personal growth. Potential outcomes could include organizational performance, rate of innovation, or customer satisfaction.

Conclusion

The objective of this chapter was to define *personal learning* and propose a model to explain the process of how personal learning is created through developmental relationships and identify potential outcomes. The majority of studies to date on mentoring have not considered the context of the relationship. We suggest that future research on mentoring take a needs-driven approach and consider how developmental relationships can best meet specific learning needs. With a learning approach, researchers can consider how developmental relationships should be structured to develop skills that facilitate knowledge management and transfer activities in a learning organization, how mentoring practices can support leadership development, and the ways in which developmental relationships can improve employees' ability to work productively in a heterogeneous workforce.

A learning approach challenges some of the traditional ways we have conceptualized, measured, and studied mentoring. One challenge to this new approach involves current measures of mentoring, which focus on what the mentor provides in the way of vocational support and psychosocial support and whether the mentor is viewed as a role model. We need to expand the focus in measures of mentoring to include learning content, such as the type of skills that are being acquired in the relationship and the knowledge that is being shared. We also need more detailed examination of specific aspects of vocational support. For example, current measures simply ask whether coaching is occurring in the relationship, but we need to know more about what exactly is being coached, and for what purpose, to really understand the learning that results from these developmental relationships. To address these questions, qualitative work, dyadic investigations, and attention to context are necessary ingredients for future work. We hope that the model in this chapter sparks creative thought about developmental relationships and personal learning and that the questions posed will result in increased research on this topic.

References

Allen, T. D., & Eby, L. T. (2003). Relationship effectiveness for mentors: Factors associated with learning and quality. *Journal of Management, 29,* 469–486.

Allen, T. D., McManus, S. E., & Russell, J. E. (1999). Newcomer socialization and stress: Formal peer relationships as a source of support. *Journal of Vocational Behavior, 54,* 453–470.

Allen, T. D., & O'Brien, K. E. (2006). Formal mentoring programs and organizational attraction. *Human Resource Development Quarterly, 17,* 43–58.

Arthur, M. B., & Rousseau, D. M. (1996). Introduction: The boundaryless career as a new employment principle. In M. Arthur & D. Rousseau (Eds.), *The boundaryless career* (pp. 3–20). New York: Oxford University Press.

Bauer, T. N., Morrison, E. W., & Callister, R. R. (1998). Organizational socialization: A review and directions for future research. *Research in Personnel and Human Resources Management, 16,* 149–214.

Becker, T. E., & Klimoksi, R. J. (1989). A field study of the relationship between organizational feedback environment and performance. *Personnel Psychology, 42,* 343–358.

Chao, G. T., O'Leary-Kelly, A. M., Wolf, S., Klein, H. J., & Gardner, P. (1994). Organizational socialization: Its content and consequences. *Journal of Applied Psychology, 79,* 730–743.

Clawson, J. G. (1996). Mentoring in the information age. *Leadership and Organization Development Journal, 17,* 6 15.

Crant, J. M. (1995). The proactive personality scale and objective job performance among real estate agents. *Journal of Applied Psychology, 80,* 532–537.

Day, D. (2000). Leadership development: A review in context. *Leadership Quarterly, 11,* 581–613.

De Janasz, S. C., Sullivan, S. E., & Whiting, V. (2003). Mentor networks and career success: Lessons for turbulent times. *Academy of Management Executive, 17*(4), 78–91.

Dymock, D. (1999). Blind date: A case study of mentoring as workplace learning. *Journal of Workplace Learning: Employee Counselling Today, 11,* 312–317.

Eby, L. T. (1997). Alternative forms of mentoring in changing organizational environments: A conceptual extension of the mentoring literature. *Journal of Vocational Behavior, 51,* 125–144.

Ellinger, A. D. (2004). The concept of self-directed learning and its implications for human resource development. *Advances in Developing Human Resources, 6,* 158–177.

Ellinger, A. D., & Bostrom, R. P. (1999). Managerial coaching behaviors in learning organizations. *Journal of Management Development, 18,* 752–771.

Feldman, D. C., & Lankau, M. J. (2005). Executive coaching: A review and agenda for future research. *Journal of Management, 31,* 829–848.

Fletcher, J. K. (1996). A relational approach to the protean worker. In D. T. Hall & Associates (Eds.), *The career is dead—Long live the career: A relational approach to careers* (pp. 105–131). San Francisco: Jossey-Bass.

Godshalk, V. M., & Sosik, J. J. (2003). Aiming for career success: The role of learning goal orientation in mentoring relationships. *Journal of Vocational Behavior, 63,* 417–437.

Granott, N. (1998). We learn, therefore we develop: Learning versus development or developing learning? In M. C. Smith & T. Pourchot (Eds.), *Adult learning and development: Perspectives from educational psychology* (pp. 15–34). Mahwah, NJ: Lawrence Erlbaum.

Hall, D. T. (1996). Long live the career—A relational approach. D. T. Hall & Associates (Eds.), *The career is dead—Long live the career: A relational approach to careers* (pp. 1–14). San Francisco: Jossey-Bass.

Hall, D. T. (2002). *Careers in and out of organizations.* Thousand Oaks, CA: Sage.

Hall, D. T., & Kahn, W. A. (2002). Developmental relationships at work: A learning perspective. In C. L. Cooper & R. J. Burke (Eds.), *The new world of work: Challenges and opportunities* (pp. 49–74). Malden, MA: Blackwell.

Hamilton, B. A., & Scandura, T. A. (2003). E-mentoring: Implications for organizational learning and development in a wired world. *Organizational Dynamics, 31,* 388–402.

Higgins, M. C., & Kram, K. E. (2001). Reconceptualizing mentoring at work: A developmental network perspective. *Academy of Management Review, 26,* 264–288.

Hirschfeld, R. R., Thomas, C. H., & Lankau, M. J. (2006). Achievement and avoidance motivational orientations in the domain of formal mentoring: Looking both ways in predicting the personal learning of mentors and protégés. *Journal of Vocational Behavior, 68,* 524–537.

James, L. R., & Mazerolle, M. D. (2002). *Personality in work organizations.* Thousand Oaks, CA: Sage.

Jordan, J., Kaplan, A., Miller J. B., Stiver, I., & Surrey, J. (1991). *Women's growth in connection.* New York: Guilford Press.

Kegan, R. (1994). *In over our heads: The mental demands of modern life.* Cambridge, MA: Prentice Hall.

Kessels, J. W. M., & Poell, R. F. (2004). Andragogy and social capital theory: The implications for human resource development. *Advances in Developing Human Resources, 6,* 146–157.

Kram, K. E. (1985). *Mentoring at work: Developmental relationships in organizational life.* Glenview, IL: Scott, Foresman.

Kram, K. E. (1996). A relational approach to career development. In D. Hall & Associates (Eds.), *The career is dead—Long live the career: A relational approach to careers* (pp. 132–157). San Francisco: Jossey-Bass.

Kram, K. E., & Hall, D. T. (1989). Mentoring as an antidote to stress during corporate trauma. *Human Resource Management, 28,* 493–510.

Kram, K. E., & Hall, D. T. (1996). Mentoring in the context of diversity and turbulence. In S. Lobel & E. Kossek (Eds.), *Managing diversity: Human resource strategies for transforming the workplace* (pp. 108–136). London: Blackwell.

Lankau, M. J., & Scandura, T. A. (2002). An investigation of personal learning in mentoring relationships: Content, antecedents, and consequences. *Academy of Management Journal, 45,* 779–790.

Maurer, T. J., Pierce, H. R., & Shore, L. M. (2002). Perceived beneficiary of employee development activity: A three-dimensional social exchange model. *Academy of Management Review, 27,* 432–444.

Maurer, T. J., Weiss, E. M., & Barbeite, F. G. (2003). A model of involvement in work-related learning and development activity: The effects of individual, situational, motivational, and age variables. *Journal of Applied Psychology, 88,* 707–724.

McCauley, C. D., & Douglas, C. A. (1998). Developmental relationships. In C. D. McCauley, R. S. Moxley, & F. Van Velsor (Eds.), *The center for creative leadership handbook of leadership development* (pp. 160–193). San Francisco: Jossey-Bass.

Merriam, S. B., & Heuer, B. (1996). Meaning-making, adult learning and development: A model with implications for practice. *International Journal of Lifelong Education, 15,* 243–255.

Mezias, J. M., & Scandura, T. A. (2005). A needs-driven approach to expatriate adjustment and career development: A multiple mentoring perspective. *Journal of International Business Studies, 36,* 519–538

Mirvis, P. H., & Hall, D. T. (1996). New organizational forms and the new career. In D. T. Hall & Associates (Eds.), *The career is dead—Long live the career: A relational approach to careers* (pp. 72–104). San Francisco: Jossey-Bass.

Mullen, E. J., & Noe, R. A. (1999). The mentoring information exchange: When do mentors seek information from their protégés? *Journal of Organizational Behavior, 20,* 233–242.

Nahapiet, J., & Ghoshal, S. (1998). Social capital, intellectual capital, and the organizational advantage. *Academy of Management Review, 23,* 242–266.

Nonaka, I., & Takeuchi, H. (1995). *The knowledge creating company.* Oxford, UK: Oxford University Press.

Ostroff, C., & Kozlowski, S. (1993). The role of mentoring in the information gathering processes of newcomers during early organizational socialization. *Journal of Vocational Behavior, 42,* 170–183.

Ragins, B. R. (1997). Diversified mentoring relationships in organizations: A power perspective. *Academy of Management Review, 22,* 482–521.

Ragins, B. R., & Verbos, A. K. (2007). Positive relationships in action: Relational mentoring and mentoring schemas in the workplace. In J. Dutton & B. R. Ragins (Eds.), *Exploring positive relationships at work: Building a theoretical and research foundation* (pp. 91–116). Mahwah, NJ: Lawrence Erlbaum.

Rogers, C. (1983). *Freedom to learn for the 80s.* Columbus, OH: Charles E. Merrill.

Scandura, T. A., & Lankau, M. J. (1996). Developing diverse leaders: A leader-member exchange approach. *Leadership Quarterly, 7,* 243–263.

Scandura, T. A., & Siegel, P. H. (1995, August). *Mentoring as organizational learning during a corporate merger.* Paper presented at the National Academy of Management Meeting, Vancouver, CA.

Seibert, K. W. (1999). Reflection-in-action: Tools for cultivating on-the-job learning conditions. *Organizational Dynamics, 27,* 54–65.

Singh, V., Bains, D., & Vinnicombe, S. (2002). Informal mentoring as an organizational resource. *Long Range Planning, 35,* 389–405.

Snyder, M. (1974). Self-monitoring of expressive behavior. *Journal of Personality and Social Psychology, 30,* 526–537.

Swap, W., Leonard, D., Shields, M., & Abrams, L. (2001). Using mentoring and storytelling to transfer knowledge in the workplace. *Journal of Management Information Systems, 18,* 95–114.

Thomas, C. H., & Lankau, M. J. (2003, November 14). *Mentoring as a competitive HR strategy in organizations: A conceptual development of the link between mentoring and social capital.* Paper presented at the Annual Meeting of the Southern Management Association, Clearwater, FL.

Thomas, D. A., & Ely, R. J. (1996). Making differences matter: A new paradigm for managing diversity. *Harvard Business Review, 74*(5), 79–90.

Yang, B. (2004). Can adult learning theory provide a foundation for human resource development? *Advances in Developing Human Resources, 6,* 129–144.

5

Mentoring Relationships From the Perspective of the Mentor

Tammy D. Allen

I n his classic study of the career development of men, mentoring others was cited by Levinson (1978) as a key developmental task for individuals in midcareer. Other career development researchers recognized that mentoring relationships were beneficial to both the mentor and to the protégé (Clawson, 1980; Dalton, Thompson, & Price, 1977; Hunt & Michael, 1983). Kram's (1985) groundbreaking research concerning developmental mentoring relationships at work emphasized the mutuality and reciprocity of mentoring relationships. As such, it is surprising that historically, the majority of empirical research has focused on the protégé, with much less attention concentrated on the mentor. However, during the past decade, this oversight has started to be addressed as research from the mentor's perspective has begun to flourish.

Research dedicated to understanding mentorship dynamics from the focal point of the mentor is important for both theoretical and practical reasons. A mentoring relationship is an inherently dyadic and complex process, with the mentor and the protégé each enacting different roles and responsibilities in the relationship. The success of any mentorship is contingent on the behaviors of both the mentor and the protégé. Accordingly, neglect of the issues unique to the role of the mentor leaves a critical gap in our understanding of the overall mentorship process and hampers theoretical development of the field. From a practice perspective, mentors play a key role in organizations as they ensure the transfer and continuation of knowledge and help prepare junior colleagues for further organizational responsibility (Kram & Hall, 1996). Moreover, high-quality and committed mentors are crucial to the success of formal mentoring programs within organizations (Allen, Eby, & Lentz, 2006b; Allen & Poteet, 1999; Ragins, Cotton, & Miller, 2000).

The purpose of the present chapter is to summarize existing research that has focused on the mentor. The review is organized around specific topics that dominate in this area, including the factors that underlie the willingness and motivation to be a mentor to others, factors that mentors consider in their selection of protégés, provision of mentoring, relationship satisfaction, and the benefits of mentoring others. The model depicted in Figure 5.1 provides a guide for viewing the process of mentoring others from the mentor's perspective. The review roughly follows the order of the proposed model. Unless specifically noted, the research reviewed is based on informal mentoring relationships or samples that consist of both formal and informal relationships. The chapter concludes with an agenda for future research.

Review of the Existing Literature

Willingness to Mentor Others and Mentor Experience

The willingness to be a mentor to others is one issue that has captured the attention of researchers interested in the mentor. Most research has focused on future mentoring intentions (e.g., "I would be willing to be a mentor in the future"), and the associated construct is typically labeled as *willingness to mentor others*. However, there is also some research examining actual experience as a mentor. These studies often compare mentors with nonmentors. Presumed predictors of willingness to mentor that have been examined include demographic factors such as gender and age, previous mentoring experience, dispositional and motivational variables, situational factors, and expected costs and benefits.

Demographic Variables

Much of the early research on mentoring was inspired by the notion that inadequate access to informal networks and mentors helped explain differences in the career advancement of men and women (Noe, 1988b; Ragins, 1989). Lack of female role models was viewed as a particular concern, as it was also theorized that women might be reluctant to assume responsibility for the mentorship of others because of perceived barriers such as time constraints, token status, and lack of self-confidence (Kram, 1985; Ragins, 1989). However, the empirical research has generally found that women have no fewer intentions to mentor others than do men (Noe, 1988b; Ragins, 1989). The research regarding perceived barriers to mentoring others is mixed. While Ragins and Cotton (1993) found that women perceived greater barriers to mentoring others than did men, Allen, Poteet, Russell, and Dobbins (1997) found no gender differences. There is some indication that organizational level may make a difference in willingness to mentor others, as well as gender. Ragins and Cotton (1993) found gender differences in willingness to mentor others and experience as a mentor among lower- and midlevel managers and employees, but Ragins and Scandura (1994) found

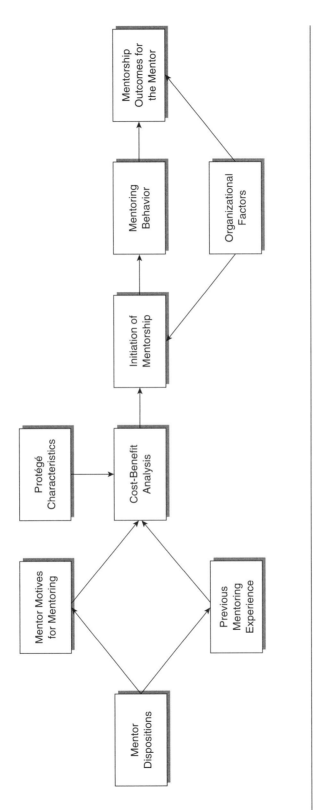

Figure 5.1 Mentoring Process Model for Mentors

no differences between executive-level men and women. Ragins and Scandura concluded that gender differences in willingness to mentor others may be a function of gender differences in rank, position, and resources.

Several studies have examined the relationship between age and mentoring others. Age and career stage models suggest that willingness to mentor others should be strongest at midcareer (Dalton et al., 1977; Levinson, 1978). However, the few studies that have examined this supposition have not been supportive. Ragins and Cotton (1993) found no support for the hypothesis that willingness to mentor others would be curvilinearly related to age. In addition, Allen, Poteet, Russell, et al. (1997) found a negative relationship between age and intention to mentor others, such that older supervisors reported fewer intentions to mentor others than did younger supervisors. However, it is important to underscore that both of these studies were based on age rather than career stage. In today's career environment, age and career stage are not as tightly entwined, in that individuals are more likely to have multiple careers across the life span (Arthur & Rousseau, 1996; Sullivan, 1999). Hence, although age may not relate to willingness to mentor, it remains to be tested whether or not career stage does.

Previous Mentoring Experience

The most tested and consistent finding in the literature regarding intentions to mentor others concerns previous mentoring experience. Previous experience as a mentor and previous experience as a protégé both positively relate to future willingness to mentor others (Allen, 2003; Allen, Poteet, & Burroughs, 1997; Allen, Poteet, Russell et al., 1997; Bozionelos, 2004; Ragins & Cotton, 1993; Ragins & Scandura, 1999). Several factors likely explain this finding. Kram (1985) noted that individuals with previous mentoring experiences likely appreciate the benefits of mentoring due to their firsthand knowledge. This finding is also consistent with the model of behavioral consistency that suggests past behavior is a reliable predictor of future behavior (Wernimont & Campbell, 1968). Finally, the impact of previous mentoring experience likely also reflects the norm of reciprocity (Gouldner, 1960). Individuals who have been protégés are motivated to reciprocate the help they have received by being mentors to others (Allen, Poteet, & Burroughs, 1997).

Dispositional Variables

Several studies have examined dispositional variables thought to relate to intentions to mentor others and to actual experience as a mentor (see Turban & Lee, Chapter 2, this volume, for a review of mentoring and personality). Aryee, Chay, and Chew (1996) reported that positive affectivity, altruism, and organization-based self-esteem were significantly correlated with motivation to mentor others. However, organization-based self-esteem was not significant in a regression equation that included all predictor variables. Allen, Poteet, & Russell et al. (1997) examined locus of control and upward striving. Results indicated that individuals with an internal locus of control were more willing to mentor others than were those with an external locus of control. In addition, mentoring others was positively associated with greater upward striving. That is, individuals who were interested in elevating their own careers were also more willing to support the careers of others through mentoring than were those less interested in upward career moves.

Allen (2003) suggested viewing mentoring others as a specific form of *organizational citizenship behavior* (OCB). Under this lens, she proposed that dispositional variables known to relate to OCB would also be applicable to the propensity to mentor others. Based on social psychological models of helping behavior, Penner and colleagues developed an inventory designed to measure individual differences in prosocial personality tendencies (Penner, Fritzsche, Craiger, & Freifeld, 1995). Their work identified two factors associated with the prosocial personality: other-oriented empathy and helpfulness. First, with regard to actual experience as a mentor, Allen found that helpfulness related to mentor experience but empathy did not. On the other hand, among the entire sample, other-oriented empathy related to greater future intentions to mentor others, but helpfulness did not. It is further noteworthy that other-oriented empathy and helpfulness explained variance in willingness to mentor others beyond career and life stage variables. The findings suggest that the variables that relate to actual experience as a mentor differ from those that relate to willingness to mentor others in the future. Helpfulness may be a better predictor of actual mentoring behavior because it has been associated with self-confidence and self-efficacy (Penner et al., 1995).

Situational Variables

Only two known studies have investigated situational variables and willingness to mentor others. Aryee et al. (1996) found that rewards for mentoring others and opportunities for interactions on the job both positively related to motivation to mentor others. Allen, Poteet, & Russell, et al. (1997) reported that willingness to mentor others related to having a high-quality relationship with one's own supervisor. In addition, although individuals who reported less job-induced stress perceived fewer barriers to mentoring than did individuals with more job-induced stress, job-induced stress was not significantly related to future intention to mentor.

Expected Costs and Benefits

Another factor that can contribute to an individual's decision to enter into a mentoring relationship involves the expected costs and rewards. Ragins and Scandura (1999) examined the expected costs and benefits associated with being a mentor among a sample of executives. Five categories of benefits were identified: rewarding experience, improved job performance, loyal base of support, recognition by others, and generativity (that is, leaving a legacy to future generations). Expected costs were that mentoring was more trouble than it was worth, the relationship could be dysfunctional, nepotism could occur, poor protégés could reflect badly on the mentor, and energy drain could result. Using total costs and benefits in the analyses, the authors found that intention to mentor was positively related to expected benefits and negatively related to expected costs. Ragins and Scandura also found that mentoring experience moderated the relationship between intention to mentor and expected costs and benefits. Although individuals lacking mentoring experience anticipated more costs associated with being a mentor than did those with mentoring experience, variations in expected costs did not affect their intention to mentor. On the other hand, among individuals with mentoring experience, lower expected costs were associated with stronger intention to mentor. The opposite effect was observed for expected benefits, in that intention to mentor related positively to expected benefits for inexperienced individuals but not for those with previous mentoring experience.

Mentor-Protégé Selection

The willingness to be a mentor to others is followed by the selection of a particular protégé. Outside of formal mentoring programs, mentors typically have complete discretion over their choice of protégé. Moreover, in most organizations, there are likely to be more individuals that desire a mentor than there are available mentors. This brings to light the important issue of what attracts mentors to their chosen protégés. However, only a limited number of studies have focused on this issue. The research that has been conducted has been driven primarily by two theories: the similarity-attraction paradigm and social exchange theory.

The *similarity-attraction paradigm* suggests that mentors will be attracted to those they perceive to be similar to themselves (Byrne, 1971). Several studies have examined the similarity-attraction hypothesis in terms of gender similarity and protégé selection. The results indicate no *expressed* preference for protégés of the same gender (Allen, 2004; Allen, Poteet, & Russell, 2000; Olian, Carroll, & Giannantonio, 1993). However, it is interesting to note that in empirical studies, same-gender mentorships typically greatly outnumber cross-gender mentorships (e.g., Allen & Eby, 2003; Ragins & Cotton, 1999; Sosik & Godshalk, 2000). The least common dyadic combination is female mentors paired with male protégés. Because of small sample problems with the female mentor/male protégé grouping, there is very limited research examining dynamics within specific gender combinations. In interviews with experienced mentors, Allen, Poteet, & Burroughs, et al. (1997) found that when mentors were asked what attracted them to their protégés, one factor that emerged was that the protégés reminded the mentors of themselves and that they had a lot in common. Thus, there is some evidence that similarity is likely to play a part in mentor-protégé selection.

Much more research regarding protégé selection has used social exchange as a framework. *Social exchange theory* suggests that individuals enter into relationships in which they believe the rewards will be greater than the costs (Blau, 1964; Homans, 1958; Thibaut & Kelley, 1959). That is, mentors will be attracted to protégés thought to bring something of value to the relationship. As described in the previous section regarding willingness to mentor, individuals develop perceptions regarding the costs and benefits associated with being a mentor (Ragins & Scandura, 1999). They likely also consider the costs and benefits associated with mentoring a particular protégé. This cost-benefit analysis takes into consideration characteristics of the protégé (Olian et al., 1993).

Research has suggested a number of different protégé characteristics preferred by mentors. Kram's (1985) research indicated that mentors are attracted to high-performing protégés with technical knowledge. Other research shows that when asked to describe the characteristics that attracted them to their protégés, interviewed mentors reported being attracted to protégés who demonstrated personality characteristics such as a "people orientation," motivational factors such as a strong work ethic and initiative, competence, and a learning orientation (Allen, Poteet, & Burroughs, 1997).

In an experimental study using vignettes, Olian et al. (1993) found that male and female banking managers were more willing to mentor others depicted as high-performing protégés than those depicted as average-performing protégés. Olian et al. also found that managers were more willing to provide career-related mentoring to male protégés if the protégé was married rather than single. The reverse was found for females. Specifically, managers intended to provide more psychosocial mentoring to single rather than married female protégés. The findings suggest that individuals may be concerned about exerting the effort to mentor female protégés who have family responsibilities. This is not surprising considering that work and family research has shown that males receive a career bonus for marriage that women do not (Landau & Arthur, 1992).

Allen et al. (2000) examined two factors that might influence protégé selection: the protégé's ability/potential and the protégé's need for help. As expected, mentors were more likely to report that they picked their protégés on the basis of protégés' ability/potential rather than protégés' need for help. The also found that female mentors were more likely than male mentors to report that they chose their protégés on the basis of ability/potential.

Allen (2004) examined the role in selection of protégé willingness to learn and ability in both a laboratory experiment and a field study. In the lab study, potential protégé profiles were developed in which protégés varied in terms of ability and willingness to learn. Participants were asked to rate their willingness to mentor each protégé in the pool of profiles. As expected, results indicated that participants were more willing to mentor protégés high in ability than low in ability and protégés high in willingness to learn than those low in willingness to learn. However, the results also revealed an interaction between the two suggesting that willingness to learn could help compensate for lower levels of ability. Individuals were agreeable to mentoring high willingness-to-learn protégés regardless of their degree of ability. Allen also found that offering rewards for mentoring others related to the type of protégé chosen. Specifically, the results suggested that when rewards for mentoring were available, mentors were less willing to mentor individuals who were not as talented or motivated. Thus, as indicated in the previous section, offering rewards for mentoring others may increase willingness to be a mentor, but it may also impact the type of protégé selected. Finally, Allen reported that mentors motivated by different factors appear to prefer certain protégé characteristics. Specifically, mentor motivation to mentor for self-enhancement was positively related to selecting a protégé based on ability. Mentors' motivation to mentor for intrinsic satisfaction was positively related to selecting a protégé based on protégé willingness to learn. Both protégé ability and willingness to learn were positively associated with mentor motivation to benefit others and the organization.

In sum, the existing research from a social exchange perspective regarding protégé selection suggests that mentors look for protégés who possess valued characteristics such as strong performance, high ability, and ample willingness to learn. There is also some evidence that gender dynamics play a role in the selection process. Specifically, male and female mentors may use different criteria for selecting their protégés, and the criteria may vary depending on the gender of the protégé. Moreover, the findings support the point of view that mentors have different motivations for mentoring others. Thus, protégé selection by mentors is likely based on a combination of demographic, motivational, and personality variables.

Provision of Mentoring

Once a mentoring relationship is formed, the career and psychosocial functions that distinguish a mentoring relationship from other forms of work relationships emerge (Kram, 1985). However, there can be a great deal of variation with regard to the extent to which the behaviors associated with mentoring occur within any given relationship. For example, some mentorships are marked by a great deal of career mentoring but little psychosocial mentoring, while others may involve a moderate amount of both. Considerable research attention has focused on identifying factors that predict the degree of career and psychosocial mentoring provided by mentors within a relationship, but it is important to note that most of this research has been based on reports of mentoring provided by protégés. Much less research has examined mentoring behavior as self-reported by the mentor. This distinction is important in that mentors and protégés may have differing perceptions of the relationship. Moreover, there may be behavior that mentors engage in on behalf of their protégés that are outside of the protégés' awareness.

In keeping with the focus of this chapter, only literature based on mentor self-reports of mentoring provided is reviewed in this section. Presumed predictors of mentor reports of mentoring that have been investigated include demographic characteristics such as mentor and protégé gender and race, interaction frequency, whether the relationship was initiated formally or informally, duration, previous mentoring experience, dispositional variables, perceived similarity, and mentor motives for mentoring others.

Demographics

The results regarding gender of the mentor and mentor reports of mentoring provided are mixed. Burke, McKeen, and McKenna (1993) found that female mentors reported providing more psychosocial and career mentoring to protégés than did male mentors. Allen and Eby (2004) found that female mentors reported providing more psychosocial mentoring than did male mentors, while male mentors reported providing more career mentoring than did female mentors. Other studies have found no differences across mentor gender and their reports of mentoring provided (Lankau, Riordan, & Thomas, 2005; Mullen, 1998).

Several studies have gone beyond mentor gender and examined the gender composition of the mentorship. Based on mentor self-reports, Allen and Eby (2004) found no differences in mentoring provided in same-gender versus cross-gender mentoring relationships. However, mentor-protégé gender interaction analyses indicated that male mentors reported providing a similar degree of psychosocial mentoring to male protégés as to female protégés. On the other hand, female mentors reported providing more psychosocial mentoring to female protégés than to male protégés. No interaction effect was found for psychosocial mentoring. Lankau et al. (2005) found that gender similarity related to mentor reports of role-modeling but not to career or psychosocial mentoring.

Only one study has examined mentor race and reports of mentoring provided. In a study limited to participants of a formal mentoring program, Lankau et al. (2005) found no differences across the psychosocial, career, and role-modeling functions with regard to mentor race. However, it should be noted that the sample size of non-White mentors was small ($n = 32$). They also found that race similarity related to mentor reports of role-modeling but not to career or psychosocial mentoring.

Interaction Frequency

It is typically thought that more frequent interaction between mentor and protégé will translate into greater mentoring provided. However, results are inconsistent. In a study of formal mentoring, Lankau et al. (2005) found that interaction time between mentors and protégés in a formal program related to mentor self-reports of providing career support but not to reports of role-modeling or psychosocial mentoring. Likewise, in a study of formal mentoring, Allen, Eby, and Lentz (2006a) found that mentor reports of interaction frequency related to career mentoring but not to psychosocial mentoring. However, in another study of formal mentoring, Ensher and Murphy (1997) found that mentor reports of number of hours of contact related to both career and psychosocial mentoring. Mullen (1998) found no relation between time spent together and mentor reports of mentoring provided.

Informal Versus Formal

Two studies have compared informal and formal mentor reports of mentoring provided. Both found no differences in mentor's self-reports of the career or psychosocial mentoring provided (Allen & Eby, 2004; Fagenson-Eland, Marks, & Amendola, 1997). However, it is important to note that the small samples of formal and informal mentors in the Fagenson-Eland et al. (1997) study limited the power to detect significant differences. Still, these findings are in noticeable contrast to research based on protégé reports of mentoring in which differences were reported, albeit inconsistently, across types of relationships (Chao, Walz, & Gardner, 1992; Fagenson-Eland et al., 1997; Ragins & Cotton, 1999; Scandura & Williams, 2001). There have been no studies in which paired mentors and protégés in both formal and informal mentorships have been simultaneously investigated.

Relationship Duration

The findings regarding duration of the relationship and mentor reports of mentoring provided are mixed. One study of seemingly informal mentoring found that longer duration related to more psychosocial mentoring but not to career mentoring (Burke et al., 1993). In contrast, two other studies consisting of a mix of formal and informal mentorships found that longer relationships related to more career mentoring but not to more psychosocial mentoring (Allen & Eby, 2004; Fagenson-Eland et al., 1997).

Previous Experience as a Mentor

Past experience as a mentor has been found to relate to mentoring provided as reported by mentors. Fagenson-Eland et al. (1997) found that more experienced mentors reported providing more career mentoring than did mentors with less experience. No relationship between previous mentoring experience and psychosocial mentoring was found. Allen and Eby (2004) also found that mentors with more previous experience as mentors reported providing more career mentoring than did those with less previous mentoring experience. Previous experience as a mentor may be confounded with rank and power within the organization, which may help explain the relationship with career mentoring.

Dispositional Variables

A few studies have examined an assortment of mentor dispositional variables and their reports of mentoring provided. Two studies have examined mentoring overall. Using a combined measure of career and psychosocial mentoring, Mullen (1998) found that mentors with greater organization-based self-esteem reported providing more mentoring to their protégés. Bozionelos (2004) found that mentor openness to experience positively related to mentor reports of providing general supervisory mentoring. The other four personality variables from the Big Five were tested, but none were significantly associated with mentoring provided. Allen (2003) distinguished between career and psychosocial mentoring. She investigated the relationship between the prosocial personality characteristics, other-oriented empathy and helpfulness, and mentoring behavior. She found that helpfulness related to career mentoring but not to psychosocial mentoring. In contrast, other-oriented empathy related to psychosocial mentoring but not to career mentoring. Allen concluded that helpfulness relates to career mentoring because it reinforces the mentor's feelings of efficacy and competence. The warmth and nurturance that are a part of psychosocial mentoring are more closely tied to other-oriented empathy. Empathetic individuals are able to foster the intimacy and trust that is critical to psychosocial mentoring.

Perceived Similarity

Two studies have examined perceived similarity in terms of factors such as personality, values, and attitudes. In both of these studies, mentors reported providing more career and psychosocial mentoring to protégés who were perceived as similar to themselves than to protégés perceived to be less similar (Burke et al., 1993; Ensher & Murphy, 1997).

Motives for Mentoring Others

Research conducted by Allen, Poteet, Russell, et al. (1997) suggests multiple reasons for mentors to engage in the act of mentoring others and that these motives relate to mentoring provided. In their qualitative study of interviewed mentors, Allen Poteet, Russell, et al. identified what they referred to as "self-focused motives" and "other-focused motives" for mentoring others. Self-focused motives were those related to improving the welfare of the self, such as the desire to increase personal learning and the gratification of developing others. Other-focused motives were those related to improving the welfare of others and included the desire to help others and to help the organization succeed.

Allen (2003) developed a measure to operationalize these motives. Factor analyses suggested a three-factor structure. Items related to other-focused mentoring loaded onto one factor, labeled *benefiting others*. Items related to self-focused motives loaded onto two independent factors. One of these factors was more extrinsically oriented and focused on *self-enhancement,* and the other factor was more intrinsically oriented and focused on *self-gratification.* Results indicated that motives for mentoring accounted for unique variation in mentors' self-reports of their career and psychosocial mentoring. Motivation to mentor for self-enhancement related positively to career mentoring but not to psychosocial mentoring. Motivation to mentor for intrinsic satisfaction related positively to psychosocial mentoring but not to career mentoring. Motivation to mentor for the purpose of benefiting others related positively to both career and psychosocial mentoring. One implication of these findings is that protégés with certain needs may be best matched with mentors motivated by different factors. For example, protégés desirous of primarily career mentoring may fit best with a mentor motivated to mentor for self-enhancement purposes.

Mentor Relationship Satisfaction

Following the provision of mentoring, the most proximal outcome of the mentorship is the participant's affective reaction or his or her overall satisfaction with the relationship. Although there have been numerous studies examining protégé satisfaction with the mentoring relationship (Allen, Eby, Poteet, Lentz, & Lima, 2004), only a few studies have examined mentor satisfaction or perceptions of the quality of the mentorship as an outcome. Several of these studies have examined gender and mentor satisfaction. In a study of formal mentorships, Noe (1988a) reported that mentors in cross-gender relationships indicated that they were more effectively utilized by their protégés than did mentors in same-gender relationships. Further examination of the data revealed that male mentors with male protégés reported a lower-quality relationship than did female mentors with female protégés and cross-gender dyads. In contrast, in a sample comprising both formal and informal mentors, Allen and Eby (2003) found no differences in mentor relationship satisfaction between same-gender and cross-gender mentorships.

Allen and Eby (2003) investigated differences in relationship satisfaction between informal and formal mentors. Although a significant correlation was observed indicating that informal mentors reported greater relationship satisfaction than did formal mentors, this effect was not significant in the regression equation controlling for mentorship duration, interaction frequency, mentor experience, mentor gender, protégé gender, occupation, gender similarity, and perceived similarity. The authors also found a positive relationship between perceived similarity and mentorship quality. That is, mentors who perceived their protégés to be similar to themselves reported the relationships to be of greater quality than did mentors with protégés perceived to be less similar. These findings were qualified by an interaction. Specifically, a stronger relationship was found between perceived similarity and mentorship satisfaction in relationships of shorter rather than longer duration. Hence, perceived similarity appears to be more important earlier in the relationship or for relationships of short duration. As the relationship develops across time, similarity becomes less important as the mentor likely takes other factors, such as complementarity, into consideration.

Young and Perrewe (2000) found that mentors were more satisfied when protégés were open to advisement and coaching and put forth effort in accomplishing work. Most recently, in a study limited to participants of formal mentoring programs, mentors who perceived that they had provided some input into who their protégés would be perceived that their mentorships were of greater quality than did mentors who perceived they had provided less input into who their mentoring partners would be (Allen, Eby, & Lentz, 2006a).

Benefits of Mentoring for the Mentor

Although a considerable amount has been written with regard to the benefits of mentoring for the mentor (e.g., Hunt & Michael, 1983; Newby & Heide, 1992), empirical research on the topic is limited. Qualitative studies examining the benefits of mentoring others suggest that mentors achieve personal satisfaction from passing knowledge and skills on to others, exhilaration from the fresh energy provided by protégés, improved job performance by receiving a new perspective on the organization from protégés, loyalty and support from protégés, and organizational recognition (Allen, Poteet, & Burroughs, 1997; Kram, 1985; Levinson, 1978). This review focuses on the more recent quantitative studies investigating the benefits of mentoring for the mentor.

Researchers are only beginning to examine how mentoring others may relate to tangible career benefits to the mentor, such as increased promotion rates and salary. Bozionelos (2004) found that general supervisory mentoring provided related to objective career success, operationalized as number of promotions, and to subjective career success among a sample of university administrators in England. Allen, Lentz, and Day (2006) compared the outcomes of individuals with no mentoring experience with those who had experience as an informal mentor. They found that experience as a mentor uniquely contributed to the variance associated with current salary, promotion rate, and subjective career success beyond the variance attributed to demographic and human capital factors often associated with career success. Allen et al. suggested that mentors may be rewarded by organizations because they are recognized as good organizational citizens. It is important to recognize that the results of both Bozionelos (2004) and Allen, Lentz, and Day (2006) were based on cross-sectional survey methodology. Thus, although the studies provide some initial evidence that mentoring others relates to career benefits for the mentor, the direction of this relationship is not clear.

Another benefit often attributed to mentoring others is that it can buffer the negative consequences associated with plateauing (e.g., Chao, 1990; Elsass & Ralston, 1989; Kram, 1985; Slocum, Cron, Hansen, & Rawlings, 1985). Although this had been suggested for decades, only recently was this tested. Lentz and Allen (2005) found little support for the notion that mentoring others moderated the relationship between plateauing and typical outcomes associated with plateauing, such as job satisfaction, affective commitment, and turnover intention. However, experience as a mentor and providing greater career and psychosocial mentoring were both associated with lesser job content plateauing than were no experience as a mentor and providing less mentoring. Thus, while mentoring others may not mitigate the effects of plateauing, it may help prevent plateauing from occurring in the first place. The authors also found that those with experience as mentors reported greater job satisfaction, greater affective organizational commitment, and fewer intentions to turnover than did those with no experience as mentors. This suggests that experience as a mentor relates to positive job attitudes.

Other recent research has examined what predicts mentor reports of benefiting from the mentoring relationship. Using a sample of both mentors and protégés, Eby, Durley, Evans, and Shockley (2005) examined three categories of predictors: relational behaviors, motivational variables, and personality variables. The mentor benefits examined were based on Ragins and Scandura's (1999) dimensions of perceived benefits to mentoring others. Eby et al. (2005) found that although all three categories of predictors related to mentor benefits, mentor and protégé personality were the weakest.

Negative Mentoring Experience

It is important to recognize that in addition to benefits associated with mentoring others, there can be problems. In Allen, Poteet, & Burroughs's (1997) qualitative research, mentors identified several negative consequences for mentors. The most frequently mentioned factor by participants was that mentoring could be a major drain on time. Other factors identified were negative fallout from coworkers who felt that protégés were being favored, protégés who abused the relationship, and personal feelings of failure if the mentorship did not work out. Feldman (1999) also noted that mentors can be hurt by destructive mentoring relationships involving "toxic" protégés and become reluctant to continue mentoring others.

Most recently, Eby and McManus (2004) examined the specific types of dysfunctional experiences that mentors report in mentoring relationships. The themes identified include negative relations involving exploitation and egocentricity, malevolent deceptions, sabotage, harassment, interpersonal difficulty, spoiling, benign deception, submissiveness, performance below expectations, and unwillingness to learn.

Review Summary and Methodological Limitations

Overall, the scholarly study of workplace mentoring is a relatively young area of inquiry, receiving serious empirical attention for only a few decades. The mentor's perspective is in an even more immature stage of development. Indeed, empirical investigation focused on the mentor might be traced only as far back as Ragins and Cotton's (1993) article concerning willingness to mentor. Thus, it should not be surprising that for most of the topics investigated from the perspective of the mentor, it is difficult to draw firm conclusions given the limited amount of research focused on a particular issue. In many cases, only two or three studies exist, and often the results are inconsistent. This literature might also be characterized as fragmented and diffuse, as researchers only begin to scratch the surface of a variety of issues of importance (again see Figure 5.1). This is also indicative of a research area in a neophyte stage of development. Nevertheless, there are a few brief summary observations that can be made on the basis of the extant research:

- With regard to willingness to mentor, it is clear that previous mentoring experience relates to future willingness to mentor.
- Individuals perceived as high potential with a strong willingness to learn are most likely to be selected as protégés.
- The motivational basis for mentoring behavior is likely driven by self-interest as well as concerns for the well-being of others.
- Structural aspects of the relationship such as relationship initiation (i.e., formal versus informal), interaction frequency, and duration of the relationship are weak and inconsistent predictors of mentoring behavior.
- Dispositional variables likely impact various parts of the mentoring process, from willingness initially to be a mentor to the type of protégé selected to the provision of mentoring behavior.
- There is initial empirical evidence that there are extrinsic and intrinsic career rewards in mentoring others.

Before turning attention to areas for future research, it is important to reflect on the methodologies commonly employed to study mentoring, to place the reviewed findings in context. The majority of studies have been based on cross-sectional designs and self-report surveys. This is characteristic of most mentoring research and is not limited just to research that has focused on the mentor. However, it leaves uncertainty regarding the causal direction of many findings (e.g., Does career success predict mentoring behavior, or does mentoring behavior predict career success?). In addition, quantitative studies of this nature are limited in the ability to assess the relational dynamics at the crux of mentoring relationships. Studies also often rely on retrospective reports versus current assessments, which can render the accuracy of responses questionable. Of course, there are limitations associated with any single research design. This calls to mind the need to employ multiple methodologies to ensure that findings are not method bound.

Future Research Directions

As the above review attests, an impressive body of research from the focal point of the mentor has begun to accumulate. However, there is considerable work yet to be done. In the following sections, areas worthy of future research that roughly follow the process model depicted in Figure 5.1 are discussed. In addition, Table 5.1 provides a summary of these ideas.

Table 5.1   Mentor Focused Research Agenda Summary

Willingness to Mentor Others

1. Link willingness to mentor others with future actual mentoring behavior.

2. Examine factors that moderate the relationship between intent to mentor others and actual mentoring behavior.

3. Incorporate aspects of diversity other than gender and age in examining willingness to mentor others (e.g., race, LGBT).

Cost-Benefit Analysis and the Decision to Mentor Others

1. Determine how the perceived costs and benefits associated with mentoring others relates to future mentoring decisions.

2. Incorporate cognitive decision-making and adult development theories into mentoring research.

Protégé Selection

1. Determine the extent that protégé selection is driven by protégé potential. Determine under what circumstances struggling protégés are mentored.

2. Examine the role of both mentor and protégé gender and the role of mentor and protégé race in the protégé selection process.

3. Examine and integrate both the social-exchange and the similarity processes that play a role in protégé selection.

Characteristics of an Effective Mentor

1. Link attributes thought to be associated with effective mentoring behavior with actual mentoring outcomes.

2. Examine whether mentor characteristics are more or less helpful for formal versus informal mentoring relationships.

3. Examine mentoring styles. For example, what are the various belief systems under which mentors operate and how do these beliefs influence mentor behavior with protégés?

(Continued)

Table 5.1 (Continued)

Role of Organizational Context

1. Investigate how workplace demands (e.g., tight production schedules, long hours) provide a barrier to facilitating an environment supportive of mentoring.

2. Examine how the organizational context influences the quality of mentoring.

3. Develop multilevel (macro, meso, and individual) frameworks for understanding the factors that influence mentoring behavior.

Providing Career and Psychosocial Mentoring Behavior

1. Develop research agendas that simultaneously take into account the needs of the protégé and consider aspects of the situation.
2. Examine the cues that mentors use to try to determine protégé needs and appropriate mentoring behavior.

3. Continue to examine and update dimensions of mentoring behavior and ensure that measures reflect both the viewpoint of the protégé and the mentor.

Outcomes Associated With Mentoring Others

1. Conduct longitudinal research examining the link between mentoring others and both objective and subjective career success outcomes.

2. Focus on learning as an outcome for mentors. What are the skills mentors learn from their mentoring relationships?

3. Examine how mentoring others benefits the psychological and physical health of the mentor.

Willingness to Mentor Others

Although a body of research has begun to develop examining intention to mentor to others (i.e., willingness to mentor) (e.g., Allen, 2003; Allen, Poteet, & Russell et al., 1997; Aryee et al., 1996; Ragins & Cotton, 1993), no studies have examined the extent to which intention to mentor others subsequently relates to actual future mentoring behavior. Although intention has been found to be a valid predictor of future behavior in areas such as turnover (e.g., Williams & Hazer, 1986), it is not clear to what extent the intention-behavior link generalizes to mentoring behavior. For example, it is possible that because of the effort mentoring others requires, the relationship between intention and behavior with regard to mentoring others may not be as strong as that observed with other constructs, such as turnover. Longitudinal research is needed to determine this relationship. A related line of research would be an examination of factors that moderate the relationship between intention and behavior. For example, an individual may want to mentor others but when faced with an actual opportunity to be a mentor may have too many time constraints to do so. Incorporation of measurement of the barriers to mentoring others (Ragins & Cotton, 1993) may be helpful in this regard.

Existing research regarding willingness to mentor others has considered few aspects of diversity other than gender and age. Examining barriers that members of racial and ethnic minority groups perceive to mentoring others may further our understanding of willingness to mentor. Similar research might be conducted regarding gay, lesbian, and transgender individuals. Moreover, it will be useful to examine a combination of demographic diversity variables. For example, for African American females, the experiences and perceived barriers to mentoring others are likely to be different from those of African American males.

Cost-Benefit Analysis and the Decision to Mentor Others

Research conducted by Ragins and Scandura (1999) demonstrates that individuals perceive both costs and benefits associated with mentoring others and that these perceptions relate to mentoring intentions. As with willingness to mentor, research is needed that determines how these perceptions relate to actual mentoring decisions. That is, under what conditions do the perceived benefits of mentoring outweigh the perceived costs and result in the initiation of a mentoring relationship? Research that incorporates cognitive-decision-making theories (e.g., March, 1994) may improve our understanding of these processes. Another useful lens for viewing perceptions regarding the costs and benefits of mentoring others would be adult development theory (see McGowan, & Stone, & Kegan, Chapter 16, this volume).

Protégé Selection

As demonstrated in the review section, only a handful of studies have examined the issue of protégé selection. Several important areas need investigation. More research is needed that determines the extent to which the initiation of mentoring relationships is driven by protégé potential. The extant research seems to suggest that preferred protégés are those who already possess the characteristics needed to achieve career success. It would be interesting to determine in what circumstances struggling individuals attract the attention of a mentor. For example, only individuals highly confident in their own career stability may be willing to assume the risk and take the time to mentor poor performers. Turbulent work environments in which job security is an issue may also create conditions that make it difficult for struggling employees to attract mentorship.

Another interesting avenue for further research is more in-depth examination of the role of gender in the protégé selection process. Although it appears that women are just as willing as men to mentor others and that women are just as likely as men to be mentored (e.g., see Ragins, 1999, for a review), some gender differences may emerge in terms of selection criteria. For example, male mentors may look for protégés who fit profiles different from those selected by female mentors. Because of their own career struggles and perceived barriers to mentoring others (e.g., Ragins & Cotton, 1993), women may be less willing than men to mentor risky protégés. Or it might be that mentor and protégé gender interact such that a woman may be more willing to mentor a risky protégé if the protégé is another woman than if the protégé is a male. Male mentors may be less attracted to female protégés with assertive or dominating personalities than to male protégés who possess the same attributes. These are all highly speculative suggestions but bring to light the need for further research regarding gender and protégé selection. Similar issues might be studied in terms of race. For example, under what conditions are mentors more or less likely to select minority protégés? Would a member of a minority group be viewed as more risky or challenging to a mentor belonging to majority group than a protégé with a demographic background similar to the mentor's?

Research that integrates the processes of similarity and social exchange would also provide needed insight into protégé selection. For example, there may be circumstances in which mentors perceive that there would be more rewards in mentoring someone different from themselves than in mentoring someone more similar (e.g., the mentor is disorganized and wants to be complemented by an organized protégé; the mentor wants to broaden his or her cultural competence and therefore selects a culturally dissimilar protégé). Alternatively, there may be situations in which the identification and similarity with a potential protégé renders probable costs that are unimportant to the mentor (e.g., the mentor wants to help someone who shares a disadvantaged background).

Characteristics of an Effective Mentor

Little is known regarding the specific characteristics that an effective mentor possesses. In a qualitative study, Allen and Poteet (1999) interviewed 27 experienced mentors regarding their opinions on the subject. Some of the most common attributes mentioned were listening and communication skills, patience, knowledge of organization and industry, and the ability to read and understand others (see also Cherniss, Chapter 17, this volume). However, there has been no empirical research linking these factors to measured mentoring outcomes. Research that includes individual assessments of mentors at the start of a mentoring relationship and then measures multiple mentorship outcomes based on multiple sources of data (e.g., protégé reports of mentoring behavior, organizational assessments of performance) would go a long way toward addressing this issue.

It is also not clear to what extent the characteristics of an effective mentor may differ for formal versus informal mentoring relationships. For example, there may be unique skills needed to be an effective mentor within a formalized program. Because formal mentorships are typically much shorter in duration than informal mentorships, formal mentors may need to be particularly adept at quickly distilling and communicating information to protégés. Moreover, the formal mentor may need a sharp ability to rapidly diagnose protégé strengths and weaknesses to best ensure that protégé needs in the relationship are met.

In addition, it may be interesting to examine mentor behavior in terms of the identification of "mentoring styles." Mentors are likely to have belief systems that impact the way they approach mentoring others and the expectations they have regarding protégé behavior. For example, some mentors may subscribe to the philosophy that protégés learn best through a "sink-or-swim" strategy. Other mentors may take a parental approach to the relationship, providing considerable advice and instruction that the mentor expects the protégé to obediently follow. The extent to which any of these styles may be more or less effective likely depends on the needs of the protégé. Research designed to reveal the belief systems under which mentors operate could be helpful in terms of increasing our understanding of mentor behavior.

The Role of Organizational Context

A relatively unexplored topic for future research is the role that the organizational environment plays in the mentoring process (see Allen, 2004; Aryee et al., 1996; Eby, Lockwood, & Butts, in press, for exceptions). Despite Kram's (1985) emphasis that organizational characteristics such as task design, performance management systems, and culture can create obstacles to the initiation and development of mentoring relationships, most research has been conducted as though mentoring relationships in organizations exist in a vacuum. Two qualitative studies based on in-depth interviews with mentors have further underscored the importance of support from the organization in creating conditions that facilitate mentoring others (Allen, Poteet, & Burroughs, 1997; Billett, 2003). These studies found that rigid organizational structures, unclear expectations, job pressures, and a competitive environment impede the mentor's ability to mentor others. Investigation is needed of how specific workplace demands, such as tight production schedules, frequent travel, long hours, and excessive deadlines, may create an environment in which individuals feel less able to mentor others. Moreover, these factors may influence the quality of the mentoring relationship. Although individuals may decide to enter a mentoring relationship despite these constraints, the extensiveness of the mentoring they are able to provide may suffer.

Research regarding the role of organizational context could be aided by the development of multilevel frameworks for understanding the factors that can influence mentoring behavior. For example, willingness to mentor others may be influenced by macrolevel factors, such as industry (e.g., more mentoring may occur in knowledge-based industries than in manufacturing environments); mesolevel factors such, as task interdependence (e.g., more mentoring may occur when there is a greater degree of task interdependence); and individual-level factors (e.g., more mentoring is likely to occur among individuals who possess prosocial personality tendencies).

Providing Career and Psychosocial Mentoring Behavior

The leadership literature has long recognized that effective leader behavior is often contingent on the situation (e.g., House, 1996). In the mentoring literature, it seems to be assumed that more psychosocial and career-related mentoring is better. Mentorship research that takes into account the needs of the protégé and aspects of the situation is needed. For example, protégés with strong peer and family social support systems may not benefit from a great degree of psychosocial mentoring. More introverted protégés who have difficulty establishing career networks may be especially needful of career mentoring. In organizations with highly structured and developed career management systems, career mentoring may be less important than in more fluid organizations without formal career systems (Dreher & Dougherty, 1997). These are just a few examples of how the characteristics of the protégé and the situation could alter the degree and type of mentoring behavior needed. In a related vein, it would be interesting to examine what cues mentors use to try to determine the needs of their protégés and subsequently alter the type of mentoring they provide. For example, inquiry by the mentor regarding the protégé's developmental network (Higgins, Chandler, & Kram, Chapter 14, this volume; Higgins & Kram, 2001) may help the mentor determine the degree of psychosocial mentoring needed. A multimethod approach that blends qualitative and quantitative research will be needed to begin to address these research questions.

Another issue related to the provision of mentoring is that none of the measures commonly used in workplace mentoring research has been tested for equivalence with mentor samples (e.g., Noe, 1988a; Ragins & McFarlin, 1990; Scandura, 1992). Fowler and Gorman (2005) recently addressed this issue. They conducted interviews with a heterogeneous group of mentors and protégés. On the basis of their interview results, they developed a new measure of mentoring functions that was validated using samples of both mentors and protégés. Eight distinct functions of mentoring were supported using both the mentor and the protégé data. The functions that were identified were personal and emotional guidance, coaching, advocacy, career development facilitation, role-modeling, strategies and systems advice, learning facilitation, and friendship. The authors found that an eight-component model provided a better fit to the data than a two-component model representing career and psychosocial functions. Although there were many similarities between the findings of the Fowler and Gorman study and Kram's (1985) original work, there were also differences. Specifically, learning facilitation is unique from the functions identified by Kram and may reflect a trend toward more mutuality in mentorships (Ragins & Verbos, 2007). In addition, the protection function included by Kram did not emerge in this study. It is not clear whether these differences arose because the nature of careers, and thus to some extent mentoring, too, has changed during the past 20 years or whether the dedicated effort to include mentors in the validation process has had some impact on the functions that have emerged. For example, protégés may not always be aware of the behaviors in which their mentors engage on their behalf. Thus, we should not expect complete congruence between mentor and protégé reports. Regardless, it is important for researchers to further examine the dimensions and measures that are used to capture mentoring behavior and to ensure that these measures represent mentoring from both the viewpoint of the protégé and the mentor.

Outcomes Associated With Mentoring Others

The frequent call for longitudinal research is again relevant in terms of investigating the career benefits associated with mentoring others. Although cross-sectional studies have provided initial support for the notion that mentoring others brings tangible as well as psychological benefits to the mentor, the direction of causality is unclear. Individuals who have achieved career success are likely to be attractive as mentors. Moreover, individuals would seemingly be more likely to engage in mentorships after achieving career success than before. Hence, there is probably a long-term dynamic process at play, such that career success helps increase an individual's attractiveness as a mentor and willingness to be a mentor, which in turn relates to mentoring others, which in turn helps further increase career success.

Much more research attention is also needed that focuses on learning as an outcome of mentoring relationships. In their qualitative study of participants in formal mentoring programs, Eby and Lockwood (2005) found that the most frequently cited benefit of participating in the program by mentors was learning. Learning was also an important outcome identified by mentors in Allen, Poteet, & Burroughs (1997). Mullen (1994) proposed viewing mentoring as a reciprocal exchange of information in which the mentor not only provides information to the protégé but also solicits knowledge from the protégé. Although Allen and Eby (2003) examined learning as an outcome, it was operationalized globally. In sum, while learning has been clearly identified as an important variable in the mentoring process for mentors, very little research has closely examined specific learning dynamics for mentors (see also Lankau & Scandura, Chapter 4, this volume).

Lankau and Scandura (2002) developed a measure that assesses learning for protégés. They identified two types of personal learning that occur in a mentorship. Based on the work of Kram and Hall (1996), one type was referred to as *relational job learning,* which involves an increased understanding regarding the interdependence of one's job with those of others. The second type of learning was labeled as *personal skill development* and was defined as the acquisition of new skills and abilities that facilitate improved working relationships. A parallel line of research is needed that more concretely identifies what it is that mentors learn from their relationships and how those forms of learning can be fostered. For example, protégés may be able to bring mentors up to speed on new trends in technology. In addition, reciprocal-learning dynamics between mentor and protégé at the dyadic level need to be studied.

Another potential benefit that has been virtually unexplored is the extent to which mentoring others can benefit the psychological and physical health of the mentor. Social health research has demonstrated that there are health benefits from both giving and receiving social support (Brown, Nesse, Vinokur, & Smith, 2003; Taylor, Klein, Gruenewald, Gurung, & Fernandes-Taylor, 2003). Moreover, research examining other specific forms of helping relationships, such as adult volunteerism, show benefits such as reduced depression, greater physical health, and increased mortality (e.g., Musick & Wilson, 2003; Oman, Thoresen, & McMahon, 1999; Thoits & Hewitt, 2001). There are several reasons why mentoring others may improve health. Giving to others brings a sense of meaning and purpose to life, which increases happiness and decreases depression (e.g., Batson, 1998; Brown et al., 2003). In addition, mentoring others may improve the functioning of the autoimmune system by enhancing control and efficacy (Penner, Dovidio, Piliavin, & Schroeder, 2005). Thus, the benefits of being a mentor may extend well beyond improved career success and favorable job attitudes (see also Dutton & Heaphy, 2003; Heaphy, 2007).

Conclusion

In recent years, the mentor has become a more frequent target of focused research attention. However, there are many potential fruitful avenues for further investigation. This is an exciting area of inquiry, with many questions yet to be answered. A continued research effort from the focal point of the mentor is needed for a complete understanding of the mentoring process. It is hoped that this chapter helps to stimulate such inquiry.

References

Allen, T. D. (2003). Mentoring others: A dispositional and motivational approach. *Journal of Vocational Behavior, 62,* 134–154.

Allen, T. D. (2004). Protégé selection by mentors: Contributing individual and organizational factors. *Journal of Vocational Behavior, 65,* 469–483.

Allen, T. D., & Eby, L. T. (2003). Relationship effectiveness for mentors: Factors associated with learning and quality. *Journal of Management, 29,* 465–486.

Allen, T. D., & Eby, L. T. (2004). Factors related to mentor reports of mentoring functions provided: Gender and relational characteristics. *Sex Roles, 50,* 129–139.

Allen, T. D., Eby, L. T., & Lentz, E. (2006a). Mentor and protégé outcomes associated with formal mentoring programs: Closing the gap between research and practice. *Journal of Applied Psychology, 91,* 567–578.

Allen, T. D., Eby, L. T., & Lentz, E. (2006b). The relationship between formal mentoring program characteristics and perceived program effectiveness. *Personnel Psychology, 59,* 125–153.

Allen, T. D., Eby, L. T., Poteet, M. L., Lentz, E., & Lima, L. (2004). Career benefits associated with mentoring for protégés: A meta-analytic review. *Journal of Applied Psychology, 89,* 127–136.

Allen, T. D., Lentz, E., & Day, R. (2006). Career success outcomes associated with mentoring others: A comparison of mentors and nonmentors. *Journal of Career Development, 32,* 272–285.

Allen, T. D., & Poteet, M. L. (1999). Developing effective mentoring relationships: Strategies from the mentor's viewpoint. *Career Development Quarterly, 48,* 59–73.

Allen, T. D., Poteet, M. L., & Burroughs, S. M. (1997). The mentor's perspective: A qualitative inquiry and future research agenda. *Journal of Vocational Behavior, 51,* 70–89.

Allen, T. D., Poteet, M. L., & Russell, J. E. A. (2000). Protégé selection by mentors: What makes the difference? *Journal of Organizational Behavior, 21,* 271–282.

Allen, T. D., Poteet, M. L., Russell, J. E. A., & Dobbins, G. H. (1997). A field study of factors related to supervisors' willingness to mentor others. *Journal of Vocational Behavior, 50,* 1–22.

Aryee, S., Chay, Y. W., & Chew, J. (1996). The motivation to mentor among managerial employees in the maintenance career stage: An interactionist's perspective. *Group & Organization Management, 21,* 261–277.

Arthur, M. B., & Rousseau, D. M. (1996). *The boundaryless career: A new employment principle for a new organizational era.* New York: Oxford Press.

Batson, C. D. (1998). Altruism and prosocial behavior. In D. T. Gilbert, S. T. Fiske, & G. Lindzey (Eds.), *Handbook of social psychology* (Vol. 2, pp. 282–316). New York: McGraw-Hill.

Billett, S. (2003). Workplace mentors: Demands and benefits. *Journal of Workplace Learning, 15,* 105–113.

Blau, P. (1964). *Exchange and power in social life.* New York: John Wiley & Sons.

Bozionelos, N. (2004). Mentoring provided: Relation to mentor's career success, personality, and mentoring received. *Journal of Vocational Behavior, 64,* 24–46.

Brown, S. L., Nesse, R. M., Vinokur, A. D., & Smith, D. M. (2003). Providing social support may be more beneficial than receiving it. *Psychological Science, 14,* 320–327.

Burke, R. J., McKeen, C. A., & McKenna, C. (1993). Correlates of mentoring in organizations: The mentor's perspective. *Psychological Reports, 72,* 883–896.

Byrne, D. (1971). *The attraction paradigm,* New York: Academic Press.

Chao, G. T. (1990). Exploration of the conceptualization and measurement of career plateau: A comparative analysis. *Journal of Management, 16,* 181–193.

Chao, G. T., Walz, P. M., & Gardner, P. D. (1992). Formal and informal mentorships: A comparison on mentoring functions and contrast with nonmentored counterparts. *Personnel Psychology, 45,* 619–636.

Clawson, J. (1980). Mentoring in managerial careers. In C. B. Derr (Ed.), *Work, family, and the career* (pp. 144–165). New York: Praeger.

Dalton, G. W., Thompson, P. H., & Price, R. L. (1977). The four stages of professional careers: A new look at performance by professionals. *Organizational Dynamics, 6,* 19–42.

Dreher, G. F., & Dougherty, T. W. (1997). Substitutes for career mentoring: Promoting equal opportunity through career management and assessment systems. *Journal of Vocational Behavior, 51,* 110–124.

Dutton, J. E., & Heaphy, E. D. (2003). The power of high-quality connections. In K. S. Cameron, J. E. Dutton, & R. E. Quinn (Eds.), *Positive organizational scholarship: Foundations of a new discipline* (pp. 263–278). San Francisco: Berrett-Koehler.

Eby, L. T., Durley, J., Evans, S. C., & Shockley, K. (2005, April). *What predicts the benefits of mentoring for mentors?* Paper presented at the 20th Annual Conference of the Society for Industrial and Organizational Psychology, Los Angeles, CA.

Eby, L. T., & Lockwood, A. (2005). Protégés and mentors' reactions to participating in formal mentoring programs: A qualitative investigation. *Journal of Vocational Behavior, 67,* 441–458.

Eby, L. T., Lockwood, A. L., & Butts, M. (in press). Perceived support for mentoring: A multiple perspectives approach. *Journal of Vocational Behavior.*

Eby, L. T., & McManus, S. E. (2004). The protégé role in negative mentoring experiences. *Journal of Vocational behavior, 65,* 255–275.

Elsass, P. M., & Ralston, D. A. (1989). Individual responses to the stress of career plateauing. *Journal of Management, 15,* 35–47.

Ensher, E. A., & Murphy, S. E. (1997). Effects of race, gender, perceived similarity, and contact on mentor relationships. *Journal of Vocational Behavior, 50,* 460–481.

Fagenson-Eland, E. A., Marks, M. A., & Amendola, K. L. (1997). Perceptions of mentoring relationships. *Journal of Vocational Behavior, 51,* 29–42.

Feldman, D. C. (1999). Toxic mentors or toxic protégés? A critical re-examination of dysfunctional mentoring. *Human Resource Management Review, 9,* 246–278.

Fowler, J. L., & O'Gorman, J. G. (2005). Mentoring functions: A contemporary view of the perceptions of mentees and mentors. *British Journal of Management, 16,* 51–57.

Gouldner, A. W. (1960). The norm of reciprocity: A preliminary statement. *American Sociological Review, 25,* 161–178.

Heaphy, E. (2007). Bodily insights: Four lenses for positive organizational relationships. In J. E. Dutton & B. R. Ragins (Eds.), *Exploring positive relationships at work: Building a theoretical and research foundation* (pp. 47–71). Mahwah, NJ: Lawrence Erlbaum.

Higgins, M. C., & Kram, K. E. (2001). Reconceptualizing mentoring at work: A developmental network perspective. *Academy of Management Review, 26,* 264–268.

Homans, G. C. (1958). Social behavior as exchange. *American Journal of Sociology, 63,* 597–606.

House, R. J. (1996). Path-goal theory of leadership: Lessons, legacy, and a reformulated theory. *Leadership Quarterly, 7,* 323–352.

Hunt, D. M., & Michael, C. (1983). Mentorship: A career training and development tool. *Academy of Management Review, 8,* 475–485.

Kram, K. E. (1985). *Mentoring at work.* Glenview, IL: Scott, Foresman.

Kram, K. E., & Hall, D. T. (1996). Mentoring in a context of diversity and turbulence. In E. E. Kossek & S. Lobel (Eds.), *Managing diversity: Human resource strategies for transforming the workplace* (pp. 108–136). Cambridge, MA: Blackwell.

Landau, J., & Arthur, M. B. (1992). The relationship of marital status, spouse's career status, and gender to salary level. *Sex Roles, 27,* 665–681.

Lankau, M. J., Riordan, C. M., & Thomas, C. H. (2005). The effects of similarity and liking in formal mentoring relationships between mentors and protégés. *Journal of Vocational Behavior, 67,* 252–265.

Lankau, M. J., & Scandura, T. A. (2002). An investigation of personal learning in mentoring relationships: Content, antecedents, and consequences. *Academy of Management Journal, 45,* 779–790.

Lentz, E., & Allen, T. D. (2005, April). *The link between mentoring and the career plateau: Addressing the empirical gap.* Paper presented at the 2005 Annual Conference of the Society for Industrial and Organizational Psychology, Los Angeles, CA.

Levinson, D. J. (with Darrow, D., Levinson, M., Klein, E. B., & McKee, B.). (1978). *Seasons of a man's life.* New York: Academic Press.

March, J. (1994). *A primer on decision-making: How decisions happen.* New York: Free Press.

Mullen, E. J. (1994). Framing the mentoring relationship as an information exchange. *Human Resource Management Review, 4,* 257–281.

Mullen, E. J. (1998). Vocational and psychosocial mentoring functions: Identifying mentors who serve both. *Human Resource Development Quarterly, 9,* 319–331.

Musick, M. A., & Wilson, J. (2003). Volunteering and depression: The role psychological and social resources in different age groups. *Social Science Medicine, 56,* 259–269.

Newby, T. J., & Heide, A. (1992). The value of mentoring. *Performance Improvement Quarterly, 5*(4), 2–15.

Noe, R. (1988a). An investigation of the determinants of successful assigned mentoring relationships. *Personnel Psychology, 41,* 457–479.

Noe, R. A. (1988b). Women and mentoring: A review and research agenda. *Academy of Management Review, 13,* 65–78.

Olian, J. D., Carroll, S. J., & Giannantonio, C. M. (1993). Mentor reactions to protégés: An experiment with managers. *Journal of Vocational Behavior, 43,* 266–278.

Oman, D., Thoresen, E., & McMahon, K. (1999). Volunteerism and mortality among the community-dwelling elderly. *Journal of Health Psychology, 4,* 301–316.

Penner, L. A., Dovidio, J. F., Piliavin, J. A., & Schroeder, D. A. (2005). Prosocial behavior: Multilevel perspectives. *Annual Review of Psychology, 56,* 365–392.

Penner, L. A., Fritzsche, B. A., Craiger, J. P., & Freifeld, T. R. (1995). Measuring the prosocial personality. In J. Butcher & C. D. Spielberger (Eds.), *Advances in personality assessment.* (Vol. 10, pp. 147–163). Hillsdale, NJ: Lawrence Erlbaum.

Ragins, B. R. (1989). Barriers to mentoring: The female manager's dilemma. *Human Relations, 42,* 1–22.

Ragins, B. R. (1999). Gender and mentoring relationships. In G. N. Powell (Ed.), *Handbook of gender in organizations* (pp. 347–370). Thousand Oaks, CA: Sage.

Ragins, B. R., & Cotton, J. L. (1993). Gender and willingness to mentor in organizations. *Journal of Management, 19,* 97–111.

Ragins, B. R., & Cotton, J. L. (1999). Mentor functions and outcomes: A comparison of men and women in formal and informal mentoring relationships. *Journal of Applied Psychology, 84,* 529–550.

Ragins, B. R., Cotton, J. L., & Miller, J. S. (2000). Marginal mentoring: The effects of type of mentor, quality of relationship, and program design on work and career attitudes. *Academy of Management Journal, 43,* 1177–1194.

Ragins, B. R., & McFarlin, D. (1990). Perception of mentor roles in cross-gender mentoring relationships. *Journal of Vocational Behavior, 37,* 321–339.

Ragins, B. R., & Scandura, T. A. (1994). Gender differences in expected outcomes of mentoring relationships. *Academy of Management Journal, 37,* 957–971.

Ragins, B. R., & Scandura, T. A. (1999). Burden or blessing? Expected costs and benefits of being a mentor. *Journal of Organizational Behavior, 20,* 493–509.

Ragins, B. R., & Verbos, A. K. (2007). Positive relationships in action: Relational mentoring and mentoring schemas in the workplace. In J. E. Dutton & B. R. Ragins (Eds.), *Exploring positive relationships at work: Building a theoretical and research foundation* (pp. 91–116). Mahwah, NJ: Lawrence Erlbaum.

Scandura, T. A. (1992). Mentorship and career mobility: An empirical investigation. *Journal of Organizational Behavior, 13,* 169–174.

Scandura, T. A., & Williams, E. A. (2001). An investigation of the moderating effects of gender on the relationships between mentorship initiation and protégé perceptions of mentoring functions. *Journal of Vocational Behavior, 59,* 342–363.

Slocum, J. W., Jr., Cron, W. L., Hansen, R. W., & Rawlings, S. (1985). Business strategy and the management of plateaued employees. *Academy of Management Journal, 28,* 133–154.

Sosik, J. J., & Godshalk, V. M (2000). The role of gender in mentoring: Implications for diversified and homogenous mentoring relationships. *Journal of Vocational Behavior, 57,* 102–122.

Sullivan, S. E. (1999). The changing nature of careers: A review and research agenda. *Journal of Management, 25,* 457–484.

Taylor, S. E., Klein, L. C., Gruenewald, T. L., Gurung, R. A. R., & Fernandes-Taylor, S. (2003). Affiliation, social support, and biobehavioral responses to stress. In J. Suls & K. A. Wallston (Eds.), *Social psychological foundations of health and illness* (pp. 314–331). Malden, MA: Blackwell.

Thibaut, J. W., & Kelley, H. H. (1959). *The social psychology of groups.* New York: John Wiley & Sons.

Thoits, P. A., & Hewitt, L. N. (2001). Volunteer work and well-being. *Journal of Health and Social Behavior, 42,* 115–131.

Wernimont, P. F., & Campbell, J. P. (1968). Signs, samples, and criteria. *Journal of Applied Psychology, 52,* 372–376.

Williams, L. J., & Hazer, J. T. (1986). Antecedents and consequences of satisfaction and commitment in turnover models: A reanalysis using latent variable structural equation models. *Journal of Applied Psychology, 71,* 219–231.

Young, A. M., & Perrewe, P. L. (2000). What did you expect? An examination of career-related support and social support among mentors and protégés. *Journal of Management, 26,* 611–632.

6

Mentoring and Leadership

Standing at the Crossroads of Theory, Research, and Practice

Veronica M. Godshalk

John J. Sosik

He who loves practice without theory is like the sailor who boards ships
without a rudder and compass and never knows where he may cast.

—Leonardo da Vinci

Anyone who has experienced a truly developmental relationship with a wise person may have considered him or her to have provided mentoring functions and to have exercised strong leadership. In fact, Bass (1985) identified mentoring as a core aspect of developmental behavior displayed by transformational leaders. Building upon this idea, researchers have begun to identify the similar developmental behaviors, functions, and outcomes between mentoring and leadership styles (e.g., Scandura & Schriescheim, 1994; Scandura & Williams, 2004; Sosik & Godshalk, 2000). A review of the literature from these two fields suggests that we have been conceptualizing and framing effective leadership with the same descriptors as those offered for effective mentors. However, this is not always the case. For example, despite all of his charm and intellectually stimulating rhetoric, Winston Churchill showed little interest in the mentoring and personal development of his staff and his own children (Burns, 1978). This example suggests that while leaders may engage in similar behaviors as mentors, there are differences between leader-subordinate and mentor-protégé relationships. At issue for researchers is how to identify and differentiate mentoring and leadership behaviors that may lead to successful personal and professional development of protégés/followers.

To begin to address this issue, this chapter attempts to answer two important questions: (a) How is mentoring truly distinct from leadership? and (b) how, when, and where are these two constructs analogous? Understanding the similarity and differences between mentoring and leadership may enable organizations to distinguish leaders/mentors from other high-ranking employees and may allow them to provide for more effective mentoring of employees.

The chapter first discusses where we are in terms of our understanding of leadership and mentoring by offering definitions of mentoring and various contemporary leadership styles. We then present the theoretical similarities and empirical distinctions between mentoring and leadership. Specifically, continua will be presented that categorize the context of current research. We then pose research questions and offer directions for future research. Finally, we conclude with ideas about how to advance the application of relevant research into practice for organizations today.

Research on Mentoring and Leadership: Where Have We Been?

After reviewing the literatures on mentoring and leadership, we realized what T. S. Eliot meant when he said, "Again, I have come back to the same place, for the first time." Sensing this feeling of déjà vu, we focused our attention on reviewing relevant research that provides a foundation for emerging streams of mentoring research. Indeed, changes in emphasis from functional to developmental forms of leadership theory may have blurred the distinction between leadership and mentoring, because leadership theory has extended its definitions to incorporate mentoring functions and relationship constructs.

Mentoring Defined

A *mentor* has been defined as an individual with advanced knowledge, usually more senior in some regard, who is committed to providing upward career mobility and assistance for the protégé (Kram, 1985; Levinson, 1978). The mentoring relationship has been characterized as an intense, sometimes intimate, professional relationship devoted to providing social support and development for the protégé's career (Carden, 1990; Sosik & Godshalk, 2000). Chao (1998) stated that mentoring relationships can be distinguished from less powerful relationships, such as sponsors, guides, and peers (Shapiro, Haseltine, & Rowe, 1978) and from typical supervisory relationships (Burke, McKenna, & McKeen, 1991).

Kram (1985) theorized the specific functions found in mentoring relationships. First, the mentor provides a vocational or career development function where he or she promotes professional growth by providing needed information, challenging assignments, exposure, visibility, and protection and by exercising organizational leverage. Second, the mentor fulfills a psychosocial function where he or she promotes personal growth through emotional support, counseling, and providing acceptance and guidance. These functions have been empirically supported (Noe, 1988; Ragins & McFarlin, 1990).

Scandura (1992) found role-modeling to represent a third distinct function. Role-modeling functions involve behaviors in which protégés identify with and emulate mentors who are trusted and respected, possess expert and referent power, and hold high standards (Gibson & Cordova, 1999; Thibodeaux & Lowe, 1996). Mentors who serve as role models encourage protégés to become involved in learning (Allen, Russell, & Maetzke, 1997), and researchers have found these developmental relationships provide for protégé learning opportunities (Godshalk & Sosik, 2003; Lankau & Scandura, 2002).

Scandura and Schriesheim (1994) conceptualized the mentoring relationship between the protégé and his or her direct supervisor as *supervisory career mentoring* (SCM). These authors defined SCM as follows:

> A transformational activity involving a mutual commitment by mentor and protégé to the latter's long-term development, as a personal, extra-organizational investment in the protégé by the mentor, and as the changing of the protégé by the mentor, accomplished by the sharing of values, knowledge, experience, and so forth. (p. 1589)

This definition is quite similar to what Burns (1978) and Bass (1985) described as *transformational leadership,* whereby the leaders become a moral agent responsible for the personal and professional development of followers into leaders in their own right.

Developmental Leadership Theories Defined

A *leadership style* can be defined as the actions or behaviors of one individual, usually in a more senior position, that influence the actions or behaviors of another to achieve organizational (Bass, 1990) or interorganizational goals (Burns, 1978; Hunt, 1991). Based on prior contributions to the literature, Yukl (1989) synthesized a leader behavior taxonomy that included both the leader's initiating structure (i.e., task-oriented actions such as planning and organizing, problem solving, clarifying roles and objectives, monitoring) and consideration (i.e., relationship-oriented actions such as supporting, developing, networking, and recognizing) activities. Some leader behaviors are primarily task oriented, while others are primarily relationship oriented.

Various theories have been offered to help us understand the mystery that surrounds leadership oriented toward developing others. For purposes of this chapter, we will focus exclusively on two such contemporary theories: transactional/transformational and leader-member exchange (LMX) leadership. We will define these theories and then identify similarities and differences between leadership and mentoring behaviors.

Transformational/Transactional Leadership Theory

Transformational leadership involves broadening and elevating followers' goals and providing them with the values, enhanced skills, and confidence to go beyond minimally acceptable expectations of performance (Bass & Avolio, 1997). *Transformational leaders* pursue organizational goals by communicating a vision that motivates employees to exert extra effort (Bass, 1990). Such leaders also show personalized attention that links individual and collective interests, resulting in commitment to the organization's vision (Hambrick, 1989). Transformational leaders are characterized by their abilities to (a) build trust by exhibiting idealized influence behaviors, (b) strive to develop followers through individualized consideration, (c) promote follower independence and critical thinking through intellectual stimulation, and (d) attach importance to human development through inspirational motivation (Sosik & Godshalk, 2000).

Transactional leaders, on the other hand, pursue a cost-benefit exchange approach with the subordinate. Such leaders set goals and provide feedback and rewards to followers as a means of assisting followers in achieving prespecified performance objectives. This approach does not necessarily strive to change or challenge the follower, but rather uses positional power to influence the subordinate to complete "contracted" work.

While transformational and transactional styles may seem antithetical, Bass (1985) noted that "while conceptually distinct, transformational and transactional leadership are likely to be displayed by the same individuals in different amounts and intensities" (p. 26). Transformational leadership adds to transactional leadership. That is, transformational leadership often explains a significant amount of incremental variance in a variety of dependent variables compare with that explained by transactional leadership alone (Bass, 1990). Sosik and Godshalk (2000) found that transformational leadership behavior was more positively related to mentoring than was transactional leadership. Therefore, we argue that transformational leadership may be a significant addition to existing frameworks investigating the developmental behavior of mentors. The transformational leadership behaviors noted by Sosik and Godshalk (2000) are representative of a mentor's behaviors toward protégés, and it appears that the leadership and mentoring literatures are converging on a similar definition for the developmental functions offered by the mentor/transformational leader to his or her protégé or follower.

LMX Theory

Graen (1976) first proposed that leaders behave differently with individuals under their supervision and therefore provide for unique relationships or exchanges to develop with each subordinate. Graen's dyadic LMX model proposes that two subgroups exist. The in-group consists of those who have high-quality exchanges with the leader, characterized by mutual respect, trust, and support; in-group members report that leaders use referent and expert power (Wayne, Liden, & Sparrowe, 1994). In contrast, out-group members experience more of a supervisory relationship and greater use of legitimate and coercive power (Graen & Cashman, 1975). Graen and Cashman noted that "in-group members [high-quality LMX relationships] received greater latitude in developing their roles, more inside information, greater influence in decision making, stronger support for their actions, and more consideration for their feelings than did out-group members" (p. 146).

Scandura and Schriesheim (1994) proposed that the LMX model of leadership is a transactional approach that describes how leaders use position power and access to organizational resources to encourage subordinates to action. Based on our review of the LMX literature, we suggest that high-quality LMX in-group relationships are more closely aligned to transformational leader-follower relationships due to their high levels of trust, identification, and information sharing, whereas LMX out-group relationships are more similar to transactional leader-follower relationships due to their contractual nature and reliance on positional forms of power.

Thibodeaux and Lowe (1996) reported convergence of in-group LMX relationships and mentoring; that is, individuals who described themselves as being in-group members also reported being mentored by their supervisors. Thibodeaux and Lowe also replicated Scandura and Schriesheim's (1994) findings, in that subordinates do not distinguish between the concepts of mentoring and high-quality exchanges. However, Scandura and Schriesheim found empirical distinctions between these constructs when mentors/leaders report. This suggests that the mentor/leader's target, the protégé, may not discern any difference in behavior whether the supervisor is acting as the mentor or the leader.

Based on the definitions noted above, high-quality LMX in-group relationships are more similar in concept to transformational leadership and mentoring relationships compared with LMX out-group relationships. The following section will expand upon the similarities and differences among the leadership and mentoring constructs.

Mentoring and Leadership Similarities/Differences

As our definition summary suggests, mentoring and transformational leadership are concepts that have overlapping characteristics depending on the individuals involved and the context within which the relationship occurs. Whether one investigates the form of the relationship (one-to-one or one-to-many), the relationship type (formal or informal), the relationship's goal focus (individual or organizational), the context within which the relationship exists (organizationally bounded or boundaryless), or the mutual identification of the roles involved (parties' agreement on mentor/leader role), the functions offered between mentor/leader and protégé/follower differ, as do the outcomes received. We will articulate the similarities and differences between mentoring and leadership given these various characteristics.

Form of Relationship

Applebaum, Ritchie, and Shapiro (1994) have suggested that perhaps the distinction between mentoring and leadership is a simple ratio difference: leadership involves one-to-many, whereas mentoring involves one-to-one. However, we believe that the difference is not so simplistic. Mentoring has traditionally been considered a dyadic form of relationship, while leadership has been characterized as a relationship between one and many (Bass, 1985; Kram, 1985). However, recent research efforts have begun to blur this distinction, as depicted in Figure 6.1. Mentoring has been described as a relationship between one mentor and many protégés, many mentors to one protégé, and many mentors to many protégés, otherwise known as a *developmental network* (Eby, 1997; de Janasz, Sullivan, & Whiting, 2003; Higgins & Kram, 2001; Higgins & Thomas, 2001; Van Emmerik, 2004). Multiple mentors at various ranks within the organization (lateral, hierarchical mentors, and group mentors) have also been posited (Burlew, 1991; Eby, 1997). Ensher, Thomas, and Murphy (2001) offered a network typology that includes the traditional mentor, the step-ahead mentor (one level higher in the organization, potentially in the position the protégé aspires to), and the peer mentor (one comparable in terms of status and experience). Higgins and Kram (2001, p. 269) suggest that all players within the protégé's developmental network are there as "developers," exclusively focused on offering career and psychosocial assistance.

Individuals who report multiple mentors have been found to have greater intentions to remain in the organization and higher work satisfaction (Higgins & Kram, 2001). Many mentors have been found to be related to enhanced career expectations (Baugh & Scandura, 1999) and both objective and subjective career success (Peluchette & Jeanquart, 2000). The key point these researchers make is that the protégé is better off with multiple mentors, since each one offers different perspectives, knowledge, and developmental advice. However, multiple mentors have been found to be related to increased role conflict (Baugh & Scandura, 1999), higher job burnout (Fagan & Walter, 1982), and lower levels of general satisfaction (Riley & Wrench, 1985).

Transformational and LMX leadership theories have similarly defined leadership as a dyadic relationship (Bass, 1990; Graen, 1976; Yukl, 1989), especially when leaders demonstrate individually considerate behavior to followers. The relationship can also be considered a many-to-one and a many-to-many form when boards of directors and top management teams show leadership and provide guidance toward specific (usually high-ranking) employees (Sosik, Jung, Berson, Dionne, & Jaussi, 2004). Mentoring received from a variety of mentor sources parallels discussions of shared-leadership systems (Avolio, 1999; Sosik, Jung et al., 2004) and network LMX assemblies (Graen & Uhl-Bien, 1995). In shared-leadership systems and networked assemblies, a group of individuals exert collective influence over each

Form of Relationship (peers, supervisors, etc.)

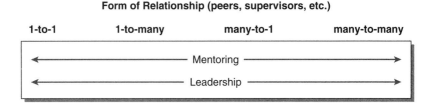

Figure 6.1 Similarities and Differences Between Mentoring and Leadership: Form of Relationship

other to work toward a common goal. The group, as a whole, shares and participates fully in the leadership and developmental tasks of the group. As the group of leaders collaborates, they challenge and develop each other's knowledge, skills, and ability, as seen in mentoring relationships.

In their review of the mentoring and leadership literatures, Sosik and Godshalk (2000) concluded that mentors may exhibit various levels of leadership behavior. Other researchers concur. Allen, Poteet, Russell, and Dobbins (1997) posited that mentoring others leads to "enhancement of leadership skills for mentors" (p. 2). Gladstone (1988) argued that mentors behave as leaders when they shape values, act as role models, and provide organizational meaning for protégés. Schein (1978) described leaders as developers and manipulators of culture, while Wilson and Elman (1990) described mentors as transfer agents of culture.

Based on this review, we believe that mentoring and leadership are more similar than different when it comes to the form of the relationship between the mentor/leader and protégé/follower. However, the social exchange that takes place between the protégé and his or her various mentors needs further investigation. Another future research opportunity includes examining how the form of the mentor/protégé (Bouquillon, Sosik, & Lee, 2005; Chao, 1998) and leader/follower (Avolio, 1999; Graen & Uhl-Bien, 1995) relationship becomes established and changes over time.

Relationship Type

As depicted in Figure 6.2, mentoring and leadership appear to be more different than alike when it comes to whether or not the relationship is formal or informal. While informal leadership may occur, leadership is typically considered a formal relationship (Bass, 1990). In contrast, mentoring has been found to be either formal or informal. Consistent with Wayne et al.'s (1994) and Graen and Cashman's (1975) leadership studies, Thibodeaux and Lowe (1996) found protégés to report greater use of referent, expert, and legitimate power by their supervisors. This suggests that while the protégés may have received mentoring from their supervisors, they identified the mentor as a formal leader as well. Scandura and Schriesheim (1994) found empirical distinctions between mentoring and leadership. They found that the protégé does not discern any difference in behavior whether the supervisor is acting as the mentor or the leader. Hence, the leader's position of formal authority seems to be a prevalent factor in the relationship.

Mentor is an informal title or role that one takes on for the career development of the protégé. Mentoring involves a long-term role model relationship that is professionally and personally development oriented (Burke et al., 1991). Informal mentoring relationships are unstructured regarding time, location, frequency, and mode of communication (Murray, 1991; Ragins, Cotton, & Miller, 2000). Leadership, on the other hand, involves a shorter-term, performance-oriented influence process. Leaders are explicitly defined by the organization, and this may be reflected in their communications with followers. Leadership may be an overt and direct influence process, while mentoring may be a more informal, subtle, and indirect influence process (Appelbaum et al., 1994).

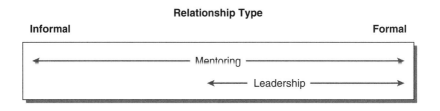

Figure 6.2   Similarities and Differences Between Mentoring and Leadership: Relationship Type

Informal mentoring relationships are often driven by developmental needs (Kram, 1985), which may be mutually beneficial to both mentor and protégé (Ragins & Verbos, 2007). The relationship may help the mentor learn, grow, and deal with midlife issues, while the protégé is developing within his or her early career stage. Mentoring also provides for "generativity," or allowing the mentor to make a significant contribution to the next generation (Levinson, 1978). Ragins (2005) stated that the mentoring relationship allows for mutually dependent, growth-driven learning and enrichment between dyad members.

Researchers have reported that informal relationships may be more focused on protégé learning and goal attainment (Godshalk & Sosik, 2003; Ragins et al., 2000). Due to the role-modeling nature of informal relationships, protégés may be more likely to be personally invested over time, so as to learn in the mentor's footsteps. Wanberg, Welsh, and Hezlett's (2003) review of the mentoring literature concluded that most studies found that informal mentoring relationships were more effective than formal relationships. Several studies found that informal relationships reported higher levels of protégés' career mentoring and higher quality relationships than their formal counterparts (Allen, Day, & Lentz, 2005; Chao, Walz, & Gardner, 1992). Fagenson-Eland, Marks, & Amendola (1997) found that informal protégés reported higher levels of psychosocial support than did formal protégés. Ragins and Cotton (1999) found that informal protégés described their relationships as offering greater mentoring functions on almost every dimension, as well as increased compensation, than those of formal protégés.

While most studies report informal relationships as more productive, Ragins et al. (2000) found that protégés who had high levels of satisfaction with their formal mentors did not differ in functions received compared with informal relationships. Wanberg et al. (2003) suggested that formal relationships may have the potential to reap the same benefits as informal relationships, based on the Ragins et al. findings. Consistent with Wanberg et al.'s suggestion, Sosik, Lee, and Bouquillon (2006) found that the efficacy of formal mentoring relationships depended upon the context in which the mentoring occurred. Formal mentoring relationships were more effective in facilitating career development, role-modeling, and organizational commitment of mentored employees in technology firms. Mentored teachers in K–12 schools benefited more from informal mentoring relationships in regard to role-modeling and organizational commitment.

Formal mentoring programs result from organizational interest in replicating informal mentoring experiences. Formal programs attempt to match mentors with protégés in terms of interests, experiences, or specific goal attainment (Noe, 1988). Murray (1991) noted that in some cases, mentors and protégés may not have met before the dyad is matched. Often, the formal program's guidelines are developed by agents outside of the dyad, and dyad members may be less motivated to participate or may place less value on the relationship because of its "forced" nature (Ragins et al., 2000; Tepper, 1995). Mentors may be less invested in the development of protégés or less likely to receive intrinsic rewards related to their efforts (Ragins et al., 2000). However, Ragins et al. (2000) noted that dyad members, particularly mentors, may participate in formal programs so as to seem involved in organizational citizens.

Protégés, too, may be involved in these relationships because of organizational expectations and therefore less personally vested in program outcomes. Poldre (1994) suggested that mentors involved in formal programs may receive explicit recognition based on their participation. This may be why Ragins and Cotton (1993) found that higher-ranking individuals reported a stronger intention to mentor and anticipated fewer drawbacks associated with mentoring than did lower-ranking individuals.

Formal mentoring programs usually have defined guidelines regarding length of relationship, location, frequency, and mode of communication (Murray, 1991; Ragins et al., 2000). In fact, some relationships have signed contracts with both dyad members agreeing to relationship specifications. Formal mentors typically focus on short-term career goals and offer specific learning to attain such goals (Geiger-DuMond & Boyle, 1995; Murray, 1991). Ragins et al. (2000) suggested that the structure of formal programs may create limitations in the formal mentor's ability to influence the protégé's work and career attitudes.

In sum, much research has focused on both informal and formal mentoring programs and has demonstrated outcomes associated with these programs (e.g., Allen, Eby, Poteet, Lentz, & Lima, 2004; Chao et al., 1992; Dreher & Ash, 1990; Fagenson, 1989; Fagenson et al., 1997; Koberg, Boss, Chappell, & Ringer, 1994; Ragins et al., 2000; Ragins & McFarlin, 1990; Ragins & Scandura, 1999; Scandura, 1992; Seibert, 1999; Tepper, 1995; Whitely, Dougherty, & Dreher, 1991). While we know about outcomes associated with informal and formal mentoring relationships, we know less about the relationships that involve leaders as mentors, regardless of whether the relationship type is informal or formal. Raabe and Beehr (2003) posited that formal mentoring programs may not share the same qualities associated with informal mentoring relationships and high-quality LMX relationships. Tepper (1995) suggested that dyad members may hold different relationship goals depending on whether the mentor was a supervisor or not and whether the relationship was informal or formal. Issues surrounding relationship type (formal versus informal) and mentor's status (supervisory or not) need further analysis. One can surmise from these studies that mentoring and leadership do, in fact, differ regarding the formality of the relationship. Whether or not leaders can have informal relationships with subordinates and what those relationships are (i.e., can we call them "mentoring relationships"?) have yet to be determined. Future research needs to focus on leaders in formal and informal mentoring relationships.

Goal Focus

Both mentoring and leadership focus on developmental opportunities, in that they promote learning, growth, and attainment of goals for both dyad members through various behaviors. As depicted in Figure 6.3, there are some subtle differences in the focus of the partners' goals. Leadership has traditionally focused on the attainment of organizational goals, while mentoring is primarily focused on the achievement of individual goals (Bass, 1990; Wanberg et al., 2003). However, research suggests some overlap in goal focus (Dansereau, Alutto, & Yammarino, 1984; Hunt, 1991; Sosik, Godshalk, & Yammarino, 2004) due to the evolving definitions of leadership.

Transformational leaders value learning and development of followers by inspiring and intellectually stimulating them. Bass (1985) suggested that mentors similarly produce developmental effects on protégés when they display transformational behaviors such as individualized consideration and idealized influence. He stated that "some [leadership] situations bring out the mentoring in superiors and their attention to the development of their protégés" (p. 94). Yukl (1989) noted that transformational leaders get followers to act on desired goals by using knowledge and experience and by "serving as coach, teacher, and mentor" (p. 211). Godshalk and Sosik (2000) suggested that the emotional attachment of followers to transformational leaders might facilitate the development of the mentoring relationship. These researchers suggest that when a supervisor takes on a leadership role, he or she plays a critical role in the development of junior organizational members' goals, just like mentors do.

Mentors also value personal learning by offering functions such as challenging job assignments that help advance the protégé's career. They provide coaching for achieving goals, recognition, and success within the organization (Kram, 1985). Transformational leadership and mentoring follow the principles of social cognitive theory (Bandura, 1986), because both mentors and transformational leaders act as role models. As role models, mentors and leaders encourage learning and development and work to develop others' self-confidence, personal identity, and well-being. Sosik, Godshalk, and Yammarino (2004) found that learning-goal-oriented mentors who exhibited high levels of transformational leadership behavior were apt to raise their learning-goal-oriented protégés' expectations for career success.

Figure 6.3   Similarities and Differences Between Mentoring and Leadership: Goal Focus

Supervisory career mentoring (SCM), mentioned previously, has been conceptualized as a transformational process in which the commitment of the mentor to the protégé's development results in enhanced protégé outcomes (Scandura & Schriesheim, 1994). SCM and transformational leadership share a common focus on goal development. Transformational leadership's idealized influence reflects high levels of respect for the protégé and focuses on personal goal achievement, which is consistent with mentoring. Individualized consideration may be promoted by frequent dyad interactions that lead to goal attainment. Individualized consideration is related to mentoring, since transformational supervisors provide one-on-one coaching, appreciate the protégé's unique talents and skills, and are attentive to the subordinate's unique developmental needs (Scandura & Williams, 2004).

Bass (1985) suggested that the individualized consideration dimension of transformational leadership would have the strongest linkage to mentoring. In addition to individualized consideration, Sosik and Godshalk (2000) argued that intellectual stimulation is offered because mentors provide protégés with challenging assignments as learning opportunities and protect protégés from the risks of making mistakes. As the protégé supports the mentor on projects, he or she also serves as "listening post" for new ideas (Zey, 1988). This sharing of ideas is consistent with intellectual stimulation and develops follower commitment. Through SCM and these noted similarities to transformational leadership, supervisors can promote high goal performance and motivate positive work attitudes of protégés. High-quality LMX leadership relationships may evolve into mentoring and may also provide for followers' goal development (Graen & Scandura, 1987).

Few studies have focused on organizational goal achievement associated with mentoring. Zey (1988) conducted one study that identified several organizational outcomes associated with mentoring: employee integration, reduced turnover, enhanced communication, employee development, managerial succession, increased productivity, and socialization. However, several studies have focused on enhanced organizational outcomes associated with strong leadership. In his review of the leadership literature, Sosik (2006) cited numerous studies making empirical connections between transformational leadership and innovation (Jung, Chow, & Wu, 2003), retention (Sosik, Jung et al., 2004), organizational commitment (Bass & Riggio, 2006; Podsakoff, MacKenzie, & Bommer, 1990), business unit goal attainment (Avolio, Howell, & Sosik, 1999), unit financial performance (Howell & Avolio, 1993), market share and customer satisfaction (Geyer & Streyrer, 1998), and occupational safety (Barling, Loughlin, & Kelloway, 2002).

This summary of the leadership and mentoring literature suggests that both leaders and mentors are concerned with individuals' goal attainment through individualized consideration, intellectual stimulation, or mentoring functions received. However, the research advocates for a relationship between leadership and organizational goal attainment more so than between mentoring and organizational goal attainment. While there is a strong relationship between mentoring and individual goals, there is also ample research suggesting relationships between transformational leadership and high-quality LMX relationships and individual goal focus. Therefore, on this continuum, there is overlap between leadership and mentoring regarding goal focus.

Context/Relationship Boundaries

While leadership is usually relegated to within the organizational context, mentoring may transcend organizational boundaries, especially when one considers extraorganizational development networks (Kram, 1985). (See Figure 6.4.) However, Chao (1998) noted a concern with prior definitions of mentoring, since it is unclear as to whether the mentor and the protégé need to reside within the same organization. Traditional definitions of mentoring assume mentor and protégé exist within the same organization. Wilson and Elman (1990) were specific when they described an "older, more experienced member of an organization takes a junior colleague 'under his or her wing,' aiding in the organizational socialization . . . and passing along knowledge . . . a mentoring relationship is said to exist" (p. 88). This internal mentoring process allows the protégé to learn the "best ways to navigate the subtleties of the organization's informal political system" (p. 89).

Similarly, transformational and high-quality LMX leadership usually occurs within organizational boundaries and is concerned with accomplishment of current organizational goals. For example, as LMX relationships develop over time, the follower's persona changes from "stranger" to "acquaintance" to "partner" as changes occur in roles, influences, exchanges, and interests. The roles of the leader and follower shift from being scripted to being negotiated. The influence shifts from one-way (leader over follower) to reciprocal, as in shared-leadership processes. The exchange develops from low- to medium- to high quality. The interest of the follower shifts from self to self/other to the group (Graen & Uhl-Bien, 1995). Transformational leadership involves influence through dyadic, group, or organizational relationships within the boundaries of the organization (Sosik, 2006). LMX leadership involves dyadic influence processes between leader and follower within an organization and focuses on the benefits that the follower and the organization derive from the relationship (Graen, 1976). For example, leaders and followers meet one on one to set goals, discuss ways to achieve goals, and provide support and feedback on the progress made toward goal achievement.

As Eby (1997) and Ragins (1997) noted, many mentoring relationships are not confined to both partners from the same organization. In fact, Wanberg et al. (2003) stated in their review of the mentoring literature that much research investigated informal mentoring relationships that span organizational boundaries. Some mentoring relationships develop in external networks that provide professional development for protégés (de Janasz et al., 2003; Higgins & Kram, 2001).

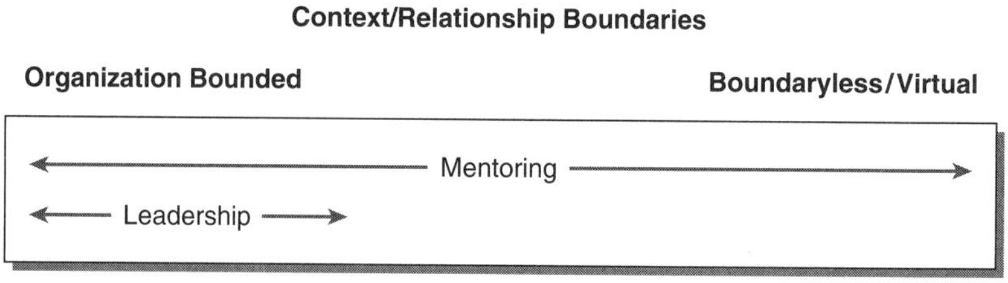

Context/Relationship Boundaries

Organization Bounded   **Boundaryless/Virtual**

← Mentoring →

← Leadership →

Figure 6.4   Similarities and Differences Between Mentoring and Leadership: Context/Relationship Boundaries

More recent investigations of boundaryless mentoring include e-mentoring or virtual mentoring. These mentoring relationships exist exclusively through electronic interactions via e-mail, instant messaging, or the Internet (Ensher, Heun, & Blanchard, 2003; Godshalk, in press; Hamilton & Scandura, 2003). E-mentoring allows for greater understanding in career and discipline-specific areas of study (Single & Muller, 2001; Single & Single, 2005), enhanced learning, increased commitment to one's profession, and a sense of renewal (MentorNet, 2002), as well as an increase in the protégé's network structural diversity, that is, the range and density of a professional's network (Higgins, 2004).

Both Scandura and Williams (2004) and Mullen (1998) noted that professional mentoring may exist, but organizational outsiders may not have the knowledge, power, and influence to effectively mentor protégés inside other organizations. Some have suggested that mentors who were external to the protégé's firm might not be able to provide protégés with the same kind of career development and psychosocial support as those who were internal to the organization (Ostroff & Kozlowski, 1993; Ragins, 1997, 1999). Silverhart (1994) found that insurance agents with internal mentors had higher first-year survival rates and sold more policies than those with external mentors.

Thibodeaux and Hays-Thomas (2005) suggested that the leadership context also varies in extraorganizational mentoring relationships and the extent to which mentors use leadership behaviors in these settings is unknown. This issue of internal versus external mentoring needs further clarification, since it may affect not only the provision of mentoring but also how and if leadership behaviors are utilized in these relationships. In sum, when contrasting mentoring and leadership on the dimension of the relationship boundaries context, mentoring appears to have no bounds, whereas leadership is bounded by the organization's legitimate borders.

Mutual Identification of Roles

Informal mentoring relationships form by mutual identification, which contributes to closeness and intimacy. Members of these relationships report a mutual attraction or chemistry, which may have sparked the relationship's development (Kram, 1985). Oftentimes, formal mentoring relationships do not achieve the same level of closeness or intimacy as do informal relationships because of the lack of partner identification. When formal mentoring dyads are paired by an external agent, there may be a level of formality associated with the relationship that disallows mutual identification of roles (Murray, 1991; Noe, 1988; Ragins et al., 2000; Tepper, 1995). Formal partners may acknowledge they have a mentor/protégé but may not self-identify as a mentor or protégé because of the lack of similarity, closeness, or role-modeling that exists in the relationship. Similarly, in informal relationships, mentors/protégés may not formally acknowledge the other partner as such due to the mentor's deep interest in the personal and professional development of the other individual. Often, these relationships may be considered friendships, sponsors, or allies (Higgins, 2004; Thomas, 1990). Therefore, because mentoring comes in formal and informal forms, dyad members may agree or disagree on whether they identify each other with the roles they play in the mentoring relationship, as depicted in Figure 6.5.

Due to the formal power position associated with the role, leadership does not lack clarity between leader and follower in the roles they play. Transformational and high-quality LMX leaders create relationships that allow for identification with the leader, because the follower views the leader as a role model who has the potential to advance his or her career. Transformational supervisors are appreciated for their coaching, their focus on followers' unique talents and skills, and their attention to followers' developmental needs (Scandura & Williams, 2004). This mutual identification process is based upon similar identities and self-concepts or agreement between the leader and the follower on important values and beliefs (Shamir, House, & Arthur, 1993). Even if the leadership style is transactional or laissez-faire, supervisors are still identified as such in the hierarchy: Regardless of leadership style, leaders and their subordinates identify high-ranking managers and agree on the identification of the leader's role in the organization. Mentoring and leadership therefore differ in the partners' mutual identification of roles.

Functions Offered

Mentoring and leadership offer similar functions for follower/protégés. However, mentoring appears to offer a broader range of functions than does leadership, as depicted in Figure 6.6. It is well documented that mentors provide psychosocial, career development, and role-modeling functions to their protégés (Noe, 1988; Ragins & McFarlin, 1990; Scandura, 1992). Leaders appear to offer role-modeling and career development through transformational and high-quality LMX relationships (Godshalk & Sosik, 2000; Scandura & Schriesheim, 1994; Sosik & Godshalk, 2004). The transformational capacity of SCM can result in the provision of mentoring functions that are different from those provided by nonsupervisors (Wanberg et al., 2003). For example, Sosik and Godshalk (2005) reported that supervisory mentors provided more career development functions than did nonsupervisory mentors. However, leaders do not appear to offer the same level of psychosocial support as mentors do (Godshalk & Sosik, 2000). It may be difficult for followers to assess how much psychosocial support they receive from leaders because of the intangible nature of the relationship (Noe, 1988). Therefore, while research in the field is still comparing the functions offered by both mentors and leaders, we believe that mentors offer a broader range of functions and support than do leaders.

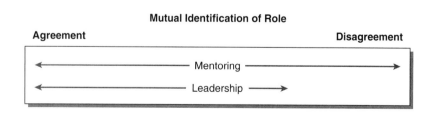

Figure 6.5   Similarities and Differences Between Mentoring and Leadership: Mutual Identification of Role

Figure 6.6   Similarities and Differences Between Mentoring and Leadership: Functions Offered

Benefits/Outcomes Received

As discussed above and depicted in Figure 6.7, mentoring appears to offer a greater range of outcomes than does leadership to the mentor, his or her protégé, and the organization. All mentoring functions (psychosocial, career development, and role-modeling) have been found to affect various protégé, mentor, and organizational outcomes. These functions are mutually beneficial for all parties, whereas leadership may provide benefits to the organization only. Individuals with mentors have been found to have higher expectations for advancement, career and job satisfaction, career commitment, and intention to stay at their organizations. They also report higher levels of compensation, salary growth, and promotions than do individuals without mentors (see Allen et al., 2004; Wanberg et al., 2003). Mentors reported that their experiences positively affected their career satisfaction and increased their self-reported career success and income (Collins, 1994; Johnson, Yust, & Fritchie, 2001). Zey (1988) found that organizations benefit from hastened employee integration, reduced turnover, increased communication, management development, succession planning, productivity, and socialization. Clearly, mentoring functions have positively affected all parties involved in these relationships.

While transformational leadership similarly offers positive outcomes for followers, such as lowering protégé job-related stress (Sosik & Godshalk, 2000), much of the leadership literature provides evidence that leadership focuses on benefiting the organization. Transformational leaders inspire followers through articulation of long-term organizational vision and motivate followers to achieve the broader firm mission through enhancing followers' belief in their being effective contributors to organizational outcomes (Shamir et al., 1993). Transformational leadership has also been found to positively affect organizations, for example, through effective military leadership (Yammarino & Bass, 1990), innovative research and development context (Howell & Avolio, 1993), and total-quality management programs (Sosik & Dionne, 1997). Sosik (2006) noted several organizational outcomes of transformational leadership, including innovation, retention, unit financial performance, market share, customer satisfaction, and occupational safety. These outcomes illustrate the use of transformational leadership as a strategic intervention for impacting organizational performance.

High-quality LMX has been found to enhance organizational performance when subordinates internalize firm values more quickly and demonstrate organizational

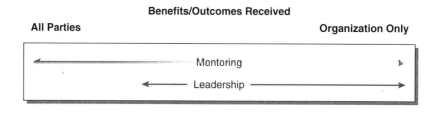

Figure 6.7   Similarities and Differences Between Mentoring and Leadership: Benefits/Outcomes Received

citizenship behavior as a result of LMX leadership (Graen & Ulh-Bien, 1995; Settoon, Bennett, & Liden, 1996; Wayne, Shore, & Liden, 1997). However, high-quality LMX behavior has also been found to improve subordinates' organizational commitment, performance ratings, promotion opportunities, turnover intention, and job satisfaction and ameliorate the effects of unmet job expectations (Gerstner & Day, 1997; Major, Kozlowski, Chao, & Gardner, 1995). Based on this review of the literature, mentoring seems to affect all parties involved in the relationship, while leadership has some effect on individuals but mostly has effects at an organizational level.

Synthesizing the Literature: Where Do We Need to Go?

It appears from this literature review that leadership researchers have found transformational leadership behaviors to supplement both high-quality LMX and transactional leadership behaviors. SCM behaviors have also been found to augment and mediate transformational leadership behaviors. Most of these studies occurred within an organization's boundaries. This suggests that within intraorganizational mentoring networks, SCM is the preferred mentor-protégé relationship (over leadership behaviors alone) for a junior employee.

Yet this raises a series of questions about what role informal relationships, nonsupervisory relationships, or developmental networks play. The literature has been almost exclusively focused (probably because of convenience samples) on variations between formal versus informal and supervisory versus nonsupervisory mentoring dyadic relationships. The focus of future research might shift to investigate the effect of mentor/leader status on the relationship and the type of influence mentors or leaders provide and consider whether these relationships are intraorganizational (i.e., within an organization's boundaries) or extraorganizational (i.e., outside the organization's boundaries). As depicted in Figure 6.8, we suggest that the outcomes associated with internal mentoring and leadership vary on the basis of whether the relationship between the dyad members is formal or informal and whether the senior dyad member is in a supervisory or nonsupervisory position. While the effect of these relationship variables needs more inquiry, we expect that mentoring will provide more provisions for protégés than will leadership behaviors.

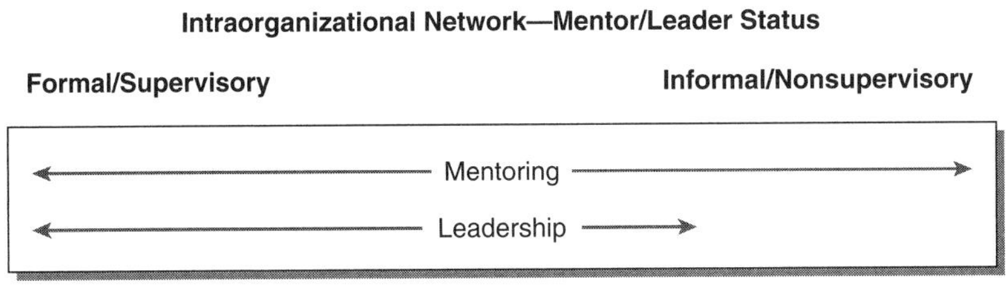

Intraorganizational Network—Mentor/Leader Status

Formal/Supervisory   **Informal/Nonsupervisory**

Mentoring

Leadership

Figure 6.8   Similarities and Differences Between Mentoring and Leadership: Intraorganizational Network—Mentor/Leader Status

Regarding extraorganizational relationships presented in Figure 6.9, we posit that outcomes associated with external mentoring and leadership vary on the basis of whether the relationship between the dyad members is formal or informal and whether the senior dyad member is in a supervisory or nonsupervisory position. An example of a formal extraorganizational relationship might be a relationship created within a formal professional association or within the local community government. Informal extraorganizational relationships may occur within your neighborhood or with friends at the gym. The question of what leadership behaviors exist in these types of relationships needs more examination. However, we expect that mentoring will provide a greater range of provisions for protégés than will leadership behaviors.

Hence, here are our first research questions:

Question 1: How do the following conditions affect intraorganizational and extraorganizational mentoring relationships?

- Formal versus informal mentoring relationship status
- Supervisory versus nonsupervisory status of mentor/leader

Question 2: What role do leadership behaviors play within these relationships?

In a similar vein, we believe that future research needs to analyze the influence processes that exist between mentor/leader and protégé/follower. Higgins and Kram (2001) noted that developmental networks span organizational boundaries. Higgins (2004) has defined these developmental network influencers as ally, friend, sponsor,

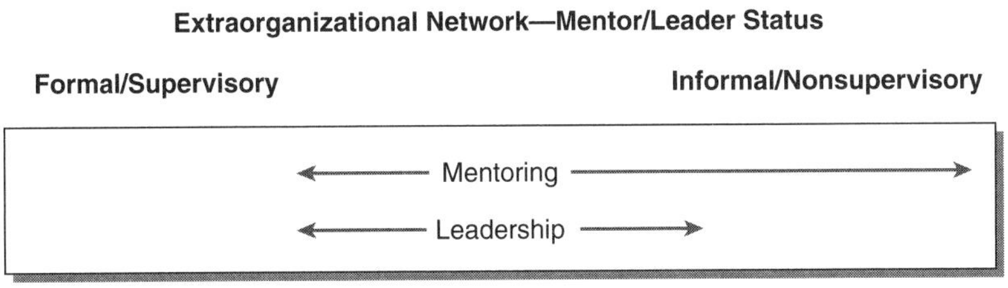

Extraorganizational Network—Mentor/Leader Status

Formal/Supervisory   **Informal/Nonsupervisory**

Mentoring

Leadership

Figure 6.9   Similarities and Differences Between Mentoring and Leadership: Extraorganizational Network—Mentor/Leader Status

and mentor. These influencers offer a range of knowledge and support for protégés. However, few studies have investigated the support protégés receive from those in their networks. Greater clarity is needed for us to understand what role allies, friends, and sponsors play in either complementing or enhancing the role that mentors and leaders fulfill for protégés. Therefore, as depicted in Figure 6.10, we propose that the outcomes associated with internal mentoring and leadership vary on the basis of whether the influence is coming from allies, friends, sponsors, or mentors. As Higgins has suggested, friends provide some psychosocial functions, while allies and sponsors provide more functions across the continuum, with mentors offering a full range of psychosocial and career development functions. We expect that mentoring will provide a greater range of these functions than will leadership behaviors.

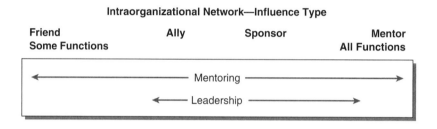

Figure 6.10   Similarities and Differences Between Mentoring and Leadership: Intraorganizational Network—Influence Type

Extraorganizational relationships are presented in Figure 6.11, and we expect that due to the fact that these relationships are occurring outside the organization's boundaries, leadership behaviors will offer a more limited range of functions than will mentoring. Most individuals have networks that include a variety of influencers—from friends to mentors—and these will be identified as some type of influencers first and may not be considered leaders. The question as to whether or not leadership behaviors exist in these types of relationships needs more investigation. Therefore, in these external relationships, we expect that mentoring will provide more functions for protégés than will leadership behaviors.

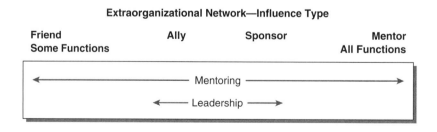

Figure 6.11   Similarities and Differences Between Mentoring and Leadership: Extraorganizational Network—Influence Type

Thus, the following research questions are offered:

Question 3: How do the following developmental influencers affect intraorganizational and extraorganizational mentoring relationships?

- Friends, allies, sponsors, and mentors

Question 4: What range of mentoring functions is offered by these influencers?

Question 5: What role do leadership behaviors play within these relationships?

Finally, while we have noted many research opportunities, we would be remiss in not including another factor that influences our lives every day—that is, technology. While a few studies have started to follow the e-commerce boom and have investigated e-mentoring (Ensher et al., 2003; Perren, 2003) and e-leadership (Avolio, Kahai, & Dodge, 2000), greater emphasis is necessary to understand how communications technology enables the mentor/leader and his or her protégé/follower to interact. Therefore, we offer the following research questions:

Question 6: How does today's technology enable or advance communication between mentor/leader and protégé/follower?

Question 7: How is frequency of communication enhanced by technology? How does frequency affect the relationship? How do written modes (e.g., e-mail or instant messaging) affect the relationship? How does less face-to-face time affect the relationship?

In synthesizing the mentoring and leadership literatures, one can see that while many issues have been addressed in helping us to comprehend these developmental relationships, there is still much that is unknown. More precision is needed in defining the mentoring relationship and in the contextual nuances we have identified. Researchers should consider the aforementioned research questions as guidelines for future investigation.

Mentoring and Leadership:
The Best Way to Get There

There has been a proliferation of research on mentoring in organizations since the publication of Kram's (1985) seminal book on mentoring. While much of the research is excellent, the field is still in a nascent stage compared with the established leadership literature. By learning from the leadership research arena, the mentoring literature will mature as it begins to adopt and integrate solid conceptual/theoretical frameworks, state-of-the-art methods and measures, and effective means for translating findings into practical applications.

Theoretical Pathways

Theoretical frameworks provide pathways for researchers to build upon knowledge that can be advanced in a verifiable manner. They are not theories, but rather blueprints of what is currently known about relationships among constructs that define a field (Sutton & Staw, 1995). Several useful frameworks for mentoring research include Kram's (1985) open systems perspective on mentoring, Koberg, Boss, and Goodman (1998) and Wanberg et al.'s (2003) conceptual process models of mentoring, and Ragin's (1997) model of diversified and homogeneous mentoring relationships. Future work should develop an overarching theoretical framework for mentoring that includes antecedents, processes, and outcomes of mentoring, including the mentor's leadership behavior and contextual facets of the relationship and their effects on the protégé.

As mentoring scholars, we observe a phenomenon and speculate about possible relationships that are likely explanations of the phenomenon. This speculation constitutes theory. Theories represent ideas about relationships among constructs within the theoretical framework (Sutton & Staw, 1995). Several specific theories often discussed in the leadership domain may be helpful in advancing the field of mentoring. These include theories of social learning (Bandura, 1986), self-awareness (Wicklund, 1975), implicit theories and the attribution process (Dweck, 1999), and positive psychological capital (Luthans & Youssef, 2004). Social learning may explain how protégés role-model their mentors' behaviors and adopt attitudes toward developing the self and others (Sosik Godshalk, & Yammarino, 2004) and coping with stress (Sosik & Godshalk, 2000). Self-awareness may account for the degree of mentor-protégé agreement on perceptions of leadership behavior displayed by the mentor and its relationship with mentoring functions provided and associated outcomes (Godshalk & Sosik, 2000; Sosik & Godshalk, 2004).

Implicit theories may differentiate healthy from dysfunctional mentoring relationships, based on whether or not mentors and protégés assume that personal attributes, such as knowledge, skills and abilities, are innate static qualities that are difficult to change or develop. If the mentor and protégé perceive personal attributes as fixed, they tend to become anxiety prone and withdraw from the relationship when faced with a challenging situation. If the mentor and protégé perceive personal attributes as malleable, they tend to remain task focused and resilient when faced with a challenging situation (Dweck, 1999). Implicit leadership theories (i.e., followers' mental models of what constitutes appropriate leadership) often account for varying degrees of leadership effectiveness (Bass, 1990; Yukl, 1989). Such differences in assumptions and attributions on the part of mentors and protégés may explain why certain mentoring relationships become dysfunctional or break up prematurely over the mentoring phases.

Theories and research stemming from the positive psychology movement (e.g., Peterson & Seligman, 2004) hold much promise for expanding what is known about mentoring. By focusing on examining the character strengths, talents, virtues, and values of mentors and protégés, we can learn how to help shape ethical, healthy, caring, and developmental mentoring relationships. Such relationships have been proposed by the literature on authentic leadership as being associated with outcomes such as high levels of trust, motivation, workplace well-being, and sustainable performance (Gardner, Avolio, Luthans, May, & Walumbwa, 2005). Research is just beginning to investigate the similarities between mentors and protégés and the relational aspects of mentoring relationships (Godshalk & Sosik, 2003; Ragins & Verbos, 2007); however, it would be worthwhile for researchers to examine the value congruence of mentors and protégés and its effects on trust and identification levels; mentoring functions received; and positive individual, dyadic, group, and organizational outcomes.

Methods and Measures

Several methodological approaches used in the leadership literature may be helpful in producing more robust mentoring study designs, including (a) multi-source data collection and analysis, (b) longitudinal designs, (c) levels of analysis specification and testing, (d) triangulated measurement of mentoring functions provided/received, and (e) use of objective performance measures.

Multisource Data Collection and Analysis

Traditional mentoring relationships are composed of both mentors and protégés. Networked mentoring relationships consist of multiple mentors and protégés. All parties influence the relationship and may perceive the dynamics of the relationship differently. Therefore, it is important to collect data from all parties in the relationship to fully account for the nature of the relationship (e.g., Godshalk & Sosik, 2003; Sosik, Godshalk, & Yammarino, 2004). Thibodeaux and Hays-Thomas (2005) even called for third parties to provide data on the perceived fairness, legitimacy, and acceptance of the mentoring relationship within the organization. Yet we still find studies that rely on self-reports of the protégé or mentor. Not only do these studies tell only part of the story, they also are subject to common method bias that artificially inflates the relationships between the independent and dependent variables (see Podsakoff, MacKenzie, Lee, & Podsakoff, 2003, to avoid these pitfalls).

Longitudinal Designs

The majority of mentoring studies to date have been correlational studies, which take a "snapshot" view of mentoring at one specific period of time. However, Kram (1985) and others have pointed out that mentoring relationships are dynamic processes that evolve over time through specific phases. While mentoring phases have been examined in prior research, few (e.g., Chao, 1998) have conducted longitudinal studies that show how mentoring antecedents, functions, and outcomes change over time. Avolio (1999) argued that all developmental relationships evolve over time and should be examined within their appropriate temporal and situational contexts. Kram (1985) similarly argued that the four stages of development of the mentoring relationship (initiation, cultivation, separation, and redefinition) provide for dynamic interchange over time between dyad members. Longitudinal empirical research places mentoring within a temporal context and allows researchers to be more precise, theoretically and practically, about when mentoring processes and their outcomes occur. It may be possible to discern leadership from mentoring behaviors when investigated over time. Therefore, we recommend that mentoring researchers collect data at multiple points in time or at least control for the length and phase of the mentoring relationship. Repeated measures or structural equation modeling may be used to test proposed relationships in longitudinal designs.

Levels of Analysis Specification and Testing

Traditional mentor-protégé relationships are assumed to be a dyadic phenomenon in which mutual learning and benefits occur. This assumption has generally not been specified explicitly in the conceptualization of mentoring, nor has it been tested explicitly in empirical work on mentoring, with the exception of Sosik, Godshalk, and Yammarino (2004). Several writers (e.g., Dansereau et al., 1984; Rousseau, 1985) have noted that levels of analysis must be a part of both conceptualization and testing of constructs. Such specification and testing using within-and-between analysis (WABA) is important for precise theory building and falsification purposes. For example, Graen and Uhl-Bien (1995) proposed that LMX theory could be framed using a multilevel analysis perspective, including the domains of leader, follower, and relationship, which could be tested using multilevel data-analytic techniques such as WABA.

Levels of analysis specification and testing also allow mentoring researchers to place appropriate boundary conditions on whether the mentoring relationships being examined operate at the individual, dyadic, group (network), organizational, or industry level of analysis. Sosik, Godshalk, and Yammarino (2004) found evidence for relationships between learning goal orientation, transformational leadership, and several career outcomes to be based either on differences between dyads or individual differences and found no evidence of mentoring processes operating at the industry level of analysis. Consistent with Higgins and Kram (2001), who noted, "It is now time to reconsider the boundaries of mentoring" (p. 283), we recommend that mentoring research be enhanced by incorporating levels of analysis as boundary conditions in conceptualization, measurement, and testing procedures.

Triangulated Measurement of Mentoring Functions Provided/Received

Another helpful recommendation is for researchers to develop more consistent and context-specific measures of mentoring functions. Most developmental leadership researchers use the MLQ-5X for transformational leadership measures (Bass & Avolio, 1997) or the LMX 7 for leader-member exchange measures (Thibodeaux & Hays-Thomas, 2005), whereas the mentoring literature is fraught with multiple mentoring measures: the Mentor Role Instrument (Ragins & McFarlin, 1990), the Mentoring Functions Scale (Noe, 1988), and Scandura's (1992) scales. Mentoring researchers need to collapse these scales into one comprehensive scale, and we suggest that Noe's and Scandura's scales, which identify the three functions mentors provide, be the focus for future use.

With the advent of electronic forms of mentoring and leadership and developmental relationships that span cultures, it seems appropriate to revisit the types of functions that mentors provide to protégés in contemporary organizations and develop more relevant measures. The explosive use of technology for interpersonal communication may influence the relationship between mentors/leaders and protégés. Researchers should also collect both quantitative and qualitative reports of functions provided by mentors and their associated leadership behavior. These reports should be tested for their degree of agreement with the protégé's perceptions of the functions provided and mentoring or leadership behaviors displayed (Godshalk & Sosik, 2000; Sosik & Godshalk, 2004). Differences in organizational and interpersonal contexts, as well as differences in gender and ethnicity, should continue to be investigated. Triangulated data collection and analyses may yield more rich, consistent, and valid conclusions about mentoring processes and outcomes.

Use of Objective Performance Measure

As noted by Ragins (1997), many of the performance outcome variables examined in intraorganizational mentoring research are perceptual in nature (e.g., career satisfaction, quality of the relationship, managerial aspirations, organizational commitment) and assessed via subjective assessments (e.g., self-reports). These measures may be biased by socially desirable responding (Paulhus, 1991) or self-serving bias (Kerlinger & Lee, 2000). It is therefore advantageous for mentoring researchers to follow the path of leadership researchers who have long advocated using objective measures of performance collected from company records, supervisors, or other independent sources. For extraorganizational relationships, reports from significant others and family members may provide similar insight. Such approaches may provide for more objective and valid measures of key outcome measures.

Training and Development

Besides their integral role in transformational leadership (Bass, 1985), mentoring relationships also provide substantial benefits to mentors, protégés, and organizations. Mentors may gain prestige, a sense of generativity, and internal satisfaction. Protégés may build social networks, develop and learn new career-related skills, and gain promotions, pay raises, and job and career satisfaction. By supporting mentoring, organizations may enhance levels of organizational commitment, retention, managerial succession and productivity (Wanberg et al., 2003), and increased communication of culture (Wilson & Elman, 1990).

In an effort to reap these benefits, a growing number of major corporations have designed and implemented formal mentoring programs involving the assigned pairing of a mentor and protégé with organizational assistance (Ragins & Cotton, 1999). While these programs appear to be generally effective, four improvements in training based are recommended. First, more attention should be paid to the characteristics and behavior of the mentor (Sosik & Godshalk, 2004). Mentor-centric approaches to selection and training could include assessments of mentors' self-awareness of leadership behavior (Godshalk & Sosik, 2000), character strengths and talents, and motivational mechanisms and techniques for leveraging diversity within the dyad (Ragins, 1997). Second, given the importance of life events to the development of mentoring relationships (Levinson, 1978), a psychodynamic evaluation of mentors' and protégés' self-concepts, critical life events, and goals may elucidate their purpose in life, thereby enhancing their authentic developmental relationship (Gardner et al., 2005).

Third, trust and commitment within mentor-protégé relationships need to be developed in formal mentoring training. Trust and commitment are key motivational mechanisms associated with the provision of psychosocial support (Bouquillon et al., 2005). These topics are especially important given the increasing number of dysfunctional mentoring relationships reported in the literature (Eby, 1997; Scandura, 1992). Training mentors and protégés in ethical decision-making frameworks, authentic transformational leadership, and positive psychology can help to enhance the quality of mentoring relationships.

Fourth, the benefits of mentoring demonstrated by prior studies may not be realized in practice if researchers continue to ignore testing the appropriate level of analysis. For example, if training for mentors and protégés on the importance of learning and continuous personal improvement as correlates of promoting transformational mentor behavior is delivered individually rather than on a dyadic basis, the benefits to the dyad and the organization will not accrue (Sosik, Godshalk, and Yammarino, 2004). Therefore, to maximize the effectiveness of formal programs, designers, trainers, and administrators of mentoring programs should be aware of how levels of analysis (e.g., individual, dyad, group/network) relate to the mentoring and leadership processes that operate in their organizations.

Conclusion

Displaying transformational and high-quality LMX leadership behavior and supervisory career mentoring is part of what effective leaders do when they provide mentoring functions to protégés. It is clear that leadership and mentoring are distinct constructs and that not all leaders are mentors and not all mentors are leaders. However, those mentors and leaders who inspire, challenge, act ethically, and advance their protégés and followers help to shape high-quality developmental relationships and build healthy and positive organizational cultures. In essence, transformational and high-quality LMX leadership and mentoring are complementary forms of development that can help organizational members to achieve high levels of professional and personal development. Such developmental relationships form the crucible that can ignite the passion for learning, excitement, and work engagement associated with creativity, innovation, and productivity. Individuals who display these mentoring and leadership behaviors set their sights on harvesting the full potential of their protégés, a vision that puts a good theory into the noble practice of making people better than they were before.

References

Allen, T. D., Day, R., & Lentz, E. (2005). The role of interpersonal comfort in mentoring relationships. *Journal of Career Development, 31,* 155–171.

Allen, T. D., Eby, L. T., Poteet, M. L., Lentz, E., & Lima, L. (2004). Career benefits associated with mentoring for protégés: A meta-analysis. *Journal of Applied Psychology, 89,* 127–136.

Allen, T. D., Poteet, M. L., Russell, J. E. A., & Dobbins, G. H. (1997). A field study of factors related to supervisors' willingness to mentor others. *Journal of Vocational Behavior, 50,* 1–22.

Allen, T. D., Russell, J. E. A., & Maetzke, S. B. (1997). Formal peer mentoring: Factors related to protégés' satisfaction and willingness to mentor others. *Group & Organization Studies, 22,* 488–508.

Applebaum, S. H., Ritchie, S., & Shapiro, B. T. (1994). Mentoring revisited: An organizational behaviour construct. *Journal of Management Development, 13,* 62–72.

Avolio, B. J. (1999). *Full leadership development: Building the vital forces in organizations.* Thousand Oaks, CA: Sage.

Avolio, B. J., Howell, J. M., & Sosik, J. J. (1999). A funny thing happened on the way to the bottom line: Humor as a moderator of leadership style effects. *Academy of Management Journal, 42,* 219–227.

Avolio, B. J., Kahai, S. S., & Dodge, G. (2000). E-leading in organizations and its implications for theory, research and practice. *Leadership Quarterly, 11,* 615–670.

Bandura, A. (1986). *Social foundations of thought and action: A social cognitive theory.* Englewood Cliffs, NJ: Prentice Hall.

Barling, J., Loughlin, C., & Kelloway, E. K. (2002). Development and test of a model linking safety-specific transformational leadership and occupational safety. *Journal of Applied Psychology, 87,* 488–496.

Bass, B. M. (1985). *Leadership and performance beyond expectations.* New York: Free Press.

Bass, B. M. (1990). *Bass and Stodgill's handbook of leadership.* New York: Free Press.

Bass, B. M., & Avolio, B. J. (1997). *Full range leadership development: Manual for the Multifactor Leadership Questionnaire.* Palo Alto, CA: Mind Garden.

Bass, B. M., & Riggio, R. E. (2006). *Transformational leadership* (2nd ed.). Mahwah, NJ: Lawrence Erlbaum.

Baugh, S. G., & Scandura, T. A. (1999). The effects of multiple mentors on protégé attitudes toward the work setting. *Journal of Social Behavior and Personality, 14,* 503–521.

Bouquillon, E. A., Sosik, J. J., & Lee, D. Y. (2005). It's only a phase: Examining trust, identification, and mentoring functions received across the mentoring phases. *Mentoring and Tutoring, 13,* 239–258.

Burke, R. J., McKenna, C. W., & McKeen, C. A. (1991). How do mentorships differ for typical supervisory relationships? *Psychological Reports, 68,* 459–466.

Burlew, L. D. (1991). Multiple mentor model: A conceptual framework. *Journal of Career Development, 17,* 213–221.

Burns, J. M. (1978). *Leadership.* New York: Harper & Row.

Carden, A. D. (1990). Mentoring and adult career development: The evolution of a theory. *Counseling Psychologist, 18,* 275–299.

Chao, G. T. (1998). Invited reaction: Challenging research in mentoring. *Human Resource Development Quarterly, 9,* 333–338.

Chao, G. T., Walz, P. M., & Gardner, P. D. (1992). Formal and informal mentorships: A comparison on mentoring functions and contract with nonmentored counterparts. *Personnel Psychology, 45,* 619–636.

Collins, P. M. (1994). Does mentorship among social workers make a difference? An empirical investigation of career outcomes. *Social Work, 39,* 413–419.

Dansereau, F., Alutto, J. A., & Yammarino, F. J. (1984). *Theory testing in organizational behavior: The variant approach.* Englewood Cliffs, NJ: Prentice Hall.

de Janasz, S. C., Sullivan, S. E., & Whiting, V. (2003). Mentor networks and career success: Lessons for turbulent times. *Academy of Management Executive, 17*(4), 78–93.

Dreher, G. F., & Ash, R. A. (1990). A comparative study of mentoring among men and women in managerial, professional, and technical positions. *Journal of Applied Psychology, 75,* 539–546.

Dweck, C. S. (1999). *Self-theories: Their role in motivation, personality, and development.* Philadelphia: Psychology Press.

Eby, L. T. (1997). Alternative forms of mentoring in changing organizational environments: A conceptual extension of the mentoring literature. *Journal of Vocational Behavior, 51,* 125–144.

Ensher, E. A., Heun, C., & Blanchard, A. (2003). Online mentoring and computer-mediated communications: New directions in research. *Journal of Vocational Behavior, 63,* 264–288.

Ensher, E. A., Thomas, C., & Murphy, S. E. (2001). Comparison of traditional, step-ahead, and peer mentoring on protégés' support, satisfaction, and perceptions of career success: A social exchange perspective. *Journal of Business and Psychology, 15,* 415–438.

Fagan, M. M., & Walter, B. (1982). Mentoring among teachers. *Journal of Educational Research, 76,* 113–118.

Fagenson, E. A. (1989). The mentor advantage: Perceived career/job experiences of protégés versus non-protégés. *Journal of Organizational Behavior, 10,* 309–320.

Fagenson-Eland, E. A., Marks, M. A., & Amendola, K. L. (1997). Perceptions of mentoring relationships. *Journal of Vocational Behavior, 51,* 29–42.

Gardner, W. L., Avolio, B. J., Luthans, F., May, D. R., & Walumbwa, F. (2005). "Can you see the real me?" A self-based model of authentic leader and follower development. *Leadership Quarterly, 16,* 343–372.

Geiger-DuMond, A. H., & Boyle, S. K. (1995). Mentoring: A practitioner's guide. *Training and Development, 49*(3), 51–54.

Gerstner, C. R., & Day, D. V. (1997). Meta-analytic review of leader-member exchange theory: Correlates and construct issues. *Journal of Applied Psychology, 82,* 827–844.

Geyer, A. L. J., & Steyrer, J. M. (1998). Transformational leadership and objective performance in banks. *Applied Psychology, 47,* 397–420.

Gibson, D. E., & Cordova, D. I. (1999). Women and men's role models: The importance of exemplars. In A. J. Murrell, F. J. Crosby, & R. J. Ely (Eds.), *Mentoring dilemmas: Developmental relationships within multicultural organizations* (pp. 121–142). Mahwah, NJ: Lawrence Erlbaum.

Gladstone, M. S. (1988). *Mentoring: A strategy for learning in a rapidly changing society.* Montreal, Canada: CEGEP John Abbot College, Research and Development Secretariat.

Godshalk, V. M. (in press). Social implications of e-mentoring: Why might e-mentoring work? In F. Li (Ed.), *Social implications and challenges of e-business.* Hershey, PA: Idea Group.

Godshalk, V. M., & Sosik, J. J. (2000). Does mentor-protégé agreement on mentor leadership behavior influence the quality of mentoring relationships? *Group & Organization Management, 25,* 291–317.

Godshalk, V. M., & Sosik, J. J. (2003). Aiming for success: The role of learning goal orientation in mentoring relationships. *Journal of Vocational Behavior, 63,* 417–437.

Graen, G. B. (1976). Role making processes within complex organizations. In M. D. Dunnette (Ed.), *Handbook of industrial and organizational psychology* (pp. 1201–1245). Chicago: Rand-McNally.

Graen, G. B., & Cashman, J. (1975). A role making model of leadership in formal organizations: A development approach. In J. G. Hunt & L. L. Larson (Eds.), *Leadership frontiers* (pp. 143–165). Kent, OH: Kent State University Press.

Graen, G. B., & Scandura, T. A. (1987). A theory of dyadic career reality. In K. Rowland & G. R. Ferris (Eds.), *Research on personnel and human resource management* (Vol. 4, pp. 147–181). Greenwich, CT: JAI Press.

Graen, G. B., & Uhl-Bien, M. (1995). Relationship-based approach to leadership: Development of leader-member exchange (LMX) theory of leadership over 25 years: Applying a multi-level multi-domain perspective. *Leadership Quarterly, 6,* 219–247.

Hambrick, D. C. (1989). Putting top managers back in the strategy picture. *Strategic Management Journal, 10,* 5–15.

Hamilton, B. A., & Scandura, T. A. (2003). E-mentoring: Implications for organizational learning and development in a wired world. *Organizational Dynamics, 31,* 388–403.

Higgins, M. (2004). *Developmental Network Questionnaire* (9-404-105). Cambridge, MA: Harvard Business School Publishing.

Higgins, M. C., & Kram, K. E. (2001). Reconceptualizing mentoring at work: A developmental network perspective. *Academy of Management Review, 26,* 264–288.

Higgins, M. C., & Thomas, D. A. (2001). Constellations and careers: Toward understanding the effects of multiple developmental relationships. *Journal of Organizational Behavior, 22,* 223–247.

Howell, J. M., & Avolio, B. J. (1993). Transformational leadership, transactional leadership, locus of control, and support for innovation: Key predictors of consolidated business-unit performance. *Journal of Applied Psychology, 78,* 891–902.

Hunt, J. G. (1991). *Leadership: A new synthesis.* Thousand Oaks, CA: Sage.

Johnson, K. K., Yust, B. L., & Fritchie, L. L. (2001). Views on mentoring by clothing and textiles faculty. *Clothing and Textiles Research Journal, 19*(1), 31–40.

Jung, D. I., Chow, C., & Wu, A. (2003). The role of transformational leadership in enhancing organizational innovation: Hypotheses and some preliminary findings. *Leadership Quarterly, 14,* 525–544.

Kerlinger, F. N., & Lee, H. B. (2000). *Foundations of behavioral research.* New York: Harcourt & Brace.

Koberg, C. S., Boss, R. W., Chappell, D., & Ringer, R. C. (1994). Correlates and consequences of protégé mentoring in a large hospital. *Group & Organization Management, 19,* 219–240.

Koberg, C. S., Boss, R. W., & Goodman, E. (1998). Factors and outcomes associated with mentoring among health-care professionals. *Journal of Vocational Behavior, 53,* 58–72.

Kram, K. E. (1985). *Mentoring at work.* Glenview, IL: Scott, Foresman.

Kram, K. (1996). A relational approach to career development. In D. T. Hall & Associates (Ed.), *The career is dead—Long live the career: A relational approach to careers* (pp. 132–157). San Francisco: Jossey-Bass.

Lankau, M. J., & Scandura, T. A. (2002). An investigation of personal learning in mentoring relationships: Content, antecedents, and consequences. *Academy of Management Journal, 45,* 779–790.

Levinson, D. J. (with Darrow, C. M., Klein, E. G., Levinson, M. H., & McKee, B.). (1978). *The seasons of a man's life.* New York: Knopf.

Luthans, F., & Youssef, C. M. (2004). Human, social, and now positive psychological capital management: Investing in people for competitive advantage. *Organizational Dynamics, 33,* 143–160.

Major, D. A., Kozlowski, S. W., Chao, G. T., & Gardner, P. D. (1995). A longitudinal investigation of newcomer expectations, early socialization outcomes, and the moderating effects of role development factors. *Journal of Applied Psychology, 80,* 418–431.

MentorNet. (2002). *2000–01 MentorNet evaluation report.* Available at http://www.mentor net.net/documents/about/results/evaluation

Mullen, E. J. (1998). Vocational and psychosocial mentoring functions: Identifying mentors who serve both. *Human Resource Development Quarterly, 9,* 319–332.

Murray, M. (1991). *Beyond the myths and magic of mentoring: How to facilitate an effective mentoring program.* San Francisco: Jossey-Bass.

Noe, R. (1988). An investigation of the determinants of successful assigned mentoring relationships. *Personnel Psychology, 41,* 457–479.

Ostroff, C., & Kozlowski, S. W. (1993). The role of mentoring in the information gathering processes of newcomers during early organizational socialization. *Journal of Vocational Behavior, 42,* 170–183.

Paulhus, D. L. (1991). Measurement and control of response bias. In J. P. Robinson, P. Shaver, & L. S. Wrightsman (Eds.), *Measures of personality and social psychological attitudes* (pp. 17–59). San Diego, CA: Academic Press.

Peluchette, J. V. E., & Jeanquart, S. (2000). Professionals' use of different mentor sources at various career stages: Implications for career success. *Journal of Social Psychology, 140,* 549–564.

Perren, L. (2003). The role of e-mentoring in entrepreneurial education and support: A meta-analytic review of the academic literature. *Education and Training, 45,* 517–525.

Peterson, C., & Seligman, M. E. P. (2004). *Character strengths and virtues: A handbook and classification.* New York: Oxford/American Psychological Association.

Podsakoff, P. M., MacKenzie, S. B., & Bommer, W. H. (1990). Transformational leader behaviors and substitutes for leadership as determinants of employee satisfaction, commitment, trust, and organizational citizenship behaviors. *Journal of Management, 22,* 259–298.

Podsakoff, P. M., MacKenzie, S. B. Lee, J. Y., & Podsakoff, N. P. (2003). Common method biases in behavioral research: A critical review of the literature and recommended remedies. *Journal of Applied Psychology, 88,* 879–903.

Poldre, P. A. (1994). Mentoring programs: A question of design. *Interchange, 25,* 183–193.

Raabe, B., & Beehr, T. A. (2003). Formal mentoring versus supervisor and coworker relationships: Differences in perception and impact. *Journal of Organizational Behavior, 24,* 271–293.

Ragins, B. R. (1997). Diversified mentoring relationships in organizations: A power perspective. *Academy of Management Review, 22,* 482–521.

Ragins, B. R. (1999). Gender and mentoring relationships: A review and research agenda for the next decade. In G. N. Powell (Ed.), *Handbook of gender and work* (pp. 347–370). Thousand Oaks, CA: Sage.

Ragins, B. R. (2005). *Towards a theory of relational mentoring.* Unpublished manuscript.

Ragins, B. R., & Cotton, J. L. (1993). Gender and willingness to mentor in organizations. *Journal of Management, 19,* 97–111.

Ragins, B. R., & Cotton, J. L. (1999). Mentor functions and outcomes: A comparison of men and women in form and informal mentoring relationships. *Journal of Applied Psychology, 84,* 529–550.

Ragins, B. R., Cotton, J. L., & Miller, J. S. (2000). Marginal mentoring: The effects of type of mentor, quality of relationship, and program design on work and career attitudes. *Academy of Management Journal, 43,* 1177–1194.

Ragins, B. R., & McFarlin, D. (1990). Perceptions of mentor roles in cross-gender mentoring relationships. *Journal of Vocational Behavior, 37,* 321–339.

Ragins, B. R., & Scandura, T. A. (1999). Burden or blessing? Expected costs and benefits of being a mentor. *Journal of Organizational Behavior, 20,* 493–509.

Ragins, B. R., & Verbos, A. K. (2007). Positive relationships in action: Relational mentoring and mentoring schemas in the workplace. In J. E. Dutton & B. R. Ragins (Eds.), *Exploring positive relationships at work: Building a theoretical and research foundation* (pp. 91–116). Mahwah, NJ: Lawrence Erlbaum.

Riley, S., & Wrench, D. (1985). Mentoring among women lawyers. *Journal of Applied Social Psychology, 15,* 374–386.

Rousseau, D. M. (1985). Issues of level in organizational research: Multi-level and cross-level perspectives. *Research in Organizational Behavior, 7,* 1–37.

Scandura, T. A. (1992). Mentorship and career mobility: An empirical investigation. *Journal of Organizational Behavior, 13,* 169–174.

Scandura, T. A. (1998). Dysfunctional mentoring relationships and outcomes. *Journal of Management, 24,* 449–468.

Scandura, T. A., & Schriesheim, C. A. (1994). Leader-member exchange and supervisor career mentoring as complementary constructs in leadership research. *Academy of Management Journal, 37,* 1588–1602.

Scandura, T. A., & Williams, E. A. (2004). Mentoring and transformational leadership: The role of supervisory career mentoring. *Journal of Vocational Behavior, 65,* 448–468.

Schein, E. H. (1978). *Career dynamics: Matching individual and organizational needs.* Reading, MA: Addison-Wesley.

Seibert, S. (1999). The effectiveness of facilitated mentoring: A longitudinal quasi-experiment. *Journal of Vocational Behavior, 54,* 483–502.

Settoon, R. P., Bennett, N., & Liden, R. C. (1996). Social exchange in organizations: Perceived organizational support, leader-member exchange, and employee reciprocity. *Journal of Applied Psychology, 81,* 219–227.

Shamir, B., House, R., & Arthur, M. (1993). The motivational effects of charismatic leadership: A self-concept based theory. *Organizational Science, 4,* 1–17.

Shapiro, E. C., Haseltine, F. P., & Rowe, M. P. (1978). Moving up: Role models, mentors, and the "Patron System." *Sloan Management Review, 19,* 51–59.

Silverhart, T. A. (1994). It works: Mentoring drives productivity higher. *Managers Magazine, 69,* 14–15.

Single, P. B., & Muller, C. B. (2001). When e-mail and mentoring unite: The implementation of a nationwide electronic mentoring program. In L. Stromei (Ed.), *Implementing successful coaching and mentoring programs* (pp. 107–122). Cambridge, MA: ASTD in Action Series.

Single, P. B., & Single, R. (2005). E-mentoring for social equity: Review of research to inform program development. *Mentoring & Tutoring, 13,* 301–320.

Sosik, J. J. (2006). Full range leadership: Model, research, extensions, and training. In C. Cooper & R. Burke (Eds.), *Inspiring leadership* (pp. 33–66). New York: Routledge.

Sosik, J. J., & Dionne, S. D. (1997). Leadership styles and Deming's behavior factors. *Journal of Business and Psychology, 11,* 447–462.

Sosik, J. J., & Godshalk, V. M. (2000). Leadership styles, mentoring functions received, and job-related stress: A conceptual model and preliminary study. *Journal of Organizational Behavior, 21,* 365–390.

Sosik, J. J., & Godshalk, V. M. (2004). Self-other rating agreement in mentoring: Meeting protégé expectations for development and career advancement. *Group & Organization Management, 29,* 442–469.

Sosik, J. J., & Godshalk, V. M. (2005). Examining gender similarity and mentor's supervisory status in mentoring relationships. *Mentoring and Tutoring, 13,* 41–54.

Sosik, J. J., Godshalk, V. M., & Yammarino, F. J. (2004). Transformational leadership, learning goal orientation, and expectations for career success in mentor-protégé relationships: A multiple levels of analysis perspective. *Leadership Quarterly, 15,* 241–261.

Sosik, J. J., Jung, D. I., Berson, Y., Dionne, S. D., & Jaussi, K. S. (2004). *The dream weavers: Strategy-focused leadership in technology-driven organizations.* Greenwich, CT: Information Age.

Sosik, J. J., Lee, D. Y., & Bouquillon, E. A. (2006). Context and mentoring: Examining formal and informal relationships in high-tech firms and K–12 schools. *Journal of Leadership and Organizational Studies, 12*(2), 94–108.

Sutton, R. I., & Staw, B. M. (1995). What theory is *not. Administrative Science Quarterly, 40,* 371–384.

Tepper, B. J. (1995). Upward maintenance tactics in supervisory mentoring and non-mentoring relationships. *Academy of Management Journal, 38,* 1191–1206.

Thibodeaux, H. F., & Hays-Thomas, R. (2005). The concept of leader-member exchange and mentoring: Core and context. In G. B. Graen & J. A. Graen (Eds.), *Global organizing designs, LMX leadership: The series* (Vol. 3, pp. 99–130). Greenwich, CT: Information Age.

Thibodeaux, H. F., & Lowe, R. H. (1996). Convergence of leader-member exchange and mentoring: An investigation of social influence patterns. *Journal of Social Behavior and Personality, 11,* 97–114.

Thomas, D. A. (1990). The impact of race on manager's experiences of developmental relationships (mentoring and sponsorship): An intra-organizational study. *Journal of Organizational Behavior, 11,* 479–492.

van Emmerik, I. J. H. (2004). The more you can get the better: Mentoring constellations and intrinsic career success. *Career Development International, 9,* 578–594.

Wanberg, C. R., Welsh, E. T., & Hezlett, S. A. (2003). Mentoring research: A review and dynamic process model. *Research in Personnel and Human Resource Management, 22,* 39–124.

Wayne, S. J., Liden, R. C., & Sparrowe, R. T. (1994). Developing leader-member exchanges: The influences of gender and ingratiation. *American Behavioral Scientist, 37,* 697–714.

Wayne, S. J., Shore, L. M., & Liden, R. C. (1997). Perceived organizational support and leader-member exchange: A social exchange theory perspective. *Academy of Management Journal, 40,* 82–111.

Whitely, W., Dougherty, T. W., & Dreher, G. F. (1991). Relationship of career mentoring and socioeconomic origin to managers' and professionals' early career progress. *Academy of Management Journal, 34,* 331–351.

Wicklund, R. (1975). Objective self-awareness. In L. Berkowitz (Ed.), *Advances in experimental social psychology* (Vol. 8, pp. 233–275). New York: Academic Press.

Wilson, J. A., & Elman, N. S. (1990). Organizational benefits of mentoring. *Academy of Management Executive, 4*(4), 88–94.

Yammarino, F. J., & Bass, B. M. (1990). The effects of transformational, transactional, and laissez-faire leadership characteristics on subordinate influencing behavior. *Basic and Applied Social Psychology, 11,* 191–203.

Yukl, G. A. (1989). *Leadership in organizations* (2nd ed.). Englewood Cliffs, NJ: Prentice Hall.

Zey, M. (1988). A mentor for all reasons. *Personnel Journal, 67*(1), 46–51.

7

Mentoring and Organizational Socialization

Networks for Work Adjustment

Georgia T. Chao

Organizational socialization is a learning and adjustment process in which the individual acquires social knowledge for a particular organizational role, understands expected behaviors of that role, and assumes the values and attitudes supported by that role. It is often described as "learning the ropes" or "fitting in" with an organization, and successful socialization is linked with positive outcomes such as job satisfaction and career development (Louis, 1980; Van Maanen & Schein, 1979). As a learning process, organizational socialization can involve formal or informal employee development strategies with a variety of mentors (Chao, Walz, & Gardner, 1992).

Understanding how mentors can facilitate the organizational socialization process is important in three ways. First, early turnover of new hires is a constant concern for employers, with about 22% of new hires voluntarily leaving their jobs within the first year (Saratoga Institute, 2003). This turnover is often due to poor organizational socialization, particularly when the new hire perceives a lack of fit between himself or herself and the organization. Arnett (2004) described how young adults often leave their jobs because the work did not mesh with their identities. Mentors can help this latest generation of workers adjust to full-time careers. Second, many career theorists argue that individuals have shifted away from a stable career within one organization to multiple career changes in multiple organizations

(Arthur & Rousseau, 1996). The U.S. Bureau of Labor Statistics (2006) reported that approximately 2.5 million Americans voluntarily quit their jobs every month. Furthermore, the average American adult between the ages of 18 and 30 has held seven to eight jobs (Arnett, 2004). This type of career mobility means that most people will experience multiple episodes of organizational socialization. Finally, the increasing diversity of today's workforce highlights a number of dimensions in which work adjustments will be required in order to promote efficient and effective operations. Current socialization tactics may be based on a historically homogeneous workforce that no longer reflects today's career entrants. Rather than assimilating new hires into an existing and potentially obsolete culture, new socialization practices can embrace diversity to enhance organizational flexibility and creativity (Nkomo & Cox, 1996). Work environments and human resource practices may require changes to accommodate people with different cultural backgrounds, work-family needs, disabilities, sexual orientations, religious preferences, and career goals. Mentors who understand how a diverse workforce can help an organization meet strategic goals could act as catalysts for organization change.

This chapter reviews the literature on organizational socialization and mentoring and charts new directions for future research. Research on organizational socialization and mentoring is organized by two general mentoring functions. First, mentoring career functions focus on organizational adjustment and career advancement. This literature review describes how mentors provide information and coaching to help protégés in their work adjustment. Second, mentoring psychosocial functions focus on the relationship and how it provides acceptance of the protégé as a valued organizational member. This literature review describes how mentors serve as key role models for their protégés. The literature reviewed in this chapter focuses on how mentors can facilitate protégé learning and adjustment within a socialization context. Although much has been written on how mentoring enhances protégé career development (Wanberg, Welsh, & Hezlett, 2003), research specifically examining mentoring and organizational socialization has emerged only in the past 15 years. Following the literature review, a developmental network perspective is used to stimulate future research. A protégé may have multiple developers who facilitate the socialization process by providing a variety of career and psychosocial functions. Different types of developers are proposed to provide specific mentoring functions based on their expertise, experience, and/or position in the organization.

Literature Review

Early research in organizational socialization has focused on the socialization process or ways by which an individual adjusts to a new organizational role. Louis (1980) described how one's expectations of a job create a framework by which people make sense of their experiences. Successful socialization is generally associated with job and career outcomes such as satisfaction, commitment, career progress, and salary progression (Bauer, Morrison, & Callister, 1998). Unsuccessful socialization is generally described as a lack of fit between the person and job and often results in dissatisfaction, strain, and turnover (Kristof-Brown, Zimmerman, & Johnson, 2005).

Various types of socialization tactics are used by organizations to help newcomers adjust to their new roles (Van Maanen, 1978; Van Maanen & Schein, 1979). These range from formal, institutionalized tactics (e.g., group orientations, specified probationary periods, available job incumbents to serve as role models) to informal, individualized tactics (e.g., individual guidance, open adjustment period, no specific hurdles to pass). Of these tactics, the *serial-disjunctive* categorization is most likely to involve mentors. In serial tactics, experienced organizational members serve as role models for newcomers; in disjunctive tactics, there are no job incumbents or role models available. Peer mentors can act as powerful role models to help newcomers learn and adjust to their new positions.

In addition to socialization processes, more recent research has focused on socialization content, or *what* is learned during the adjustment period. Chao, O'Leary-Kelly, Wolf, Klein, and Gardner (1994) identified six content areas of organizational socialization. People were better socialized into their organizational roles when they learned about (a) performance proficiency, or learning to perform the job successfully; (b) specific language related to organizational acronyms and jargon; (c) relationships and how to get along with other organizational members; (d) power structures and organizational politics; (e) organizational goals and values, and (f) the history of their specific organizational units as well as general organizational history. Learning in these six content areas was related to socialization outcomes such as job satisfaction, organizational commitment, and career development. More recent research continues to show how learning in these socialization content areas is related to role clarity, job satisfaction, and organizational commitment (Klein, Fan, & Preacher, 2006; Wesson & Gogus, 2005).

Mentoring relationships can develop between newcomers and organizational members who help them adjust. Louis, Posner, and Powell (1983) surveyed recent college graduates who were in new jobs on the kinds of socialization practices they experienced and the helpfulness of those practices. Only 45% of the sample reported having mentors, but these new hires rated their mentors moderately helpful to becoming an effective organizational member. Furthermore, a mentor's help was significantly correlated with a protégé's job satisfaction.

Many organizations make formal mentoring a part of their orientation programs for new employees, although few report results from these programs (e.g., Horowitz, 1999). The general purpose of orientation programs is to help socialize newcomers into organizational members by providing critical information about the organization's operations and culture. Although some orientation programs have been shown to be effective (Klein & Weaver, 2000), the wide range of program quality requires conclusions to be program-specific. Cawyer and Friedrich (1998) surveyed new faculty and found that a mentoring program was identified as an activity that would have enhanced their socialization experiences. Heimann and Pittenger (1996) examined the effects of formal mentorship on newcomer socialization of university faculty and found a positive relationship between a protégé's report of the interpersonal closeness of the mentorship and value of the program to organizational socialization and commitment. Gagen and Bowie (2005) described how a mentor training workshop could improve the effectiveness of mentoring for new teachers.

Thus, the socialization literature identifies mentoring as a potentially powerful agent of organizational socialization. The following literature review is organized in two parts to highlight how career and psychosocial mentoring functions aid the socialization process. Although most of the mentoring research takes a traditional definition of *mentoring,* that is, a senior-level-mentor and a junior-level-protégé dyad within an organization, more recent investigations of mentoring have broadened the definition to include any relationship that provides career-related or psychosocial support to the protégé (see Higgins, Chandler, & Kram, Chapter 14, this volume; Higgins & Kram, 2001). Following the literature review, examinations of traditional and networked forms of mentoring are provided as a foundation for future research in organizational socialization.

Mentoring Career Function and Organizational Socialization

A mentor's career functions are conceptualized as "those aspects of the relationship that enhance learning the ropes and preparing for advancement in an organization" (Kram, 1985, p. 22). Research on specific career functions related to organizational socialization generally center on coaching. Employees often lack necessary information that can help them be more competent and effective in their organizations (Lankau & Scandura, 2002). Mentors can serve as coaches, providing information and advice for the protégé to meet or exceed job expectations. Within an organizational socialization context, coaching may involve teaching newcomers specific socialization content so they can transition into successful organizational members.

Chao et al. (1992) compared formally mentored, informally mentored, and nonmentored employees on self-reports of organizational socialization, satisfaction, and salary. Comparisons between the two types of mentoring showed no differences in reported psychosocial support, but informally mentored protégés reported significantly more career-related support than did formally mentored protégés. For all content areas of organizational socialization, informally mentored subjects learned more about organizational goals and values, politics, people, language, history, and performance proficiency than did nonmentored subjects. Formally mentored subjects tended to report levels of organizational socialization inbetween those reported by informally mentored protégés and nonmentored subjects. With regard to socialization outcomes of job satisfaction and salary, informally mentored protégés were significantly higher than nonmentored subjects for both outcomes and significantly higher than formally mentored protégés on salary. Chao et al. concluded that mentoring is associated with better organizational socialization. Swap, Leonard, Shields, and Abrams (2001) interviewed mentors and protégés and also found mentors to be effective socialization agents, particularly with tacit knowledge. Informal lessons often included organizational stories to illustrate how organizational values influence decision making and actions.

Career functions are intended to aid a protégé's career advancement, and the general mentoring research has supported positive relationships between career mentoring and salary, satisfaction, and promotions (Seibert, Kraimer, & Liden, 2001). Some studies in organizational socialization did not measure socialization content, but examined mentoring and socialization outcomes related to the career function. Silverhart (1994) found that newly hired insurance agents who had mentors in their organizations were associated with higher retention, higher productivity, and more positive job attitudes than agents with no mentors or agents whose mentors were outside the organizations. Schrodt, Cawyer, and Sanders (2003) compared academic socialization of new faculty members who reported having a mentor with those who were not mentored. Results showed that protégés reported significantly stronger ownership in their departments, were more connected to their work environments, and had more information about research, teaching, and service expectations than did their nonmentored counterparts. Mentoring was concluded to enhance the socialization process for new faculty and to build loyalty to the institution where they work. These results suggest that mentoring has mutual benefits to the organization and its employees by effectively helping new employees adapt and become organizational members.

Mentoring Psychosocial Function and Organizational Socialization

A mentor's psychosocial functions are conceptualized as role-modeling and developing a newcomer's identity as an organizational member and as a professional. Early work on social learning theory (Bandura, 1977) provides a theoretical framework for how role models and mentors can help socialize newcomers into an organization. Social learning theory explains how individuals learn from observations of other people. Interactions between the person, behavior, and environment define the social context for modeling. Kram (1985) found that role-modeling was the most frequently reported psychosocial function mentors provided for their protégés. In fact, Scandura (1992) found that role-modeling was a separate dimension of mentor functions. It is a conscious process in which the protégé identifies with the mentor and aspires to be like the mentor. It is also a nonconscious process when the mentor may be unaware of setting an example for the protégé and the protégé may be unaware of tacit knowledge gained from the mentorship.

As noted earlier, the serial socialization tactic provides role models for organizational newcomers. Cable and Parsons (2001) found a positive relationship between the extent to which organizations used serial tactics and newcomer perceptions of person-organization fit. Furthermore, newcomers with role models were more likely to change their personal values to be more congruent with their perceptions of the organization's values. Ostroff and Kozlowski (1993) focused on how traditional mentoring affected the information-gathering processes during early organizational socialization. They compared mentored and nonmentored newcomers in a longitudinal study and found different patterns of information acquisition. Although both groups relied on observation of others, mentors served as role models for their protégés to observe, whereas nonmentored newcomers observed their coworkers. Furthermore, mentored newcomers learned more about organizational practices and issues than did their nonmentored counterparts.

Filstad (2004) interviewed and observed several newly hired real estate agents and concluded that many newcomers used several role models as partial models to fill different needs. Successful agents identified best sellers as their most important role models; however, they also used supervisors as motivational models. Furthermore, average agents and staff personnel served as survivor models by providing information and solutions to practical day-to-day problems. Rarely was one individual considered a total role model to emulate in all ways. More likely, newcomers selected different behaviors from different models to suit their own personalities and performance expectations. Filstad concluded that the successful organizational socialization of these newcomers was dependent on their choices of role models and the quality of observations and interactions with these models. More successful newcomers had multiple success models and integrated the lessons from all their models better than below-average agents. Thus, "multiple contingent role models" are used by newcomers in the organizational socialization process. The idea of multiple role models will be further discussed in the section on networks and mentoring.

Social learning is more likely to occur when the observer identifies with the model, the model has admired status, and the behavior has functional value (Bandura, 1977). These conditions often incorporate demographic information, and the matching of mentors and protégés can be partially based on race, gender, age, and so on (see Blake-Beard, O'Neill, & McGowan, Chapter 25, this volume). Only a few studies examining mentoring and organizational socialization have been conducted with a focus on diversity issues. As noted in the introduction, the increasing diversity of domestic workforces as well as the growth of global organizations make the successful integration of new personnel into an organization a critical competitive advantage. Formal mentoring programs have often been implemented in organizations committed to developing and promoting women and ethnic minorities. However, within an organizational socialization context, these programs must also consider adjustment needs for specific groups.

In a qualitative study of African American new faculty in predominantly White institutions of higher education, Burden, Harrison, and Hodge (2005) identified a need for mentoring programs to facilitate newcomer socialization into the organization. African American members of the faculty were concerned that their White colleagues might try to socialize them to comply with and protect dominant Eurocentric ideologies and pedagogies. Diversity training and promotion of culturally sensitive pedagogies were suggested as training needs for mentors. Furthermore, mentors may also need to be sensitive to how African American faculty adjust to predominantly White student populations. Finally, mentors may have to help African American faculty make sense out of unfair situations, such as double standards for promotion and tenure, marginalization of faculty of color, and biases against Black scholars.

In a laboratory study, Thomas, Hu, Gewin, Bingham, and Yanchus (2005) asked White college students to read 12 potential protégé profiles and rated how willing they were to peer mentor each. The profiles varied on race (Black/White), gender (male/female), and level of proactive socialization attempts (low, moderate, high). Overall, Thomas et al. found a strong effect for socialization proactivity. Regardless of a potential protégé's race or gender, the more that person was portrayed as interested in forming new relationships and seeking information and feedback from staff members, the more likely the subject was to be willing to mentor him or her. However, if the potential protégé's level of proactivity was low, subjects were more willing to mentor a White male or Black female compared with a White female or Black male. Thomas et al. concluded that a potential protégé's proactive socialization behaviors can attract a peer mentor and suggested that organizational orientation programs should encourage newcomer proaction in forming a mentoring relationship.

Within an international context, Feldman, Folks, and Turnley (1999) examined interns who had recently completed overseas assignments. They found that interns who differed from their mentors in nationality or gender were less likely to receive task-, social-, and career-related support from their mentors. In addition, interns who did not receive much mentoring were likely to be poorly socialized into their assignments, learned less about international business, and received fewer job offers from their internship employers compared with interns with substantial mentoring. These results highlight concerns of organizational socialization within a diverse workforce. Marginalization of a demographically different newcomer is more likely when the current organizational members are relatively homogeneous, hold negative stereotypes against the newcomer, and have higher status and skill levels than the newcomer (Jackson, Stone, & Alvarez, 1993).

Summary

Mentors can be powerful socializing agents as an individual adjusts to a new job or organization. They may serve directly as role models of exemplary organizational members, and they may identify other appropriate role models for their protégés. As protégés learn about their roles within the organization, mentors can help them correctly interpret their experiences within the organization's expectations and culture. An individual's adjustment is more likely to be successful with a mentor's psychosocial and career-related support. Current research has supported the effectiveness of formal and informal mentors on the socialization process; and higher-quality mentoring is associated with greater positive outcomes (see Baugh & Fagenson-Eland, Chapter 10, this volume).

More research is needed on how mentoring can help facilitate the organizational socialization of special groups. Currently, most of the literature examines the organizational socialization of newcomers. Socialization theory recognizes multiple socialization episodes as individuals not only change organizations but also change jobs within organizations. Socialization needs may differ for a newly hired entry-level employee and a newly promoted executive. The effects of a well-established mentorship on the socialization of a senior-level protégé have yet to be explored. Furthermore, little is currently known about mentoring effects for various demographic groups. Wanberg et al. (2003) reviewed some research examining gender and race effects, but more is needed, particularly studies on race that go beyond Black/White comparisons (see Blake-Beard, Murrell, & Thomas, Chapter 9, this volume). Research on mentoring and organizational socialization that includes examinations of age, disabilities, sexual orientations, religion, and other background characteristics is needed to better understand how these individuals adjust to organizations in which some members hold preconceived notions about individuals' backgrounds. In addition, there is a need to understand how organizational socialization tactics may need to change, as traditional models for assimilating employees may not be appropriate for newcomers with diverse cultural values and expectations.

Finally, almost all of the literature reviewed here has assumed only positive outcomes. Research on gender, race, and nationality differences between the mentor and protégé have identified some potential problems, and these issues may be more salient when the protégé is new to the organization and struggling to fit in. In addition, there is little research on how relational problems can result in minor, taxing, or serious outcomes for either party (see Eby, Chapter 13, this volume). Organizational socialization is a dynamic adjustment process. Changes in the mentoring relationship are likely as the adjustments unfold, resulting in negative as well as positive episodes of mentoring.

Developmental Networks, Mentoring, and Organizational Socialization

The current literature supports mentoring as an effective socializing process. Almost all of the literature reviewed here has assumed a traditional mentoring relationship of a senior mentor and junior protégé within an organization. More research is needed to examine how multiple mentors and multiple kinds of mentorships can help a protégé's organizational socialization. If one mentor is good, are two mentors better? A developmental network perspective is used to expand our understanding of mentoring and organizational socialization. Different mentors may be able to address different socialization needs of protégés in order to facilitate the work adjustment process.

Filstad (2004) observed that most newcomers had multiple role models that served different needs during the socialization process. Although most of the mentoring research has focused on only one mentor-protégé relationship, Kram (1985) recognized "relationship constellations" that provide multiple sources of developmental support for a protégé. Higgins, Chandler, and Kram provide a theoretical framework to reconceptualize mentoring in Chapter 14 of this handbook. Their typology of developmental networks is described by two dimensions: (a) the diversity of social systems from which protégés draw upon to form developmental relationships and (b) the strength of these relationships. Traditional mentoring is represented as a strong developmental relationship within one social system (e.g., the organization). Alternative forms of mentoring are described as developmental relationships, with the term *developer* instead of *mentor* applied to an individual who provides career-related and/or psychosocial support to a protégé.

Within an organizational socialization context, a matrix of developers and development functions is proposed to guide future research and practice. This matrix is defined by types of developers and types of mentoring functions relevant to organizational socialization and is shown in Table 7.1. The matrix is intended to illustrate the kinds of developer/function options that may be available to an organizational newcomer; it is not intended to be an exhaustive list of all possible options.

Table 7.1 Matrix of Types of Developers and Development Functions in Organizational Socialization

	Developer Is Organizational Superior to Newcomer	Developer Is Organizational Peer to Newcomer	Developer Is Organizational Subordinate to Newcomer	Demographic Match	Professional/ Interest Area Match	Geographic Location Match
Career-Related Mentoring: Teach newcomer to become proficient in his/her job performance. Socialization content areas: performance proficiency, language	+	0	−	0	+	0
Career-Related Mentoring: Enhance newcomer's exposure and visibility in the organization. Socialization content areas: people, politics	+	+	−	+	+	+
Career-Related Mentoring: Protect newcomer from potentially negative contacts with other organizational members. Teach newcomer about organizational politics. . Socialization content area: politics	+	+	0	0	0	0
Psychosocial Mentoring: Role-model desired attitudes, values, and behavior for newcomer to emulate. Socialization content area: organizational goals/values	+	+	−	0	0	0
Psychosocial Mentoring: Help newcomer's acceptance and confirmation as organizational member. Socialization content areas: people, politics	+	+	0	+	+	+
Psychosocial Mentoring: Enhance newcomer's identity as an organizational member. Socialization content areas: history, organizational goals/values	+	+	+	+	+	+

"+" = likely function for this type of developer; "0" = possible function for this type of developer; "−" = unlikely function for this type of developer.

Types of Developers

In organizational socialization, *developers* are agents who provide career-related and/or psychosocial support to a protégé as he or she adjusts to the new organization. These developers are generally described by two category schemes: (a) their hierarchical relationship with the newcomer and (b) the key feature(s) that attract the developer and newcomer to engage in a professional relationship. From a hierarchical perspective, the developer may be the newcomer's direct or indirect superior, peer, or subordinate. Direct relationships are closely tied to the newcomer's formal lines of authority, current job assignment, and performance expectations; thus, these relationships are better positioned to help the newcomer adjust to the job. Indirect relationships generally cross one or more lines of authority or business units; thus, these relationships are better positioned to help the newcomer adjust to the general organization and culture.

Developers who are organizational superiors to the protégé have power to affect the protégé's job assignments and visibility. They may also be in a position to protect the protégé from early mistakes or to shield the protégé from negative organizational members who intend to exploit the protégé. Developers who are peers or subordinates of the protégé are less likely to have organizational power, but the protégé may be more comfortable seeking help from these kinds of developers. Peer developers often support each other in the socialization process and share lessons learned. Their similar positions in the organization and shared need to adjust efficiently provide a common ground for developmental relationships. Subordinate developers can be rich sources of information about people and procedures. Newcomers may be more comfortable asking subordinates for help because subordinates are less threatening and their evaluations of the newcomer are generally not as important as superior and peer evaluations. For example, a doctor who is a new intern at a hospital is more likely to ask a nurse how to insert a syringe than to ask other doctors or their supervisors.

In addition to categorizing developmental relationships by place in the organization's hierarchy, these relationships can be distinguished by the key criteria that link a developer with a newcomer. A key feature of the initiation stage of mentoring is the belief that the mentor and protégé share common values related to work and individual development (Kram, 1985). These common values can serve as attractors in potential matches between developers and newcomers. Common values are often shared among members of a particular culture; thus, cultural similarities between a developer and newcomer can attract these individuals into a developmental relationship. *Culture* is defined here in the broadest sense, as implicit and explicit values and understandings shared by a group of people. Culture can be a source of social identity and a catalyst for two people to initiate a relationship (Turner, 1982). An individual's social network is likely to include links to people with similar cultural values, and these people are potential developers for that individual's organizational socialization.

Chao and Moon (2005) described a metatheory for understanding multiple cultural identities within an individual. Aside from general conceptualizations of culture tied to nationality or ethnicity, other cultures may be identified from demographic, geographic, and associative features. With demographic cultural features, a developer and newcomer may share common physical features, such as race, sex, age, or ethnicity. Research on gender-as-culture or cultural value differences across age cohorts supports these demographic cultural distinctions. Consequently, some formal mentoring programs may match up a mentor and protégé based on these features, as opposed to work-related interests. Diversity programs often make use of this strategy to help newly hired women and minorities efficiently adjust to the organization (see Blake-Beard et al., Chapter 25, this volume).

Along with demographically defined cultures, Chao and Moon (2005) also described geographically defined cultures. Different cultures have been identified in coastal versus inland areas, temperate versus tropical climates, and urban versus rural environments. Within an organizational socialization context, geographically defined cultures can influence the developer-newcomer relationship in two ways. First, they may serve as the attracting feature for both individuals. For example, a Texan newcomer in a New York office might want to seek out another "transplanted" Texan for help in the socialization adjustment process. Second, different geographic locations may offer more suitable types of developers for newcomers. Within large global organizations, developmental relationships need not be confined within the bounds of a single site location. Although face-to-face meetings may be more conducive for mentoring, Overman (2004) and Ensher and Murphy (see Chapter 12, this volume) described how mentoring can also take place electronically, via e-mail, telephone, and computer-mediated communication. Expanding the pool of possible mentors to all geographic locations will maximize the likelihood of a good mentor-protégé match, especially for individuals who are not members of a dominant culture. Newcomers may be interested in a developer who is not at the same location, for several reasons. The location may not have enough mentors or developers to satisfy the needs of all newcomers. The location may not have developers with whom particular newcomers can identify with. For example, expatriate newcomers may benefit more with a developer from the home country than with developers only in the host country. Furthermore, if a newcomer is to be transferred to another location, he or she may benefit from early contact with a developer in that location. Mezias and Scandura (2005) described how expatriates can benefit from multiple mentors as they adjust to all phases of an international assignment, from predeparture to repatriation.

Finally, associative features of cultural identities highlight group identities that an individual deems important. Within the organizational socialization context, an individual's professional identity is a prime example of an associative culture. Developers who share a newcomer's professional identity can be powerful socialization agents, even if they do not share organizational membership with the newcomer. Lessons from organizational outsiders can teach a newcomer about general strategies for job success that would be valuable, regardless of unique characteristics of the newcomer's organization. Furthermore, these lessons can be complemented by lessons from organizational members who can give more specific help on adjusting to the organization's formal and informal rules, expectations, and policies.

Multiple cultural identities within every individual offer multiple ways to link with other people. A young African American mother starting an academic career may benefit from one developer who is in her profession, another who is an African American professional, and yet another who is balancing work and family priorities. Thus, three developers can comprehensively cover most of the protégé's socialization needs. As their links to the protégé vary, their abilities to offer specific career-related and psychosocial support will also vary.

Types of Developer Functions for Organizational Socialization

Within a mentoring context, two major functions, career-related and psychosocial, are used to identify how developers help socialize a newcomer into an organization. Three career-related and three psychosocial functions are described in Table 7.1. The table identifies which functions are most likely, possible, or unlikely for a particular type of developer. It also identifies specific socialization content areas that are likely to be learned for a particular career-related or psychosocial function.

Of the career-related functions, coaching a newcomer to meet job expectations is the most important for successful socialization and job performance. Newcomers who are unable or unwilling to meet job expectations are unlikely to stay in the organization. These job expectations may be explicit performance criteria and part of a formal appraisal process, or they may be implicit expectations of organizational behavior that conform to the existing organizational culture. Lessons learned during this socialization process can range from simple explanations of the organization's idiosyncratic language, terms, and acronyms to more complex lessons on how newcomers can become proficient in their job performance. Developers who are in direct contact with the newcomer and who can observe and provide feedback on the newcomer's performance are most likely to coach the newcomer to meet or exceed job expectations. However, any developer who understands the newcomer's performance requirements and current knowledge, skills, and abilities may be able to coach that individual on his or her job performance.

A second career-related function involves enhancing the newcomer's exposure and visibility in the organization. Developers within the organization can use their networks to link newcomers to organizational members outside their immediate work environment. Kram (1985) describes how exposure and visibility serve as socializing forces. As new employees are exposed to people and units outside their work environment, they learn more about their organizations. Learning about people and organizational politics can help newcomers understand who can be helpful and who can be harmful. This information can help the newcomer evaluate his or her fit with the organization, recognize appropriate adjustment behaviors, and identify relevant career paths for the future. Furthermore, a newcomer's visibility to other organizational members, particularly powerful ones, increases attention to that newcomer and could result in new opportunities. Other organizational members are more likely to consider a newcomer for special projects, position openings, development opportunities, and so on if they are aware of that person's capabilities and potential.

A third career-related function important in organizational socialization involves developers protecting the newcomer. This protection can be proactive when developers steer a newcomer away from other organizational members who are manipulative and exploitative. This protection can also be reactive when developers shield a newcomer from undue criticism or repercussions from "beginners' mistakes" or poor performance. Although too much protection may be undesirable (Kram, 1985), some protection can help the newcomer feel like a valued organizational member. Developers who are knowledgeable about organizational politics can teach newcomers how to navigate political waters to enhance their organizational standing.

Three psychosocial functions are briefly described here to illustrate how these mentoring functions can help developers socialize newcomers into an organization. First, developers can serve as role models of successful organizational members to newcomers. Kram (1985) noted, "For the individual in early career years, role-modeling is critical for learning the ropes of an organization" (p. 113). Role models can teach a variety of socialization content areas to newcomers; yet shared organizational goals and values are likely to forge stronger ties between the two parties. Most developers can serve as role models, although it may be less feasible if the newcomer cannot directly observe the role model (i.e., newcomer and developer are not in the same location), and it may be less appropriate if the newcomer has a higher organizational status or rank than the developer. As noted earlier, individuals are more likely to identify several role models who address different needs, as opposed to adopting only one role model to completely emulate (Filstad, 2004).

Developers also help support newcomers by accepting them and confirming their organizational membership. Mutual respect and liking between developers and newcomers can expedite the socialization process and maximize the perceived fit between a newcomer and an organization. Developers who are highly familiar with many organizational members are in a better position to help newcomers establish their own networks. Furthermore, friendships that spring from developmental relationships often function as mutual support systems in times of threat or trouble. All developers who offer friendship in the relationship are in a position to provide general acceptance and confirmation. Chao et al. (1994) found that newcomers who learned more about people and politics in the organization were better socialized than newcomers who learned little in these areas.

Most developers can counsel newcomers to build positive and satisfying work relationships. The key to a developer's potential with this function rests in the size and depth of his or her own organizational network. In addition to network building, developers can also help new employees build competencies that are required for current job success as well as future career development. Developers who are familiar with the newcomer's career field, whether it be as an expert, senior member, or peer, are most likely to understand the required knowledge, skills, and abilities for current and future success. Finally, developers who share common demographic characteristics with the newcomer are most likely to be viewed as role models who successfully balance work and family demands. Thus, a newly hired single parent may find support and guidance from established single parents in the organization. Lessons learned from these developers can help newcomers balance their own work-family priorities.

Finally, a third psychosocial function important to organizational socialization involves the newcomer's identity as an organizational member. Developers can teach the newcomer about the organization's general history, as well as the history of the newcomer's particular unit. This information provides a background for newcomers to better understand how they fit into the organization and what may be likely in the future. In addition, if newcomers learn about and accept the organization's goals and values as their own, this value congruence will support the newcomer's identity as an accepted organizational member.

The types of mentoring functions illustrated in Table 7.1 are provided to stimulate future research—it is not an exhaustive list. Similarly, types of developers are not limited to those listed in Table 7.1. Additional matches between newcomers and developers on complementary individual differences could significantly enhance the relationship. For example, Chandler and Kram (2005) described how developmental stage theory can be used to examine mentoring networks. They submit that an individual's level of adult development (the complexity of a person's cognitive, social, and emotional growth) has implications for that individual's relationships with developers, the structure of the developmental network, and likely outcomes from this network. Thus, a protégé at an advanced developmental stage who is matched with a mentor at a lower developmental stage is unlikely to receive appropriate help and support. Although Table 7.1 lists several types of developers, it must be recognized that developers can be described by more than one category. Thus, a developer who is an organizational superior to the newcomer and who shares several important demographic features and professional interests with the newcomer is better positioned to help that individual adjust to the organization than a developer who has fewer ties with the newcomer.

The identification of which type of developer is likely to provide which type of function is provided to stimulate development of future research hypotheses. Exceptions to rules are likely, but understanding who is most likely to provide specific developmental help can provide guidance in the design and implementation of formal mentoring programs. A network perspective of developers recognizes that a newcomer can have more than one developer facilitate the socialization process. Current organizational practices allow for group mentoring in which one mentor has several protégés (see P-Sontag, Vappie, & Wanberg, Chapter 24, this volume), and the next step is to design a corresponding matrix of newcomers who can learn from a network of developers.

Some empirical research has already examined developmental networks. Morrison (2002) found organizational newcomers' informational networks were related to learning in organizational knowledge, task mastery, and role clarity. In addition, she found that characteristics of the newcomers' friendship networks were related to greater organizational knowledge. Van Emmerik (2004) found that the size of a developmental network was related to perceived intrinsic career success. Results from other network characteristics—range of network, emotional intensity, frequency of communications, and years acquainted—were less conclusive. Dobrow and Higgins (2005) measured the density of developmental networks in a longitudinal study. *High-density networks* were described as networks with many links among members (i.e., most people in the network knew other network members, thus making some resources redundant). In contrast, low-density networks involved people who did not know each other; thus, each developer offered advice and resources that were not influenced by other developers. Dobrow and Higgins found that developmental network density was negatively related to an individual's clarity of professional identity. Thus, the low-density network provided more variety of information and resources than a high-density, redundant network, and these resources stimulated professional identity exploration and growth. Dobrow and Higgins advised early careerists to build a diverse developmental network and to change their networks as their professional identities mature.

Future Research Directions

Research on developmental networks is an emerging area in mentoring and organizational socialization. Molloy (2005) reviewed the network literature as it pertains to mentoring and found a distinct shift away from an exclusive focus on a single mentoring relationship to a consideration of multiple concurrent developmental relationships. For example, Higgins and Thomas (2001) compared the effects of a primary developer (i.e., mentor) with an individual's developmental network and found the entire constellation of developers to better predict an individual's long-term career outcomes. More attention on developmental networks is needed as workforces evolve to be increasingly mobile, more diverse, and more likely to use advanced technologies that facilitate communications and interactions among people all over the world (Molloy, 2005).

Early research has been criticized for treating all developers as if they were the same by operationalizing the network as a simple number of developers or as a subjective measure of provided support (Molloy, 2005). Future research can avoid this problem by describing the different types of developers a newcomer may encounter and the lessons learned from each. Instead of describing the network's average level of psychosocial support, cumulative effects of what is learned may be better predictors of a newcomer's socialization. For example, learning across six content areas of organizational socialization (Chao et al., 1994) may vary with different developers. Senior developers are more likely to teach a newcomer about the history of the organization or work unit, whereas developers who are demographically similar to the newcomer may be more likely to share their experiences with organizational politics. Future research should examine how newcomers synthesize and integrate the lessons learned from multiple developers. Mentoring schemas, or mental representations of mentor and protégé roles, formed from previous or current relationships can shape expectations and behaviors in current and future mentorships (Ragins & Verbos, 2007). In addition, more research is needed to identify other socialization content areas about which developers may be uniquely positioned to teach. Results from this research will extend current theory in organizational socialization and in developmental networks.

At the applied level, formal mentoring programs may benefit from recognition of developmental networks. Instead of assigning one mentor to one protégé for general career development, formal socialization programs can identify multiple developers for a newcomer who has multiple developmental needs. For example, an organizational superior can be the newcomer's primary coach to meet job expectations;

a subordinate can volunteer to help the newcomer identify with the organization; and a successful peer who shares professional interests with the newcomer can serve as a good role model. Within the network, developers can focus on their strengths in the relationship and can refrain from offering advice outside their areas of expertise and experience. Rather than relying on a single mentor, multiple developmental areas are met by multiple developers. Assigning more than one developer to a newcomer recognizes the multiple dimensions of organizational socialization. Furthermore, if formal developers are encouraged to stay within their areas of expertise, they may be able to coach more than one newcomer. Thus, a formal socialization program with a developmental network perspective focuses on critical developmental needs and matches developers and newcomers on the basis of these needs.

The beginning of this chapter described three characteristics in today's workforce of young adults: significant early turnover, high career mobility, and increasing diversity. Each poses new challenges in organizational socialization. Current research has supported efficient and effective adjustment to a new position as a predictor of job satisfaction and career success (Bauer et al., 1998). A network of developers has been presented as a guide for future research and practice in organizational socialization. Multiple developers can provide simultaneous career-related and psychosocial mentoring functions to help a newcomer adjust to his or her position. The developmental network recognizes that individual developers hold different strengths of expertise and experience to serve as role models, coaches, advisors, and supporters for organizational socialization. Future research and practice in developmental networks and organizational socialization can enhance newcomers' learning curves as they actively seek a variety of adjustment lessons from many developers who can help them.

References

Arnett, J. J. (2004). *Emerging adulthood: The winding road from the late teens through the twenties.* New York: Oxford University Press.

Arthur, M. B., & Rousseau, D. M. (1996). Introduction: The boundaryless career as a new employment principle. In M. B. Arthur & D. M. Rousseau (Eds.), *The boundaryless career: A new employment principle for a new organizational era* (pp. 3–20). New York: Oxford University Press.

Bandura, A. (1977). *Social learning theory.* Englewood Cliffs, NJ: Prentice Hall.

Bauer, T. N., Morrison, E. W., & Callister, R. R. (1998). Organizational socialization: A review and directions for future research. *Research in Personnel and Human Resources Management, 16,* 149–214.

Burden, J. W., Jr., Harrison, L. Jr., & Hodge, S. R. (2005). Perceptions of African American faculty in kinesiology-based programs at predominantly White American institutions of higher learning. *Research Quarterly for Exercise and Sport, 76,* 224–237.

Cable, D. M., & Parsons, C. K. (2001). Socialization tactics and person-organization fit. *Personnel Psychology, 54,* 1–23.

Cawyer, C. S., & Friedrich, G. W. (1998). Organizational socialization: Processes for new communication faculty. *Communication Education, 47,* 234–245.

Chandler, D. E., & Kram, K. E. (2005). Applying an adult development perspective to developmental networks. *Career Development International, 10,* 548–566.

Chao, G. T., & Moon, H. (2005). The cultural mosaic: A metatheory for understanding the complexity of culture. *Journal of Applied Psychology, 90,* 1128–1140.

Chao, G. T., O'Leary-Kelly, A. M., Wolf, S., Klein, H. J., & Gardner, P. D. (1994). Organizational socialization: Its content and consequences. *Journal of Applied Psychology, 79,* 730–743.

Chao, G. T., Walz, P. M., & Gardner, P. D. (1992). Formal and informal mentorships: A comparison on mentoring functions and contrast with nonmentored counterparts. *Personnel Psychology, 45,* 619–636.

Dobrow, S. R., & Higgins, M. C. (2005). Developmental networks and professional identity: A longitudinal study. *Career Development International, 10,* 567–583.

Feldman, D. C., Folks, W. R., & Turnley, W. H. (1999). Mentor-protégé diversity and its impact on international internship experiences. *Journal of Organizational Behavior, 20,* 597–611.

Filstad, C. (2004). How newcomers use role models in organizational socialization. *Journal of Workplace Learning, 16,* 396–409.

Gagen, L., & Bowie, S. (2005). Effective mentoring: A case for training mentors for novice teachers. *Journal of Physical Education, Recreation & Dance, 76*(1), 40–45.

Heimann, B., & Pittenger, K. K. S. (1996). The impact of formal mentorship on socialization and commitment of newcomers. *Journal of Managerial Issues, 8,* 108–117.

Higgins, M. C., & Kram, K. E. (2001). Reconceptualizing mentoring at work: A developmental network perspective. *Academy of Management Review, 26,* 264–288.

Higgins, M. C., & Thomas, D. A. (2001). Constellations and careers: Toward understanding the effects of multiple developmental relationships. *Journal of Organizational Behavior, 22,* 223–247.

Horowitz, A. S. (1999). Up to speed—fast. *Computerworld, 33*(7), 48.

Jackson, S. E., Stone, V. K., & Alvarez, E. B. (1993). Socialization amidst diversity: The impact of demographics on work team oldtimers and newcomers. *Research in Organizational Behavior, 15,* 45–109.

Klein, H. J., Fan, J., & Preacher, K. J. (2006). The effects of early socialization experiences on content mastery and outcomes: A mediational approach. *Journal of Vocational Behavior, 68,* 96–115.

Klein, H. J., & Weaver, N. A. (2000). The effectiveness of an organizational-level orientation training program in the socialization of new hires. *Personnel Psychology, 53,* 47–66.

Kram, K. E. (1985). *Mentoring at work: Developmental relationships in organizational life.* Glenview, IL: Scott, Foresman.

Kristof-Brown, A. L., Zimmerman, R. D., & Johnson, E. C. (2005). Consequences of individuals' fit at work: A meta-analysis of person-job, person-organization, person-group, and person-supervisor fit. *Personnel Psychology, 58,* 281–342.

Lankau, M. J., & Scandura, T. A. (2002). An investigation of personal learning in mentoring relationships: Content, antecedents, and consequences. *Academy of Management Journal, 45,* 779–790.

Louis, M. R. (1980). Surprise and sense making: What newcomers experience in entering unfamiliar organizational settings. *Administrative Science Quarterly, 25,* 226–251.

Louis, M. R., Posner, B. Z., & Powell, G. N. (1983). The availability and helpfulness of socialization practices. *Personnel Psychology, 36,* 857–866.

Mezias, J. M., & Scandura, T. A. (2005). A needs-driven approach to expatriate adjustment and career development: A multiple mentoring perspective. *Journal of International Business Studies, 36,* 519–538.

Molloy, J. C. (2005). Development networks: Literature review and future research. *Career Development International, 10,* 536–547.

Morrison, E. W. (2002). Newcomers' relationships: The role of social network ties during socialization. *Academy of Management Journal, 45,* 1149–1160.

Nkomo, S. M., & Cox, T. H., Jr. (1996). Diverse identities in organizations. In S. R. Clegg, C. Hardy, & W. R. Nord (Eds.), *Handbook of organization studies* (pp. 338–356). London: Sage.

Ostroff, C., & Kozlowski, S. W. J. (1993). The role of mentoring in the information gathering processes of newcomers during early organizational socialization. *Journal of Vocational Behavior, 42,* 170–183.

Overman, S. (2004). Mentors without borders. *HR Magazine, 49*(3), 83–86.

Ragins, B. R., & Verbos, A. K. (2007). Positive relationships in action: Relational mentoring and mentoring schemas in the workplace. In J. E. Dutton & B. R. Ragins (Eds.), *Exploring positive relationships at work: Building a theoretical and research foundation* (pp. 91–116). Mahwah, NJ: Lawrence Erlbaum.

Saratoga Institute (2003). *Workforce Diagnostic System (WDS) benchmarking reports.* New York: PricewaterhouseCoopers LLP.

Scandura, T. A. (1992). Mentorship and career mobility: An empirical investigation. *Journal of Organizational Behavior, 13,* 169–174.

Schrodt, P., Cawyer, C. S., & Sanders, R. (2003). An examination of academic mentoring behaviors and new faculty members' satisfaction with socialization and tenure and promotion processes. *Communication Education, 52,* 17–29.

Seibert, S. E., Kraimer, M. L., & Liden, R. C. (2001). A social capital theory of career success. *Academy of Management Journal, 44,* 219–237.

Silverhart, T. A. (1994). It works: Mentoring drives productivity higher. *Managers Magazine, 69*(10), 14–15.

Swap, W., Leonard, D., Shields, M., & Abrams, L. (2001). Using mentoring and storytelling to transfer knowledge in the workplace. *Journal of Management Information Systems, 18*(1), 95–114.

Thomas, K. M., Hu, C., Gewin, A. G., Bingham, K., & Yanchus, N. (2005). The roles of protégé race, gender, and proactive socialization attempts on peer mentoring. *Advances in Developing Human Resources, 7,* 540–555.

Turner, J. C. (1982). Towards a cognitive redefinition of the social group. In H. Tajfel (Ed.), *Social identity and intergroup relations* (pp. 15–40). Cambridge, UK: Cambridge University Press.

U.S. Department of Labor Bureau of Labor Statistics. (2006). *Job openings and labor turnover: November 2005* (USDL 06–39). Washington, DC: Author.

Van Emmerik, I. J. H. (2004). The more you can get, the better: Mentoring constellations and intrinsic career success. *Career Development International, 9,* 578–594.

Van Maanen, J. (1978). People processing strategies for organizational socialization. *Organizational Dynamics, 7,* 8–36.

Van Maanen, J., & Schein, E. H. (1979). Towards a theory of organizational socialization. In B. M. Staw (Ed.), *Research in organizational behavior* (Vol. 1, pp. 209–264). Greenwich, CT: JAI Press.

Wanberg, C. R., Welsh, E. T., & Hezlett, S. A. (2003). Mentoring research: A review and dynamic process model. *Research in Personnel and Human Resources Management, 22,* 39–124.

Wesson, M. J., & Gogus, C. I. (2005). Shaking hands with a computer: An examination of two methods of organizational newcomer orientation. *Journal of Applied Psychology, 90,* 1018–1026.

8

Gender and Mentoring

Issues, Effects, and Opportunities

Carol McKeen

Merridee Bujaki

I t is well documented in the literature that mentoring relationships are important for all managers, regardless of gender. Most studies on the outcomes of mentoring have focused on outcomes for protégés, however, rather than on outcomes for mentors or organizations (Wanberg, Welsh, & Hezlett, 2003). There are many benefits reported to accrue to individuals who are mentored, to a greater extent than to those who are not mentored (Allen, Eby, Poteet, Lentz, & Lima, 2004; Noe, Greenberger, & Wang, 2002). The beneficial outcomes of mentoring can be classified as having either a career or personal impact. These have been described as *distal* and *proximal outcomes* by Wanberg et al. (2003). Career or distal benefits can be either subjective or objective. Objective career benefits include the following: more promotions (Dreher & Ash, 1990); greater compensation (Chao, 1997; Dreher & Ash, 1990); more career mobility (Scandura, 1992); and faster advancement (Dreher & Ash, 1990; Whitely, Dougherty, & Dreher, 1991). Subjective career benefits include more career satisfaction (Fagenson, 1989); more career commitment (Bachman & Gregory, 1993; Colarelli & Bishop, 1990); more career planning (Chao, 1997); more organizational socialization (Chao, 1997; Ostroff & Kozlowski, 1993); more self-esteem at work (Koberg, Boss, & Goodman, 1998); more job satisfaction (Bahniuk, Dobos & Hill, 1990; Chao 1997); more job involvement (Koberg et al., 1998); lower turnover intentions (Laband & Lentz, 1995; Viator & Scandura, 1991); more organizational power (Fagenson, 1988); and relational attributes described as *growth-in-connection* (Fletcher & Ragins, Chapter 15, this volume).

The literature also contains a great deal of information about why mentoring relationships are essential (not just important) for the success of women in organizations (Burke & McKeen, 1990; Noe 1988b; O'Neill, Horton, & Crosby, 1999; Ragins, 1989, 1997a, 1997b, 1999). Mentors help women to overcome barriers to advancement that are unique to their gender (Morrison, White, & Van Velsor, & the Center for Creative Leadership, 1987). A trusted guide, sponsor, and interpreter—a mentor—is critical to (a) assisting women in decoding the masculine culture in organizations, (b) promoting women's successful functioning and advancement in organizations, and (c) enhancing women's feelings of safety and belonging in such an environment. Women indicate that being mentored means they have someone who truly cares about them and acts in their best interests: They experience a feeling of connection; they have their sense of worth affirmed; and they feel less isolated (Gibson, 2004).

Wanberg et al. (2003) proposed a conceptual process model of formal mentoring. Their schema incorporates the antecedents and outcomes of mentoring relationships, reflecting the important questions of how and why mentoring relationships are formed and what the effects are of participation in a mentoring relationship. The mentoring relationship itself is influenced by the interaction of the organizational context, the characteristics of the protégé, the characteristics of the mentor, and the characteristics of the dyad. Which mentoring functions are provided and what the mentoring outcomes will be (for the protégé, the mentor, and the organization) will be determined by the unique intersection of these factors, as well as the factors leading to the formation of the mentoring relationship. This model illustrates the complexity of mentoring relationships and hints at the challenges in conducting research on mentoring.

Gender appears in the model as a key characteristic of both protégés and mentors. The issues, effects, and opportunities arising from the study of gender and mentoring are complex, particularly since the concept of "gender" operates on multiple levels. These levels include the individual (mentor, protégé, or researcher), the dyad (mentor-protégé pair), the organizational level (corporate masculinity; Maier, 1991), and the societal level (reflecting how women and their contributions are valued by society). The gender of the protégé and/or the gender of the mentor may influence the reasons mentoring relationships are formed (the antecedents). For example, the gender of the mentor may influence the skills, resources, and expectations the mentor brings to the relationship, and what these expectations are may be different depending on the gender of the protégé. Similarly, the gender of the protégé may affect what the protégé needs, seeks, or expects and how the relationship is interpreted, and these things may also vary depending on the gender of the mentor. A mentoring relationship takes place in the context of organizational cultures, structures, policies, and procedures—which themselves have gendered dimensions. The outcomes of the mentoring relationship may vary on the basis of any of these gender factors, and, indeed, the value attached to various outcomes may also be influenced by gender. In terms of how mentoring relationships are studied, even the selection of research method and level of analysis may be influenced by the gender preferences, views, and priorities of mentoring researchers.

In addition to operating on multiple levels, the study of gender and mentoring employs a number of gender lenses (Fletcher & Ragins, Chapter 15, this volume).

For example, a masculine model of mentoring considers the relationship from an instrumental perspective—what the relationship can do—while a feminine model of mentoring looks at the relationship from an affective or relational point of view— what the relationship can be. Ragins and Verbos (2007) described mentoring in relational, rather than instrumental, terms; in these terms, outcomes involving "mutual growth, learning and development in personal, professional and career domains" (Ragins & Verbos, 2007, p. 92) are envisaged. They suggested that the traditional approach to mentoring research ignores the reciprocal nature of mentoring relationships and "takes a hierarchical and perhaps stereotypically masculine approach to the relationship" (p. 95), which does not address relational outcomes or processes.

Despite the challenges, the role of gender in mentoring must be addressed. Successful mentoring relationships convey so many benefits that we must enhance our understanding of gender and mentoring to ensure that all individuals, regardless of gender, and all organizations understand the issues surrounding mentoring relationships and have access to the beneficial effects and opportunities that arise with mentoring.

A Review of Gender and Mentoring Research

Catalyst is a leading research organization that works with businesses and professions to expand opportunities for women at work. Its research has included studying the impact of mentoring on helping women to break through the glass ceiling. That the glass ceiling still exists is evident from recent statistics from Catalyst indicating that women made up 14% of corporate officers in Canada in 2002, and this increased only fractionally, to 14.4%, in 2004 (Catalyst, 2004). In 2005 in the United States, only eight women were included among the *Fortune* 500 CEOs; only 5.2% of the *Fortune* 500 top earners were women; only 7.9% of the *Fortune* 500 highest titles were held by women; and only 15.7% of the *Fortune* 500 corporate officers were women (Diversity Best Practices, Business Women's Network, 2005). Research by Catalyst also found that mentoring was an effective strategy for overcoming the glass ceiling among female executives (Ragins, Townsend, & Mattis, 1998), women lawyers (Catalyst, 2001b), and women in financial services (Catalyst, 2001a). In its study of women in corporate leadership, Catalyst (1996) reported that 37% of senior-level female executives said an influential mentor or sponsor was a critical ingredient for success, and 80% said this was at least somewhat important to career advancement. In the same study, 91% of successful female executives reported having had a mentor and identified mentoring as a key success strategy (Ragins et al., 1998). Similar results have been found in Canada and in the United Kingdom (Catalyst, 1998, 2000), and 47% of women of color cited "lack of an influential mentor" as their number one barrier to advancement (Catalyst, 1999).

Thus, the managerial literature clearly identifies mentoring as important in helping women to break through the glass ceiling. Why and how mentoring helps women and others with this and other distal outcomes (Wanberg et al., 2003) have been investigated in the academic literature. To understand why these distal outcomes arise, it is necessary to understand why mentoring relationships are formed, what types of and how much mentoring is received, and what proximal outcomes are experienced as a result of mentoring (Wanberg et al., 2003). Wanberg et al.'s conceptual process model of mentoring looks at all these aspects of mentoring. We use their model as a broad organizing framework for a detailed review of gender and mentoring research.

Proximal Outcomes

Mentors help women to succeed by assisting them in identifying and addressing key success factors and in overcoming barriers to success. Protégés can change themselves or their behaviors (through higher levels of cognitive, skill-based, or affective learning), develop new social networks (Wanberg et al., 2003), and experience relational outcomes such as interdependence and connection (Fletcher & Ragins, Chapter 15, this volume). Mentors make important contributions in defining performance expectations, in helping women develop a style with which male managers are comfortable with, in ensuring that women are included in informal networks, in assisting women in selecting (or requesting) appropriate assignments, and in overcoming discrimination.

Performance Expectations. Seventy-seven percent of senior-level women ranked the ability to exceed performance expectations as their number one success factor (Catalyst, 1996). Clearly, women need to understand those performance expectations, but this is often difficult, as such expectations become increasingly subtle at more-senior levels. Mentors may assist senior women in determining what these performance expectations are (Catalyst, 2002).

Finding a Style With Which Men Are Comfortable. Sixty-one percent of senior-level women (Catalyst, 1996) cited the necessity of developing a style with which male managers are comfortable. The low number of women near the top of organizations gives women a minority status and makes it more difficult for them to fit in (Kanter, 1977). There are also few other women to act as role models or to learn from. The subtleties of a style men are comfortable with can be learned only from someone who knows the culture and is willing to help a woman understand this (Catalyst, 2002; Allen, Day, & Lentz, 2005).

Gaining Access to Informal Networks. Half of the senior women in the Catalyst study (1996) reported feeling excluded from informal communication networks. Not only are women likely to be excluded from networks, they are also less likely to get the supports offered by networks from their own direct supervisors (Cianni & Romberger, 1995; Ohlott, Ruderman, & McCauley, 1994). In informal networks, women and men are able to learn about the predominant organizational culture and become known in a broader context than is usually afforded by everyday workplace interactions. Exclusion from these networks is particularly detrimental when an individual is a minority surrounded by a dominant culture that he or she doesn't fully understand. Ibarra (1993) referred to the need to negotiate trade-offs so as to develop "useful" networks. However, women are known to employ different negotiation strategies than men. According to Ragins (1997b), the minority status arising from being female means that women have "to exert more effort and establish different and acceptable power bases by employing such strategies as developing specialized expertise and credentials, joining external and internal power coalitions, and demonstrating exceptional job performance" (p. 489). Mentors may help minority members to gain access to important informal networks.

Challenging Assignments. Successful women also noted the necessity to seek out challenging (stretch) assignments that give them opportunities to develop and showcase their skills (Catalyst, 1996). Mentors have a role in advising women about which assignments to take and why and in offering support and guidance during the assignment (keeping in mind that women need to exceed performance expectations on these challenging assignments) (Catalyst, 2002). Women's communication styles are more indirect than men's, and women are more likely to downplay their own contributions in order to minimize status differences within a work group (Tannen, 1995). Women managers may therefore be less likely to engage in self-promotional activities and may benefit from a mentor who will do this for them.

Overcoming Stereotypes. Mentors also help women overcome both overt and covert forms of discrimination and thus help them figure out how to get to the top (Burke & McKeen, 1990; Ragins, 1989, 1997a, 1997b). Mentors can confer legitimacy on their protégés; mentors can challenge stereotypical preconceptions that disadvantage women; and mentors' "reflected power" (Kanter, 1977) can convey the message that their protégés have their powerful support.

In terms of the work/life interface, women's careers are typically characterized by career interruptions (Ibarra, 1993; Ragins, 1997b) and increased rates of turnover (Ibarra, 1993). Both these circumstances mean that the development and maintenance of relationship ties are complicated by a lack of time (since women still bear primary responsibility for second-shift activities (Hochschild, 1989). However, women may need mentoring relationships all the more to help them successfully negotiate conflicts between family and work (Ensher & Murphy, Chapter 12, this volume; Greenhaus & Singh, Chapter 21, this volume; Neilson, Carlson, & Lankau, 2001). A mentor may be helpful to women in overcoming the stereotype that they are seen as less committed to their careers and their organizations once they have children. In this case, the mentor's role might be to promote the woman's commitment to others, as well as to advise her on how to negotiate this part of her career. In other words, mentors may be well-placed to help women minimize the challenges of stereotypes and realities related to work-family issues.

Other Factors. Despite research findings that male and female mentors provide similar mentoring functions to their protégés, the research examining the connection between the gender of the mentor and outcomes for the protégé has yielded inconsistent results. Ragins & McFarlin (1990) noted evidence that protégés perceive that male mentors bring more power to the relationship. Dreher and Cox (1996) found that protégés with female mentors or mentors of color earn less money than those with White male mentors. The greater organizational power that men have means that male mentors are better able to provide more positive career outcomes and career development functions (Ragins & Sundstrom, 1989). Corroborating this, Ragins and Cotton (1999) found that protégés with histories of male mentors received more financial compensation than those with histories of female mentors. Ragins (1999) suggested that because women define themselves in terms of inter-dependent relationships (Gilligan, 1982), female mentors may provide more psychosocial mentoring functions than do male mentors.

Participant/Relationship Antecedents

Despite the critical importance of mentors to women's careers, mentors are not always easy to find. In the financial services sector, only 35% of women reported having mentors, and 50% were dissatisfied with the availability of mentors (Catalyst, 2001a). Wilson and Elman (1990) noted that the increasing diversity of the workforce adds another dimension to the mentor-protégé matching problem: difficulties inherent in the establishment of relationships between people who do not closely identify with one another. The fact that women and men generally do not closely identify with each other is cited as a reason that women are not included in mentoring relationships with senior-level men (Ibarra, 1993). Furthermore, the complexities of managing cross-gender mentoring relationships are outlined by several authors (Clawson & Kram, 1984; Hurley & Fagenson-Eland, 1996; Kram, 1985; Ragins, 1989). Thus, current organizational demographics may make the establishment and maintenance of mentoring relationships more difficult for women than for men—at the same time that mentoring relationships are even more important for women than for men. Despite the fact that women face greater barriers to forming formal mentoring relationships, they are actually as likely to develop informal mentoring relationships. This suggests that women with informal mentors have recognized the importance of such relationships and have worked particularly hard to develop them.

Numerous studies (cited by O'Neill, 2002) conclude that a person's gender does not affect the likelihood of that person becoming a protégé. This finding is inter-esting considering that Ragins and Cotton (1991) found that more women than men in their study said they needed a mentor and perceived more barriers to obtaining one. Viator (2001) found similar results for African Americans, in that they perceive greater barriers to obtaining a mentor and they were less likely to obtain an informal mentor. It is not known whether women's and men's percep-tions of the difficulty in obtaining a mentor (or their willingness to report such dif-ficulties) confounded these findings or whether the barriers that women perceived were real and they found ways to overcome them. If the former is the case, this has implications for potential bias in reporting in many of the studies undertaken, and if the latter is the case, the extra effort expended by women who succeed in obtain-ing a mentor is worth recognizing and addressing.

Characteristics of the Protégé. Fagenson (1988) found that the probability of being a protégé was much greater for high-level workers than for low-level workers, regard-less of gender. Given the persistent skew of organizational demographics (with men being in more-senior positions, on average, than women), this suggests the necessity to control for the protégé's organizational position or rank when addressing issues relating to the likelihood of being mentored.

Ragins (1989) suggested that the gender of the protégé may influence the type of mentoring received by the protégé. That is, female protégés may seek more socioemotional support from mentors, while male protégés may seek more instrumental help. Others have suggested that mentors give psychosocial help to men and instrumental help to women (Burke, 1984; Burke & McKeen, 1990, 1995; Burke, McKeen, & McKenna, 1990; Burke, McKenna, & McKeen, 1991). Tharenou (2005) found that the gender of both protégé and mentor are factors in determining the type of supports provided in a mentoring relationship: Both male and female mentors provided the same amount of career support to protégés, regardless of gender; however, female mentors provided more psychosocial support than did male mentors, particularly to female protégés. These findings raise the question of whether the types of support mentors give is influenced by what protégés seek.

The role of gender role orientation may be greater than the role of gender itself in predicting the presence and functions of a mentor. Scandura and Ragins (1993) found that men and women with androgynous and masculine role orientations were more likely to have a mentor than those with feminine orientations. In fact, gender role orientation accounted for more of the variance in mentorship roles than did biological sex (Scandura & Ragins, 1993). Androgynous people reported more career development and psychosocial support than did those with either masculine or feminine role orientations.

Most of what we know about gender and mentoring is based on studies of White women managers or professionals and their mentoring relationships. To date, relatively little is known about race and mentoring (Blake-Beard, Murrell, & Thomas, Chapter 9, this volume; Cox & Nkomo, 1991; Kalbfleisch & Davies, 1991), and less is known about the interaction of gender and race in mentoring relationships. Catalyst (1999) examined the experiences of women of color in corporate management, but little research has focused yet on the unique interactions of gender, race, and culture (for example, African American, Latina, and Asian American women) in mentoring relationships

Characteristics of the Mentor. Although there has been comparatively less research on mentoring from the mentor's perspective than from the protégé's, theory suggests that female managers may face more obstacles to becoming mentors than do male managers (Ragins 1989, 1997a). Among midlevel managers, Ragins and Cotton (1993) found that men were nearly twice as likely to be mentors as women, even though women expressed equivalent intentions to mentor despite anticipating more drawbacks. However, in an extension to this study with senior, rather than midlevel, executives, women were found to be as likely as men to be mentors, and women expressed intentions to mentor in the future that were equivalent in number to men's intentions (Ragins & Scandura, 1994). Other studies on the likelihood of being a mentor have suggested that the role of gender may be directly affected by the organization's climate and the potential mentor's rank in the organization (Ragins, 1999).

There has been little research investigating the impact of gender on the costs and benefits associated with being a mentor. Parker and Kram (1993) speculated that women trying to break the glass ceiling might benefit from the support and influence gained by being a mentor. However, Kanter (1977) suggested that women's token status in most organizations increases their visibility and the pressure to perform. This may make potential women mentors less willing to take on the risk of a protégé whose failure would reflect noticeably on the mentor (Parker & Kram, 1993). As Ragins (1999) noted, the female mentor/female protégé relationship is the most visible of all gender and mentoring combinations and faces the greatest risks (Tharenou, 2005). Female mentors who are midlevel managers are seen to be in the most risky position, since they are both highly visible and struggling to advance. They may have greater freedom to mentor only after they break through the glass ceiling (Ragins, 1999). This suggests the mentor's rank should be controlled when investigating the role of gender in mentoring.

Work-family issues as well as other obstacles to advancement that women face may make the time involved in becoming a mentor hard for women to justify as they struggle to advance their own careers (Ragins & Sundstrom, 1989). E-mentoring, which can take place in one's own space, according to one's own schedule, has the potential to address this issue (Ensher & Murphy, Chapter 12, this volume). However, e-mentoring may be less visible within the organization and therefore less likely to be noticed and rewarded.

Sosik and Godshalk (2005) examined the influence of the mentor's status, supervisor versus nonsupervisor, on the protégé's perception of mentoring functions and outcomes. Protégés perceived that supervisory mentors provided more career development functions than did nonsupervisory mentors. This is consistent with earlier research (Fagenson-Eland, Marks, & Amendola, 1997; Tepper, 1995). Sosik and Godshalk (2005) also found that the mentor's status interacted with mentor-protégé gender similarity to influence psychosocial support, career development, and career satisfaction.

Dyad Characteristics. It has been suggested that the gender composition of the mentoring relationship may have a significant effect on the functions and outcomes of the relationship (Ragins 1997a, 1997b; Sosik & Godshalk, 2000, 2005; Tharenou, 2005). There are several issues that require investigation: Are there differences between same-gender and cross-gender mentoring relationships? If so, what are the effects of each of the four possible gender compositions (female mentor/female protégé, female mentor/male protégé, male mentor/male protégé, male mentor/female protégé)? There is also a need to consider whether and how each of these four combinations interacts with other factors. Sosik and Godshalk (2000) investigated the effects of the gender composition of the relationship on the protégé's perception of the mentoring functions received. They found female mentors were perceived to provide more role-modeling and less career development than were male mentors. Male protégés perceived more psychosocial support from female than from male mentors. Female protégés with male mentors perceived more career development functions than did protégés in any other relationships.

O'Neill and Blake-Beard (2002) identified "six possible gender-related barriers to female mentor-male protégé relationships: organizational demographics, relational demography, sexual liaisons, gender stereotypes, gender behaviors, and power dynamics" (p. 53). A shortage of female mentor/male protégé pairs may arise as a result of the relative shortage of senior-level women. In addition, there is evidence showing that men may not select female mentors because women are perceived to have less power (thus, less to offer as a mentor) than men (Ragins, 1997a). It is also possible that senior-level women perceive that there will be a limit to the psychosocial and role-modeling functions they can provide in mentoring relationships if they mentor men (Ragins, 1999). In addition, male protégés may want to model their behavior on the behavior of male mentors because this fits their image of the successful executive (Schein & Davidson, 1993).

For a variety of reasons, women are more likely than men to be in cross-gender mentoring relationships (Burke et al., 1990; Ragins & Cotton, 1991). Cross-gender mentoring relationships face numerous challenges—both in reality and in the perceptions of those relationships by others. These challenges include the absence of role-modeling, intimacy concerns, gender stereotyping that limits individual growth, public scrutiny of the relationship, and possible peer resentment (Kram, 1985). Cross-gender relationships can be more difficult to manage than same-gender relationships (Allen et al., 2005; Clawson & Kram, 1984; Hurley & Fagenson-Eland, 1996; Kram, 1985; Ragins, 1989). Ragins (1999) noted that "compared to cross-gender mentoring relationships, same-gender mentoring relationships between people who are presumed to be heterosexual by others are less susceptible to sexual innuendoes and rumors and have less potential to develop into romantic relationships" (p. 365). Corroborating this, Fitt and Newton (1981) found that sexual tension was an issue in cross-gender relationships and that 10% of their cross-gender pairs had been romantically involved. Bowen (1985) found that jealous spouses and resentful coworkers were a problem. Ragins and Cotton (1991) found women more likely to report that they hesitated to initiate a cross-gender mentoring relationship for fear this would be misconstrued as a sexual advance by the mentor or others. However, the challenges posed by cross-gender mentoring relationships can be addressed more successfully if both mentor and protégé are high on emotional intelligence (Cherniss, Chapter 17, this volume). In fact, interpersonal competence was seen as a more important factor influencing the attractiveness of a mentor than either the mentor's gender or age (Olian, Carroll, Giannantonio, & Feren, 1988). In addition, e-mentoring offers the possibility of mitigating some of these challenges (Ensher & Murphy, Chapter 12, this volume).

Protégés generally prefer mentors of the same gender, although this preference may not be consistent across genders; for example, men may seek male mentors to a greater extent than women seek female mentors. Burke and McKeen (1995) found that women who did not have male mentors did not express a preference for female mentors, nor did they see problems with male mentors. However, women who had actually experienced having male mentors reported more concerns. For example, O'Neill (2002) suggested that women's greater participation in cross-gender relationships may provide them with qualitatively different mentoring experiences than those of their male colleagues. Participants in such cross-gender relationships may assume more sex-stereotypical roles (Clawson & Kram, 1984; Kram, 1985). Since women are more likely than men to be in cross-gender mentoring relationships and these are more difficult to manage than same gender mentoring relationships, this contributes to an unlevel playing field for managerial and professional women (Bradford, 1992), making advancement even more difficult.

Ragins and Cotton (1999) found that relationships consisting of a male mentor and a male protégé lead to more financial compensation than any other mentor-protégé combination and that male protégés with female mentors reported less satisfaction with their mentors than in all other gender combinations. Further, male protégés with female mentors were less likely than protégés in all other combinations to report that their mentors provided challenging assignments and exposure in the organization. They also found that female protégés were more likely to report engaging in after-work activities when they had female rather than male mentors.

In terms of the impact of mentor support on career advancement, Tharenou (2005) determined that career support positively predicted career advancement for women; however, psychosocial support was either not related to career advancement or reduced career advancement (based on measures such as salary, management level, and time since promotion). These relationships varied depending on the gender of mentor and protégé. According to Tharenou (2005), "The positive links of career support and the negative links of psychosocial support consistently arose for women with female mentors, inconsistently for women with male mentors, and overall not for men with male or female mentors" (p. 99). Noe (1988a) found that mentors in cross-gender relationships reported that their protégés used the relationships more effectively than did mentors with same-gender protégés. In particular, male mentors with male protégés reported less effective use of the mentoring relationship by their protégés than did female mentors with female protégés or mentors in cross-gender relationships. What is clear is that the gender composition of the mentoring dyad is critical to several aspects of the relationship.

Mentoring Received

Most research on the receipt of mentoring functions has focused on the two categories of mentoring functions suggested by Kram (1985): career functions and psychosocial functions (Allen & Eby, 2004; Tharenou, 2005). Allen et al. (2004) found evidence that "mentoring is more strongly related to subjective indicators of career success, such as career and job satisfaction, than it is to objective career success indicators" (p. 133). However, they also found evidence that objective career success is more highly related to career mentoring than to psychosocial mentoring. Research on the receipt of mentoring functions by gender of the protégé has yielded mixed and inconsistent results (O'Neill, 2002). Dreher and Ash (1990) found that female business school graduates were more likely than male business school graduates to report that their mentors conveyed empathy. Given our current understanding of the communication styles of women and men (Tannen, 1995), it is likely that women, more than men, would be more aware of and place more value on empathy. This is explored by Fletcher and Ragins (Chaper 15, this volume) in their discussion of the gendered assumptions of traditional mentoring perspectives. In their study of protégés' perceptions of mentor functions, Sosik and Godshalk (2000) found that female mentors were perceived to provide more role-modeling, less career development, and more psychosocial support and the role-modeling provided was perceived to be the greatest in cross-gender pairs with female mentors. In a later study of protégés' perceptions, they found that protégés in cross-gender mentoring relationships reported receiving more psychosocial support than did those in same-gender relationships (Sosik & Godshalk, 2005).

Ragins (1999) questioned "whether reports of mentoring are influenced by social desirability or self-perceptions related to gender" (p. 351). Ragins noted that differences in men's and women's self-construals may lead to gender differences in willingness to mentor in same- or cross-gender relationships, in perceptions of work relationships, and in how these relationships are reported to others. It is possible there are certain aspects of relationships (such as empathy) that men may notice less or report less than women because these aspects are not consistent with the independent self-construals of men. That is, it may be possible that men feel less comfortable admitting they received help from mentors and may underreport these relationships. Gender and mentoring researchers need to investigate potential differences in reporting behaviors, because research findings based on self-reports may be distorted by differences in reporting behaviors.

Allen and Eby (2004) examined mentoring functions provided as reported by mentors. Male mentors reported providing more career mentoring functions to protégés, while female mentors indicated they provided more psychosocial mentoring functions. In terms of the gender composition of the mentor-protégé pairing, Allen and Eby (2004) found that female mentors provided more psychosocial mentoring functions to female rather than male protégés. As noted earlier, however, the provision of psychosocial supports by female mentors may actually hinder the career advancement of female protégés (Tharenou, 2005).

Relational mentoring has much to add to our thinking about mentoring functions. Ragins and Verbos (2007) have suggested that relational mentoring goes beyond the psychosocial and career development functions to include relational processes such as reciprocity, mutual learning, and empathetic teaching and relational behaviors such as empathy, disclosure, sensitivity, and empowerment. They believe that relational mentoring is the highest-quality mentoring state and communal norms are critical for reaching this state.

Relatively little research has focused on the mentoring relationship from the mentor's perspective. One area that has been investigated is the relationship between the gender of the mentor and the functions of the relationship (Allen & Eby, 2004). As with the likelihood of becoming a mentor, at least one study reported by O'Neill (2002) suggested that the rank of the mentor affects the type of help that is received by the protégé, with more senior mentors providing more instrumental help (consistent with greater organizational power). Again, the current skew in organizational demographics, coupled with the finding that more-senior mentors are more likely to dispense more instrumental help, may make it appear that male mentors provide more instrumental help. In fact, it may be the rank, not the gender, of the mentor that is relevant to the provision of instrumental help. This possibility requires further investigation.

Whether female mentors provide more psychosocial functions than do male mentors is unclear. Brefach (1986) found that female protégés with female mentors were more likely than those with male mentors to report that their mentors helped them integrate personal and professional aspects of their lives. Quinn (1980), however, found that male mentors were perceived as providing more assistance in integrating personal and professional self-concepts than were female mentors. Burke, McKeen, and McKenna (1993) found that female mentors reported providing more psychosocial and career development functions than did male mentors and that all mentors reported providing more psychosocial functions to female than to male protégés. This was corroborated by Allen and Eby (2004). Ensher and Murphy (1997) found no support for the proposition that female mentors are perceived as providing more psychosocial functions. Burke and McKeen (1997) found that the gender of the mentor did not affect protégés' reports of mentor functions. However, Burke and McKeen did find that women with female mentors were more involved in their jobs, while at the same time, women with female mentors reported greater intention to quit than did women with male mentors.

Organizational Context

Research by Ragins and Cotton (1999) suggested that whether the mentoring relationship is formal or informal confounds the findings about the provision of mentor functions. They reported that protégés with formal mentors received fewer career development and psychosocial functions than did protégés with informal mentors but that this was not the same for men and women. Women with formal mentors received less coaching, role-modeling, and friendship and fewer social interactions than those with informal mentors, but this difference was not found for men. Ragins, Cotton, and Miller (2000) addressed the impact of mentoring relationships on work and career attitudes. While they found that male and female protégés reported equal attitudinal benefits from informal mentoring, women with formal mentors actually reported less career commitment than did individuals who had no mentors. Overall, these findings suggest that formal mentors may be more beneficial for male protégés than for female protégés.

An Agenda for Gender and Mentoring Research

There is still much that we do not know about gender and mentoring. We propose here an agenda for gender and mentoring research that addresses two broad aspects of this research. First, we identify methodological issues that should be addressed. Second, we discuss a number of specific research questions that need to be addressed by future research.

Methodological Issues in Gender and Mentoring Research

Levels of Analysis. To date, most research on gender and mentoring has focused on the individual level of analysis—specifically, the impact of mentoring on protégés. The need to conduct research at various levels of analysis has been noted. Ibarra (1993) called for analysis at both personal and organizational levels. Others have indicated that individual, interpersonal, organizational, and social levels of analysis should all be addressed (Fletcher, 1998; Ragins 1997b; Wanberg et al., 2003). Future research needs to focus on mentors, the functioning of the mentoring dyad, the organizational costs and benefits, and the social implications of mentoring activities.

Research Approach. A combination of quantitative and qualitative research is needed (Ibarra, 1993). Some gender and mentoring research is at the stage of proposing and beginning to test models of the antecedents and consequences of mentoring (Higgins & Kram, 2001; Ibarra, 1993; Wanberg et al., 2003). An appropriate methodological approach for such hypothesis testing—one that would also address concerns over the validity and reliability of mentoring measures—may be structural equation modeling (Noe et al., 2002). In contrast, from a feminine research perspective, additional qualitative inquiry, perhaps more storytelling, is appropriate (Allen, Poteet, & Burroughs, 1997; Gibson, 2004), as is additional research based upon theories of women's ways of relating (Fletcher, 1998; Fletcher & Ragins, Chapter 15, this volume; Gersick, Bartunek, & Dutton, 2000).

Research Methods. The concern that too much mentoring research is based upon self-reports of protégés, which gives rise to common-method bias (Dougherty & Dreher, Chapter 3, this volume), needs to be addressed. This is a particular concern because women and men are likely to have different biases in their self-reports (Ragins, 1999; Wanberg et al., 2003). Multiple methods of data collection would help to address these concerns. Future research can benefit from a multiplicity of research methods, including collecting additional objective data (e.g., on career success measures), along with subjective data from multiple perspectives (protégé, mentor, peers, supervisors, etc.). These methods would help to answer questions about whether and how reports of mentoring (by protégés and mentors) are influenced by social desirability or self-construals related to gender.

Longitudinal Studies. Ibarra (1993) and Ragins (1997b) identified difficulties in disentangling cause and effect in mentoring relationships. For example, does mentoring lead to career success, or are protégés selected because of their already occurring success? The only way to separate cause and effect in mentoring research will be to engage in longitudinal research (Allen et al., 2004). Longitudinal studies will also be appropriate to study the formation, course, and dissolution of mentoring relationships, as well as the transition from mentoring to peer relationships (Gersick et al., 2000; Ragins & Verbos, 2007). In longitudinal studies of mentoring relationships, it will be of interest to see whether women and men seek different types of mentoring.

For example, do female mentors seek mentoring relationships that reflect greater equality and interdependence between mentor and protégé (in accordance with a great emphasis on relational activities; Fletcher & Ragins, Chapter 15, this volume), and do male mentors seek more hierarchical mentoring relationships that will provide them with greater status and recognition (Ragins, 1999)?

Research Questions in Gender and Mentoring

In addition to methodological issues in gender and mentoring research, numerous research questions in gender and mentoring have yet to be fully explored. A number of these questions are summarized in Table 8.1.

Research Subject. Most mentoring research to date has focused on the impact of the mentoring relationship on the protégé (Wanberg et al., 2003). In the future, more research focus should be directed to the issues, effects, and opportunities that mentoring provides to mentors. The gender dimension of this research will also be of interest—in other words, do the antecedents and outcomes of mentoring differ for male and female mentors? In particular, what are the unique needs of women that encourage them to take on a mentoring role, and what do they seek from their mentoring experiences? There is also a need for more research on mentoring relationships across the full range of mentor-protégé gender combinations and on the impact of gender on the types of mentoring functions provided by mentors to protégés.

Organizational Context. Fletcher and Ragins (Chapter 15, this volume) advocate treating gender as a systemic- rather than an individual-level phenomenon. Comparative research (Ibarra, 1993) will help determine the impact of variation in organizational contexts on mentoring relationships. Since some organizational contexts are more masculine than others, such research will address the impact of gender at organizational as well as individual levels.

Negative Mentoring Consequences. Additional research is needed to address potentially negative effects of mentoring relationships (Eby, Chapter 13, this volume; Gersick et al., 2000). Most research to date assumes that mentoring relationships are beneficial for the participants and their organizations. Ragins and Verbos (2007) identify a dysfunctional relationship as one that is characterized by violation of norms of exchange and community and that may instead use exploitative norms for personal gain, disregarding the other's needs and interests. They conclude that "dysfunctional mentoring states can lead to negative or even harmful outcomes" (p. 98; also see Eby, Butts, Lockwood & Simon, 2004). Research to identify conditions in which the costs of mentoring exceed the benefits and how this varies with the gender composition of the dyad will be particularly helpful in designing mentoring programs to ensure that adverse effects of mentoring are not disproportionately borne by members of one gender.

Mentoring and Diversity. Mentoring research can also address ways in which gender and other aspects of diversity interact to affect mentoring processes and outcomes.

Table 8.1   An Agenda for Future Research

Mentoring Question	Gender and Mentoring Question
What are the antecedents and outcomes of mentoring relationships? (Fletcher & Ragins, Chapter 15; Ibarra, 1993; Ragins, 1997b)	Are the antecedents and outcomes the same for women and men? Should outcomes include more relational factors?
Can a calculus of mentoring be defined in terms of the cost-benefit trade-offs both mentor and protégé make? (Fletcher & Ragins, Chapter 15; Ragins & Scandura, 1994)	Is this calculus different for women and men?
Do current measures of mentoring capture all its dimensions? (Higgins & Kram, 2001)	Do women and men focus differently on the quantity versus the quality of mentoring relationships? Do women and men focus on different factors when they consider a mentoring relationship?
Does race affect mentoring relationships? (Cox & Nkomo, 1991; Kalbfleisch & Davies, 1991; Ragins, 1997b)	How do race and gender interact in mentoring relationships?
Do other aspects of diversity (sexual orientation, physical ability, age, etc.) impact mentoring relationships?	How do gender and other aspects of diversity (sexual orientation, physical ability, age, etc.) interact in mentoring relationships?
Why do mentors mentor? (Allen & Eby, 2004; Ragins, 1999)	Do women have unique needs that encourage them to mentor? Do women seek something different than men from their experiences as a mentor? Do women face different costs and benefits from mentoring?
Are all mentoring relationships equal? (Ensher & Murphy, Chapter 12; O'Neill & Blake-Beard, 2002; Ragins, 1997a, 1997b; Sosik & Godshalk, 2000, 2005)	Do female mentor/female protégé, female mentor/male protégé, male mentor/female protégé, and male mentor/male protégé relationships differ? How? Why? What are the moderating effects of e-mentoring on these differences?
Do communication styles affect mentoring relationships? (Ragins, 1999)	Do women's and men's different communication styles impact the formation, processes, outcomes, and meaning of mentoring interactions?
Does having a mentor affect perceptions of competence and performance attributions? (Ragins, 1999)	Are perceptions of women's and men's competence and attributions of performance differentially influenced by having a mentor? What is the role of gender in these perceptions?
Do mentoring relationships affect perceptions of equity and justice in organizations? (Ragins, 1999)	Are perceptions of equity and justice different when women or men benefit from mentoring relationships?

(Continued)

Table 8.1 (Continued)

Mentoring Question	Gender and Mentoring Question
Do the status, power, and influence of mentors and protégés have an impact on mentoring relationships? (Ragins, 1999)	Do differences in the status, power, and influence of mentors and protégés affect women and men in mentoring relationships differently? Does gender affect assumptions of status, power, and influence?
Do mentoring relationships evolve over time? Is the time to progress through mentoring stages predictable? (Chao, 1997; Ragins, 1997b)	Is this evolution different for women and men? Do same-gender and cross-gender mentoring relationships evolve differently?
	Do women progress more quickly through certain mentoring stages than men? What are the effects of nonlinear career paths (more common for women) on the formation, functions, and evolution of mentoring relationships?
What is the process by which transitions from mentor/protégé to peer relationships take place? (Fletcher & Ragins, Chapter 15; Gersick et al., 2000)	Do these transitions differ for women and men?
How does mentoring fit into the overall development of both mentors and protégés as they seek to resolve the underlying challenges of adult development? (Fletcher & Ragins, Chapter 15; Kram & Isabella, 1985)	Is this development different for women and men? Do differences in career aspirations influence women's and men's mentoring relationships?
Are certain mentoring functions linked to early or late career stages?	Are these links different for women and men?
Do career interruptions and breaks influence the experience of mentoring?	Do career interruptions and breaks differentially impact women's and men's mentoring experiences?
Do changing employment patterns (second careers, delayed retirement) influence mentoring relationships?	Do changing employment patterns differentially affect women's and men's mentoring relationships?
Do definitions of career and life success influence the desire for specific types of mentoring functions?	Do women's and men's definitions of career and life success differentially influence the mentoring functions they desire?
Are mentoring and values related?	Is there a relationship between gender, values, and mentoring?
What factors (personal, organizational and systemic) lead to negative mentoring experiences? (Eby, 2007; Fletcher & Ragins, Chapter 15; Gersick et al., 2000)	Are the factors leading to negative mentoring experiences different for women and men? Are they different depending on the gender composition of the mentor-protégé dyad?

Mentoring Question	Gender and Mentoring Question
How is dissatisfaction with a mentoring relationship expressed? (Ibarra 1993; Withey & Cooper, 1989)	Do women and men express dissatisfaction with their mentoring relationship differently?
Do various aspects of organizational context influence mentoring relationships? (Ibarra, 1993)	Do variations in corporate culture (including corporate masculinity) influence mentoring relationships differently for women and men? How?
What organizational training and support can facilitate successful mentoring?	Do women and men need different training and support from their organizations for successful mentoring?
Do mentoring functions, antecedents, and outcomes differ in e-mentoring? Is e-mentoring governed by principles of homophily? (Ensher et al., 2003; Ensher & Murphy, Chapter 12; Hamilton & Scandura, 2003)	Does e-mentoring have differential effects on women and men? Is cross-gender mentoring less problematic in e-mentoring relationships?
Is mentoring a reciprocal or a unidirectional relationship? (Fletcher & Ragins, Chapter 15; Gersick et al., 2000; Ibarra, 1993; Kram & Isabella, 1985; Ragins, 1997b)	In what ways is the nature of this relationship affected by the gender composition of the relationship?
Does mentoring fit within a broader set of developmental and relational networks? (Higgins & Kram, 2001; Higgins et al., Chapter 14).	Does the concept of mentoring as a developmental or relational network apply equally to women's and men's experience of mentoring?

For example, how are race and gender related in mentoring relationships (see Blake-Beard et al., Chapter 9, this volume)? There is some suggestion that race may have more of an effect than gender on mentoring relationships (Cox & Nkomo, 1991; Kalbfleisch & Davies, 1991), and this finding should be pursued. Further, it will be important to look at the combined impact of the gender and racial composition of mentoring relationships (Ragins, 1997b). Of particular interest will be the pairings of female mentors of color (minority individuals) with either female (minority) or male (majority) protégés.

Extensions to current mentoring research could also address the interaction of gender and sexual orientation in mentoring relationships. Further, cross-cultural gender and mentoring research could examine the impact of national cultures (not just organizational cultures) on antecedents, processes, and outcomes of mentoring.

E-Mentoring. With the advent of the Internet and widespread use of e-mail, mentors and protégés are no longer constrained by requirements for physical proximity. Virtual mentors and distance-mentoring relationships now exist (Ensher, Heun, & Blanchard, 2003; Ensher & Murphy, Chapter 12, this volume; Hamilton & Scandura, 2003). How are mentoring relationships, functions, antecedents, and outcomes different in virtual mentoring? Ensher & Murphy (Chapter 12) have observed that e-mentoring relationships are typically more egalitarian than face-to-face relationships and there is an equalization of status in addition to a decreased emphasis on demographics (as they are not visible). This attenuation of status dif ferentials allows more focus on deeper levels of connection rather than on surface similarity. These factors may have differential impacts on women and men. The literature suggests that women prefer more egalitarian relationships and that one of the major barriers to women in organizations and in mentoring relationships involves negative stereotypes. Worries about cross-gender mentoring may be reduced in e-mentoring relationships, as there may be less concern about the possibility of inappropriate sexual behavior within the context of the mentoring relationship. Important research questions include the following: Are the formation of e-mentoring relationships governed by principles of homophily? What behaviors are required of protégés to initiate these relationships (see Higgins, Chandler, & Kram, Chapter 14, this volume)? What are the effects of gender on e-mentoring relationships and outcomes?

Mentoring Measures. Most empirical studies focus on the amount of mentoring that protégés receive (Higgins & Kram, 2001), whereas there is some suggestion for women that the amount is not as critical as the relationship itself. In addition, the dependent measures in most mentoring research are seemingly objective measures such as salary, increase in pay, position title, and number of promotions. These measures are consistent with a masculine definition of career success. Van Emmerick (2004) hoped to address some of these concerns by including measures of intrinsic career success, but this still does not capture the full range of factors (life satisfaction, work-life balance, health) that may be included in women's definitions of success. To the extent that women and men define career success differently, these variables may not capture the relevant consequences for women. If women and men seek different outcomes from their careers, they may seek different benefits from their mentoring relationships. For example, female protégés may seek role models or help in balancing work-life demands. Alternatively, female mentors may take on the role of mentor to fill their relational needs (especially if their own career success came at a personal price). For a full discussion of these issues see Fletcher and Ragins (Chapter 15, this volume) and Ragins and Verbos (2007).

Mentoring as an Adult Relationship. Issues of gender and mentoring at various career stages (Ragins 1997b) should also be examined. The career stages to be investigated could be linked to theories of adult development, adult relationships, and Stone Center Relational Theory (Fletcher & Ragins, Chapter 15, this volume). Kram and Isabella (1985) suggested, "The field of adult relationships is one that deserves greater attention. Investigation of relationships with peers, mentors, and subordinates at different career stages and in diverse organizational settings are preliminary steps toward a better understanding of adult relationships at work" (p. 131). Research on mentoring at various career stages may be made more challenging by changes in traditional career stages. Individuals are changing careers more frequently, and these changes are occurring, voluntarily and involuntarily, at all ages.

Many individuals are choosing to work later in life and to delay or phase in retirement. Research questions that could be addressed in this evolving environment include the following: How will the role of mentors change when people start and end their careers later in life? Are particular mentoring functions tied primarily to early or late career stages? How will demographic changes impact such mentoring relationships? Might they become truly reciprocal—each member of a mentoring dyad serving as a mentor to the other—one for career functions, the other for psychosocial functions? Will men's mentoring relationships become more like women's current mentoring relationships, since women's careers have traditionally tended to have more interruptions and changes to accommodate their other life interests?

Mentoring and Life Values. Women have indicated that one of the primary reasons they change employers is to seek organizations with compatible values (Catalyst, 1998). Thus, it would be beneficial to research the relationship between gender, values, and mentoring to address how values affect women's and men's interest in mentoring (Fletcher & Ragins, Chapter 15, this volume). Organizations might be particularly interested in learning how they can signal compatible values through their mentoring and other organizational policies and practices.

Concepts of Mentoring. Kram's (1985) definition of mentoring indicates that it is to be a developmental experience for the protégé in terms of both career development and personal development. However, much mentoring research has focused almost exclusively on the instrumental role of mentoring in career development and the achievement of career success. If mentoring is defined to include personal growth, it supports additional research along the lines that mentoring is a relational activity (Fletcher, 1998; Fletcher & Ragins, Chapter 15, this volume; Ragins & Verbos, 2007) or a subset of social network relationships (Higgins & Kram, 2001; Ibarra, 1993). Fletcher and Ragins (Chapter 15, this volume) have suggested that because mentoring theory originated with the experience of White male professionals, it reflects this dominant identity. They argue that traditional mentoring theory is not neutral and reifies the masculine and devalues or ignores the feminine and may not fit women's needs or experiences (Fletcher, 1998; Ragins & Verbos, 2007, as cited in Fletcher & Ragins, Chapter 15, this volume). If, in contrast, mentoring is defined more narrowly as focusing on career growth (Ragins 1997b), then additional research based upon social exchange theory and theories of leader-member exchange, justice, or power may be more appropriate (Noe et al., 2002).

According to Higgins and Kram (2001), "Individuals receive mentoring assistance from many people at any one point in time, including senior colleagues, peers, family, and community members" (p. 264). They indicated that factors such as reduced loyalty to organizations, less-hierarchical organizations, and alternative work styles (e.g., telecommuting) are expected to be responsible for increasingly diversified developmental networks. Van Emmerick (2004) referred to the variety of mentors and developmental networks a person has as "mentoring constellations." She described developmental networks using two variables: diversity (the number of types of contacts in the network and their uniqueness) and strength (the level of emotional affect, reciprocity, and frequency of communication). Her research found that women have more diverse networks and their developmental relationships are stronger. Corroborating this, Thomas (2001), noted that racial minority managers need to develop a constellation of support systems rather than one developmental relationship in order to succeed. Women may also find this approach necessary.

How developmental relationships begin is addressed by Higgins, Chandler, & Kram in Chapter 14 of this handbook. They propose a third dimension of developmental networks, "relational engagement," which is described as a set of behaviors by the protégé at the beginning of a relationship. How these behaviors vary by the gender composition of the relationship and the organizational context, as well as research on the role of gender in broader networks, will become increasingly important in the future.

Gender and Mentoring: A Vision for the Future

Implicit in most studies of mentoring is an underlying belief that appropriate goals for mentoring programs are increased organizational power, greater upward mobility, higher rates of compensation, and additional prestige. However, mentoring programs may not have the intended consequences if women and men differ in their underlying motivations, either for work itself or for their participation in mentoring relationships. For example, if women do not believe, in accordance with expectancy theory (Vroom, 1964), that their efforts will lead to organizational rewards or, more important, if women do not believe that the available organizational rewards are valued, then mentoring relationships will not lead to similar outcomes for women and men. Thus, one of our key concerns for much of the existing gender and mentoring research is that it accepts masculine definitions of success and fails to address aspects of relationships important to women. Future gender and mentoring research needs to consider that these traditional definitions may not be appropriate to women, nor indeed to all men (Fletcher & Ragins, Chapter 15, this volume).

From our knowledge of the broader literature on women in management, we know that careers play different roles in the lives of many women and men and that their definitions of "success" may vary widely (Gersick & Kram, 2002). In addition, the adult development literature indicates that women and men face some unique developmental challenges, often according to different time lines. The approaches women and men take to resolving developmental dilemmas may vary in part based upon variation in their underlying priorities and value systems (Gersick & Kram, 2002; Pringle & McCulloch Dixon, 2003). Men have typically been socialized to define their masculinity as dependent upon the achievement of career success. Women's definitions of success tend to be multidimensional and include both career and life success (MacDermid, Lee, Buck, & Williams, 2001). Thus, it may be necessary to propose distinct theories of mentoring as an aid to career development for men but a theory of mentoring for women that has both career and personal elements. This is evident in research that has indicated that women desire more psychosocial and role-modeling functions (in addition to career support) from their mentors (Burke et al., 1990). In fact, Ibarra (1993) explicitly recognized that "women differ from men in their preferences for strong, supportive, intimate relationships and lack of instrumental orientation in developing those relationships" (p. 77). In other words, many women value relationships for their own sake (Gibson, 2004), not just what the relationship can do for them. Relational mentoring has much to offer in conceptualizing mentoring for all individuals, but specifically for women. Relational mentoring specifically addresses the reciprocal nature of mentoring, which has been ignored in the hierarchical and masculine focus of traditional mentoring research (Ragins & Verbos, 2007).

By midcareer, women's career aspirations are lower than the aspirations of men at midcareer (Ibarra, 1993). It is not known whether these lower aspirations are due to personal factors (for example, a broad definition of success, only one aspect of which addresses career advancement) or a realization by midcareer of the more limited opportunities for advancement that women face. There is a need to examine the impact of differences in career aspirations on the formation of, and benefits arising from, mentoring relationships. If mentoring is narrowly defined as providing guidance for career success, then this definition itself may mean that mentoring will be less beneficial for women. In fact, some existing research seems to suggest that gender-specific models of mentoring may be necessary. For example, Gersick et al. (2000) found that although both women and men identified helpful and harmful themes in recounting their mentoring stories, *help* and *harm* had different meanings for women and men.

A clearer understanding of how mentoring differs for women and men is needed. The models of mentoring that apply to men (either protégés or mentors) may not be applicable to women in their roles as protégés or mentors (Tharenou, 2005). Future research will need to examine what women seek (and gain) from same-gender and cross-gender mentoring relationships and how this is different from what men seek (and gain) from such relationships.

Conclusion

Research on gender and mentoring may be intended to develop policies and prescriptions for mentoring programs to maximize organizational effectiveness, to enhance our understanding of gender and mentoring phenomena simply for the sake of knowledge, to aid individual women in maximizing their career success by encouraging them to learn ways of coping with corporate masculinity, or to foment change in the very patriarchal organizational and societal systems that now constrain women's achievements.

Gender and mentoring research has the potential to enhance our understanding of the antecedents and consequences of mentoring for women and men. In turn, this understanding may help to develop more effective mentoring programs and to lead to greater levels of achievement by both individuals and organizations. However, we hope for even greater results from a broader understanding of the issues, effects, and opportunities arising from research on gender and mentoring. Traditionally, mentoring seems intended to assimilate women into the dominant masculine corporate culture. Women who successfully break thorough the glass ceiling, in part as a result of mentoring relationships, may choose assimilation. Alternatively, they may choose a strategy that allows them to integrate, in themselves and their organizations, the best of masculine and feminine characteristics. In this way, we hope the current culture of masculinity is itself transformed into a more accepting, more welcoming, more balanced, and, ultimately, more rewarding environment in which to live and work.

References

Allen, T. D., Day, R., & Lentz, E. (2005). The role of interpersonal comfort in mentoring relationships. *Journal of Career Development, 31,* 155–169.

Allen, T. D., & Eby, L. T. (2004). Factors related to mentor reports of mentoring functions provided: Gender and relational characteristics. *Sex Roles, 50,* 129–139.

Allen, T. D., Eby, L. T., Poteet, M. L., Lentz, E., & Lima, L. (2004). Career benefits associated with mentoring for protégés: A meta-analysis. *Journal of Applied Psychology, 89,* 127–136.

Allen, T. D., Poteet, M. L., & Burroughs, S. M. (1997). The mentor's perspective: A qualitative inquiry and future research agenda. *Journal of Vocational Behavior, 51,* 70–89.

Bachman, S. I., & Gregory, K. (1993, April). *Mentor and protégé gender: Effects on mentoring roles and outcomes.* Paper presented at the Society for Industrial and Organizational Psychology Conference, San Francisco.

Bahniuk, M. H., Dobos, J., & Hill, S. K. (1990). The impact of mentoring, collegial support, and information adequacy on career success: A replication. *Journal of Social Behavior & Personality, 5,* 431–451.

Bowen, D. D. (1985). Were men meant to mentor women? *Training and Development Journal, 39*(2), 31–34.

Bradford, D. L. (1992). *A level playing field? (Barriers to the inclusion of women and minorities in today's organizations).* Unpublished manuscript.

Brefach, S. M. (1986). *The mentor experience: The influences of female/male mentors on the personal and professional growth of female psychologists.* Unpublished doctoral dissertation, Boston University.

Burke, R. J. (1984). Mentors in organizations. *Group & Organization Studies, 9,* 353–372.

Burke, R. J., & McKeen, C. A. (1990). Mentoring in organizations: Implications for women. *Journal of Business Ethics, 9,* 317–332.

Burke, R. J., & McKeen, C. A. (1995). Do managerial women prefer mentors? *Psychological Reports, 76,* 688–690.

Burke, R. J., & McKeen, C. A. (1997). Benefits of mentoring relationships among managerial and professional women: A cautionary tale. *Journal of Vocational Behavior, 51,* 43–57.

Burke, R. J., McKeen, C. A., & McKenna, C. (1990). Sex differences and cross-sex effects on mentoring: some preliminary data. *Psychological Reports, 67,* 1011–1024.

Burke, R., McKeen, C. A., & McKenna, C. (1993). Correlates of mentoring in organizations: The mentor's perspective. *Psychological Reports, 72,* 883–896.

Burke, R. J., McKenna, C. S., & McKeen, C. A. (1991). How do mentorships differ from typical supervisory relationships? *Psychological Reports, 68,* 459–467.

Catalyst. (1996). *Women in corporate leadership: Progress and prospects.* New York: Author.

Catalyst. (1998). *Closing the gap: Women's advancement in corporate and professional Canada.* New York: Author.

Catalyst. (1999). *Women of color in corporate management: Opportunities and barriers.* New York: Author.

Catalyst. (2000). *Breaking the barriers: Women in senior management in the UK.* New York: Author.

Catalyst. (2001a). *Women in financial services: The word on the street.* New York: Author.

Catalyst. (2001b). *Women in law: Making the case.* New York: Author.

Catalyst. (2002). *Creating successful mentoring programs: A Catalyst guide.* New York: Author.

Catalyst. (2004). *Women and men in U.S. corporate leadership: Same workplace, different realities?* New York: Author.

Chao, G. T. (1997). Mentoring phases and outcomes. *Journal of Vocational Behavior, 51,* 15–28.

Cianni, M., & Romberger, B. (1995). Perceived racial, ethnic, and gender differences in access to developmental experiences. *Group & Organization Management, 20,* 440–459.

Clawson, J. G., & Kram, K. E. (1984). Managing cross-gender mentoring. *Business Horizons, 27*(3), 22–32.

Colarelli, S. M., & Bishop, R. C. (1990). Career commitment: Functions, correlates, and management. *Group & Organization Studies, 15,* 158–176.

Cox, T. H., & Nkomo, S. M. (1991). A race and gender-group analysis of the early career experience of MBAs. *Work and Occupations, 18,* 431–446.

Diversity Best Practices, Business Women's Network. (2005). *Women and diversity WOW! Facts.* Washington, DC: Author.

Dreher, G. F., & Ash, R. A. (1990). A comparative study of mentoring among men and women in managerial, professional, and technical positions. *Journal of Applied Psychology, 75,* 539–546.

Dreher, G. F., & Cox, T. H. (1996). Race, gender, and opportunity: A study of compensation attainment and the establishment of mentoring relationships. *Journal of Applied Psychology, 81,* 297–308.

Eby, L. T., Butts, M., Lockwood, A., & Simon, S. A. (2004). Protégés' negative mentoring experiences: Construct development and nomological validation. *Personnel Psychology, 57,* 411–447.

Ensher, E. A., Heun, C., & Blanchard, A. (2003). On-line mentoring and computer mediated communication: New directions in research. *Journal of Vocational Behavior, 63,* 264–288.

Ensher, E. A., & Murphy, S. E. (1997). Effects of race, gender, perceived similarity, and contact on mentor relationships. *Journal of Vocational Behavior, 50,* 460–481.

Fagenson, E. A. (1988). The power of a mentor: Protégés' and nonprotégés' perceptions of their own power in organizations. *Group & Organization Studies, 13,* 182–194.

Fagenson, E. A. (1989). The mentor advantage: Perceived career/job experiences of protégés versus non-protégés. *Journal of Organizational Behavior, 10,* 309–320.

Fagenson-Eland, E. A., Marks, M. A., & Amendola, K. L. (1997). Perceptions of mentoring relationships. *Journal of Vocational Behavior, 51,* 29–42.

Fitt, L. W., & Newton, D. A. (1981). When the mentor is a man and the protégée is a woman. *Harvard Business Review, 59*(2), 56–60.

Fletcher, J. K. (1998). Relational practice: A feminist reconstruction of work. *Journal of Management Inquiry, 7,* 163–186.

Gersick, C. J. G., Bartunek, J. M., & Dutton, J. E. (2000). Learning from academia: The importance of relationships in professional life. *Academy of Management Journal, 43,* 1026–1044.

Gersick, C. J. G., & Kram, K. E. (2002). High-achieving women at midlife: An exploratory study. *Journal of Management Inquiry, 11,* 104–127.

Gibson, S. K. (2004). Being mentored: The experience of women faculty. *Journal of Career Development, 30,* 173–188.

Gilligan, C. (1982). *In a different voice: Psychological theory and women's development.* Cambridge, MA: Harvard University Press.

Hamilton, B. A., & Scandura, T. A. (2003). E-mentoring: Implications for organizational learning and development in a wired world. *Organizational Dynamics, 31,* 388–403.

Higgins, M. C., & Kram, K. E. (2001). Reconceptualizing mentoring at work: A developmental network perspective. *Academy of Management Review, 26,* 264–289.

Hochschild, A. R. (1989). *The second shift: Working parents and the revolution at home.* New York: Viking Press.

Hurley, A. E., & Fagenson-Eland, E. A. (1996). Challenges in cross-gender mentoring relationships: Psychological intimacy, myths, rumours, innuendoes and sexual harassment. *Leadership & Organization Development Journal, 17,* 42–49.

Ibarra, H. (1993). Personal networks of women and minorities in management: A conceptual framework. *Academy of Management Review, 18,* 56–87.

Kalbfleisch, P. J., & Davies, A. B. (1991). Minorities and mentoring: Managing the multicultural institution. *Communication Education, 40,* 266–271.

Kanter, R. M. (1977). *Men and women of the corporation.* New York: Basic Books.

Koberg, C. S., Boss, R. W., & Goodman, E. (1998). Factors and outcomes associated with mentoring among health-care professionals. *Journal of Vocational Behavior, 53,* 58–72.

Kram, K. E. (1985). *Mentoring at work.* Glenview, IL: Scott, Foresman.

Kram, K. E., & Isabella, L. A. (1985). Mentoring alternatives: The role of peer relationships in career development. *Academy of Management Journal, 28,* 110–132.

Laband, D. N., & Lentz, B. F. (1995). Workplace mentoring in the legal profession. *Southern Economic Journal, 61,* 783–802.

MacDermid, S. M., Lee, M. D., Buck, M., & Williams, M. L. (2001). Alternative work arrangements among professionals and managers: Rethinking career development and success. *Journal of Management Development, 20,* 305–317.

Maier, M. (1991). The dysfunctions of corporate masculinity: Gender and diversity issues in organizational development. In K. Keef (Ed.), *Human capital development* (pp. 147–169). Alfred, NY: Alfred University School of Business.

Morrison, A. M., White, R. P., Van Velsor, E., & the Center for Creative Leadership. (1987). *Breaking the glass ceiling: Can women reach the top of America's largest corporations?* Reading, MA: Addison-Wesley.

Neilson, T. R., Carlson, D. S., & Lankau, M. J. (2001). The supportive mentor as a means of reducing work-family conflict. *Journal of Vocational Behavior, 59,* 364–381.

Noe, R. A. (1988a). An investigation of the determinants of successful assigned mentoring relationships. *Personnel Psychology, 41,* 457–479.

Noe, R. A. (1988b). Women in mentoring: A review and research agenda. *Academy of Management Review, 13,* 65–78.

Noe, R. A., Greenberger, D. B., & Wang, S. (2002). Mentoring: What we know and where we might go. *Research in Personnel and Human Resources Management, 21,* 129–173.

Ohlott, P. J., Ruderman, M. N., & McCauley, C. D. (1994). Gender differences in managers' developmental job experiences. *Academy of Management Journal, 37,* 46–67.

Olian, J. D., Carroll, S. J., Giannantonio, C. M., & Feren, D. M. (1988). What do protégés look for in a mentor? Results of three experimental studies. *Journal of Vocational Behavior, 33,* 15–37.

O'Neill, R. M. (2002). Gender and race in mentoring relationships: A review of the literature. In D. Clutterbuck & B. R. Ragins (Eds.), *Mentoring and diversity: An international perspective* (pp. 1–22). Oxford, UK: Butterworth-Heinemann.

O'Neill, R. M., & Blake-Beard, S. D. (2002). Gender barriers to the female mentor-male protégé relationship. *Journal of Business Ethics, 37,* 51–63.

O'Neill, R. M., Horton, S., & Crosby, F. J. (1999). Gender issues in developmental relationships. In A. J. Murrell, F. J. Crosby, & R. J. Ely (Eds.), *Mentoring dilemmas: Developmental relationships within multicultural organizations* (pp. 69–80). Mahwah, NJ: Lawrence Erlbaum.

Ostroff, C., & Kozlowski, S. W. (1993). The role of mentoring in the information gathering processes of newcomers during early organizational socialization. *Journal of Vocational Behavior, 42,* 170–183.

Parker, V. A., & Kram, K. E. (1993). Women mentoring women: Creating conditions for connection. *Business Horizons, 36*(2), 42–51.

Pringle, J. K., & McCulloch Dixon, K. (2003). Re-incarnating life in the careers of women. *Career Development International, 8,* 291–300.

Quinn, B. S. C. (1980). *The influence of same-sex and cross-sex mentors on the professional development and personality characteristics of women in human services.* Unpublished doctoral dissertation, Western Michigan University.

Ragins, B. R. (1989). Barriers to mentoring: The female manager's dilemma. *Human Relations, 42,* 1–22.

Ragins, B. R. (1997a). Antecedents of diversified mentoring relationships. *Journal of Vocational Behavior, 51,* 90–109.

Ragins, B. R. (1997b). Diversified mentoring relationships in organizations: A power perspective. *Academy of Management Review, 22,* 482–521.

Ragins, B. R. (1999). Gender and mentoring relationships: A review and research agenda for the next decade. In G. N. Powell (Ed.), *Handbook of gender and work* (pp. 347–370). Thousand Oaks, CA: Sage.

Ragins, B. R., & Cotton, J. (1991). Easier said than done: Gender differences in perceived barriers to gaining a mentor. *Academy of Management Journal, 34,* 939–951.

Ragins, B. R., & Cotton, J. L. (1993). Gender and willingness to mentor in organizations. *Journal of Management, 19,* 97–111.

Ragins, B. R., & Cotton, J. L. (1999). Mentor functions and outcomes: A comparison of men and women in formal and informal mentoring relationships. *Journal of Applied Psychology, 84,* 529.

Ragins, B. R., Cotton, J. L., & Miller, J. S. (2000). Marginal mentoring: The effects of type of mentor, quality of relationship, and program design on work and career attitudes. *Academy of Management Journal, 43,* 1177–1194.

Ragins, B. R., & McFarlin, D. (1990). Perception of mentor roles in cross-gender mentoring relationships. *Journal of Vocational Behavior, 37,* 321–339.

Ragins, B. R., & Scandura, T. A. (1994). Gender differences in expected outcomes of mentoring relationships. *Academy of Management Journal, 37,* 957–971.

Ragins, B. R., & Sundstrom, E. (1989). Gender and power in organizations: A longitudinal perspective. *Psychological Bulletin, 105,* 51–88.

Ragins, B. R., Townsend, B., & Mattis, M. (1998). Gender gap in the executive suite: CEOs and female executives report on breaking the glass ceiling. *Academy of Management Executive, 12*(1), 28–42.

Ragins, B. R., & Verbos, A. K. (2007). Positive relationships in action: Relational mentoring and mentoring schemas in the workplace. In J. E. Dutton & B. R. Ragins (Eds.),

Exploring positive relationships at work: Building a theoretical and research foundation (pp. 91–116). Mahwah, NJ: Lawrence Erlbaum.

Scandura, T. A. (1992). Mentorship and career mobility: An empirical investigation. *Journal of Organizational Behavior, 13,* 169–174.

Scandura, T. A., & Ragins, B. R. (1993). The effects of sex and gender role orientation on mentorship in male-dominated occupations. *Journal of Vocational Behavior, 43,* 251–265.

Schein, V. E., & Davidson, M. J. (1993). Think manager, think male. *Management Development Review, 6*(3), 24–29.

Sosik, J. J., & Godshalk, V. M. (2000). The role of gender in mentoring: Implications for diversified and homogeneous mentoring relationships. *Journal of Vocational Behavior, 57,* 102–122.

Sosik, J. J., & Godshalk, V. M. (2005). Examining gender similarity and mentor's supervisory status in mentoring relationships. *Mentoring and Tutoring, 13,* 39–52.

Tannen, D. (1995). The power to talk: Who gets heard and why. *Harvard Business Review, 73*(5), 138–148.

Tepper, B. J. (1995). Upward influence tactics in supervisory mentoring and nonmentoring relationships. *Academy of Management Journal, 38,* 1191–1205.

Tharenou, P. (2005). Does mentor support increase women's career advancement more than men's? The differential effects of career and psychosocial support. *Australian Journal of Management, 30,* 77–109.

Thomas, D. A. (2001). The truth about mentoring minorities: Race matters. *Harvard Business Review, 79*(2), 98–112

Van Emmerik, I. J. H. (2004). The more you can get the better: Mentoring constellations and intrinsic career success. *Career Development International, 9,* 578–594.

Viator, R. E. (2001). An examination of African Americans' access to public accounting mentors: Perceived barriers and intentions to leave. *Accounting, Organizations, and Society, 26,* 541–561.

Viator, R. E., & Scandura, T. A. (1991, September). A study of mentor-protégé relationships in large public accounting firms. *Accounting Horizons, 5,* 20–30.

Vroom, V. (1964). *Work and motivation.* New York: John Wiley & Sons.

Wanberg, C. R., Welsh, E. T., & Hezlett, S.A. (2003). Mentoring research: A review and dynamic process model. *Research in Personnel and Human Resources Management, 22,* 39–124.

Whitely, W., Dougherty, T. W., & Dreher, G. F. (1991). Relationship of career mentoring and socioeconomic origin to managers' and professionals' early career progress. *Academy of Management Journal, 34,* 331–351.

Wilson, J. A., & Elman, N. S. (1990). Organizational benefits of mentoring. *Academy of Management Executive, 4*(4), 88–93.

Withey, M. J., & Cooper, W. H. (1989). Predicting exit, voice, loyalty, and neglect. *Administrative Science Quarterly, 34,* 521–539.

9

Unfinished Business

The Impact of Race on Understanding Mentoring Relationships

Stacy D. Blake-Beard

Audrey Murrell

David Thomas

> *The problem of the twentieth century is the color line.*
>
> —W. E. B. DuBois

W. E. B. DuBois's 1903 words are prophetic, as he proclaims the importance of an issue with which we are still grappling in the 21st century—race. As contributors to this volume, we were asked to focus on the relationship between race and mentoring. What do we learn about this important developmental relationship by examining the research on race and mentoring? Like DuBois, we believe that the analysis of race is fundamental within our society. Race continues to be a critical factor as we examine relationships in organizations, particularly if we are located in a U.S.-based context. Race is a socially embedded phenomenon that affects just about every aspect of our lives, and as such

AUTHORS' NOTE: The authors thank Jessica Porter and Ayesha Kanji for their assistance in the identification and analysis of articles for this review.

provides a valuable lens with which to examine the mentoring literature (Thomas & Alderfer, 1989).

Now, more than ever, is a timely moment in our history to examine the influence of race in the extant literature on a critical topic such as mentoring. Foreman (2000) described race as "America's major piece of unfinished business" (p. 30). Race is clearly "unfinished business" because of the plethora of emotions that are unleashed as we approach the taboo (Thomas, 1989). This tension speaks to the importance of this chapter as we explore the issue of mentoring as embedded within the social context of race within today's dynamic and diverse organizations. First, we delineate several important reasons why it is critical to discuss mentoring and race. We explore how race has been positioned within the literature to provide a context for our review of how the mentoring literature has discussed (and omitted) race as a key factor. We ask a critical question in this review: What do we know about the intersection of mentoring and race in organizations? Finally, we explore some of the unfinished business concerning race and mentoring and present a model to drive future research in this important area.

Why Examine Race and Mentoring?

Understanding interactions across different racial groups is critical given the changing nature of organizations and the composition of the people within them. These diverse interactions will certainly have implications for the intersection of race and mentoring. Several trends and themes underscore the need for us to more fully explore the intersection of race and mentoring.

Clearly, organizations are undergoing significant changes that are relevant to the relationship between race and mentoring. One change is an increasingly diverse workforce (Bell, 2006; Blake-Beard, 2003; Cox & Blake, 1991; Thomas & Ely, 1996). The non-White population is growing more rapidly than the total population, according to the most recent census figures. From 1990 to 2008, the Black population will grow by 31%, compared with 11% for the White population and 25% for the total population. The White population will grow by only 3.2% between 2005 and 2010, according to recent census data and projections (U.S. Census Bureau, 2005). Adding to this diversity, the Latino population will grow at a rate of 14.4%, Asian Americans/Pacific Islanders at 15.4%, while the growth rate for the overall population during that time frame will be about 4.2%. Nearly 67 million people of Latino origin are expected to be added to the nation's population between 2000 and 2050. Their numbers are projected to grow from 35.6 million to 102.6 million, an increase of 188%. Their share of the nation's population should nearly double, from 12.6% to 24.4% (U.S. Census Bureau, 2005).

Yet another trend affecting this discussion is increasing workforce diversity. Firms must address how to support and enable relationships among people who come from diverse cultures, backgrounds, and perspectives. Organizations must grapple with how to engage this diverse population in a common enterprise among disparate groups who "do not share a common history or culture" (Caproni, 2005, p. 269). The impact of race on mentoring relationships is an important question to raise, first and foremost because the changing composition of the workforce means that individuals will experience more cross-race (and cross-cultural) interactions within organizations of today and tomorrow (Murrell & James, 2001).

While diversity in workforce participation is increasing, we still see a glass ceiling that effectively keeps the top levels absent of the same diversity that exists throughout the middle and lower levels of the organization. According to the Catalyst organization, while the number of women of color in the workforce has increased, they still represent only 1.1% of corporate officers in *Fortune* 500 firms (Catalyst, 2001). Their research outlines some of the barriers that are faced, particularly by women of color, who often have a "double disadvantage" within traditional organizations (Bell, 1990; Murrell, 2000). According to the U.S. Equal Employment Opportunity Commission (EEOC, 2003), African Americans accounted for 7.2% and Latinos 5.0% of professionals, whereas Whites accounted for 84.5%. The traditional "glass ceiling" has been recast as a concrete ceiling—an impermeable barrier that keeps women and people of color effectively locked out of the corridors of power in organizations across industries and professions (Catalyst, 2001; Tomlinson, 2001). Work by Thomas (Thomas & Alderfer, 1989; Thomas & Gabarro, 1999) clearly shows the power of mentoring in helping people of color (in their work, specifically African Americans) "break though" to senior levels within the organization. Thus, understanding the intersection of race and mentoring may outline a process for changing the dynamics of power and, in turn, break down the barriers that keep women and people of color from attaining leadership positions within organizations.

Finally, work by Thomas (1989, 1993) made it clear that the nature and outcomes of interracial dynamics embedded within the organization's culture can provide revealing information about the state of racial affairs within the firm. In fact, some argue that people of color may act as a "miner's canary"—an indicator of conditions that are challenging not only for numerical minorities but also for majority groups in that same organization (Guinier & Torres, 2002). The presence of dissatisfaction, frustration, and high turnover among people of color is perhaps a precursor to future problems that will be experienced by majority group members if the issues facing these more vulnerable groups are not resolved. Thus, the issue of race and mentoring may not be just an outcome of shifting workforce demographics or a process for altering interracial dynamics in the workplace, but may also be a predictor of the overall health and strength of the organization. This potential predictive power means that understanding the intersection of mentoring and race is critical to expanding our knowledge of diverse organizational dynamics, as these relationships may serve as an outcome, a process, and a metric related to diversity in organizations.

Examining Race in Organizational Research: A Few Caveats

As we delve into examining the issue of mentoring within the context of race in organizations, it is helpful to briefly review the context of how race has been conceptualized and studied within the management literature. In the late 1980s and early 1990s, Nkomo and Cox (Cox & Nkomo, 1986, 1990; Nkomo, 1992; Nkomo & Cox, 1990) provided a powerful evaluation and critique of how management scholars have typically underconceptualized race in the organizational behavior research. Nkomo (1992) described the research on race as "narrowly focused, ahistorical and decontextualized" (p. 497). Thus, a key issue for addressing the intersection of race in the mentoring literature must be one of inclusion. Our most highly regarded models, theories, and empirical studies either exclude race as a factor or include samples that lack diversity such that race is relegated to "unexplained variance."

When we gather a great deal of information about one group and use that information to generate theories and policy that we then apply to other groups, this exclusion inevitably leads to faulty generalization or incomplete models and theories (Minnich, 1991; Nkomo, 1992). Not only do we focus on one group's experiences and cast it as the norm, we view differences as "exceptions" or anomalies to this biased normative data. Acknowledgment of this bias is important because while there may be substantial research and theories on the topic of mentoring in organizations, there is significantly less research that directly examines mentoring in the context of race. Race is often excluded rather than included in organizational research, and that also applies to research on the topic of mentoring. Thus, our review is restricted to a relatively small amount of literature that explicitly includes race as a factor within the research methodology or theoretical model.

There is still an additional caveat that must be stated as we review the extant literature. Within the existing research that addresses race and mentoring, the focus is often on understanding why the experiences of "others" (i.e., non-Whites) do not follow the standard model (i.e., those based on primarily White samples). Thus, assimilation becomes a preferred lens through which we have examined race in organizations, including within the mentoring literature. *Assimilation* is "conceptualized as a one-way process that requires non-European, non–English speaking groups to change to fit the dominant culture" (Nkomo, 1992, p. 496; see also Feagin, 1987). An underlying assumption of assimilation is that there should be little difference between the experiences of racial minorities and Whites. Whether or not a group successfully assimilates into the mainstream must then be explained, often by differences in individual-level factors such as psychological or personality characteristics of Whites and people of color. Those groups that differ from the norm and need to assimilate are the ones that "have race"; the dominant group is presented as the standard or implicit benchmark. As a result, race has been addressed methodologically to a large extent via comparative studies. As Cox and Nkomo (1990) noted, the explicit research question often compares or pits one group versus another (e.g., of Blacks versus Whites). Thus, we know very little about the unique experiences for people of color, especially in the context of mentoring in organizations.

Unfortunately, the treatment of race within organizational research often offers explanations of differential experiences without really delving into why we see these differences or, more important, challenging the existing models in response to the experiences of different groups. As Brief and Hayes (1997) noted, organizational scientists have not fulfilled their obligation to deepen our understanding of workplace race relations. Rarely do scholars provide the conclusion that because their findings do not hold for people of color, the popular or prevailing model should be invalidated or at least questioned and revised. In addition, according to Nkomo (1992), research on race "provides little insight into the complexity of the psychological, organizational and societal variables that may account for such findings" (p. 498) such as differences in the experiences of Whites and racial minorities. Thus, while we rely on existing data that explicitly examine race within the context of mentoring relationships, we provide these caveats to acknowledge the limitations of existing work, which leaves many "unanswered questions" to be discussed later in this chapter.

These limitations notwithstanding, we explore the importance of race in enhancing our understanding of diverse mentoring relationships. To organize our review of the existing literature, we attempt to answer three key questions: How does race influence *access* to mentoring relationships? How does race impact the *interactions* between mentors and protégés? How does race influence the *outcomes* of mentoring relationships?

Race and Mentoring: Challenging Access

Mentoring has gained increasing attention as a powerful tool to enable the careers of those advancing through the ranks in organizations (Blake-Beard, 1999; Dreher & Ash, 1990; Dreher & Chargois, 1998; Murrell, Crosby, & Ely, 1999; Thomas & Gabarro, 1999). A *mentor* is generally defined as a more senior individual who uses his or her influence and experience to help with the advancement of a protégé (Kram, 1988). Those with access to mentoring have been consistently shown to benefit from their involvement in these relationships; they report higher salaries, increased promotion rates, greater career satisfaction, higher organizational commitment, and less intention to leave the organization, as well as lower levels of turnover (Blake-Beard, 1999; Crosby, 1999; Dreher & Cox, 1996; O'Neill, 2002; Ragins, 1999; Scandura, 1992; Viator, 2001; Wanberg, Welsh, & Hezlett, 2003). Race clearly influences overall access in two ways: access to any type of mentoring relationship and who has access to as a mentor. A common perception is that people of color will have a more challenging time gaining access to mentoring relationships (Ford & Wells, 1985; Herbert, 1989; Hyun, 2005; Kaplan, Keinath, & Walo, 2001; Thomas, 1990; Viator, 1999). Findings from Cox and Nkomo's (1991) study of 729 Black and White MBAs supported this perception; they found that Black MBAs reported significantly less access to mentors than did White MBAs. Catalyst's (1999, 2001) groundbreaking series of studies of women of color in the corporate sector highlighted the importance of access to mentoring for positive career outcomes. Lack of access to mentors was cited as one of the top four barriers to career success among the women of color surveyed. Many of the women who were then interviewed in a later follow-up study still indicated difficulty in gaining access to mentors, and those who gained access revealed that their mentors were predominantly White males. These results were supported by earlier work from Dreher and Cox (1996), who tracked the career experiences of Black and Hispanic MBA graduates from top business schools within the United States. Their findings indicated that these MBAs of color are significantly less likely than Whites to establish relationships with White mentors. Other work also supported the notion that people of color find difficulty in gaining access to mentoring relationships (Catalyst, 2001; Viator, 2001).

Interestingly, a few studies do not find any differences by race in gaining access to mentoring relationships. For example, Thomas (1990) examined Black and White managers and found no statistically significant differences with regard to access to mentoring; in his study, Whites and Blacks both reported an average of 2.4 developmental relationships. Blake-Beard's (1999) research on career outcomes for Black and White women also did not find any significant differences in these two groups' access to mentoring. Koberg, Boss, Chappell, & Ringer's (1994) study of skilled, professional, and managerial hospital employees found that mentoring was actually higher among minority employees than among White employees. Koberg and her colleagues suggested that their unexpected results may be a result of the impact of antidiscrimination legislation dominant within the profession they studied and this hospital's dedication and involvement in programs and practices related to increasing diversity within their organization. Each of these findings suggests that while some people of color may find difficulty in gaining access to any type of mentoring relationships, the issue of access may be a function of the specific attributes of mentors whom protégés of color receive (or select) along with the organizational context that either supports or acts as a barrier to the formation of interracial development relationships.

Gaining access to mentors of the same race may be difficult for people of color because of their low numbers within higher levels in the organization (Catalyst, 1999; Sims, 2002). Access to White males may be limited because of dissimilar backgrounds, perceived risk, or other interpersonal and organizational barriers. Thomas (1990, 1993) found that when mentoring relationships were present, White males predominated as mentors for White females, Black males, and Black females. More important, for protégés of color to gain access to mentors of color, they had to go outside of their own departments/units (Thomas, 1990). Lancaster (1997) described this complexity in access to mentoring relationships for people of color as due to White males occupying the "predominate mentoring class."

Gaining access to mentoring means that people of color to a greater degree than Whites are thrust into interracial dynamics embedded within the organization (Sims, 2002; Thomas, 1990). Access to mentors of the same race is not as available to people of color within their organizations without crossing additional boundaries, such as level, location, or function or seeking these relationships outside of their own organizations (Murrell, Blake-Beard, Porter, & Williamson, 2006). In either case, there is an additional burden, or what we call a "mentoring tax," on these developmental relationships that is clearly a function of race. People of color may find it difficult to access mentors of any type, and when they do, they must overcome critical barriers within the relationship, such as differences in race, gender, job level, function/profession, or organizational environment.

What this challenge suggests is that access (overall availability and race of mentor) to mentoring may be driven by the types of relationships and social networks that people of color cultivate within organizations. For example, Ibarra's (1993) study of the informal networks of White and minority managers found that minority managers had networks with significantly lower levels of homophily than those of their White counterparts. In addition, career advancement for minority managers was related to the configuration of their networks; Ibarra (1995) found that the networks of low-potential minorities tended to be dominated by Whites (cross-race relationships), while the networks of high-potential minorities were composed of a balance of same-race and cross-race relationships. Her research speaks to the importance of the pattern and composition of relationships that are developed both within and across racial boundaries. People of color often develop two complementary networks: one set of relationships with Whites who may provide access to resources and opportunities and another set of relationships with people of color who provide psychosocial and emotional support. Whites, on the other hand, don't have to include people who are racially different from them within their networks. An interesting implication of these different patterns is the suggestion that for people of color, same-race and interracial mentoring serve very different purposes, or what Kram (1985) would label as "mentoring functions." Thus, the pattern of access to developmental relationships is clearly tied to the nature, type, and strength of these relationships, which may vary as a function of race

Race and Mentoring: A Function of Interactions

Interracial dynamics within organizations have been examined extensively, and both the complexity as well as the range of positive and negative dynamics are well documented (Alderfer & Thomas, 1988; James, 2000; Murrell & James, 2001). Interestingly, the complexity of these relationships impacts both parties involved in the interaction. Tsui, Egan, and O'Reilly's (1992) research on work teams showed that Whites in heterogeneous teams experience greater dissatisfaction and lower organizational commitment than Whites in racially homogeneous groups. Their earlier work showed related findings: Whites with African American superiors experience greater role ambiguity and conflict than their White counterparts with White superiors (Tsui & O'Reilly, 1989). Thus, cross-race interactions can negatively impact satisfaction, trust, and commitment for both parties involved in the relationships.

It makes sense that the complexity of interracial dynamics should spill over into mentoring relationships. Early work by Thomas (1989) showed that racial differences were often an obstacle for White mentors forming relationships and identifying positively with their African American protégés. African American managers who had White mentors early in their careers were more dissatisfied with their advancement than those who had African American mentors (Murray, 1982). The differential experience of the mentoring relationship speaks to the importance of race in shaping developmental interactions. Effective mentoring has its foundation in the willingness of partners to authentically engage one another, share strengths, and provide developmental opportunities. Building trust becomes more challenging as mentoring partners cross lines of race. Thomas (1989) acknowledged the challenges of building effective mentoring relationships across dimensions of race. He stated that the changing environment and racial dynamics that we are facing in organizations "engenders the deeper difficulties that we face in creating a climate of authentic collaboration" among Whites and people of color (p. 280).

In addition to producing challenging interpersonal dynamics, race places a role in the type of mentoring relationships that occurs. Kram's (1983, 1985) ground-breaking work on mentoring functions has significantly shaped how we look at the nature of interactions within developmental relationships. She found that mentoring interactions can be described as providing two primary functions: career (instrumental) support and psychosocial (emotional) support. Career functions include exposure and visibility, sponsorship, coaching, protection, and access to challenging assignments. In contrast, psychosocial functions include role-modeling, acceptance and confirmation, counseling, and friendship.

Using the conceptual model outlined by Kram, Thomas (1990) hypothesized that based on high levels of similarity and ability to trust and identify with one another, respondents involved in same-race relationships will report greater levels of psychosocial support. His survey of more than 450 developmental relationships confirmed this hypothesis; Blacks reported experiencing more psychosocial support from same-race versus cross-race relationships. However, these same-race relationships were more often with peers, located outside of the department, and what Thomas labeled "skip-level" relationships. Interestingly, Thomas's work did not find any differences by protégé race in the amount of career support that was provided. Similarly, James's (2000) study of Black and White managers in a *Fortune* 500 services firm mirrored Thomas's results. James found that Black and White managers did not report differential levels of career support but there was a difference in receipt of psychosocial support. Black managers reported less psychosocial support than their White counterparts.

Steinberg and Foley's (1999) study of Army senior noncommissioned officers and commissioned officers produced two interesting findings. First, the authors found three functions, not the two traditionally seen in studies of mentoring. Steinberg and Foley called their functions "personal development," "career sponsoring," and "job coaching." The authors suggested that the unique environment of the Army, which stresses basic skill development as a critical skill for soldiers, explains the emergence of "job coaching" as a separate function. Second, Steinberg and Foley noted that there was not a significant difference in the mentoring functions that majority and minority members received. While race was not a trigger for differential receipt of functions, rank of the protégé was an important predictor.

Clearly, this is a critical area that requires more empirical work and attention. The limited amount of research that examines race and the functions of mentoring have produced some conflicting findings. Some studies have found differences in the experiences of people of color that cut across the psychosocial and career functions originally outlined by Kram (1985). However, recent work has challenged the original two-category classification scheme (career versus psychosocial) as being exhaustive (e.g., Scandura, 1992). We believe that for people of color, career functions may need to precede psychosocial functions for effective and beneficial cross-race mentoring relationships to occur. The more complex longitudinal work needed to tease apart these relationships has not yet been done, but it will provide vital data to better understand the relationship between race and interactions across different mentoring functions. Despite the need for further research, it is clear that both career and psychosocial functions of mentoring are important drivers of career outcomes that often differ by race.

Race and Mentoring: Outcomes Matter

A great deal of research has focused on the impact that race has on career outcomes such as job satisfaction, commitment, earnings, advancement, and a variety of career experiences (Alderfer & Thomas, 1988; Daly, 1996; Dickens & Dickens, 1982; Essed, 1991; James, 2000; Ortiz-Walters & Gilson, in press). Typically, this research has focused on outcomes along two dimensions: objective and subjective (Higgins & Thomas, 2001; Turban & Dougherty, 1994). Objective outcomes include variables such as promotion and compensation, while subjective outcomes include satisfaction variables, such as compensation satisfaction or supervisor satisfaction; involvement, commitment; and other work-related attitudes.

While a substantial amount of attention has been devoted to the impact of race on subjective versus objective outcomes, there is still some disagreement on whether race has a differential impact on these two types of outcomes. In her study of Black and White professional women, Blake-Beard (1999) examined the impact of protégé race on four outcome variables, two objective and two subjective. While she did not see a difference between Black and White women in terms of the objective outcomes, there were differences between the two groups in terms of the subjective outcomes. White respondents reported higher levels of compensation satisfaction and greater satisfaction with their career progress. The research that Catalyst has done on women of color suggests that we may want to pay attention to potential differential relationships between race and outcome variables. In their work, Catalyst (2006) found striking differences among women of color in relation to key outcomes. African American women reported higher levels of exclusion from the workplace in comparison to Latinas and Asian Americans.

Although the distinction of objective versus subjective outcomes provides a useful categorization, is does not capture the nature of these outcomes in terms of their cost versus benefit for the mentor or the protégé. Thus, a wide variety of research looks at the outcomes of mentoring in terms of positive versus negative consequences for those involved in the relationship (see reviews by Ragins, 1999; O'Neill, 2002; Wanberg et al., 2003). What is clear from this research is that we have a great deal of evidence on the positive impact of mentoring as a function of race, but little work that examines the negative impact of the presence of mentoring relationships (versus lack of access to mentoring). The small and growing literature on negative mentoring (Eby & Allen, 2002; Eby, Butts, Lockwood, & Simon, 2004; Eby, McManus, Simon, & Russell, 2000; Scandura, 1998) has been characterized by samples that are predominantly White. For example, Eby and her colleagues have published several studies on negative mentoring, but their samples are 95% to 97% Caucasian. While the work coming from this team of researchers is adding to our extant knowledge about the impact of negative mentoring, the racially homogeneous samples mean that we learn nothing about the experiences of people of color.

Dickens and Dickens (1982) argued that people of color (specifically African Americans) are often not able to reap the benefits of mentoring relationships because the issue of race and the dynamics of race relationships act as critical obstacles. In this view, race somehow blocks the well-established "ROI" (return on investment) of mentoring relationships in organizations. Thomas and Kram (1988) examined the benefits and outcomes of developmental relationships: "While it is clear that race is a significant predictor of some career outcomes, we know little about the specific mechanism that mediates observed differences" (p. 489). Thus, more attention is needed to understand when and why we see hypothesized positive outcomes of mentoring relationships, particularly within the context of racial dynamics

Regardless of whether we focus on objective versus subjective or on positive versus negative outcomes of mentoring, the focal target of these outcomes as a function of race is another perspective that should be addressed within this area of work. Previous mentoring research has focused almost exclusively on the mentee or protégé as the target of outcomes of mentoring relationships (Ragins & Scandura, 1999). Perhaps this is because there are a limited number of mentors of color who are available within organizations. These small numbers notwithstanding, there is some limited evidence that the experiences of mentors of color are quite different from their White counterparts. For example, in a study examining the experiences of 1,660 young women and their mentors, MentorNet (2004) found that mentors of color reported a number of outcomes at higher levels than did their White counterparts. Mentors of color reported increased self-confidence, improved supervisory skills, improved skills for recruiting new talent, better networking skills, and renewed commitment to their fields.

Finally, an important distinction between outcomes for individuals versus outcomes for organizations is an emerging focus within the mentoring literature. Within the work on diversity in organizations (see Ragins's 1997a, 1997b, research on diversified mentoring relationships), the conceptual link between mentoring and benefits for the firm has been well established (Alleman & Clark, 2000; Blake-Beard & Murrell, 2006; Perrone, 2003; Wilson & Elman, 1990). However, empirical evidence on the organizational benefits of diverse mentoring relationships is limited.

Clearly, the outcomes of mentoring and the impact of race vary as a function of the categorization employed. While we know a great deal about objective versus subjective outcomes of mentoring and race, there is still much to be developed in areas such as negative outcomes of mentoring, the impact of race on outcomes for the mentor, along with empirical evidence on the organizational outcomes of mentoring as a function of race. While there has been an emerging body of work on the impact of race on outcomes along with access and interactions of mentoring relationships, there are still a number of questions to be answered, leaving a great deal of unfinished business within this area of research.

Race and Mentoring: Some Unfinished Business

From our analysis of the extant research on race and mentoring, we identify a number of challenges and opportunities that should guide future work in this area. These challenges and opportunities are driven not only by unanswered questions in the existing research but, also by emerging issues raised by the changing nature of careers and organizations. Clearly, factors such as the changing relationship between individuals and the firm, which Arthur and Rousseau (1996) labeled the "new employment principle," raise a number of questions about how we approach the study of race and mentoring in the future. Within this new employment contract, Thomas and Higgins (1996) argued that both people of color and majority individuals will be challenged by the "psychological instability that emanates from a work context that does not affirm salient and important aspects of one's personal identity, or provide sufficient information and guidance to sustain one's career growth and development" (p. 273). Clearly, we have a number of things to learn about and from the intersection of race and mentoring in organizations.

One of the areas that provides both a primary opportunity for research and a significant challenge to the advancement of knowledge in this area concerns the fundamental issue of how we define mentoring within the context of race. As our review and reviews by others (see Fletcher & Ragins, Chapter 15, this volume) of the empirical literature has revealed, the mentoring literature is fraught with broad generalizations because of the ways in which race has been both excluded and misconceptualized in previous work (Minnich, 1991; Nkomo, 1992). Given the changing demographics of today's organizations, we must examine the assumptions and methodologies that help to generate existing definitions and typologies of mentoring to more directly test how they may or may not apply within the context of race.

While published research that includes a diverse representation of individuals within our samples has increased, the dominant racial group within organizational research has traditionally been White men. Because other racial groups are seen as "minority" groups, the experiences and perspectives of the dominant racial group have become the dominant or default conceptual models within mentoring research. The original work conducted by Kram (1985) relied on rigorous in-depth qualitative interviews on the functions served by mentors across a number of different organizations. However, the functions served by mentors did not explicitly explore differences by race or gender in crafting this original conceptual model. Later research has examined differences in the frequency of or experience with these various functions (e.g., Clawson & Kram, 1984), but no empirical research to date has grappled with whether Kram's overall model of mentoring and its classification of developmental functions is fundamentally different for people of color. In fact, since the majority of research examines differences only between the experiences of African Americans and Whites, we know very little about the way mentoring is defined that is based on the experience of other racial groups outside of those interviewed within the original sample. This point of critique is quite similar to issues raised among early Black psychologists who argued that we should not generalize existing models of human behavior to racial groups who were absent from the sample used to define and shape the dominant theories (see Jones, 1991).

One of the clear implications of excluding race from this early conceptual framework concerns ways in which we now measure and operationalize the mentoring construct. Independent of the dimension of race, a number of scholars have raised concerns with the wide variety of measurement tools and operationalizations used in the field (e.g., Allen, Eby, Poteet, Lentz, & Lima, 2004). Some studies use an overall index of mentoring; others measure the broad categories of career and psychological functions; whereas a few attempt to differentiate between the specific mentoring functions identified in Kram's original interviews. In addition, current measures are not easily adapted to situations involving multiple mentoring relationships, group mentoring, interorganizational mentoring, and emerging forms of mentoring such as "e-mentoring" (see Ensher & Murphy, Chapter 12, this volume).

Recent findings raise questions about whether the classic two-dimensional model of mentoring is, in fact, robust. Scandura and her colleagues (Lankau & Scandura, 2002; Scandura, 1992; Scandura & Viator, 1994) have found evidence for three broad categories of mentoring functions: career, psychosocial, and role-modeling. Similarly, Gibson (2004) has focused on defining and measuring role models as a separate and distinct construct from mentoring (rather than a function of overall mentoring as Kram's model articulates). Gibson distinguished between close and distant role models, such that distant role models are a "cognitive representation" of behaviors that drive goals and aspirations of the individuals that neither involve nor require direct contact with the individual (role model). Murrell and Zagenczyk (in press) have offered a similar argument concerning gender, race, and, role model status. Despite the influence of Kram's model in shaping mentoring research, there is significant variability in both the measurement and operationalization of what we mean by the concept of mentoring.

According to Allen et al. (2004), while the dominant literature thus far is consistent in the position that psychosocial and career functions are the "primary, distinct, and reliable" dimensions of mentoring, it can be argued that additional research on this question is needed. Perhaps the mental models of mentors and protégés in Kram's original sample would—if this sample included people of color—reveal some different functions of mentoring, other categories and functions, or a different overall structure of mentoring experiences. For example, the labeling of what determines "career" versus "psychosocial" could vary depending on the experience and perspective of those being interviewed. As Kram (1985) articulated, career functions are those aspects of the relationship that enhance career advancement. This suggests that the labeling of these mentoring functions as career versus psychological is driven by expected outcomes already known to vary as a function of race.

We argue that any typology that attempts to capture the functions or activities of the mentor-protégé relationship must be understood within the context of race. This statement is based on the wide variety of empirical and theoretical work that shows race to be embedded within the organizational context (Alderfer & Thomas, 1988), a consistent driver of work attitudes and outcomes (Murrell & James, 2001), and a moderator of the ROI employees receive from training and other developmental activities (James, 2000). In addition, given that relational aspects of the work experience have been shown to be critical drivers of career outcomes and attitudes for minorities (Cox & Blake, 1991), perhaps what is typically labeled as "psychosocial support" should really be seen as fundamental (and essential) career support for people of color. It may be the case that the distinction between career versus psychosocial is itself socially constructed as part of the mentor-protégé relationship rather than an absolute or universal (and externally determined) classification scheme.

A key challenge for future research on mentoring is to move beyond the faulty assumption that the experience of race within organizations does not shape, alter, and drive the mentoring relationship. In addition, scholars must acknowledge that within their own mentoring research, it is inappropriate to assume that the experiences of one group adequately and accurately capture the experiences of other groups. When we accept models that have been defined on basis of the experience of one dominant racial or ethnic group (unless this is explicitly stated as part of the research model), we silence our ability to articulate the authentic dynamics of mentoring relationships within a diverse organizational context. Instead of drawing conclusions that bring us closer to the truth about human behavior in organizations, we are drawing artificial distinctions that move us further away from this true understanding.

Our appeal for a greater inclusion of race within the context of mentoring research is quite consistent with Ragins's (1997a, 1997b) notion of "diversified mentoring relationships." She has made it clear from the perspective of power dynamics within organizations that there is an inextricable link between mentoring and diversity. As Ragins (1997b) stated, "Micro-theories for each marginalized group ignore the implications of multiple group membership, and take a limited piecemeal perspective toward explaining diversity in mentoring relationships" (p. 483). In fact, one can argue that when people of color are excluded from the sample or race effects are left as unexamined variance within our data, we are assuming that only people of color have "race" and that examining the experiences of Whites means that we are not conducting research on race in organizations.

Ragins's notion of diversified mentoring relationship raises another important point relevant to our review of work in this area. Her focus on the critical role that power dynamics plays in shaping mentoring relationships challenges the traditional interpersonal attraction paradigm that underlies most mentoring research. The classic view of mentoring based on the similarity-attraction paradigm (Berscheid, 1985) assumes that similarity at the individual level is the primary driver of mentoring relationships. However, issues of rank, power, organizational structure, and social identity are crucial factors that shape the outcomes and experiences of people in organizations. In addition, as structural, organizational, and social forces, they operate independently of (and sometimes in opposition to) attraction at the individual level. Last, viewing mentoring exclusively from an interpersonal-attraction perspective ignores the idea that developmental relationships also involve group identity and the exchange of power, knowledge as well as social (versus human) capital.

Current models that define mentoring purely at the individual or interpersonal levels are limited in today's organization context. Power dynamics and the social construction of racial group identity are clearly embedded within organizations and within society (Alderfer, 1987). In fact, social identity theory is based on a fundamental assumption that one cannot extrapolate from the interpersonal level to the intergroup level of analysis in order to understand how identity shapes behavior and attitudes (Tajfel & Turner, 1986). For example, Erkut and Mokros (1984) found that both male and female students avoided selecting female faculty as mentors because they were viewed as less powerful within the organization and profession. Similarly,

Clawson and Kram (1984) noted external reputation and public image as key drivers of cross-gender mentoring. Murrell and Tangri (1999) discussed a similar dynamics concerning race and mentoring within an academic environment. Clearly, this work suggests that something other than interpersonal similarity or attraction is an important driver within the context of formal and informal mentoring relationships (Viator & Pasewark, 2004).

We echo Ragins's challenge that work on mentoring must include an understanding of diversified mentoring relationships. However, we extend her original notion that diversified relationships occur only when a mentor and protégé differ in group memberships that are associated with power as defined by their common organization. Her argument highlights the importance of seeing diversity as a continuous rather than a categorical variable and the importance of understanding both the strength of identification and the context of power within the organization. However, viewing diversified mentoring relationships only within the context of a single organization ignores the significance of race in our broader society.[1] We include what Thomas and Higgins (1996) call a "cosmopolitan orientation" toward mentoring that takes into account dynamics that cut across interpersonal and intergroup boundaries as well as factors internal and external to the organization. This allows us to produce robust models of mentoring relationships that cut across racial identity groups as well as firm-defined work groups. Given the nature of the emerging and boundaryless organization, the distinction between power dynamics that are bound by a single context is less normative and provides only a limited scope.

We see that a key challenge and opportunity for future research is how to examine the dual effects of diversity and embeddedness of mentoring relationships. This clearly poses a challenge for current measures and methodologies that dominate how mentoring research was conducted in the past. Future research must move past simple between group comparisons of central tendencies to understand the unique dynamics that exist within different racial groups and how that drives interactions between different racial groups over time. While it is important to validate the unique experience of people of color in terms of access to and benefits from mentoring (e.g., Thomas, 1993), future research models should challenge our thinking and measurement tools to include the interaction of multiple group identities (e.g., race, gender, work group), in both formal and information relationships, across multiple (e.g., internal, external) organizational contexts. We must also acknowledge that regardless of whether it is explicitly measured within our specific data, race is both constant and embedded within the social and organizational contexts (see Eddleston, Baldridge, & Veiga, 2004) that shape mentoring relationships (Alderfer & Thomas, 1988). Thus, we must build models of race and mentoring that are dynamic, interactive, and multilevel.

We acknowledge some recent steps in this direction, foreshadowed by Kram (1985) and her call for a "constellation" of support. Building on Kram's work, Higgins and her colleagues (Higgins & Kram, 2001; Higgins & Thomas, 2001) expanded mentoring theory to encompass their notion of "mentoring constellations." Regardless of whether one considers mentoring relationships that are primary or secondary, single or multiple, hierarchical or peer, the importance of these constellations or networks provides an opportunity for future research to capture the richness and the complexity of mentoring. In addition, the recent integration of mentoring research within a social networks framework opens up a range of opportunities in terms of conceptual models, measurements tools, and methodological techniques. For example, some recent work on race and social networks has found that centrality, as a traditional networks measure, is an important index that helps to explain differences in the experience of people of color (and women) in organizations (e.g., Ibarra, 1993, 1995). In addition, Friedman's work on affinity or social network groups and race examined the strength of ties among African Americans that extend outside their current organizations yet impact careers and work attitudes inside their current organizations (Friedman, 1996; Friedman, Kane, & Cornfield, 1998).

Unfortunately, only a limited number of empirical studies have explored not only the differences between developmental networks of different racial groups but also study the unique features of social networks within racial groups. We see this as an opportunity to develop race-specific, or what we will call "race-inclusive," research of mentoring and career outcomes. For example, Ibarra (1993) found that minorities have a very different "opportunity context" for the cultivation of developmental relationships. Similarly, James (2000) concluded that there may be an as yet undiscovered race-specific model of workplace attainment that involves different drivers for Blacks compared with Whites. What is unclear at this point is the extent to which the drivers of these different opportunity contexts or work attainment models are a function of individual preferences (i.e., similarity-attraction), structural barriers (i.e., discrimination), or intergroup power dynamics (i.e., social identity maintenance).

In addition, within the current research on social networks, there is some debate on the types of relationships that are the most effective in driving career outcomes versus social relationships within the firm. Raider and Burt (1996) positioned this question within the context of social capital that they have argued is "generally important, but more important for people at the social frontier—people at the interface of different social worlds" (p. 189). This suggests that people of color may rely on the benefits of social capital to a greater extent do than their White counterparts. However, little current research helps to examine the types of social networks that are the most productive as a function of the dynamics of race in organizations. Burt and his colleagues would argue that differences in social networks account for performance differences among individuals who are equivalent in terms of experience, education, and ability (Burt, 1992; Raider & Burt, 1996). This suggests that strong social capital helps some individuals to experience a better return than others on their human capital. Consistent with Burt, mentoring relationships can be viewed as a competitive advantage for individuals as well as a primary source of social capital for the individual and for the firm.

However, little research to date has teased apart the specific network structure and social capital pattern necessary for people of color to succeed. One notion is that network structures that are large and comprise disconnected contacts are the best for producing social capital. This idea of "structural holes" has been shown to drive career outcomes for majority individuals within organizations (see Burt,

1992); however, we know little about the impact on the experiences of people of color of networks comprising disconnected individuals. There is much to be debated about the impact of strong versus weak ties for career and organizational outcomes. From a social network perspective, ties may vary in strength along a continuum from weak to strong. *Tie strength* is defined as "the amount of time, the emotional intensity, the intimacy (mutual confiding) and reciprocal services that characterize the tie" (Granovetter, 1973, p. 1361). Individuals who maintain strong ties are likely to have similar attitudes, backgrounds, experiences, and access to resources (Burt, 1992). In contrast to strong ties, exchanges that occur through weak ties are less frequent and less intimate. Weak ties are based on infrequent interaction, usually with individuals who reside outside the focal individual's network. Weak ties are significant because they allow access to different sources of information or resources that an individual does not receive through strong ties (Burt, 1992; Granovetter, 1973).

We cannot assume, however, that a single type of developmental constellation that produces social capital for majority individuals will have the same impact and operate by the same processes for people of color. In fact, based on recent challenges to Burt's notion of structural holes (see Leana & Van Buren, 1999), one might caution people of color against building networks of weak ties and disconnected parties as a strategy for career advancement and success. We clearly see opportunities for interesting empirical questions, based on the integration of mentoring, diversity, and embedded intergroup relations, that utilize the emerging methodologies and tools within social network analysis as fruitful for future research.

Race and Mentoring Relationships: A Revised Model

To advance our thinking and research on the intersection between race and mentoring, we revised Thomas's (1993) model on racial dynamics in cross-race development relationships. This redeveloped model tried to draw a link between strategies for managing racial differences and the type of relationships that emerge.

Clearly, this early model was based on the assumption that the interracial interactions within the mentoring relationship were a function of racial dynamics embedded within the organizational environment. The major contribution of this early model was in identifying a variety of different strategies that emerge from differences in the perspective of Whites and African Americans involved in cross-race mentoring relationships. Thomas (1993) argued that cross-race perspectives, and their subsequent impact on relationship management, may be either complementary or noncomplementary. By *complementary relationships,* Thomas referred to interactions where both parties' racial perspectives are mutually supportive and they prefer the same strategy for managing racial difference. In contrast, *noncomplementary relationships* are characterized by different strategy preferences for managing racial difference being held by each party. We retain the notion of complementary versus noncomplementary as an intervening process for these

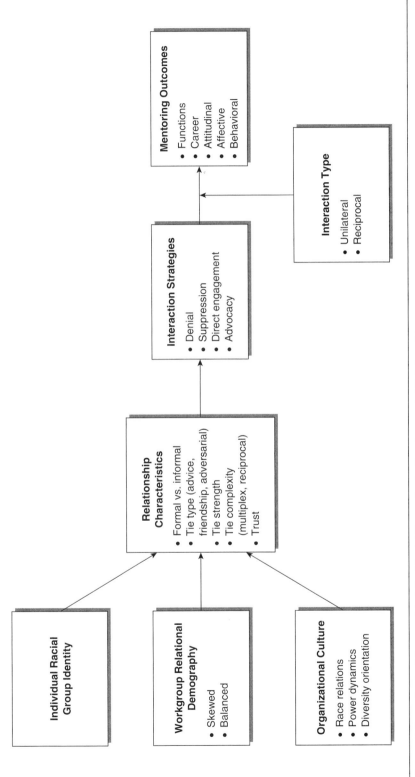

Figure 9.1 Revised Process Model of Racial Dynamics in Developmental Relationships

SOURCE: Thomas (1993).

strategies. Clearly, having similarity in the preferred strategy between the mentor and protégé is as important as the need to match stakeholder influence strategy to the target audience (see Frooman & Murrell, 2005).

In addition, we extend the model developed by Thomas (1993) on the basis of current knowledge and research on race and mentoring, as discussed herein. Our revised model (see Figure 9.1) includes the interaction strategy preferences originally developed by Thomas, with two changes. First, given the work that has emerged on the connection between mentoring and diversity, we include *advocacy* as a possible strategy that moves beyond direct engagement within the relationship, toward engagement in the process of change throughout the organization. The experience of cross-mentoring relationships can create a desire for change surrounding diversity either because of positive experiences or equally because of negative ones (Thomas & Ely, 1996). Second, based on Frooman and Murrell's (2005) work on stakeholder influence strategies, our revised model separates the concepts of denial and suppression as two distinct interaction responses. In fact, Thomas (1993) acknowledged that these two options may not be interchangeable: "These protégés' reticence and/or discomfort about race seems to contribute to a tendency to suppress and perhaps even deny the salience of race in their cross-race development relationships" (p. 179). Our revised model includes four distinct interactions strategies that can occur as a result of various developmental relationship characteristics: denial, suppression, direct engagement, or advocacy.

Furthermore, we extend Thomas's model by expanding the drivers of these strategy preferences (see Figure 9.1). Work by Helms (1990), Cross (1991), and Murrell (1997) has shown the importance of racial group identity through understanding its impact on interracial dynamics. Recent work has moved well beyond the assumption that the mere presence of a racial categorization results in identification with and actions based on a particular racial group membership. Building on the work of social identity theory (Tajfel & Turner, 1986), it is important to not simply place individuals into a racial category, but to understand the strengths of their individual levels of racial group identity and how this drives race-relevant relationships and behaviors. For example, Thomas (1993) found that the dynamics of cross-race interactions are influenced by what he labeled the "racial awareness" of both parties involved in the relationship. Thus, our revised model places individual racial group identity as a precursor to the preferred interaction strategies that may drive the type of relationships formed, as well at the outcomes. In addition, individuals tend to identify with people who are like them on important or salient identity group characteristics (Miller & Dreger, 1973; Murrell, 1997). Thus, individual racial group identity is included as an important antecedent to relationship characteristics and preferred interaction strategies (see Figure 9.1).

Our revised model also includes two important contextual variables: workgroup relational demography and organizational culture surrounding power and race relations. Work by Tsui and her colleagues (Tsui & O'Reilly, 1989; Tsui et al., 1992) and by Jackson and Ruderman (1995) clearly showed the importance of relational demography and work group composition on key outcomes. We argue that both of these variables provide the embedded social context for interracial mentoring relationship in line with the original conceptual model developed by Thomas (1999). As key contextual variables, they both shape and drive the types of relationships that can and do occur both within and between different racial groups. In addition, according to Thomas and Ely (1996), the different models or perspectives on power and diversity shape the overall context for cross-race relationships within any given organization. We include these two variables as additional antecedents within our revised model of racial dynamics within mentoring relationships.

The original model proposed by Thomas (1993) predicted a direct relationship between racial perspective and strategy interaction preferences. However, our revised model reflects the substantial work that has been done showing that the type of social network influences the nature and outcomes of mentoring relationships and that these networks are impacted by race (Ibarra 1993, 1995). Social networks are important in terms of whether these ties are based on formal or informal mentoring relationships, the strength of ties (Granovetter, 1973), the content of social ties (e.g., advice, friendship, adversarial), and the complexity of ties (reciprocal, multiplex). *Reciprocal ties* are defined as relationships in which there is mutuality within the social tie (e.g., we both give and receive advice from one another). *Multiplex ties* are those in which relationships cut across more than one content (e.g., friendship ties that are also advice ties). All of these dimensions have been shown to impact the nature of social networks as well as the outcomes.

Last, we include trust as an important dimension of these relationship characteristics. Although some social network models include trust-related variables as a dimension of strength (Marsden, 1988; Marsden & Campbell, 1984), the nature of previous work on mentoring relationships suggests that trust deserves a focal point as a dimension of relationship characteristics. Thomas's (1990) work clearly showed that mutuality and trust are important in distinguishing between what he labeled as the "mentor-protégé" versus the "sponsor-protégé" relationship.

Thus, our revised model includes the nature of racial identity perspectives, work group composition, and organizational culture as antecedents to the specific characteristics of social ties involving developmental relationships. The strength of social ties, formality, content, complexity, and trust are proposed as important dimensions of these relationships. Similar to the original model proposed by Thomas (1993), these relationship characteristics drive a preferred interaction strategy between the mentor and protégé. Denial and suppression are avoidance strategies that can emerge because of negative relationship characteristics driven by individual racial identity or contextual factors (group composition, organizational culture). On the other hand, direct engagement and advocacy are proactive strategies that are related to positive relationships characteristics. These preferred interaction strategies produce a range of different outcomes, including mentoring functions (psychosocial, career), attitudinal (satisfaction, commitment), career (advancement, salary), and behavioral (intention to stay, relationship cultivation, relationship separation). However, the impact of these preferred interaction strategies on various outcomes is moderated by the degree to which these strategies are complementary (mentors and protégés share the same strategy) versus noncomplementary (the parties have different strategy preferences). Thus, the type of interaction strategy is believed to interact with whether it is shared by both parties involved, and this interaction impacts a range of different outcomes typically studied within mentoring research (see Figure 9.1).

Race and Mentoring: Some Final Thoughts

The study of race and mentoring represents unfinished business for organizational scholars, managers, and practitioners. As Nkomo (1992) suggested, the way that research on race has been conceptualized "provides little insight into the complexity of the psychological, organizational and societal variables that may account for such findings" (p. 498) of differences between the experiences of Whites and racial minorities. We see research on race and mentoring as providing an extraordinary opportunity to help us answer some of the persistent and vital questions concerning the dynamics of race in organizations. Similar to the classic work on school desegregation and the contact hypothesis (see Hewstone, Rubin, & Willis, 2002, for an excellent review of this work), we see mentoring as providing a comparable opportunity to understand the dynamics of interpersonal contact, learning, and social mobility across racial boundaries in work settings. Clearly, we have a number of things to learn about and to learn from the intersection of race and mentoring in organizations. Our revised model provides an initial attempt to help structure some critical questions for future research. Regardless of the theoretical model devised, we must acknowledge and act on the basis of the understanding that regardless of whether it is explicitly measured within our specific data proposed in our conceptual models, race is embedded within both the social and organizational contexts that shape mentoring relationships (Thomas & Alderfer, 1989).

Note

1. For the current discussion, we focus on race within a U.S. context because of the unique historical, social, and economic factors that uniquely define racial interactions within this country. Other discussions of mentoring within a global context can be explored by Clutterbuck and Ragins (2002).

References

Alderfer, C. P. (1987). An inter-group perspective on group dynamics. In J. W. Lorsch (Ed.), *Handbook of organizational behavior* (pp. 190–222). Englewood Cliffs, NJ: Prentice Hall.

Alderfer, C. P., & Thomas, D. A. (1988). The significance of race and ethnicity for understanding organizational behavior. In C. L. Cooper & I. T. Robertson (Eds.), *International review of industrial and organizational psychology* (pp. 1–42). London: John Wiley & Sons.

Alleman, E., & Clark, D. L. (2000). Accountability: Measuring mentoring and its bottom line impact. *Review of Business, 21,* 62–67.

Allen, T. D., Eby, L. T., Poteet, M. L., Lentz, E., & Lima, L. (2004). Career benefits associated with mentoring for protégés: A meta-analysis. *Journal of Applied Psychology, 89,* 127–136.

Arthur, M. B., & Rousseau, D. M. (1996). *The boundaryless career: A new employment principle for a new organizational era.* New York: Oxford University Press.

Bell, E. L. (1990). The bicultural life experience of career-orientated Black women. *Journal of Organizational Behavior, 11,* 459–477.

Bell, M. P. (2006). *Diversity in organizations.* Mason, OH: Thomson South-Western.

Berscheid, E. (1985). Interpersonal attraction. In G. Lindzey & E. Aronson (Eds.), *The handbook of social psychology* (pp. 413–484). New York: Random House.

Blake-Beard, S. (1999). The costs of living as an outside within: An analysis of the mentoring relationships and career success of Black and White women in the corporate section. *Journal of Career Development, 26,* 21–36.

Blake-Beard, S. D. (2003). Critical trends and shifts in the mentoring experiences of professional women. *CGO Insights, No. 15.* Boston: CGO, Simmons School of Management.

Blake-Beard, S. D., & Murrell, A. J. (2006). *The Executive Leadership Council's (ELC) guide to effective mentoring.* Washington, DC: Executive Leadership Council.

Brief, A. P., & Hayes, E. L. (1997). The continuing "American Dilemma": Studying racism in organizations. In C. L. Cooper & D. M. Rousseau (Eds.), *Trends in organizational behavior* (pp. 89–106). Chichester, UK: John Wiley & Sons.

Burt, R. S. (1992). *Structural holes.* Cambridge, MA: Harvard University Press.

Caproni, P. J. (2005). Managing cultural diversity. *Management skills for everyday life: The practical coach* (2nd ed.). Upper Saddle River, NJ: Pearson Prentice Hall.

Catalyst. (1999). *Women of color in corporate management: Opportunities and barriers.* New York: Author.

Catalyst. (2001). *Women of color executives: Their voices, their journeys.* New York: Author.

Catalyst. (2006). *Connections that count: The informal networks of women of color in the United States.* New York: Author.

Clawson, J. G., & Kram, K. E. (1984, May/June). Managing cross-gender mentoring. *Business Horizons,* pp. 22–32.

Clutterbuck, D., & Ragins, B. R. (2002). *Mentoring and diversity: An international perspective.* Oxford, UK: Butterworth-Heinemann.

Cox, T. H., & Blake, S. (1991). Managing cultural diversity: Implications for organizational competitiveness. *Academy of Management Executive, 5,* 45–56.

Cox, T., & Nkomo, S. (1986). Differential performance appraisal criteria: A field study of Black and White managers. *Group & Organization Studies, 11,* 101–119.

Cox, T., & Nkomo, S. M. (1990). Invisible men and women: A status report on race as a variable in organization behavior research. *Journal of Organizational Behavior, 11,* 419–431.

Cox, T. H., & Nkomo, S. M. (1991). A race and gender-group analysis of the early career experiences of MBAs. *Work and Occupation, 18,* 431–446.

Crosby, F. J. (1999). The developing literature on developmental relationships. In A. J. Murrell, F. J. Crosby, & R. J. Ely (Eds.), *Mentoring dilemmas: Developmental relationships within multicultural organizations* (pp. 3–20). Mahwah, NJ: Lawrence Erlbaum.

Cross, W. (1991). *Shades of Black: Diversity in African-American identity.* Philadelphia: Temple University Press.

Daley, D. M. (1996). Paths of glory and the glass ceiling: Differing patterns of advancement among women and minority federal employees. *Public Administration Quarterly, 20,* 143–162.

Dickens, F., & Dickens, L. (1982). *The Black manager.* New York: Amacom.

Dreher, G. F., & Ash, R. A. (1990). A comparative study of mentoring among men and women in managerial, professional, and technical positions. *Journal of Applied Psychology, 75,* 539–546.

Dreher, G. F., & Chargois, J. A. (1998). Gender, mentoring experiences, and salary attainment among graduates of historically Black universities. *Journal of Vocational Behavior, 53,* 401–416.

Dreher, G. F., & Cox, T. H. (1996). Race, gender, and opportunity: A study of compensation attainment and the establishment of mentoring relationships. *Journal of Applied Psychology, 81,* 297–308.

Eby, L. T., & Allen, T. D. (2002). Further investigation of protégés' negative mentoring experiences: Patterns and outcomes. *Group & Organization Management, 27,* 456–479.

Eby, L. T., Butts, M., Lockwood, A., & Simon, S. A. (2004). Protégés' negative mentoring experiences: Construct development and nomological validation. *Personnel Psychology, 57,* 411–447.

Eby, L. T., McManus, S., Simon, S. A., & Russell, J. E. A. (2000). An examination of mentoring from the protégé's perspective. *Journal of Vocational Behavior, 57,* 42–61.

Eddleston, K. A., Baldridge, D. C., & Veiga, J. F. (2004). Towards modeling the predictors of career success: Does gender matter? *Journal of Managerial Psychology, 19,* 360–385.

Erkut, S., & Mokros, J. R. (1984). Professors as models and mentors for college students. *American Educational Research Journal, 21,* 399–417.

Essed, P. (1991). *Understanding everyday racism: An interdisciplinary theory.* Newbury Park, CA: Sage

Feagin, J. R. (1987). Changing Black Americans to fit a racist system? *Journal of Social Issues, 41,* 85–89.

Ford, D. L., & Wells, L. (1985). Upward mobility factors among Black public administrators: The role of mentors. *Centerboard: Journal of the Center for Human Relations, 3,* 33–48.

Foreman, C. H. (2000). Facing up to racial disparity. *Brookings Review, 8,* 29–30.

Friedman, R. (1996). Defining the scope and logic of minority and female network groups: Does separation enhance integration? In G. Ferris (Ed.), *Research in personnel and human resource management* (pp. 307–349). Greenwich, CT: JAI Press.

Friedman, R., Kane, M., & Cornfield, D. B. (1998). Social support and career optimism: Examining the effectiveness of network groups among Black managers. *Human Relations, 5,* 1155–1177.

Frooman, J., & Murrell, A. J. (2005). Stakeholder influence strategies: The roles of structural and demographic determinants. *Business and Society, 44,* 3–31.

Gibson, D. E. (2004). Role models in career development: New directions for theory and research. *Journal of Vocational Behavior, 65,* 134–156.

Granovetter, M. (1973). The strength of weak ties. *American Journal of Sociology, 78,* 1360–1380.

Guinier, L., & Torres, G. (2002). *The miner's canary: Enlisting race, resisting power and transforming democracy.* Cambridge, MA: Harvard University Press.

Helms, J. E. (1990). *Black and White racial identity.* New York: Greenwood.

Herbert, J. (1989). *Black entrepreneurs and adult development.* New York: Praeger Press.

Hewstone, M., Rubin, M., & Willis, H. (2002). Intergroup bias. *Annual Review of Psychology, 53,* 575–586.

Higgins, M. C., & Kram, K. E. (2001). Reconceptualizing mentoring at work: A developmental network perspective. *Academy of Management Review, 26,* 264–298.

Higgins, M. C., & Thomas, D. A. (2001). Constellations and careers: Toward understanding the effects of multiple developmental relationships. *Journal of Organizational Behavior, 22,* 223–247.

Hyun, J. (2005). *Breaking the bamboo ceiling: Career strategies for Asians.* New York: HarperCollins.

Ibarra, H. (1993). Personal networks of women and minorities in management: A conceptual framework. *Academy of Management Review, 18,* 56–87.

Ibarra, H. (1995). Race, opportunity, and diversity of social circles in managerial networks. *Academy of Management Journal, 38,* 673–703.

Jackson, S. E., & Ruderman, M. N. (1995). *Diversity in work teams: Research paradigms for a changing workplace.* Washington, DC: American Psychological Association.

James, E. H. (2000). Race-related differences in promotions and support: Underlying effects of human and social capital. *Organizational Science, 11,* 493–508.

Jones, R. E. (1991). *Black psychology* (3rd ed.). Hampton, VA: Cobb & Henry.

Kaplan, S. E., Keinath, A. K., & Walo, J. C. (2001). An examination of perceived carriers to mentoring in public accounting. *Behavior Research in Accounting, 13,* 195–220.

Koberg, C. S., Boss, R. W., Chappell, D., & Ringer, R. C. (1994). Correlates and consequences of protégé mentoring in a large hospital. *Group & Organization Management, 19,* 219–239.

Kram, K. E. (1983). Phases of the mentor relationship. *Academy of Management Journal, 26,* 608–625.

Kram, K. E. (1985). *Mentoring at work.* Glenview, IL: Scott, Foresman.

Kram, K. E. (1988). *Mentoring at work: Developmental relationships in organizational life.* Lanham, MD: University Press of America.

Lancaster, H. (1997, April 1). Managing your career: How women can find mentors in a world with few role models. *Wall Street Journal,* p. B1.

Lankau, M. J., & Scandura, T. A. (2002). An investigation of personal learning in mentoring relationships: Content, antecedents, and consequences. *Academy of Management Journal, 45,* 779–790.

Leana, C., & Van Buren, H. (1999). Organizational social capital and employment practices. *Academy of Management Review, 24,* 538–555.

Marsden, P. V. (1988). Homogeneity in confiding relations. *Journal of Social Networks, 10,* 57–76.

Marsden, P. V., & Campbell, K. E. (1984). Measuring tie strength. *Social Forces, 63,* 482–501.

MentorNet. (2004). *E-mentoring for women of color in engineering and science: Final report to the engineering information foundation.* New York: Author. Available at http://www.mentornet.net/documents/files/WomenofColorFinalReportMay2004.pdf

Miller, K. S., & Dreger, R. M. (1973). *Comparative studies of Blacks and Whites in the United States.* New York: Seminar Press.

Minnich, E. K. (1991). Discussing diversity. *Liberal Education, 77,* 2–7.

Murray, M. (1982). *The middle years of life of middle-class Black men: An exploratory study.* Unpublished doctoral dissertation, University of Cincinnati.

Murrell, A. J. (1997). To identify or not to identity: Preserving, ignoring, and sometimes destroying social identity. In S. Fiske & J. Eberhardt (Eds.), *Racism: The problem and the response* (pp. 18–201). Thousand Oaks, CA: Sage.

Murrell, A. J. (2000). Career and family. In N. J. Burgess & E. Brown (Eds.), *African American women: An ecological perspective* (pp. 173–194). New York: Falmer Press.

Murrell, A. J., Blake-Beard, S. D., Porter, D. M., & Williamson, A. (2006). *Inter-organizational formal mentoring: An innovative approach for cultivating diverse organizations.* Unpublished manuscript.

Murrell, A. J., Crosby, F. J., & Ely, R. J. (1999). *Mentoring dilemmas: Developmental relationships within multicultural organizations.* Mahwah, NJ: Lawrence Erlbaum.

Murrell, A. J., & James, E. H. (2001). Gender and diversity within organizations. *Sex Roles, 45,* 243–257.

Murrell, A. J., & Tangri, S. S. (1999). Mentoring at the margin. In A. J. Murrell, F. Crosby, & R. J. Ely (Eds.), *Mentoring dilemmas: Developmental relationships within multicultural organizations* (pp. 211–224). Mahwah, NJ: Lawrence Erlbaum.

Murrell, A. J., & Zagenczyk, T. (in press). Gender, race, and role model status: Exploring the impact of informal developmental relationships on management careers. In M. Karsten (Ed.), *Gender, ethnicity, and race in the workplace*. Westwood, CT: Greenwood Press/ Praeger.

Nkomo, S. M. (1992). The emperor has no clothes: Rewriting "race in organizations." *Academy of Management Review, 17*, 487–513.

Nkomo, S. M., & Cox, T. (1990). Factors affecting the upward mobility of Black managers in private sector organizations. *Review of Black Political Psychology, 18*, 39–43.

O'Neill, R. M. (2002). Gender and race in mentoring relationships: A review of the literature. In D. Clutterbuck & B. R. Ragins (Eds.), *Mentoring and diversity: An international perspective* (pp. 1–22). Thousand Oaks, CA: Sage.

O'Neill, R. M., & Blake-Beard, S. D. (2002). Gender barriers to the female mentor-male protégé relationship. *Journal of Business Ethics, 37*, 51–63.

Ortiz-Walters, R., & Gilson, L. L. (in press). Mentoring in academia: An examination of the experiences of protégés of color. *Journal of Vocational Behavior*.

Perrone, J. (2003). Creating a mentoring culture. *Healthcare Executive, 18*(3), 84–85.

Raider, H. J., & Burt, R. S. (1996). Mentoring and the boundaryless career: Lessons from the minority experience. In M. B. Arthur & D. M. Rousseau (Eds.), *The boundaryless career: A new employment principle for a new organizational era* (pp. 187–200). New York: Oxford University Press.

Ragins, B. R. (1997a). Antecedents of diversified mentoring relationships. *Journal of Vocational Behavior, 51*, 90–109.

Ragins, B. R. (1997b). Diversified mentoring relationships: A power perspective. *Academy of Management Review, 229*, 482–521.

Ragins, B. R. (1999). Gender and mentoring relationships: A review and research agenda for the next decade. In G. Powell (Ed.), *Handbook of gender and work* (pp. 347–370). Thousand Oaks, CA: Sage.

Ragins, B. R., & Scandura, T. A. (1999). Burden or blessing? Expected costs and benefits of being a mentor. *Journal of Organizational Behavior, 20*, 493–509.

Scandura, T. A. (1992). Mentorship and career mobility: An empirical investigation. *Journal of Organizational Behavior, 13*, 169–174.

Scandura, T. A. (1998). Dysfunctional mentoring relationships and outcomes. *Journal of Management, 24*, 449–467.

Scandura, T. A., & Viator, R. E. (1994). Mentoring in public accounting firms: An analysis of mentor-protégé relationships, mentoring functions, and protégé turnover intentions. *Accounting, Organizations, and Society, 19*, 717–734.

Sims, A. D. (2002). *An inter-group examination of African-American executives' mentoring relationships: Traversing the invisible hurdles of corporate America*. Unpublished doctoral dissertation, Rutgers, the State University of New Jersey.

Steinberg, A. G., & Foley, D. M. (1999). Mentoring in the army: From buzzword to practice. *Military Psychology, 11*, 365–379.

Tajfel, H., & Turner, J. (1986). The social identity of intergroup. In S. Worchel & W. G. Austin (Eds.), *Psychology of intergroup relations* (pp. 7–24). Chicago: Nelson.

Thomas, D. A. (1989). Mentoring and irrationality: The role of racial taboos. *Human Resource Management, 28*, 279–290.

Thomas, D. A. (1990). The impact of race on managers' experiences of developmental relationships. *Journal of Organizational Behavior, 11*, 479–492.

Thomas, D. A. (1993). Racial dynamics in cross-race developmental relationships. *Administrative Science Quarterly, 38*, 169–194.

Thomas, D. A. (1999). Beyond simple demography—power hypothesis: How Blacks in power influence White-mentor/Black-protégé developmental relationships. In

A. J. Murrell, F. J. Crosby, & R. J. Ely (Eds.), *Mentoring dilemmas: Developmental relationships within multicultural organizations* (pp. 157–170). Mahwah, NJ: Lawrence Erlbaum.

Thomas, D. A., & Alderfer, C. (1989). The influence of race on career dynamics theory and research on minority career experiences. In M. B. Arthur, D. T. Hall, & B. S. Lawrence (Eds.), *Handbook of career theory* (pp. 133–158). New York: Cambridge University Press.

Thomas, D. A., & Ely, R. J. (1996, September–October). Making differences matter: A new paradigm for managing diversity. *Harvard Business Review,* pp. 79–90.

Thomas, D. A., & Gabarro, J. J. (1999). *Breaking through: The making of minority executives in corporate America.* Boston: Harvard Business School Press.

Thomas, D. A., & Higgins, M. (1996). Mentoring and the boundaryless career: Lessons from the minority experience. In M. B. Arthur & D. M. Rousseau (Eds.), *The boundaryless career: A new employment principle for a new organizational era* (pp. 268–281). New York: Oxford University Press.

Thomas, D. A., & Kram, K. E. (1988). Promoting career enhancing relationships: The role of the human resource professional. In M. London & E. More (Eds.), *Employee career development and the human resource professional* (pp. 49–66). Westport, CT: Greenwood Press.

Tomlinson, A. (2001, December 17). Concrete ceiling harder than glass to break for women of color. *Canadian HR Reporter,* pp. 7, 13.

Tsui, A. S., Egan, T. D., & O'Reilly, C. A. (1992). Being different: Relational demography and organizational attachment. *Administrative Science Quarterly, 37,* 549–579.

Tsui, A. S., & O'Reilly, C. A. (1989). Beyond simple demographic effects: The importance of relational demography in superior-subordinate dyads. *Academy of Management Journal, 32,* 402–423.

Turban, D. B., & Dougherty, T. W. (1994). Role of protégé personality in the receipt of mentoring and career success. *Academy of Management Journal, 37,* 688–702.

U.S. Census Bureau. (2005). *Fact sheet for race, ethnic, ancestry group.* Available at http://www.factfinder.census.gov

U.S. Equal Employment Opportunity Commission. (2003). *Table 1: Occupational employment in private industry by race/ethnic group/sex and by industry, United States.* Available at http://www.eeoc.gov/stats/jobpat/2003/national.html

Viator, R. E. (1999). An analysis of formal mentoring programs and perceived barriers to obtaining a mentor at large public accounting firms. *Accounting Horizons, 12,* 37–53.

Viator, R. E. (2001). An examination of African Americans' access to public accounting mentors: Perceived barriers and intentions to leave. *Accounting, Organizations, and Society, 26,* 541–561.

Viator, R. E., & Pasewark, W. R. (2004). Mentoring separation tension in the accounting profession: The consequences of delayed structural separation. *Accounting, Organizations, and Society, 20,* 371–387.

Wanberg, C. R., Welsh, E. T., & Hezlett, S. A. (2003). Mentoring research: A review and dynamic process model. *Research in Personnel and Human Resource Management, 22,* 39–124.

Wilson, J. A., & Elman, N. S. (1990). Organizational benefits of mentoring. *Academy of Management Executive, 4,* 88–94.

10

Formal Mentoring Programs

A "Poor Cousin" to Informal Relationships?

S. Gayle Baugh

Ellen A. Fagenson-Eland

The topic of mentoring has increased in popularity in recent years in both the academic and the popular literature. A search of the PsycInfo database using the keyword *mentor* resulted in over 1,000 publications appearing in the past 25 years, with over 250 of them published in the past 3 years. Clearly, this topic has attracted a great deal of attention.

The literature on the benefits of mentoring has been carefully reviewed in earlier chapters (see especially Allen, Chapter 5; Dougherty & Dreher, Chapter 3; and Lankau & Scandura, Chapter 4). The advantages resulting from the mentoring relationship have been most clearly established for protégés, but mentors can also gain from the dyadic relationship. Organizations, too, have been identified as beneficiaries of mentoring, with outcomes like enhanced communication and commitment and reduced turnover suggested in the literature (Butyn, 2003; Hegstad, 1999; Perrone, 2003). Given all of the potential benefits of mentoring, it is not surprising that organizations have begun to develop mentoring programs in order to ensure that such advantageous relationships are developed and maintained, rather than relying on happenstance (Barbian, 2002a).

AUTHORS' NOTE: This chapter as well as this book are dedicated to Ellen, my coauthor and my friend. She is greatly missed.

Formal mentoring relationships are those that are initiated through some orga-nizational program that assigns mentors and protégés and facilitates and supports developmental relationships within the assigned dyads for a specified period of time (Wanberg, Walsh, & Hezlett, 2003). While formal mentoring relationships may take the traditional, hierarchical, one-on-one approach to mentoring, mentor-ing programs have evolved over the past two decades. Formal mentoring rela-tionships now may also take the form of peer relationships, team mentoring or mentoring circles, and structured networks (Douglas & McCauley, 1999; Kram & Hall, 1996; McManus & Russell, Chapter 11, this volume). As noted by Ensher and Murphy (Chapter 12, this volume), further variation in mentoring relationships results from the reliance on electronic communication rather than face-to-face interaction as an alternative or even the exclusive method of communication in mentoring relationships, including formal mentoring relationships.

It is important to determine whether such organizationally sponsored formal mentoring relationships offer benefits similar to those accruing to informal rela-tionships (see Dougherty & Dreher, Chapter 3, this volume). Formal mentoring relationships may also provide distinctive benefits not available from informal relationships. Organizational practices and program features need to be identi-fied that facilitate the ability of formal mentoring relationships to provide ben-efits equivalent to those of informal relationships, as well as conditions that allow organizations to capitalize on any advantages unique to formal relation-ships. This chapter will examine the issues associated with formal mentoring programs.

We must first turn our attention to the structural differences between formal and informal mentoring. Formal mentoring programs may be developed to address a variety of organizational needs, so it is important to delineate the purposes that formal mentoring programs may serve. We will next compare formal and informal mentoring relationships with respect to the mentoring functions performed, as well as looking at the benefits to the protégés in formal relationships relative to protégés in informal relationships or individuals who have not been mentored. While out-comes for mentors have been less well researched (see Allen, Chapter 5, this vol-ume), our summary of the benefits specific to informal relationships, as well as the negative or dysfunctional outcomes for both parties (see Eby, Chapter 13, this vol-ume), suggests many unanswered questions. Looking at both the positive and neg-ative outcomes of mentoring for both parties leads us to try to identify those program features associated with program success, and from this standpoint we develop an agenda for future research on formal mentoring.

The research that is specific to formal mentoring is limited, relative to research on informal mentoring or that which does not identify the nature of the relation-ship or confounds formal and informal mentoring dyads. Despite the paucity of research, there has been no lack of practitioner-oriented publications that provide anecdotal evidence with respect to the requisite features of successful formal men-toring programs. The suggestions for future research activity that will be offered have been influenced by the apparent "disconnect" between the need for informa-tion on the part of program developers and the scant research data on which to base program recommendations.

Features of Formal Mentoring Programs and Relationships

The touted benefits of informal mentoring for both mentors and protégés did not go unnoticed within organizations, and many developed formal programs in order to reap similar benefits. Structural features of formal mentoring programs impinge upon the resulting formal relationships, however, rendering them inexact copies of informal relationships. Some of the aspects of formal programs, along with resulting differences between formal and informal relationships, are important in considering the effectiveness of formal mentoring.

Formal mentoring programs exhibit great variation in structural aspects, just as there is great variety in the types of informal mentoring relationships that develop. There are two essential differences between formal and informal mentoring relationships that involve the initiation and the duration of the relationship (Ragins & Cotton, 1999). The first distinction is that formal relationships are developed with organizational assistance, whereas informal relationships are developed as a result of mentor-protégé interaction and are driven by the needs and desires of the two parties (Allen, Day, & Lentz, 2005; Lyons & Oppler, 2004). The second difference is that formal relationships develop within a limited time frame, usually set by the program manager and rarely longer than 1 year. Informal relationships will continue as long as the parties remain involved, although the nature of the relationship may change over time (Kram, 1983).

Formal mentoring programs vary with respect to the mechanisms used in matching mentors and protégés. Matching techniques range from the careful matching processes used by MENTTIUM (detailed by Sontag, Vappie, & Wanberg, Chapter 24, this volume) to something described as "blind dates" (Blake-Beard, O'Neill, & McGowan, Chapter 25, this volume), in which case the parties themselves must identify the unique needs they can fulfill for one another. Formal relationships usually have a set of organizationally prescribed goals. The goals of informal relationships, if they exist, are specified by the parties themselves rather than being imposed by external sources, as is the case for formal mentoring programs (Allen & Eby, 2003).

Informal mentoring relationships are relatively unconstrained with respect to frequency, length, or content of meetings between the parties, and interactions may vary in length and content. These exchanges could appear to an observer to be casual meetings, although it is likely that the members of the dyad have established their own norms with respect to appropriate meeting configurations. Formal dyads may be bound by some programmatic prescription of a minimum number of meetings of a certain length, and the program requirements may even specify or suggest the content of some of the meetings. Alternatively, the program may require that the parties themselves formally agree on the frequency, duration, or even content of meetings for the length of the program. Informal mentoring relationships last as long as both parties continue to benefit from them, although the nature of the relationships may change over time (Chao, 1997; Kram, 1983; Pollock, 1995). Formal mentoring relationships have a specified duration, which is usually shorter than the typical informal relationship (Allen et al., 2005). This reduced time frame for relationship development has implications for the progress of formal relationships through the various stages of mentoring relationships (Kram, 1983). Formal relationships that endure beyond the time boundaries of the informal program may well evolve into informal mentoring relationships.

A distinction that has been less frequently noted is that informal relationships can be less visible than formal relationships. Formal programs are normally accompanied by at least some internal publicity, which serves to make formal mentoring dyads more visible in the organization. There are also differences in the preparation that the parties bring to their roles in formal and informal relationships. Some mentoring programs provide extensive training to either the mentors or the protégés or both, so that their expectations of the relationship are more congruent with one another and with the goals of the program, whereas informal dyads develop their relationship on the basis of the expectations that the two parties bring to the liaison (Ragins & Verbos, 2007). Another feature of formal mentoring programs that has received scant attention is that in formal programs, the mentors and protégés may all be known to one another as a result of formal group activities that are part of the program. There is more potential for information sharing among protégés and mentors as groups than is the case for informal mentoring. Mentoring may even take a different form than the traditional, one-on-one, hierarchical relationships that are explored in the empirical literature. Unfortunately, research on such nontraditional formal mentoring programs has not progressed to the point where it can be coherently discussed within this chapter.

Finally, formal mentoring relationships have risks, some of which are the same as those of informal relationships, such as a poorly performing protégé reflecting badly on the mentor, and some of which are more closely associated with formal relationships, such as the potential for formal evaluation based on one's performance in the relationship. These risks coupled with the enhanced visibility of formal relationships due to the associated publicity might result in formal relationships that are qualitatively different from informal ones. Nonetheless, the potential benefits to the participants and to the organization are also very attractive. As a result, organizations are motivated to try to replicate informal mentoring relationships through the mechanism of formal mentoring programs.

Benefits of Mentoring to the Organization

Most of the early research in this field focused on the benefits to the protégé as a result of being mentored, concentrating on informal rather than formal relationships (e.g., Allen, Eby, Poteet, Lentz, & Lima, 2004; Baugh, Lankau, & Scandura, 1996; Fagenson, 1988, 1989; Kram 1985b; Scandura, 1992). As the field developed, more attention was directed to benefits for the mentor (e.g., Allen, 2003; Allen, Poteet, & Burroughs, 1997; Ragins & Scandura, 1999). But the practitioner literature is replete with suggestions that organizations that sponsor the development of formal mentoring relationships will see benefits resulting from their investment. Most of these suggestions are based on generalizing the benefits of informal mentoring relationships to the formal setting, an approach that will be examined in more detail later in this chapter.

One of the most commonly cited benefits of formal mentoring programs is enhanced socialization of relatively new employees (Benabou & Benabou, 2000; Gibb, 1999; Hegstad, 1999; Singh, Bains, & Vinnicombe, 2002). Mentoring relatively new organizational entrants should result in those individuals having a better understanding of the organization's mission, values, formal structure, and informal systems, leading to improved performance on the job. Related goals include development of organizational commitment and improved retention of new hires (Butyn, 2003; Gray & Gray, 1990; Jossi, 1997; Singh et al., 2002; Tyler, 1998). If mentoring enhances the socialization of new employees, then these individuals should have a stronger commitment to the organization as a result of the investment made in them, which should lead in the long run to better retention (Payne & Huffman, 2005).

Organizations are also expected to benefit from enhanced performance on the part of protégés relative to nonprotégés (Barbian, 2002a; Benabou & Benebou, 2000; Gibb, 1999; Hegstad, 1999; Jossi, 1977; Perrone, 2003; Tyler, 1998). Improved performance may result in increased organizational learning (Jossi, 1997; Perrone, 2003) and will likely positively affect career planning and development on the part of both the organization and the protégé (Benabou & Benabou, 2000; Gray & Gray, 1990). Mentoring is especially effective in facilitating the transfer of learning to the job, as protégés can request support with respect to specific job challenges (Benabou & Benabou, 2000; Hegstad, 1999; Lankau & Scandura, Chapter 4, this volume).

Early identification of management talent and leadership development are frequently cited benefits associated with formal mentoring programs (Hegstad, 1999; Perrone, 2003; Singh et al., 2002). Utilizing formal mentoring programs to "fast-track" some individuals into management positions will lead to earlier development of their aptitude and better planning for how to utilize it within the organization (Barbian, 2002b). Companies using this approach can be accused of favoritism or discrimination, however, and are usually cautioned to use care in selecting protégés for these types of programs (Forret, Turban, & Dougherty, 1996; McDonald & Hite, 2005).

Formal mentoring programs have frequently been targeted toward women and minorities, with the goal of enhancing diversity within the management ranks (Barbian, 2002a; Benabou & Benabou, 2000; Gibb, 1999; Jossi, 1997). Programs directed toward women and minorities provide access to mentoring for members of these underrepresented groups, offer legitimacy for diversified mentoring relationships, foster upward mobility for the protégés, and provide education for the mentors with respect to challenges faced by women and minorities in organizations (Kram & Bragar, 1992; Ragins, 2002; Zielinski, 2000). Such targeted programs will encounter issues related to mentoring in diversified dyads, such as those that have been identified by Ragins (1997).

Improved organizational communication may also result from mentoring programs (Singh et al., 2002). Linking senior and junior employees in a dyadic relationship will enhance the flow of information from higher levels of the organization downward, as well as from lower levels of the organization upward. Mentoring a more junior colleague will provide the mentor with greater insight into the types of problems and frustrations that are typically encountered by lower-level managers (Butyn, 2003; Gaskill, 1993; Zielinski, 2000).

The many claims of organizational benefits resulting from mentoring programs have yet to attract much empirical attention, however. Two studies included interviews with the individuals responsible for the development of formal mentoring programs (Gaskill, 1993; Hegstad & Wentling, 2004). In both cases, the program developers rated their programs as at least moderately successful. Another survey of organizations utilizing formal developmental relationships, more than half of which were traditional mentoring relationships, indicated that the program managers rated them as effective in meeting goals and objectives (Douglas & McCauley, 1999). In this instance, no difference was found between organizations utilizing formal developmental relationships for employee development and those that did not on sales volume, 3-year sales trend, or 3-year employment trend, suggesting that it might be difficult to capture a relationship between formal mentoring programs and more distal organizational outcomes. Generally, the empirical study of formal mentoring outcomes has not included the outcomes expected to accrue to the organization (the qualitative study by Eby & Lockwood, 2005, is an exception). Admittedly, organizational outcomes are difficult to influence through human resource interventions (Wanberg et al., 2003), but claims and anecdotal reports of organizational benefits, including increased revenues and reduced turnover, continue to appear in the literature (e.g., Wolosky, 2005).

The dearth of evidence of program effectiveness from an organizational standpoint is a concern with respect to the development of formal mentoring programs. Such programs involve a commitment of management time and of financial resources. Companies need evidence that investments in formal mentoring programs actually pay some kind of dividend.

Mentoring Functions in Formal and Informal Relationships

If organizations are to enjoy any benefits from formal mentoring programs, it is important to establish that mentoring is actually taking place within the relationships facilitated by the programs. If protégés do not believe that the traditional mentoring functions are actually being provided to them, then organizations can hardly expect that any of the benefits of formal mentoring programs will materialize. Several studies have addressed the extent to which protégés in formal relationships report receiving the traditional mentoring functions of vocational (or career) support and psychosocial support relative to their informally mentored counterparts.

The evidence on the difference between formal and informal protégés with respect to mentoring functions received is mixed. Several studies have found that formal protégés report less vocational support than do informal protégés (Allen et al., 2005; Chao, Walz, & Gardner, 1992; Ragins & Cotton, 1999; Scandura & Williams, 2001), whereas others found no such differences (Fagenson-Eland, Marks, & Amendola, 1997; Sosik, Lee, & Bouquillon, 2005; Tepper, 1995). There is also a tendency for formal protégés to report less psychosocial support than do informal protégés (Fagenson-Eland et al., 1997; Ragins & Cotton, 1999; Scandura & Williams, 2001; Sosik et al., 2005), but three studies reported no difference in the level of psychosocial support received based on relationship type (Allen et al., 2005; Chao et al., 1992; Tepper, 1995). While some studies indicate that informal protégés receive more mentoring than formal protégés and others that formal and informal protégés receive equivalent amounts, no study has suggested that formal protégés receive levels of support superior to informal protégés.

The evidence with respect to differences between formal and informal protégés on mentoring received does not fit easily with findings from studies focusing only on formal relationships. In general, individuals in formal mentoring relationships report more psychosocial support than career support (Allen, McManus, & Russell, 1999; Noe, 1988; Raabe & Beehr, 2003; Waters, McCabe, Kiellerup, & Kiellerup, 2002). This finding is underscored by a finding that formal mentors rated psychosocial support as more important than vocational support (Smith, Howard, & Harrington, 2005). There is no corresponding research on differences in level of functions provided for informal protégés for comparison. Given that formal protégés generally report more psychosocial support than career support, however, one might expect to find little difference between formal and informal protégés on psychosocial functions. From the research summarized, it does not appear that this is the case.

The inconsistency in the empirical results leads to speculation as to the reasons for such disparity. There are, of course, methodological differences between studies, including differences in the measures used to assess mentoring functions, lack of control for the stage of the relationships studied, and differences in research design (concurrent, longitudinal, or retrospective). The differences in the programs involved in the research also offer some explanation for disparate findings. Programmatic differences that may account for varying results include the length of the formal mentoring program, the amount of participant training offered, the degree of structure with respect to meeting frequency and content, and the extent of interaction among protégé and mentor groups. There are two additional issues, however, that deserve attention.

The research to date aimed at comparing mentoring functions in formal and informal relationships has been predicated on measures that were developed to assess mentoring functions provided in informal relationships. There has been no corresponding development of measures specifically derived from and directed toward mentoring functions within formal relationships. Formal and informal mentoring are not identical phenomena, however, and it is essential to direct some attention toward delineating the differences in the nature of relationships that develop within a formal as compared with an informal context. Assessing the quality of formal relationships by the measures developed for informal relationships may not be an appropriate comparison, and the inconsistency in empirical results may be due to incorrectly assuming equivalence in functions.

A second potential explanation for variation in results is that there may be differences in expectations for mentoring functions provided that are attributable to the nature of the mentoring relationship. It may be that protégés have generally lower expectations of a formal mentoring relationship simply because it is not "natural" (i.e., the mentor was induced to participate, rather than freely selecting the protégé as somehow worthy of investment). By contrast, protégés may anticipate better outcomes from formal relationships because their expectations are raised by the fact that they are selected for special attention. Protégé expectations may be strongly influenced by the organizational goals specified for the formal mentoring program and may be further modified by training provided within formal programs. Some investigation of protégés' expectations at the initiation stage of the relationship will shed some light on these questions.

One study conducted within a CPA firm, while not specifically exploring expectations, did look at preferences for formal and informal mentoring relationships. Results suggested that junior-level individuals reported a preference for formal mentoring relationships, whereas senior-level employees preferred informal relationships (Siegel & Reinstein, 2001). The results might reflect preferences with respect to flexibility in the frequency and timing of meetings. That is, junior-level employees might find that the requirement for regular meetings imposed by a formal mentoring program is to their benefit, whereas senior-level employees might find such a requirement to be an encroachment on their time (or, more specifically, on their billable hours) (Wolosky, 2005).

Protégé Benefits From Formal Mentoring Relationships

The research reviewed with respect to mentoring functions is suggestive of poorer-quality relationships for formal mentorships than for informal relationships. If formal mentoring relationships are less rich with respect to mentoring functions, then it follows that protégés engaged in formal relationships should enjoy fewer benefits associated with mentoring than do informal protégés, while still perhaps being advantaged relative to their nonmentored peers.

The evidence with respect to differences between formal and informal protégés is complex. No differences were found between formal and informal protégés on organizational commitment, career involvement, or job satisfaction in two studies (Chao et al., 1992; Sosik et al., 2005). But assessing the quality of the mentorship is important in determining relationships with outcome variables. Ragins, Cotton, and Miller (2000) found that protégés in satisfying formal mentoring relationships reported greater organizational commitment, career commitment, job satisfaction, organization-based self-esteem, and organizational justice, as well as lower turnover intentions, than individuals in less satisfying informal relationships. Further, reported quality of the mentoring relationship accounted for more variance in outcomes than either presence of a mentor or type of mentoring relationship (formal versus informal). Positive mentoring experiences seem to be associated with positive protégé assessments of the work environment, regardless of whether the relationship was initiated with or without organizational intervention.

Only one study compared formal and informal protégés with respect to role outcomes (Viator, 2001). The researcher found a negative relationship between vocational support and role conflict among individuals with a formal mentor, whereas the relationship was positive for those with an informal mentor among a sample of CPAs. Formal mentors appeared to be more helpful than informal mentors with respect to reducing role conflict, perhaps because the formal designation confers on the mentor more formal power to intervene in the protégé's work assignments.

With respect to external indicators of career success, informal mentoring has been associated with higher salaries than has formal mentoring (Chao et al., 1992). Individuals with histories of informal mentors over a 10-year period received higher levels of compensation than those with histories of formal mentors, but no difference was found for promotions (Ragins & Cotton, 1999). Informal mentoring was associated with higher levels of self-reported job performance on the part of the protégé than was formal mentoring, but neither form of mentoring was related to turnover intentions (Viator, 2001). None of these studies included any measure of relationship quality or relationship satisfaction, so variation in the quality of mentoring relationships may explain differences in reported outcomes (Ragins et al., 2000).

Comparisons between formally mentored and nonmentored individuals with respect to outcomes have also resulted in complex findings. A cross-sectional study of formal protégés as compared with nonmentored individuals found no difference in job satisfaction, but after 1 year, formal protégés reported greater job satisfaction than did nonmentored individuals (Seibert, 1999). No differences were found between the two groups with respect to organizational commitment, work role stress, or self-esteem (Seibert, 1999). With respect to outcomes, quality of the relationship once again played an important role. Protégés who reported higher-quality relationships indicated higher organizational commitment, career commitment, and organization-based self-esteem than did nonmentored individuals, but protégés in low-quality formal relationships did not significantly differ from nonmentored individuals (Ragins et al., 2000).

Relationship satisfaction within formal mentoring dyads may be a function of frequency of contact. Three studies examined the influence of frequency of contact within formal relationships, and all three found positive effects. Opportunity to interact predicted the reported quality of the relationship (Heimann & Pittenger, 1996), including greater satisfaction and less disappointment with the relationship (Lyons & Oppler, 2004; Viator, 1999). Of course, satisfying relationships may lead participants to interact more frequently than those in less fulfilling relationships, and the cross-sectional nature of the research does not permit the elimination of reverse or even reciprocal causality.

These results with respect to the effect of type of relationship on protégé outcomes parallel those for mentoring functions. Protégés in formal relationships do not fare as well as informal protégés, with perhaps the exception of reduction of role conflict, although they may be advantaged relative to nonprotégés. The quality of the relationship developed is an important moderating variable, however, with protégés in high-quality, satisfying formal relationships reporting outcomes as good as or better than those in marginal informal relationships. Further, time is a crucial element in mentoring research, as different relationship outcomes may emerge over time and formal and informal relationships have different time schedules with respect to their development. Finally, the absence of attention to the organizational goals of formal programs causes some concern. A collection of respondents who identified themselves as current or previous participants in some formal mentoring program formed the sample of formal protégés in most of the research reported. The formal protégés may well have participated in programs with differing goals, resulting in differing outcomes, thus producing inconsistent results when outcomes for protégés in formal programs were compared with those for informal protégés.

Mentor Benefits in Formal Programs

Mentors are key participants in mentoring relationships, whether formal or informal, so it is reasonable to anticipate that a great deal of attention would be directed toward the mentor's perceptions and experience of the mentoring relationship. Contrary to expectation, very little research has been focused specifically on mentors (see Allen, Chapter 5, this volume). Even less attention has been paid specifically to mentors in formal relationships, despite the fact that organizations for the most part depend on individuals to volunteer to be mentors (see Sontag, Vappie, & Wanberg, Chapter 24, this volume).

It appears that mentors and protégés in formal relationships do not necessarily agree on the level of mentoring functions provided to the protégés. In one study, mentors reported that they provided more vocational than psychosocial support, whereas protégés reported more psychosocial than vocational support received (Raabe & Beehr, 2003). Similarly, Fagenson-Eland and colleagues (1997), using unmatched samples of protégés and mentors, found that formal protégés reported receiving less psychosocial support than did informal protégés, whereas mentors reported no differences in functions they provided based on relationship type, but less frequent communication with formal than informal protégés.

In a study examining the effect of relationship type on mentors' perceptions of relationship effectiveness, no differences were found in relationship quality between formal and informal relationships (Allen & Eby, 2003). Duration of the relationship was positively correlated with relationship quality for formal but not informal relationships, however. Formal mentors reported lower relationship quality than did informal mentors early in the relationship, but the perceptions of relationship quality increased among formal mentors over time to match those of informal mentors, suggesting that formal relationships may become more like informal relationships over time (Allen & Eby, 2003).

A qualitative study of reactions to formal mentoring (Eby & Lockwood, 2005) showed that mentors and protégés received different benefits from participating in the mentoring program, with protégés indicating more benefits from the relationship than did mentors. Both parties identified learning about other areas of the organization as the most important outcome of the relationship, which was one of the goals of the program. Mentors reported personal gratification and enhanced managerial skills as additional benefits not suggested by protégés (Eby & Lockwood, 2005).

This summary of research on formal mentors indicates relatively low levels of agreement between mentors and protégés on the nature of their relationships. While conceptual models of mentoring suggest that mentors should receive benefits from the relationship (Ragins & Verbos, 2007) and the literature on informal mentoring implies that they do (e.g., Allen, Chapter 5, this volume; Allen et al., 1997; Pullins & Fine, 2002; Ragins & Scandura, 1999), there is only a limited basis to begin to build a taxonomy of the types of benefits that formal mentors should expect to enjoy.

The absence of a well-developed literature on mentors in formal relationships is puzzling. Mentor motivation to participate in a formal mentoring program is a very important topic to pursue. It is particularly important to determine whether there are benefits to the mentor resulting from formal relationships that are different from those that can flow from informal relationships. A qualitative research approach, obtaining rich and in-depth information from informal as well as formal mentors, would seem to be the appropriate empirical approach, as it does not tie the researcher to constructs that have already been developed in the context of informal mentoring. Identification of mentor benefits from formal relationships is critical in order to offer mentors some potential incentives for participating in formal programs. Formal mentoring programs would not be possible without willing volunteer mentors, as coerced participation in such programs can defeat their purpose.

Negative Outcomes of Formal Mentoring Relationships

Mentoring relationships are generally construed as positive pairings that offer both parties opportunities for growth and development. Interpersonal relationships are very rarely uniformly positive, however, and recently, attention has turned to some of the negative effects that can occur in mentoring relationships (Eby, Chapter 13, this volume; Scandura, 1998). Due to the fact that formal mentoring relationships do not occur "naturally," one might predict that more dysfunctions would be found in formal than informal mentoring relationships. The partners in a formal mentoring dyad may feel more organizational pressure to persist in trying to make the relationship "work" beyond the point when an informal relationship would have withered for lack of attention (Feldman, 1999), thus causing members in formal dyads to accept less satisfying relationships and more negative outcomes without terminating the relationships than would members of informal dyads.

Recognizing that formal relationships will range in quality from highly satisfying to marginal, there has been some study of negative outcomes as well as benefits in formal mentoring. A qualitative study examined relational problems in formal mentoring relationships. Several concerns were shared by both protégés and mentors, including mentor-protégé mismatch, scheduling difficulties, and geographical barriers. Protégés reported a few unique concerns, such as unmet expectations, neglect or lack of interest on the part of their mentors, and structural separation. Mentors reported feelings of inadequacy stemming from the mentoring relationship as the only unique problem experienced (Eby & Lockwood, 2005). These problems were reported, though, along with several benefits that were acknowledged by the participants, indicating that the relationships were imperfect, but hardly dysfunctional.

A second study examined the differences between formal and informal protégés with respect to the level of negative experiences reported (Eby, Butts, Lockwood, & Simon, 2004). Formal protégés reported that their mentors engaged in more distancing behavior than that reported by informal protégés and were more likely to find their mentors to be lacking in needed expertise than were informal protégés. No differences were found between formal and informal protégés with respect to the interpersonal comfort or dyadic mismatch reported in their relationships (Allen et al., 2005; Eby et al., 2004). While there are greater reported difficulties in formal than informal relationships, they do not seem to be severe.

Formal mentoring dyads do not report more problematic relationships than do informal pairs, despite a great deal of expressed concern (e.g., Kizilos, 1990). Most practitioner-oriented discussions of formal mentoring programs indicate that there must be an "escape" for participants in dissatisfying mentoring relationships, although there is rarely much guidance for how to arrange a separation without engendering hurt feelings, loss of self-esteem, and concerns about public admissions of failure (Burke & McKeen, 1989; Gaskill, 1993; Tyler, 1998; Zey, 1985). As a result, partners may seek to dissolve a formal relationship only when it is truly dysfunctional, whereas participants in a marginally satisfying formal mentoring relationship may persist in trying to make the relationship "work" despite some negative outcomes (Feldman, 1999).

Mentors are the more experienced and established members of mentoring dyads and are usually at least one, and sometimes more, hierarchical levels above their protégés in an organization (e.g., Klauss, 1981). As a result, the literature on dysfunctional mentoring relationships tends to cast the mentor in the role of the "villain" (Feldman, 1999). Nonetheless, mentors may also expect some negative effects from engaging in mentoring relationships, including demands on time and emotional energy, disloyalty from protégés, and loss of status due to poor protégé performance (Allen et al., 1997; Eby, Chapter 13, this volume; Ragins & Scandura, 1999). It is, once again, surprising that almost no research has been directed toward the mentor as the key individual in formal mentoring relationships. The dearth of information about both positive and negative experiences of mentors in formal relationships suggests great potential for future research.

Designing Effective Formal Mentoring Programs

The evidence presented thus far supports the view that formal mentoring is a less desirable substitute for informal relationships, with participants in formal relationships less advantaged than their counterparts in informal relationships. Such conclusions are based on comparisons of formal and informal mentoring relationships that utilize measures that are appropriate to informal relationships and fail to acknowledge that formal mentoring programs are frequently developed to accomplish specific goals. These goals include making mentoring a natural part of the organizational culture (Barbian, 2002b; Clutterbuck, 2004), extending the benefits of mentoring to those who for whom informal mentoring might not be available (Fagenson-Eland & Baugh, 2001; Kram & Bragar, 1992; Olian, Carroll, & Giannantonio, 1993), or developing leadership potential within the organization (Forret et al., 1996; Giscombe, Chapter 22, this volume; Gray & Gray, 1990; Kram & Hall, 1996). If a formal mentoring program is to be offered, then attention must be given to the features that lead to effective programs. While the best practices in formal mentoring programs will be carefully reviewed in another chapter (see Sontag, Vappie, & Wanberg, Chapter 24, this volume), the literature on effective formal mentoring programs will be briefly summarized here. There is a great deal of literature offering advice to program developers with respect to the design features of the program (e.g., Benabou & Benabou, 2000; Butyn, 2003; Gibb, 1999; Tyler, 1998; Zey, 1985) based on very limited research and large doses of anecdotal evidence.

Formal mentoring programs should be designed with specific goals (Butyn, 2003; Eby & Lockwood, 2005) that are linked to the company's strategic objectives (Kram & Bragar, 1992). In the absence of clear goals, program effectiveness cannot be ascertained. The only research study examining the effect of program goals indicated that protégés were generally more satisfied with promotional opportunities if the program was directed toward career development rather than socialization (Ragins et al., 2000).

The program's goals may determine the individuals eligible for the program, but mentors and protégés must still be selected from among the candidates. Suggestions for criteria for selection of protégés include willingness to learn, curiosity, work involvement, and some level of communication competency (Hale, 2000; Kalbfleisch & Davies, 1993; Pittenger & Heimann, 2000). Both interpersonal and business skills are suggested as important in the selection of mentors (Gaskill, 1993; Kalbfleisch & Davies, 1993). Participation in formal mentoring programs is generally voluntary, as pressure to engage is viewed as detrimental to participant commitment (Kram & Bragar, 1992; Tyler, 1998). There is evidence to suggest that voluntary participation does increase participant satisfaction (Ragins et al., 2000).

The process of matching mentors and protégés is important, as poor matching may result in dysfunctional or failed relationships. Evidence suggests that allowing participants input into the matching process will result in a more positive experience (Allen, Eby, & Lentz, 2006; Klauss, 1981; Ragins et al., 2000; Viator, 1999). Similarity of the members of the dyad, especially with respect to interests and values, may result in a better quality relationship (Allen & Eby, 2003; Klauss, 1981; Lankau, Riordan, & Thomas, 2005), although the importance of similarity may decrease over time (Allen & Eby, 2003). It may be that other aspects of the mentoring program are equally important as or even more important than dyadic matching (Lankau & Scandura, 2002).

Frequency of interaction between the mentor and protégé within informal relationships has a positive effect on participant reactions (Noe, Greenberger, & Wang, 2002). Available research suggests that setting guidelines for frequency of meetings leads to more positive responses to the program (Allen et al., 2006; Ensher & Murphy, 1997; Heimann & Pittenger, 1996; Ragins et al., 2000; Seibert, 1999; Viator, 1999). Length of the program is a different issue, with most recommendations falling between 6 months and 1 year (e.g., Butyn, 2003; Tyler, 1998). However, a survey of organizations with formal mentoring programs found that the duration of such relationships varied from 10 weeks to 4 years (Gaskill, 1993), while Douglas and McCauley (1999) found reports of formal developmental relationships as short as 1 day. There appears to be little agreement among program developers on the minimal length of time required for the emergence of mentoring relationships.

There is more agreement with respect to training, which is strongly recommended for good mentoring programs (Allen et al., 1997; Clutterbuck, 2002; Forret et al., 1996; Kram, 1985a; Noe et al., 2002). Allen and her colleagues (2006) found that the quality of the training provided is of greater importance than simply providing training to mentoring program participants. Lankau and Scandura (Chapter 4, this volume) have made a strong case that training participants about learning processes and styles is an important aspect of any effective mentoring program. Training in interpersonal skills and clarifying goals and expectations are generally endorsed in the literature, as well. There are few recommendations about the process of training, however. There is a similar lack of information about handling mismatched mentor-protégé dyads and program evaluation, despite the fact that these issues are frequently cited as important to program success (Butyn, 2003; Gibb, 1999; Tyler, 1998; Zey, 1985). The many innovations in mentoring programs, including peer mentoring, structured networks, mentoring circles, and group mentoring, have yet to be empirically explored, along with the effects of computer-mediated communication in formal mentoring relationships. There is a wealth of opportunity for research on formal mentoring programs.

Directions for Future Research

Our discussion of future research directions will be guided by Figure 10.1. This diagram shows that the structure of a mentoring program must first be developed; then, protégés and mentors, who come with their own sets of demographic and personal characteristics, must be matched into pairs (or perhaps networks) and provided with training of some kind. They develop dyadic relationships (or relationship networks) based on their own current and past experiences in developmental relationships and in the context of organizational features, which either support or impede their efforts. The quality of the mentoring relationships developed will, in turn, influence the amount and type of outcomes experienced by protégés, mentors, and the organization itself.

Structural features of formal mentoring programs affect the process of matching protégés and mentors, which, in turn, influences the relationships developed within the program and the outcomes available to the participants. Mentoring programs are generally designed to achieve some kind of goal or organizational outcome, although in some cases, the objective might not be very well articulated. It is not clear from the current research on formal mentoring as to the extent to which the program goals influence the relationship development process or the extent to which goal acceptance among participants is required. The approach planned with respect to frequency, type (electronic or face to face), and content of meetings will influence

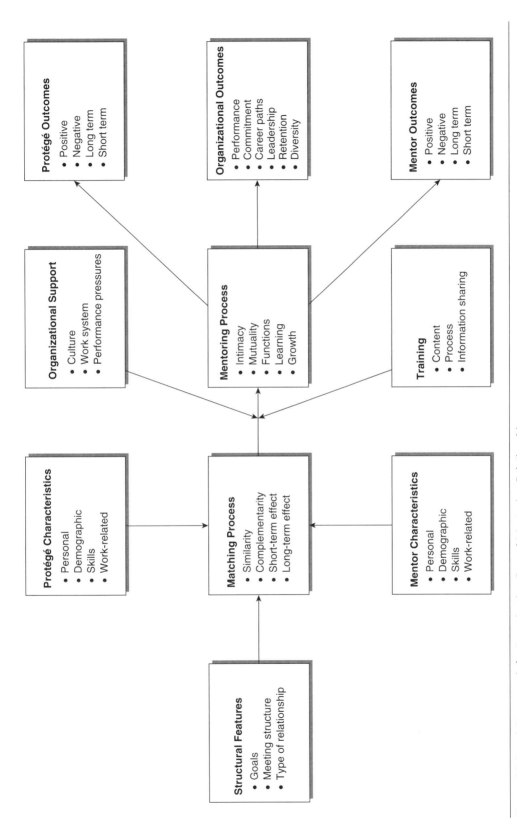

Figure 10.1 A Framework for Investigating Formal Mentoring Relationships

the requirements with respect to matching mentors and protégés and the mentoring relationships developed. In some programs, participating dyads are given much latitude to develop their own structures for how their relationships are enacted, whereas in others, participants are provided with guidelines or even directives with respect to their meetings. While it would seem that greater latitude might result in formal mentoring relationships that are more like informal relationships, this question has not been pursued in research to date. Finally, the type of relationship that the program is designed to initiate is a key factor affecting the mentoring process. While the research to date on formal mentoring has focused on traditional, hierarchical, one-on-one mentoring relationships, there are alternative structures that some organizations are currently utilizing. Clearly, much more research should be directed at peer mentoring, group mentoring, structured networks, and other alternatives to traditional mentoring relationships in order to determine the strengths and drawbacks of these newer approaches to developmental relationships.

Participant characteristics directly affect the matching process, as indicated in Figure 10.1, and may also have an influence on the mentoring relationships developed. The research on mentor and protégé characteristics emphasizes gender (e.g., Lankau et al., 2005; Ragins et al., 2000), but investigation of other demographic variables is needed. Research on personal characteristics (such as interests and values) and work-related variables (such as skills, including interpersonal skills, work involvement, and work-family conflict) should prove fruitful. Both mentor and protégé also are influenced by their history of previous developmental relationships, in that previous experience builds expectations for current relationships and also affects the level of interpersonal skill that the participants bring with them. The effect of these variables on the perceived "goodness of fit" from the perspective of both mentors and protégés should be examined, as well as the effect on the quality of the relationships developed.

The matching process deserves much more empirical consideration than it has received to this point (see Blake-Beard, O'Neill, & McGowan, Chapter 25, this volume). Matching can take the form of similarity or complementarity, with differing effects on the mentoring relationship. Further, matching processes may have different effects over short versus long time periods, indicating a need for longitudinal research. Finally, the potential mediating effect of training and the organizational context on the relationship between mentor-protégé matching and the quality of the relationship (indicated in Figure 10.1) have yet to be explored.

The effect of participant training and of information sharing among participants on program outcomes deserves attention. It is possible that excellent training can enhance or even replace a detailed matching process (indicated in Figure 10.1), although it is not a substitute for the selection of good mentors. Nonetheless, the effect of content and process of the training offered on the quality of the relationship developed should be investigated. Information sharing among program participants is unique to the formal mentoring process. Mentor and protégé groups can be brought together through the course of the formal mentoring program to learn from one another about capitalizing on opportunities and managing conflicts. By contrast, participants in informal relationships are left to their own resources when concerns or questions arise. If this potential has been exploited in practice, it has not been reported in the literature.

Organizational context can also influence the relationship development process. A culture that is supportive of learning and development, a work system that emphasizes collaboration rather than competition, a reward system for employee development, and the absence of rigorous individual performance pressure are features of the organization that will enhance a formal mentoring program (Wanberg et al., 2003). Context variables have rarely been included in research on formal mentoring programs (Sosik et al., 2005, is an exception) but are crucial in understanding their success or failure.

The focal point of formal mentoring programs is the mentoring relationship itself, as shown in Figure 10.1. Research on formal mentoring programs, like all research on mentoring, must confront the problem of defining a mentoring relationship. The fact that a relationship is developed within the context of a formal mentoring program does not necessarily mean that it is a mentoring relationship. Both conceptual and empirical work are needed to develop the parameters of mentoring relationships with respect to the requisite levels of intimacy, mutuality, functions, and frequency of contact, as well as the minimum length of relationship necessary to acknowledge a relationship as "mentoring" and not some other kind of support. It makes little sense to investigate the outcomes of formal mentoring programs if the relationships developed within them are impoverished with respect to the level of mentoring that occurs and might best be characterized as some other form of work-related support or assistance. The temporal constraints of formal mentoring programs may preclude the development of "true" mentoring relationships, or perhaps formal mentoring relationships are qualitatively or quantitatively different from informal relationships. The recent trend toward looking at "constellations" of developmental relationships (e.g., Higgins & Kram, 2001; Higgins & Thomas, 2001) highlights the importance of carefully defining both informal and formal mentoring, lest it become confused with other types of developmental relationships.

A clearer definition of the requisite characteristics of a mentoring relationship, including a more precise delineation of the differences between formal and informal mentoring relationships, will facilitate evaluation of the effectiveness of formal mentoring programs. Currently, evaluations that indicate limited effectiveness for formal mentoring programs may be reporting on relationships that are not mentoring at all. Further, these evaluations are based on functions and outcomes that are associated with informal mentoring relationships, with little explicit recognition that formal mentoring relationships may be qualitatively different. Thus, while formal mentoring appears to be a "poor cousin" to informal mentoring, it may instead be that comparisons are being made between informal mentoring and a variety of other types of supportive relationships or that differences in the nature of formal and informal relationships render comparisons inappropriate.

Along the same lines, it is necessary to look at the quality of relationships in judging the effectiveness of formal mentoring relationships and programs. The quality of relationships developed within formal mentoring programs will vary, and the quality of the relationships developed is likely to be the result of the care and attention paid to the development and maintenance of the program. Relationship quality includes the variables listed in Figure 10.1—intimacy, mutuality, functions, growth, and learning—but is discussed in more depth by Fletcher and Ragins (Chapter 15, this volume). Future research on formal mentoring relationships should include some assessment of relationship quality.

Most of the attention to the outcomes of mentoring has been focused on the positive outcomes for protégés, with some attention to negative effects. Further emphasis should be placed on the outcomes for mentors, including negative outcomes, as mentors are key participants in formal programs. If individuals are reluctant or unwilling to become mentors, then formal mentoring programs will falter. Mentors may be more motivated to serve if they are aware of the potential benefits and are offered strategies to avoid potential pitfalls.

A serious deficiency with respect to research on formal mentoring programs is the absence of a delineation of the benefits and drawbacks of such programs to the organization itself. While it is true that evidence with respect to the influence of informal mentoring on organizational outcomes has not yet been presented, companies must invest financial and other resources (including managerial time) in formal programs. Investments must be evaluated on the basis of anticipated gains. The many assertions of mentoring's benefits to organizations have yet to be supported with evidence. Organizations must base expectations for the benefits of formal mentoring programs on something more than unsubstantiated claims. In addition, organizations need to be informed about potential problems in order to develop program designs to best avoid them.

As has been noted elsewhere in this book, there is a desperate need for longitudinal research on mentoring, and that need is equally great with respect to formal programs. Mentoring relationships unfold and evolve over time, offering different benefits and disadvantages at different stages. Formal programs, which are by nature time limited, may have a different process of relationship development than informal relationships, so that stage models that are appropriate for informal mentoring relationships may not fit the development of formal relationships. Longitudinal research will serve to shed some light on the process issues, which have, up to this point, received inadequate consideration. Longitudinal research, especially long-term evaluation, may be necessary in order to determine what, if any, organization-level benefits emerge from formal mentoring relationships. Conducting this important and necessary research will require a partnership between business and academe. On the business side, companies must make a long-term commitment to open sharing of information, including some personnel-related information like salaries, promotions, and performance evaluations. On the academic side, researchers must be willing to work within a research team, and at least some of the team members must be willing to focus a major portion of their research efforts on one area.

Conclusion

Many organizations have developed formal mentoring programs in an attempt to capture the benefits resulting from informal relationships. Formal mentoring programs also offer some unique benefits to organizations, including incorporating mentoring into the organizational culture, extending mentoring relationships to underserved groups, and exploiting the potential of mentoring for leadership development. The evidence to date suggests that formal relationships, while beneficial, are not truly on par with informal relationships with respect to individual outcomes, whereas the organizational-level outcomes have rarely been assessed. It is evident, however, that the quality of the relationship developed matters a great deal with respect to the outcomes to be expected, so the program features that promote the development of high-quality relationships must be identified. Unfortunately, although prescriptions for effective programs abound, most are based on anecdotal evidence.

There is also a growing need to integrate formal mentoring programs with other types of developmental relationships. This area is as yet undeveloped in the current literature on formal mentoring, although companies are developing innovative programs that include peer mentoring, group mentoring, structured networks, e-mentoring, and other nontraditional forms of mentoring. In this instance, research needs to catch up with practice!

There is a great need for research that is explicitly focused on formal mentoring relationships and programs. We have proposed a framework for viewing formal mentoring relationships that can guide theory, research, and practice in the future. Using this framework, we have indicated areas of research that have been relatively unexplored but are likely to lead to findings that can be utilized to enhance the effectiveness of formal mentoring programs. We hope that this framework will prove useful to future researchers and practitioners with an interest in formal mentoring programs.

References

Allen, T. D. (2003). Mentoring others: A dispositional and motivational approach. *Journal of Vocational Behavior, 62,* 134–154.

Allen, T. D., Day, R., & Lentz, E. (2005). The role of interpersonal comfort in mentoring relationships. *Journal of Career Development, 31,* 155–169.

Allen, T. D., & Eby, L. T. (2003). Relationship effectiveness for mentors: Factors associated with learning and quality. *Journal of Management, 29,* 469–486.

Allen, T. D., & Eby, L. T., & Lentz, E. (2006). Mentorship behaviors and mentorship quality associated with formal mentoring programs: Closing the gap between research and practice. *Journal of Applied Psychology, 91,* 567–578.

Allen, T. D., Eby, L. T., Poteet, M. L., Lentz, E., & Lima, L. (2004). Career benefits associated with mentoring for protégés: A meta-analysis. *Journal of Applied Psychology, 89,* 127–136.

Allen, T. D., McManus, S. E., & Russell, J. E. A. (1999). Newcomer socialization and stress: Formal peer relationships as a source of support. *Journal of Vocational Behavior, 54,* 453–470.

Allen, T. D., Poteet, M. L., & Burroughs, S. M. (1997). The mentor's perspective: A qualitative inquiry and future research agenda. *Journal of Vocational Behavior, 51,* 70–89.

Barbian, J. (2002a). A little help from your friends. *Training, 39*(3), 38–60.

Barbian, J. (2002b). The road best traveled. *Training, 39*(5), 38–42.

Baugh, S. G., Lankau, M. J., & Scandura, T. A. (1996). An investigation of the effects of protégé gender on responses to mentoring. *Journal of Vocational Behavior, 49,* 309–323.

Benabou, C., & Benabou, R. (2000). Establishing a formal mentoring program for organizational success. *National Productivity Review, 19*(4), 1–8.

Burke, R. J., & McKeen, C. A. (1989). Developing formal mentoring programs in organizations. *Business Quarterly, 53*(3), 76–79.

Butyn, S. (2003). Mentoring your way to improved retention. *Canadian HR Reporter, 16*(2), 13–15.

Chao, G. T. (1997). Mentoring phases and outcomes. *Journal of Vocational Behavior, 51,* 15–28.

Chao, G. T., Walz, P. M., & Gardner, P. D. (1992). Formal and informal mentorships: A comparison on mentoring functions and contrast with nonmentored counterparts. *Personnel Psychology, 45,* 619–336.

Clutterbuck, D. (2002). Establishing and sustaining a formal mentoring programme for working with diversified groups. In D. Clutterbuck & B. R. Ragins (Eds.), *Mentoring and diversity: An international perspective* (pp. 45–86). Oxford, UK: Butterworth-Heinemann.

Clutterbuck, D. (2004). Making the most of informal mentoring. *Development and Learning in Organizations, 18*(4), 16–17.

Douglas, C. A., & McCauley, C. D. (1999). Formal developmental relationships: A survey of organizational practices. *Human Resource Development Quarterly, 10,* 203–220.

Eby, L., Butts, M., Lockwood, A., & Simon, S. A. (2004). Proteges' negative mentoring experiences: Construct development and nomological validation. *Personnel Psychology, 57,* 411–447.

Eby, L. T., & Lockwood, A. (2005). Protégés' and mentors' reactions to participating in formal mentoring programs: A qualitative investigation. *Journal of Vocational Behavior, 67,* 441–458.

Ensher, E. A., & Murphy, S. E. (1997). Effects of race, gender, perceived similarity, and contact on mentoring relationships. *Journal of Vocational Behavior, 50,* 460–481.

Fagenson, E. A. (1988). The power of a mentor: Protégés' and nonprotégés' perceptions of their own power in organizations. *Group & Organization Studies, 13,* 182–194.

Fagenson, E. A. (1989). The mentor advantage: Perceived career/job experiences of protégés vs. non-protégés. *Journal of Organizational Behavior, 10,* 309–320.

Fagenson-Eland, E. A., & Baugh, S. G. (2001). Personality predictors of protégé mentoring history. *Journal of Applied Social Psychology, 31,* 2502–2517.

Fagenson-Eland, E. A., Marks, M. A., & Amendola, K. L. (1997). Perceptions of mentoring relationships. *Journal of Vocational Behavior, 51,* 29–42.

Feldman, D. C. (1999). Toxic mentors or toxic protégés: A critical re-examination of dysfunctional mentoring. *Human Resource Management Review, 9,* 247–278.

Forret, M. L., Turban, D. B., & Dougherty, T. W. (1996). Issues facing organizations when implementing formal mentoring programs. *Leadership and Organizational Development Journal, 17,* 27–30.

Gaskill, L. R. (1993). A conceptual framework for the development, implementation, and evaluation of formal mentoring programs. *Journal of Career Development, 20,* 147–160.

Gibb, S. (1999). The usefulness of theory: A case study in evaluating formal mentoring schemes. *Human Relations, 52,* 1055–1075.

Gray, M. M., & Gray, W. (1990). Planned mentoring: Aiding key transitions in career development. *Mentoring International, 4*(2), 27–32.

Hale, R. (2000). To match or mis-match? The dynamics of mentoring as a route to personal and organizational learning. *Career Development International, 5,* 223–234.

Hegstad, C. (1999). Formal mentoring as a strategy for human resource development: A review of research. *Human Resource Development Quarterly, 10,* 383–390.

Hegstad, C. D., Wentling, R. M. (2004). The development and maintenance of exemplary formal mentoring programs in Fortune 500 companies. *Human Resource Development Quarterly, 15,* 421–448.

Heimann, B., & Pittenger, K. K. S. (1996). The impact of formal mentorship on socialization and commitment of newcomers. *Journal of Managerial Issues, 8,* 108–117.

Higgins, M. C., & Kram, K. E. (2001). Reconceptualizing mentoring at work: A developmental network perspective. *Academy of Management Review, 26,* 264–289.

Higgins, M. C., & Thomas, D. A. (2001). Constellations and careers: Toward understanding the effects of multiple developmental relationships. *Journal of Organizational Behavior, 22,* 223–247.

Jossi, F. (1997). Mentoring in changing times. *Training, 34*(8), 50–54.

Kalbfleisch, P. J., & Davies, A. B. (1993). An interpersonal model for participation in mentoring relationships. *Western Journal of Communication, 57,* 399–415.

Kizilos, P. (1990). Take my mentor, please! *Training, 27*(4), 49–55.

Klauss, R. (1981). Formalized mentor relationships for management and executive development in the federal government. *Public Administration Review, 41,* 489–496.

Kram, K. E. (1983). Phases of the mentoring relationship. *Academy of Management Journal, 26,* 608–625.

Kram, K. E. (1985a). Improving the mentoring process. *Training and Development Journal, 39*(4), 40–43.

Kram, K. E. (1985b). *Mentoring at work: Developmental relationships in organizational life.* Glenview, IL: Scott, Foresman.

Kram, K. E., & Bragar, M. C. (1992). Development through mentoring: A strategic approach. In D. H. Montross & C. J. Shrinkman (Eds.), *Career development: Theory and practice* (pp. 221–254). Springfield, IL: Charles C Thomas.

Kram, K. E., & Hall, D. T. (1996). Mentoring in a context of diversity and turbulence. In E. Kossek & S. Lobel (Eds.), *Managing diversity: Human resources strategies for transforming the workplace* (pp. 108–136). Cambridge, MA: Blackwell.

Lankau, M. J., Riordan, C. M., & Thomas, C. H. (2005). The effects of similarity and liking in formal relationships between mentors and peers. *Journal of Vocational Behavior, 67,* 252–265.

Lankau, M. J., & Scandura, T. A. (2002). An investigation of personal learning in mentoring relationships: Content, antecedents, and consequences. *Academy of Management Journal, 45,* 779–790.

Lyons, B., & Oppler, E. S. (2004). The effects of structural attributes and demographic characteristics on protégé satisfaction in mentoring programs. *Journal of Career Development, 30,* 215–229.

McDonald, K. S., & Hite, L. M. (2005). Ethical issues in mentoring: The role of HRD. *Advances in Developing Human Resources, 7,* 569–582.

Noe, R. A. (1988). An investigation of the determinants of successful assigned mentoring relationships. *Personnel Psychology, 41,* 457–479.

Noe, R. A., Greenberger, D. B., & Wang, S. (2002). Mentoring: What we know and where we might go. *Research in Personnel and Human Resources Management, 21,* 129–173.

Olian, J. D., Carroll, S. J., & Giannantonio, C. M. (1993). Mentor reactions to protégés: An experiment with managers. *Journal of Vocational Behavior, 43,* 266–278.

Payne, S. C., & Huffman, A. H. (2005). A longitudinal examination of the influence of mentoring on organizational commitment and turnover. *Academy of Management Journal, 48,* 158–168.

Perrone, J. (2003). Creating a mentoring culture. *Healthcare Executive, 18*(3), 84–85.

Pittenger, K. K. S., & Heimann, B. A. (2000). Building effective mentoring relationships. *Review of Business, 21,* 28–42.

Pollock, R. (1995). A test of conceptual models depicting the developmental course of informal mentor-protégé relationships in the workplace. *Journal of Vocational Behavior, 46,* 144–162.

Pullins, E. B., & Fine, L. M. (2002). How the performance of mentoring activities affects the mentor's job outcomes. *Journal of Personal Selling and Sales Management, 22,* 259–271.

Raabe, B., & Beehr, T. A. (2003). Formal mentoring vs. supervisor and coworker relationships: Differences in perceptions and impact. *Journal of Organizational Behavior, 24,* 271–293.

Ragins, B. R. (1997). Antecedents of diversified mentoring relationships. *Journal of Vocational Behavior, 51,* 90–109.

Ragins, B. R. (2002). Understanding diversified mentoring relationships: Definitions, challenges, and strategies. In D. Clutterbuck & B. Ragins (Eds.), *Mentoring and diversity: An international perspective* (pp. 23–53). Oxford, UK: Buttterworth-Heinemann.

Ragins, B. R., & Cotton, J. L. (1999). Mentor functions and outcomes: A comparison of men and women in formal and informal mentoring relationships. *Journal of Applied Psychology, 84,* 529–550.

Ragins, B. R., Cotton, J. L., & Miller, J. S. (2000). Marginal mentoring: The effects of type of mentor, quality of relationship, and program design on work and career attitudes. *Academy of Management Journal, 43,* 1177–1194.

Ragins, B. R., & Scandura, T. A. (1999). Burden or blessing? Expected costs and benefits of being a mentor. *Journal of Organizational Behavior, 20,* 493–509.

Ragins, B. R., & Verbos, A. K. (2007). Positive relationships in action: Relational mentoring and mentoring schemas in the workplace. In J. E. Dutton & B. R. Ragins (Eds.), *Exploring positive relationships at work: Building a theoretical and research foundation* (pp. 91–116). Mahwah, NJ: Lawrence Erlbaum.

Scandura, T. A. (1992). Mentorship and career mobility: An empirical investigation. *Journal of Organizational Behavior, 13,* 169–174.

Scandura, T. A. (1998). Dysfunctional mentoring relationships and outcomes. *Journal of Management, 24,* 449–467.

Scandura, T. A., & Williams, E. A. (2001). An investigation of the moderating effects of gender on the relationship between mentorship initiation and protégé perceptions of mentoring functions. *Journal of Vocational Behavior, 59,* 342–363.

Seibert, S. (1999). The effectiveness of facilitated mentoring: A longitudinal quasi-experiment. *Journal of Vocational Behavior, 54,* 482–502.

Siegel, P. H., & Reinstein, A. (2001). An exploratory study of mentor relationships in a large CPA firm. *Scandinavian Journal of Management, 17,* 421–436.

Singh, V., Bains, D., & Vinnicombe, S. (2002). Informal mentoring as an organizational resource. *Long Range Planning, 35,* 389–405.

Smith, W. J., Howard, J. T., & Harrington, K. V. (2005). Essential formal mentor characteristics and functions in governmental and non-governmental organizations from the program administrator's and the mentor's perspective. *Public Personnel Management, 34,* 31–58.

Sosik, J. J., Lee, D., & Bouquillon, E. A. (2005). Context and mentoring: Examining formal and informal relationships in high tech firms and K–12 schools. *Journal of Leadership and Organization Studies, 12*(2), 94–108.

Tepper, B. J. (1995). Upward maintenance tactics in supervisory mentoring and nonmentoring relationships. *Academy of Management Journal, 38,* 1191–1205.

Tyler, K. (1998). Mentoring programs link employees and experienced execs. *HRMagazine, 43*(5), 98–103.

Viator, R. E. (1999). An analysis of formal mentoring programs and perceived barriers to obtaining a mentor in a large public accounting firm. *Accounting Horizons, 13,* 37–53.

Viator, R. E. (2001). The association of formal and informal public accounting mentoring with role stress and related job outcomes. *Accounting, Organizations, and Society, 26,* 73–93.

Wanberg, C. R., Welsh, E. T., & Hezlett, S. A. (2003). Mentoring research: A review and dynamic process model. *Research in Personnel and Human Resources Management, 22,* 39–124.

Waters, L., McCabe, M., Kiellerup, D., & Kiellerup, S. (2002). The role of formal mentoring on business success and self-esteem in participants of a new business start-up program. *Journal of Business and Psychology, 17,* 107–121.

Wolosky, H. W. (2005). Mentoring: The formal approach pay-off. *Practical Accountant, 38*(1), 28–32.

Zey, M. G. (1985). Mentor programs: Making the right moves. *Personnel Journal, 64*(2), 53–57.

Zielinski, D. (2000). Mentoring up. *Training, 37*(10), 136–140.

11

Peer Mentoring Relationships

Stacy E. McManus

Joyce E. A. Russell

Traditional one-on-one mentoring from a more senior person can help increase a protégé's advancement, compensation, and job and career satisfaction (e.g., Allen, Eby, Poteet, Lentz, & Lima, 2004; Russell, 2004), yet flatter organizational structures with fewer hierarchical levels reduce the already relatively low number of potential traditional senior-level mentors available in organizations. As a consequence, individuals must make use of multiple sources of developmental support, especially to succeed in turbulent business environments where layoffs, career plateaus, and limited promotion opportunities can derail the careers of even the most promising employees (Arthur & Rousseau, 1996; Eby, 1997; Higgins & Kram, 2001; Sullivan, 1999). Peer mentors are one such important source of key developmental assistance (e.g., Kram, 1985; Kram & Isabella, 1985).

While much has been written about the traditional senior- and junior-level mentoring relationship, relatively little is known about the value of alternative sources of mentoring, such as peer mentors. This chapter examines peer mentoring in the context of developmental networks, reviews the literature on peer mentoring, develops a working definition of the construct, and differentiates peer mentoring from other types of mentoring and developmental relationships. We consider the challenges and opportunities specific to peer mentoring relationships and the unique benefits individuals can derive from peer mentoring. Finally, we raise theoretical issues associated with the study of peer mentoring and offer several propositions for future research.

AUTHORS' NOTE: The authors contributed equally to the preparation of this chapter.

Peer Mentoring in the Context of Developmental Networks

Sources of Work-Related Support

Traditionally, a mentor has been defined as someone senior in age and experience who provides guidance and assistance to help a protégé in his or her professional and personal development (e.g., Kram, 1985; Levinson, 1978; Ragins & Cotton, 1999). This traditional conceptualization has driven most of the research on organizational mentoring, though Kram (1985) suggested early on that individuals rely on multiple individuals for developmental support. She noted that in addition to mentors, other people who are part of an individual's relationship constellation, such as family members, supervisors, peers/coworkers, subordinates, and friends, can provide developmental assistance. This idea has been elaborated on recently in the literature (Allen & Finkelstein, 2003; Eby, 1997; Higgins & Kram, 2001). Eby (1997) suggested that a variety of hierarchical and lateral relationships, including coworkers, team members, and even professional organizations, could fulfill traditional mentoring functions to help people gain and improve skills related to both their jobs and their careers. These relationships are thought to be particularly helpful in difficult circumstances such as domestic and international relocations and layoff survival.

Allen and Finkelstein (2003) conducted qualitative research to find out what sources of support were used by 88 professional, nonfaculty university employees. They defined *support* as that which "has helped you learn, grow, and develop on the job" (Allen & Finkelstein, 2003, p. 349). Table 11.1 indicates the sources of support they found, in order of reported frequency, along with how Allen and Finkelstein's findings relate to those of Kram (1985) and Eby (1997).

Taken together, these studies have helped to highlight the possible sources of developmental support individuals might use in relation to their work lives. They

Table 11.1 Sources of Work-Related Support

Allen & Finkelstein (2003)	Kram (1985)	Eby (1997)
1. Coworkers	✓	✓
2. Education and training		✓
3. Membership in professional associations		✓
4. Family members	✓	
5. Outside friends	✓	
6. Self-instruction		
7. Supervisors	✓	✓
8. Subordinates and support staff	✓	
9. Religion		

also indicate that the most consistently identified sources of work-related support are coworkers and supervisors, which makes sense given that these are the people with whom individuals would share the most work-relevant information and interpersonal contact.

Structures of Developmental Networks

Higgins and Kram (2001) examined how people used these various sources of support. They applied a social network perspective to create a taxonomy of developmental relationship structures based on network diversity and relationship tie strength. They defined a *developmental network* as "the set of people a protégé names as taking an active interest in and action to advance the protégé's career by providing developmental assistance" (Higgins & Kram, 2001, p. 268), which includes both career and psychosocial support as traditionally defined in the mentoring literature. *Network diversity* is an indicator of the number of different support domains, such as those listed in Table 11.1, that individuals tap for job- and career-related support, while *relationship tie strength* is related to the extent to which affective bonding and interactions are central to the relationship. Higgins and Kram suggested four different developmental network profiles from the primary developmental beneficiary's perspective: *receptive,* characterized by low network diversity and weak ties; *opportunistic,* indicated by high network diversity and weak ties; *entrepreneurial,* consisting of high diversity and strong ties; and *traditional,* marked by low diversity and strong ties. The "traditional" quadrant of this 2×2 taxonomy represents established conceptualizations of mentoring relationships, in which a protégé has strong developmental relationships with only one or two mentors.

Both Eby (1997) and Higgins and Kram (2001) pointed out that alternatives to traditional mentoring relationships could be inter- or extraorganizational, occur between people at the same or different hierarchical levels, focus on both job/organization functions and career/personal functions, and involve multiple relationships occurring simultaneously. Those individuals with multiple sources of work-related developmental support have been found to experience greater organizational commitment, job and work satisfaction, career expectations, actual and perceived career success, promotions, perceptions of alternative employment, and continual access to and acquisition of career-related knowledge, along with reduced turnover intentions and work-role ambiguity (Baugh & Scandura, 1999; de Janasz, Sullivan, & Whiting, 2003; Higgins & Thomas, 2001; Peluchette & Jeanquart, 2000). These results have led researchers to recommend that individuals obtain developmental assistance from a diverse set of sources (de Janasz & Sullivan, 2004; Russell, 2004).

As Higgins and Kram (2001) noted,

Individuals beyond a primary senior person seldom have been considered as mentors in research on mentoring. . . . The provision of career and psychosocial support is still of primary interest, but *who* provides such support and how such support is provided are now more in question. (pp. 265, 267)

Peers are one such source of developmental assistance, though there is relatively little research on the topic of peer mentoring, particularly in business contexts. Having reviewed peer support in the context of individuals' work-relevant developmental relationship constellations, we next review research on organizational peer relationships to lay the foundation for further developing the construct of peer mentoring.

The Nature of Organizational Peer Relationships

Peer relationships in organizations were not extensively studied until Kram and Isabella's (1985) groundbreaking work,[1] which identified the functions that peers provide each other and created a taxonomy of different types of peer relationships. Working with the human resources staff at a large manufacturing firm in the northeastern United States, the authors identified possible participants such that the group would meet the following sampling criteria: early, middle, and late career stages were represented proportionately; the sample was gender balanced; participants had been with the firm for at least 3 years, which was deemed enough time to form significant peer relationships; and individuals on the list of possible participants included only those who sincerely wanted to share their experiences with the researchers.

Using those criteria, 15 people were selected and agreed to participate in the research. Those individuals chose 1 or 2 other people in the firm with whom they had established supportive relationships, a process that resulted in 25 pairs of people (11 participants selected 2 supportive others, 3 selected 1, and 1 selected none). The researchers interviewed the 15 focal participants about those supportive relationships, concentrating on the relationship history, thoughts and feelings over time about the relationship(s), and how the relationship(s) affected the focal person's career trajectory. Each significant other was interviewed as well. Kram and Isabella used the biographical interviewing technique employed by Levinson (1978) and Glaser and Strauss's (1967) grounded theory approach to understand the data. They looked for similarities across cases, identified categories that reflected those similarities, and then ensured that data within categories were highly similar while data across categories were as different as possible.

Their findings shed a great deal of light on how peer relationships at work could, and could not, fulfill functions provided by traditional mentors. The functions provided by traditional mentors, as listed in Table 11.2, were identified by Kram (1985), in her seminal research on mentoring relationships at work. As Kram and Isabella (1985), concluded, comparing traditional mentoring functions with those that peers enacted indicated that traditional mentors provide more career functions than do peers, while the two types of relationships provide the same number of psychosocial support functions. This observation has been supported by subsequent quantitative research (e.g., Ensher, Thomas, & Murphy, 2001). Peers, then, can compensate for an absence of traditional mentors with respect to psychosocial functions, but not career functions. Those who have the benefit of challenging work assignments, sponsorship, protection, and exposure and visibility are likely to reap more job and career benefits than are individuals who do not have that type of career-related support. Note also the similarities between developmental functions provided by peer relationships in Kram and Isabella's (1985) study and those provided by coworkers in Allen and Finkelstein's (2003) research: skill development, coaching, support, feedback, providing a new perspective, affirmation, and networking. This convergence makes sense given that coworkers are often at the same organizational level and likely consider each other peers.

In addition to identifying the kinds of support people received from peers, Kram and Isabella (1985) also identified three types of peer relationships that vary along a continuum based on trust, commitment level, relationship intensity, issues addressed, and needs satisfied. Each of these peer relationships served various primary functions. For example, the *information peer's* primary function is information sharing. The relationship is social but is limited in sharing personal experiences and providing information regarding career opportunities. The main functions of the *collegial peer* are career strategizing, job-related feedback, and friendship. Information is shared, and there are increasing levels of self-disclosure and trust. The main functions of the *special peer* are confirmation, emotional support, personal feedback, and friendship. The relationship is characterized as having a "best friend," with a strong sense of bonding and a wide range of support for family and work issues. Kram and Isabella further described the dominant themes of peer relationships at successive career stages (establishment, advancement, middle career, late career) and noted that peers seem to be important across career stages, while traditional mentors are particularly important during early career. Close peer relationships are especially meaningful to people in later career stages, because they provide a sense of continuity and connection while creating a protected forum for

Table 11.2   Developmental Functions in Mentoring and Peer Relationships

Mentoring Relationships	*Peer Relationships*
Career-Related Functions • Sponsorship • Coaching • Exposure and visibility • Protection • Challenging work assignments	Career-Related Functions • Information sharing • Career strategizing • Job-related feedback
Psychosocial Functions • Acceptance and confirmation • Counseling • Role-modeling • Friendship	Psychosocial Functions • Confirmation • Emotional support • Personal feedback • Friendship
Special Attribute • Complementarity	Special Attribute • Mutuality

SOURCE: Kram and Isabella (1985).

discussing significant work and life transitions as people move toward "second careers" or retirement.

Research on Peer Mentoring

So far, we have set peer relationships in the context of developmental relationship constellations and reviewed Kram and Isabella's (1985) research on organizational peer relationships that revealed how peers can meet each other's developmental needs. It is important to note that their work focused on understanding peer relationships at work, discovering along the way that peers can serve some of the same functions traditional mentors do. We now turn to research specifically designed to study peer mentoring relationships.

McDougall and Beattie (1997) solicited participation for their research on peer mentoring relationships from individuals enrolled either part-time or full-time in postgraduate management education programs. Each person who agreed to participate in the project provided access to an individual which whom the participant felt he or she had a peer mentoring relationship, resulting in a total of 28 informal peer mentor pairs. Most pairs (79%) were made up of women, while the rest were mixed-gender pairs. McDougall and Beattie conducted qualitative work with these pairs, using a combination of semistructured interviews and critical incidents to collect data about the nature of the relationships. The data were then subjected to content analysis to develop a typology of peer mentoring. They defined *peer mentoring* as "a process where there is mutual involvement in encouraging and enhancing learning and development between two peers, where peers are people of similar hierarchical status or who perceive themselves as equals" (McDougall & Beattie, 1997, p. 425). This definition was used when asking respondents to describe their peer mentoring relationships. McDougall and Beattie's work resulted in a typology of peer *mentorships* that is quite similar to the typology of peer *relationships* developed by Kram and Isabella (1985). The two sets of findings are juxtaposed in Table 11.3.

From Table 11.3, we can see a fairly robust convergence of findings. As we move along the continuum from basic information sharing to more-nuanced interactions, relationships become both deeper and broader. Information is disclosed more extensively within the work domain as relationships progress toward extensive sharing within the personal life domain as well. As is clear from the category names chosen by McDougall and Beattie, the sharing of basic work-related information and limited personal information is typical of a regular coworker relationship that does not qualify as a peer mentorship. As relationships progress, we are likely to see an increased prevalence of "mentoring episodes" (Fletcher & Ragins, Chapter 15, this volume), which are short-term developmental interactions. Over time, as more and more mentoring episodes come to characterize the relationship, the nature of the relationship transforms into a mentorship. Exactly where the inflection point occurs may be difficult to define—doing so would likely require very frequent and long-term data collection coupled with analyses that could take into account nonlinear shifts in the state of the relationship (e.g., catastrophe

Table 11.3   Types of Peer Mentoring Relationships

Kram & Isabella (1985)		McDougall & Beattie (1997)	
Type of Peer	Relationship Characteristics and Primary Functions	Type of Peer	Behaviors, Values, and Focus
Information peer	• Demands little, but offers many benefits • Social relationship, but limited in sharing of personal experiences • Increases individual's eyes and ears to organization (work only) • Source of information regarding career opportunities • Primary function is information sharing	Coworker	• Cognitive behaviors (e.g., explaining, advising, sharing information, developing ideas, and bouncing them off each other) • Communicative behaviors (e.g., collaborating, listening, questioning, discussion) • Share basic day-to-day work information and some limited personal information • Value experience and accessibility in the peer • Focus on basics of work rather than development
Collegial peer	• Information sharing joined by increasing levels of self-disclosure and trust • Allows for greater self-expression • Limited support for exploration of family and work issues • Provides direct and honest feedback • Primary functions are career strategizing, job-related feedback, and friendship	Utilitarian peer mentor	• Cognitive and communicative behaviors • Learning behaviors (e.g., facilitating, reflecting, taking on different perspectives, role-modeling, coaching) • Affective behaviors (e.g., helping, supporting, encouraging, reaffirming, understanding, calming) • Value trust, friendship, support, sense of humor, and knowing where you stand with your peer

(Continued)

Table 11.3 (Continued)

Kram & Isabella (1985)		McDougall & Beattie (1997)	
Type of Peer	Relationship Characteristics and Primary Functions	Type of Peer	Behaviors, Values, and Focus
			• Generally a moderate focus on both work and personal development
Special peer	• Equivalent of best friend • Strong sense of bonding • Wide range of support for family and work issues • Offers chance to express one's personal and professional dilemmas, vulnerabilities, and individuality • Primary functions include confirmation, emotional support, personal feedback, and friendship	Holistic peer mentor	• Cognitive, communicative, learning, and affective behaviors • Challenging behaviors (e.g., constructive criticism, productive disagreement) • Value trust, friendship, support, sense of humor, constructive challenges, nonjudgmental stance, ability to express personal and professional vulnerabilities and have those concerns heard in a supportive, helpful way • Strong focus on both work and personal development

SOURCE: Kram and Isabella (1985, Table 3, p. 120); McDougall and Beattie (1997, pp. 428–431).

modeling). Once the peer relationship becomes a peer mentorship, it is character-ized by increasing amounts of intimacy, vulnerability, and authenticity that span both work and personal domains. This differs from close friendships because there is a conscious focus on work and career development, though that is not the exclu-sive focus of the relationship. Interestingly, the same process that occurs for peer mentoring relationships (i.e., increasing mentoring episodes until it is a mentoring relationship) is likely to be true of traditional mentoring relationships as well. So, what differentiates peer mentorships from traditional mentorships other than the source of support? In the next section, we consider some key concepts that help us to see the differences.

Complementarity, Mutuality, and Reciprocity in Peer Mentorships

Traditionally, mentoring relationships have been studied as largely providing one-way benefits from the mentor to the protégé. While the mentor does benefit from the relationship, often those benefits result directly from the mentor's own actions rather than from something the protégé provides independently. For instance, by virtue of helping a protégé, mentors can satisfy their need for generativity (to pass on what they have learned to others) and be recognized by the organization as a developer of talent (e.g., Allen, Poteet, Russell, & Dobbins, 1997; Kram, 1985). This works well for the protégé, whose need for guidance is complementary to the mentor's generativity need. In this type of situation, satisfying one's own need necessarily requires addressing the need of another. This type of interaction is complementary so long as the other accepts the effort directed toward him or her. In this type of example, the individuals' needs arise from their stage of psychological development, and the needs themselves are psychological in nature. Kram viewed such complementary relationship needs as a special attribute of traditional mentorships.

Individuals may also have complementary knowledge, skills, and abilities that emerge in a relationship as offsetting strengths and weaknesses. For instance, respondents in the McDougall and Beattie (1997) study indicated this type of *complementarity* was an important characteristic of holistic peer mentoring. By this they meant that while the peers shared core values in common, each individual had different styles and skills the other lacked or could improve (i.e., they were each able to address each other's developmental needs). In both perspectives of complementarity, putting the two people together in some way creates a whole. The difference between the two points of view is that in the first case, the mentor needs to express X and in so doing would satisfy a need Y of the protégé. In the second case, both people would like to be strong at A and B, but one of them is better at A while the other is better at B, and they realize they can use their own strengths to help develop each other's relative weakness. There is no necessary satisfaction of one's own needs in the satisfaction of the other's needs.

Kram (1985) also expressed another point of view about complementarity in peer relationships, suggesting it takes the form of empathy and the mirroring of one's own experiences in the other. This was also observed in the McDougall and Beattie (1997) study and is congruent with the idea that people in peer mentorships are engaged in a process of development that is directionally parallel. That is, the two people are at similar developmental stages yet can benefit each other emotionally and tactically. Mirroring and empathy come about as a result of the real developmental similarities the peers experience, potentially allowing them to better understand each other. Thus, we propose several propositions for future research:

Proposition 1: Complementarity as (a) an expression of empathy and mirroring and (b) having offsetting strengths and weaknesses will be a relational characteristic of peer mentorships.

Proposition 2: Complementarity as an expression of empathy and mirroring will persist over the course of a peer mentorship.

A related set of concepts that have been discussed in terms of mentoring relationships are mutuality and reciprocity. *Mutuality* can have two different meanings: one encompasses reciprocity, as in mutual assistance, and the other means to share things in common, as in mutual interests or a mutual understanding. Kram and Isabella (1985) used the former meaning when identifying mutuality as a special attribute of peer relationships. They specifically conceptualized mutuality as both members of the dyad being able to fluidly trade off taking the roles of learner and expert, making it possible for both people to give and receive mentoring functions during mentoring episodes. This type of fluid expertise is a key skill required for all mutually high-quality interactions, according to the Stone Center Relational Theory (SRT) that Fletcher and Ragins (Chapter 15, this volume) applied to understanding mentoring relationships. According to SRT, all high-quality relationships are mutual and reciprocal, fostering interdependence, connection, and relational skill development. Both peer and traditional mentoring relationships can be relational in this way, though the content of the growth, learning, and development likely differs. Traditional mentors grow by learning how to develop others effectively, for instance, having gained experience that they can use to help another who has not yet had those experiences. There is an inherent asymmetry to the developmental needs of the two people. On the other hand, in peer mentoring situations, their developmental needs are more in parallel with each other, and they are able to mutually support each other psychologically, emotionally, and in their careers, to achieve their objectives. As Fletcher and Ragins (Chapter 15, this volume) point out, the less the hierarchical difference between mentoring partners—as is the case with peer mentoring—the more likely the relationship is to become a high-quality one.

This point of view is consonant with the results of McDougall and Beattie's (1997) research, in which "mutual involvement" was a key part of the peer mentoring definition. Their results indicated that relative to traditional hierarchical mentoring relationships, peer mentorships are experienced as being more reciprocal and equitable, with both members contributing to the other's development. Because they are able to both help each other grow and develop in meaningful ways, those in peer mentoring relationships feel less like a burden and more like they have a right to receive the benefits offered by their partners. Taken together, this leads us to propose the following:

Proposition 3: Mutuality will be more commonly found in peer mentorships than in traditional mentorships.

In addition to complementarity and mutuality, *reciprocity* is a third important relational characteristic. We were able to find only one study that empirically examined perceptions of reciprocity in different types of mentoring relationships. In a study of informal mentoring relationships, Ensher et al. (2001) surveyed 142 participants about their mentoring relationships. The respondents were evenly split between men and women who were generally well-educated individuals and had not yet broken into the managerial ranks of their organizations. Ensher et al. (2001) asked each respondent to think of his or her most influential mentor and then categorize that person as one of three types: a peer mentor, or "someone at the same level (i.e., a coworker) who provides support"; a step-ahead mentor, or "someone who is a little more experienced and only one or two levels above in their career"; and a traditional mentor, or "someone who is much more experienced and further ahead in their career than the protégé" (pp. 426–427). Respondents were asked to think of this one most influential mentor while responding to the rest of the questionnaire.

Ensher et al. (2001) operationalized reciprocity as respondents' perception of "an equal give-and-take" in the relationship, with both members putting in equal amounts of effort and time in the relationship, and respondents' belief that the relationship should have an equal exchange of benefits. Controlling for relationship duration and mentor and protégé race and gender, Ensher et al. found that protégés' perceptions of relationship reciprocity predicted satisfaction with their mentors and that all three types of mentors were perceived as having provided similar amounts of reciprocity in the mentoring relationships. These results are interesting because they suggest that reciprocity itself may not be more common in peer mentorships. It is likely, as Ensher et al. mentioned, that the *nature* of what is reciprocated may differ across types of mentorships. Social exchange theory (Blau, 1964; Homans, 1958) posits that people weigh costs against benefits when deciding whether to engage in a relationship. This implicit mental calculus answers the question of whether the other person brings enough to the table to offset any costs (e.g., opportunity costs, drawbacks of the other person) of the relationship. As part of this assessment, individuals evaluate the extent to which another is likely to be willing and able to reciprocate positive behaviors. As the probability of reciprocity increases, the greater is the likelihood that the two individuals will decide to engage in a relationship.

Reciprocity can involve two individuals giving and receiving identical benefits to each other. For instance, if one person treats the other for dinner one night, the other person will treat the next time the two go out to eat together. Reciprocity has also been conceptualized as appropriate responses to another's overtures. This view, based on Homans's (1958) work, was used by Young and Perrewe (2000, 2004) in their studies of exchanges in traditional mentorships. They considered as reciprocal those exchanges in which a mentor provides supportive behaviors, such as inviting a protégé to a networking event, and the protégé provides a reciprocal behavior, such as "putting forth effort in attending functions as requested" (Young & Perrewe, 2004, p. 111). As this conceptualization shows, the social exchange is made up of completing a cycle by responding in kind to an overture.

Adopting another point of view would allow us to consider different currencies of exchange that go beyond the identical or the directly responsive. In elaborating on the nature of reciprocity, Gouldner (1960) suggested that reciprocal exchanges are mutually dependent and perceived as equal or near equal in value. Several factors determine value: the status of the individuals, the cost to the giver, the level of need of the receiver, and the giver's freedom of choice in deciding to reciprocate. For instance, those who have less (e.g., fewer options or less of any one option) can give less on an absolute basis, yet it can still be perceived as equivalent to someone of a higher status giving more because the relative cost to each party is roughly the same. Similarly, value increases when parties can freely choose not to reciprocate and when the need of the receiver is high. Thus, we can see that reciprocity occurs when people give and receive benefits of essentially equal value, opening up the possibility for exploring different currencies of exchange used by different people. Take, for instance, the case of traditional mentoring relationships. The types of functions a mentor can provide, for example, exposure and visibility, or protection, are often unlikely to be the kinds of functions that a protégé can provide in exchange beyond active acceptance. However, the protégé may be able to provide a different currency in exchange for protection, for example, loyalty. If we were to assign loyalty a lower absolute value than protection, it would still be possible for the exchange to be perceived as equivalent if the loyalty was given freely, if the protégé's motivation was expressive (e.g., loyalty out of gratitude) rather than instrumental (e.g., providing loyalty in order to obtain further protection), and if the mentor needed more loyal people to count on at work. Thus, we can see how the currencies of exchange each participant has to offer can differ substantially, while still creating a reciprocal exchange.

On the other hand, currencies of exchange between peers are much more likely to be similar and to go beyond active receipt of another's supportive behaviors. If the two individuals are at a high enough organizational level, they may be able to exchange career functions like exposure and visibility with each other. If they are at lower levels, they may be more limited to psychosocial exchanges (e.g., friendship) or less risky career-related exchanges (e.g., advice about career strategies). Thus, reciprocity may look different in traditional versus peer mentorships, leading us to propose the following:

> *Proposition 4:* As individuals move up the organizational hierarchy, they will have more currencies of social exchange available to use.

> *Proposition 5:* In traditional mentorships, mentors will have (a) more available currencies of social exchange (e.g., career functions) than protégés and (b) will be able to offer more risky currencies of exchange (e.g., protection).

> *Proposition 6:* In traditional mentorships, mentors and protégés will be able to reciprocally exchange psychosocial functions to a greater extent than career functions.

> *Proposition 7:* In peer mentorships, individuals will have similar currencies of social exchange in both the (a) psychosocial and (b) career domains that are equally likely to be reciprocally exchanged.

Learning in Peer Mentorships

As part of the exchange that occurs between traditional mentors and protégés or between peer mentors, individuals in the relationship are expected to be learning, growing, and developing both personally and professionally. Learning is facilitated when people have a sense of *psychological safety,* the perception that interpersonal risks in the workplace can be taken without fear that proximal others will reject or try to embarrass the risk taker (Edmondson, 1999). Initially studied as a local phenomenon occurring in work teams, psychological safety also occurs in dyads (e.g., Edmondson & Woolley, 2003) and fosters learning by providing an interpersonal context of trust and mutual respect that is conducive to experimentation and questioning. When dyads are characterized by higher psychological safety, the individuals are better able to have productive conversations around performance and work itself, as well as around career and personal aspirations. However, when there is a greater power differential between two people, the likelihood of perceived safety to take learning-related risks could be lower for both people than when the individuals are roughly equal in power (Edmondson, 1996). Because there is by definition a smaller power and status gap between peers than between traditional mentors and protégés, we can expect peers to be more willing to reveal areas of difficulty and challenge to each other with fewer fears of reprisal or negative consequences.

This dovetails with the relational skills both people need to create high-quality interactions as outlined in Stone Center Relational Cultural Theory (RCT) (i.e., authenticity, being competent emotionally and empathically, and being willing to be vulnerable in a relationship, as described by Fletcher & Ragins, Chapter 15, this volume). As with psychological safety, we see an emphasis on being able to be one's true self, with the expectation that the other individual would be able to understand one's situation and respond respectfully, truthfully, and with compassion. SRT further posits that *fluid expertise*—the ability to easily and authentically switch between learner and expert roles as appropriate—is another key relational skill for high-quality interactions. As discussed earlier, this maps well to Kram's (1985) characterization of effective developmental peer relationships. The ability to trade off these roles should also enhance individuals' sense of safety with each other, since each person regularly experiences being in the more vulnerable position over time. The ability (a) to reveal one's shortcomings and developmental needs and (b) to have those needs recognized and addressed in a nonjudgmental and supportive fashion are critical for the kind of growth and learning individuals can expect to gain from mentoring relationships.

Learning behaviors such as reflection and taking on different perspectives offered by the peer mentor were important in differentiating between coworkers and peer mentors in McDougall and Beattie's (1997) work. Further, they found that the deepest and broadest peer mentoring relationship (the holistic peer mentorship) was uniquely characterized by the partners' willingness to be vulnerable to each other around both personal and professional issues, trusting that their concerns would be heard in a supportive, nonjudgmental, reassuring way. These results suggest that the holistic peer mentorships studied by McDougall and Beattie might have been characterized by higher-quality relationships and greater psychological safety than utilitarian mentorships or coworker relationships. In sum, we propose the following:

Proposition 8: Mentorships characterized as psychologically safe will result in more learning for both members of the dyad.

Proposition 9: Mentorships characterized by high-quality interactions (i.e., where both people demonstrate authenticity, emotional and empathic competence, and vulnerability) will be experienced by the individuals as more psychologically safe than relationships characterized by lower-quality interactions.

Proposition 10: Peer mentorships will be characterized as more psychologically safe than traditional mentorships.

Proposition 11: Consequently, peer mentorships may be characterized by broader and deeper learning than that experienced in traditional mentorships.

Additional Research on Developmental Peer Relationships

Up to this point, we have reviewed the scant literature on peer relationships and relational peer mentoring that involves complementarity, mutuality, and reciprocity. We have used other theoretical perspectives to inform propositions about the nature of these peer mentorships. Other research has been conducted on developmental peer relationships that are unidirectional in nature. By this we mean that the peer mentorships studied involved individuals at the same hierarchical level in organizations with different degrees of job or organizational tenure, where the more senior member had responsibility for providing assistance to the more-junior member. To distinguish these from peer mentors who are engaged in a mutually developmental relationship (i.e., relational peer mentoring), we identified two different types of unidirectional peer mentorships that have been studied in the literature: informal *unidirectional peer mentorships* and *formal socializing peer mentoringships.*

Informal Unidirectional Peer Mentorships

Work in this area defines *peers* as those who occupy the same space in the organizational hierarchy but have different degrees of job tenure. Fine and Pullins (1998) provided a typical example of how peer mentoring is defined in this type of situation: Peer mentoring occurs when "a more experienced salesperson (the mentor) takes responsibility for the development and guidance of a less experienced salesperson (the protégé)" (p. 89). Using this definition, they studied the peer mentoring experiences as reported by salespeople working for an office products manufacturer that did not have a formal mentoring program. Focusing on the perceived benefits of this mentoring, Fine and Pullins (1998) found that men perceived more benefits to this type of relationship than did women. In same-sex relationships, women reported receiving more counseling and coaching than men reported. Relative to women in cross-sex relationships, female protégés in same-sex relationships reported more job motivation, and female mentors reported more job involvement.

In another study of informal unidirectional peer mentoring, Pullins and Fine (2002) examined how being a mentor was beneficial to an individual's own job outcomes. From a national sample of real estate agents, 138 individuals stated that they were mentors, based on the following definition: "a more experienced agent who *provides* help and support to a less experienced agent (peer or colleague)" (Pullins & Fine, 2002, p. 270). The unidirectionality of the support was made even more clear by the addition of a definition of a protégé as "a less experienced agent who *receives* help and support from a more experienced agent (peer or colleague)" (p. 270). These mentors experienced a sense of career rejuvenation when they provided exposure for their protégés. Mentors also experienced enhanced performance and greater satisfaction with their own advancement opportunities when they provided skill development assistance to their protégés.

Taken together, we can see that peer protégés experience benefits such as counseling, coaching, and job motivation and that there are some gender differences in the benefits perceived. Further, peer mentors benefit from the relationships by gaining enhanced job involvement and a generally more positive outlook on their own careers. Finally, we see that people may be more likely to become informal unidirectional peer mentors to others when they have more experience in the organization and are satisfied with their jobs.

It should be noted that while we call these "informal unidirectional peer mentorships," it is clear that the mentors do receive benefits from engaging in the relationship. The key differentiating factor is that the intention of the relationship is for the more junior member to benefit from the more senior member's experience and expertise, similar to what we see in traditional mentoring. The benefits such unidirectional peer mentors are able to offer may, however, be more limited than traditional mentorships because, as peers, these mentors may not be able to influence key career functions such as challenging assignments or protection. However, unidirectional peer mentors may be in an advantageous position to provide more helpful job-related functions, such as tips about how to increase hit rates with sales calls, how to manage challenging clients, and other situations that they themselves are in over the course of executing their jobs. This leads us to propose the following:

Proposition 12: Informal unidirectional peer mentors will provide more job-related than career-related functions to their protégés.

While the above review involves peer mentoring of junior organizational members, another body of research examines the role of formal peer mentoring programs in contributing to newcomer socialization. Interestingly, most of this work has been conducted in academic settings in which advanced students help new students adjust to their new schools or academic programs. The research in this area is reviewed below.

Formal Socializing Peer Mentorships

Allen, Russell, and Maetzke (1997) studied the experiences of 68 first-year MBA students who were part of a formal peer mentoring program. First-year students worked in teams of five or six members. Two or three second-year MBA volunteers were randomly assigned as mentors to the first-year student teams. Allen et al. found that protégés were more satisfied with their second-year mentors when they spent more time together and received both career-oriented and psychosocial support. In turn, greater satisfaction with the mentors was positively related to individuals' willingness to serve as a mentor to others in the future. Also, women were somewhat more willing than men to report being willing to mentor others in the future.

In another study of 64 different MBA students involved in a similar formal peer mentoring program, Allen, McManus, and Russell (1999) found that assigned mentors were important in facilitating organizational socialization. Specifically, both psychosocial and career mentoring were positively related to general socialization. Psychosocial mentoring was positively related to politics and performance proficiency aspects of socialization. Career mentoring was positively related to people socialization (e.g., that others in the program liked them). Both types of mentoring were related to reported help received in dealing with stress, but neither was associated with actual stress experienced. Protégés also reported receiving more psychosocial than career support from their peer mentors, a finding that is consistent with Kram and Isabella's (1985) qualitative work. These two studies are interesting because they do not involve one-to-one peer mentoring assignments in a formal program. This suggests that it may be useful to provide options within boundaries to people in terms of who they connect with in a peer mentoring relationship.

Grant-Vallone and Ensher (2000) studied 29 peer mentors and protégés participating in a formal peer mentoring program for graduate students in psychology, with similar results. The more time they spent with each other, the more both peer mentors and protégés reported psychosocial and career functions being provided to the newcomer, with psychosocial functions being provided more than career functions. More mentoring support was positively related to peer mentor relationship satisfaction and satisfaction with the graduate program but was not related to experienced stress levels. This study is particularly valuable because it includes the perspectives of both peer mentors and peer protégés, demonstrating strong convergence between the two points of view about what the newcomers receive from their program experiences.

To better understand why individuals choose to serve as peer mentors in similar types of programs, Thomas, Hu, Gewin, Bingham, and Yanchus (2005) conducted a laboratory investigation of how race, gender, and proactive socialization behaviors on the part of a paper (fictitious) "new student" affected current students' (freshmen through seniors) willingness to serve as formal peer mentors to the stimulus person (i.e., the mentor pairs would be assigned by academic department heads). The goal of the fictitious program was to help new students "become socialized and integrated into the department" that was to become their academic home once they declared a major (Thomas et al., 2005, p. 545). They found that female participants were more likely than males to report being willing to serve as peer mentors to incoming students. Participants were more willing to mentor paper students who were described as being more proactive. Interestingly, when the paper student's proactivity was described as low, participants were more willing to mentor the student if he or she was a White male (compared with a Black male or White female) or a Black female (compared with a White female). Thus, belonging to the dominant demographic class (White male) seems to be advantageous in securing a peer mentor, at least when proactivity is low.

All of these are studies of formal programs in which the goal has been to engage peers to help socialize organizational newcomers to an educational institution and/or program. These studies together suggest that such formal peer mentorships can help newcomers become better socialized to their new organizations and give newcomers relatively more psychosocial than career support, especially when the peers spend more time together. Such programs may help newcomers feel as if they are getting more help dealing with the stress of entering a new organization, but they may not actually reduce the stress the newcomers experience. The more time the peers spend together, the more benefits the newcomer appears to receive, including feelings of satisfaction with the formal peer program and the academic program they have entered. It appears that women are more likely than men to be willing to serve as formal peer mentors and that attractive newcomers are those who are proactive, with White men possibly having an advantage in attracting this source of support.

Another use of formal developmental peer support that goes beyond newcomer socialization efforts is the use of *peer learning coaches* in leadership development programs (e.g., Center for Creative Leadership; McCauley & Guthrie, 2005). Even in short-term leader development programs, formal relationships can be established, and mentoring functions such as coaching, acceptance and confirmation, and role-modeling can be built in to augment traditional mentoring relationships. Peer learning partners are dyads or small groups of participants who help each other with their ongoing learning during the course of a program (e.g., observing and giving feedback; McCauley & Guthrie, 2005). Organizations have also used peer coaching as a management development initiative along with one-on-one mentoring, team coaching, executive coaching, action learning, and structured networks (Douglas & McCauley, 1999). Other configurations might involve group mentoring, such as a group of peers who mentor each other or facilitated peer development circles that use the expertise of more-senior mentors for the benefit of a group of protégés who may or may not also serve as peer mentors to each other. We mention these additional alternatives to help clarify the range of different types of developmental support that involve peers.

At this point, we have now reviewed the literature and developed some research propositions for three types of peer mentorships: (a) relational peer mentorships, in which individuals fluidly swap the learner and expert roles to provide complementary, mutual, and reciprocal developmental support to each other; (b) informal unidirectional peer mentorships, in which a more senior peer provides support to a more junior peer in a reciprocal relationship; and (c) formal socializing peer mentorships, in which more-experienced peers help organizational newcomers adjust to their new surroundings. While there is little evidence regarding reciprocation in this third type of relationship, it is likely that organizational newcomers provide something to their formal peer mentors, even if it is nothing more than gratitude and potential friendship. Given this categorization of peer mentoring relationships, we turn now to briefly consider some additional issues for future study, including an understanding of the conditions that foster peer mentoring.

Conditions Fostering Peer Mentoring

Various types of conditions seem to foster peer mentoring in organizations. These include significant events in individuals' careers, such as entry into an organization and job relocation, as well as the nature of the corporate culture. In addition, several individual factors may be related to the degree to which employees look for peer relationships. These include perceived similarity between mentor and protégé, demographic background (race, gender), and attitudes toward authority and competitiveness.

At least in academic settings, it has been recognized that formal peer mentoring programs can serve a vital role in helping socialize new students in their academic programs and institutions. McDougall and Beattie (1997) pointed out that organizational entry was a time when informal peer mentors also could be very helpful. Just as organizational entry is a significant event that can be eased with developmental assistance, other significant events may lead individuals to reach out to their peers for help. For instance, Eby (1997) postulated that significant work changes such as relocation, in both expatriation and repatriation experiences, can motivate individuals to seek guidance and assistance from their peers. In these cases, peers can provide a better picture of "how things really work around here" and may be more willing to provide candid information to their colleagues than superiors might be willing to provide. Thus, we propose the following:

> *Proposition 12:* Disruptive organizational events will serve as triggers for peers to turn to each other for developmental support.

In addition to identifiable organizational events, the general organizational culture may also be more or less conducive to the development of peer mentorships. For instance, a paternalistic culture may be a friendly environment for traditional mentorships to spontaneously grow and flourish, while an entrepreneurial culture that values individuals making their own way with little guidance from superiors might be more conducive to the development of peer mentorships. Firms with collaborative corporate cultures that encourage cross-functional teams, for example, foster the conditions necessary for extended peer interactions on multiple projects that set the stage for the emergence of informal peer mentoring relationships. We propose the following:

> *Proposition 13:* Organizational cultures that are collaborative and entrepreneurial will be more conducive than paternalistic organizational cultures to the organic growth of peer mentorships.

In addition to external circumstances that may motivate peers to turn to each other for developmental support, individual difference variables may also play a role in the development of peer mentorships. For instance, mentoring scholars have begun investigating perceived similarity as a contributing factor to mentorship quality. Byrne's (1971) similarity-attraction paradigm posited that when two individuals see more similarities between themselves, the attraction between the two people is strengthened, which increases the likelihood of them forging a relationship. This is particularly true when individuals believe they are similar to each other in terms of their values, attitudes, and beliefs. As noted by Ragins (1997a, 1997b), such perceived similarity is likely to enhance interpersonal comfort and shared social identification, which should increase the likelihood of relationship formation and result in better relationship quality. Research on traditional mentoring relationships has demonstrated that mentors give more support to protégés whom they perceive as similar to themselves in terms of intelligence, approach to procedures, personality, background, ambition, education, and activities outside of work (Burke, McKeen, & McKenna; 1993), while protégés who perceive themselves as being more similar to their mentors also report more liking, satisfaction, and contact with their mentors (Ensher & Murphy, 1997). Further, protégés' perceived attitudinal similarity, but not demographic similarity, is positively related to their reports of vocational support, psychosocial support, role-modeling, and satisfaction with their mentors (Ensher, Grant-Vallone, & Marelich, 2002; Turban, Dougherty, & Lee, 2002).

Allen and Eby (2003) found that mentors who perceive their protégés as similar to themselves also report greater mentorship quality and more learning from the mentorship. These relationships are moderated by mentorship duration such that stronger associations between perceived similarity and both quality and learning are found in mentorships of shorter duration, which is congruent with Turban at al.'s (2002) findings. Further, Allen and Eby (2003) also investigated gender similarity, finding no association between it and mentors' assessments of either relationship quality or learning. Studies that evaluated both demographic and perceived similarity found that perceived similarity is more important than demographic similarity in predicting assessments of relationship quality (Allen & Eby, 2003; Ensher et al., 2002; Turban et al., 2002).

When considering peer mentorships, it is possible that perceived similarity is a stronger predictor of relationship engagement than for traditional mentorships. Since traditional mentors are likely to be more able than peers to provide certain career functions (e.g., challenging assignments, protection) that can lead to valuable outcomes for protégés (e.g., promotions, greater compensation), individuals may seek out traditional mentors in part to gain those resulting tangible benefits. Interpersonal comfort may take a backseat to the benefits the mentor can offer. With peers, on the other hand, interpersonal comfort may be the primary concern when people consider engaging in a mutually developmental relationship. People generally are more comfortable with those who are similar to themselves because the situation helps meet their needs for inclusion and equality (see Duck, 1988, for a brief review). It may be worthwhile to trade off having these needs met for tangible benefits such as those obtained from a traditional mentor, but may not be worth foregoing if the primary set of benefits are more psychosocial in nature, as with peer mentorships. We propose the following:

Proposition 14: Perceived similarity will predict peer mentorship formation to a greater extent than it will predict traditional mentorship formation.

Proposition 15: As with traditional mentorships, peer mentorships characterized by greater perceived similarity will be evaluated as higher-quality relationships by the participants than those in which perceived similarity is lower.

There are more White males at the higher levels of organizations than there are women or people of color. This means that those people who have faced challenges related to gender, race, or ethnicity and are looking for developmental relationships simply have fewer options to choose from when searching for a traditional mentor. When this lack of options is coupled with the fact that individuals generally tend to form relationships with others who are experienced as being familiar and similar (e.g., Duck, 1988), it suggests that peer mentorships may be a particularly viable and attractive option for women and people of color. For example, Thomas (1990, 2001) cited evidence that professionals of color may be more likely than White professionals to seek peer mentors for psychosocial support, noting that a lack of interpersonal comfort in both cross-race and cross-gender relationships generally limits the depth of those relationships. This could lead women to experience the same sort of need for psychosocial support from other women, and, in fact, many large organizations today have professional women's networks that may foster peer mentorship development. In sum,

> *Proposition 16:* Women and people of color will be more likely than White men to develop peer mentorships to fulfill psychosocial functions.

Kram (1985) discussed several attitudes that could influence the quality of traditional mentorships, and some of those may also influence whether an individual would prefer to have a traditional mentor or a peer mentor. For instance, those whose attitudes toward authority are antagonistic may prefer to seek assistance from peers since they can mutually trade off the roles of expert and learner, thereby reducing the authority attributed to the developmental partner. On the other hand, those who seek approval from authority figures may be more likely to seek out traditional mentors. Attitudes toward competition could also affect individuals' preferences for peers over traditional mentors. For instance, highly competitive individuals may prefer to seek developmental assistance from traditional mentoring sources because there is a substantially lower probability that the two people would both be under consideration for the same advancement opportunities. It may also be true that those who are highly competitive would actively avoid revealing weaknesses to their peers to reduce the risk that the peers might exploit their competitive advantage. In sum,

> *Proposition 17:* Those with antagonistic attitudes toward authority and those who are less competitive may prefer peer mentorships over traditional mentorships as sources of developmental support.

Defining *Peers*

Future research on any type of peer mentoring should be careful to specify what is meant by *peers*. Most research of the past has used hierarchical level as the major defining characteristic of who a peer is. In more hierarchical organizations of the past, peers were those who were at the same organizational rank in terms of pay, status, and job responsibilities (e.g., Kram & Isabella, 1985). People who were at the same level in the company were likely to also be about the same age, be at the same life stage, have about the same level of work experience, and be at the same career stage (e.g., Levinson, 1986; Super, 1980). Today, however, that may not be the case.

Flattened organizations mean larger numbers of people at fewer hierarchical levels, and so there is likely to be a significant amount of variation among individuals within rank in terms of status, job responsibilities, and pay. In addition, individuals in today's workforce take more personal responsibility for directing their careers compared with people in the past who relied on their organizations to provide the next promotion and long-term employment stability. This "boundaryless career" (Arthur & Rousseau, 1996) comes with many more job and career changes than people used to make a few decades ago. These changes mean that individuals jumping into new careers might be lower in an organizational hierarchy than others of their same age, general work experience, or life stage.

Finally, demographic changes mean that the relationships between age, life stage, and career stage are changing as well, especially for women. As people are marrying and starting families later than they did decades ago, earlier life stages are matching up with later career stages. For instance, starting a new family may no longer happen along with career exploration and instead may occur during career establishment or reevaluation. For women with higher education levels, these stage and age connections may be even more complex, since more-educated women tend to marry later and, if they have children, to do so later as well. These trends together suggest that processes for identifying individuals who are peers—whether intra- or interorganizationally—should take into account these more granular indicators, because organizational level can no longer serve as the proxy it once did.

Conclusion

In this chapter, we described the state of the current research on peer mentoring and suggested avenues for future research. Clearly, much more research is needed on the value and effectiveness of peer mentoring before strong conclusions can be reached. With the changing nature of work, careers, and organizations, it seems that multiple mentors will be increasingly important to employees and that peers may provide a valuable source of this psychosocial and career support. More research is needed that examines the relative effectiveness and benefits of alternative sources of mentoring (supervisor, peer, etc.) to protégés. It would be beneficial to know the types of differential benefits provided by mentors who are supervisors, peers, and other higher-level managers. To date, very few studies have been conducted in this area (Russell, 2004).

In addition to documenting the benefits that occur for the mentor and the protégé from peer mentoring, it is also important to examine the costs associated with peer mentoring. Eby and her colleagues (Eby, Chapter 13, this volume; Eby & Allen, 2002; Eby, McManus, Simon, & Russell, 2000) have demonstrated that a wide variety of negative mentoring experiences exist from both the mentor's and protégé's points of view in traditional mentorships. It would be interesting to see whether negative experiences are different in peer relationships and in traditional mentoring relationships. Given the greater power differential between higher-level mentors and protégés versus peer mentors and protégés, we might expect more negative issues to arise with traditional mentoring relationships. On the other hand, jealousies might be more likely to occur if peer mentoring resulted in better outcomes for the protégé relative to the peer mentor. In addition to jealousy, difficulties could arise in peer mentorships if peers are more likely to reveal significant performance challenges to each other. To the extent that performance issues are related to various counterproductive behaviors, peer mentors may be exposed to more dysfunctional interactions than are traditional mentors. More research, however, is needed to examine this.

It will also be important to examine the types of mentoring relationships that are more or less important over a protégé's career. At each stage (early, middle, late) of an individual's career, a different type of mentoring may be needed. Perhaps relationships with more-senior mentors are more important early on in protégés' career and peers become more important at later stages in their career development. Or, as Kram (1983) noted decades ago, peer relationships might be more important to protégés during the early or middle career period, since there may be fewer higher-level managers available to serve as traditional, formal mentors. Also, peers might be able to provide needed socialization and support during the early career stage. As Allen, Russell, & Maetzke (1997) found, psychosocial functions were important during the protégé's early career period. In another study, Peluchette and Jeanquart (2000) found that faculty at different levels (assistant professors, associate professors, full professors) utilized different sources of mentors, and this was related to their objective career success. More research should examine the value of mentors at varying career stages using other populations as well.

Greenhaus and Singh (Chapter 21, this volume) suggest that the skills, insights and other resources derived from a mentoring relationship can help protégés balance their work and family lives more effectively. This would seem to be particularly true for peer mentoring. Peers may share ideas with one another (psychosocial support, career-enhancing tips) about how they manage and integrate their work and personal lives. Research has already shown that individuals with mentors report less work-family conflict than those without mentors (Nielson, Carlson, & Lankau, 2001). More research is needed, however, to document the specific role that peer mentors play in alleviating work-family conflict.

In sum, peer mentors can be an important part of an individual's developmental network and should not be viewed as the only or best source of developmental support. Repeatedly, researchers have suggested that individuals who have multiple sources of support fare better than those who do not (e.g., Baugh & Scandura, 1999; Burlew, 1991; de Janasz & Sullivan, 2004; de Janasz et al., 2003; Higgins & Thomas, 2001; Peluchette & Jeanquart, 2000; Russell, 2004). Note that throughout this chapter, we have focused on relationships that *began* as peer relationships rather than those that *became* peer relationships after a period of traditional mentorship. While it is beyond the scope of this work to delineate the similarities and differences between these two types of peer relationships, it is an interesting area worth exploring in future research.

Note

1. This work also formed the basis for Chapter 6 in Kram's (1985) book *Mentoring at Work*.

References

Allen, T. D., & Eby, L. T. (2003). Mentoring benefits for mentors: Career, learning, and quality outcomes. *Journal of Management, 29,* 465–486.

Allen, T. D., Eby, L. T., Poteet, M. L., Lentz, E., & Lima, L. (2004). Career benefits associated with mentoring for protégés: A meta-analysis. *Journal of Applied Psychology, 89,* 127–136.

Allen, T. D., & Finkelstein, L. M. (2003). Beyond mentoring: Alternative sources and functions of developmental support. *Career Development Quarterly, 51,* 346–356.

Allen, T. D., McManus, S. E., & Russell, J. E. A. (1999). Newcomer socialization as stress: Formal peer relationships as a source of support. *Journal of Vocational Behavior, 54,* 453–470.

Allen, T. D., Poteet, M. L., Russell, J. E. A., & Dobbins, G. H. (1997). A field study of factors related to supervisors' willingness to mentor others. *Journal of Vocational Behavior, 50,* 1–22.

Allen, T. D., Russell, J. E. A., & Maetzke, S. B. (1997). Formal peer mentoring: Factors related to protégés' satisfaction and willingness to mentor others. *Group & Organization Management, 22,* 488–507.

Arthur, M. B., & Rousseau, D. M. (1996). *The boundaryless career: A new employment principle for a new organizational era.* New York: Oxford University Press.

Baugh, S. G., & Scandura, T. A. (1999). The effect of multiple mentors on protégé attitudes toward the work setting. *Journal of Social Behavior and Personality, 14,* 503–521.

Blau, P. (1964). *Exchange and power in social life.* New York: John Wiley & Sons.

Burke, R. J., McKeen, C. A., & McKenna, C. S. (1993). Correlates of mentoring in organizations: The mentor's perspective. *Psychological Reports, 72,* 883–896.

Burlew, L. D. (1991). Multiple mentor model: A conceptual framework. *Journal of Career Development, 17,* 213–221.

Byrne, D. (1971). *The attraction paradigm.* New York: Academic Press.

de Janasz, S. C., & Sullivan, S. E. (2004). Multiple mentoring in academe: Developing the professorial network. *Journal of Vocational Behavior, 64,* 263–283.

de Janasz, S. C., Sullivan, S. E., & Whiting, V. (2003). Mentor networks and career success: Lessons for turbulent times. *Academy of Management Executive, 17,* 78–91.

Douglas, C. A., & McCauley, C. D. (1999). Formal developmental relationships: A survey of organizational practices. *Human Resource Development Quarterly, 10,* 203–220.

Eby, L. T. (1997). Alternative forms of mentoring in changing organizational environments: A conceptual extension of the mentoring literature. *Journal of Vocational Behavior, 51,* 125–144.

Eby, L. T., & Allen, T. D. (2002). Further investigation of protégés negative mentoring experiences. *Group & Organization Management, 27,* 456–479.

Eby, L. T., McManus, S., Simon, S. A., & Russell, J. E. A. (2000). An examination of negative mentoring experiences from the protégé's perspective. *Journal of Vocational Behavior, 57,* 42–61.

Edmondson, A. (1996). Learning from mistakes is easier said than done: Group and organizational influences on the detection and correction of human error. *Journal of Applied Behavioral Science, 32,* 5–32.

Edmondson, A. (1999). Psychological safety and learning behavior in work teams. *Administrative Science Quarterly, 44,* 350–383.

Edmondson, A. C., & Woolley, A. W. (2003). Understanding outcomes of organizational learning interventions. In M. Easterby-Smith & M. Lyles (Eds.), *International handbook of organizational knowledge management* (pp. 185–211). London: Blackwell.

Ensher, E. A., Grant-Vallone, E. J., & Marelich, W. D. (2002). Effects of perceived attitudinal and demographic similarity on protégés support and satisfaction gained from their mentoring relationships. *Journal of Applied Social Psychology, 32,* 1407–1430.

Ensher, E. A., & Murphy, S. E. (1997). Effects of race, gender, perceived similarity, and contact on mentor relationships. *Journal of Vocational Behavior, 50,* 460–481.

Ensher, E. A., Thomas, C., & Murphy, S. E. (2001). Comparison of traditional, step-ahead, and peer mentoring on protégés support, satisfaction, and perceptions of career success: A social exchange perspective. *Journal of Business & Psychology, 15,* 419–438.

Fine, L. M., & Pullins, E. B. (1998). Peer mentoring in the industrial sales force: An exploratory investigation of men and women in developmental relationships. *Journal of Personal Selling and Sales Management, 18*(4), 89–103.

Glaser, B. G., & Strauss, A. L. (1967). *Discovery of grounded theory: Strategies for qualitative research.* Chicago: Aldine.

Gouldner, A. W. (1960). The norm of reciprocity: A preliminary statement. *American Sociological Review, 25,* 161–178.

Grant-Vallone, E. J., & Ensher, E. A. (2000). Effects of peer mentoring on types of mentor support, program satisfaction and graduate student stress. *Journal of College Student Development, 41,* 637–642.

Higgins, M. C., & Kram, K. (2001). Reconceptualizing mentoring at work: A developmental network perspective. *Academy of Management Review, 26,* 264–289.

Higgins, M. C., & Thomas, D. A. (2001). Constellations and careers: Toward understanding the effects of multiple developmental relationships. *Journal of Organizational Behavior, 22,* 223–247.

Homans, G. C. (1958). Social behavior as exchange. *American Journal of Sociology, 63,* 597–606.

Kram, K. E. (1983). Phases of the mentor relationship. *Academy of Management Journal, 26,* 608–625.

Kram, K. E. (1985). *Mentoring at work: Developmental relationships in organizational life.* Glenview, IL: Scott, Foresman.

Kram, K. E., & Isabella, L. A. (1985). Mentoring alternatives: The role of peer relationships in career development, *Academy of Management Journal, 28,* 110–132.

Levinson, D. J. (with Darrow, C. N., Klein, E. B., Levinson, M. A., & McKee, B.). (1978). *Seasons of a man's life.* New York: Knopf.

Levinson, D. J. (1986). A conception of adult development. *American Psychologist, 41,* 3–13.

McCauley, C. D., & Guthrie, V. (2005, August). *Designing relationships for learning into leader development programs.* Paper presented at symposium, "Creating New Visions of Mentoring: Building Bridges and Making Waves" (B. R Ragins & K. Kram, Chairs), Academy of Management, Honolulu, HI.

McDougall, M., & Beattie, R. S. (1997). Peer mentoring at work: The nature and outcomes of non-hierarchical developmental relationships. *Management Learning, 28,* 423–437.

Nielson, T. R., Carlson, D. S., & Lankau, M. J. (2001). The supportive mentor as a means of reducing work-family conflict. *Journal of Vocational Behavior, 59,* 364–381.

Peluchette, J. V., & Jeanquart, S. (2000). Professionals' use of different mentor sources at various career stages: Implications for career success. *Journal of Social Psychology, 140,* 549–564.

Pullins, E. B., & Fine, L. M. (2002). How the performance of mentoring activities affects the mentor's job outcomes. *Journal of Personal Selling & Sales Management, 22,* 259–272.

Ragins, B. R. (1997a). Antecedents of diversified mentoring relationships. *Journal of Vocational Behavior, 51,* 90–109.

Ragins, B. R. (1997b). Diversified mentoring relationships in organizations: A power perspective. *Academy of Management Review, 22,* 482–521.

Ragins, B. R., & Cottton, J. L. (1999). Mentor functions and outcomes: A comparison of men and women in formal and informal mentoring relationships. *Journal of Applied Psychology, 84,* 529–550.

Russell, J. E. A. (2004). Mentoring. *Encyclopedia of Applied Psychology, 2,* 609–615.

Sullivan, S. E. (1999). The changing nature of careers: A review and research agenda. *Journal of Management, 25,* 457–484.

Super, D. E. (1980). A life-span, life-space approach to career development. *Journal of Vocational Behavior, 16,* 282–298.

Thomas, D. A. (1990). The impact of race on mangers' experiences of developmental relationships (mentoring and sponsorship): An intra-organizational study. *Journal of Organizational Behavior, 11,* 479–492.

Thomas, D. A. (2001). The truth about mentoring minorities: Race matters. *Harvard Business Review, 79*(4), 98–112.

Thomas, K. M., Hu, C., Gewin, A. G., Bingham, K., & Yanchus, N. (2005). The roles of protégé race, gender and proactive socialization attempts on peer mentoring. *Advances in Developing Human Resources, 7,* 540–555.

Turban, D. B., Dougherty, T. W., & Lee, F. K. (2002). Gender, race, and perceived similarity effects in developmental relationships: The moderating role of relationship duration. *Journal of Vocational Behavior, 61,* 240–262.

Young, A. M., & Perrewe, P. L. (2000). The exchange relationship between mentors and protégés: The development of a framework. *Human Resource Management Review, 10,* 177–209.

Young, A. M., & Perrewe, P. L. (2004). The role of expectations in the mentoring exchange: An analysis of mentor and protégé expectations in relation to perceived support. *Journal of Managerial Issues, 16,* 103–126.

12

E-mentoring

*Next-Generation Research
Strategies and Suggestions*

Ellen A. Ensher

Susan Elaine Murphy

W hat do Ray Charles, Tom Brokaw, Oprah Winfrey, and Deepak Chopra all have in common? They had mentors who influenced them, and you can read all about these important career relationships by visiting the Harvard Mentoring Project online (http://www.whomentoredyou.org). In fact, in collaboration with MENTOR/National Mentoring Partnership Act, Harvard's Mentoring Project implemented a national mentoring month in January 2002. These efforts are a testament to the burgeoning prevalence and widespread acceptance of mentoring. Recently, in our own research with 50 senior executive mentors and their protégés, we found that having a mentor in today's work environment is more important than ever before (Ensher & Murphy, 2005).

Couple the growing popular reliance on mentoring with the fact that now there are approximately 1 billion users of the Internet worldwide (Hof, 2005) and the increase in a new, technology-based form of mentoring seems inevitable. We predict that a growing emphasis on the use of computer-mediated communication (CMC) in mentoring relationships will lead to increasing use of to a unique form of mentoring known as *electronic mentoring* or *e-mentoring. Computer-mediated communication* refers to media such as e-mail, chat rooms, newsgroups, mailing lists, interactive Web sites, blogs, and text-based virtual environments (Parks & Roberts, 1998). In the past several years, there has been a surge of articles describing various e-mentoring programs, suggesting that this is a phenomenon whose time has come (Knouse, 2001; Knouse & Webb, 2000; O'Neill & Harris, 2004; Single & Single, 2005). However, although there are a number of articles that describe programs, there are far fewer articles that provide empirical evidence of their overall effectiveness. This gap between the prevalence of programs and a dearth of research on them represents an area of considerable opportunity for academics to partner with practitioners to make exciting scholarly and practical contributions.

Purpose and Definition of E-mentoring

The purpose of this chapter is to provide an in-depth look at e-mentoring. In this chapter, we provide a definition and brief history of e-mentoring. In addition, we trace its prevalence and proliferation and provide a summary of the research thus far. We spend the bulk of our efforts in this chapter introducing a conceptual model that provides specific recommendations for research propositions and future research.

It is helpful to begin by defining the concept of e-mentoring, which is alternatively known as *online mentoring, virtual mentoring,* or *telementoring.* We prefer the term *e-mentoring,* as it more consistent with the vernacular used to describe other types of electronic relationships; however, the above-mentioned terms are often used as synonyms. Early definitions of e-mentoring can be found in the work of leaders in e-mentoring research such as Single and Muller (2001), as well as other scholars (Bierema & Merriam, 2002; Ensher, Heun, & Blanchard, 2003; Hamilton & Scandura, 2003; Headlam-Wells, 2004). After studying these various definitions, we suggest one that represents an accurate compilation. Therefore, we define *e-mentoring* as a mutually beneficial relationship between a mentor and a protégé, which provides new learning as well as career and emotional support, primarily through e-mail and other electronic means (e.g., instant messaging, chat rooms, social networking spaces, etc.). Our definition reflects two unique aspects of e-mentoring. First, these relationships typically cut across internal and external organizational boundaries as well as geographic boundaries and time zones and have the capacity to be more egalitarian than face-to-face (FtF) mentoring. Second, e-mentoring demonstrates that the electronic medium has particular utility for various other forms of mentoring, such as peer mentoring, group mentoring, and reverse mentoring (i.e., where a younger employee mentors a more organizational advanced person, usually in technology-related topics). This definition integrates what we believe e-mentors do as well as the context in which they communicate. E-mentoring occurs either as part of a formal mentoring program or in the context of informal mentoring and can occur outside of an organization either formally or informally.

A definition of e-mentoring would not be complete without a discussion of the continuum of e-mentoring relationships. Ensher and colleagues (2003) suggested that there are three types of e-mentor relationships that exist along a continuum in terms of the degree to which computer-mediated communication is used. These types are CMC-only, CMC-primary, and CMC-supplemental. *CMC-only* refers to relationships in which all communication is mediated electronically, often only through e-mail. An excellent example is MentorNet, an e-mentoring program that to date has paired nearly 18,000 graduate and undergraduate students in technical fields with industry professionals (MentorNet, 2007). This same type of model describes the many support networks that take place online and pair individuals in particular careers with others looking to make career changes. Dow Chemical and other companies use a Web-based mentoring program called "Open Mentoring," which combines the protégé/mentor-driven matching process with the support tools of a formal program (Overman, 2004). Most of the initial pairing and "meeting" is done over the Internet. Once a relationship is established, the extent to which CMC is used for this particular program and others like it will vary depending on preferences of the individuals in the relationship and their geographic distance.

CMC-primary are those relationships in which the majority of interactions are conducted virtually but can also be supplemented by in-person meetings or phone calls. For example, because many mentoring relationships take place within different geographically located offices for IBM, much of the mentoring is done by electronic means. Also, many business incubators, such as the Women's Technology Cluster in the San Francisco Bay area, give women high-tech entrepreneurs access to mentors (Ensher & Murphy, 2005). A majority of these mentoring relationships occur electronically, with follow-up phone calls and a few in-person meetings (Whiting & de Janasz, 2004). CMC-primary mentoring programs are also utilized by colleges that encourage current students to pair up with alumni interested in mentoring.

In *CMC-supplemental* relationships, the majority of mentoring is done in person, yet the relationship interactions may be augmented with the use of technology. Many formal and informal mentoring relationships in today's organizations probably use CMC-supplemental, although no research exists that quantifies the prevalence. Many times, CMC-supplemental relationships begin as FtF relationships and then evolve into e-mentoring relationships due to mutual convenience or geographic incompatibility (Ensher et al., 2003). It seems likely that these formal and informal relationships will easily transition into e-mentoring. For example, in conversations with Disney/ABC employees, they talked about how most of the formal mentoring relationships begin as FtF but are also supplemented with e-mails to follow up on ideas or ask quick questions about a particular work challenge (Ensher & Murphy, 2005). Informal relationships were augmented readily with e-mail communication.

This typology of e-mentoring represents considerable opportunities for future researchers. It seems as though most of the formal e-mentoring relationships are CMC-only and CMC-primary, which is what the bulk of the available literature addresses. In contrast, it is likely that informal e-mentoring relationships are CMC-supplemental, but much less has been written about these types of relationships (Ensher et al., 2003). Both informal and formal mentoring relationships are most likely also CMC-supplemental, because it would be difficult to find individuals who did not use e-mail for at least some portion of their communication with others.

Where Have We Been? A Review of Past Research

Many researchers have been interested in studying the ways in which technological advances are affecting how work is completed in organizations (Mohrman, 1998). Research on the effectiveness of virtual teams and virtual organizations takes into account the effects of asynchronous communication for employees who work in different time zones and in different locations who rarely meet FtF, if ever. In addition to touting a number of important benefits of virtual interactions (e.g., global access to talent, reduced real estate expenses, increased customer satisfaction, and environmental benefits), the research also points to shortcomings in virtual teams and organizations, including reduced attachment to the organization, difficulties in cross-cultural communication, and feelings of isolation (e.g., Spreitzer, 2003).

This research on virtual teams, organizations, and individual interactions is still in its early phases, and e-mentoring research is no exception. Many practical and conceptual advances in the field of e-mentoring have been made by scholars and practitioners in the field of education. Both Single and Single (2005) and Hof (2005) trace the ascent of the Internet to the early 1980s, when e-mail became a popular application for connecting individuals. In particular, America Online (AOL) increased access to e-mail, an application that had previously been limited to specialized populations such as university scholars and researchers. In 1993, the Web browser emerged and developed into a broadcast medium that enabled masses of people to communicate, giving rise to emerging business applications.

Early applications of e-mentoring programs arose to address issues of social inequity and were focused mainly on serving youth. The model of partnering with corporations to provide mentoring to underserved populations was taken a step further with the advent of MentorNet in 1997. MentorNet (http://www.mentor net.net) grew out of the desire of its founder, Carol Muller, to provide a means for women students (both undergraduate and graduate) to succeed in science disciplines (this includes science, technology, engineering, and mathematics) for which student retention rates are low. Today, MentorNet serves primarily women, and to a lesser extent men, by matching college students with mentors in leading technology organizations (e.g., AT&T, IBM, Cisco). MentorNet has been nationally recognized as a best-practice formal e-mentoring program.

More recently, we have seen corporations partner with nonprofits to create their own e-mentoring programs for their employees to connect with youth or other young professionals. One advantage that many companies find in adopting these programs is that their employees become quite familiar with the concept of e-mentoring and understand the advantages and limitations of mentoring relationships conducted electronically. Also, from a quick review of the research, those companies who are technology-intensive usually are the ones who promote this type of mentoring for helping youth, and we would assume they would be most likely to promote e-mentoring for employees. For example, IBM promotes mentoring of high school and college interns or students interested in technology careers, in addition to encouraging mentoring at all levels of the organization. Mentoring is included in manager performance appraisals as a job responsibility. Given the geographic diversity of the company, most e-mentoring may be at the CMC-augmented level, with some international mentoring relationships taking on a CMC-only level.

Several authors (Ensher et al., 2003; Hamilton & Scandura, 2003; Knouse, 2001; Knouse & Webb, 2000) have presented various other examples of e-mentoring programs. Currently, there are many different types of e-mentoring that serve different populations, and some authors have also suggested various categories of existing programs (Bierema & Merriam, 2002; Headlam-Wells, 2004). We build on their work here to present a categorization of e-mentoring programs in Table 12.1.

Table 12.1　　E-mentoring Categories and Examples

Category of Program	Examples
Corporate-sponsored programs for employees	Dow Chemical has a global e-mentoring program for employees to connect with one another internationally (Overman, 2004).
Corporate-sponsored programs for students	MentorPlace program is a program sponsored by IBM that focuses on engaging Hispanic elementary school children with IBM employees (Davis, 2004). According to the National Mentoring Partnership (http://www.mentoring .org), there are about 70 e-mentoring programs sponsored and supported by various organizations (Field, 2003). Another example is the Bethpage Federal Credit Union that partners employees with high school students (Ochalla, 2004).
Entrepreneurs	The Service Corps of Retired Executives provides expertise to small-business owners and entrepreneurs through online mentoring (Knouse & Webb, 2000).
Health care	The American Society of Health-System Pharmacists Virtual Mentoring Exchange partners seasoned pharmacists with newer members and future leaders of the pharmacy profession (ASHP, 2004). A second example is the American College of Healthcare Executives and their Leadership Mentoring Network, which creates virtual mentoring partnerships between health care executives (Hofmann & Noblin, 2002).
Higher education and alumni	Goizeta Business School has an e-mentoring program that pairs its alumni with currently enrolled MBA students (Carter, 2002).
K–12 education professionals	Education Minnesota has an e-mentoring program that enables new teachers to connect with more-experienced teachers ("E-Mentoring Opens Doors," 2004). The National Association of Secondary School Principals has a virtual mentor program, which links principals, assistant principals, and aspiring principals to recognized leaders in their field (McCampbell, 2002).
Public relations professionals	The Public Relations Society of America has a PRSA College of Fellows online mentoring program that matches new public relations professionals with those who are more experienced (Phair, 2000).

(Continued)

Table 12.1 (Continued)

Category of Program	Examples
Science, technology, engineering, and mathematics	MentorNet is the largest e-mentoring program that pairs primarily women undergraduate and graduate students with professionals in these areas (MentorNet, 2007).
Special populations	The Society for the Advancement of Chicanos and Native Americans in Science (SACNAS) has an e-mentoring program that partners research scientists and K–12 educators (Kurzwell, 2004).
State and federal government	The Society of American Foresters has an online mentoring program that enables natural resource professions to learn from more-experienced professionals ("Gain and Share Knowledge," 2002). Another example is the U.S. Office of Personnel Management e-mentoring service, which pairs federal workers with subject matter experts in their fields (Lisagor, 2005).

The list certainly does not represent the entire universe of e-mentoring programs, but it is our attempt to create a categorization of what is available after conducting a thorough search of business and education databases. The table shows that programs exist for professionals and corporate and government employees. Table 12.1 also includes examples of organizations extending e-mentoring to help youth and college students (or potential employees). We are certain that many existing formal mentoring programs are augmented by one or more forms of e-mentoring. Unfortunately, there is no accurate estimate of the number of programs. Also, this list does not begin to address the many informal e-mentoring relationships, a limitation noted earlier. However, it is a reasonable starting place to examine the effectiveness of existing formal e-mentoring programs.

Advantages of E-mentoring

The rapid proliferation of e-mentoring programs indicates a number of important advantages to these types of programs. Ensher and colleagues (2003) suggested the five major advantages to e-mentoring are (a) greater access to mentors, as e-mentoring reduces the barriers of geography or time; (b) reduced costs in terms of administering the mentoring program, conducting training, and reproducing materials; (c) equalization of status or attenuation of salient differences due to the less intimidating nature of the medium; (d) decreased emphasis on demographics, as participants in e-mentoring programs often initially lack clear knowledge of each other's age, race, or other physical characteristics (although revealing hints about one's age or names that reveal ethnic or cultural backgrounds can give information); and (e) a record of interactions. Other authors have found several additional advantages as well.

Hamilton and Scandura (2003) suggested that e-mentoring overcomes barriers typically associated with FtF mentoring. For example, e-mentoring can enable individuals to overcome personality barriers such as low assertiveness, poor social skills, or simply shyness or fear to initiate contact. The electronic medium can render these first encounters much less risky than a FtF initiation.

Single and Single (2005) build on these ideas by proposing that e-mentoring provides two additional unique benefits: impartiality and interorganization connections. Many times, individuals in e-mentoring programs connect with those who have no managerial responsibility over them, and often, they even connect with those outside of their organizations. In these cases, the impartiality of the questions and feedback received can be very helpful to both the mentors and the protégés, as it is free of political issues or internal agendas. Likewise, e-mentoring can provide an important avenue for networking with those in different organizations. As discussed by Higgins, Chandler, and Kram (Chapter 14, this volume), as well as Ensher and Murphy (2005), mentoring for today's professionals is best accomplished through a network of mentors who provide different types of support.

Advantages of e-mentoring may differ by the type of CMC, whether it is CMC-only, CMC-primary, or CMC-supplemental. For example, a CMC-supplemental relationship would likely only aid a typical informal relationship as just one more method of communication, helping a mentoring pair coordinate meetings and share information quickly or possibly develop a relationship relatively quickly. This type of e-mentoring would be less likely to provide a network for networking within other organizations that either CMC-only or CMC-primary could afford. However, CMC-supplemental might aid in a formal mentoring relationship to give individuals who are just getting to know one another a less threatening way to check in with one another. There are many other differences we might expect along the continuum of e-mentoring; therefore, most of this chapter will focus on the benefits of formal and informal CMC-only or CMC-primary relationships.

Potential Disadvantages

Of course, e-mentoring is not without its disadvantages. The major disadvantages suggested by Ensher and her colleagues (2003) are (a) increased likelihood of miscommunication due to reliance on asynchronous communication and inability to communicate nonverbally as effectively; (b) slower development of relationships online than in FtF relationships, as trust and rapport may take a longer time to become established; (c) varying degrees of competency in written communication or with technical skills; (d) computer malfunctions or Internet connectivity issues; and (e) increased concern regarding betrayals of privacy and confidentiality.

Bierema and Merriam (2002) also suggested that e-mentoring relationships can be characterized by less commitment, as the individuals involved can easily disengage, with few of the unpleasant social cues found in FtF relationships. Indeed, Whiting and de Janasz (2004) found this to be true in an e-mentoring assignment given to their students. Also, the digital divide may represent a barrier, as typically, economically disadvantaged groups of people are less likely to have access to the Internet and e-mail, thus restricting access for those who could truly benefit a great deal from mentoring. Recent research suggests that comfort level with computers and online relationships may be another issue. Bozionelos (2004) found that socio-economic background was positively related to computer experience and negatively related to anxiety in using computers. If individuals of lower socioeconomic status are less likely to feel comfortable using computers and are more anxious using them, this certainly would have a direct impact on their comfort levels when engaging in e-mentoring relationships.

Other issues are associated with the faceless interaction that occur in e-mentoring, with respect to gender, race, and even age diversity. In diverse relationships, we would expect that individuals may overuse stereotype information once the partner's gender or race becomes known, rather than getting to know the person as an individual. Or, alternatively, race and gender differences may be ignored to such an extent in these faceless interactions that the protégé may feel something is missing in the relationship. Thomas (1993), for example, found that in more successful cross-race mentoring relationships, acknowledging race was important. Age differences may reveal differences in communication style with e-mail that might be overcome in FtF interactions. Clearly, there is much to be considered in researching e-mentoring programs. In the next section, we will consider a number of research propositions.

Research on teleworking and virtual offices suggests that individuals working under these conditions are likely to feel less commitment to their organizations and learn less tacit knowledge required to move up the organizational career ladder (Workman, Kahnweiler, & Bommer, 2003). What are the implications of these findings for e-mentoring? Individuals who telework most likely will establish e-mentoring relationships as a way to offset some of the isolating effects of telework. Moreover, the research on telework highlights some of the issues associated with information-poor communication. Although many major communication cues are obvious, subtle social cues may be more difficult to discern. For example, research on e-leadership focuses on how leaders can be as effective using a communication medium with less-than-optimal richness (Avolio & Kahai, 2003). Although research on e-leadership shows that the effects of transactional and transformational leadership can be transmitted to followers and affect group effectiveness and creativity, the nonverbal aspects of FtF communication are lost and leaders must take care to ensure that all aspects of leadership impact the group or the organization (see research by Sosik, 1997; Sosik, Avolio, & Kahai, 1997, 1998; Sosik, Kahai, & Avolio, 1998). For mentoring, this research highlights the steps in investigating the how, why, and when for transmitting interpersonal influence and places in which it may fall short of its intended impact.

Where Do We Need to Go?
Suggestions for Future Research

Previously, we set the foundation by describing the various types of e-mentoring programs and providing a summary of their major advantages and disadvantages. Next, we offer a conceptual model and specific set of suggestions for future research related to e-mentoring.

Introduction to the Conceptual Model

The model presented in Figure 12.1 provides a number of ideas for a future research. It takes into account general research on mentoring and knowledge of e-mentoring. Naturally, it does not represent all possibilities for future research or all variables that might impact e-mentoring, but we think it does present many ideas that we hope will intrigue researchers to further examine this phenomenon. Although it may be applied generally to the continuum of CMC e-mentoring relationships, the model developed here focuses explicitly on CMC-only relationships. The model also can be applied to formal and informal e-mentoring relationships, but we note places where differences are expected between these two types of programs with respect to the model.

Antecedents to E-mentoring: Why Engage in E-mentoring?

In this section, we suggest five major variables that could be examined to determine why protégés and mentors might engage in e-mentoring relationships. One important variable that is unique to protégés is their own perceived access to FtF mentors. We suggest four other variables that should be examined by future research in relation to determining why mentors and protégés might engage in e-mentoring: (a) past experience with mentoring, (b) comfort with CMC, (c) organizational culture/support, and (d) desire for expanding developmental network. After briefly reviewing existing research literature on each of these variables, we present research propositions. We focus on formal and informal mentoring relationships that are accomplished predominately through electronic communication, rather than on developing specific hypotheses for the three forms of CMC we discussed earlier.

Access to FtF Mentors. A large and well-developed body of research provides evidence that nearly everyone could benefit from mentoring (see Ensher & Murphy, 2005, for a complete discussion, and other reviews such as the meta-analysis by Allen, Eby, Poteet, Lentz, & Lima, 2004, and descriptive review by Wanberg, Welsh, & Hezlett, 2003). The question of whether certain groups of people such as women and people of color have more difficulty obtaining mentors at all, and powerful high-quality mentors in particular, has received much investigation. As is often the case, various researchers have reached different conclusions based upon the available data. In Wanberg, et al.'s (2003) comprehensive literature review, they concluded that the findings are mixed regarding whether women and people of color have greater difficulty finding mentors. In a recent review of the literature, Ragins (2007) concluded that while women and people of color report greater barriers to obtaining mentors than do their White male counterparts, race and gender have different effects in the actual ability to attract mentors. Women are as likely as men to obtain mentors, but some studies have found that people of color are less likely than European Americans to have mentors (Ragins, 2007).

However, there are exceptions to these findings that have not been researched, but nevertheless are important to consider. For example, women in male-dominated

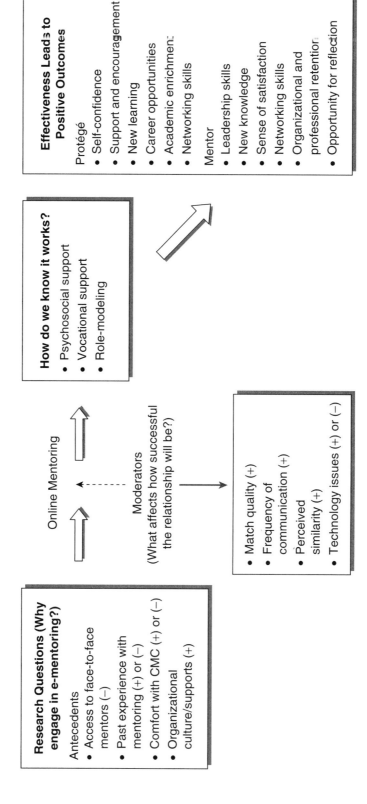

Figure 12.1   Conceptual Model for E-mentoring Research Agenda

occupations, such as technology, may have a much harder time obtaining mentors. For example, a recent study by the Catalyst (2003) organization found that women in technology companies in the *Fortune* 500 represent only 9.3% of board seats and 11% of corporate officer positions, which is substantially lower than in other *Fortune* 500 companies. The organization's evaluation attributed this finding to many factors, including women's lack of mentors, participation in professional networks, and available role models (Catalyst, 2003). This finding was also supported by a recent review by Clutterbuck and Ragins (2002). Moreover, Thomas (2001) and Thomas and Gabarro (1999) suggested that a strong network and a portfolio of mentors are critical to the advancement of people of color and that there are many barriers to finding the right mentors. Members of other groups, such as gays and lesbians, may also find it more difficult to obtain high-quality mentors because of stereotypes and discrimination (Ragins & Cornwell, 2001; Ragins, Cornwell, & Miller, 2003). Finally, others who are simply shy, geographically isolated, or just too busy with other life demands might also find it difficult to find a good FtF mentor. Therefore, e-mentoring, with its reduced emphasis on superficial characteristics and wide access to a global community, offers a way to overcome these barriers. These findings suggest the following proposition:

> *Proposition 1:* Protégés who perceive themselves as having poor access to FtF mentors will be likely to seek out e-mentoring relationships. Specifically, members of nondominant groups should be more likely than members of dominant groups to seek e-mentoring relationships.

Past Experience With Mentoring. How much do one's past experiences impact one's future behavior? Psychologists would say quite a lot. In fact, there has been some research in the FtF mentoring literature that suggests that past experience with mentoring is an excellent predictor of the likelihood of one engaging in future mentoring relationships (Allen, Russell, & Maetzke, 1997; Ragins & Cotton, 1993). As noted by Ragins, Cotton, and Miller (2000), as well as others, mentoring relationships fall along a continuum from "very positive" to "very negative," with what they have termed "marginal mentoring" falling somewhere in between. Moreover, negative experiences with mentors have been shown to be related to less positive outcomes (Eby, Chapter 13, this volume; Eby & Allen, 2002; Eby, Butts, Lockwood, & Simon, 2004; Eby, McManus, Simon, & Russell, 2000). The range of past experiences with mentoring is expected to be predictive of acceptance of e-mentoring, specifically as follows:

> *Proposition 2:* Past experiences with mentoring will positively affect mentors' and protégés' likelihood of engaging in e-mentoring.

Comfort With CMC. Although there has been no published research, we are aware of that specifically examines whether comfort with CMC impacts e-mentoring, there are several reasons we suspect this may be an intriguing and important variable to study. First, we look toward the CMC literature. Torkzadeh, Pflughoeft, and Hall (1999) examined the impact of positive and negative user attitude toward computers on training program effectiveness. They found that users' initial attitudes significantly affected their online learning experiences, as those who were positive to start with had better experiences than those who were not. In a recent investigation of online mentoring relationships, Ensher, de Janasz, & Heun (2007) found that comfort with CMC was predictive of protégés' satisfaction and effectiveness of their relationships with their mentors. This would be the case for mentors as well. One could imagine, however, that if the CMC comfort of the mentor and the protégé were incongruous, the relationship overall might be perceived as less satisfactory.

Proposition 3: A higher degree of comfort with CMC will positively impact mentors' and protégés' likelihood of engaging in e-mentoring.

Organizational Culture/Support. Thus far, it is clear that technology organizations (e.g., IBM, Hewlett-Packard, and others) have led the way in sponsoring e-mentoring programs (MentorNet, 2007). In general, it is likely that organizations in which technology and/or mentoring are valued, rewarded, or supported are more likely to be places in which employee engage in e-mentoring. Because individuals in these organizations most likely are familiar and comfortable with leading-edge, technology-aided communication, as they market these tools extensively to their customers, they would accept e-mentoring more readily than would employees of companies that lag in technology. As we found in our own research, mentors who worked in technology were quite comfortable using e-mail and instant messaging to keep in touch with their various protégés but realized the limitations associated with that communication mode (Ensher & Murphy, 2005).

Proposition 4: Mentors and protégés in organizations that support mentoring and technology (as well as individuals who use e-mail as a primary method for accomplishing work) will be more likely to engage in e-mentoring and have more positive outcomes than individuals from organizations in which support is lower.

Desire to Establish a Developmental Network. Mentoring relationships today have changed. Rather than a protégé having an exclusive relationship with one mentor, many individuals realize that complex career problems require a developmental network of mentors (Ensher & Murphy, 2005; Higgins & Kram, 2001; Higgins Chandler, & Kram, Chapter 14, this volume). The mentors can fulfill the traditional role, with an older, more experienced person mentoring a younger, less experienced person; or alternative roles such as peer mentors, step-ahead mentors, or perhaps boss mentors could all be within an individual's developmental network.

Proposition 5: We expect that individuals who have experience with multiple mentors will be more likely to engage in e-mentoring.

The antecedents of mentoring also could include other components, such as mentor and protégé personality types. For example, in FtF mentoring, high need for achievement (Fagenson, 1992) and learning goal orientation in protégés may lead such individuals to seek out mentors more often. Similarly, mentors with prosocial personalities, which include high levels of helping behavior and empathy (Allen, 2003), or those mentors with an internal locus of control (Allen, Poteet, Russell, & Dobbins, 1997) have been shown to be more willing to mentor others (see Turban & Lee, Chapter 2, this volume, for a review of the many personality characteristics that predict who seeks out mentors and who is more likely to mentor others). Moreover, personality might also predict how well individuals adapt to e-mentoring.

Moderators of E-mentoring: What Affects How Successful the Relationship Will Be?

A number of variables may impact the effectiveness of the mentoring relationship. We hope that future researchers will be inspired to address any number of interesting potential moderators. Based on our past work, we suggest that immediate research address four potential variables, including (a) frequency of communication, (b) match quality (particular to formal programs), (c) level of perceived similarity, and (d) technology issues.

Frequency of Communication

Past research in FtF mentoring has found empirical evidence supporting a positive relationship between frequency of interaction and mentoring effectiveness. Specifically, Allen, Russell, and Maetzke (1997) examined MBA students participating in a formal mentoring program and found that students who spent more time with their mentors were more satisfied than those who spent less time. In a later study, Grant-Vallone and Ensher (2000) reported that doctoral students participating in peer mentoring programs experienced higher degrees of both emotional and career support from relationships characterized by frequent interaction than from those with less interaction.

Program evaluations conducted by e-mentoring program administrators have found similar results (Lewis, 2002; MentorNet, 2007). For example, both mentors and protégés engaged in relationships through MentorNet agreed that frequent e-mails were critical to maintain a good flow of communication. Recent research by Ensher et al. (2007) with graduate and undergraduate students engaged in e-mentoring relationships as part of a class assignment found that protégés who interacted more frequently with their mentors were significantly more satisfied than those who interacted less frequently. In their recent review of the literature on e-mentoring, Single and Single (2005) also pointed out that the frequency and duration of e-mentoring interactions is the one variable consistently related to positive outcomes (Asgari & O'Neill, 2004; Bennett, Hupert, Tsikalas, Meade, & Honey, 1998). This makes sense, given that one of the disadvantages to e-mentoring is that it is an impersonal medium and due to the perceived anonymity, it is easy to ignore people online. Therefore, we recommend that the following research proposition be investigated by future researchers:

Proposition 6: Mentors and protégés who interact more frequently online will be more satisfied overall and will report greater relationship effectiveness than those who interact less frequently.

One caveat in thinking about interaction frequency and relationship satisfaction is that individuals may interact more frequently when relationship quality is high and the match is successful. Conversely, less frequent interaction would occur in low-quality, mismatched relationships. However, frequency of interaction, if required, could actually lead to more relationship satisfaction and quality and, in turn, increase frequency. The relationship between frequency and relationship and match quality needs further investigation.

Match Quality

This is an elusive, yet highly sought-after component of a formal mentoring program. The way in which mentors and protégés in formal e-mentoring programs become paired with one another is integral to the ultimate success of the relationships. A review of the literature in FtF formal mentoring programs provides a number of beneficial guidelines, such as pairing people based on similar interests, values, and goals (Chao, Walz, & Gardner, 1992; Ensher & Murphy, 1997; Fagenson-Eland, Marks, & Amendola, 1997; Noe, 1988). Mentoring program developers and experts suggest that participants be given a choice in whom they are partnered with to achieve successful matches (Murray, 2001), although some research has shown that choice in match makes no difference in satisfaction (Ragins et al., 2000). In electronic mentoring, choice may be less of an issue since it may be difficult for mentors and protégés to differentiate between potential partners. Newer research by Ensher and Murphy (2005) suggested that the importance of complementary skills also be considered when matching mentors and protégés. This qualitative study showed that many mentors were interested in protégés who could give them business or organizational insights they might not currently have access to in their jobs. This was especially true for reverse mentoring relationships, in which both parties were hoping to gain knowledge.

It is difficult enough to match mentors and protégés in FtF settings, in which they often share at least some basics like organizational affiliation and geography. How, then, can match quality be maximized in an online setting, where mentors and protégés can be paired with one another completely outside their circles of familiarity? This problem is a grossly underresearched area that definitely bears further investigation by future researchers. We suggest that as a starting place, researchers look to MentorNet and the methods the organization uses to match mentors and protégés.

In MentorNet, mentors and protégés both complete profiles with their interests and preferences. Basically, the program gives both the mentor and the protégé suggestions based on common preferences, such as majors, disciplines, and gender/ethnicity. This profile also identifies a protégé's preferences for a mentor, such as gender, field of work, location, and ethnicity. Mentors and protégés are also asked about their comfort in discussing common mentoring topics, such as work-life balance, career knowledge, and gender issues. Then, through a sophisticated computer algorithm, protégés are presented with five potential matches and are given the choice to pick one of the matches or let MentorNet choose. The results speak for themselves, as evaluations of mentor and protégé satisfaction have been consistently high, as approximately 95% of participating protégés and mentors indicated that they would recommend MentorNet to others. Future researchers would be well-advised to look at the specific variables used by MentorNet and determine whether they are feasible in their own program evaluations. A more detailed look at the matching process could parse out which variables are more critical than others, particularly within varied populations.

We strongly encourage future researchers to look closely at online matching systems and carefully consider the importance of choice in determining how mentors and protégés are paired with one another. This area of matching represents intriguing possibilities to partner with our colleagues in industrial psychology and information technology. The success of other online matching services outside of mentoring (e.g., online dating services, such as Match.com, eHarmony, or online coaching Web sites), all of which use similar algorithms and offer the element of choice suggest that the quality of the online match is very important. We also expect that the frequency of interaction will be a mediating variable in the relationship between match quality and effectiveness. Therefore, we suggest the following research propositions under conditions in which mentors and protégés have a voice in choosing their partners:

Proposition 7: Match quality will have a significant moderating effect on the relationship between mentor and protégé characteristics and the effectiveness of e-mentoring relationships. Match quality will be based on personality factors and mentoring expectations.

Proposition 8: Initial match quality will be related to the frequency of interaction, which, in turn, will impact later satisfaction with the match.

Perceived Similarity

This is an area of research that has attracted considerable attention in the FtF mentoring literature. In fact, Wanberg and colleagues (2003), in their recent mentoring review of the literature, identified this area as one that warranted much further attention by researchers. We agree. The research thus far has indicated that in FtF relationships, demographic characters such as race and gender matter quite a bit in the initial stages of impression formation (Bell & Nkomo, 2001; Ensher & Murphy, 1997; Ragins, 1999; Turban, Dougherty, & Lee, 2002), yet, as people get to know each other better, demographic differences become less salient, and perceived similarity becomes more important. Harrison, Price, and Bell (1998) make the distinction between *surface-level diversity,* which refers to superficial differences such as age, race, gender, or physical ability, and *deep-level diversity,* which refers to values, goals, and thoughts.

The distinction between surface- and deep-level diversity becomes very important when we consider e-mentoring. CMC researchers have found that electronic communication can be advantageous in some settings because it lacks the visual clues that can lead to bias, stereotypes, and discrimination. Not only are electronic partners free of visual clues related to surface demographics, but they are also somewhat free of visual reminders of status differences (Sproull & Kiessler, 1999; Turkle, 1995). This attenuation of status differences can enable mentors and protégés to focus on deep levels of similarity in values, attitudes, and goals, rather than surface-level similarity. This represents considerable opportunity for anyone who is not a member of a majority group to be seen for who he or she really is, rather than categorized as a member of a protected class or special interest group. Therefore, we suggest the following research propositions:

Proposition 9: E-mentors and protégés will be more likely to depend on aspects of deep-level similarity rather than surface level-similarity in forming impressions of one another.

Proposition 10: Status differences (e.g., organization level, experience, age) between e-mentors and protégés will be less apparent in e-mentoring relationships than in FtF relationships.

Technology Issues

Previous authors (Ensher et al., 2003; Hamilton & Scandura, 2003) have identified several issues that apply specifically to technology that may affect the quality of the relationship and overall mentoring effectiveness. These include but are not limited to (a) foibles of CMC caused by lack of nonverbal communication and contextual cues that can lead to miscommunication, such as disinhibition and flaming; (b) computer or Internet malfunctions; and (c) issues of privacy and confidentiality.

These inherent problems with CMC in general and e-mentoring in particular have been addressed by recent authors in education who suggest implementing a series of support mechanisms and infrastructure tools to remedy these problems. Kasprisin, Single, Single, and Muller (2003) examined the effectiveness of e-training to improve e-mentoring program effectiveness. These researchers used a control group experimental design that randomly assigned one group of protégés in an e-mentoring program to mandatory e-training. The purpose of the training was to improve their communication with their mentors. The rest of the participants were assigned to a group where e-training was optional. Their results indicated that those who were received the mandatory e-training exchanged more frequent e-mails with their mentors, thus resulting in a better overall experience with the e-mentoring program. These findings suggest that e-training and coaching could be used to specifically address some of the aforementioned problems related to miscommunication.

Another study, by Single, Muller, Cunningham, and Single (2000), investigated the use of electronic communities as a means of providing additional support for mentors and protégés engaged in e-mentoring programs. The electronic discussion lists allowed mentors and protégés to engage with the entire community of professionals and students online to discuss important issues such as work-life balance, job search and retention strategies, and other pertinent career-related matters. They found that these lists offered a way for mentors to provide each another with peer mentoring and provide group mentoring for the protégés, as they had access to a wide variety of ideas and resources. This represents another innovative aspect made possible with e-mentoring, as once dyads are paired, electronic communities and entire networks can easily be formed as well. This can also help alleviate the problem of relying solely on one mentor for all forms of support.

How Do We Know E-mentoring Works?

General mentoring effectiveness is typically examined in two major ways. First, research attempts to determine the extent to which mentored individuals in different types of programs receive adequate mentoring. That is, are protégés (and mentors) satisfied with mentoring relationships, and are mentors providing expected mentoring functions (e.g., instrumental/career support, psychosocial support, and role-modeling support)? Furthermore, are the protégés providing benefits to the mentors (e.g., information exchange, access to a wider network, a chance to share knowledge, etc.)? The second major question is this: To what extent do individuals (and their organizations) involved in mentoring relationships actually benefit from these relationships in terms of promotions, salary increases, career satisfaction, job satisfaction, and organizational commitment? Function and benefits are the typical indicators of mentoring effectiveness, and for e-mentoring relationships, there may be additional factors to consider, but in this section, we focus on these two most commonly considered outcomes of e-mentoring relationships: functions and benefits.

Mentor Functions

Although there is some debate in the FtF mentoring literature around what exactly constitutes mentoring (Eby, 1997; Ensher & Murphy 2005; Higgins & Kram, 2001), there is considerable agreement around the issue of what mentors do and the functions they perform. There is general consensus that mentors provide psychosocial or emotional support, career or instrumental support, and in most cases serve as role models as well. Measures for these functions have been well validated in a number of studies (Noe, 1988; Ragins & McFarlin, 1990; Scandura, 1992; Scandura & Ragins, 1993).

One of the key questions as we move forward in studying e-mentoring is the following: To what degree do these same mentor functions found in FtF mentoring also apply in e-mentoring? Preliminary results indicate that e-mentors may provide career and emotional support just as effectively as FtF mentors (Hamilton & Scandura, 2003; Single, 2004) but might be less effective in providing role-modeling, particularly in CMC-only relationships (Ensher et al., 2003; Ensher et al., 2007). E-mentoring may provide additional areas of support, such as access to others through the mentor (e.g., "Hey, let me e-mail my friend in accounting about that issue and have her get back to you"), more specific industry knowledge, or other important functions not found through the confines of FtF mentoring. We suggest the following propositions:

Proposition 11: E-mentors will provide career and emotional support to protégés just as effectively as FtF mentors.

Proposition 12: E-mentors may be less effective at providing role modeling than FtF mentors.

Proposition 13: E-mentors may provide additional categories of support, including specific industry knowledge for both the mentor and protégé. In other words, we expect that there might be slightly higher levels of information exchange in e-mentoring relationships compared with FtF.

Outcomes of E-mentoring

There has been some recent evidence suggesting that protégés and mentors engaged in e-mentoring receive many of the same benefits that protégés gain in FtF mentoring relationships. We review findings from several different e-mentoring programs as a way to highlight some of these benefits. Given the specific nature of the various programs and their populations, we urge caution in generalizing these findings to all populations. Though these findings are promising, future research needs to replicate and extend these early findings. In addition, although the benefits we outline are very important, more traditional mentoring outcomes, such as increased job satisfaction, career advancement, organizational commitment, career commitment, salary increase, and reduction of turnover costs for organizations, are more distal outcomes researchers may consider evaluating as e-mentoring programs are evaluated. Other unique outcomes might include access to information or career advancement opportunities, developmental and educational opportunities, and access to a broad network of potential mentors or colleagues.

A program evaluation of MentorNet, which addresses undergraduate and graduate science, technology, engineering, and math students, showed positive outcomes for both protégés and mentors. In an integration of MentorNet program evaluations since the organization's inception in 1997, Muller and Barsion (2003) found that five consistent themes emerged, supported by both quantitative and qualitative data in regard to protégé benefits. MentorNet protégés reported receiving the following benefits from their mentors: (a) encouragement, reassurance, moral support, and confidence boosting; (b) career information, alternatives, and inspiration; (c) academic advice and support that were able to relate academic work to the workplace; (d) advice for women and that provided them with female role models in engineering and science; and (e) options for balancing work and family. Not only did the MentorNet protégés report receiving important benefits, but the mentors found their participation to be very helpful as well.

Next, we examine the limited although initially promising evidence regarding protégé and mentor benefits found among e-mentoring programs that focus on senior-level professionals mentoring more-junior professionals. Headlam-Wells (2004) published one of the few empirical studies in the management literature on an e-mentoring program. They reported the results of an e-mentoring program that paired 28 aspiring managers or women on career breaks with current women managers in a variety of professions. They found that many of the benefits experienced by the participants were the same as those found in previous research in FtF mentoring programs, including support, guidance, professional friendships, career development, new perspectives, networking skills, and personal development. Mentors reported that they gained as well and that they had the opportunity to increase their own skills and knowledge, enjoyed the opportunity to give back, and were provided with valuable opportunities for reflection.

McCampbell (2002) described the Virtual Mentoring Program available through National Association of Secondary School Principals, in which experienced principals provide online mentoring to new or would-be principals. According to McCampbell, protégés gain a number of benefits, including (a) increase in knowledge of educational leadership skills and practices, (b) development of broader perspectives on leadership, and (c) the opportunities to network with successful role models. McCampbell (2002) suggested that mentors involved in the Virtual Mentoring Program gain a number of important benefits as well, which are similar to those of the MentorNet mentors. Descriptions of other e-mentoring programs (American Society of Health-System Pharmacists [ASHP], 2004; Carter, 2002; Hoffman & Noblin, 2002) report similar findings for mentor and protégé benefits and suggest the following research propositions.

Proposition 14: Protégés who are engaged in effective e-mentoring relationships will be likely to gain a number of positive benefits, including self-confidence, support and encouragement, new learning, career opportunities, academic enrichment, and networking skills. For protégés in the nondominant group, we expect there would be a greater gain in benefits than for those in the dominant group.

Proposition 15: Mentors who are engaged in effective e-mentoring relationships will be likely to gain a number of positive benefits, including leadership skills, new knowledge, sense of satisfaction, networking skills, organizational and professional retention, and opportunity for reflection. Mentors in the nondominant group may gain greater benefits than mentors in the dominant group.

In sum, not only do mentors and protégés engaged in e-mentoring gain considerable benefits that appear to echo those found in FtF programs, but organizations that support these programs are likely to stand to benefit as well. It seems likely that organizations that support e-mentoring increase their employees' organizational commitment, loyalty, and retention. E-mentoring can serve as an efficient and cost-effective means of orientation and socialization and can help to develop the talent pipeline.

Conclusion

E-mentoring has the potential to provide to a wider audience the already well-established benefits that come from formal and informal mentoring. However, because e-mentoring takes place in a specialized environment, it may be difficult to ensure that all the richness of full FtF mentoring relationships is captured. Looking at e-mentoring as an optional relationship within a developmental network is one way to understand the added career benefits it provides.

Research in other areas of electronically mediated communication, including e-leadership, group processes, virtual work groups, and virtual organizations, highlights a few of the drawbacks associated with this specialized communication medium. It may be that e-mentoring will always be a supplemental form of mentoring and possibly never a replacement for FtF mentoring relationships. However, given that e-mentoring can take place across asynchronous time and place, it has potential to provide additional benefits that are limited in some FtF interactions. It is important to consider the vast opportunities for e-mentoring, tempered with the acknowledgment of possible drawbacks, and to know when and where it will be best utilized. This can be accomplished by specific research designed to evaluate the efficacy of e-mentoring.

Figure 12.1 serves as a preliminary starting point for additional research on e-mentoring. We begin identifying situations in which e-mentoring makes sense and might supplant or augment traditional FtF mentoring relationships. These situations include characteristics of the mentor, the protégé, and the organization, as well as the opportunity for FtF mentoring interactions. Additional factors to consider might be (a) personality factors that make mentors or protégés more, or less, willing to engage in any form of e-mentoring and (b) more understanding of the organizational factors that support these efforts.

To examine outcomes of e-mentoring, we suggest including not only traditional aspects such as mentor functions and more bottom-line measures but also some benefits that may be more characteristic of e-mentoring than those found in typical FtF mentoring interactions. Of course, it will be important to consider moderator and mediating variables in understanding the effectiveness of e-mentoring. We point out factors such as match quality, frequency of communication, and perceived similarity as affecting relationship quality. In addition, current mentoring relationships, formal or informal, would influence whether an individual would seek out an e-mentoring relationship. We expect that e-mentoring could be a natural extension of a current FtF relationship or could serve as an additional relationship in an individual's developmental network. Also, those involved in previous FtF relationships may be more likely to seek out e-mentoring relationships because they feel more comfortable with mentoring in general.

The conceptual model presented is generic to some extent, allowing for research on either formal or informal e-mentoring as a key moderator in the relationship between inputs and mentoring relationship quality. Although more e-mentoring research is being published, most research has focused on formal mentoring programs, not on spontaneously developed mentoring relationships. In future research, it will be important to compare the relative benefits associated with formal e-mentoring against those of informal e-mentoring relationships. In addition, the typology of e-mentoring should be more fully investigated within the context of both formal and informal mentoring relationships. It may be that different modes of e-mentoring (CMC-only, primary, supplemental) work well in certain situations and not in others. The research question may be whether there are effective differences with respect to mentoring outcomes. Also, research may identify additional benefits and also underscore whether new measures will be necessary to adequately capture the range of benefits expected from e-mentoring relationships. Traditional measures of mentor functions may also need to be modified. With proper research and a focus on providing organizational improvements, e-mentoring is a tool that will be used effectively to provide the vast benefits of mentoring to a wider audience than ever before.

References

Allen, T. D. (2003). Mentoring others: A dispositional and motivational approach. *Journal of Vocational Behavior, 62,* 134–154.

Allen, T. D., Eby, L. T., Poteet, M. L., Lentz, E., & Lima, L. (2004). Career benefits associated with mentoring for protégés: A meta analysis. *Journal of Applied Psychology, 89,* 127–136.

Allen, T. D., Poteet, M. L., Russell, J., & Dobbins, G. H. (1997). A field study of factors related to supervisors' willingness to mentor others. *Journal of Vocational Behavior, 50,* 1–22.

Allen, T. D., Russell, J. E. A., & Maetzke, S. B. (1997). Formal peer mentoring: Factors related to protégés satisfaction and willingness to mentor others. *Group and Organization Management, 22,* 488–507.

Asgari, M., & O'Neill, K. (2004, April). *What do they mean by "success?" Contributors to perceived success in a telementoring program for adolescents.* Paper presented at the American Educational Research Association, San Diego, CA.

American Society of Health-System Pharmacists. (2004). Virtual mentoring exchange program. Q & A. *American Journal of Health-System Pharmacy, 61,* 238.

Avolio, B. J., & Kahai, S. (2003). Placing the "E" in e-leadership: Minor tweak or fundamental change. In S. Murphy & R. Riggio (Eds.), *The future of leadership development* (pp. 49–70). Mahwah, NJ: Lawrence Erlbaum.

Bell, E. L. J. E., & Nkomo, S. M. (2001). *Our separate ways: Black and White women and the struggle for professional identity.* Boston: Harvard Business School Press.

Bennett, D., Hupert, N., Tsikalas, K., Meade, T., & Honey, M. (1998). *Critical issues in the design and implementation of telementoring environments.* New York Center for Children and Technology. Retrieved June 14, 2005, from http://www2.edc.org/CCT/admin/publications/report/09_1998.pdf

Bierema L., & Merriam, S. (2002). E-mentoring: using computer mediated communication to enhance the mentoring process. *Innovative Higher Education, 26,* 211–227.

Bozionelos, N. (2004). Socio-economic background and computer use: The role of computer anxiety and computer experience in their relationship. *International Journal of Human-Computer Studies.* Retrieved February 12, 2005, from http://www.elsevier.com/locate/ijhcs

Carter, C. (2002, Spring). Mentoring in an electronic age: Long-distance mentors help pay it forward. *Goizueta,* pp. 10–13.

Catalyst. (2003). *Bit by bit: Catalyst's guide to advancing women in high tech companies.* New York: Author.

Chao, G. T., Walz, P. M., & Gardner, P. D. (1992). Formal and informal mentorships: A comparison of mentoring functions and contrast with nonmentored counterparts. *Personnel Psychology, 45,* 1–16.

Clutterbuck, D., & Ragins, B. R. (2002). *Mentoring and diversity: An international perspective.* Woburn, MA: Butterworth-Heinemann.

Davis, M. (2004). E-Mentoring. *Triangle Business Journal, 19*(40), 3.

Eby, L. T. (1997). Alternative forms of mentoring in changing organizational environments: A conceptual extension of the mentoring literature. *Journal of Vocational Behavior, 61,* 125–144.

Eby, L. T., & Allen, T. D. (2002). Further investigation of proteges' negative mentoring experiences. *Group & Organization Management, 27,* 456–479.

Eby, L. T., Butts, M., Lockwood, A., & Simon, S. A. (2004). Protégés negative mentoring experiences: Construct development and nomological validation. *Personnel Psychology, 57,* 411–447.

Eby, L. T., McManus, S. E., Simon, S. A., & Russell, J. E. A. (2000). An examination of negative mentoring experiences from the protégé's perspective. *Journal of Vocational Behavior, 57,* 42–61.

E-mentoring opens doors in academics. (2004). *American Scientist Research Triangle Park, 92*(2), 200.

Ensher, E. A., de Janasz, S. C., & Heun, C. (2007). *E-mentoring: Virtual relationships and real benefits.* Manuscript submitted for publication.

Ensher, E. A., Heun, C., & Blanchard, A. (2003). Online mentoring and computer-mediated communication: New directions in research. *Journal of Vocational Behavior, 63,* 264–288.

Ensher, E. A., & Murphy, S. E. (1997). Effects of race, gender, perceived similarity, and contact on mentor relationships. *Journal of Vocational Behavior, 50,* 460–481.

Ensher, E. A., & Murphy, E. (2005). *Power mentoring: How mentors and protégés get the most out of their relationships.* San Francisco: Jossey-Bass.

Fagenson, E. A. (1992). Mentoring—Who needs it? A comparison of protégés' and non-protégés' needs for power, achievement, affiliation, and autonomy. *Journal of Vocational Behavior, 41,* 4860.

Fagenson-Eland, E. A., Marks, M. A., & Amendola, K. L. (1997). Perceptions of mentoring relationships. *Journal of Vocational Behavior, 51,* 29–42.

Field, A. (2003, March 3). No time to mentor? Do it online. *Business Week,* p. 126.

Gain and share knowledge, skills, and expertise—At your computer. (2002). *Journal of Forestry, 100*(1), 7.

Grant-Vallone, E. J., & Ensher, E. A. (2000). Effects of peer mentoring on types of mentor support, program satisfaction, and graduate student stress: A dyadic perspective. *Journal of College Student Development, 41,* 637–642.

Hamilton, B., & Scandura, T. (2003). E-Mentoring: Implications for organizational learning and development in a wired world. *Organizational Dynamics, 31,* 388–402.

Harrison, D. A., Price, K. H., & Bell, M. (1998). Beyond relational demography: Time and the effects of surface and deep level diversity of work group cohesion. *Academy of Management Journal, 41,* 96–107.

Headlam-Wells, J. (2004). E-mentoring for aspiring women managers. *Women in Management Review, 19,* 212.

Higgins, M. C., & Kram, K. E. (2001). Reconceptualizing mentoring at work: A developmental network perspective. *Academy of Management Review, 26,* 264–288.

Hof, R. (2005, June 20). The power of us. *Business Week,* p. 75.

Hofmann, P., & Noblin, J. (2002). Mentoring dialogue: Critical questions and answers. *Healthcare Executive Chicago, 17*(6), 8–13.

Kasprisin, C., Single, P., Single, M., & Muller, C. (2003). Building a better bridge: Testing e-training to improve e-mentoring programs in higher education. *Mentoring & Tutoring, 11,* 67–78.

Knouse, S. (2001). Virtual mentors: Mentoring on the Internet. *Journal of Employment Counseling, 38,* 162–168.

Knouse, S., & Webb, S. (2000). Unique types of mentoring for diverse groups in the military. *Review of Business, 21*(1/2), 48–52.

Kurzweil, J. (2004). SACNAS love at first sight . . . and ever after. *The Hispanic Outlook in Higher Education Paramus, 15*(5), 35.

Lewis, C. (2002). *International telementor program (ITP) report: Evaluation results from teacher surveys.* Retrieved April 15, 2005, from http://www.telementor.org

Lisagor, M. (2005). E-mentoring: A tool for federal workers. *Federal Computer Week, 19*(2), 50.

McCampbell, B. (2002). Virtual mentoring: Using the Web to support mentoring and coaching. *Principal Leadership, 2*(5), 63–65.

MentorNet. (2007, May 1). Available at http://www.mentornet.net

Mohrman, S. A. (1998). The contexts for geographically dispersed teams and networks. In C. Cooper & D. Rousseau (Eds.), *Trends in organizational behavior* (pp. 63–80). New York: John Wiley & Sons.

Muller, C., & Barsion, S. (2003, June). *Assessment of large-scale e-mentoring network for women in engineering and science: Just how good is MentorNet?* WEPAN 2003 Conference, Chicago.

Murray, M. (2001). *Beyond the myths and magic of mentoring: How to facilitate an effective mentoring program* (Rev. ed.). San Francisco: Jossey-Bass.

Noe, R. A. (1988). An investigation of the determinants of successful assigned mentoring relationships. *Personnel Psychology, 41,* 457–479.

Ochalla, B. (2004). Credit Union introduces e-mentoring program. *Credit Union Management, 27*(7), 7.

O'Neill, D., & Harris, J. (2004). Bridging the perspectives and developmental needs of all participants in curriculum-based telementoring programs. *Journal of Research on Technology in Education, 37,* 111–128.

Overman, S. (2004). Mentors without borders. *HRMagazine, 49*(3), 83–86.

Parks, M. R., & Roberts, L. D. (1998). "Making MOOsic": The development of personal relationships online and a comparison to their off-line counterparts. *Journal of Social and Personal Relationships, 15,* 517–537.

Phair, J. (2000). Fellows extend mentoring program online. *Public Relations Tactics, 7*(10), 6.

Ragins, B. R. (1999). Gender and mentoring relationships: A review and research agenda for the next decade. In G. N. Powell (Ed.), *Handbook of gender and work* (pp. 347–370). Thousand Oaks, CA: Sage.

Ragins, B. R. (2007). Diversity and workplace mentoring: A review and positive social capital approach. In T. D. Allen & L. T. Eby (Eds.), *Blackwell handbook of mentoring: A multiple perspectives approach* (pp. 281–300). Oxford, UK: Blackwell.

Ragins, B. R., & Cornwell, J. M. (2001). Pink triangles: Antecedents and consequences of perceived workplace discrimination against gay and lesbian employees. *Journal of Applied Psychology, 86,* 1244–1261.

Ragins, B. R., Cornwell, J. M., & Miller, J. S. (2003). Heterosexism in the workplace: Do race and gender matter? *Group and Organization Management, 28,* 45–74.

Ragins, B. R., & Cotton, J. L. (1993). Gender and willingness to mentor in organizations. *Journal of Management, 19,* 97–111.

Ragins, B. R., Cotton, J. L., & Miller, J. S. (2000). Marginal mentoring: The effects of type of mentor, quality of relationship, and program design on work and career attitudes. *Academy of Management Journal, 43,* 1177–1194.

Ragins, B. R., & McFarlin, D. B. (1990). Perception of mentor roles in cross-gender mentoring relationships. *Journal of Vocational Behavior, 37,* 321–339.

Scandura, T. A. (1992). Mentorship and career mobility. An empirical investigation. *Journal of Organizational Behavior, 13,* 169–174.

Scandura, T. A., & Ragins, B. R. (1993). The effects of sex and gender role orientation on mentorship in male-dominated occupations. *Journal of Vocational Behavior, 43,* 251–265.

Single, P. B. (2004, June). *Expanding our use of mentoring: Reflection and reaction.* Paper presented at the symposium on "Mentoring Scholars in Gender Equity Studies: Strengthening the Journey and Building an Inclusive Knowledge Base," at the Annual Meeting of the American Educational Research Association, San Diego, CA.

Single, P. B., & Muller, C. (2001). When e-mail and mentoring unite: The implementation of a nationwide electronic mentoring program. In L. Stromei (Ed.), *Implementing successful coaching and mentoring programs* (pp. 107–122). Cambridge, MA: American Society for Training & Development (ASTD) in Action Series.

Single, P. B., Muller, C., Cunningham, C., & Single, R. (2000). Electronic communities: A forum for supporting women professionals and students in technical and scientific fields. *Journal of Women and Minorities in Science and Engineering, 6,* 115–129.

Single, P., B., & Single, R. (2005). E-mentoring for social equity: Review of research to inform program development. *Mentoring and Tutoring, 13,* 301–320.

Sosik, J. J. (1997). Effects of transformational leadership and anonymity on idea generation in computer-mediated groups. *Group & Organization Management, 22,* 460–487.

Sosik, J. J., Avolio, B. J., & Kahai, S. S. (1997). Effects of leadership style and anonymity on group potency and effectiveness in a group decision support system environment. *Journal of Applied Psychology, 82,* 89–103.

Sosik, J. J., Avolio, B. J., & Kahai, S. S. (1998). Inspiring group creativity: Comparing anonymous and identified electronic brainstorming. *Small Group Research, 29,* 3–31.

Sosik, J. J., Kahai, S. S., & Avolio, B. J. (1998). Transformational leadership and dimensions of creativity: Motivating idea generation in computer-mediated groups. *Creativity Research Journal, 11,* 111–121.

Spreitzer, G. (2003). Leadership development in the virtual workplace. In S. Murphy & R. Riggio (Eds.), *The future of leadership development* (pp. 71–86). Mahwah, NJ: Lawrence Erlbaum.

Sproull, L., & Kiessler, S. (1999). Computers, networks, and work. *Scientific American, 265*(3), 116–123.

Thomas, D. A. (1993). Racial dynamics in cross-race developmental relationships. *Administrative Science Quarterly, 38,* 169–194.

Thomas, D. A. (2001). The truth about mentoring minorities: Race matters. *Harvard Business Review, 79*(4), 98–107.

Thomas, D. A., & Gabarro, J. J. (1999). *Breaking through: The making of minority executives in corporate America.* Boston: Harvard Business School Press.

Torkzadeh, G., Pflughoeft, K., & Hall, L. (1999). Computer user attitudes, training effectiveness, and self-efficacy: An empirical study. *Behaviour & Information Technology, 18,* 299–309.

Turban, D. B., Dougherty, T. W., & Lee, F. K. (2002). Gender, race and perceived similarity effects in developmental relationships: The moderating role of relationship duration. *Journal of Vocational Behavior, 61,* 240–262.

Turkle, S. (1995). *Life on the screen.* New York: Simon & Schuster.

Wanberg, C. R., Welsh, E. T., & Hezlett, S. A. (2003). Mentoring research: A review and dynamic process model. *Research in Personnel and Human Resources Management, 22,* 39–124.

Whiting, V., & de Janasz, S. C. (2004). Mentoring in the 21st century: Using the Internet to build skills and networks. *Journal of Management Education, 28,* 275–293.

Workman, M., Kahnweiler, W., & Bommer, W. (2003). The effects of cognitive style and media richness on commitment to telework and virtual teams. *Journal of Vocational Behavior, 63,* 199–219.

13

Understanding Relational Problems in Mentoring

A Review and Proposed Investment Model

Lillian T. Eby

Mentoring scholarship has focused heavily on the positive aspects of mentor-protégé relationships. This includes examining the objective and subjective benefits of mentoring for protégés (for a review, see Allen, Eby, Poteet, Lentz, & Lima, 2004), the actual and anticipated benefits of mentoring for mentors (e.g., Allen, Poteet, & Burroughs, 1997; Eby, Durley, Evans, & Ragins, 2006; Fletcher & Ragins, Chapter 15, this volume; Ragins & Scandura, 1999; Ragins & Verbos, 2007), and the benefits associated with participation in formal mentoring programs (e.g., Eby & Lockwood, 2005; Ragins & Cotton, 1999; Ragins, Cotton, & Miller, 2000). Comparatively less research has examined problems that can exist in mentoring relationships. This is surprising since, like all interpersonal relationships, mentoring is subject to difficulties, disappointments, and even at times serious relational dysfunctions (Eby & McManus, 2004; Eby, McManus, Simon, & Russell, 2000; Ragins & Scandura, 1997). In fact, in both Levinson (1978) and Kram's (1985) seminal studies of mentoring, relationship problems such as jealousy, sabotage, betrayal, psychological abuse, and overdependence were noted and cautions given to not overlook the potentially negative relational dynamics that can emerge between mentors and protégés.

This chapter maps the landscape of problems in mentoring relationships by defining the construct of *relational problems* and discussing what we know about relational problems in mentoring. This sets the stage for the presentation of a continuum of relational problems that classifies such problems in terms of their severity. The next section incorporates the preceding review of relational problems with the literature on the known benefits of mentoring to propose an integrative model of mentoring relationships. In the final section of this chapter, an agenda for future research is presented.

Relational Problems in Mentoring

Numerous definitions have been put forward to describe problems in mentoring relationships. Often, these definitions focus on the extent to which the mentoring *relationship* is "destructive" (Kram, 1985, p. 10), "dysfunctional" (Feldman, 1999, p. 253; Ragins & Scandura, 1999, p. 498; Scandura, 1998, p. 449), or "marginal" (Ragins et al., 2000, p. 1178) or the extent to which the relationship leads to "negative consequences" (Allen et al., 1997, p. 78) or "negative outcomes" (Hunt & Michael, 1983, p. 478). For example, a mentoring relationship may fail to meet one or both parties' needs or be a source of distress, frustration, conflict, or dissatisfaction (Feldman, 1999; Johnson & Huwe, 2002; Kram, 1985; Ragins et al., 2000; Scandura, 1998). Likewise, a mentoring relationship may leave one or both individuals feeling as though the overall costs associated with the relationship outweigh the benefits (Feldman, 1999; Johnson & Huwe, 2002) or that mentoring is more trouble than it is worth (Ragins & Scandura, 1999).

Other definitions of mentoring problems focus on *specific experiences* in the mentoring relationship, referring to "negative mentoring experiences" (Eby et al., 2000, p. 3; Eby, Butts, Lockwood, & Simon, 2004, p. 412) or "dysfunctional psychological reasons for (relationship) termination" (Ragins & Scandura, 1997, p. 946). This includes specific events in the relationship, such as sabotage, deception, and exploitation, as well as characteristic patterns of mentor or protégé behavior, such as overdependence, jealousy, personality clashes, and unwillingness to learn (Eby & Allen, 2002; Eby et al., 2000; Eby et al., 2004; Ragins & Scandura, 1997). These differing definitions are not trivial; some refer to the mentoring relationship as a whole, whereas others refer to specific experiences in the mentoring relationship.

In this chapter, I argue that an understanding of problems in mentoring relationships necessitates an in-depth understanding of specific experiences between mentor and protégé that contribute to the one's overall perception of the relationship. This is consistent with Higgins, Chandler, and Kram's (Chapter 14, this volume) call for a focus on mentor-protégé interactions as a way to understand overall relational engagement and disengagement. Thus, in this chapter, *relational problems* are defined as real or perceived aspects of mentor-protégé interactions that minimize, negate, or undermine the personal and professional growth of one or both members. This definition has the specific mentoring experience or "mentoring episode" (Ragins & Fletcher, Chapter 15, this volume) as the point of reference and provides a platform for understanding problematic mentoring relationships in terms of the culmination of specific relational experiences.

Consistent with emerging perspectives on mentoring (Eby & McManus, 2004; Fletcher & Ragins, Chapter 15, this volume; Ragins et al., 2000; Ragins & Verbos,

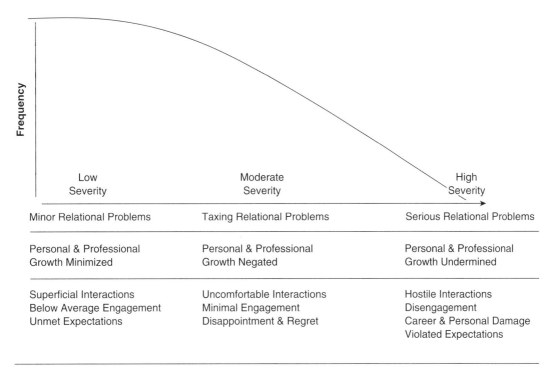

Figure 13.1   Continuum of Relational Problems

2007; Simon & Eby, 2003), relational problems are proposed as existing on a continuum of severity (see Figure 13.1). This continuum is marked by three types of relational problems, each with unique characteristics.

One end of the continuum is anchored by *minor relational problems.* An example of a minor relational problem is mentor or protégé skill deficits. This might include low job performance, specific technical skills deficits, or relatively minor interpersonal deficits (e.g., poor communication skills). Another example of a minor relational problem is personal problems that interfere with work-related performance and have the potential to strain the mentorship. For example, in the Eby et al. (2000) study, a protégé discussed a situation in which his or her mentor had personal and family problems outside of work that interfered with the mentor's ability to provide support. Similarly, a mentor in Eby and McManus's (2004) study talked about a protégé who experienced difficulty handling situations positively at work following a divorce, which made it difficult for the mentor to provide mentoring support. As shown in Figure 13.1, minor relational problems are expected to *minimize* the personal and professional growth of one or both individuals. Minor relational problems are also characterized by superficial interactions between mentor and protégé, below-average engagement, and unmet expectations.

Somewhat more serious are *taxing relational problems* (see Figure 13.1). These problems reflect fundamental and often ongoing difficulty relating to one another, as well as failure of one or both parties to fully engage in the relationship, psychologically or behaviorally. Specific problems include mentor-protégé mismatches in personality, values, and work styles, as well as mentor neglect and protégé unwillingness to learn (Eby et al., 2000; Eby & McManus, 2004). As shown in Figure 13.1, taxing relational problems are expected to *negate* the personal and professional growth of one or both individuals. Moreover, taxing relational problems are associated with uncomfortable interactions, minimal engagement, and feelings of disappointment and regret.

At the other end of the continuum are *serious relational problems* (see Figure 13.1). These problems include experiences such as sabotage, exploitation, harassment, deception, and manipulation. Interestingly, both mentors and protégés report experiencing serious relational problems, although in some cases the problem may manifest differently. For instance, due to their greater power and influence, mentors are more likely to directly sabotage protégés' careers, whereas protégés may engage in more "behind-the-scenes" sabotage, by spreading rumors about their mentors or badmouthing them to others (Eby & McManus, 2004). As another illustration, mentors may engage in exploitation by having protégés do their "grunt work" and taking credit for their protégés' accomplishments (Eby et al., 2000). In contrast, protégés may directly exploit their mentors by entering into the relationship only for personal gain or engage in indirect exploitation by taking advantage of those around them to get ahead (Eby & McManus, 2004). As shown in Figure 13.1, serious relational problems are expected to *undermine* an individual's personal and professional growth. Such problems are also associated with hostile interactions, disengagement (e.g., exit relationship, organizational turnover), career and personal damage (e.g., blocked promotion, lowered self-esteem), and violated expectations.

As shown by shape of the distribution in Figure 13.1, there are expected differences in the relative frequency of these three types of relational problems. Minor relational problems are expected to be more common than taxing relational problems, which should be more common than serious relational problems. This reflects conventional wisdom that highly dysfunctional mentoring is probably uncommon (Ragins et al., 2000; Ragins & Verbos, 2007; Scandura, 1998). It is also consistent with findings from Eby and McManus's (2004) study of mentoring problems from the mentor's perspective, in which marginally effective relationship experiences were reported most frequently, followed by ineffective relationship experiences, and then dysfunctional relationship experiences.

What We Know About Relational Problems in Mentoring

Figure 13.1 provides a useful backdrop to review what we know about relational problems in mentoring. Three bodies of scholarship are discussed that have contributed to our understanding of relational problems in mentoring: organizational mentoring, student-faculty mentoring, and clinical supervisory relationships. Where adequate literature exists, relational problems are discussed from the perspectives of the mentor and the protégé. This is important since each individual has a unique role in the mentoring relationship (Eby & McManus, 2004). After discussing what we know about relational problems in these three bodies of scholarship, a summary and integration section is provided.

Overview

Organizational mentoring, student-faculty mentoring, and clinical supervisory relationships all exist in work settings and involve a more senior or more experienced individual (the mentor) providing guidance and support to a more junior or less experienced individual (the protégé). In addition, in all three types of mentoring relationships, the protégé may receive both career-related support and psychosocial support from the mentor, and the mentor also stands to gain from the relationship (Eby, Durley, et al., 2006; Fletcher & Ragins, Chapter 15, this volume; Kram, 1985; Levinson, 1978; Ragins & Verbos, 2007). However, there are differences across these three types of mentoring. Student-faculty and clinical supervisory relationships adopt an apprentice model of learning, whereby the mentor has specific technical expertise to impart upon the protégé, knowledge that cannot be easily learned in other ways (Jacobi, 1991; Powell & Brodsky, 1993). In contrast, the learning and development that happens in organizational mentoring tends to be more general and less technically oriented (Kram, 1985). Student-faculty mentoring is unique from the other forms of mentoring because it is more time bound (students enter programs and graduate within a certain time frame). Likewise, clinical supervisory relationships are unique because they are typically assigned (formal) relationships in which the mentor has dual responsibility for protégé development and evaluation (Powell & Brodsky, 1993). However, clinical supervision is distinct from supervision in general because a primary job duty of clinical supervisors is coaching, developing, training, and mentoring supervisees (Powell & Brodsky, 1993).

Organizational Mentoring

Much of what we know about relational problems comes from research on organizational mentoring. These relationships may develop spontaneously through mutual attraction or be formally arranged by a third party within the organization (Ragins & Cotton, 1999).

Protégé and Mentor Perspective. Several scholars provide theoretical discussions of mentoring problems, concentrating primarily on serious relational dysfunctions. Scandura (1998) adapts Duck's (1994) typology of the dark side of close personal relationships to propose seven distinct types of relationship dysfunctions in mentorships. Scandura discusses four types of "destructive (mentoring) relationships" (p. 454), including those marked by negative relations (bullies, enemies), sabotage (revenge, silent treatment, career damage), difficulty (conflict, binds), and spoiling (betrayal, regret). She further notes that protégé submissiveness, mentor or protégé deception, and harassment are other types of dysfunctional behavior in mentoring relationships. While a few dysfunctions are proposed as originating from one party (e.g., mentor bullying), mentoring problems are primarily discussed without reference to the mentor or protégé perspective. However, Scandura provides a conceptual model that outlines how both mentor and protégé characteristics may contribute to dysfunctional mentoring, which, in turn, may lead to a wide range of outcomes, such as relationship termination, reduced self-esteem, turnover, and stress. Feldman's (1999) theoretical article highlights the mutuality and reciprocity of mentoring relationships, making the important point that both mentor and protégé can contribute to problems. He notes that while protégés can be victimized by mentors, protégés can "bring dysfunctional mentoring upon themselves" (p. 252) and even engage in behavior that is damaging to their mentors (e.g., badmouthing).

Protégé Perspective. Several empirical studies provide insight into relational problems in organizational mentoring from the protégé's perspective. The first of these studies examined protégés' reported reasons why their mentoring relationships ended (Ragins & Scandura, 1997). These authors found that ex-protégés reported several dysfunctional psychological reasons for relationship termination, including mentor jealousy, dependency, and lack of support/unrealistic mentor expectations. In a subsequent qualitative study that focused more generally on relational problems in mentoring, Eby et al. (2000) found that the most common mentoring problem was mismatch in values, personalities, and work styles. This was followed by distancing behavior, which included mentor neglect and lack of interest in the relationship. A third problem was mentor manipulation, such as wielding power tyrannically, inappropriately under- or overdelegating work, and engaging in self-interested political behavior at the expense of the protégé (e.g., taking undue credit for a protégé's work). Lack of mentor technical and interpersonal skills was another mentoring problem. A final problem was mentor dysfunctionality, which refers to problems external to the relationship (e.g., marital problems) that inhibit one's ability to be an effective mentor. In a later study, Eby and Lockwood (2005) found that protégés participating in a formal mentoring program also reported some mentoring problems, including mentor neglect and mentor-protégé mismatches.

In terms of correlates, some relational problems are more frequently reported in the separation phase of the mentoring relationship, among protégés in formal mentorships, among protégés in less complementary relationships, and in organizations where there is less support for mentoring (Eby, Lockwood, & Butts, 2006; Eby et al., 2004). Moreover, as protégés' reports of mentoring problems increase, so does stress, intentions to leave both the organization and mentorship, psychological job withdrawal, and depressed mood, while job satisfaction and relational learning decrease (Eby & Allen, 2002; Eby et al., 2004). Also demonstrating how mentoring problems can influence protégés, Ragins et al. (2000) found that those in marginal or dissatisfying mentorships reported lower job satisfaction, career and organizational commitment, satisfaction with promotional opportunities, organization-based self-esteem, and procedural justice, as well as higher intentions to quit. In fact, protégés who were in dissatisfying mentorships reported higher intentions to leave the organization than their nonmentored counterparts.

Mentor Perspective. Since mentors are in positions of greater power and are charged with helping protégés develop professionally and personally, it is not surprising that they report some unique problems with protégés. For example, Ragins and Scandura (1999) found that executives anticipate several possible costs from mentoring others. This includes concerns that the mentorship will be more trouble than it is worth, that it will become dysfunctional in some way (e.g., exploitive or back-stabbing protégé), that the protégé will be a bad reflection on the mentor, and that mentoring will be an energy drain. Allen et al. (1997) identified some similar concerns by mentors, most notably the time requirements associated with mentoring and protégé abuse of the relationship for personal gain.

In an attempt to examine the range of mentoring problems that mentors report with protégés, Eby and McManus (2004) analyzed narrative accounts of mentoring experiences from 103 mentors. They found that the most common types of problems typify marginally effective relationships and include working with a protégé who is unwilling to learn or does not meet the mentor's performance expectations. This dovetails with the finding that mentors are attracted to protégés who display a learning orientation, motivation, and competency (Allen et al., 1997; Allen, Poteet, & Russell, 2000; Olian, Caroll, & Giannantonio, 1993). A second category of problems identified by Eby and McManus corresponds to ineffective relationships and includes difficulty (conflicts, disagreements), spoiling (real or perceived disloyalty or disappointment), benign deception (protégé impression management), protégé submissiveness, and general dysfunctionality (e.g., protégé nonwork problems that interfere with the mentoring relationship). A final group of problems are those that represent dysfunctional relationship experiences, including negative relations (protégé exploitation and egomania), malevolent deception (protégé lying), protégé sabotage, protégé harassment, and protégé jealousy/competition (Eby & McManus, 2004). A study of mentors participating in a formal mentoring program identified some similar problems from the mentor's perspective, including difficulty relating interpersonally and disappointment in the mentorship (Eby & Lockwood, 2005).

Almost no empirical research has examined the correlates of mentors' problems with protégés. However, some initial evidence suggests that when relational problems represent more of a typical pattern of interacting with the protégé, such problems have more of a negative impact on the mentorship. Moreover, as the perceived impact on the mentorship increases in severity, satisfaction with the relationship declines (Eby & McManus, 2004).

Student-Faculty Mentoring

Mentoring relationships in academia are important for students' personal development and professional training (Austin, 2002; Clark, Harden, & Johnson, 2000). Faculty members indoctrinate students into a profession, and this type of mentoring can have lasting effects on students (Austin, 2002; Ellis, 1992; Johnson, 2007). Notwithstanding the potentially positive influence that faculty can have on students, Kalbfleisch (1997) found that one half of both undergraduate and graduate students reported at least one significant conflict event with their mentors.

While some research has examined the types of mentoring problems experienced in student-faculty mentoring relationships, little, if any, empirical research exists on correlates of relational problems.

Student and Faculty Perspective. Several mentoring problems are applicable to both students and faculty members. Johnson and Huwe (2002) note that mismatches in personality, communication style, relationship preference, career stage, and career interest (i.e., research versus practice) can make it difficult to initiate and sustain effective academic mentorships. Other potential problems involve conflict on substantive issues (e.g., writing style, authorship, role expectations), boundary violations that may impair the objectivity of the mentor or make the student or faculty member uncomfortable (e.g., faculty assuming parental role, student disclosing personal issues), and emotional or sexual attraction (Johnson & Huwe, 2002). In rare cases, a graduate student may have sexual contact with a faculty member (Johnson, 2003).

Student Perspective. Scholars are often critical of mentoring in higher education, noting that faculty members have competing obligations, such as teaching, research, and service activities, which reduce their ability to provide organized, high-quality developmental experiences for students (Austin, 2002; Levinson, 1978). In addition, reward and recognition systems in most universities provide few incentives for faculty to develop strong mentoring relationships (Austin, 2002). This, coupled with heavy faculty role demands, means that mentor neglect can occur (Johnson, 2007; Levinson, 1978). In fact, faculty neglect is one of the most often cited sources of student dissatisfaction in graduate training (Clark et al., 2000). Lack of mentoring support also raises potential ethical issues, particularly when faculty members oversee student training, internship, or practicum experiences (Goodyear, Crego, & Johnston, 1992). Other forms of unethical, or even illegal, behavior on the part of faculty can create mentoring problems. This includes fraudulent behavior (e.g. faking research data, altering research findings), wrongly taking credit for students' work, failing to provide recognition for student contributions, exploiting students emotionally or financially, sharply criticizing students, publicly humiliating students, stealing from university funds, and plagiarizing others' work (including students') (Clark et al., 2000; Goodyear et al., 1992; Fallow & Johnson, 2000; Johnson & Huwe, 2002). Other mentoring problems include working with a faculty member who lacks technical or relational skills, overinvolvement in students' career decisions, and faculty abandonment due to death or job change (see Johnson & Huwe, 2002).

Faculty Perspective. As with the literature on organizational mentoring, far less has been written about faculty mentors' unique problems with student protégés. Only one such study was found, and it indicated that faculty mentors report that heavy time demands and excessive dependency by students can cause problems in student-faculty mentorships (Busch, 1985). Other potential protégé problems have been noted, including overdependence on the mentor, the need for excessive reassurance and direction, incompetence, unwillingness to learn, and disloyalty (Bruss & Kopala, 1993; Johnson & Huwe, 2002). Protégé impression management, especially if used to gain entry into a mentorship, may also lead to relational problems if the mentor later learns that the protégé does not possess those qualities or is not truly interested in the mentor's research (Johnson & Huwe, 2002).

Clinical Supervisory Relationships

Clinical supervisory relationships occur among individuals in health-related service settings, such as psychological clinics, women's shelters, drug abuse treatment centers, rehabilitation centers, and campus counseling centers. As with the types of mentoring described previously, effective clinical supervisory relationships help supervisees develop both personally and professionally (Powell & Brodsky, 1993).

Supervisee Perspective. Reports of relational problems in clinical supervision are common. Moskowitz and Rupert (1983) found that almost 40% of trainees reported a major conflict with a clinical supervisor. A more recent study of psychiatric supervisees found that 58% reported neglect in training and 50% reported emotional neglect (Kozlowska, Nunn, & Cousens, 1997). Several recent qualitative studies shed light on the specific types of problems experienced by supervisees, including supervisor neglect or disinterest (Culbreth & Borders, 1998; Kozlowska et al., 1997; Magunson, Wilcoxon, & Norem, 2000; Nelson & Friedlander, 2001; Ramos-Sánchez et al., 2002), technical inadequacy (Culbreth & Borders, 1998; Magunson et al., 2000; Nelson & Friedlander, 2001; Ramos-Sánchez et al., 2002), lack of trustworthiness and acceptance (Culbreth & Borders, 1998; Gray, Ladany, Walker, & Ancis, 2001; Magunson et al., 2000; Nelson & Friedlander, 2001), tyrannical behavior, and supervisor politicking (e.g., scapegoating, sabotage) (Kozlowska et al., 1997; Magunson et al., 2000; Nelson & Friedlander, 2001). Other problems discussed by supervisees include having differing worldviews or therapeutic perspectives than their supervisors (Kozlowska et al., 1997; Nelson & Friedlander, 2001; Ramos-Sánchez et al., 2002) and supervisors' failure to provide ongoing support (Culbreth & Borders, 1998; Gray et al., 2001; Ramos-Sánchez et al., 2002).

Some studies have examined correlates of supervisees' reported problems with clinical supervisors. For instance, problems in supervision can damage the working alliance between supervisee and supervisor by weakening supervisee trust, reducing emotional connectedness, decreasing the likelihood of open communication and disclosure, and reducing overall satisfaction with the supervisor (Gray et al., 2001; Kozlowska et al., 1997; Ramos-Sánchez et al., 2002). Supervisees describing problems with their supervisors also often report lower self-efficacy (Gray et al., 2001; Ramos-Sánchez et al., 2002), heightened stress (Kozlowska et al., 1997; Nelson & Friedlander, 2001), less satisfaction with the clinical training experience (Ramos-Sánchez et al., 2002), and reduced career commitment (Ramos-Sánchez et al., 2002). Finally, several studies note that problems in clinical supervision can negatively affect supervisees' relationships with their own clients (Gray et al., 2001; Ramos-Sánchez et al., 2002) and in some cases may be an impetus for changing career fields all together (Nelson & Friedlander, 2001; Ramos-Sánchez et al., 2002; Unger, 1999).

Clinical Supervisor Perspective. There is far less research on clinical supervisors' problems with supervisees. However, the literature on clinical supervision discusses how supervising others' clinical work can be stressful, frustrating, disappointing, and lead to supervisor burnout (Powell & Brodsky, 1993). Transference can also create relational problems, as supervisees may project anxious, ambivalent, and sometimes hostile feelings about their own parents on their supervisors (e.g., view supervisors as overly critical or demanding) (Pearson, 2000). Supervisors may also find supervisees acting in ways that mirror client behavior, for example, being highly dependent, manipulative, or defiant (Pearson, 2000). Another common problem involves difficulty maintaining appropriate boundaries with the supervisee. In some cases, clinical supervision can turn into supervisee therapy, particularly in fields such as substance abuse treatment, where many supervisees are in recovery themselves (Todd & Heath, 1992).

Summary and Integration

The types of mentoring problems reported in these three types of mentoring relationships share some similarities. For example, in all three bodies of scholarship, mentor neglect, mentor-protégé mismatches, mentor skill shortages, and mentor manipulation are noted. Further, problems associated with unmet role expectations and boundary violations are consistently identified. It also appears as if the relational problems experienced in each of the three types of mentoring can be minor, taxing, or serious (see Figure 13.1).

Notwithstanding these similarities, there are unique aspects of these three types of mentoring. One could argue that in both student-faculty and clinical supervisory mentoring, the relational stakes may be higher than in organizational mentoring. Clinical supervisors spend about half of their time providing evaluative feedback, guidance, and coaching to supervisees. They also interact daily with supervisees and play a pivotal role in their professional development (Powell & Brodsky, 1993). In addition, clinical supervisors are typically assigned to supervisees and are responsible for their performance evaluations. This increases supervisors' power base over supervisees. Academic mentors also wield considerable power and influence over student protégés, acting as the gatekeeper for important resources (e.g., assistantships, internships), evaluating their performance, and serving as an important resource for their professional development. Moreover, in many academic institutions, students "sign up" to work with a particular faculty mentor, making it difficult to exit a mentorship if problems arise.

Adding to the potential vulnerability of protégés in clinical supervisory and academic mentoring relationships is the lack of preparation of both clinical supervisors and faculty members for the role of mentor (Austin, 2002; Powell & Brodsky, 1993). This is in contrast to organizational mentors, who often have previous experience managing employees and may have more resources at their disposal to hone their mentoring skills (e.g., financial support for personal development, access to relevant training). Further, in organizational settings, individuals rarely enter mentoring relationships completely against their will (Allen, Eby, & Lentz, 2006); this contrasts with clinical supervision and academia, where individuals are expected to mentor individuals as part of their formal role requirements.

An Investment Model of Mentoring Relationships

Up to this point, the discussion has focused on defining relational problems and reviewing the extant literature from various scholarly perspectives. The next logical step is to develop a conceptual model that places relational problems in the context of the mentoring relationship as a whole. In developing such a model, it is important to remember that relational problems do not exist in a vacuum. Like other types of relationships, mentorships are likely to be marked by both positive experiences and relational problems (Eby et al., 2004). For example, consider how relationships with friends, spouses, lovers, and family members (e.g., parent-child, sibling-sibling) can be fulfilling, enriching, and supportive yet also disappointing, conflict laden, and emotionally draining (Wood & Duck, 1995). Therefore, it is important not to artificially dichotomize a mentoring relationship as "good" or "bad," since this is an oversimplification; while most mentoring experiences are probably positive, over the course of the relationship, there are likely to be conflicts, disappointments, unmet expectations, and perhaps even acts of perceived betrayal or sabotage. In this section, I use an established theory of close relationships to understand how relational problems and positive relational experiences jointly determine one's satisfaction in the mentoring relationship and how relationship satisfaction, along with several other key relational variables, influences the stability of the mentoring relationship.

Broadening our view of mentoring to simultaneously consider relational problems and positive experiences has several advantages. First, it provides a more comprehensive perspective on mentoring. It acknowledges that a powerful yet aloof mentor may provide a protégé with outstanding exposure and visibility yet seem uninterested in spending time talking to the protégé about his or her professional development. Or a likeable yet mediocre-performing protégé may provide a mentor with companionship and loyalty yet be a source of frustration by not living up to the mentor's expectations. Second, this perspective helps us understand why individuals may stay in mentoring relationships even though they report relational problems or why even in the face of relational problems, some mentors and protégés may still report that their relationships are satisfying. Finally, such a perspective leads to more realistic view of mentoring. This is important, since mentoring is not a career cure-all or panacea; assuming so creates unrealistic expectations for both mentors and protégés (e.g., Eby et al., 2004; Kram, 1985), which may lead to negative outcomes for both individuals (e.g., less favorable work attitudes) and organizations (e.g., higher intentions to turnover, reduced work effort).

Theoretical Overview

One of the most widely studied and well-supported theories of close relationships is Rusbult's investment model (Rusbult, 1980a, 1980b, 1983). It is derived from interdependence theory, which suggests that the interaction between individuals is the essential component of all close relationships (Thibaut & Kelly, 1978). Interaction involves the exchange of tangible resources (e.g., instrumental support such as reviewing a résumé or coaching a protégé through a presentation, helping a mentor solve a complicated technical problem) and intangible resources (e.g., emotional support, such as providing encouragement or praise), both of which yield relational benefits. However, relational interactions also create costs. Tangible costs include relational interactions that require time, physical energy, and other personal resources (e.g., going to lunch, sharing personal experiences), whereas intangible costs include psychological and emotional energy expended on the relationship (e.g., worrying about a problem experienced by a protégé) as well as frustration or relational friction associated with mentor-protégé exchanges (e.g., difficulty interacting, real or perceived acts of sabotage or betrayal). According to interdependence theory, the cost-benefit ratio associated with a relationship is a key driver of relationship satisfaction. Furthermore, accumulated relational benefits increase one's dependence on the relationship, whereas relational costs decrease dependence.

Rusbult (1980a, 1980b, 1983) extended interdependence theory by noting that the magnitude and importance of resources associated with the relationship (i.e., relationship investments) also predict relationship dependence (Rusbult, Martz, & Agnew, 1998). For example, an individual invests time, emotional energy, and other resources in a relationship that cannot be recovered if the relationship dissolves. For instance, the time a mentor spends coaching a protégé cannot be regained when the relationship ends. In effect, the act of investing in the relationship increases the costs associated with leaving. Rusbult further explains that the more individuals believe that others outside the relationship are able to meet their needs, the less dependent they are on the relationship. If few alternatives exist or the quality of those alternatives is low, individuals may remain dependent on the current relationship. Taken together, this provides an elegantly simple explanation for why individuals sometimes stay in relationships with heavy costs. For example, some benefits (e.g., companionship, financial stability), coupled with investments (e.g., children, shared assets) and few alternatives (e.g., no alternative means of financial support) predict abused wives' decisions to remain with their abusers (Rusbult & Martz, 1995). A final extension of interdependence theory is the suggestion that relational dependence is reflected in feelings of relationship commitment, which, in turn, predicts the stability or longevity of the relationship.

Application of the Investment Model to Mentoring Relationships

The investment model is ideally suited for understanding mentoring since it includes both the positive (i.e., benefits) and the negative (i.e., costs) aspects of a relationship and links these exchanges to relational processes and outcomes. The conceptual model presented in Figure 13.2 maps investment model predictions on to mentoring relationships. The general pattern of relationships depicted in Figure 13.2 is supported in studies of adult friendships (e.g., Rusbult, 1980b), adult heterosexual dating relationships and marriages (e.g., Rusbult, 1980a, 1983; Rusbult, Johnson, & Morrow, 1986), and gay and lesbian relationships (e.g., Duffy & Rusbult, 1986). The investment model is also supported in longitudinal studies of relational commitment (e.g., Bui, Peplau, & Hill, 1996) and is generalizable across cultures (Lin & Rusbult, 1995; Van Lange et al., 1997).

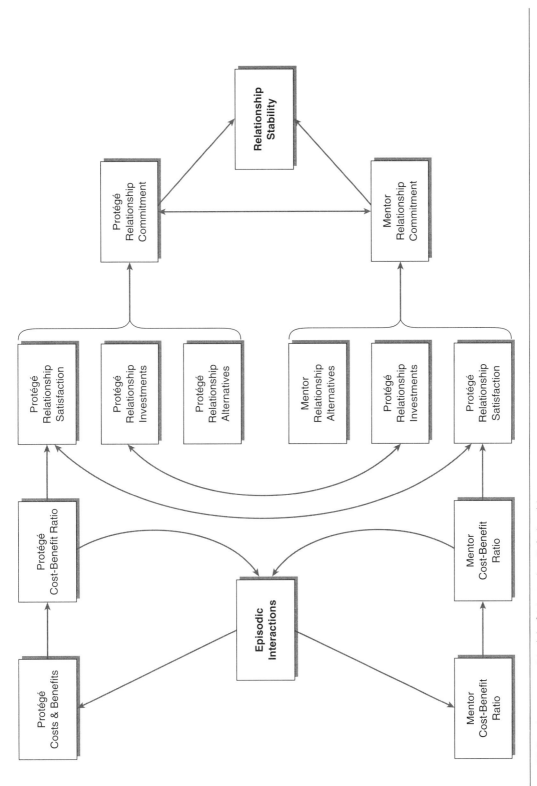

Figure 13.2   Investment Model of Mentoring Relationships

Before describing the specific elements in Figure 13.2, a few issues should be noted. First, the model depicts parallel relationships among conceptual variables for protégés and mentors alike. For example, the perceived cost-benefit ratio associated with the mentoring relationship leads to relationship satisfaction for protégés as well as mentors. Second, there are crossover effects that reflect dyadic interactions. For instance, a protégé's perceptions of the cost-benefit ratio associated with the mentorship influences subsequent episodic interactions with the mentor, which, in turn, affect the costs and benefits experienced by the mentor. Third, the proposed framework is limited to explicating the process and outcomes associated with relational exchanges, not identifying the predictors of such exchanges (see Fletcher & Ragins, Chapter 15, this volume; Ragins & Verbos, 2007). Finally, no moderators are depicted in Figure 13.2, for the sake of parsimony. However, since such effects are likely, several potential moderators are discussed in the final section of this chapter.

While Figure 13.2 is based on Rusbult's (1980a, 1980b, 1983) investment model, there are several extensions to her original model. Most notably, Rusbult's model did not simultaneously consider both partners' perspectives. Rather, it focused on one individual's perception of the relationship. The model shown in Figure 13.2 recognizes that both the protégé's and mentor's perspectives are important to consider, which is consistent with emerging research on mentoring (Allen, Chapter 5, this volume; Eby, Durley, et al., 2006; Fletcher & Ragins, Chapter 15, this volume; Ragins & Verbos, 2007). Moreover, the model in Figure 13.2 extends Rusbult's work by including crossover effects between relational partners and including the construct of episodic interactions to illustrate how perceptions of the cost-benefit ratio of the relationship influence future interactions. These expansions of Rusbult's original model provide a more comprehensive treatment of the relational dynamics that occur in mentoring relationships, while emphasizing the importance of relational costs and benefits as drivers of subsequent processes and outcomes.

Definitional Issues. The *costs* associated with the relationship include the relational problems experienced in the mentorship. These costs are experienced by each individual and can run the gamut from minor relational problems to serious relational problems (see Figure 13.1). The *benefits* associated with the relationship include the positive relational experiences as reported by the mentor or the protégé. For protégés, this includes specific positive experiences associated with the broad categories of career-related (e.g., coaching, exposure, and visibility) and psychosocial (e.g., friendship, counseling) support (e.g., Kram, 1985; Ragins & McFarlin, 1990). For mentors, the benefits include personal satisfaction, organizational recognition, the development of a base of support within the organization from developing relationships with protégés, and technical support (see Allen, Chapter 5, this volume).

The accumulated costs and benefits determine the perceived *cost-benefit ratio* associated with the relationship at a whole. If one individual believes that the overall mentoring benefits outweigh the costs, the relationship has a positive valence. In contrast, if one believes that the costs outweigh the benefits, the relationship has a negative valence. As such, the perceived cost-benefit ratio exists on a continuum and is a dynamic property of the mentorship; with the passage of time, benefits (costs) can accrue and change the cost-benefit ratio (Rusbult, 1983). Conceptualizing the mentoring relationship in terms of its cost-benefit ratio moves the level of analysis from the specific relational event or episode (the focus earlier in this chapter) to the mentoring relationship in its totality.

Other key variables in Figure 13.2 include relationship satisfaction, relationship investments, relationship alternatives, relationship commitment, and relationship stability. *Relationship satisfaction* refers to affective reactions to the mentoring relationship. *Relationship investments* refer to the extent of time, physical energy, and other resources (e.g., money, psychological energy) invested in the relationship. *Relationship alternatives* include other individuals who could fulfill the role of mentor or protégé as well as other sources of developmental support in one's network (Higgins & Kram, 2001). Finally, *relationship stability* refers to the durability or longevity of the relationship.

Proposed Pathways. As shown in Figure 13.2, the costs (relational problems) and benefits (positive experiences) associated with a mentoring relationship determine the perceived cost-benefit ratio of the mentoring relationship. Both protégés and mentors develop cost-benefit-ratio perceptions based on their positive and negative experiences in the relationship. This overall cost-benefit perception influences both subsequent episodic interactions and relationship satisfaction. In terms of the former, one's action toward a partner will be influenced by perceptions of the cost-benefit ratio. For example, if the costs of the relationship are viewed as greatly outweighing the benefits for Person 1, this person may withhold assistance, retaliate passively or actively, or disengage psychologically or behaviorally from the other person. These actions by Person 1 toward Person 2 would subsequently heighten Person 2's perception of relational costs and ultimately influence this person's perception of the cost-benefit ratio. With this series of events set in motion, Person 2 might engage in an episodic interaction with Person 1 that is viewed negatively by that person and incurs additional relational costs that influence his or her perceived cost-benefit ratio. In effect, the actions of Person 1 and Person 2 toward one another create an interpersonal process that is dynamic and mutually reinforcing or punishing (see left side of Figure 13.2).

This dynamic process of costs, benefits, and episodic interactions fuels each person's satisfaction with the relationship. Consistent with research on other types of close relationships, it is expected that relationship satisfaction along with relationship investments and relationship alternatives lead to relationship commitment (Rusbult, 1980a, 1980b, 1983; Rusbult & Martz, 1995). Figure 13.2 also introduces crossover effects, whereby one partner's relationship satisfaction is reciprocally related to the other's relationship satisfaction. This is consistent with the idea of "growth-fostering interactions" (Fletcher & Ragins, Chapter 15, this volume), in which repeated positive interactions between mentor and protégé fuel a mutually satisfying, high-quality mentoring relationship. The model in Figure 13.2 takes this a step further by illustrating that repeated negative interactions may create a mutually dissatisfying, low-quality mentoring relationship.

Reciprocal relationships are also expected with relationship investments; as one partner reports greater (or lesser) investments, so too should the other partner

(Huston & Burgess, 1979). This is because many investments in the mentoring relationship are marked by mutuality; both individuals are investing in the relationship when meeting together, sharing ideas, learning, interacting with each other, and so on. In contrast, no crossover effects are expected with relationship alternatives. The availability of relationship alternatives for one person is not dependent on the other person's relationship alternatives. For instance, a mentor may not have many other protégés to choose from if the current relationship were to terminate, whereas a protégé may have many other sources of developmental support available.

The final pathways in Figure 13.2 are associated with relationship commitment. Perceived commitment to the mentorship by both the protégé and the mentor jointly and uniquely influence the stability of the mentoring relationship. As each individual's commitment to the relationship increases, so will the likelihood that the relationship will continue. This is in line with empirical tests of the investment model (e.g., Rusbult, 1983; Rusbult & Martz, 1995). Moreover, crossover effects are expected for relationship commitment such that as a mentor's perceived commitment to the relationship increases, so too will protégé's perceived commitment to the relationship. This is consistent with the notion of reciprocity and mutuality in close relationships (Huston & Burgess, 1979).

Agenda for Future Research

The model presented in Figure 13.2 provides a starting place for future research on mentoring problems yet raises many new questions. In this final section, an agenda for future research is presented that builds on the ideas presented in Figure 13.2. Table 13.1 summarizes these ideas.

Accumulation and Weighting of Relational Costs and Benefits

A core component of the proposed model involves the dyadic dynamic processes associated with relationship costs and relationship benefits. This raises several important issues for future research. One is the accumulation and weighting of relational costs and benefits. Given the continuum of problems depicted in Figure 13.1, it seems likely that more-serious relational problems are weighted more heavily than minor relational problems in determining the overall cost-benefit ratio of the relationship. In fact, minor problems might accrue indefinitely and have minimal impact on the overall cost-benefit ratio, whereas all it might take is one serious relational problem (e.g., one real or perceived act of sabotage) for an individual to change his or her perception of the cost-benefit ratio. There is also some evidence that "bad" events carry more weight than "good" events in everyday life, as well as in close relationships (see Baumeister, Bratslavsky, Finkenauer, & Vohs, 2001). If so, it may not be appropriate to equally weigh "costs" and "benefits" when determining the overall cost-benefit ratio of a mentoring relationship. Likewise, the relationship between costs and benefits and the subsequent cost-benefit ratio may be nonlinear. Perhaps there are relationship "tipping points" at which one (perhaps minor) event is the "straw that broke

Table 13.1   Topics for Future Research

1. Accumulation and Weighting of Relational Costs and Benefits
   - How do perceived costs and benefits accrue over time in mentoring relationships?
   - How are perceived costs and benefits weighted in determining the overall cost-benefit ratio of a mentoring relationship?
   - Are perceived costs weighed more heavily than perceived benefits in determining the overall cost-benefit ratio of a mentoring relationship?
   - Are there common relationship "tipping points" and, if so, what are they?

2. Expand Criterion Space
   - Is the perceived cost-benefit ratio *directly* related to career, job, and work outcomes for the protégé?
   - Is the perceived cost-benefit ratio *indirectly* related to career, job, and work outcomes for the protégé?
   - Is the perceived cost-benefit ratio *directly* related to career, job, and work outcomes for the mentor?
   - Is the perceived cost-benefit ratio *indirectly* related to career, job, and work outcomes for the mentor?
   - Can "high cost" mentoring relationships lead to individual growth in the long haul? If so, under what conditions?

3. Examine Moderator Variables
   - How does phase of the mentoring relationship influence the relationships depicted in Figure 13.2?
   - How does relationship initiation influence the relationships depicted in Figure 13.2?
   - How do the quantity and quality of previous mentoring experiences influence the relationships depicted in Figure 13.2?

the camel's back" and forever alters the mentoring relationship. This is consistent with Duck's (1992) analogy of a wave in discussing how negative relational events can accumulate in a nonlinear manner and lead to abrupt relationship decline.

Expand Criterion Space

Another area for future research involves expanding the criteria examined in relation to perceived relationship costs and benefits. While Figure 13.2 focuses on relationship outcomes, it is reasonable to expect that cost-benefit assessments may also directly or indirectly influence other outcomes. This follows from research linking protégés' reactions to, and experiences in, mentoring relationships with career outcomes, job attitudes, and work outcomes (see Allen et al., 2004). While less extensive, there is also some literature linking mentors' mentoring experiences to similar outcomes (see Allen, Chapter 5, this volume). It is also recommended that researchers examine the possibility that mentoring relationships that are viewed by mentors or protégés as "high cost" may be viewed later on as positive growth experiences. This would follow from research that finds that individual learning can occur following major life crises, such as divorce, physical illness, and job loss (Latack & Dozier, 1986; Schaefer & Moos, 1992).

Examine Moderator Variables

A final next step for future research is to examine possible moderator variables that may be operating in Figure 13.2. While there are many possibilities, three variables are discussed here: relationship phase, relationship initiation, and previous mentoring experience. Phase of the mentoring relationship may be important to consider, since with the passage of time, the relationship changes, as do the potential relationship benefits and costs (Rusbult, 1983; Kram, 1985). As such, some of the associations depicted in Figure 13.2 may vary by *relationship phase*. For example, the perceived cost-benefit ratio may have a particularly strong effect on relationship satisfaction early in the relationship, since during this time, individuals may be more likely to use social exchange norms to evaluate relationship quality (Levinger, 1979). Later in the relationship, individuals are more likely to develop mutual goals and have repeated and sustained interactions (Huston & Burgess, 1979), both of which may reduce the importance of cost-benefit "scorekeeping" as a predictor of episodic interactions or relationship satisfaction.

Relationship initiation can influence subsequent relational processes as well as relationship outcomes (Chao, Walz, & Gardner, 1997; Eby et al., 2004; Ragins & Cotton, 1999), suggesting it may also be important to consider as a moderator variable. For example, individuals in informal mentoring relationship come together spontaneously based on mutual attraction and liking (Ragins & Cotton, 1999). If informal relationships are marked by more interpersonal chemistry, liking, and closeness, the relationship may more resilient to the potentially negative effects of relational problems. Likewise, the relational processes that brought the mentor and protégé together in informal relationships may make the links between relationship commitment and relationship stability stronger for those in informal, compared with formal, mentoring relationships.

A final potential moderator variable is the *previous experience* of the mentor and protégé in mentoring relationships. Individuals enter into relationships with both general and specific expectations that are shaped by their previous relational experiences (Planalp, 1985, 1987). In the context of mentoring relationships, these are referred to as "mentoring schemas" (Ragins & Verbos, 2007, p. 101), cognitive scripts that guide individual behavior in mentoring relationships. Since direct experience influences mentoring schemas (Ragins & Verbos, 2007), it stands to reason that previous experience as a mentor and/or as a protégé may influence some of the associations depicted in Figure 13.2. For instance, individuals who have substantial experience in mentoring relationships (as mentors or as protégés) may have an easier time "weathering the storm" if the relationship runs into trouble than those with little or no previous mentoring experience. This is consistent with the finding that those with more previous experience in mentoring relationships anticipate fewer costs and greater benefits in subsequent mentoring relationships (Ragins & Scandura, 1999). The nature of previous mentoring experiences may also be important to consider, as this can color one's interpretation of relational events. Consider two protégés, one with previous experience with a dictatorial, neglectful mentor and the other with previous experience with an altruistic, committed mentor. These two protégés may evaluate specific relational experiences with a new mentor very differently, based on their previous experience.

Conclusion

The emerging literature on relational problems provides a unique perspective on mentoring relationships. We are beginning to understand the different manifestations of mentoring problems and, in some cases, their associated outcomes. In this chapter, it is argued that relational problems exist on a continuum of severity (see Figure 13.1) and that to understand the processes and outcomes of mentoring relationships, it is important to consider both positive experiences and relational problems (see Figure 13.2). Much work is yet to be done to fully understand the "ups and downs" of mentoring relationships, and it is hoped that this chapter sparks future research on the problems in mentoring relationships and expands scholars' thinking on the benefits and drawbacks of these important developmental relationships.

References

Allen, T. D., Eby, L. T., & Lentz, E. (2006). The relationship between formal mentoring program characteristics and perceived program effectiveness. *Personnel Psychology, 59,* 125–153.

Allen, T. D., Eby, L. T., Poteet, M. L., Lentz, E., & Lima, L. (2004). Career benefits associated with mentoring for protégés: A meta-analysis. *Journal of Applied Psychology, 89,* 127–136.

Allen, T. D., Poteet, M. L., & Burroughs, S. M. (1997). The mentor's perspective: A qualitative inquiry. *Journal of Vocational Behavior, 51,* 70–89.

Allen, T. D., Poteet, M. L., & Russell, J. E. A. (2000). Protégé selection by mentors: What makes the difference? *Journal of Organizational Behavior, 21,* 271–282.

Austin, A. E. (2002). Preparing the next generation of faculty. *Journal of Higher Education, 73,* 94–122.

Baumeister, R. F., Bratslavsky, E., Finkenauer, C., & Vohs, K. D. (2001). Bad is stronger than good. *Review of General Psychology, 5,* 323–370.

Bruss, K. V., & Kopala, M. (1993). Graduate school training in psychology: Its impact upon the professional development of identity. *Psychotherapy: Theory, research, practice, training, 30,* 685–691.

Bui, K. T., Peplau, L. A., & Hill, C. T. (1996). Testing the Rusbult model of relationship commitment and stability in a 15-year study of heterosexual couples. *Personality and Social Psychology Bulletin, 22,* 1244–1257.

Busch, J. W. (1985). Mentoring in graduate schools of education: Mentors' perceptions. *American Educational Research Journal, 22,* 257–265.

Chao, G. T., Walz, P. M., & Gardner, P. D. (1992). Formal and informal mentorships: A comparison on mentoring functions and contrast with nonmentored counterparts. *Personnel Psychology, 45,* 619–636.

Clark, R. A., Harden, S. L., & Johnson, W. B. (2000). Mentor relationships in clinical psychology doctoral training: Results of a national survey. *Teaching of Psychology, 27,* 262–268.

Culbreth, J. R., & Borders, L. D. (1998). Perceptions of the supervisory relationship. *Journal of Substance Abuse Treatment, 15,* 345–352.

Duck, S. (1992). The role of theory in the examination of relationship loss. In. T. L. Orbuch (Ed.), *Close relationship loss: Theoretical approaches* (pp. 3–27). New York: Springer-Verlag.

Duck, S. (1994). Stratagems, spoils, and a serpent's tooth: On the delights and dilemmas of personal relationships. In W. R. Cupach & B. H. Spitzberg (Eds.), *The dark side of interpersonal relationships* (pp. 3–24). Hillsdale, NJ: Lawrence Erlbaum.

Duffy, S., & Rusbult, C. E. (1986). Satisfaction and commitment in homosexual and heterosexual relationships. *Journal of Homosexuality, 12,* 1–23.

Eby, L. T., & Allen, T. D. (2002). Further investigation of protégés' negative mentoring experiences: Patterns and outcomes. *Group & Organization Management, 27,* 456–479.

Eby, L. T., Butts, M. M., Lockwood, A., & Simon, S. A. (2004). Protégés' negative mentoring experiences: Construct development and nomological validation. *Personnel Psychology, 57,* 411–447.

Eby, L. T., Durley, J. R., Evans, S. C., & Ragins, B. R. (2006). The relationship between short-term mentoring benefits and long-term mentor outcomes. *Journal of Vocational Behavior, 69,* 424–444.

Eby, L. T., & Lockwood, A. (2005). Protégés' and mentors' reactions to participating in a formal mentoring program: A qualitative inquiry. *Journal of Vocational Behavior, 67,* 441–458.

Eby, L. T., Lockwood, A., & Butts, M. M. (2006). Perceived support for mentoring: A multiple perspectives approach. *Journal of Vocational Behavior, 68,* 267–291.

Eby, L. T., & McManus, S. E. (2004). The protégé's role in negative mentoring experiences. *Journal of Vocational Behavior, 65,* 255–275.

Eby, L. T., McManus, S. E., Simon, S. A., & Russell, J. E. A. (2000). The protégé's perspective regarding negative mentoring experiences: The development of a taxonomy. *Journal of Vocational Behavior, 57,* 1–21.

Ellis, H. C. (1992). Graduate education in psychology: Past, present, and future. *American Psychologist, 47,* 570–576.

Fallow, G. O., & Johnson, W. B. (2000). Mentor relationships in secular and religious professional psychology programs. *Journal of Psychology and Christianity, 19,* 363–376.

Feldman, D. C. (1999). Toxic mentors or toxic protégés? A critical re-examination of dysfunctional mentoring. *Human Resource Management Review, 9,* 247–278.

Goodyear, R. K., Crego, C. A., & Johnston, M. W. (1992). Ethical issues in the supervision of student research: A study of critical incidents. *Professional Psychology: Research and Practice, 23,* 203–210.

Gray, L. A., Ladany, N., Walker, J. A., & Ancis, J. R. (2001). Psychotherapy trainees' experience of counterproductive events in supervision. *Journal of Counseling Psychology, 48,* 371–383.

Higgins, M. C., & Kram, K. E. (2001). Reconceptualizing mentoring at work: A developmental network perspective. *Academy of Management Review, 26,* 264–268.

Hunt, D. M., & Michael, C. (1983). Mentorship: A career training and development tool. *Academy of Management Review, 8,* 475–485.

Huston, T. L., & Burgess, R. L. (1979). Social exchange in developing relationships: An overview. In T. L. Huston & R. L. Burgess (Eds.), *Social exchanges in developing relationships* (pp. 3–28). New York: Academic Press.

Jacobi, M. (1991). Mentoring and undergraduate academic success: A review of the literature. *Review of Educational Research, 61,* 505–532.

Johnson, W. B. (2003). A framework for conceptualizing competence to mentor. *Ethics and Behavior, 13,* 127–151.

Johnson, W. B. (2007). The benefits associated with student-faculty mentoring relationships. In T. D. Allen & L. T. Eby (Eds.), *Blackwell handbook of mentoring: A multiple perspectives approach* (pp. 211–231). Malden, MA: Blackwell.

Johnson, W. B., & Huwe, J. M. (2002). Toward a typology of mentorship dysfunction in graduate school. *Psychotherapy: Theory, Research, Practice Training, 39,* 44–55.

Kalbfleisch, P. J. (1997). Appeasing the mentor. *Aggressive Behavior, 23,* 389–403.

Kozlowska, K., Nunn, K., & Cousens, P. (1997). Adverse experiences in psychiatric training: Part 2. *Australian and New Zealand Journal of Psychiatry, 31,* 641–652.

Kram, K. E. (1985). *Mentoring at work.* Glenview, IL: Scott, Foresman.

Latack, J. C., & Dozier, J. B. (1986). After the ax falls: Job loss as career growth. *Academy of Management Review, 11,* 375–392.

Levinger, G. (1979). A social exchange view on the dissolution of pair relationships. In R. L. Burgess & T. L. Huston (Eds.), *Social exchanges developing relationships* (pp. 169–196). New York: Academic Press.

Levinson, D. J. (with Darrow, D., Levinson, M., Klein, E. B., & McKee, B.). (1978). *Seasons of a man's life.* New York: Academic Press.

Lin, Y. H., & Rusbult, C. E. (1995). Commitment to dating relationships and cross-sex friendships in America and China: The impact of centrality of relationship, normative support, and investment model variables. *Journal of Social and Personal Relationships, 12,* 7–26.

Magnuson, S., Wilcoxon, S. A., & Norem, K. (2000). A profile of lousy supervision: Experienced counselors' perspectives. *Counselor Education and Supervision, 39,* 189–202.

Moskowitz, S. A., & Rupert, P. A. (1983). Conflict resolution within the supervisory relationship. *Professional Psychology: Research and Practice, 14,* 632–641.

Nelson, M. L., & Friedlander, M. L. (2001). A close look at conflictual supervisory relationships: The trainees' perspective. *Journal of Counseling Psychology, 48,* 384–395.

Olian, J. D., Caroll, S. J., & Giannantonio, C. M. (1993). Mentor reactions to protégés: An experiment with managers. *Journal of Vocational Behavior, 43,* 266–278.

Pearson, Q. M. (2000). Opportunities and challenges in the supervisory relationship: Implications for counselor supervision. *Journal of Mental Health Counseling, 22,* 283–294.

Planalp, S. (1985). Relational schemas: A test of alternative forms of relational knowledge as guides to communication. *Human Communication Research, 12,* 3–29.

Planalp, S. (1987). Interplay between relational knowledge and events. In R. Burnett, P. McGhee, & D. Clark (Eds.), *Accounting for relationships: Explanations, representation, and knowledge* (pp. 175–191). New York: Metheun.

Powell, D. J., & Brodsky, A. (1993). *Clinical supervision in alcohol and drug abuse counseling: Principles, models, methods.* New York: Lexington/Macmillian.

Ragins, B. R., & Cotton, J. L. (1999). Mentor functions and outcomes: A comparison of men and women in formal and informal mentoring relationships. *Journal of Applied Psychology, 84,* 529–550.

Ragins, B. R., Cotton, J. L., & Miller, J. S. (2000). Marginal mentoring: The effects of type of mentor, quality of relationship, and program design on work and career attitudes. *Academy of Management Journal, 43,* 1177–1194.

Ragins, B. R., & McFarlin, D. B. (1990). Perceptions of mentor roles in cross-gender mentoring relationships. *Journal of Vocational Behavior, 37,* 321–339.

Ragins, B. R., & Scandura, T. A. (1997). The way we were: Gender and the termination of mentoring relationships. *Journal of Applied Psychology, 82,* 945–953.

Ragins, B. R., & Scandura, T. A. (1999). Burden or blessing: Expected costs and benefits of being a mentor. *Journal of Organizational Behavior, 20,* 493–509.

Ragins, B. R., & Verbos, A. K. (2007). Positive relationships in action: Relational mentoring and mentoring schemas in the workplace. In. J. E. Dutton & B. R. Ragins (Eds.), *Exploring positive relationships at work: Building a theoretical and research foundation* (pp. 91–116). Mahwah, NJ: Lawrence Erlbaum.

Ramos-Sánchez, L., Esnil, E., Goodwin, A., Riggs, S., Touster, L. O., Wright, L. K., et al. (2002). Negative supervisory events: Effects on supervision satisfaction and supervisory alliance. *Professional Psychology: Research and Practice, 33,* 197–202.

Rusbult, C. E. (1980a). Commitment and satisfaction in romantic associations: A test of the investment model. *Journal of Experimental Social Psychology, 16,* 172–186.

Rusbult, C. E. (1980b). Satisfaction and commitment in friendships. *Representative Research in Social Psychology, 11,* 96–105.

Rusbult, C. E. (1983). A longitudinal test of the investment model: The development (and deterioration) of satisfaction and commitment in heterosexual involvements. *Journal of Personality and Social Psychology, 45,* 101–117.

Rusbult, C. E., Johnson, D. J., & Morrow, G. D. (1986). Predicting satisfaction and commitment in adult romantic involvements: As assessment of the generalizability of the investment model. *Social Psychology Quarterly, 49,* 81–89.

Rusbult, C. E., & Martz, J. M. (1995). Remaining in an abusive relationship: An investment model analysis of nonvoluntary dependence. *Personality and Social Psychology Bulletin, 21,* 558–571.

Rusbult, C. E., Martz, J. M., & Agnew, C. R. (1998). The investment model scale: Measuring commitment level, satisfaction level, quality of alternatives, and investment size. *Personal Relationships, 5,* 357–391.

Scandura, T. A. (1998). Dysfunctional mentoring relationships and outcomes. *Journal of Management, 24,* 449–467.

Schaefer, J. A., & Moos, R. H. (1992). Life crises and personal growth. In B. N. Carpenter (Ed.), *Personal coping: Theory, research, and practice* (pp. 149–170). Westport, CT: Praeger.

Simon, S. A., & Eby, L. T. (2003). A multidimensional scaling study of negative mentoring experiences. *Human Relations, 56,* 1083–1106.

Thibaut, J. W., & Kelley, H. H. (1978). *The social psychology of groups.* New York: John Wiley & Sons.

Todd, T. C., & Heath, A. W. (1992). Supervision of substance abuse counselors. In C. E. Stout, J. L. Levitt, & D. H. Ruben (Eds.), *Handbook for assessing and treating addictive disorders* (pp. 313–323). Westport, CT: Greenwood Press.

Unger, D. (1999, August). *Core problems in clinical supervision: Factors related to outcomes.* Paper presented at symposium, "Psychotherapy Supervision: For Better or for Worse" (M. L. Friedlander, Chair), 107th Annual Meeting of the American Psychological Association, Boston.

Van Lange, P. A., Rusbult, C. E., Drigotas, S. M., Arriaga, X. B., Witcher, B. S., & Cox, C. L. (1997). Willingness to sacrifice in close relationships. *Journal of Personality and Social Psychology, 72,* 1373–1395.

Wood, J. T., & Duck, S. (1995). Off the beaten track: New shores for relationship research. In J. T. Wood & S. Duck (Eds.), *Under-studied relationships: Off the beaten track* (pp. 1–21). Thousand Oaks, CA: Sage.

PART III

Mentoring Theory

Applying New Lenses and Perspectives

Section Purpose and Structure

The goal of this section is to stimulate new theoretical perspectives on mentoring by integrating and applying related theoretical perspectives and disciplines. To achieve this objective, we invited a group of stellar scholars from a variety of disciplines to apply their theoretical lenses to the field of mentoring. The authors were asked to address three objectives in their chapters. First, they were asked to introduce the reader to the theoretical lenses that they have applied to the field of mentoring. Second, they were asked to explain why their theoretical lenses are useful to the field of mentoring and how they can be used for developing and enriching mentoring theory. Toward that end, the authors developed new theoretical models and frameworks and offered specific research propositions. Last, they were asked to identify methodological challenges that may be encountered in empirically testing the new theory and to give recommendations for meeting these challenges.

Overview of Chapters

This section begins with a chapter by Monica Higgins, Dawn Chandler, and Kathy Kram that broadens the horizon of mentoring theory by applying a social network perspective to the mentoring literature. Their chapter first offers an overview of established network structures involving diversity and strength of ties and then introduces developmental initiation as a new dimension of developmental networks. Developmental initiation involves a set of development-seeking behaviors undertaken to enhance knowledge, skills, performance, and/or learning. The authors draw upon the help-seeking, feedback-seeking, and information-seeking literatures to explain how development-seeking behaviors influence the initiation of mentoring relationships and developmental networks. The chapter offers propositions, a research agenda, and a discussion of methodological challenges encountered in applying social network perspectives to the mentoring arena.

Next, Joyce Fletcher and Belle Rose Ragins use a developmental theory of relational interactions, the Stone Center Relational Cultural Theory (RCT), to examine and refine the construct of high-quality relational mentoring. RCT views connection as the primary site of human growth and development and offers the critical perspective that relational processes are nested within the context of gender, diversity, and societal power dynamics. The authors develop an RCT model of relational mentoring that examines the relational skills, conditions, and behaviors that influence mentoring relationships and short-term mentoring interactions or episodes. The chapter offers research propositions and an agenda for future research that promises to enhance our understanding of the antecedents, processes, and outcomes of high-quality mentoring.

Using an adult development theory lens, Eileen McGowan, Eric Stone, and Robert Kegan offer the field of mentoring rich new insight into the role development plays in mentoring relationships. Their chapter uses constructive-developmental theory as a mechanism for examining how developmental cognitive structures affect mentoring relationships. Constructive-developmental theory holds that individuals construct the meaning of their environments and that these meaning-making structures proceed in a predictable, successive sequence throughout adulthood. The authors examine the role that meaning-making structures play in the dynamics of mentoring relationships and potential outcomes for both parties at different stages of adult development. They offer propositions, examine methodological challenges, and propose a research agenda that explores how mentoring relationships may contribute to individuals' developmental progression across the adult life span.

In his chapter, Cary Cherniss examines a key component of effective mentoring relationships that has not been examined in the literature: emotional intelligence. *Emotional intelligence* is defined as the ways in which individuals perceive, express, understand, and manage emotion in themselves and others. The author examines two key themes related to mentoring and emotional intelligence. First, he examines how the emotional intelligence of mentors and protégés affects the quality of their relationships by helping them manage their emotions. Second, he explores how relational quality influences the ability of mentors and protégés to develop their emotional intelligence by enhancing self-awareness, self-regulation, empathy, and social skills. The chapter offers propositions for future research and a model that examines how organizational culture and emotional intelligence influences mentoring behaviors, processes, and outcomes.

Richard Boyatzis offers the field keen insight into how mentoring relationships can support meaningful personal change by applying intentional change theory (ICT) to the mentoring arena. ICT describes the components and process of desirable and sustainable change in individual's behaviors, thoughts, feelings, and perceptions. The author examines the specific role mentors play in helping protégés achieve self-discoveries and the psychophysiological benefits mentors obtain as a result of this process. He explores the role of emotions in the mentoring process and presents the idea of mentoring as a form of compassion and a way to obtain the "ideal self." The chapter poses research questions and identifies challenges for future research on mentoring as an essential element of the personal intentional change process.

Tim Hall and Dawn Chandler apply exciting new perspectives in the career literature to mentoring relationships. Their chapter applies new models of career learning to examine how developmental relationships influence career learning cycles. The authors explain that careers are made up of a series of short learning cycles that involve exploration, learning, and experimentation. Their chapter offers a model of relationally driven career learning that examines the types and qualities of developmental relationships that trigger, facilitate, or hinder task and personal learning as individuals progress through career learning cycles. The chapter presents propositions that guide future research on how career cycles influence mentoring, developmental relationships, and individual learning and development.

Next, Pamela Kalbfleisch offers a cross-disciplinary perspective on mentoring by applying theoretical perspectives from the communication and interpersonal relationship fields to the mentoring arena. Her chapter presents and applies mentoring enactment theory, which proposes that individuals use strategic and routine communication strategies to initiate, develop, maintain, and repair their mentoring relationships. The author examines the role of personal filters and relational life cycles in the communication process and offers propositions that explore how relationship variables affect communication requests at various points in mentoring relationships. The chapter systematically examines several predictable communication challenges in mentoring relationships and offers guidelines for future research on how communication processes influence the initiation of relationships, as well as their maintenance and repair over time.

In the last chapter of this section, Jeffrey Greenhaus and Romila Singh break important new ground by applying a work-family perspective to the study of mentoring relationships. Their chapter offers a comprehensive model that explains how mentors may help or hinder their protégés' attempts to achieve work-family balance. The authors propose that mentors hold a work-family lens, a type of mentoring schema that influences the career and psychosocial functions provided to protégés. These functions, in turn, affect the protégé's work-related demands and resources and his or her subsequent experience of work-family conflict or work-family enrichment. The authors' model examines the antecedents to the work-family lens and explores how contextual and individual factors moderate the enactment of the lens and the relationship between lens enactment and work-family outcomes. The chapter offers specific propositions and directions for future research on the role of mentoring in work-family outcomes, involving areas such as balance, stress, satisfaction, performance, and well-being.

By applying and integrating theories from related fields to mentoring, this section offers mentoring scholars important new theoretical models that help to explain how, why, and under what conditions the potential of developmental relationships may be realized. Most important, these authors help us to think outside the current landscape of mentoring theory and plant new seeds that promise to enhance our efforts to tend the garden of mentoring in the future.

14

Developmental Initiation and Developmental Networks

Monica C. Higgins

Dawn E. Chandler

Kathy E. Kram

This chapter's dual purposes are to illuminate the value of utilizing a social network perspective to examine mentoring and to extend a theoretical application of network theory by introducing a new dimension to our understanding of "developmental networks": *developmental initiation.*

Since Higgins and Kram's (2001) application of a network lens to mentoring, research on "developmental networks" has begun to proliferate (e.g., Chandler & Kram, 2005; Dobrow & Higgins, 2005; Molloy, 2005). In that article, a developmental network perspective was introduced and compared with traditional conceptualizations of mentoring, and two dimensions from social network research were employed to aid in the description of possible developmental network structures: *diversity,* which refers to the range of sources from which individuals receive developmental help, and *strength of ties,* which refers to emotional closeness and frequency of communication.

Here, we identify a third dimension that is relevant to the application of a social network perspective to developmental networks: developmental initiation. We define *developmental initiation* as "a set of development-seeking behaviors undertaken by a focal individual that are intended to enhance his or her skills, knowledge, task performance, and/or personal learning." Although developmental initiation is not necessarily linked to developmental relationship formation, more frequent development-seeking behaviors are likely to lead to situations in which developmental relationships begin. In the mentoring and social network literatures, relationship formation is a relatively unexplored phenomenon (Kram, 1985; McGowan, 2004; Mullen, 1994; Scandura & Williams, 1998, 2001). The concept of developmental initiation is offered to begin to fill this literature gap as it relates to mentoring.

The chapter begins with a brief tour of a social network perspective and its relevance to the mentoring literature. Next, we explain the conceptual shift in the mentoring literature from a focus on the relationship between a senior mentor and junior protégé to an emphasis on multiple relationships within a developmental network. We elaborate on the current state of the mentoring literature to highlight how the research in this domain has made a general shift toward examination of developmental networks rather than single, hierarchical mentoring relationships. Recently, researchers and practitioners have become increasingly interested in the individual and organizational factors that result in developmental networks, that is, in sets of relationships that may include much more than a senior person in an individual's place of employment (e.g., peers, subordinates, customers, family, and community members). Further, researchers have begun to examine how such developmental network structures are likely to foster individual performance and professional growth and development (e.g., Dobrow & Higgins, 2005; Higgins & Thomas, 2001).

We then review some studies that offer insight into developmental relationship initiation and then introduce the notion of developmental initiation as a way to further understand how these career-enhancing relationships are cultivated. We draw upon the help-seeking, feedback-seeking, and information-seeking literatures to help explain development-seeking behaviors that influence the relationship origination. We develop four propositions relating demographic antecedents—age, socioeconomic status (SES), gender, and nationality—to developmental initiation and another developmental network dimension, diversity, which has been studied by mentoring scholars in the past (e.g., Dobrow & Higgins, 2005; Higgins, 2001). Consistent with social network research, we define developmental network diversity as the range of sources from which individuals receive help (e.g., professional association, employer, family).

The chapter ends with a future research agenda on developmental networks and developmental initiation and includes a discussion of methodological challenges researchers may face when using social network methods to develop valid insights, theory, and practical applications for the study of mentoring.

Incorporating a Social Network Perspective

Studies on social networks highlight that individual action is embedded within a social context (e.g., Granovetter, 1973, 1983; see also Brass, Galaskiewicz, Greve, & Tsai, 2004). In contrast to economic models that suggest that individual decisions and actions occur in the isolation of the environment, a social network perspective illuminates that an individual's network of relationships provide opportunities and constraints for behavior (e.g., Brass et al., 2004; Burt, 1992). A quarter century of network research—which includes studies at the interpersonal, intraorganizational, and interorganizational levels—has resulted in an impressive body of literature on the antecedents and consequences of social networks (for a recent review of the network literature, see Brass et al., 2004).

An evolution of mentoring toward a network perspective can be roughly traced to research in the 1990s and the turn of the millennium, as scholars began to explore the nature and consequences on career growth and personal learning of having *multiple mentors*. This work built directly upon Kathy Kram's (1985) original assertion that individuals have "constellations" of mentors in their careers. Recent research has begun to examine multiple concurrent relationships (e.g., Baugh & Scandura, 1999; Higgins, 2000, 2001; Higgins & Thomas, 2001; Kram & Hall, 1996; Thomas, 1990) and has been strongly influenced by two factors: first, the recognition of a reality that existed since mentoring was introduced into the organizational literature in the late 1970s and early 1980s (e.g., Kram, 1983, 1985; Levinson, 1978) that a focal individual actually draws upon support from multiple sources and, second, the recognition of changes in the career context that may further necessitate the need for multiple sources of support in one's career (e.g., Arthur & Rousseau, 1996; Hall & Associates, 1996; Kram & Hall, 1996). We assert here that a convergence has occurred between these two factors: Whereas individuals have always drawn upon more than one individual at a given point in time for support, today, the social context in which careers are embedded has become increasingly turbulent (Kegan, 1994), thus strengthening the necessity of network assistance to enhance career development. And, indeed, mentoring and the importance of networks have been increasingly incorporated into public awareness, although the application to mentoring remains in its infancy.

A growing focus on multiple mentors has marked a shifting conceptualization of mentoring in recent research. Although Kram's (1985) work two decades prior introduced the notion of a "constellation" of developmental relationships—individuals from various social spheres, including one's peer group, family, community affiliations, and place of employment—early mentoring research focused on the dyad between a younger, less experienced protégé and a senior, seasoned mentor.

The first formal application of a social network perspective occurred when Higgins & Kram (2001) introduced the notion of a "developmental network." A developmental network is an "egocentric network" (Ibarra & Smith-Lovin, 1997) and so is composed of developers. This network of developmental relationships is identified by a protégé, limited to individuals who in a general sense are instrumental to his or her career development and personal learning. A developmental network is not everyone an individual talks to; rather, it is a subset of an individual's entire set of social ties, since it consists of only those ties that provide varying degrees of developmental support (Higgins & Kram, 2001; Higgins & Thomas, 2001).

A *developmental network,* defined as "a group of people who take an interest in and action to advance a focal individual's career" (Higgins & Kram, 2001, p. 268), has been described using two dimensions drawn from the social network literature: the *diversity* of individuals constituting the network and the *strength of tie* of the constituting relationships. A network's diversity can be determined on the basis of either the *range* of the social arenas from which individuals have relationships (e.g., employer, community, family) or its *density,* which measures the degree to which individuals in the network know one another (Brass, 1995; Burt, 1983; Higgins & Kram, 2001). A relationship's strength of tie refers to the degree of closeness and/or frequency of communication between a focal individual and his or her developer (Granovetter, 1973).

In their discussion of developmental networks, Higgins and Kram (2001) introduced a typology of four possible networks that result from a combination of strong and weak ties, and high and low network diversity: receptive, traditional, opportunistic, and entrepreneurial networks. Each developmental network type, they proposed, is likely to be associated with certain outcomes, such as career change, personal learning, work satisfaction, and organizational commitment (Higgins & Kram, 2001).

As Higgins and Kram (2001) proposed, viewing mentoring from a developmental network perspective provides a new lens on mentoring at work. From this vantage point, an individual receives help from multiple dyadic relationships, not one, and from individuals whose help may span organizational boundaries as well as hierarchical lines of authority. Thus, the developmental network conceptualization broadened the mentoring field, opening numerous avenues for theoretical and empirical exploration and for the application of social network methodologies.

Recent Research on Developmental Networks and Mentoring Networks

Since the formal reconceptualization of mentoring, theoretical and empirical research examining developmental networks and mentoring networks has been gaining momentum.[1] Mentoring networks are a subset of developmental networks; they focus specifically on relationships with mentors, as opposed to "developers," as Higgins and Kram (2001) call them, who may come from social arenas that extend beyond the protégé's place of work. Recent theoretical research includes Mezias and Scandura's (2005) extension of mentoring networks to an international context; de Janasz, Sullivan, and Whiting (2003) and de Janasz and Sullivan's (2004) research on multiple mentors; and Chandler & Kram's (2005) research that applied an adult development lens to the study of developmental networks.

Empirical studies of developmental networks have begun to emerge as well. For example, Dobrow and Higgins's (2005) longitudinal study suggests that there tends to be a negative relationship between network density (the degree to which developers know each other) and professional identity over time. Also, recent research by Cummings and Higgins (2006) showed how the composition of ties within one's developmental network changes over time, furthering an understanding of developmental network properties and dynamics. Prior empirical work has examined the relationships between developmental network properties and career change (Higgins, 2001), organizational retention and promotion (Higgins & Thomas, 2001), and work satisfaction (Higgins, 2001).

A Tumultuous Career Context

As noted earlier, a focus on multiple developmental relationships constituting a network is consistent with today's turbulent career environment (Eby, 1997;

Lankau & Scandura, 2002). Forces such as technological sophistication, globalization, and organizational downsizing have coincided to foster short-term concurrent relationships between individuals within and outside of their employing organizations (e.g., Higgins & Kram, 2001; Kram & Hall, 1996). Individuals today are likely to experience "boundaryless" careers that span organizational boundaries. In the past, organizations could be expected to drive career development, given that an individual's tenure within a given employer could span decades (Arthur, Claman, DeFillippi, & Adams, 1995; Arthur & Rousseau, 1996). Now, individuals must drive their own career growth, enacting a "protean" career (Hall, 2002, 2004; Hall & Mirvis, 1996). Since individuals cross organizational boundaries more frequently than in the past, protégés cannot expect mentors to be available for long-term relationships (de Janasz et al., 2003). Further, given the pace of change and globalization, it is unlikely that any mentor could meet all of a protégé's needs, thus necessitating multiple relationships for growth (de Janasz et al., 2003). In sum, a developmental network as a medium for career growth mirrors individuals' career experiences and expectations today. The application of a social network lens to mentoring has aided alignment between research and people's career realities.

The Value of a Social Network Perspective

In addition to fostering alignment between the mentoring literature and individuals' career experiences, a developmental network perspective furthers the mentoring literature in three key ways. First, drawing upon social network theory, Higgins and Kram's (2001) theoretical approach offers insight into different ways of conceptualizing and, in the future, testing the benefits of mentoring at work. By incorporating theory that addresses both tie strength and network diversity, scholars have new ways of understanding the quality and benefits of mentoring.

Second, social network methodologies allow quantitative measurement of network structure dimensions, facilitating network comparisons across individuals (e.g., Dobrow & Higgins, 2005). Third, a network perspective makes it possible to examine the unique characteristics of a network's structure. For example, Cummings and Higgins (2006) found evidence for an "inner-outer core" across individual networks in which the ties that remain intact over time, and populate an "inner core" to one's network, are those that provide high psychosocial support and low career support. This research contrasts with the vast majority of mentoring research, which considers only singular ties or independent multiple mentors at a given point in time.

Developmental Initiation

As the foregoing discussion suggests, research on developmental networks is becoming more pervasive as scholars begin to answer questions opened by the application of a social network perspective to mentoring. Still, relatively little is known about how developmental networks are formed (Cummings & Higgins, 2006). Further, in the mentoring literature, although there has been a significant amount of research on the initiation of mentoring relationships (e.g., Kram 1985; McGowan, 2004; Mullen, 1994; Scandura & Williams, 1998, 2001; Turban & Dougherty, 1994), quite a bit remains unknown as to what constitutes those interaction behaviors. Much of the prior research on the formation of mentoring relationships has been exploratory, leaving open the opportunity for theoretical development. Finally, we know relatively little about the antecedents to initiation behaviors and to developmental network formation. Scandura & Williams (2001) asserted,

> It is important to consider how initiation affects the development of mentorship. First impressions may drive the initial interactions that occur and the way that each party approaches each other may well determine the nature of the relationship that evolves. (p. 344)

In this chapter, we develop theory regarding the kinds of behaviors that may influence those initial interactions between an individual and potential developers and how that "developmental initiation," as we call it, affects the structure of developmental networks that are formed.

Although this chapter focuses on the antecedents as opposed to the outcomes of developmental initiation and developmental network formation, we agree with Scandura and Williams that examining how relationships begin may yield important insights into the consequences for the protégé, the mentor or developer, and the relationship itself. Each encounter between the protégé and developer influences the next in terms of perceived investment, liking, and complementarity.

We offer the concept of developmental initiation to address this gap in the mentoring literature associated with the formation of developmental relationships. We define *developmental initiation* as a set of development-seeking behaviors undertaken by a focal individual that are intended to enhance his or her skills, knowledge, task performance, and/or personal learning (see Box 14.1 for relevant definitions). We expect that an individual's level of developmental initiation (the frequency with which he or she enacts development-seeking behaviors) with others will influence whether developmental relationships are formed. For example, an individual who exhibits a high level of developmental initiation will frequently engage with others in pursuit of assistance, help, advice, and feedback, and therefore have more opportunities for developmental relationships with others to form.

BOX 14.1   Relevant Terms

Developmental initiation: development-seeking behaviors undertaken by a focal individual that are intended to enhance his or her skills, knowledge, task performance, and/or personal learning.

Level of initiation: the extent to which an individual enacts development-seeking behaviors.

A high level of initiation is characterized by frequent enactment of development-seeking behaviors.

A low level of initiation is characterized by infrequent enactment of development-seeknig behaviors.

Of course, ultimately, relationship formation and consequences for the individual (protégé), the developer, and the relationship will depend both upon the individual as well as the potential developer's perceptions and behaviors over time. So, for example, an individual may demonstrate a high level of developmental initiation and yet do so in such a way as to leave others annoyed or perceiving the individual as overly needy. Alternatively, an individual may act in an emotionally intelligent, respectful, and appreciative manner in seeking out developmental opportunities and still be rebuffed by an individual who is too busy to offer assistance. Whether the individual developmentally initiates in ways that are perceived positively be a potential developer, while important to understand, is beyond the scope of this chapter. Here, we focus specifically on factors that affect how much and where an individual is likely to engage in developmental initiation. In this way, we further researchers' understanding of how developmental networks are cultivated.

Specifically, our propositions focus on antecedents to either high levels of developmental initiation, in which an individual exhibits frequent development-seeking behaviors, or low levels of developmental initiation, in which an individual exhibits development-seeking behaviors with a low degree of frequency. As we propose, several individual-difference demographic factors may play a role in determining not only the level of developmental initiation a focal individual engages in but also the diversity of developers with whom he or she forms relationships. Thus, these two dimensions, developmental initiation and developmental network diversity, are the central focus of the development of our propositions.

Developmental initiation represents a third dimension that is useful to describing developmental networks, and it complements Higgins & Kram's (2001) work that introduced the dimensions of developmental network diversity and strength of tie.

Development-Seeking Behaviors

Individuals, depending upon personal factors and organizational constraints, will engage in behaviors intended to elicit developmental support from others. These behaviors may be purposely aimed at fostering a developmental relationship or generally intended to further one's development and personal learning from "mentors in the moment" (Scandura & Williams, 1998).

Development-seeking behaviors can come in many forms, including information-seeking, help-seeking, feedback-seeking, and initiating behaviors. All of these behaviors are beneficial to the focal individual in that they either enhance the likelihood of cultivating a developmental relationship or facilitate immediate skill development. Over time, the frequency with which an individual enacts these behaviors along with the potential mentor's or developer's reactions to such behaviors have implications for whether and how the relationship develops. Indeed, whether these are fleeting or lasting relationships that an individual develops is an important area for future research. Here, we simply propose that there are certain antecedents one can point to that might affect not only the amount of development-seeking behaviors but also where he or she seeks out help.

Information seeking facilitates knowledge flow and relates to an individual's tasks, role, and workgroup and an organization's culture, and it is sought from an individual's supervisor, formal mentor, and peers (Morrison, 1993; Ostroff & Kozlowski, 1993). By seeking out information, an individual can gain familiarity with persons who can serve as developers and/or support from existing developers (Mullen, 1994). Similarly, *help seeking* enables an individual to secure developmental support from potential developers. In fact, individuals who arouse a developer's desire to help are perceived as appealing as protégés (Allen, Poteet, & Russell, 2000). *Feedback seeking,* which allows an individual to assess his or her task or role performance (Ashford & Cummings, 1983), also facilitates interaction with existing or possible developers.

Antecedents of Developmental Initiation

In this chapter, we consider in particular the factors that affect the extent to which individuals will tend to exhibit high levels of developmental initiation. We expect that different individuals will tend to exhibit different levels of developmental initiation. For our purposes, then, we define an individual's *level of developmental initiation* as the frequency with which he or she enacts development-seeking behaviors, on average, with others. A high level of initiation is characterized by frequent enactment of development-seeking behaviors. In contrast, a low level of initiation is characterized by infrequent enactment of development-seeking behaviors.

Diversity, in this discussion, is considered to be the degree to which developers in a network are from a range of different social arenas. The diversity in an individual's developmental network, as explained earlier, influences the likely breadth of new ideas and information provided to a protégé (Dobrow & Higgins, 2005; Higgins, 2001; Ragins, 1997). Relationships crossing organizational, hierarchical, and physical boundaries can positively impact an individual's ability to complete work (Cross & Cummings, 2004). In the following section, we consider how four demographic individual-level factors—SES, gender, age, and nationality—affect an individual's overall level of developmental initiation and the diversity of his or her developmental network.

Socioeconomic Status

How does individuals' SES influence their levels of developmental initiation and the diversity of their developmental networks? Homophily and entitlement theories offer insight into this question.

First, research has suggested that individuals with higher SES may benefit more than other employees from mentoring due to the effects of *homophily* (Pfeffer, 1977; Whitely, Dougherty, & Dreher, 1991). High-level managers will likely come from high-SES origins (Blau & Duncan, 1967; Stinchcombe, 1965; Whitely et al., 1991). Homophily arguments and the similarity-attraction theory (e.g., Berscheid & Reis, 1998; Bryne & Nelson, 1965) suggest that similarity breeds interpersonal liking and tie formation (Kanter, 1977). Senior managers from high-SES origins may seek out protégés who come from similar backgrounds whom they perceive to share the same values and skills (Whitely et al., 1991). Senior management, in functioning as an elite "inner circle" (Useem, 1984), may seek to preserve status by aligning with junior mentors who remind them of themselves (Whitely et al., 1991). High-SES-background individuals might convey their socioeconomic backgrounds to senior mangers by conversing about, among other things, elite neighborhoods in which they grew up, expensive private schools they attended, high-ticket items they received as gifts as young adults, or second homes their families own.

Using arguments grounded by the notion of homophily, Whitely et al. (1991) found that SES moderated the relationship between mentoring and career progress. Higher-SES employees with mentors received more promotions than their counterparts from lower-SES backgrounds (Whitely et al., 1991). The foregoing discussion suggests that high-SES protégés may not perceive the need for a high level of initiation because they are sought out as protégés and therefore may be relatively passive in seeking out assistance, information, or advice from others.

What does homophily suggest about the relationship between SES and network diversity? If high-SES individuals are in relatively high-level positions within an organization and thus are well positioned to provide valuable career support to a protégé, it is likely that high-SES individuals will not seek out help more broadly—that is, they will not develop diverse developmental networks. Further, high-SES developers, once identified by high-SES protégés, may sponsor and provide visibility to their protégés by introducing them to other senior managers, thus initiating other possible network ties, likely those that are similar in kind (versus diverse). As a result, high-SES individuals may develop networks that are low diversity in kind. Taken together, we expect high-SES protégés to be associated with low-diversity networks and low developmental initiation.

A second explanation for high-SES networks is based on the notion of *entitlement,* which involves "the expectation of a reward as the result of a social contract" (Campbell, Bonacci, Shelton, Exline, & Bushman, 2004, p. 31). By virtue of their relationships to individuals who possess social and human capital, such as family and friends, high-SES individuals may feel that positive benefits from others are warranted irrespective of their own effort. If the high-SES individual continually "inherits" the ties of significant others, he or she may over time fail to value hard work and instead rely on others' "graciousness." Ultimately, entitlement may lead to a developmental network composed of low diversity and characterized by low developmental initiation on the part of the protégé.

Taken together, we suggest the following:

Proposition 1: Individuals with higher SES will tend to develop less diverse networks through the use of low developmental initiation.

Stated differently, higher-SES individuals will tend to develop networks with a narrow range of developers through infrequent development-seeking behaviors.

Gender

Gender expectations, macrostructural constraints, homophily, and relational outcome preferences offer theoretical explanations for differences in levels of developmental initiation and network diversity between men and women. First, some research suggests that women tend to be passive in relationship initiation and men tend to be aggressive (Maccoby & Jacklin, 1974; Scandura & Williams, 1998). Thus, in fulfilling societal expectations, men are likely to be assertive in establishing relationships (Scandura & Williams, 2001). Women, on the other hand, may wait for developers to initiate relationships due to apprehensiveness about being perceived as "pushy" or due to concerns regarding the potential for misinterpretation of such cross-gender relationships (Ragins & Cotton, 1991; Scandura & Williams, 2001, p. 348). This hypothesis is consistent with Allen's review of the mentor's perspective, which speculates, "Male mentors may be less attracted to female protégés with assertive or dominating personalities than to male protégés who possess the same attributes" (Chapter 5, this volume).

In addition, research on similarity, attraction, and homophily suggest that male mentors are naturally more likely to establish relationships with other men (Berscheid & Reis, 1998; Bryne & Nelson, 1965) as they seek out "similar selves." Moreover, research suggests that male mentors tend to be more inclined to initiate relationships that lead to instrumental support than are female mentors, who prefer mutual initiation with a protégé (Gaskill, 1991; Scandura & Williams, 2001). Further, given complications that can arise from having a close professional relationship with the opposite gender (Clawson & Kram, 1984; George & Kummerow, 1981; Ragins & Cotton, 1991), male mentors may be more inclined to respond to initiation attempts made by other men, versus women. Men may also find it easier than women to initiate relationships with other men given the comfort level and understanding that results from gender similarities.

Other research suggests that gender differences may be due to differences in opportunity structures within a firm. For example, organizational studies have long suggested that managerial positions tend to be highly populated by men (Kanter, 1977; Morrison & Von Glinow, 1990), thus leading to a larger potential pool of male (versus female) senior mentors.

Given the greater availability of potential male (versus female) developers who are interested in pursuing relationships with same-gender protégés, male protégés may find that a high level of developmental initiation is a by-product of homophily and structural availability. Male developers are more available and visible (than female developers) to male protégés who want information, help, and feedback and can read developers' signals. Women, on the other hand, may find it more difficult to actively engage because the available pool of male developers may be more hesitant to respond to their efforts at initiating. Further, as suggested earlier, women may prefer to wait for male developers to initiate relationships with them or be less aggressive so as to allow for a mutual initiation (Scandura & Williams, 2001).

Scandura and Williams's (2001) study on gender as a moderator between relationship initiation and perceptions of mentoring functions found that male protégés received more mentoring functions than did females in protégé-initiated relationships. On the other hand, female protégés received more mentoring functions in mentor-initiated and mentor- and protégé-initiated relationships. Scandura and Williams's findings suggest that "protégé initiation is more beneficial for male protégés. . . . Therefore, for males, assertive behavior may produce the greatest benefits from mentoring" (p. 359). However, this study did not account for the gender composition of the relationships. So, although males reportedly received more mentoring than women when they initiated the relationship, the study's findings may reflect a comparison of male protégés in same-gender relationships and female protégés in cross- and same-gender relationships. Scandura and Williams's research showed that although the ratio of male to female protégés was 1 to 1, the ratio of male to female mentors was 3 to 1, suggesting that men made up a significant percentage of the mentor pool. Scandura & Williams's (2001) research is consistent with Forret & Dougherty's (2004) study, which found that involvement in networking behaviors—attempts to develop and maintain relationships with others who have the potential to assist them in their work or career—was more beneficial for men's career progress than for women's.

These findings suggest that gender effects may also reflect the gender composition of the relationship, which is often further complicated by the scarcity of cross-gender relationships involving male protégés with female mentors. Consequently, men may experience the greatest benefits from developmental initiation to the extent that they are reaching out to other men, who are likely to perceive initiating attempts positively.

Macrostructural constraints and homophily arguments similarly suggest that men tend to have low-diversity networks. To the extent that male protégés are engaged with males who are more likely than women to be in high-ranking positions in organizations, men perceive themselves as having useful networks (see Ibarra, 1995, on perceived network utility), reducing the range of their help seeking. As some research suggests, men tend to receive more overall functional support from their ties to male developers than women receive from their female developers, because the structural context limits the size of women's same-gender networks compared with men's (Rothstein, Burke, & Bristor, 2001).

Further, research shows that men often seek more instrumental as opposed to developmental outcomes from their relationships, thus affecting the kinds of ties they develop (Ragins, 1989; Ragins & Verbos, 2007). Since relationships with male mentors have been shown to yield greater compensation and promotions, men, in seeking instrumental outcomes, may restrict their networks because their relationships with other men offer the desired support (Dreher & Ash, 1990; Ragins & Cotton, 1991).

Consequently, men may feel that their developmental needs can be met by male managers within organizational boundaries and across fewer hierarchical levels than is the case with women. An intraorganizational network that spans few levels is less diverse than one that spans organizations and levels, and so represents low developmental network diversity. Women, on the other hand, tend to have networks that have greater vertical range (and hence, diversity) because the opportunity context requires crossing greater organizational boundaries to develop same-gender ties (Ibarra, 1992; Rothstein et al., 2001). Therefore,

Proposition 2a: Men will tend to develop low-diversity developmental networks through the use of high developmental initiation.

Stated differently, men will tend to develop networks with a narrow range of developers through frequent development-seeking behaviors. While this proposition may hold for most organizations today, which tend to be male dominated rather than female dominated, the following addendum is useful in recognition of the role that opportunity structure may play in the kinds of developmental networks men (versus women) develop:

Proposition 2b: Men will tend to develop low-diversity developmental networks through the use of high developmental initiation, particularly when the protégé is working in a male-, rather than female-, dominated organization.

Age

An adult development perspective is also useful when considering an individual's level of developmental initiation. Certain adult development theories posit that individuals face "developmental tasks" at various ages, suggesting that younger individuals, those in their 20s, for example, may be attractive to midlife adults in more-senior positions who have excelled in their careers and now have a desire to mentor (Levinson, 1978; Levinson, & Levinson, 1996). These older adults, who perceive the younger individuals to be youthful versions of themselves, may more actively engage in the relationship (Allen et al., 2000). Protégés are therefore likely to be more passively (than actively) engaged, given that their developers are more likely to seek them out.

A consistent conclusion would be drawn using a help-seeking perspective. Young people, having recently entered the workforce, may feel uncomfortable asking for help. Given their novice status, they may feel that to ask for help is to suggest that they are unable to tackle problems and challenges on their own. In an effort to maintain a positive impression, they may tend toward autonomy in their work (Goffman, 1959). Further, younger people will have fewer prior experiences in developmental relationships. Consequently, they may not recognize that they have something to offer a developer or understand the behavioral repertoire that aids relationship formation, leading as well to lower developmental initiation.

Adult development theories can also lend insight into why younger individuals may have high-diversity networks (e.g., Erikson, 1963; Levinson, 1978; Levinson & Levinson, 1996). First, certain adult development theories (e.g., Levinson, 1978; Levinson, & Levinson, 1996) describe developmental tasks that individuals must meet at certain ages. The key developmental task of early adulthood is to "enter into the adult world" and separate from one's parents (Levinson, 1978). Research suggests that when asked to identify a developmental network, a young adult (early 20s to age 30) will name a (or both) parents as well as peers (Chandler, 2006; Higgins, 2001). The foregoing suggests that in identifying one's parent(s), the young individual will have greater diversity in his or her network.

Further, younger individuals, having not long ago emerged from high school and college, are more likely than older individuals to be embedded in the institutions and relationships that have shaped their early adulthood (Kegan, 1982), thus increasing the diversity of social arenas from which ties may form. Whereas an older individual may have "lost touch" with college and high school friends (which would represent varying social spheres from which to draw support), the younger individual may identify individuals from these social spheres as part of their developmental networks. Both of these groups represent social spheres that enhance network diversity (see Higgins, 2001).

Proposition 3: Young adults, in comparison to adults in their midlife or later, will tend to develop high-diversity developmental networks through the use of low developmental initiation.

Expatriates

Here, we look at those who live and work in places other than their home countries: expatriates. As stated earlier, an individual is more likely to ask for help under conditions of high psychological safety and perceptions of control (Fisher, Nadler, & Whitcher-Alagna, 1982), the latter of which may be related to an individual's self-esteem (Bandura, 1986; Nadler, 1987, 1991). By extension, it may be that an individual's decision to study or work abroad is positively related to his or her level of developmental initiation. Self-esteem has been shown to be positively correlated with networking behaviors by individuals (Forret & Dougherty, 2001). High self-efficacy and self-esteem will likely lead to proactive behaviors (Bateman & Crant, 1993), including engaging others for assistance, information, and feedback, which is characteristic of a high level of developmental initiation.

Research on international mentoring is consistent with this line of reasoning. Studies suggest that employees who are chosen for international assignments may be self-confident and self-reliant, enjoy meeting new people, have an openness to new ideas and diverse opinions, and handle unfamiliar situations adeptly (e.g., Mendenhall & Oddou, 1986; Oddou, 1991). If employees are chosen on the basis of these criteria, expatriates may have the confidence to reach out to others for learning opportunities. Further, it may be that "interested and willing" expatriate candidates are those who possess the foregoing qualities (Oddou, 1991, p. 302), thus enhancing the likelihood of developmental experiences abroad.

Moreover, given the diversity of their own prior living experience, expatriates may be more accustomed to actively reaching out for assistance of a variety of kinds in order to meet their own needs. To adapt to new work environments and to acclimate to new cultures, expatriates may have developed skills in seeking out help across various levels within the organization (e.g., supervisors, peers, and subordinates), across departments, and outside the organization (e.g., within the expatriate community). Consequently, expatriates may embrace a more cosmopolitan (than local) orientation in their careers, leading to a high-diversity developmental network (Gouldner, 1958). Ultimately, the success with which expatriates cultivate relationships depends upon the skill with which they seek out information, assistance, and help. While expatriates may feel confident and accustomed to reaching out to others, they may or may not do so in ways that build the trust, rapport, and mutuality to ensure that developmental relationships are fostered.

Homophily arguments lead to a similar conclusion regarding the relationship between network diversity and nationality. Prior research has suggested that minorities are underrepresented in private sector managerial positions (e.g., Cox, 1991; Morrison & Von Glinow, 1990). While organizational demography is becoming increasingly diverse, expatriates are similarly underrepresented in most organizations. The structural context, therefore, leads to a situation in which expatriates will, like women, engage developmental relationships with dissimilar individuals, yielding high-diversity networks. Taken together, the foregoing discussion suggests the following:

Proposition 4: Expatriates will tend to develop high-diversity developmental networks through the use of high developmental initiation.

Beyond Developmental Network Formation: Individual and Organizational Implications

Mentoring research strongly suggests that having a mentor or developer positively impacts a focal individual's career. As asserted by Hill (1991), rather than seeking a perfect mentor, an individual should become the "perfect protégé." The reconceptualization of mentoring (Higgins & Kram, 2001) illuminates that the perfect protégé will engage and maintain a "portfolio" (Higgins, 2000, 2001) of informal and formal developmental relationships as vehicles for learning in a tumultuous environment.

Although the emphasis of this chapter has been on the very early stages of relationship formation and in particular the kinds of developmental networks that different kinds of individuals form, the longer-term implications of such beginnings are important to consider as well. Indeed, the foregoing discussion suggests that the degree to which the protégé is invested in the initiation of a relationship may have implications for interactions and outcomes at later phases of the relationship (Kram, 1983). The theory presented here implies, therefore, that individuals should consider their level of developmental initiation, and its impact on their ability to build mutually enhancing relationships, as well as a developmental network that is responsive to their needs.

We acknowledge that the cultivation of developmental relationships is an interactive process. Therefore, what we have offered here is a somewhat limited view of how developmental relationships are formed. Still, we believe the concept of developmental initiation and the propositions suggested here begin to pave the way for future mentoring research that embarks on understanding both the protégé's and the developer's roles in developmental relationship formation.

Individuals should ask themselves questions such as the following: To what extent do I initiate conversations with potential developers? To what extent do I reach out others for assistance and/or information? To what extent do I seek out feedback related to my job performance? A protégé's answers to these questions and the ways in which he or she responds to them may lend insight well beyond development-seeking behaviors, to certain kinds of relationship-enhancing behaviors that can affect the later cultivation and maintenance stages of their developmental relationships.

In addition, given the significance of developmental initiation suggested in this chapter, we propose that individuals spend time contemplating their career goals, needs, and interests so that they are prepared before seeking out help (Claman, 2002). Doing so will enable them to select compatible developers that can offer them valuable and lasting career and psychosocial assistance. When an individual has a sense of his or her career "path with a heart" (Shepard, 1984), that person is better positioned to help a developer help him or her, which can ultimately result in deeply satisfying relationships for professional and personal growth.

The ideas presented here also offer new insight into how organizations can develop programs that can better educate individuals as they embark on building developmental networks. Organizational programs that are focused on the protégé may help participants by describing and training individuals so that they engage effectively, and not simply frequently, in development-seeking behaviors. Indeed, whereas this chapter focuses on the kinds of networks that the level of developmental initiation may produce, the real value to organizations and people over time will be found in figuring out how to effectively cultivate relationships in one's network over time, in order to satisfy the needs of both protégés and their developers. Human resource and executive development professionals should have ongoing dialogues that encourage individuals to reflect on their progress toward cultivating a responsive network, engaging in active developmental initiation in developmental relationships, and enhancing the mutuality of developmental relationships.

Many of the arguments behind our propositions suggest as well that a firm's opportunity structure and climate can affect the course of developmental relationships. Thus, management and human resource professionals should also consider whether the organizational environment is conducive to nurturing relationships across departments and levels and with stakeholders, such as suppliers, who are critical to its functioning (Lengnick-Hall & Lengnick-Hall, 2004). For example, consideration should be given to fostering "communities of practice" within and outside the organization that emphasize collaboration (Lengnick-Hall & Lengnick-Hall, 2004).

Future Research

Developmental Initiation

In this chapter, we have offered developmental initiation as a concept to bridge the gap in our understanding of how and what kinds of networks of developmental relationships are formed. Our discussion also has reciprocal implications for the social network literature given that a similar paucity of research on initiation exists (for exceptions, see Gulati & Gargiulo, 1999; Kim & Higgins, in press).

This chapter has developed theory to undergird the notion of developmental initiation from the extant mentoring, social networks, and relevant literatures. Construct development begins with the derivation of dimensions from the existing literature or, in absence of relevant studies, an inductive qualitative approach (in-depth interviews) to unearth dimensions (Schwab, 1980). The next step involves refining and validating these ideas.

To develop and refine the propositions suggested here, qualitative research is initially appropriate, given the need to explore and capture the rich interactions between protégés and their developers early on. For example, it is uncertain whether high-SES individuals are not highly engaged because of entitlement or because they are uncomfortable asking for assistance and initiating relationships. Here, we offered both explanations. Once qualitative research has been conducted and construct dimensions refined, a survey instrument could be developed to measure developmental initiation across individuals.

Our chapter has described the level of initiation, defined by the frequency with which an individual enacts development-seeking behaviors, as important to relationship and network functioning. Subsequent research should examine the "optimal" level of initiation. This would lend insight into the quality of developmental initiation and how this affects important outcomes. At some point, a protégé risks being overly engaged to the point of annoying developers and undermining perceptions of the protégé's ability. Therefore, future research may ask the following question: What is the "tipping point" at which information seeking and other types of initiation behavior damages a relationship? Tipping points may also vary by relationship stage, such that early stages are more susceptible to overload; once a relationship is committed, a developer may not mind more frequent requests for help.

Future research should be dedicated to understanding how personal characteristics such as a focal individual's relational skills or emotional intelligence (see Cherniss, Chapter 17, and Fletcher & Ragins, Chapter 15, this volume) influence the level and quality of developmental initiation. Research of this kind would complement our chapter, which is concerned with the level of developmental initiation, by aiding an understanding of individuals' differing abilities to initiate with effectiveness. We imagine, for example, that emotionally intelligent individuals who enact a high level of developmental initiation would be more favorably perceived than those who are less emotionally intelligent (Cherniss, Chapter 17, this volume). Building from Ragins & Verbos's (2007) theoretical research, a study on how relational schemas—cognitive maps that guide mentor and protégé behaviors—influence developmental initiation would inform what cognitive processes underpin individuals' development-seeking efforts.

Coupling the level and quality of developmental initiation efforts aids our understanding of which protégé behaviors will lead to a series of "relational mentoring episodes" (Fletcher & Ragins, Chapter 15, this volume). Individuals who engage in a series of relational mentoring episodes—mutually enhancing growth interactions—are likely to experience a deepening commitment to the relationship (Fletcher & Ragins, Chapter 15, this volume).

Also important is an understanding of how an individual's style plays a role in developmental initiation. An individual's *interactional style* has been suggested to impact the types of relationships he or she is able develop (e.g., Higgins & Kram, 2001; Ibarra, 1992). For example, a trusting, mutual relationship is more likely to result from an *expressive interactional style* (Miller & Stiver, 1997) that results in a developer feeling valued and respected (Higgins & Kram, 2001). An expressive style, stemming from an interest in securing developmental assistance beyond career advancement, is likely to lead to more authentic behaviors and thus leave the impression that an individual is interested in the interaction for developmental rather than purely instrumental gains (Giacalone & Rosenfeld, 1989; Goffman, 1959). In contrast, a purely *instrumental interaction style,* stemming from an interest in securing career advancement, will likely lead to behaviors that are perceived as strategic and self-serving, thus resulting in a target individual feeling patronized or bothered, and will likely undermine the relationship (Giacalone & Rosenfeld, 1989; Goffman, 1959; Higgins & Kram, 2001). In addition, congruency of expectations may affect the course of the relationships cultivated in one's developmental network (see Ragins & Verbos, 2007).

Future research could also empirically examine the consequences of developmental initiation and/or developmental network diversity. As mentioned earlier, such an undertaking would require examining the needs, reactions, and perceptions of developers in the protégé's network. It could be that the developer's interpretation of the protégé's behaviors fully mediates any relationships between protégé actions and consequences. It may also be the case that the developer's own needs, skills, and history in developmental relationships will affect how productive and beneficial that protégé's initial behaviors will be. Further, although prior mentoring research has considered how protégé characteristics (Allen, Poteet, & Burroughs, 1997; Allen et al., 2000; Aryee, Lo, & Kang, 1999; Burke & McKeen, 1997; Fagenson, 1989; Levinson, 1978; Levinson, & Levinson, 1996; Turban & Dougherty, 1994) and behaviors (e.g., Waldron, 1991) impact the benefits of having mentoring relationships and how different developmental network structures affect a protégé's career (e.g., Higgins & Kram, 2001; Higgins & Thomas, 2001), there is no research that considers both—that is, how protégé behaviors and developmental network characteristics together affect outcomes that are of significance to a protégé (or to his or her developers). The idea of developmental initiation and the propositions offered here open up an exciting new area of inquiry: How do the two dimensions of developmental initiation and network diversity interact to affect the career of the protégé as well as the careers of the developers within the protégé's developmental network? Does high developmental initiation lead to perceived higher relational quality with developers?

Additional questions to be addressed with future research include the following: Does a high level of developmental initiation mitigate challenges facing diversified relationships within and across one's developmental network? On the flip side, one could ask whether diversified relationships (e.g., cross-gender or race relations) require greater levels of developmental initiation in the beginning stages to build the foundation for a long-lasting and mutually beneficial relationship. Does developmental initiation in and of itself lead to greater career-related self-efficacy? Is developmental initiation associated with personal learning for the protégé, or for his or her developers (Lankau & Scandura, Chapter 4, this volume)? How does developmental initiation affect the kinds of behaviors in which developers engage as they seek out help in their own careers?

Future research should also theoretically and empirically explore other antecedents and consequences of developmental initiation. For example, common observation suggests that irrespective of demographics, some individuals are more adept at reaching out for developmental support. Future research could examine which individual attributes are associated with assertive behaviors that are perceived positively by potential developers. Research on emotional competencies (Boyatzis, Chapter 18, this volume; Cherniss, Chapter 17, this volume; Goleman, 1995; Goleman, Boyatzis, & McKee, 2002), for example, suggests that individuals who possess greater empathy and self-awareness are more likely than those with lesser competency development to enact high-quality development-seeking behaviors. For example, individuals who are able to empathize with others are likely to be able to seek out assistance with an understanding of how others will perceive development-seeking efforts and will therefore adjust actions accordingly.

In addition, the developers' perspective is an important ingredient and remains to be explored as well. In their review of the mentoring literature, Wanberg, Welsh, and Hezlett (2003) stated that "research on how mentors and protégés interact is limited" (p. 80). Given the importance of a developer's investment to the relationship, future research should examine whether and how developmental initiation impacts a developer's perception of the protégé and relationship possibilities. It may also be the case that a developer's own needs, skills, interests, and experience in mentoring relationships will affect the extent to which he or she responds favorably to development-seeking behaviors on the part of the protégé, affecting the entire course of the developmental relationship far beyond the initiation stage.

Future Research Applying a Social Network Lens to Developmental Networks

In addition to the specific dimension of developmental initiation, many avenues exist for research on developmental networks more generally. Higgins and Kram (2001), Molloy (2005), and Chandler and Kram (in press) provided research agendas for future work on developmental networks that is attentive to antecedents, network structure, and outcomes. For example, and building upon the present work, it is critical to explore individual factors other than demographic variables that explain variations in network structure and the value they provide to a protégé. Specifically, which mutable, competency-based attributes affect the degree and quality with which individuals seek out relational assistance? More generally, how do such attributes affect the way individuals experience their networks and the relationships that constitute them?

Much research is needed to understand what types of networks exist, as well as the career implications of differing developmental network structures. Studies should consider how network properties, such as the density and range of the relationships that make up the developmental network, may vary in different contexts, such as different ethnic and national cultures. For example, Mezias and Scandura's (2005) theoretical research has laid the foundation for an empirical exploration of expatriate developmental networks. In addition, studies that examine the nature and implications of changing developmental networks properties remain in their infancy (for exceptions, see Cummings & Higgins, 2006; Dobrow & Higgins, 2005).

Researchers should be aware of, and informed by, prior and concomitant research on social networks. Research on social networks has proliferated in the past 25 years, resulting in a literature abundant in empirical and theoretical studies, increasingly sophisticated methodologies, and a healthy research agenda from which to draw applications to the field and practice of mentoring.

The literatures on positive organizational scholarship (Cameron, Dutton, & Quinn, 2003) and on developing close relationships (Dindia & Duck, 2000; Duck, 1994; Rogers & Escudero, 2004) are also of value in guiding future theoretical and empirical research on developmental networks. The positive organizational scholarship literature emphasizes relationships as sources of vitality, generativity, resilience, and energy (Cameron et al., 2003; Dutton & Ragins, 2006). Emerging perspectives on mentoring underpinned by positive organizational scholarship enables the view of developmental networks as high-quality connections and sources of social capital (Dutton & Heaphy, 2003; Ragins, 2007; Ragins & Verbos, 2007) and points to relational dynamics—thriving and resiliency—and reciprocal outcomes that have not been closely examined to date (e.g., Ragins & Verbos, 2007).

Research on close relationships can illuminate how developmental relationships continually unfold and shared meanings are produced as individuals and their developers interact (e.g., Duck, 1994). Consistent with this chapter, close relationship perspectives help to fill the gap in our understanding of relational interactions and the cultivation and evolution of relationships.

Conclusion

This chapter has introduced a novel dimension—developmental initiation—that is relevant to a social network application to mentoring. Based on the extant literature, we identified and described the kinds of development-seeking behaviors that characterize developmental initiation. Then, drawing upon mentoring, social psychology, and social networks literatures, we focused on how certain individual-level characteristics may affect the level of protégé developmental initiation and also the range or diversity of assistance he or she may seek out. Finally, to generate ideas for future research, we discussed ways in which a protégé's level of developmental initiation in the initiation phase may influence the relationship's later functioning and subsequent outcomes, which, when extrapolated to the level of a developmental network, may have significant implications for the protégé's personal and professional development.

In particular, we focused on the development of testable propositions associated with the antecedents of an individual's level of developmental initiation vis-à-vis the relationships in his or her developmental network. We suggested that different demographic factors will differentially impact an individual's level of initiation as well as the diversity of his or her developmental network. We hope that this chapter has illuminated the practical implications of developmental initiation and will stimulate other researchers to apply a social network perspective to mentoring. Given that the notion of a developmental network mirrors one's career reality, we hope such efforts will serve to broaden and strengthen the mentoring literature.

Note

1. To our knowledge, research on mentoring networks (e.g., de Janesz et al., 2003) considers a *mentor* to be an individual who provides high levels of psychosocial and career support, consistent with Kram's (1985) description of a mentor. As an exception, Mezias and Scandura (2005) referred to mentoring networks that include individuals who provide varying degrees of psychosocial and career support. We consider a developmental network to be distinct from a mentoring network, in that it can include all types of developmental relationships, not exclusively those characterized as true mentors (see Higgins & Kram, 2001).

References

Allen, T. D., Poteet, M. L., & Burroughs, S. M. (1997). The mentor's perspective: A qualitative inquiry and future research agenda. *Journal of Vocational Behavior, 51,* 70–89.

Allen, T. D., Poteet, M. L., & Russell, J. E. A. (2000). Protégé selection by mentors: What makes the difference? *Journal of Organizational Behavior, 21,* 271–282.

Arthur, M. B., Claman, P. H., DeFillippi, R. J., & Adams, J. (1995). Intelligent enterprise, intelligent careers. *Academy of Management Executive, 9*(4), 7–22.

Arthur, M., & Rousseau, D. M. (Eds.). (1996). *The boundaryless career: A new employment principle for a new organizational era.* New York: Oxford University Press.

Aryee, S., Lo, S., & Kang, I.-L. (1999). Antecedents of early career stage mentoring among Chinese employees. *Journal of Organizational Behavior, 20,* 563–576.

Ashford, S. J., & Cummings, L. L. (1983). Feedback as an individual resource: Personal strategies for creating information. *Organizational Behavior and Human Performance, 32,* 370–389.

Bandura, A. (1986). *Social foundations of thought and action: A social cognitive theory.* Englewood Cliffs, NJ: Prentice Hall.

Bateman, T. S., & Crant, J. M. (1993). The proactive component of organizational behavior: A measure and correlates. *Journal of Organizational Behavior, 14,* 103–118.

Baugh, S. G., & Scandura, T. A. (1999). The effects of multiple mentors on protégé attitudes toward the work setting. *Journal of Social Behavior and Personality, 14,* 503–521.

Berscheid, E., & Reis, H. T. (1998). Attraction and close relationships. In D. T. Gilbert, S. T. Fiske, & G. Linzey (Eds.), *Handbook of social psychology* (pp. 193–281). New York: McGraw-Hill.

Blau, P. M., & Duncan, O. D. (1967). *The American occupational structure.* New York: John Wiley & Sons.

Brass, D. J. (1995). A social network perspective on human resources management. *Research in Personnel and Human Resources Management, 13,* 39–79.

Brass, D. J., Galaskiewicz, J., Greve, H., & Tsai, W. (2004). Taking stock of networks and organizations: A multilevel analysis. *Academy of Management Journal, 47,* 795–819.

Burke, R. J., & McKeen, C. A. (1997). Benefits of mentoring relationships among managerial and professional women: A cautionary tale. *Journal of Vocational Behavior, 51,* 43–57.

Burt, B. S. (1983). Range. In R. S. Burt & M. J. Minor (Eds.), *Applied network analysis: A methodological introduction* (pp. 176–194). Thousand Oaks, CA: Sage.

Burt, B. S. (1992). *Structural holes.* Cambridge, MA: Harvard University Press.

Byrne, D., & Nelson, D. (1965). Attraction as a linear function of proportion of positive reinforcements. *Journal of Personality and Social Psychology, 1,* 659–663.

Cameron, K. S., Dutton, J. E., & Quinn, R. E. (Eds.). (2003). *Positive organizational scholarship: Foundations of a new discipline.* San Francisco: Berrett-Koehler.

Campbell, W. K., Bonacci, A. M., Shelton, J., Exline, J. J., & Bushman, B. J. (2004). Psychological entitlement: Interpersonal consequences and validation of a new self-report measure. *Journal of Personality Assessment, 83,* 29–45.

Chandler, D. E. (2006). *Beyond the organization: The role of the outside developer.* Unpublished manuscript.

Chandler, D. E., & Kram, K. E. (2005). Applying an adult development perspective to developmental networks. *Career Development International, 10,* 548–566.

Chandler, D. E., & Kram, K. E. (in press). Mentoring in the new career context. In M. Peiperl & H. Gunz (Eds.), *Handbook of career studies.* Thousand Oaks, CA: Sage.

Claman, P. H. (2002). *Ask: How to get what you want and need at work.* Boston: Insights.

Clawson, J. G., & Kram, K. E. (1984). Managing cross-gender mentoring. *Business Horizons, 27*(3), 22–32.

Cox, T. (1991). The multicultural organization. *Academy of Management Executive, 5*(2), 34–47.

Cross, R., & Cummings, J. N. (2004). Tie and network correlates of individual performance in knowledge-intensive work. *Academy of Management Journal, 47,* 928–937.

Cummings, J. N., & Higgins, M. C. (2006). Developmental instability at the network core: Support dynamics in developmental networks. *Social Networks, 28*(1), 38–55.

de Janasz, S. C., & Sullivan, S. E. (2004). Multiple mentors in academe: developing a professional network. *Journal of Vocational Behavior, 64,* 263–283.

de Janasz, S. C., Sullivan, S. E., & Whiting, V. R. (2003). Mentor networks and career success: Lessons for turbulent times. *Academy of Management Executive, 17*(4), 78–91.

Dindia, K., & Duck, S. (2000). *Communication in personal relationships.* New York: John Wiley & Sons.

Dobrow, S. R., & Higgins, M. C. (2005). Developmental networks and professional identity: A longitudinal study. *Career Development International, 10,* 567–583.

Dreher, G. F., & Ash, R. A. (1990). A comparative study of mentoring among men and women in managerial, professional, and technical positions. *Journal of Applied Psychology, 81,* 539–546.

Duck, S. (1994). *Meaningful relationships: Talking, sense and relating.* Thousand Oaks, CA: Sage.

Dutton, J. E., & Heaphy, E. D. (2003). The power of high-quality connections. In K. S. Cameron, J. E., Dutton, & R. E. Quinn (Eds.), *Positive organizational scholarship: Foundations of a new discipline* (pp. 263–278). San Francisco: Berrett-Koehler.

Dutton, J. E., & Ragins, B. R. (2006). *Exploring positive relationships at work: Building a new theoretical and research foundation.* Mahwah, NJ: Lawrence Erlbaum.

Eby, L. T. (1997). Alternative forms of mentoring in changing organizational environments: A conceptual extension of the mentoring literature. *Journal of Vocational Behavior, 51,* 125–144.

Erikson, E. H. (1963). *Childhood and society.* New York: Norton.

Fagenson, E. A. (1989). The mentor advantage: Perceived career/job experiences of protégés versus non-protégés. *Journal of Organizational Behavior, 10,* 309–320.

Fisher, J. D., Nadler, A., & Whitcher-Alagna, S. (1982). Recipient reactions to aid. *Psychological Bulletin, 91,* 27–54.

Forret, M. L., & Dougherty, T. W. (2001). Correlates of networking behavior for managerial and professional employees. *Group & Organization Management, 26,* 283–311.

Forret, M. L., & Dougherty, T. W. (2004). Networking behaviors and career outcomes: Differences for men and women? *Journal of Organizational Behavior, 25,* 419–437.

Gaskill, L. R. (1991). Same-sex and cross-sex mentoring of female protégés: A comparative analysis. *Career Development Quarterly, 40,* 48–63.

George, P., & Kummerow, J. (1981). Mentoring for career women. *Training, 18*(2), 44–49.

Giacalone, R. A., & Rosenfeld, P. (1989). *Impression management in the organization.* Hillside, NJ: Lawrence Erlbaum.

Goffman, E. (1959). *The presentation of self in everyday life.* Garden City, NJ: Doubleday.

Goleman, D. (1995). *Emotional intelligence.* New York: Bantam Books.

Goleman, D., Boyatzis, R. E., & McKee, A. (2002). *Primal leadership: Realizing the power of emotional intelligence.* Cambridge, MA: Harvard Business School Publishing.

Gouldner, A. W. (1958). Cosmopolitans and locals: Towards an analysis of latent social roles. *Administrative Science Quarterly, 2,* 444–80.

Granovetter, M. (1973). The strength of weak ties. *American Journal of Sociology, 78,* 1360–1380.

Granovetter, M. (1983). The strength of weak ties: A network theory revisited. *Sociological Theory, 1,* 201–233.

Gulati, R., & Gargiulo, M. (1999). Where do interorganizational networks come from? *American Journal of Sociology, 104,* 1439–1493.

Hall, D. T. (2002). *Careers in and out of organizations.* Thousand Oaks, CA: Sage.

Hall, D. T. (2004). The protean career: A quarter century journey. *Journal of Vocational Behavior, 65,* 1–13.

Hall, D. T., & Associates (Eds.). (1996). *The career is dead—Long live the career: A developmental relational approach to careers.* San Francisco: Jossey-Bass.

Hall, D. T., & Mirvis, P. H. (1996). The new career: Psychological success and the path with a heart. In D. T. Hall & Associates (Eds.), *The career is dead—Long live the career: A developmental relational approach to careers* (pp. 15–45). San Francisco: Jossey-Bass.

Higgins, M. C. (2000). The more, the merrier? Multiple developmental relationships and work satisfaction. *Journal of Management Development, 19,* 277–296.

Higgins, M. C. (2001). Career change: A social influence perspective. *Journal of Organizational Behavior, 22,* 595–618.

Higgins, M. C., & Kram, K. E. (2001). Reconceptualizing mentoring at work: A developmental network perspective. *Academy of Management Review, 26,* 264–268.

Higgins, M. C., & Thomas, D. A. (2001). Constellations and careers: Toward understanding the effects of multiple developmental relationships. *Journal of Organizational Behavior, 22,* 223–247.

Hill, L. (1991). *Beyond the myth of the perfect mentor: Building a network of developmental relationships* (Harvard Business School Case No. 9-491-096). Boston: Harvard Business School Publishing.

Ibarra, H. (1992). Homophily and differential returns: Sex differences in network structure and access in an advertising firm. *Administrative Science Quarterly, 37,* 422–447.

Ibarra, H. (1995). Race, opportunity, and diversity of social circles in managerial networks. *Academy of Management Journal, 38,* 673–704.

Ibarra, H., & Smith-Lovin, L. (1997). *Creating tomorrow's organization: A handbook for* future research in organizational behavior. Sussex, UK: John Wiley & Sons.

Kanter, R. M. (1977). *Men and women of the corporation.* New York: Basic Books.

Kegan, R. (1982). *The evolving self: Problem and process in human adult development.* Cambridge, MA: Harvard University Press.

Kegan, R. (1994). *In over our heads: The mental demands of modern life* (2nd ed.). Cambridge, MA: Harvard University Press.

Kim, J., & Higgins, M. C. (in press). Where do alliances come from? The effects of upper echelons on alliance formation. *Research Policy, 36,* 499–514.

Kram, K. E. (1983). Phases of the mentor relationship. *Academy of Management Journal, 26,* 608–625.

Kram, K. E. (1985). *Mentoring at work: Developmental relationships in organizational life* (Rev. ed.). Glenview, IL: University Press of America.

Kram, K. E., & Hall, D. T. (1996). Mentoring in a context of diversity and turbulence. In E. E. Kossek & S. A. Lobel (Eds.), *Managing diversity: Human resource strategies for transforming the workplace* (pp. 108–136). Boston: Blackwell.

Lankau, M. J., & Scandura, T. A. (2002). An investigation of personal learning in mentoring relationships: Content, antecedents, and consequences. *Academy of Management Journal, 45,* 779–790.

Lengnick-Hall, M. L., & Lengnick-Hall, C. A. (2004). HR's role in building relationship networks. *Academy of Management Executive, 17*(4), 53–63.

Levinson, D. J. (with Darrow, D., Levinson, M., & McKee, B). (1978). *Seasons of a man's life.* New York: Knopf.

Levinson, D. J., & Levinson, J. (1996). *Seasons of a woman's life.* New York: Knopf.

Maccoby, E. E., & Jacklin, C. N. (1974). *The psychology of sex differences.* Stanford, CA: Stanford University Press.

McGowan, E. M. (2004). *Relationship work: A descriptive theory of a faculty-to-faculty formal mentoring program in higher education.* Unpublished doctoral dissertation, Harvard University, School of Education.

Mendenhall, M., & Oddou, G. (1986). Acculturation profiles of expatriate managers: implications for cross-cultural training programs. *Columbia Journal of World Business, 21*(4), 73–79.

Mezias, J. M., & Scandura, T. A. (2005). A needs-driven approach to expatriate adjustment and career development: A multiple mentoring perspective. *Journal of International Business Studies, 36,* 519–538.

Miller, J. B., & Stiver, I. P. (1997). *The healing connection: How women form relationships in therapy and in life.* Boston: Beacon.

Molloy, J. C. (2005). Developmental networks: Literature review and future research. *Career Development International, 10,* 536–548.

Morrison, A., & Von Glinow, M. A. (1990). Women and minorities in management. *American Psychologist, 45,* 200–208.

Morrison, E. W. (1993). Newcomer information feedback seeking: Exploring types, modes, sources, and outcomes. *Academy of Management Journal, 36,* 557–589.

Mullen, E. J. (1994). Framing the mentoring relationship as an information exchange. *Human Resource Management Review, 4,* 257–281.

Nadler, A. (1987). Determinants of help-seeking behavior: The effects of helper's similarity, task centrality, and recipient's self-esteem. *European Journal of Social Psychology, 17,* 57–67.

Nadler, A. (1991). Help-seeking behavior: Psychological costs and instrumental benefits. *Review of Personality and Social Psychology, 19,* 81–123.

Oddou, G. (1991). Managing your expatriates: What the successful firms do. *Human Resource Planning, 14,* 301–308.

Ostroff, C., & Kozlowski, S. W. (1993). The role of mentoring in the information gathering processes of newcomers during early organizational socialization. *Journal of Vocational Behavior, 42,* 170–183.

Pfeffer, J. (1977). Effects of an MBA and socioeconomic origin on business school graduate salaries. *Journal of Applied Psychology, 62,* 688–705.

Ragins, B. R. (1997). Diversified mentoring relationships in organizations: A power perspective. *Academy of Management Review, 22,* 482–521.

Ragins, B. R. (1989). Barriers to mentoring: The female manager's dilemma. *Human Relations, 42*, 1–22.

Ragins, B. R. (2007). Diversity and workplace mentoring relationships: A review and positive social capital approach. In T. D. Allen & L. T. Eby (Eds.), *Blackwell handbook of mentoring: A multiple perspectives approach* (pp. 281–300). Oxford, UK: Blackwell.

Ragins, B. R., & Cotton, J. L. (1991). Easier said than done: Gender differences in perceived barriers to gaining a mentor. *Academy of Management Journal, 34*, 939–951.

Ragins, B. R., & Verbos, A. (2007). Relational mentoring and mentoring schemas in the workplace. In J. Dutton & B. R. Ragins (Eds.), *Exploring positive relationships at work: Building a theoretical and research foundation* (pp. 91–116). Mahwah, NJ: Lawrence Erlbaum.

Rogers, L. E., & Escudero, V. (Eds.). (2004). *Relational communication: An interactional perspective to the study of process and form.* Mahwah, NJ: Lawrence Erlbaum.

Rothstein, M. G., Burke, R. J., & Bristor, J. M. (2001). Structural characteristics and support beliefs in the interpersonal networks of women and men in management. *International Journal of Organizational Analysis, 9*, 4–25.

Scandura, T. A., & Williams, E. A. (1998, November). Initiating mentoring: Contrasting the reports of protégés in assigned and informal relationships. *Southern Management Association proceedings* (pp. 140–142). New Orleans, LA: Southern Management Association Meeting.

Scandura, T. A., & Williams, E. A. (2001). An investigation of the moderating effects of gender on the relationships between mentorship initiation and protégé perceptions of mentoring functions. *Journal of Vocational Behavior, 59*, 342–363.

Schwab, D. P. (1980). Construct validity in organizational behavior. In B. M. Straw & L. L. Cummings (Eds.), *Research in organizational behavior* (pp. 3–43). Greenwich, CT: JAI Press.

Shepard, H. A. (1984). On the realization of human potential: A path with a heart. In M. B. Arthur, L. Bailyn, D. J. Levinson, & H. A. Shepard (Eds.), *Working with careers* (pp. 25–46). New York: Columbia University School of Business.

Stinchcombe, A. L. (1965). Social structure and organizations. In J. G. March (Ed.), *Handbook of organizations* (pp. 142–193). Chicago: Rand McNally & Company.

Thomas, D. A. (1990). The impact of race on managers' experiences of developmental relationships (mentoring and sponsorship): An intra-organizational study. *Journal of Organizational Behavior, 2*, 479–492.

Turban, D. B., & Dougherty, T. W. (1994). Role of protégé personality in receipt of mentoring and career success. *Academy of Management Journal, 34*, 331–351.

Useem, M. (1984). *The inner circle.* Oxford, UK: Oxford University Press.

Waldron, V. R. (1991). Achieving communication goals in superior-subordinate relationships: The multifunctionality of upward maintenance tactics. *Communication Monographs, 58*, 289–306.

Wanberg, C. R., Welsh, E. T., & Hezlett, S. A. (2003). Mentoring research: A review and dynamic process model. *Research in Personnel and Human Resources Management, 22*, 39–124.

Whitely, W. T., Dougherty, T. W., & Dreher, G. F. (1991). Relationship of career mentoring and socioeconomic origin to managers' and professionals' early career progress. *Academy of Management Journal, 34*, 331–351.

15

Stone Center Relational Cultural Theory

A Window on Relational Mentoring

Joyce K. Fletcher

Belle Rose Ragins

Mentoring scholars are just beginning to explore the processes, functions, and outcomes that distinguish different levels of quality in mentoring relationships. Mentoring relationships fall along a continuum (see Ragins, Cotton, & Miller, 2000), and while significant theoretical and empirical inroads have been made in understanding negative forms of mentoring (Eby, Chapter 13, this volume; Eby & Allen, 2002; Eby, Butts, Lockwood, & Simon, 2004; Scandura, 1998), little attention has been placed on the positive end of the relationship continuum. Inspired by the positive psychology movement (Seligman & Csikszentmihalyi, 2000; Snyder & Lopez, 2002) and the emerging field of positive organizational scholarship (Cameron, Dutton, & Quinn, 2003; Dutton & Ragins, 2007), there has been a recent call to examine the characteristics, processes, and outcomes of high-quality mentoring. In response, the construct of relational mentoring has been offered as a way to capture high-quality mentoring relationships and distinguish high-quality from average or marginal forms of mentoring (Ragins, 2005; Ragins & Verbos, 2007).

As a new concept, relational mentoring offers substantial promise for the field of mentoring and has been enriched by applying theoretical lenses of positive social capital (Baker & Dutton, 2007; Ragins, 2007) and psychological theories of cognitive processes in relationships (Baldwin, 1992, 1999; Ogilvie & Ashmore, 1991; Planalp, 1985; Ragins & Verbos, 2007). This chapter expands the construct of relational mentoring further by drawing on the theoretical lens of Stone Center Relational Cultural Theory (Miller, 1976; Jordan, Kaplan, Miller, Stiver, & Surrey, 1991). Stone Center Relational Cultural theory (RCT) offers a unique framework to delineate the processes and outcomes associated with high-quality interactions and relationships and analyze them within the larger cultural and societal contexts in which they occur. By viewing mentoring relationships through the lens of RCT, this chapter offers a framework for examining the conditions, processes, and outcomes associated with high-quality mentoring and expands the theoretical foundation of relational mentoring.

The chapter is organized as follows. First, we define relational mentoring and contrast it with traditional perspectives on mentoring. Next, we provide a brief review of the history of RCT. We then examine the key tenets of RCT and apply them to relational mentoring. We offer propositions for future research and present an RCT framework for relational mentoring. Finally, we offer recommendations for future research and theory on relational mentoring.

Traditional and Relational Perspectives on Mentoring

Traditionally, *mentoring* has been defined as a relationship between an older, more experienced mentor and a younger, less experienced protégé for the purpose of developing and helping the protégé's career (Hunt & Michael, 1983; Kram, 1985; Noe, 1988; Ragins, 1989). This traditional perspective has been questioned by scholars in both the mentoring (Higgins & Kram, 2001; Kram & Hall, 1996; McManus & Russell, Chapter 11, this volume) and positive relationships at work (Dutton & Heaphy, 2003; Dutton & Ragins, 2007; Ragins & Dutton, 2007) research arenas. These scholars point out that this one-directional, hierarchical view of mentoring does not capture the full range of processes, mechanisms, and outcomes of developmental relationships. Thus, new, more relational perspectives on mentoring have surfaced (McGowan, 2001; 2004; Ragins, 2005; Ragins & Verbos, 2007). In contrast to traditional perspectives, relational perspectives widen the lens to include interdependent and mutual processes that result in a full range of relational outcomes for both mentors and protégés (Ragins, 2005). *Relational mentoring* represents the relationship state of high-quality mentoring (Ragins & Verbos, 2007) and is defined as "an interdependent and generative developmental relationship that promotes mutual growth, learning and development within the career context" (Ragins, 2005, p. 10). A relational approach does not dismiss traditional approaches, but rather challenges some of the assumptions embedded in traditional mentoring perspectives and expands the constructs and dynamics open to study.

Mentoring scholars have identified three limitations in traditional perspectives that can be addressed by relational mentoring (see Ragins, 2005; Ragins & Verbos, 2007). First, a relational approach challenges the view of mentoring as a one-sided relationship in which a higher-ranking mentor provides for the career needs of the protégé by performing career development and psychosocial functions. Although Krams (1985) original work explored benefits for mentors, with few exceptions (see Allen, Chapter 5, this volume; Ragins & Scandura, 1999) most existing research examines mentoring from the protégé's side of the relationship (see reviews by Allen, Eby, Poteet, Lentz, & Lima, 2004; Noe, Greenberger, & Wang, 2002; Wanberg, Welsh, & Hezlett, 2003). The concept of relational mentoring makes visible the reciprocal and mutual nature of high-quality relationships and highlights areas of mentoring research that call for more exploration, such as specific *outcomes* that accrue to the mentor, the *functions* provided by the protégé, and the relational *microprocesses* that can generate growth, learning, and development for both mentors and protégés.

The second challenge relational mentoring presents to the traditional perspective is in the delineation of outcomes associated with the relationship. Traditionally, the success of the relationship has been assessed through outcomes that reflect traditional indicators of career success, such as advancement and the achievement of autonomy, independence, and differentiation from others (Fletcher, 1996a; Kram, 1996). This contrasts with more recent relational perspectives that view career development as a process that leads to increasingly complex states of interdependence and connection with others, as well as to the acquisition of relational skills and competencies (Fletcher, 1996a; Kram, 1996). Relational mentoring challenges the practice of using independence and autonomy to reflect career success and instead points to outcomes that reflect the ability to operate effectively in a context of interdependence and connection (Fletcher, 1996a; Kram, 1996; Ragins & Verbos, 2007).

The third challenge relational mentoring presents to traditional perspectives is that it highlights the role of power in interactions (Miller, 1976, 2003; Walker, 2002). Relational perspectives emphasize mutual learning and influence—a model that has been called "power with" (Follett, 1924; Miller, 1976). This contrasts with "power over" modes of influence that characterize hierarchical work relationships. By viewing the mentor as the prevailing source of power, influence, and expertise in the relationship, traditional perspectives underestimate protégés as a source of influence and expertise (e.g., protégés having more technical expertise than mentors). By releasing mentors and protégés from the rigid hierarchical roles of "teacher" and "student," relational mentoring challenges us to think more expansively about mutual influence in high-quality learning relationships and allows us to examine our assumptions about power in the relationship. This also allows us to explore potential conflicts that might arise between influence based on hierarchical power compared with other sources (e.g., French & Raven, 1959) and identify the relational skills needed to enact a model of "power with" within the confines of hierarchical work relationships.

In sum, relational mentoring offers mentoring scholars not only a new range of antecedents, processes, and outcomes to explore but also broadens our view of mentoring to incorporate the full range of developmental relationships. As displayed in Table 15.1, relational mentoring does not reject traditional forms of mentoring, but extends this perspective to capture the core processes and outcomes of high-quality mentoring relationships.

Table 15.1 A Comparison of Traditional and Relational/RCT Perspectives on Mentoring

Traditional Perspectives on Mentoring	Relational Mentoring Using an RCT Lens
Self	Self-in-Relation
One-directional learning	*Two-directional* learning
Hierarchical mode of influence	*Nonhierarchical* mode of influence
Focus on individual achievement leads to implicit goal of increased *independence* of protégé	Focus on growth-in-connection leads to goal of increased proficiency for both mentor and protégé in acting in context of *interdependence*.
Increased ability (of protégé) to function in context of *separation and independence*	Increased ability (of protégé and mentor) to function in context of *interdependence*
Mentor skills in teaching and coaching; Protégé skills in learning and being coached	Mentor *and* protégé must have skills in teaching and learning
Focus on mentor functions, behaviors, skills, and experience	Focus on mentor *and* protégé functions behaviors, skills, and experience
Static expertise	*Fluid* expertise
Social identity as *individual* variable (e.g., sex differences)	Social identity as *systemic* variable (e.g., systemic gender dynamics)
Power as *individual* variable	Power as *systemic* variable
Preeminence of one mentoring *relationship*	A continuum of mentoring *episodes*
Focus on protégé outcomes	Focus on outcomes for protégés *and* mentors

In this chapter, we use a particular theory of relational interactions, RCT (Jordan et al., 1991; Miller, 1976), to further define and examine the new construct of relational mentoring. We believe RCT can enhance our understanding of relational mentoring at two broad levels. First, at a microlevel, RCT's carefully nuanced delineation of the processes, outcomes, characteristics, and skills associated with relational interactions highlights the microprocesses within social interactions that lead to developmental outcomes. While relational mentoring challenges one-directional models of growth and suggests that future research explore mentoring from a two-directional perspective, the specific microprocesses embedded in two-directional mentoring have not been fully identified (see Ragins & Verbos, 2007). As discussed later, these microprocesses present a significant area of future research possibilities for relational mentoring.

Second, RCT situates these microlevel concepts within the larger, societal contexts of gender and power in which they occur. Thus, while relational mentoring challenges traditional models of hierarchical power, RCT goes further to suggest that societal-level systemic forces and social identity combine to play a key role in relational interactions.

In the following sections, we provide a brief review of the history of RCT. We then describe three key tenets of RCT and examine their implications for the field of mentoring.

Stone Center Relational Cultural Theory (RCT)

RCT is a model of human growth developed by psychologists and psychiatrists at the Stone Center for Developmental Services and Studies at Wellesley College (Jordan 1986; 1991; Jordan et al., 1991; Miller, 1976; Miller & Stiver, 1997; Surrey, 1985). While most theories of human development include the role of relationships (e.g., Levinson, 1978, Kegan, 1994), the hallmark of RCT is that it privileges connection as the primary site of human growth, carefully delineating the relational processes that account for this growth while exploring the gender and power dynamics underlying the relationship

The Theory's History Is Feminist

In the early 1970s, psychiatrist Jean Baker Miller noted that models of mental health were inadequate in capturing much of human experience. Listening to and learning from women's experience, she offered something new, a relational theory of human growth and development that she called "growth-in-connection." The central precept of this theory is that human growth, rather than occurring primarily through the processes of separation and individuation, occurs primarily in a context of relational connection with others. Working with Stone Center colleagues, Miller (1976) identified the relational skills and attributes essential to this type of growth and observed that this growth-in-connection model revealed important truths not only about women's psychological growth, but about all human development.

There are two historical aspects of RCT that distinguish it from more recent relational ideologies (e.g., Draft, 2001; Duck, 1994; Hosking, Dachler, & Gergen 1995; McNamee & Gergen, 1999). First, RCT explicitly sought to recast relational attributes (e.g., empathy and the capacity to experience vulnerability) as strengths that should be developed in all as opposed to deficiencies that are evidence of weakness or greater emotional need in some (the need to be liked, for example). With the advent of concepts like emotional intelligence (Goleman, 1995), it is easy to forget how radical a concept this was in the 1970s. As RCT has developed, it has gone beyond noting that relational attributes are strengths and has delineated the microprocesses within relational interactions where these competencies are used.

Second, RCT is distinct from other theories in its incorporation of gender and cultural context. Unlike other developmental theories (e.g., Kegan, 1994; Levinson, 1978; Loevinger, 1976) and conceptualizations of relational skills, such as emotional intelligence (Goleman, 1995), RCT treats gender as a cultural rather than an individual-level phenomenon. That is, RCT calls attention to the gendered nature of mainstream theories of human growth and development, focusing not on the question of differences between men and women, but rather on the masculine nature of the theories themselves. Specifically, Miller (1976) noted that mainstream theories characterize relational attributes as feminine traits associated with women's greater emotional needs. She noted that in Western society, men are socialized to devalue and deny in themselves the relational skills needed to survive psychologically, and they rely on women to provide these attributes. Women are socialized to provide these skills, usually invisibly and without acknowledgment that these attributes are needed and valuable. Women therefore become the "carriers" of relational strengths in Western society, responsible for creating relational connections for others and meeting basic relational needs without calling attention to the needs themselves. Rather than strengths, these relational attributes are surrounded by what Miller (1976) called a "language of deficiency" (e.g., emotionally needy, codependent or overly dependent on relationships, low ego strength, etc.) and are often characterized as a source of psychological problems rather than strength. Miller observed that the invisibility and devaluing of relational activity allows society to perpetuate a myth of self-reliance and independence, even though most people have a network of others who support their "individual" achievement.

Over time, RCT deepened its cultural analysis beyond gender, to broader systemic categories of power and social identity. While other developmental theories, such as stage theories (e.g., Kegan, 1982, 1994, Loevinger, 1976), explore growth as an individual-level phenomenon that develops over time regardless of social identity and societal-level power dynamics, RCT includes this broader context. In fact, Stone Center theorists recently changed the name of the theory from "Stone Center Relational Theory" to "Relational Cultural Theory" (Miller, 2004) to highlight the point that relational interactions must always be understood within the broader social context in which they occur.

Applying the Tenets of RCT to Relational Mentoring

In this section, we examine the key tenets of RCT, apply these tenets to the mentoring arena, and offer propositions for future research. An application of the critical tenets of RCT theory to relational mentoring is diagrammed in Figure 15.1.

Tenet #1: Interdependent Self-in-Relation

A key tenet of RCT is its view of the self. As many have noted (see Kegan, 1994; Watkins & Marsick, 2003; Miller, 1976; Miller & Stiver, 1997), traditional concepts of self are rooted in theories that reflect Western models of adult development. These concepts envision growth as a process of becoming increasingly proficient at separating and individuating oneself from others in an implicit move from dependence to independence. Stone Center relational theorists (Miller, 1976; 1984; Miller & Stiver, 1997; Surrey, 1985) were at the forefront in challenging these traditional models. They also challenged the very conceptualization of "self," asserting that it does not adequately capture the fluid, two-directional flow of mutual influence that

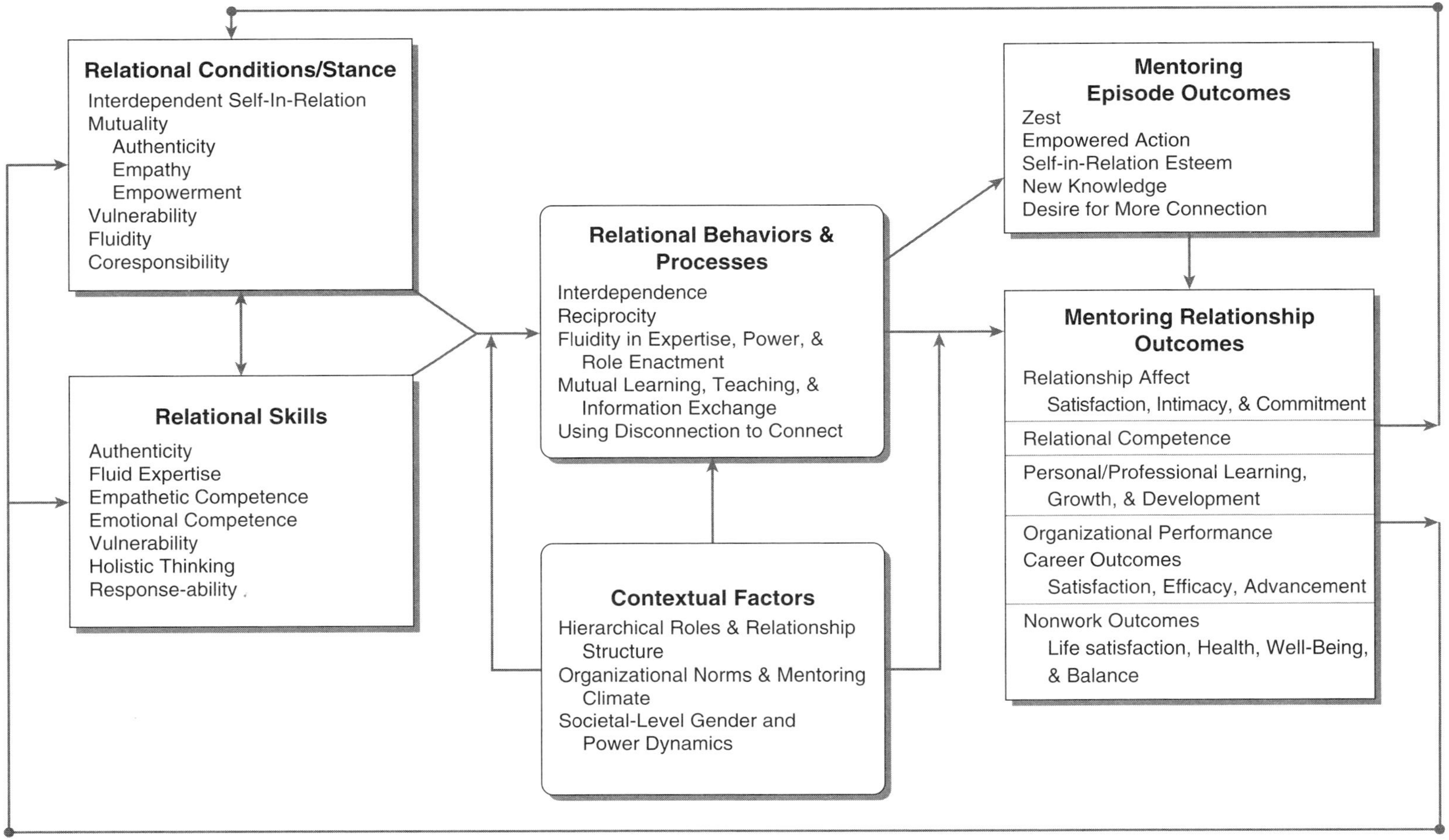

Relational Conditions/Stance
Interdependent Self-In-Relation
Mutuality
Authenticity
Empathy
Empowerment
Vulnerability
Fluidity
Coresponsibility
Relational Skills
Authenticity
Fluid Expertise
Empathetic Competence
Emotional Competence
Vulnerability
Holistic Thinking
Response-ability
Relational Behaviors & Processes
Interdependence
Reciprocity
Fluidity in Expertise, Power, & Role Enactment
Mutual Learning, Teaching, & Information Exchange
Using Disconnection to Connect
Contextual Factors
Hierarchical Roles & Relationship Structure
Organizational Norms & Mentoring Climate
Societal-Level Gender and Power Dynamics
Mentoring Episode Outcomes
Zest
Empowered Action
Self-in-Relation Esteem
New Knowledge
Desire for More Connection
Mentoring Relationship Outcomes
Relationship Affect
Satisfaction, Intimacy, & Commitment
Relational Competence
Personal/Professional Learning, Growth, & Development
Organizational Performance
Career Outcomes
Satisfaction, Efficacy, Advancement
Nonwork Outcomes
Life satisfaction, Health, Well-Being, & Balance

Figure 15.1 An RCT Model of Relational Mentoring

characterizes interactions. They cited research (e.g., Beebe & Lachman, 1988; Tronick, 1989) indicating that even in the earliest days of life, an infant influences the emotional field between self and caretaker and begins to develop an interacting sense of self. Thus, RCT theorists suggested that every relational interaction should be studied and understood as two-directional. In addition, they asserted that the word *self* needs to be replaced to better capture the human developmental process. Drawing on earlier theorists (e.g., Chodorow, 1978), they offered a replacement: *self-in-relation* (Surrey, 1985).

The concept of self-in-relation, which is congruent with current thinking in the cognitive sciences domain (see Brewer & Gardner, 1996; Cross & Madson, 1997; Ogilvie & Ashmore, 1991) has direct utility for understanding the processes involved in high-quality mentoring because it highlights how personal growth for both mentors and protégés is inextricably connected to their partners. Traditional perspectives on mentoring cast the mentor in the role of "protector" and the protégé in the role of "dependent," with the implicit goal of moving the protégé to an increased state of independence and self-sufficiency. The concept of self-in-relation recasts the goal of the relationship by suggesting that positive relationships involve movement toward increased competence in enacting both members' self-in-relation and increasing their abilities to operate effectively in a context of interdependence.

Other psychological perspectives on relational identity (Brewer & Gardner, 1996; Brickson & Brewer, 2001) and interdependent self-construals (Cross, Bacon, & Morris, 2000; Cross & Madson, 1997) hold that individuals vary in the degree to which they define themselves by their relationships with others. In contrast, the concept of self-in-relation holds that all individuals are selves-in-relation and what varies is the extent to which we either accept and enact that reality—or deny it and operate as if we were discrete beings independent of others. Nonetheless, it is reasonable to assume that (for a variety of individual- and systemic-level reasons) the extent to which one accepts and enacts one's self-in-relation will vary and that this variance will have an impact on the motivation to engage in relational-mentoring interactions. It is also reasonable to expect that the process of engaging in relational-mentoring interactions will reinforce and increase one's acceptance of one's identity as an interdependent self-in-relation. Finally, the quality of mentoring interactions should be positively influenced by the degree to which members of the relationship acknowledge their self-in-relation identities.

Applying this RCT lens to the relational-mentoring domain yields the following set of propositions:

Proposition 1a: The degree to which one acknowledges one's identity as an interdependent self-in-relation will predict one's motivation to engage in relational-mentoring interactions.

Proposition 1b: The degree to which members in relational-mentoring interactions acknowledge their interdependent selves-in-relation will predict the quality of the interaction.

Tenet #2: Specific Criteria Define ✗
Growth-Fostering Interactions

The second key tenet of RCT is its identification of the specific conditions, skills, and outcomes that define a mutually (i.e., two-directional) *growth-fostering interaction*. That is, RCT does not simply assert that growth and learning are dependent on social interactions. Rather than casting all relational and dialogic interactions as occasions where human agency can be accomplished interactively (e.g., Della Noce, 1999; Hosking et al., 1995; McNamee & Gergen, 1999), RCT differentiates growth-fostering interactions from non-growth-fostering interactions. By analyzing relational quality at the level of a single interaction, RCT offers a framework for studying developmental relationships at the level of one interaction, or what we call a *mentoring episode*. As noted in the subtenets below, RCT not only delineates the two-directional microprocesses within social interactions that lead to growth and learning but also offers a set of evaluative criteria that can be used to determine whether growth and learning occurred within a given interaction, thus allowing us to classify the interaction as mutually growth fostering or not.

The concept of mentoring episodes makes an important contribution to mentoring research, as it has the potential to bring clarity to one of the tenets of mentoring that has become muddied in recent years. With the advent of concepts such as peer mentoring, lateral mentoring, and developmental networks (Eby, 1997; Ensher, Thomas, & Murphy, 2001; Higgins, Chandler, & Kram, Chapter 14, this volume; Higgins & Kram, 2001; McManus & Russell, Chapter 11, this volume), the issue of what constitutes a mentoring relationship has surfaced (see also Dougherty & Dreher, Chapter 3, this volume). As Ragins (1999b) noted, a frequent methodological problem in mentoring research is the assumption that all relationships that engage in developmental behaviors are mentoring relationships. Mentoring episodes offer mentoring scholars a way to distinguish between a short-term interaction that occurs at a specific point in time and a mentoring relationship. In essence, although all mentoring relationships involve mentoring episodes, individuals can engage in mentoring episodes without being in mentoring relationships. Moreover, the concept of mentoring episodes captures the dynamic and fluid nature of relationships (Boyatzis, Chapter 18, this volume; Duck, 1994) and may provide insight into how some relationships are transformed into mentoring relationships. For example, an increase in mentoring episodes may create a "tipping point" in which members come to view their work relationship as a mentoring relationship.

The notion of mentoring episodes also offers a more fine-grained understanding of relational mentoring and the continuum of mentoring relationships. According to RCT, high-quality relational-mentoring episodes are those in which the criteria for a mutually growth-fostering interaction (which are discussed below) are met. It is reasonable to assume that the frequency and quality of these episodes will predict a deepening connection and commitment between the parties and may over time evolve to what both may acknowledge as a high-quality mentoring relationship. RCT therefore gives us a way of envisioning a full continuum of possible mentoring interactions—from episodic to continuous—as well as a way to differentiate among them in order to study and articulate unique characteristics and outcomes of relational mentoring. Mentoring relationships that are characterized by a high number of mutually growth-fostering relational-mentoring episodes should be more likely to be experienced as high-quality, relational mentoring.

This discussion can be summarized by the following propositions:

Proposition 2a: High-quality mentoring relationships consist of a series of high-quality (mutually growth-fostering) relational-mentoring episodes that occur over time.

Proposition 2b: The frequency, duration, and intensity of high-quality relational-mentoring episodes will predict the degree to which members of the relationship acknowledge it as a high-quality mentoring relationship.

While RCT offers us a way to study mentoring at the level of one relational interaction, it also notes that not every interaction in a growth-fostering relationship is likely to be a mutually growth-fostering episode. Indeed, RCT notes that individual relational interactions may be one-directional or even characterized by disconnection and the absence of growth. However, according to RCT theory, one of the conditions for the continuation of a growth-in-connection relationship is that members have the skills, desire, and ability to move from and through episodes of disconnection back to connection. This process is complicated by what RCT theorists call "relational paradox" (Miller & Stiver, 1997). This refers to the tendency to disconnect oneself from the relationship (e.g., moving away from authenticity, being silent, moving away from one's own expertise) because of the fear that being authentic might damage the relationship or forestall future interactions. This can lead to relational interactions that result in disconnection rather than connection. If not addressed, this can lead to a downward spiral of disconnection and ultimately a growth-deadening rather than a growth-fostering relationship. However, if such disconnections are addressed, they can lead to an even deeper connection and result in the capacity for increased growth-in-connection.

Thus, RCT offers relational mentoring not only the idea of a continuum of mentoring episodes but also a way of thinking about how a series of episodes evolve over time to create a high-quality mentoring relationship.

Proposition 2c: The frequency with which episodes of disconnection are addressed effectively within a mentoring relationship will determine the quality of that relationship.

A key implication of this perspective is that mentoring relationships exist along a continuum of quality that reflects the discrete experience of mentoring episodes; a given episode may or may not be mutual. While high-quality mentoring relationships are characterized by a preponderance of mutually growth-fostering episodes, not every interaction in the relationship is likely to meet that standard. RCT specifies a set of evaluative criteria that can be used to determine whether mutual growth and learning occurred within a given interaction, thus allowing us to classify the episode as mutually growth fostering or not. According to RCT theory, mutually growth-fostering interactions meet three sets of criteria: (a) the *conditions* (i.e., set of beliefs or stance) that must be present, (b) the relational *skills* required to achieve these conditions, and (c) the *outcomes* that must be mutually achieved for the interaction to be defined as mutually growth fostering. These criteria are listed as subtenets below.

Subtenet #2a: Conditions of mutually growth-fostering interactions. According to RCT, a growth-in-connection episode is characterized by the construct of mutuality in which the boundary between one's self and one's partner is fluid and multi-directional. The process involves movement toward mutual authenticity (bringing one's authentic self to the interaction), to mutual empathy (whereby one can hold onto one's self but also experience the other's reality), and finally to mutual empowerment (whereby each person is in some way influenced or affected by the other, so that something new is created) (Jordan, 1986, 1991). RCT posits that this kind of mutuality depends on both parties operating from a self-in-relation stance, a condition in which both members of the interaction recognize vulnerability as part of the human condition, approach the interaction expecting to grow from it, and feel a responsibility to contribute to the growth of the other. That is, when growth-in-connection is happening, the process is always multidirectional and characterized by fluidity and coresponsibility.

RCT offers useful insights into the conditions needed for relational-mentoring episodes. Applying RCT tenets on relational stance, high-quality mentoring should be more likely to emerge when both members approach their interactions (i.e., mentoring episodes) from a position of vulnerability, thereby accepting it as one of the conditions for growth and learning.

> *Proposition 3a:* The quality of a mentoring episode will be predicted by the degree to which each member approaches the interaction from a position of vulnerability.

It is important to note that a stance of vulnerability, especially for the mentor, contradicts established hierarchical roles that prevail in traditional work relationships. Applying an RCT view, relational mentoring requires that mentors and protégés need to be willing and able to put aside hierarchical roles in order to enter the mentoring episode from a place of mutual vulnerability. This raises issues not only of risk but also of identity, role expectations, and the ability to curtail impression management "face-saving gambits." RCT suggests that relational mentoring involves egalitarian practices of power that de-emphasize or disavow the power associated with members' positions or group memberships. For example, to achieve mutual growth-in-connection, mentors must be comfortable showing their own needs, lack of competence, and vulnerability, while protégés must be able to acknowledge their own sources of expertise and be willing to share this expertise with their mentors. These behaviors conflict with conventional prescriptions for organizational roles in hierarchical contexts. This discussion is summarized by the following propositions:

> *Proposition 3b:* Mentoring episodes are most likely to evolve to high-quality mentoring relationships when both members have the ability to resist hierarchically prescribed roles and adopt a relational stance.

Table 15.2   Relational Skills and Competencies

Skill/Competency	Definition
Authenticity	Ability to access and express one's own thoughts and feelings
Fluid Expertise	Ability to move easily from expert to nonexpert role Ability to acknowledge help and give credit to others with no loss of self-esteem
Empathic Competence	Ability to understand other's experience and perspectives
Emotional Competence	Ability to understand, interpret, and use emotional data
Vulnerability	Ability to admit "not knowing," to seek help and expertise with no loss of self-esteem
Holistic Thinking	A synthesis of thinking, feeling, and acting
Response-Ability	Ability to hold onto one's own perspective while at the same time fully engaging with another's to allow mutual influence

SOURCE: Fletcher (1998).

Subtenet #2b: Relational skills are required to put conditions into practice. According to RCT, a key condition for growth-fostering interactions is that participants approach the interaction expecting to grow, learn, and be changed by it and feel a responsibility—and a desire—to contribute to the growth of the other. Putting this stance into practice requires relational skills such as empathy, listening, and emotional competence (Fletcher, 1999). These skills are listed in Table 15.2.

The skills and conditions identified by RCT are useful to relational mentoring in at least three ways. First, in contrast to traditional one-directional approaches to mentoring, RCT highlights the two-directional nature of growth-fostering interactions, such as mentoring episodes, and identifies the set of relational skills and competencies both parties need to put such a two-directional model of growth into practice (Fletcher, 1999; Jordan, 1999; Miller & Stiver, 1997).

Second, these skills highlight the role of relational competence in mentoring relationships. While the notion of relational skills figures prominently in Kram's work (Chandler & Kram, 2005; Kram, 1985, 1996), there has been a subsequent lack of theory and empirical research on this topic (see review by Wanberg et al., 2003). RCT reinforces early views of mentoring by predicting that relational skills and competence will play a key role in relational mentoring.

Proposition 4a: The relational skills held by the mentor and protégé will predict the quality of their mentoring episode and the ultimate quality of their mentoring relationship.

Third, by emphasizing the two-directional nature of growth-in-connection interactions, RCT reinforces and resurrects early perspectives that both mentors and protégés need to be responsible for and committed to the growth and development of their partners (see Kram, 1985). Subsequent research has focused on the mentor's behaviors and functions and largely ignores the skills, behaviors, and functions of the protégé (see Wanberg et al., 2003). Although relational mentoring theory emphasizes the protégé's role in the relationship (Ragins & Verbos, 2007), RCT offers this perspective a typology of conditions, skills, and outcomes that can be used to assess relational growth-in-connection in mentoring relationships.

In particular, RCT offers key insights into mutual role enactment processes in mentoring relationships. The role of the protégé in relational mentoring is related to RCT concepts such as fluid expertise, interdependence, reciprocity, and mutuality (Fletcher, 1998). Although the overall level of expertise between mentor and protégé may be asymmetrical, growth-in-connection models allow for a state of fluidity in which expertise shifts within a given mentoring episode. For example, an academic mentor may provide the protégé with strategies for publication, but the protégé may provide the mentor with the latest information on statistical software. Another example is cross-race mentoring relationships, in which protégés of color offer dominant-group mentors the opportunity to learn about diversity in very personal and powerful ways (Ragins, 1997, 2002). RCT therefore allows us to examine episodes in which the protégé empowers or enables the mentor to develop new forms of knowledge and skills. This suggests that future research on relational mentoring should focus on delineating the functions, tasks, and "work" of being a protégé and the specific ways in which mentors learn from the protégé. In essence, while traditional perspectives on mentoring focus on static role designations, a relational perspective offers the possibility of less-discrete and more-fluid role relationships in high-quality mentoring relationships. It is therefore reasonable to expect that fluidity in moving from role of expert to nonexpert characterizes high-quality mentoring relationships and episodes.

Proposition 4b: The degree to which mentors and protégés engage in fluid expertise will predict the quality of mentoring episodes and relationships.

Finally, it is important to consider the role organizational context plays in the display and practice of relational skills in mentoring relationships. For example, Miller (1976) asserted that the characterization of relational skills as strengths is a challenge to conventional wisdom, which views vulnerability and the skills associated with enacting it as signs of personal inadequacy rather than competencies. Despite recent, more relational models of leadership (e.g., Kouzes & Posner, 2002; Pearce & Conger, 2003), there may be organizational forces (Fletcher & Kaeufer, 2003; Fletcher, 2004) that undermine the goals of relational mentoring, because enacting relational practices flies in the face of conventional wisdom about what competent leadership (i.e., heroic, individualistic models) and competent management practice entail (i.e., having answers, not showing vulnerability). This suggests that organizational norms and climate influence the development of high-quality mentoring relationships. In particular, from an RCT perspective, it is reasonable to expect that organizational framing of managerial competence will influence the development and sustainability of relational mentoring.

Table 15.3   The "Five Good Things": Outcomes of Growth-Fostering Interactions

Criteria	Definition
Zest.	Connection with the other that gives both members a sense of increased energy and vitality.
Empowered Action:	Motivation and ability to put into practice some of what was learned or experienced in the relational interaction.
Increased Sense of Worth (Self-in-Relation Esteem):	Increased feelings of worth that come from the experience of having used one's "self-in-relation" to achieve mutual growth in connection.
New Knowledge:	Learning that comes from the ability to engage in "fluid expertise," fully contributing one's own thoughts and perspective while at the same time being open to others.
Desire for More Connection:	A desire to continue this particular connection and/or establish other growth-fostering connections, leading to a spiral of growth that extends outward, beyond the initial participants.

Proposition 4c: The degree to which organizations adhere to one-directional, nonrelational images of competence will influence the degree to which relational mentoring can flourish in that environment.

Subtenet #2c: Outcomes of growth-fostering interactions: The five good things. RCT offers specific evaluative criteria with which to differentiate growth-fostering inter-actions from other types of social interactions. Specifically, Miller and Stiver (1997) theorized that when mutual learning and growth have occurred, parties in the interaction achieve "five good things," which are defined in Table 15.3.

RCT theory holds that all five of these episode outcomes must be mutual in order for connection, learning, and growth to occur in a given interaction (Miller & Stiver, 1997). According to RCT, it is not enough for only one member of the rela-tionship to experience the five good things. If the outcomes are not mutual, the ideal of generative growth has not been achieved. Thus, RCT views mutual growth-in-connection as a binary state. In a given interaction, either it has occurred or it has not. Applied to mentoring episodes, this means that if, for example, a protégé is not moved to empowered action, but instead feels disempowered or exploited in an interaction or if a mentor does not achieve some level of new knowledge or does not experience a desire for more connection, a truly mutual relational-mentoring episode has not been achieved.

Therefore, an application of RCT to mentoring episodes yields the following proposition:

Proposition 5a: Mutual growth-in-connection mentoring episodes are those in which both members experience some level of zest, empowered action, increased sense of worth, new knowledge, and the desire for more connection.

Mentoring episodes in which the standard of mutual growth-in-connection has been met (i.e., the five good things) can be expected to have a cumulative effect on both protégés and mentors as the mentoring relationship evolves. This offers promise for the study of relational mentoring as occurring along a continuum of quality (Ragins & Verbos, 2007). For example, it is possible that the number of mentoring episodes that qualify as mutually growth fostering (i.e., all five outcomes are mutually achieved) might be the measure of where a mentoring relationship is located on a continuum of quality. Although RCT holds that all five outcomes must be mutually achieved for an interaction to be considered growth fostering, future research should test this perspective in mentoring relationships. In particular, future studies could examine the degree to which one or both members experience the five outcomes and determine the specific links to quality. Perhaps some outcomes or combinations of outcomes are more important than others for determining whether or not a mentoring episode is experienced as mutually growth fostering. That is, while RCT theory views mutual growth-in-connection in one interaction as binary (mutual growth has or has not occurred) and makes no differentiation in importance among the five outcomes, future research could examine whether this binary standard holds true for mentoring episodes.

In the same vein, it is reasonable to assume that repeated episodes in which the five good things are mutually achieved will lead to increasing levels of relational competence in both members of the relationship. *Relational competence* can be defined as the ability to operate effectively in a context of connection and interdependence (Fletcher, 1999). Relational competence depends on the ability to enact relational skills with increasing levels of proficiency. Once achieved, relational competence is transferable across other relationships and settings. Like emotional intelligence (see Cherniss, Chapter 17, this volume), relational competence is inextricably related to instrumental outcomes such as organizational effectiveness, achievement, learning, and leadership (Fletcher, 1999; Goleman, 1998).

The concept of relational competence has direct utility for mentoring. Although Kram's (1985) work points to the importance of relational competence, most empirical mentoring research examines instrumental outcomes associated with the relationship (see Allen et al., 2004) and does not consider the skills and competencies derived from the relationship that yield these outcomes. According to RCT, relational competence is one vehicle through which positive career outcomes are achieved. Members' relational competence increases as a consequence of repeated episodes of interactions in which the five good things are mutually achieved. An increase in their relational competence will, in turn, lead to an increase in their work performance and ability to obtain a range of career outcomes, such as advancement, career satisfaction, and career self-efficacy.

Proposition 5b: Relational competence achieved in a high-quality mentoring relationship will spill over to other work relationships and increase the overall competence and effectiveness of both mentor and protégé.

Proposition 5c: Increases in overall competence and effectiveness will be likely to lead to enhanced career outcomes, such as advancement, satisfaction, and efficacy for both mentor and protégé.

It should be noted that increases in relational competence also influence the development of the relationship by enhancing the relational skills and conditions that are antecedents to relational-mentoring episodes. This is represented by the reinforcing feedback loop in Figure 15.1. Thus, relational competence is an outcome that reinforces the antecedent skills and conditions required to engage relational processes and behaviors.

Another key outcome of growth-fostering interactions is increased positive affect. At the level of mentoring episode, positive affect is embedded in the last of the five good things: the desire for more and deeper connection, which is experienced as an affective behavioral state (Fletcher, 1998). Applying RCT to mentoring relationships, it is reasonable to assume that as mentoring episodes evolve to a relationship, repeated experiences of positive affective behavioral states will increase the intimacy, closeness, satisfaction, and commitment experienced by both members of the relationship. This increase in positive affect will, in turn, increase both the quality and desire for additional relational episodes.

Conceptualizing positive affect as a by-product or outcome of the relationship has important implications for understanding relational mentoring. Scholars who have applied RCT to work settings observe that affection is not a required antecedent to the ability and desire to engage in growth-fostering workplace interactions (Fletcher, 1996b, 1999). Thus, even individuals with no prior attraction have the ability to engage in authentic, mutually growth-fostering interactions and achieve relational outcomes. This is an important distinction for mentoring, which was first studied as an informal relationship occurring between individuals who were naturally attracted to one another (Kram, 1985). As a result of this initial perspective, positive affect has traditionally been viewed as an optimal condition for the development of effective mentoring relationships. RCT suggests that while positive affect may be an antecedent to the motivation to enter a mentoring relationship, it is not required for quality outcomes to occur. Other factors, such as members' relational skills and their ability to adopt a relational stance, may be even more important than prior intimacy for the quality of the relationship.

However, the explication of positive affect as an outcome is not meant to minimize or dismiss its role on the quality of the relationship. As illustrated in a feedback loop in Figure 15.1, it is likely that members who experience positive affective outcomes will experience an increase in their desire and ability to engage in future mutually growth-fostering interactions.

Proposition 5d: Positive affect is not a required antecedent to the initial ability and desire to engage in high-quality mentoring episodes.

Proposition 5e: Increased positive affect (i.e. intimacy, satisfaction, commitment) is a relationship outcome achieved through multiple relational-mentoring episodes experienced over time.

Proposition 5f: As an outcome, positive affect reinforces the desire to engage in additional relational-mentoring episodes and enhances the quality of those episodes.

Finally, drawing on holistic approaches that incorporate the effects of work relationships on life states and experiences (Ragins, 2005, in press; Ragins & Dutton, 2007), we expect that relational mentoring will influence nonwork experiences such as life satisfaction, psychological and physical health, well-being, and balance (see Dutton & Heaphy, 2003; Heaphy, 2007).

There are at least three ways in which relational mentoring may spill over into the nonwork domain. First, since relational competence (Fletcher, 1999) is not limited to the organization's boundaries, the relational competence achieved in high-quality mentoring relationships may facilitate members' development of other high-quality nonwork relationships involving friends, family, and members of their personal and professional communities (see also Greenhaus & Singh, Chapter 21, this volume). Individuals in high-quality mentoring relationships may also realize the benefits of growth-fostering relationships and seek other generative relationships outside the work setting (Ragins, 2005). Second, because the work domain has become such an intrinsic part of the life domain (Ragins, in press), career and job satisfaction may spill over to life satisfaction, physical health, and well-being (Heaphy, 2007). Finally, relational mentoring is holistic in focus and scope (Ragins & Verbos, 2007), and the creation of authentic identities and balance across life domains may be a key focus of high-quality mentoring relationships (Ragins, 2007).

> *Proposition 5g:* The effects of relational mentoring relationships within the workplace will spill over to nonwork relationships, leading to positive life outcomes, such as life satisfaction, health, well-being, and balance.

Tenet #3: Systemic Power

RCT highlights how traditional concepts of self as an independent entity and growth as a process of separation from others contribute to what Jean Baker Miller (1976) called the "myth of individual achievement." This belief that independence is a state that can be achieved belies the essentially *interdependent* nature of the human condition. Moreover, RCT asserts that this myth operates as a discursive exercise of power, whereby some in society are expected to provide the collaborative subtext of life invisibly, so others can enact the "myth of individual achievement" without acknowledging that this collaborative subtext of support is needed and important. The theory points out that both a gender/patriarchic power and a more general power dynamic are involved in sustaining these so-called myths of independence and individual achievement.

Gender. RCT places the construct of relationality within the discourse on the social construction of gender (West & Zimmerman, 1991), highlighting the fact that relationality is not a gender-neutral concept. On the contrary, gender socialization, especially in Western society, assigns to women the task of creating the relational conditions under which human growth-in-connection can occur (Chodorow, 1978; Fairbairn, 1952; Miller, 1976; Miller & Stiver, 1997; Winnicott, 1958). Thus, using relational skills and adopting a self-in-relation stance is likely to be, at some deep, perhaps even unconscious level, associated with femininity.

Power. The fact that in systems of unequal power (i.e., race, class, gender, sexual orientation), those with less power are required to develop relational skills in order to be attuned to and anticipate the needs, desires, and implicit requests of the more powerful means that at some deep, perhaps unconscious level, these skills are associated with powerlessness (Bartolome & Laurent 1988; Miller, 1976).

The RCT perspective on gender and power dynamics places the construct of relational mentoring within a larger societal context and makes visible the ways in which relational activity is subject to systemic dynamics outside of the relationship itself. This perspective offers several implications for mentoring. The first is related to gender. RCT suggests that because mentoring theory (like developmental theory) has origins in the experience of White male professionals in the Western world, it reflects the attributes, values, life experiences, and gender role expectations of this dominant identity (see also Thomas & Alderfer, 1989). Thus, RCT supports the idea that traditional perspectives on mentoring constitute a body of knowledge that Joan Acker (1990) called "gendered" (i.e., knowledge that implicitly reifies the masculine and devalues or ignores the feminine). It is reasonable to assume, therefore, that traditional perspectives on mentoring may not fit the needs, experiences, or role expectations of women (Fletcher, 1994; Ragins, 1995, 1997, 1999a, 2007) and may cause special problems and dilemmas for them. For example, because women have been expected to be the "carriers" of relational strengths for society, those who have broken through the glass ceiling often face intense pressure to mentor lower-ranking women in their organizations (see Giscombe, Chapter 22, this volume; McKeen & Bujaki, Chapter 8, this volume; Ragins, Townsend, & Mattis, 1998; Ragins, 1999a). In the same vein, women who choose not to mentor violate these gendered assumptions about femininity and what "good women" do and may subsequently face harsh judgments and recriminations (Ragins, 1989; Ragins & Scandura, 1994).

On the other hand, RCT suggests that because women are socialized to be the carriers of relational strengths for society, they may be likely to adopt the relational stance required to effectively engage in high-quality relational-mentoring episodes and relationships.

This leads to the following proposition:

Proposition 6a: Traditional perspectives on mentoring may not serve the needs and experience of women well and may cause special problems and dilemmas for them.

Proposition 6b: Relational perspectives on mentoring may be more likely than traditional perspectives to serve the needs and experiences of women and other nondominant groups.

The second implication of RCT's perspective on gender and power dynamics for mentoring addresses the impact of group membership on role expectations and processes in mentoring relationships. RCT proposes that other social identity characteristics add to and interact with gender to affect one's mentoring experiences. As noted earlier, RCT asserts that because people with less power are required to develop relational skills in order to anticipate and respond to the needs of the more powerful, power dynamics inherent in dominant and non-dominant social identity groups influence relational interactions. For example, while women may be expected to take on the mantle of mentoring as an expression of their femininity, the situation may be exacerbated for African American women, who face an additional set of role expectations (e.g., to serve others selflessly) that stems from a history of slavery and oppression (see Blake-Beard, Murrell, & Thomas, Chapter 9, this volume; Thomas, 1989). By the same token, the experience of being a mentor or protégé may be quite different for White men and men of color. While White male mentors may be viewed as exemplary organizational citizens for providing mentoring to "needy" women and people of color, men of color may be expected to "help their own," even though their mentoring may be valued less because they have less power and may be less able to sponsor their protégés' advancement (see Dreher & Chargois, 1998; Dreher & Cox, 1996). Mentors of color may face stereotypes that undercut their ability to develop relationships with dominant-group protégés (Collins, Kamya, & Tourse, 1997; Johnson-Bailey & Cervero, 2004; Ortiz-Walters & Gilson, 2005; Thomas, 1993); and protégés of color may find it difficult to offer their expertise and engage in mutual exchanges with dominant-group mentors because of racial stereotypes and attributions that denigrate their competence (see Kalbfleisch & Davies, 1991; Thomas, 1990; Thomas & Gabarro, 1999; Viator, 2001).

RCT therefore suggests that systemic power dynamics at the societal level (i.e., the legacies of patriarchal laws, slavery, and homophobic secrecy) need to be taken into account when studying mentoring relationships. In particular, RCT theory predicts that the interaction—or what Holvino (2001) called the "simultaneity" of social identity characteristics—within as well as between members of the relationship will affect mentoring episodes and the ability of the relationship to reach the high-quality state of relational mentoring.

This suggests that mentoring research and models of relational mentoring pay attention not only to hierarchical power and status differences between mentors and protégés but also to the power associated with their group memberships, which is brought with them into the relationship (see Ragins, 1997; Ragins & Sundstrom, 1989). Accordingly, an RCT perspective predicts that power influences the expectations, roles, and behaviors in mentoring relationships and is a key contextual factor that affects the development and outcomes of relational-mentoring episodes and relationships.

Proposition 6c: The social identity of the mentor and protégé and the history of power relations between their identity groups will have an impact on their relational interactions, on their mentoring experiences, and on their ability to achieve high-quality relational-mentoring episodes and relationships

In summary, RCT provides a powerful window for framing and understanding relational mentoring. Let us now offer a brief agenda for future research in this area.

Conclusion and Directions for Future Research

There are a number of fruitful avenues for future research and theory development on relational mentoring. To start, mentoring scholars could delineate the specific functions or behaviors enacted by protégés in high-quality relational-mentoring episodes and relationships. The framework presented here offers some insights into the skills and behaviors of both members of the relationship, but a finer analysis of the specific functions the protégé provides would be useful. For example, a key function of protégés may be the provision of information and the facilitation of colearning in the relationship (see Kram, 1996). Mullen and her colleagues (Mullen, 1994; Mullen & Noe, 1999) identified five types of information that mentors may receive from their protégés: information on role demands, expected behaviors, technical information, performance feedback, and social feedback. Other mentoring scholars point to the personal learning (Higgins & Kram, 2001; Kram, 1996) and job-related learning (Lankau & Scandura, 2002; also, Chapter 4, this volume) that occur in mentoring relationships. Mentor's reports of the benefits they receive from the relationship can also provide insight into functions protégés may provide in high-quality relationships (Allen, Chapter 5, this volume; Allen & Eby, 2003; Allen, Poteet, & Burroughs, 1997; Ragins & Scandura, 1999). In addition to providing generativity and fulfillment, protégés may increase the mentor's visibility and recognition in the organization, offer a loyal base of support, serve as an advocate for the mentor, and help the mentor become a more effective member of the organization. Future research could provide an in-depth examination of these and other protégé functions.

The propositions offered in this chapter offer a foundation for future research, but three additional areas for research could be highlighted here. First, future research could examine the relationship between mentoring episodes and mentoring relationships. For example, it would be useful to assess the "tipping point" at which mentoring episodes become mentoring relationships and the antecedents that determine this relational transition. Second, our chapter discusses relational stance as a key antecedent of high-quality mentoring relationships, but future research could examine the factors that lead to this relational stance. Mentoring schema theory (Ragins & Verbos, 2007) could be integrated into this approach, as well other theoretical perspectives on high-quality connections and relationships at work (Dutton, 2003; Dutton & Heaphy, 2003). Third, the RCT perspective on gender and power dynamics in mentoring relationships offers a unique opportunity to untangle the effects of multiple dimensions of diversity on the processes, behaviors, and outcomes of high-quality mentoring relationships (see Ragins, 2007). One avenue for exploration would be to undertake a feminist critique of mentoring theory. Feminist critiques (see Calàs & Smircich, 1993; Fletcher, 1994; Martin & Knopoff, 1995; Mumby & Putnam, 1992) start from the premise that knowledge about a particular subject is gendered (Acker, 1990), reifying certain (masculine) sources of knowledge and experience and devaluing others (feminine). Such a critique could explore the concept of mentoring from women's experiences, not trying to fit that experience into current conceptualizations, but seeking to create an alternative model.

Mentoring scholars also need to grapple with a key methodological question: When is a mentoring relationship a mentoring relationship? While some are clearly mentoring relationships, with both parties agreeing on the nature of the relationship, others are constrained by ambiguity or divergent perceptions about the relationship. The concept of mentoring episodes may offer some clarity; individuals may have engaged in multiple mentoring episodes but vary in their perceptions of whether the relationship is a mentoring relationship. Although our chapter has begun to untangle this issue from a conceptual perspective, broader methodological questions remain. For example, although dyadic methods can and should be used to assess mutual perceptions of the relationship, to what extent does perceptual congruency matter in determining relationship outcomes? Along similar lines, if members do not agree on whether the relationship is a mentoring relationship but the outcomes and processes reflect mentoring, is it a mentoring relationship? This points to the importance of considering mentoring schemas, or the cognitive maps that guide the perceptions, expectations, and behaviors of mentors and protégés (Ragins & Verbos, 2007). Members of the relationship may hold congruent or incongruent mentoring schemas, which may influence their expectations, behaviors, and evaluations of the relationship. Finally, mentoring scholars will surely grapple with the methodological challenge of measuring relational processes in mentoring relationships.

Finally, RCT offers important insight into formal mentoring programs. One common criticism of formal mentoring is that it lacks the "chemistry" or mutual attraction that enhances the development of informal relationships (Baugh, & Fagenson-Eland, Chapter 10, this volume; Chao, Walz, & Gardner, 1992; Ragins & Cotton, 1999). However, RCT suggests that the quality of a mentoring relationship is derived not from initial attraction, but rather from the relational skills, conditions, and stance of its members. Thus, formal mentoring relationships may not be inherently inferior to naturally occurring relationships, but may instead require relational training and skill building to succeed. Future research could examine whether formal programs that emphasize mutual benefits of relational mentoring and offer training in relational competence are more successful in establishing high-quality relationships than are programs informed by traditional perspectives.

In conclusion, Stone Center Relational Cultural Theory offers an effective framework for understanding the antecedents, processes, and outcomes of high-quality mentoring episodes and relationships. An application of this theoretical lens to the mentoring arena offers scholars a rich agenda for future research that promises a deeper understanding of relational mentoring and other developmental relationships.

References

Acker, J. (1990). Hierarchies, jobs, bodies: A theory of gendered organizations. *Gender & Society, 4,* 139–158.

Allen, T. D., & Eby, L. T. (2003). Relationship effectiveness for mentors: Factors associated with learning and quality. *Journal of Management, 29,* 469–486.

Allen, T. D., Eby, L. T., Poteet, M. L., Lentz, E., & Lima, L. (2004). Career benefits associated with mentoring for protégés: A meta-analysis. *Journal of Applied Psychology, 89,* 127–136.

Allen, T. D., Poteet, M. L., & Burroughs, S. M. (1997). The mentor's perspective: A qualitative inquiry and future research agenda. *Journal of Vocational Behavior, 51,* 70–89.

Baker, W. E., & Dutton, J. E. (2007). Enabling positive social capital at work. In J. E. Dutton & B. R. Ragins (Eds.), *Exploring positive relationships at work: Building a theoretical and research foundation* (pp. 325–345). Mahwah, NJ: Lawrence Erlbaum.

Baldwin, M. W. (1992). Relational schemas and the processing of social information. *Psychological Bulletin, 112,* 461–484.

Baldwin, M. W. (1999). Relational schemas: Research into social-cognitive aspects of interpersonal experience. In D. Cervone & Y. Shoda (Eds.), *The coherence of personality: Social cognitive bases of consistency, variability, and organizations* (pp. 127–154). New York: Guilford Press.

Bartolome, F., & Laurent, A. (1988). Managers: Torn between two roles. *Personnel Journal, 67*(10), 72–83.

Beebe, B., & Lachman, F. (1988). The contribution of mother-infant mutual influence to the origins of self and object representation. *Psychoanalytic Psychology, 5,* 305–337.

Brewer, M., & Gardner, W. (1996). Who is this "we"? Levels of collective identity and self representations. *Journal of Personality and Social Psychology, 71,* 83–91.

Brickson, S., & Brewer, M. (2001). Identity orientation and intergroup relations in organizations. In M. A. Hogg & D. J. Terry (Eds.), *Social identity processes in organizational contexts* (pp. 49–66). Philadelphia: Taylor & Francis.

Calàs, M. B., & Smircich, L. (1993, March–April). Dangerous liaisons: The "feminine-in-management" meets "globalization." *Business Horizons, 36,* pp. 73–83.

Cameron, K. S., Dutton, J. E., & Quinn, R. E. (2003). Foundations of positive organizational scholarship. In K. S. Cameron, J. E. Dutton, & R. E. Quinn (Eds.), *Positive organizational scholarship: Foundations of a new discipline* (pp. 3–13). San Francisco: Berrett-Koehler.

Chandler, D. E., & Kram, K. E. (2005). Applying an adult development perspective to developmental networks. *Career Development International, 10,* 548–566.

Chao, G. T., Walz, P. M., & Gardner, P. D. (1992). Formal and informal mentorships: A comparison on mentoring functions and contrast with nonmentored counterparts. *Personnel Psychology, 45,* 619–636.

Chodorow, N. (1978). *The reproduction of mothering.* Berkeley: University of California Press.

Collins, P. M., Kamya, H. A., & Tourse, R. W. (1997). Questions of racial diversity and mentorship: An empirical investigation. *Social Work, 42,* 145–152.

Cross, S. E., Bacon, P. L., & Morris, M. L. (2000). The relational-interdependent self-construal and relationships. *Journal of Personality and Social Psychology, 78,* 791–808.

Cross, S. E., & Madson, L. (1997). Models of the self: Self-construals and gender. *Psychological Bulletin, 122,* 5–37.

Della Noce, D. (1999). Seeing theory in practice: An analysis of empathy in mediation. *Negotiation Journal, 15,* 271–301.

Draft, W. (2001). *The deep blue sea.* San Francisco: Jossey-Bass.

Dreher, G. F., & Chargois, J. A. (1998). Gender, mentoring experiences, and salary attainment among graduates of a historically black university. *Journal of Vocational Behavior, 53,* 401–416.

Dreher, G. F., & Cox, T. H. (1996). Race, gender, and opportunity: A study of compensation attainment and the establishment of mentoring relationships. *Journal of Applied Psychology, 81,* 297–308.

Duck, S. (1994). *Meaningful relationships: Talking, sense, and relating.* Thousand Oaks, CA: Sage.

Dutton, J. E. (2003). *Energize your workplace: How to build and sustain high-quality connections at work.* San Francisco: Jossey-Bass.

Dutton, J. E., & Heaphy, E. D. (2003). The power of high-quality connections. In K. S. Cameron, J. E. Dutton, & R. E. Quinn (Eds.), *Positive organizational scholarship: Foundations of a new discipline* (pp. 263–278). San Francisco: Berrett-Koehler.

Dutton, J. E., & Ragins, B. R. (Eds.). (2007). *Exploring positive relationships at work: Building a theoretical and research foundation.* Mahwah, NJ: Lawrence Erlbaum.

Eby, L. T. (1997). Alternative forms of mentoring in changing organizational environments: A conceptual extension of the mentoring literature. *Journal of Vocational Behavior, 51,* 125–144.

Eby, L. T., & Allen, T. D. (2002). Further investigation of protégés' negative mentoring experiences: Patterns and outcomes. *Group & Organization Management, 27,* 456–479.

Eby, L. T., Butts, M., Lockwood, A., & Simon, S. A. (2004). Protégés' negative mentoring experiences: Construct development and nomological validation. *Personnel Psychology, 57,* 411–447.

Ensher, E. A., Thomas, C., & Murphy, S. E. (2001). Comparison of traditional, step-ahead, and peer mentoring on protégés support, satisfaction, and perceptions of career success: A social exchange perspective. *Journal of Business and Psychology, 15,* 419–438.

Fairbairn, W. D. R. (1952). *An object relations theory of personality.* New York: Basic Books.

Fletcher, J. K. (1994). Castrating the female advantage. *Journal of Management Inquiry, 3,* 74–82.

Fletcher, J. K. (1996a). A relational approach to developing the protean worker. In D. T. Hall & Associates (Eds.), *The career is dead—Long live the career: A relational approach to careers* (pp. 105–131). San Francisco: Jossey-Bass.

Fletcher, J. K. (1996b, August). *What's love got to do with it? Relational theory's challenge to affection-based models of relational practice.* Paper presented at symposium, "Dismantling the Dichotomy Between Public and Private Life: Emotional and Relational Practices at Work" (J. Martin, Chair), Academy of Management, Cincinnati, Ohio.

Fletcher, J. K. (1998). Relational practice: A feminist reconstruction of work. *Journal of Management Inquiry, 7,* 163–187.

Fletcher, J. K. (1999). *Disappearing acts: Gender, power, and relational practice at work.* Cambridge: MIT Press.

Fletcher, J. K. (2004). The paradox of postheroic leadership: An essay on gender, power, and transformational change. *Leadership Quarterly, 15,* 647–661.

Fletcher, J. K., & Kaeufer, K. (2003). Shared leadership: Paradox and possibility. In C. Pearce & J. Conger (Eds.), *Shared leadership: Reframing the hows and whys of leadership* (pp. 21–47). Thousand Oaks, CA: Sage.

Follett, M. P. (1924). *Creative experience.* New York: Longmans. Green.

French, J. R. P., & Raven, B. H. (1959). The bases of social power. In D. Cartwright (Ed.), *Studies in social power* (pp. 150–167). Ann Arbor: University of Michigan, Research Center for Group Dynamics, Institute of Social Research.

Goleman, D. (1995). *Emotional intelligence.* New York: Bantam Books.

Goleman, D. (1998). *Working with emotional intelligence.* New York: Bantam Books.

Heaphy, E. (2007). Bodily insights: Four lenses for positive organizational relationships. In J. E. Dutton & B. R. Ragins (Eds.), *Exploring positive relationships at work: Building a theoretical and research foundation* (pp. 47–71). Mahwah, NJ: Lawrence Erlbaum.

Higgins, M. C., & Kram, K. E. (2001). Reconceptualizing mentoring at work: A developmental network perspective. *Academy of Management Review, 26,* 264–288.

Holvino, E. (2001). *Complicating gender: The simultaneity of race, gender, and class in organization change(ing)* (CGO Working Paper #13). Boston: Center for Gender in Organizations, Simmons School of Management,

Hosking, D., Dachler, H. P., & Gergen, K. J. (Eds.). (1995). *Management and organization: Relational alternative to individualism.* Aldershot, UK: Ashgate.

Hunt, D. M., & Michael, C. (1983). Mentorship: A career training and development tool. *Academy of Management Review, 8,* 475–485.

Johnson-Bailey, J., & Cervero, R. M. (2004). Mentoring in black and white: The intricacies of cross-cultural mentoring. *Mentoring and Tutoring, 12,* 7–22.

Jordan, J. (1986). *The meaning of mutuality* (Working Paper No. 23). Wellesley, MA: Wellesley Centers for Women, Wellesley College.

Jordan, J., Kaplan A., Miller J. B., Stiver, I., & Surrey, J. (1991). *Women's growth-in-connection.* New York: Guilford Press.

Jordan, J. V. (1991). *The movement of mutuality and power* (Working Paper No. 53). Wellesley, MA: Wellesley Centers for Women, Wellesley College.

Jordan, J. V. (1999). *Toward connection and competence* (Working Paper No. 83). Wellesley, MA: Wellesley Centers for Women, Wellesley College.

Kalbfleisch, P. J., & Davies, A. B. (1991). Minorities and mentoring: Managing the multicultural institution. *Communication Education, 40,* 266–271.

Kegan, R. (1982). *The evolving self: Problem and process in human adult development.* Cambridge, MA: Harvard University Press.

Kegan, R. (1994). *In over our heads: The mental demands of modern life.* Cambridge, MA: Harvard University Press.

Kouzes, J. M., & Posner, B. Z. (2002). *The leadership challenge* (3rd ed.). San Francisco: Jossey-Bass.

Kram, K. (1985). *Mentoring at work: Developmental relationships in organizational life.* Glenview, IL: Scott, Foresman.

Kram, K. (1996). A relational approach to career development. In D. T. Hall & Associates (Eds.), *The career is dead—Long live the career: A relational approach to careers* (pp. 132–157). San Francisco: Jossey-Bass.

Kram, K. E., & Hall, D. T. (1996). Mentoring in a context of diversity and turbulence. In E. E. Kossek & S. A. Lobel (Eds.), *Managing diversity: Human resource strategies for transforming the workplace* (pp. 108–136). Cambridge, MA: Blackwell.

Lankau, M. J., & Scandura, T. A. (2002). An investigation of personal learning in mentoring relationships: Content, antecedents, and consequences. *Academy of Management Journal, 45,* 779–790.

Levinson, D. (with Darrow, C., Klein, E., Levinson, M., & McKee, B.). (1978). *The seasons of a man's life.* New York: Knopf.

Loevinger, J. (1976). *Ego development.* San Francisco: Jossey-Bass.

Martin, J., & Knopoff, K. (1995). The gender implications of apparently gender-neutral theory: Re-reading Max Weber. In E. Freeman & A. Larson (Eds.), *Women's studies and business ethics: Toward a new conversation* (pp. 30–49). Oxford, UK: Oxford University Press.

McGowan, E. M. (2001). *Texts and contexts of reciprocity: Five models of mentoring.* Unpublished manuscript, Harvard University, Cambridge, MA.

McGowan, E. M. (2004). *Relationship work: A descriptive theory of a faculty-to-faculty formal mentoring program in higher education.* Unpublished doctoral dissertation, Harvard University, Cambridge, MA.

McNamee, S., & Gergen, K. J. (1999*). Relational responsibility: Resources for sustainable dialogue.* Thousand Oaks, CA: Sage.

Miller, J. B. (1976). *Toward a new psychology of women*. Boston: Beacon Press.

Miller, J. B. (1984). *The development of women's sense of self* (Working Paper No. 12). Wellesley, MA: Wellesley Centers for Women, Wellesley College.

Miller, J. B. (2003). *Telling the truth about power* (Working Paper No. 100). Wellesley, MA: Wellesley Centers for Women, Wellesley College.

Miller, J. B. (2004). Preface. In J. Jordan, L. Hartling, & M. Walker (Eds.), *The complexity of connection* (pp. i–iv). New York: Guilford Press.

Miller, J. B., & Stiver, I. (1997). *The healing connection*. Boston: Beacon Press.

Mullen, E. J. (1994). Framing the mentoring relationship as an information exchange. *Human Resource Management Review, 4*, 257–281.

Mullen, E. J., & Noe, R. A. (1999). The mentoring information exchange: When do mentors seek information from their protégés? *Journal of Organizational Behavior, 20*, 233–242.

Mumby, D., & Putnam, L. (1992). The politics of emotion: A feminist reading of bounded rationality. *Academy of Management Review 17*, 465–486.

Noe, R. A. (1988). An investigation of the determinants of successful assigned mentoring relationships. *Personnel Psychology, 41*, 457–479.

Noe, R. A., Greenberger, D. B., & Wang, S. (2002). Mentoring: What we know and where we might go. *Research in Personnel and Human Resources Management, 21*, 129–173.

Ogilvie, D. M., & Ashmore, R. D. (1991). Self-with-other representation as a unit of analysis in self-concept research. In R. C. Curtis (Ed.), *The relational self: Theoretical convergences in psychoanalysis and social psychology* (pp. 282–314). New York: Guildford Press.

Ortiz-Walters, R., & Gilson, L. L. (2005). Mentoring in academia: An examination of the experiences of protégés of color. *Journal of Vocational Behavior, 67*, 459–475.

Pearce, C. L., & Conger, J. A. (Eds.). (2003). *Shared leadership: Reframing the hows and whys of leadership*. Thousand Oaks, CA: Sage.

Planalp, S. (1985). Relational schemata: A test of alternative forms of relational knowledge as guides to communication. *Human Communication Research, 12*, 3–29.

Ragins, B. R. (1989). Barriers to mentoring: The female manager's dilemma. *Human Relations, 42*, 1–22.

Ragins, B. R. (1995). Diversity, power, and mentoring in organizations: A cultural, structural, and behavioral perspective. In M. Chemers, M. Costanzo, & S. Oskamp (Eds.), *Diversity in organizations* (pp. 91–132). Thousand Oaks, CA: Sage.

Ragins, B. R. (1997). Diversified mentoring relationships: A power perspective. *Academy of Management Review, 22*, 482–521.

Ragins, B. R. (1999a). Gender and mentoring relationships: A review and research agenda for the next decade. In G. Powell (Ed.), *Handbook of gender and work* (pp. 347–370). Thousand Oaks, CA: Sage.

Ragins, B. R. (1999b). Where do we go from here and how do we get there? Methodological issues in conducting research on diversity and mentoring relationships. In A. Murrell, F. J. Crosby, & R. Ely (Eds.), *Mentoring dilemmas: Developmental relationships within multicultural organizations* (pp. 227–247). Mahwah, NJ: Lawrence Erlbaum.

Ragins, B. R. (2002). Understanding diversified mentoring relationships: Definitions, challenges, and strategies. In D. Clutterbuck & B. R. Ragins, *Mentoring and diversity: An international perspective* (pp. 23–53). Oxford: Butterworth-Heinemann.

Ragins, B. R. (2005). *Towards a theory of relational mentoring*. Unpublished manuscript.

Ragins, B. R. (2007). Diversity and workplace mentoring: A review and positive social capital approach. In T. D. Allen & L. T. Eby (Eds.), *Blackwell handbook of mentoring: A multiple perspectives approach* (pp. 281–300). Oxford, UK: Blackwell.

Ragins, B. R. (in press). Disclosure disconnects: Antecedents and consequences of disclosing invisible stigmas across life domains. *Academy of Management Review*.

Ragins, B. R., & Cotton, J. L. (1999). Mentor functions and outcomes: A comparison of men and women in formal and informal mentoring relationships. *Journal of Applied Psychology, 84,* 529–550.

Ragins, B. R., Cotton, J. L., & Miller, J. S. (2000). Marginal mentoring. The effects of type of mentor, quality of relationship, and program design on work and career attitudes. *Academy of Management Journal, 43,* 1177–1194.

Ragins, B. R., & Dutton, J. E. (2007). Positive relationships at work: An introduction and invitation. In J. E. Dutton & B. R. Ragins (Eds.), *Exploring positive relationships at work: Building a theoretical and research foundation* (pp. 3–25). Mahwah, NJ: Lawrence Erlbaum.

Ragins, B. R., & Scandura, T. A. (1994). Gender differences in expected outcomes of mentoring relationships. *Academy of Management Journal, 37,* 957–971.

Ragins, B. R., & Scandura, T. A. (1999). Burden or blessing? Expected costs and benefits of being a mentor. *Journal of Organizational Behavior, 20,* 493–509.

Ragins, B. R., & Sundstrom, E. (1989). Gender and power in organizations: A longitudinal perspective. *Psychological Bulletin, 105,* 51–88.

Ragins, B. R., Townsend, B., & Mattis, M. (1998). Gender gap in the executive suite: Female executives and CEOs report on breaking the glass ceiling. *Academy of Management Executive, 12*(1), 28–42.

Ragins, B. R., & Verbos, A. K. (2007). Positive relationships in action: Relational mentoring and mentoring schemas in the workplace. In J. E. Dutton & B. R. Ragins (Eds.), *Exploring positive relationships at work: Building a theoretical and research foundation* (pp. 91–116). Mahwah, NJ: Lawrence Erlbaum.

Scandura, T. A. (1998). Dysfunctional mentoring relationships and outcomes. *Journal of Management, 24,* 449–467.

Seligman, M. E. P., & Csikszentmihalyi, M. (2000). Positive psychology: An introduction. *American Psychologist, 55,* 5–14.

Snyder, C. R., & Lopez, S. J. (Eds.). (2002). *Handbook of positive psychology.* New York: Oxford University Press.

Surrey, J. (1985). *The self in relation* (Working Paper No. 13). Wellesley, MA: Wellesley Centers for Women, Wellesley College.

Thomas, D. A. (1989). Mentoring and irrationality: The role of racial taboos. *Human Resource Management, 28,* 279–290.

Thomas, D. A. (1990). The impact of race on managers' experiences of developmental relationships (mentoring and sponsorship): An intra-organizational study. *Journal of Organizational Behavior, 11,* 479–491.

Thomas, D. A. (1993). Racial dynamics in cross-race developmental relationships. *Administrative Science Quarterly, 38,* 169–194.

Thomas, D. A., & Alderfer, C. P. (1989). The influence of race on career dynamics: Theory and research on minority career experiences. In M. B. Arthur, D. T. Hall, & B. S. Lawrence (Eds.), *Handbook of career theory* (pp. 133–158). Cambridge, UK: Cambridge University Press.

Thomas, D. A., & Gabarro, J. J. (1999). *Breaking through: The making of minority executives in corporate America.* Boston, MA: Harvard Business School Press.

Tronick, E. (1989). Emotions and emotional communication in the infant. *American Psychologist, 44,* 112–119.

Viator, R. E. (2001). An examination of African Americans' access to public accounting mentors: Perceived barriers and intentions to leave. *Accounting, Organizations, and Society, 26,* 541–561.

Walker, M. (2002). *Power and effectiveness: Envisioning an alternative paradigm* (Working Paper No. 94). Wellesley, MA: Wellesley Centers for Women, Wellesley College.

Wanberg, C. R., Welsh, E. T., & Hezlett, S. A. (2003). Mentoring research: A review and dynamic process model. *Research in Personnel and Human Resources Management, 22,* 39–124.

Watkins, K. E., Marsick, V. J. (2003). *Sculpting the learning organization.* San Francisco: Jossey-Bass.

West, C., & Zimmerman, D. (1991). Doing gender. In J. Lorber & S. Farrell (Eds.), *The social construction of gender* (pp. 13–37). Newbury Park, CA: Sage.

Winnicott, D. W. (1958). *The maturational process and the facilitating environment.* New York: International Universities Press.

16

A Constructive-Developmental Approach to Mentoring Relationships

Eileen M. McGowan

Eric M. Stone

Robert Kegan

I n this chapter, we explore how a constructive-developmental theoretical lens can enhance our understanding of the potentials, demands, and dynamics of mentoring relationships. Our belief is that best practices in developmental relationships depend upon understanding the meaning-making structures of the individuals involved. To better grasp the needs and expectations of protégés and mentors and understand how to optimize their relationships, we may need to extend our view of mentoring relationships to include an understanding of the deep, pervasive mental structures that shape how we construct our experience.

Our understanding of mentoring is grounded in the notion that it is a reciprocal, developmental relationship (Kram, 1985; Levinson, 1978) that develops between persons relatively more experienced (mentors) and less experienced (protégés) (Mullen, 1994). While some mentoring relationships emerge spontaneously or "informally" between individuals, others are the result of organizational intervention or "formal" programs. In this chapter, we link what we have learned about adult development to current knowledge of mentoring relationships. Employing a constructive-developmental theoretical lens (Kegan, 1982, 1994; Kegan & Lahey,

2001), we examine the role human meaning-making structures play in mentoring relationships and address the complexities of *support* and *challenge* for adults at various stages of development. Notions of support, challenge, and continuity are integral to the conceptualization of the "holding environment," a construct that better allows us to understand growth-enhancing surroundings. Our hope is that by gaining new insight into the dynamics of mentoring relationships and how adult meaning-making systems may affect mentoring capacities, practitioners can make more informed decisions when establishing formal mentoring programs or when navigating informal relationships. Within this chapter, we put forth five propositions and identify areas for future research at the intersection of adult development and mentoring theory and practice.

Constituents of Adult Development

Within the field of personality psychology, the literature has been predominately focused on unhealthy aspects of development that derail or subvert us from achieving our goals (Freud & Josef, 2004). Research concentrates primarily on the analysis of risk factors, such as genetic predisposition to psychological illness (Faraone, Tsuang, & Tsuang, 1999), environmental deprivation (Mazure, 1995), or addiction (Hilarski, 2005). Occasionally, the literature considers mitigating factors that support resilience (Bowlby, 2004), but for the most part, it is overoriented toward maladjustment. Less prevalent are works that take a substantive approach to assessing *healthy* adult development—what it looks like, how it is experienced, how it is supported, and how it is encouraged.

During the past 50 years, a new line of empirical work has emerged that focuses on the study of healthy human development through exploration of the phases of our lives, what we hope for and what is required of us at different stages in our developmental journeys (Erikson, 1963; Hall & Kram, 1982; Levinson, 1978; Schein, 1990; Vaillant, 2002). This work starts to consider the importance of role, society, hierarchical position, gender, and voice in influencing our identities and expectations. While life phase literature recognizes the differing demands that the world makes upon each of us and the critical fact that all individuals are not equally successful in meeting these demands, from a developmental perspective, it does not account for vast discrepancies in basic coping capacities found in people within the same life phase (Kegan, 1994). The existence of such stark inconsistencies in ability suggests that development is not necessarily attributable simply to the passage of time, but rather is influenced by capacities that enable individuals to see things in qualitatively different ways.

Although rarely credited in this regard, the emerging field of "positive psychology" (Cloninger, 2004; Linley & Stephen, 2004; Seligman, 1990) and the turn to the study of healthy psychological development (Kohlberg, 1981; Selman, 1980) has its origins in the work of Jean Piaget (1936/1952, 1937/1954, 1948, 1969), who turned from the study of children as error makers and reality distorters to an appreciation of the wholeness, consistency, dignity, and harmony in the way children construct experience. Piaget's breakthrough research laid the foundation for constructive-developmental psychology, including Perry's (1970) work on intellectual and ethical development, Kohlberg's (1981) studies on moral development, social perspective taking by Selman (1980), and the ego-developmental work of Kegan (Kegan, 1982, 1994; Kegan & Lahey, 2001). We use this chapter to explore how the lens of adult development, based on Kegan's (1982, 1994) neo-Piagetian Constructive-Developmental Theory may enhance our understanding of adult developmental relationships.

Constructive-Developmental Theory

Constructive-developmental theory is premised on two distinct, big ideas (Kegan, 1982). A *constructivist* perspective proposes that humans do not simply happen upon reality, but rather are continually engaged in an active process of constructing that reality. The way in which we experience the world is dependent upon how we mentally organize it. A *developmental* perspective proposes that organic systems evolve through qualitatively different periods of growth, based upon alternative periods of stability and change. It suggests that there are consistent and predictable elements within the human developmental journey that we can observe, analyze, and benefit from studying further. *Constructive-developmentalism* integrates these two fundamental concepts in a theory on the evolution (or development) of meaning making (constructing reality), not only in childhood, but throughout adulthood (Kegan, 1982).

Constructive-developmental theory posits that the evolutionary movement of the psyche occurs as individuals step away from, take control over, or integrate earlier aspects of themselves that formerly controlled them. As young children, we are captive to our own impulses ("subject" to them), but as we develop, we construct a more complex self that is, of course, still full of impulses but is increasingly able to control them (take them as "object"), on behalf of goals, needs, and purposes that are not so in-the-moment. Later in childhood, we are subject to the fulfillment of these individual needs until we are gradually able to take them as object and integrate them with the needs of others. During adolescence, we identify ourselves with our relationships, to family and partners, and with those inherited belief systems that define us (i.e., we are subject to them). For many, this definition of self accompanies us throughout our lifetimes and describes Kegan's third stage, the "Socialized Self." For others, another shift of identity occurs when relationships become something we "have" (object) rather than identifiers of self (subject). At this stage, we make self-authoring choices about what we believe, and we take responsibility for those selections (Kegan's fourth stage, the "Self-Authorizing Self"). A final shift in subject-object relations occurs in a relatively small percentage of the population when individuals begin to develop the capacity to take a perspective on their own belief systems and commitments and then eventually can include within the self a number of different ideologies at once (Kegan's fifth, or "Self-Transforming" stage). These individuals are no longer captive of a single ideology.

For the purposes of this chapter, we will concentrate on discussing the stages of adult development (Stages 3, 4, and 5) and the transitions that occur between them.

For shorthand purposes, and in ways that will prove useful when differentiating among mentoring relationships, we can consider the various ways these different developmental positions (Stage 3, the transition between 3 and 4, Stage 4, the transition between 4 and 5, and Stage 5) "hang" with others—that is their different "pendencies":

Stage 3: Dependent

3–4 Transition: Counterdependent

Stage 4: Independent

4–5 Transition: Suspendent

Stage 5: Interdependent.

Because we are particularly interested in the ways in which developmental relationships can purposefully facilitate evolutionary movement in adulthood, we will begin by exploring the interaction of the individual with his or her surroundings. We will consider the kinds of environmental supports that facilitate development before proceeding to a more detailed description of the internal processes and stages that constitute development. In this next section, we consider what we know about growth-enhancing surroundings, or holding environments, and how they may contribute to a better understanding of mentoring relationships.

Holding Environments

Although constructive-developmental theory focuses on the individual's meaning-making and growth process, it would be inaccurate to portray development as occurring in isolation or somehow separated from the surrounding environment. In fact, it is precisely because constructive-developmental theory is premised on the continual renegotiation of boundaries between self and other that our personal development should be understood as more than merely intrapsychic change isolated from situational or contextual influences. Rather, inherent in constructive-developmentalism is the acknowledgement that our individual development is heavily influenced by contact with the world in which we exist. Development is affected (encouraged, challenged, supported, or thwarted) by the unique interaction of our individual needs/strengths and the particular situational forces or *holding environments* in which we are situated (Winnicott, 1965).

As we move through life, we do so surrounded by people, communities, and environments, which can either support or thwart our development. While factors contributing to growth are present to at least some extent in almost any situation, it is the uniquely balanced combination of ingredients of a supportive holding environment that actually facilitates, as opposed to merely permits, evolutionary movement. Integrating subject-object theory with the conceptualization of a holding environment suggests that as we continually renegotiate the boundaries between the self and others, we are striving for balance between that which we see as a part of ourselves and that from which we are separating. In reality, "There is never just an individual" (Winnicott, 1965) developing in isolation, but rather there is a person who is in the process of evolving or actively resolving the subject-object balance (Kegan, 1982). Because of this inevitable linkage between internal growth and external surroundings, we now explore in more detail the conceptualization of an effective holding environment and speculate as to how mentoring relationships may contribute to healthy development.

Holding environments have three fundamental dimensions: confirmation, contradiction, and continuity (Kegan, 1982). Each dimension is familiar and found in the most fundamental human experiences of comfort and stress. A *confirming environment* provides a sense of comfort in which the evolutionary movement of the self is acknowledged and affirmed. Just as an infant must be physically held and psychologically "attached" to a primary caretaker, so too must developing adults feel understood and accepted by others. Even in the midst of conflict or challenge, a developing adult needs to be held or confirmed, not as the problem or anxiety with which they are wrestling at the moment, but as the person who is currently undergoing the challenge. Our understanding of the world must be confirmed or held in some way in order for us to continue to grow.

Yet confirmation by itself is not sufficient to stimulate change. For development to occur, we must experience some degree of stress or challenge to our existing approach to meaning making (order/stage) in order to eventually move beyond it. If we are not challenged to view the world differently, we risk lacking the impetus to change and develop. The notions of *confirmation* (being affirmed or "holding on" to current meaning-making structures) and *contradiction* (being challenged or "letting go" of a stationary balance) may initially seem at odds with each other, but upon further evaluation are actually quite complementary. For example, a wise parent constantly prepares the child for independence, while simultaneously ensuring the child's sense of safety and protection. A developmentally healthy approach to "holding on" sets the stage for eventual separation.

As for the third dimension, *continuity,* a successful holding environment is steadfast, remaining firmly in place amidst periods of turmoil and relative calm. It is reliable, consistent, and dependable. During periods of evolution, a stable holding environment enables us to develop, establish new and qualitatively different meaning-making structures, reestablish a sense of balance, and resolve the subject-object conflict with which we continually wrestle. A holding environment provides a safe space in which the self can grow, change, and evolve. It "sticks around" even as the developing individual is in the process of moving beyond it. And while it can be uncomfortable for the "holder" to have someone push away, staying in relationship is critical so that the person can progress at his or her own pace.

The ingredients of successful holding environments include a balance of confirmation, contradiction, and continuity, according to the specific requirements of one's stage of development. Thus, for a mentoring relationship to be experienced as effective, whether functioning in isolation or in conjunction with other systems of support, the holding environment must be tailored to the protégé's meaning-making structure and must meet the needs of that particular developmental stage. In other words, our perceptions of what actually constitutes support and challenge differ based on how we understand the world. Linking this understanding of a holding environment to mentoring theory suggests that there is no one "right" or "wrong" commonly shared set of behaviors that a mentor can provide that constitutes an ideal holding environment. Rather, the value that specific mentor behaviors contribute will be based upon the needs and cognitive structure of the protégé. Good mentoring can involve good "holding" (confirmation), good "letting go" (contradiction), or reliable "sticking around" as the relationship is reconstructed as one between colleagues (continuity) or all three.

The consistency of a supportive holding environment provides the individual with an anchor—something to hold on to amidst other shifting life forces. Oftentimes, a mentor can be this anchor, enhancing an individual's ability to move forward and to grow. There may be times in which this relationship itself is sufficient to support developmental movement and other times when it is most effective when experienced in conjunction with other supportive relationships or environments. We conclude this section on holding environments by suggesting that a mentoring relationship will not necessarily provide all the influence necessary for a protégé's development. Instead, it is far more likely that a single relationship will contribute various elements to larger, more extensive systems of support composed of many influences, including work cultures, family and social support structures, spiritual communities, and educational environments.

Now that we have considered the kinds of environmental supports that best facilitate development and the possible roles that mentoring relationship can play in these processes, we will detail the stages of developmental movement across adulthood, relate these meaning-making structures to the particular conceptualizations of confirmation, challenge, and continuity that accompany them, and, finally, describe how these ideas align with successful mentoring relationships.

Stages of Adult Development

Stage 3: The Socialized Mind ("Dependence")

Typically, by the end of adolescence, individuals have entered into a Stage 3 "Socialized Self," in which the alignment of the self within relationships or externally provided belief systems take precedence over the fulfillment of personal needs. Parents gratefully appreciate when their teenager makes this transition, characterized by the ability to take some control over personal wants and needs and to balance them with the desires of others in decision making. This capacity enables a different level of engagement and, for the first time, allows the conceptualization of self-sacrifice to emerge in the service of relational development. For individuals in this stage, the question of "Who are you?" is answered: "I *am* that to which I am faithful or loyal (experienced relationally, ideationally, or both). I *am no longer* my needs." Personal needs can now be viewed as "object"—"something that I have," not "something that I am." "Because I can now take a perspective on my needs, I can make decisions about their relative importance and have control over them rather than being controlled by them." While this is a significant developmental advancement and suggests positive implications for participation in healthy mentoring relationships, understanding the limitations of this meaning-making stage is critical to furthering our knowledge of mentoring dynamics. Individuals functioning in Stage 3 often experience difficulty separating out the self from the relationship or in establishing relational boundaries. They are typically identified (and identify themselves) by their relationships, along with their commitments and loyalties. This relational fusion resists separation or individuality. Expressions of deep difference are experienced as threatening to the continuation of the relationship.

For those firmly situated in the Socialized Balance, or third order of consciousness, personal expectations are strongly shaped by perceptions of the surrounding environment and are highly reflective of cultural, familial, and organizational norms. Because this stage is typically ascendant in later adolescence and early adulthood, at a time when young adults are first entering the workforce, it is reasonable to assume that many protégés will enter into mentoring relationships possessing a third-order way of organizing and understanding the world. While many adults eventually evolve beyond this stage, a significant segment of the population does not and, instead, continues to understand the world from a third-order perspective well into and throughout adulthood. So, while it is likely that this stage more characteristically represents the meaning-making stage of protégés, it is possible (yet somewhat less likely) that a mentor may also be located here.

Protégés at this level of development will likely expect a career mentor to be an authority in his or her field, providing instruction, definitions of reality, performance assessment, and expert guidance. For mentors who are interested in providing meaningful supports for development to a Stage 3 protégé, they will share desired guidance, while at the same time encouraging protégés to think and act independently. Effective mentors to Stage 3 protégés confirm their socialized way of meaning making, while simultaneously encouraging protégés to eventually develop and embrace self-authoring behaviors. Such a mentor will confirm the protégé's ability to engage in mutually reciprocal relationships, resist the protégé's third-order necessity to be fused or embedded in the mentoring relationship, demand that the protégé assume responsibility for decision making, and encourage the protégé's independence while staying in the relationship. The greatest temptation for mentors of third-order protégés is to fully accept the reality-defining powers that the protégé is all too happy to confer upon the mentor. In anticipation of this chapter's unfolding, readers may want to consider how the mentor's own developmental position may or may not equip him or her to resist this temptation.

In Figure 16.1, the conceptualizations of confirmation, challenge, and continuity are explored according to a Stage 3 meaning-making structure. The types of behaviors associated with these constructions are suggested on the basis of ways in which they may be provided by mentoring relationships, other relationships, or environmental factors.

The 3-to-4 Transition (Counterdependence)

Development through the stages includes substantial periods of transition through and between stages, some of which may last several years. During these

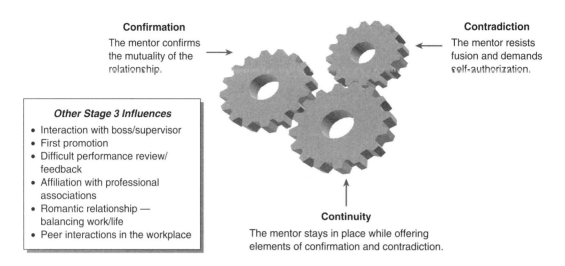

Confirmation
The mentor confirms the mutuality of the relationship.

Contradiction
The mentor resists fusion and demands self-authorization.

Other Stage 3 Influences
- Interaction with boss/supervisor
- First promotion
- Difficult performance review/ feedback
- Affiliation with professional associations
- Romantic relationship — balancing work/life
- Peer interactions in the workplace

Continuity
The mentor stays in place while offering elements of confirmation and contradiction.

Figure 16.1   Components of a Holding Environment for Protégés in Stage 3: The Interactivity of Confirmation, Contradiction, and Continuity for the Socialized Balance

transitions, individuals may feel particularly "imbalanced" as they strive to negotiate qualitatively different ways of understanding their surroundings. Mentors can help protégés navigate transitional periods, typically marked by uncertainty. Protégés in the 3-to-4 transition often struggle to come to terms with redefining their loyalties to traditions of family, religion, culture, and organizational norms, while at the same time navigating and solidifying their "self-loyalties" to newly emerging beliefs of their own, which may be distinct from those with which they have long been affiliated. Protégés may experience this challenge in the form of tension between competing commitments to what "has been" and what "can be." The accompanying emotions often range from feelings of disloyalty to eventual invigoration and independence upon emergence from being the "receiver" to the "constructor" of one's own life. Mentoring an individual through this transition is particularly challenging because the protégé's needs and expectations are continually evolving and the mentor is often the subject of the protégé's rebellion, as he or she seeks to differentiate from the mentor.

Effective mentors to protégés between Stages 3 and 4 stay in place during the transition, are able to contain the protégé's sense of anxiety and imbalance, and simultaneously encourage the protégé's desire to move toward self-authorization. In creating an effective holding environment, the mentor will generate opportunities for "provisional" identities that allow the protégé to "try on" a new self while simultaneously retaining his or her "old" form. For example, one young man at a software firm was successfully honing his skills as a marketing professional. Unexpectedly invited by a mentor in the company (not his direct supervisor) to help out with a partnership negotiation, the protégé assumed the provisional identity of a business development professional, for the first time leading a group of his peers and superiors in an area in which he had little prior knowledge. (See Figure 16.2.)

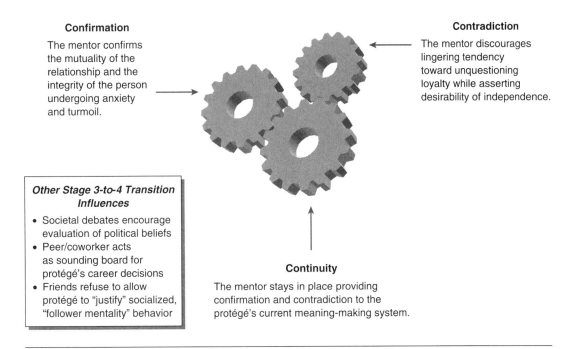

Confirmation

The mentor confirms the mutuality of the relationship and the integrity of the person undergoing anxiety and turmoil.

Contradiction

The mentor discourages lingering tendency toward unquestioning loyalty while asserting desirability of independence.

Other Stage 3-to-4 Transition Influences

• Societal debates encourage evaluation of political beliefs
• Peer/coworker acts as sounding board for protégé's career decisions
• Friends refuse to allow protégé to "justify" socialized, "follower mentality" behavior

Continuity

The mentor stays in place providing confirmation and contradiction to the protégé's current meaning-making system.

Figure 16.2   Components of a Holding Environment for Protégés in Stage 3-to-4 Transition: The Interactivity of Confirmation, Contradiction, and Continuity for Transition Between the Socialized and Self-Authoring Balance

Stage 4: The Self-Authoring Mind ("Independence")

Stage 4 is characterized by the emergence a "self-authoring" meaning system. Individuals at this stage come to understand their roles as constructors, not receivers, of their lives and subsequently accept responsibility for internal feelings, decision making, and behavior. A firmly entrenched Stage 4 individual possesses a strong sense of personal identity, based upon a self-guided system of beliefs. For adults in this stage, the question of "Who are you?" is answered: "I *am* my independent self, the governor or regulator of my life. I *am not* made up by my relationships or beliefs. I make up (author) my relationships and beliefs." Individuals at this stage are no longer dependent upon others to define themselves, but rather are able to articulate and negotiate clear relational boundaries. Personal relationships can now be viewed as "object"—"something that I have," not "something that I am." "Because I am now able to take a perspective on my relationships, I can now be actively involved in making decisions *about* them rather than being controlled *by* them."

The capacity to take a perspective on relationships is a valuable tool for transcending one's overidentification with a mentoring partner. This level of functioning enables independence of judgment and consideration of a broad range of options. For example, a mentor could initially react disapprovingly to a protégé's decision to leave the company in favor of a compelling offer at a competitive firm. The protégé's departure could have a number of potential negative ramifications, ranging from the immediate loss of manpower within the mentor's firm to the mentor's disappointment at the loss of daily camaraderie with the protégé. While this may be the initial reaction of many mentors, a Stage 4 mentor will have the capacity to take a perspective on that reaction. Because the mentor no longer *is* the relationship, but instead *has* the relationship, its potential loss does not put the mentor's sense of identity at stake. Instead, the mentor has the capability to envision a range of possible outcomes, any one of which could present a perfectly viable alternative to the current situation. Instead of feeling devastated or threatened by the separation, the mentor can choose to react differently. As is true with all forms of personal growth, this new frame of reference represents a hard-earned developmental advancement.

At the same time, the self-authoring meaning-making structure has its limitations. Individuals at this stage have great difficulty questioning their deeply held beliefs, because they *are* those beliefs. Having worked so diligently to develop an independent value system, they tend to identify completely with it. In this instance, challenges to one's ideology pose a threat to one's sense of self.

Upon entering the Stage 4 of development, we become comfortable with our own authority. Having developed a relationship to traditions and norms (religion, family, culture, and external expectations), we no longer hold on to these norms out of a sense of obligation or mere identification. If we do decide to subscribe to these factors, we do so as a matter of independent, personal choice. We develop the capacity to construct our own "institution" or belief system. Decisions are guided by internal judgment, not external authority. The self-authoring individual takes responsibility for those judgments, speaking and behaving with independence and self-regulation. Research indicates that this level of development is attained by less than 40% of the adult population (Kegan, 1994).

At the fourth order of meaning making, the protégé's preference for a mentor is likely to be for a senior ally who respects the integrity and efficacy of a person's own "way." This ally will assist in the protégé's journey toward a self-constructed system—and, possibly, when protégés are reaching the conclusion of the self-authoring stage, become a mentor who invites protégés to see themselves as "bigger" than their current systems, theories, or ways of making meaning. Mentors to Stage 4 protégés should be respectful of the integrity of the protégé's "institution," while at the same time suggesting its possible limitations and opportunities for alternate perspective taking. In creating an effective holding environment, the mentor will confirm the protégé's capacity for independence and responsibility for self, question the protégé's need to judge solely on basis of the institutional-self's values, and encourage the protégé's ideological expansion, while remaining actively involved in the relationship. (See Figure 16.3.)

The 4-to-5 Transition ("Suspendence")

Perhaps less than 10% of adults undergo the transition between Stages 4 and 5, and those that do often do so later in life (typically as a mentor rather than as a protégé) (Kegan, 1994). Having obtained a sense of self-authorization and

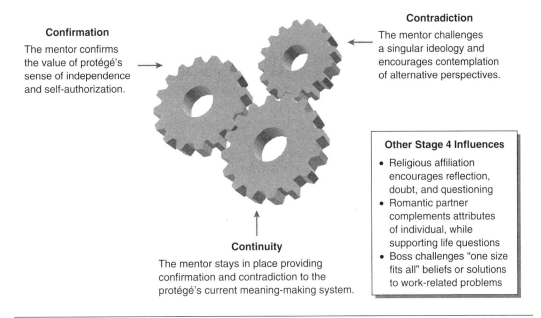

Confirmation

The mentor confirms the value of protégé's sense of independence and self-authorization.

Contradiction

The mentor challenges a singular ideology and encourages contemplation of alternative perspectives.

Other Stage 4 Influences

- Religious affiliation encourages reflection, doubt, and questioning
- Romantic partner complements attributes of individual, while supporting life questions
- Boss challenges "one size fits all" beliefs or solutions to work-related problems

Continuity

The mentor stays in place providing confirmation and contradiction to the protégé's current meaning-making system.

Figure 16.3   Components of a Holding Environment for Protégés in Stage 4: The Interactivity of Confirmation, Contradiction, and Continuity Producing Evolutionary Movement for Protégés in Self-Authoring Balance

comfort with personal meaning making, we begin to recognize that while our "institution" may function quite productively, it is not complete or whole. Our accomplishments do not reflect the full potential of the self. Aspects of who we are as an adult remain underdeveloped and incomplete, and we aspire to bring all elements of the self to fulfillment. We are able to suspend, step back from, or be critical of our once-vaunted personal ideologies. Both mentors and protégés approaching the world at this level of complexity bring an expansive approach to developmental engagement and likely represent worthy partners in personal and professional exploration. In creating an effective holding environment, the mentor will confirm the protégé's capacity for independence, while acknowledging the need for adult interdependence and staying in the relationship as beneficial to both parties. (See Figure 16.4.)

Stage 5: The Self-Transforming Mind ("Interdependence")

Individuals at Stage 5, the "Self-Transforming" stage, begin to see not just the limitations inherent in taking any one perspective, but can hold within the self the contradictions and tensions of competing ideologies. Ideas and commitments with which they were previously identified can now be viewed as "object," or evaluated from a distance, thus enabling a Stage 5 mentor to take perspective on and react to closely held ideas or commitments. The answer to the question of "Who are you?"

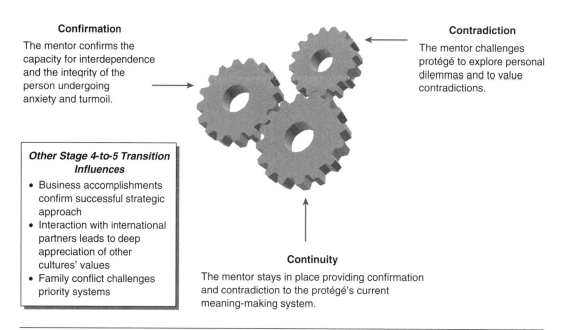

Confirmation

The mentor confirms the capacity for interdependence and the integrity of the person undergoing anxiety and turmoil.

Contradiction

The mentor challenges protégé to explore personal dilemmas and to value contradictions.

Other Stage 4-to-5 Transition Influences

- Business accomplishments confirm successful strategic approach
- Interaction with international partners leads to deep appreciation of other cultures' values
- Family conflict challenges priority systems

Continuity

The mentor stays in place providing confirmation and contradiction to the protégé's current meaning-making system.

Figure 16.4   Components of a Holding Environment for Protégés in 4-to-5 Transition: The Interactivity of Confirmation, Contradiction, and Continuity Producing Evolutionary Movement for the Transition Between the Self-Authoring and Self-Transforming Balance

at Stage 5 is more expansive and incorporative than at previous stages: "I *am not* my ideology" (which can now be viewed as "object"), "something that I have," not "something that I am." "I *am* bigger than any one system and open to new perspectives." The self-transforming approach to meaning making is a uniquely advanced level of personal development that relatively few are able to achieve in their lifetimes. Mentors at this level of development have the potential to offer protégés at any level of development an enormous capacity for full relational engagement. Self-transforming mentors are no longer captive to their own favorite theories and preferred approaches and can therefore be available to concentrate on the needs of protégés; they are no longer overidentified with the relationship as an extension of their own agendas and thus can offer engagement without an agenda; they are no longer held by a singular belief system and hence are able to offer a dialectic form of engagement.

Summary of Developmental Stages

In summary, we have offered an abbreviated version of a complex theory of adult development, in which the evolutionary movement of the psyche is characterized as a progression through a series of qualitatively different meaning-making stages in which the fundamental task is resolving a progressively sophisticated and nuanced subject-object balance. While this trajectory may appear straightforward and linear in theory, in reality, this movement may take years to accomplish and may be punctuated by long periods of imbalance or transition between levels. The transition between levels is often characterized by a precarious sense of uncertainty, including the ongoing questioning of one's current meaning-making structures while simultaneously wrestling with the adoption of new ones. In this sense, developmental movement can be quite disorienting. It comes with risks, and often costs. The existence of these risks and costs provides a compelling reason for both better understanding the evolutionary movement of the psyche and for integrating this knowledge into the field of developmental relationships. It is precisely because developmental progress is so difficult, risky, and challenging that we need the supports mentoring relationships can provide to accompany and guide us on our developmental journey.

Propositions for Future Research

Based on our interest in the interrelationship between adult development and the functioning of developmental relationships, we offer the following five testable propositions (see Table 16.1).

> *Proposition 1:* The ways in which protégés and mentors form expectations of, and understand their experience in, mentoring relationships will be heavily influenced by their developmental meaning-making structures.

Our belief is that because developmental meaning-making structures are pervasive in influencing the ways in which we approach and perceive our life experiences, some consistency in approaches to and experiences of mentoring can be identified on the basis of stage location. We propose that participants in mentoring relationships who can be identified as sharing the same level of development would predictably hold some similar expectations and understandings of this relationship, which would, in turn, differ from those of others in different developmental locations. Testing this proposition is relatively straightforward: Researchers could identify the developmental stage for a discrete number of mentors and protégés through the use of the Subject-Object Interview (Kegan, 1994).[1] A second qualitative, "mentoring experience interview" would be conducted, using carefully constructed questions and follow-ups that delved into how subjects understood their experiences and expectations of their mentoring relationships. Analysis would then be conducted to identify and compare how, if at all, developmental stage location is associated with common features of subjects' understandings.

We propose that a person in Stage 3, who views the world through a socialized meaning-making structure, experiences a kind of relational embeddedness within the mentoring context. Given this level of development, this individual is strongly identified with the relationship, finds a compelling sense of affirmation in its positive functioning, and feels significant distress when problems occur. Expectations of closeness with and similarity to the mentoring partner characterize entry into the relationship. If both mentor and protégé are in Stage 3,

Table 16.1   Research Propositions Based on a Constructive-Developmental Theoretical Framework

Proposition 1	The ways in which protégés and mentors form expectations of, and understand their experience in, mentoring relationships will be heavily influenced by their developmental meaning-making structures.
Focus	Studies in this area would focus on identifying the developmental stage locations of the mentors and protégés and linking that to the corresponding expectations, experiences, and meaning that the participants attach to their experiences of the relationships.
Nature of Questions	What expectations do protégés and mentors at differing stages of development bring to the relationships?
	How does the stage location of a mentor or protégé influence his or her experience of the relationship?
Proposition 2	A person's developmental location may be an important filter in identifying benefits and satisfaction derived as a result of participation in the relationship.
Focus	Studies in this area would "zero in" on the specific feelings of satisfaction and identification of benefits that mentors and protégés attribute as outcomes of the relationship, in order to study the degree to which those located at the same developmental stage experience it in similar ways.
Nature of Questions	What benefits do protégés and mentors at different stages of development derive from participation in mentoring relationships?
	How does the stage location of a mentor or protégé influence his or her feelings of the multiple types of satisfaction that can be derived from participation in the relationships?
Proposition 3	The interaction of the mentor's and protégé's developmental locations impacts the functioning of the relationships, and certain combinations may offer more promise than others.
Focus	Developmental stage of mentor/protégé
Nature of Questions	What impact do the interactions of various stages have upon mentoring experiences and outcomes for protégés and mentors?
	Are we able to identify stage combinations that hold more probability of success than others?
	How can mentoring programs use a developmental lens when addressing matching issues?
Proposition 4	The final phase of mentoring relationships, redefinition, widely documented within the literature as posing the greatest challenge to both mentorship participants, places cognitive and affective demands upon mentors. The manner in which these challenges are experienced and managed will differ according to the developmental location of the mentor.
Focus	Developmental stage of mentor
Nature of Questions	What is the nature of the demands experienced by mentors at Stage 3, the socialized stage of development, as the relationship enters its final phase of redefinition?

	How are these the same as or different from those demands experienced by mentors at Stages 4 and 5?
	What do these results tell us about the kinds of supports they need to bring the relationships to a successful conclusion?
Proposition 5	While some mentoring relationships may provide all the necessary elements to support a protégé's development, most mentoring relationships serve as partial contributors to a larger developmental network of relationships, which together constitute a growth-enhancing or effective holding environment.
Focus	Developmental stage of protégé
Nature of Questions	Research into this question will focus not only on individual protégés and their mentoring relationships but also on the larger developmental network of relationships in which they are immersed. These studies will look at the necessary constituents of a successful holding environment (issues of confirmation, contradiction, and continuity) and investigate the sources beyond the mentoring interaction of support and their possible interaction with the mentoring relationship.

personal boundaries are apt to be unclear. As long as both partners share this relational orientation, this fusion is not experienced as problematic; however, if one partner shifts into a different way of viewing the world (such as moving to a 3-to-4 transition), relational difficulties may arise. The blurring of personal boundaries, acceptable to mentors and protégés in Stage 3, will most likely be experienced as intrusive and uncomfortable for individuals in the Self-Authorizing fourth stage. The following case, taken from our practice, provides concrete examples of how the functioning of mentoring relationships can be better understood through the lens of constructive-developmental theory and illustrates Proposition 1 in action.

> *During her college years, Laura attracted two highly skilled yet very different mentors. Rose, the director of human resources at Laura's college, employed her as a work-study student, took a personal interest in her career development, and assigned her projects with high visibility. Rose was proud of Laura and regularly complimented her on her performance. Laura was reliant on her mentor's affirmation and found that it motivated her to undertake increasingly challenging tasks. Over time, Laura's and Rose's relationship developed into a personal friendship. Rose was quite opinionated about the professional path she believed Laura should follow and frequently offered unsolicited, yet welcome advice on how Laura should proceed with her career. Laura recognized in hindsight that she was dependent upon Rose for approval and eagerly accepted her mentor's direction without much questioning.*

At the same time that Laura was being mentored by Rose, she developed a relationship with one of her teachers, Professor Eleanor Wharton. Laura joined a study group in which Professor Wharton refused to provide the students with concrete, definitive answers to their questions, but rather challenged the students to form their own responses and opinions by inevitably turning questions back upon the questioner, "Well, it doesn't matter if I like your paper or not—what do you think?" Laura found the professor's approach to self-directed learning to be utterly frustrating. She could not obtain from Professor Wharton the clear direction or explicit judgment she sought.

Over the next 15 years, Laura maintained a relationship with both mentors. As Laura matured, she came to find Rose's desire and efforts to influence her decision making to be increasingly uncomfortable, and eventually unacceptable. While she valued Rose's opinions, she no longer felt compelled to follow her mentor's advice without questioning. As Laura pushed back, Rose responded hurtfully, interpreting her protégé's inquisitiveness as personal attacks. In response, Laura increasingly distanced herself from Rose's mentorship and instead concentrated on strengthening their friendship. At the same time, Laura found herself turning more and more to Professor Wharton when wrestling with important life decisions. Laura chose to make decisions for herself, but not always by herself. She began to rely on Professor Wharton to help distill complex situations, to ask tough and relevant questions, and to be respectful (but not always approving) of her personal decisions. While both women remain an important part of Laura's life, it is Professor Wharton who continues to function as a mentor.

Laura's approach to meaning making during her college years reflects her understanding of the world at a third order, or socialized stage. During this period, Laura was capable of fully participating in these mutually beneficial relationships and located her identity in association to her mentors. While in Stage 3, Laura was comfortable being *identified with* and *defined by* Rose. This embedded connectedness confirmed her feelings of security and confidence. She blossomed amidst Rose's attention, reinforcement, and praise. Our understanding from Laura's interviews years later is that Rose likely also made sense of the world from a third-order vantage point. Details of their relationship reveal evidence that Rose merged the roles of mentor and friend, mixing her own needs for comfort and reassurance into the relationship in a manner that did not support Laura's transition from Stage 3 to 4.

At the same time, Professor Wharton's at least fourth-ordered way of responding to Laura created a set of demands Laura was not capable of meeting at her current stage of development. Professor Wharton encouraged Laura to be a self-authorizing individual: to determine who she was and what she thought, what she wanted and how she wanted to achieve it. Professor Wharton was ready to provide the necessary supports for Laura to think on her own but refused to make decisions for the young woman. Professor Wharton challenged Laura to become her own source of authorization, to enter into the fourth-ordered balance. Because Laura was not initially ready to assume this challenge, she experienced Professor Wharton's mentorship style as demanding, frustrating, and not particularly supportive. As Laura moved out of Stage 3 and into Stage 4, she grew "beyond" the holding environment provided by Rose and sought a different type of confirmation, challenge, and consistency that could be provided only by a more advanced stage mentor. As Laura developed increasingly complex cognitive systems and capacities for self-authoring behavior, her respect for Professor Wharton's mentoring style grew. Her initial frustration evolved into an appreciation for the independence and respect that these challenges engendered. The satisfaction and benefits that Laura derived from these two different relationships evolved in parallel with her development or meaning-making structures.

Studies in this area could provide insight into beneficial mentoring functions to offer protégés at differing stages and also provide a sense of the progression of support necessary to continue to meet protégés' needs as they change and develop. Research into meaning-making structures can alternatively explore the outcomes of the relationships and the ways in which mentoring partners at different stages of development experience positive effects. These ideas direct our attention to our next proposition.

Proposition 2: A person's developmental location may be an important filter in identifying benefits and satisfaction derived as a result of participation in the relationship.

If meaning-making structures heavily influence expectations of and experiences in mentoring relationships, it is reasonable to assume that the sense of satisfaction derived from participation in mentoring relationships and the identification of benefits may also be directly related to developmental stage. Future research into this area could focus on mentors and protégés who identify past relationships as successful and are willing to reflect on the beneficial outcomes and the sense of satisfaction that they derived. Questions could probe for a better understanding of the nature of the outcomes they experienced and the ways in which they felt they benefited from participation.

Given our constructive-developmental perspective, we propose that mentors and protégés in Stage 3 derive satisfaction from the experience of similarity and agreement and actually require a sense of closeness and togetherness. Stage 3 mentors are pleased with protégés who keep in close contact, are dependent upon them for advice, and value their expertise. They find fulfillment in having protégés who emulate their example. Stage 3 protégés require mentors who are recognized experts in their fields, provide concrete answers, affirm their instincts, maintain consistent and reliable communication, and share similar goals. They find pleasure in pleasing their mentors and meeting their expectations.

On the other hand, Stage 4 mentors and protégés would probably express very different perceptions of success and satisfaction. Based on a constructive-developmental perspective, Stage 4 mentors and protégés derive satisfaction in coming to know themselves well within the relational context. They feel comfortable asserting beliefs, even if these beliefs differ significantly from those of their partners. Stage 4 mentors experience satisfaction in seeing the values to which they are committed perpetuated, as long as protégés are not supporting them solely out of a sense of loyalty. At the same time, these mentoring participants experience difference as stimulating and are able to see the ways in which discussions across differences help clarify their relative positions. Mentors and protégés in Stage 4 appreciate the uniqueness each other's perspective brings and the richness that it adds to their relationships. Stage 4 protégés value relationships that challenge them to think for themselves, question, and pose alternative solutions. They derive satisfaction from meeting self-constructed goals. Mentors experience satisfaction with protégés who are eager to find themselves, as opposed to simply emulating their role-modeling. Yet as a result of the ability of Stage 4 mentors to put relationships in perspective, if this does not occur, they are flexible in adapting their goals to those of the particular protégé with whom they are engaged. So, if paired with protégés at Stage 3, Stage 4 mentors demonstrate the capacity to adjust their expectations. They derive satisfaction from positive outcomes emanating from the relationship, regardless of whether or not the relationship continues. Since their identities are not linked to the relationship, stages of separation and redefinition are not necessarily stressful and perceptions of satisfaction can endure even through a difficult ending.

While age constructions are not determinative of level of development, stage-level testing suggests that Stage 4 is rarely attained before midlife. Therefore, we would not expect the majority of protégés to be at this level. Moreover, protégés at Stage 5 would be even rarer, and thus our description of this stage is confined to mentors.

Stage 5 mentors derive satisfaction from the uniqueness of each relationship and are open to new ways of connecting. They relish opportunities for different outcomes and appreciate the ways in which the relationships enhance previously unexplored or underdeveloped aspects of the self (which they may identify in protégés). Able to disassociate from one particular ideology or way of viewing the world, Stage 5 mentors are welcoming of ideas to challenge their preferred ways of doing things. If heavily invested in professional development, they may especially appreciate thinking about the integration of personal goals with career aspirations. They might resist formulaic patterns of engagement, with predictable outcomes and expected benefits, and instead prefer more adventurous explorations. Stage 5 mentors could potentially be ideal partners in diversified relationships that would fully tap their capacities for interpersonal connection. Being open to questioning their own ideological perspectives, they would bring openness to cross-cultural exploration and learning, not achievable by mentors at lower stages.

While this chapter has concentrated primarily on the development of the protégé, consideration of constructive-developmental theory expands the range of outcomes possible for the mentor within this evolutionary sequence. The theory's view of adult development as movement in service of psychological capacity building presents a far more expansive spectrum of beneficial outcomes and growth opportunities available for mentors than has been previously explored.

A related area for further inquiry involves the possibility that Stage 4 mentors may be encouraged toward their own 4-to-5 transitions by needing to cope with the very independence that they foster in their protégés. Mentors at Stage 4, often dedicated to the perspectives they have worked hard to formulate, may find the serious questioning by an independent protégé to be provocative. While it is possible these challenges might evoke feelings of frustration in a strongly self-authoring mentor (unlike Stage 3 mentors, who would be captive to those feelings), fourth-ordered mentors can have a relationship to their own reactions. These mentors are able to step away from and assess their potential feelings of frustration, taking responsibility for the role that they play in the relationship and for the relational imbalance. This perspective taking allows mentors to transform both the way they internally understand the interaction and the way they externally manage it. Mentors who are able to embrace this challenge may find reward in increased capacity and personal development. As guides to a younger generation of adults who question, probe, and openly contradict the most sacred of constructs, mentors may be challenged to consider the partiality of their own belief systems, no matter how attached they are to such beliefs or how well these systems have become entrenched during adulthood. The openness to reconsider firmly established beliefs and to grow in unanticipated ways reinforces the potential of mentoring alliances to nurture mutual growth across multiple stages of development.

Propositions 1 and 2 carry important implications for better understanding the functioning of mentoring relationships. Insights from a constructive-developmental theoretical lens suggest that no single set of mentoring behaviors will be experienced as "best practice" by all protégés. Instead, perceptions of effective mentoring are highly dependent upon the individual and interactive levels of cognitive complexity operating among the participants. Constructive-developmental theory provides insight into how individuals' meaning-making structures at different levels of development influence their participation and interaction within mentoring relationships. Proposing the idea of qualitatively different ways of experiencing mentoring relationships based on predictable developmental stages begs the question of ideal matches. If we (a) have an idea of what individuals at different stages of development generally expect and need from mentoring relationships, (b) possess insight into which behaviors will likely be experienced as satisfying to different protégés or mentors based on their orders of mind, and (c) can anticipate what the particular challenges will be that individuals face according to their meaning-making structures, then we can make some informed decisions about which protégés and mentors should be matched with one another, which existing partnerships are likely to fail, and which partnerships are likely to succeed. Consideration of the "optimal match" as the basis for future study leads us to our next proposition:

Proposition 3: The interaction of the mentor's and protégé's developmental locations impacts the functioning of the relationships, and certain combinations may offer more promise than others.

Constructing effective mentoring relationships between individuals who possess evolving meaning-making systems is a complicated dynamic that is subject to constantly shifting dialogues of evolving world perceptions. While it is tempting to propose simple models of mentor and protégé pairs who are simultaneously engaged in movement toward increasingly complex ways of understanding the world, we are not able to be predictive to this level of granularity. For example, we cannot take for granted that mentors at lower levels of development than their protégés are necessarily ineffective as personal or professional guides. And although we suspect that greater cognitive complexity is associated with increased competency, it does not guarantee successful relational engagement any more than functioning at high levels of development guarantees happiness. Evaluating *how* an individual will use the tools that development affords to nurture relationships, cultivate happiness, or create a meaningful life, constructive-developmental theory suggests that advances in development increase the *kinds and number of tools* that individuals have at their disposal to attain these goals. For example, although learning to talk does not guarantee effective dialogue, it is nevertheless reasonable to assume that language acquisition is an effective tool in increasing communication skills. Likewise, while higher levels of personal development in mentors do not ensure more successful mentoring relationships, it is reasonable to assume that mentors who possess capacities such as perspective taking, continual questioning of their own beliefs, and taking responsibility for their actions are able to bring a wider variety of tools and growth-enhancing forces to the relationship.

Future researchers should consider focusing on how the limits and capacities of different meaning-making structures in adult development interact within the context of mentoring relationships. How does a mentor's and protégé's development influence one another's learning during the course of the relationship? Are there optimal combinations of mentor and protégé developmental stages? Can successful mentoring relationships exist when the mentor is at a lower stage of development than his or her protégé? And can a mentor provide effective guidance and a healthy holding environment while going through a significant personal developmental transition? Research into these questions would involve following or interviewing pairs of individuals in various stage combinations. This could be done longitudinally by following individual pairs as they progress through their relationships or interviewing pairs of individuals at various levels of development, at different stages of the relationship.

> *Proposition 4:* The final phase of mentoring relationships, redefinition, widely documented within the literature as posing the greatest challenge to both mentorship participants, places cognitive and affective demands upon mentors. The manner in which these challenges are experienced and managed will differ according to the developmental location of the mentor.

Substantial relational changes due to separation, redefinition, or the termination of relationships often present significant challenges to those involved. It is not easy, nor is it well understood, how to negotiate the many cognitive and emotional changes both mentors and protégés face as mentoring relationships end. We propose that cognitive-developmental theory offers a useful lens for anticipating the nature of these challenges, specifically for mentors, depending upon developmental location.

For Stage 3 mentors, participating in a positively functioning mentoring relationship confirms their capacity for contribution to and self-sacrifice for the benefit of others. It affirms their ability to fully engage in a mutually beneficial relationship. If paired with a protégé who also views the world from this perspective, they may experience the relationship in a very positive and supportive way. In another case, as a protégé enters into a 3-to-4 transition and begins to "outgrow" what the mentor offers, how might we expect a Stage 3 mentor to react? A Stage 3 mentor is likely to describe a deep sense of abandonment as the relationship in which he or she is embedded changes. Because the relationship *is* the identity for such a mentor, threats to its continued existence may ultimately be perceived as a threat to his or her identity. In subject-object terms, the mentor is embedded in the relationship and is subject to it. Hence, its loss can be experienced by a Stage 3 mentor as the loss of self. Aligning this particular meaning-making structure with the final phase of the relationship suggests that the demands placed upon Stage 3 mentors are substantial. In this situation, certain behaviors can be anticipated, the most obvious being the mentor's resistance to separation, which inevitably leads the relationship into redefinition.

A mentor at Stage 4, on the other hand, brings the capacity to take a perspective on the relationship (as opposed to being embedded within it). Because the termination of a relationship is not associated with the identity of a Stage 4 mentor, its conclusion is experienced with less trauma and distress. The maintenance of clear relational boundaries, which are necessary for a mentor at Stage 4 to be comfortable while in the relationship, facilitates an easier progression through separation and redefinition. At the same time, a Stage 4 mentor demonstrates the capacity to take responsibility for behaviors that might cause stress and those that could be more responsive to a protégé's difficulty in terminating. An enhanced capability for perspective taking allows Stage 4 mentors to interact in a personalized way, tailoring mentoring behaviors to the developmental needs of the protégé. This ability affords the mentor the capacity to either accommodate the demands of the protégé in a more effective way, thereby increasing the possibility that the relationship can continue, or to bring the relationship to a successful conclusion, without experiencing stress or trauma.

Effective and aware mentors stay mindful that they themselves may play a role in the drama of reconstructed loyalties and identification and may themselves be "pushed against" toward the closing phase of the mentoring relationship. Difficult conclusions to mentoring relationships are well documented in the literature (Kram, 1985; Levinson, 1978), and it may be easier for mentors to experience, and even assist in, the reflection and redefinition that can accompany the 3-to-4 transition, if mentors are themselves at the self-authoring stage (or beyond).

> *Proposition 5:* While some mentoring relationships may provide all of the necessary elements to support a protégé's development, most mentoring relationships serve as partial contributors to a larger developmental network of relationships, which together constitute a growth-enhancing or effective holding environment.

Understanding the role and potential of a protégé's extended holding environment is essential to grasping the various contributions mentoring can provide in encouraging adult development. While it is possible, and in some instances desirable, for a mentoring relationship to serve as a self-contained holding environment (offering elements of confirmation, contradiction, and continuity), it is also possible for the relationship to contribute only one or some of these elements to larger, more complex networks of support that we, as adults, create and mold around ourselves (Chandler & Kram, 2005). An example of this network configuration might be found in viewing a young (Stage 3) professional woman's support system as a holding environment in which she identifies (a) her spouse and family as providing the sense of confirmation she needs by validating her current self as a highly valued relational being, (b) her formal mentor as providing the challenge she requires in demanding higher levels of self-authoring behaviors in terms of decision making within the work context, and (c) her constellation of colleagues who stay in accompaniment with her as she grows and changes, both personally and professionally, thereby providing continuity. Note that in this example, the woman's mentor does not provide all three elements required in a successful holding environment, but merely contributes a single element that is supplemented by others.

Initial work in this arena has already begun. Chandler and Kram (2005) have explored the interactions between the meaning-making stage of the individual and its impact on types of networks created. They have also explored the particular role these specifically constructed networks play in supporting development (Chandler & Kram, 2005; Higgins, Chandler, & Kram, Chapter 14, this volume; Higgins & Kram, 2001). Consideration of this phenomenon adds further complexity to the existing evaluation of mentoring relationships by extending the range of influences on the individual to the entire psychosocial environment within which the relationship is functioning. Research into this conceptualization holds the promise of providing a sound theoretical basis for the advantages which a "constellation" of mentors (Higgins & Kram, 2001) affords, each offering a variety of developmental combinations that can be supportive, challenging, or both. Many of the issues engaged in this chapter, along with other related propositions (Chandler & Kram, 2005), are the first signs of testable hypotheses that will contribute to future research.

Methodological Challenges

Constructive-developmental theory may offer an innovative lens through which to view the mentoring relationship and to pursue new questions for further study. Mentoring relationships have long been viewed from a phase theory perspective as one of the primary supports for development in adulthood for both mentors and protégés (Levinson, 1978). Complementary in nature, mentoring relationships have been shown to simultaneously fulfill the salient developmental needs of both the mentor and the protégé (Kram, 1985). Given a constructive-developmental perspective, future research can build upon this foundation to further our understanding of how mentoring relationships may contribute to developmental progression across the adult life span in a way that more accurately differentiates the developmental locations of both mentors and protégés.

To move this research agenda forward, new research studies must be constructed with care to match the kinds of questions asked with the methodological strategies employed. For those studies in which it is necessary to determine an individual's precise stage location in order to make claims of capacities and limitations, the researcher will need a thorough understanding of constructive-developmental theory and the use of the Subject-Object Interview (Lahey, Souvaine, Kegan, & Felix, 1988). While it is tempting to make quick evaluations of individuals' orders of mind, the subtleties involved for even the most seasoned developmental researchers require the use of a reliable instrument.

However, for researchers whose purpose does not involve pinpointing the precise stage of development achieved by mentoring participants, it is possible to pose questions in such a way that broad stances toward individuation, self-authorization, responsibility taking, and other indicators of developmental location in adulthood can be elicited. Because we know that the majority of adults will fall somewhere on a Stage 3-to-4 continuum, it is reasonable to construct research protocols that target the capacities and limitations associated with progression through and location within these stages. Enhancing our understanding of the strengths and limitations of these various meaning-making structures and their interactions within mentoring relationships could provide insight into an entire spectrum of relational configurations not yet considered within the current mentoring literature.

Conclusion

Our knowledge and understanding of adult development is constantly evolving. As we live longer, we are coming to understand that cognitive and affective capacities in adulthood may actually develop in ways previously unimaginable. Whereas prior thinking suggested that our mental ability, like our physical growth, reaches its fullest height by the end of life's second decade, current research indicates that mental capacity can qualitatively change through adulthood. Increasingly complex cognitive systems contribute to our ability to meet the growing demands of the modern world (Kegan, 1994). The dynamic interplay between increasing societal demands and pressures on human mental capacity drives the need for continued research on factors or relationships that may support and even facilitate this developmental transformation. This chapter addresses the importance of recognizing the fundamentals of adult development as it pertains to mentoring when trying to understand, create, and implement intentionally supportive adult developmental relationships.

Results of this initial conversation between the fields of mentoring and constructive-developmental theory suggest areas of opportunity, learning, and future research. For example, constructive-developmental theory posits that what constitutes support and challenge differs depending upon individual approaches to meaning making. This understanding has multiple implications for the field of mentoring. It suggests that there is no one "right" way to approach mentoring. "Best practices" are highly dependent upon the meaning-making structures of the individuals involved and must be understood accordingly. Also, issues of matching are similarly affected by an understanding of this theory. The interaction of aligned or misaligned mental systems adds layers of complexity not previously considered in such depth when selecting and forming mentoring pairs.

In the end, our survival and development as humans depend upon our capacity to recruit the invested attention of others to us and, at the same time, on others' willingness and capacity to be recruited (Kegan, 1982). Mentoring relationships, both formal and informal, are premised on this need. Integrating the most current understanding of what constitutes development, and how it is supported, with our understanding of the relational dynamics of mentoring relationships represents an important contribution to both fields.

Note

1. For further information on reliability and validity, see the Appendix in the *Guide to the Subject-Object Interview* (Lahey, Souvaine, Kegan, & Felix, 1988). Interrater reliability across studies has ranged from .75 to .90, with one study reporting test-retest reliability of .83. In addition, a longitudinal study suggests that this instrument has the capacity to capture individuals' gradual changes in subject-object relationships over time in the anticipated developmental direction.

References

Bowlby, R. (2004). *Fifty years of attachment theory*. London: Karnac.

Chandler, D. E., & Kram, K. E. (2005). Applying an adult development perspective to developmental networks. *Career Development International, 10,* 548–566.

Cloninger, C. R. (2004). *Feeling good: The science of well-being*. New York: Oxford University Press.

Erikson, E. H. (1963). *Childhood and society*. New York: Norton.

Faraone, S. V., Tsuang, M. T., & Tsuang, D. W. (1999). *Genetics of mental disorders: A guide for students, clinicians, and researchers*. New York: Guilford Press.

Freud, S., & Josef, B. (2004). *Studies in hysteria* (L. Nicola, Trans.). New York: Penguin Books.

Hall, D. T., & Kram, K. E. (1982). Development in mid-career. In D. Montross & C. Shinkman (Eds.), *Midcareer in career development in the 1980's: Theory and practice* (pp. 406–423). Springfield, IL: Charles C Thomas.

Higgins, M. C., & Kram, K. E. (2001). Reconceptualizing mentoring at work: A developmental network approach. *Academy of Management Review, 26,* 264–288.

Hilarski, C. (Ed.). (2005). *Addiction, assessment, and treatment with adolescents, adults and families*. Binghamton, NY: Haworth Social Work Practice Press.

Kegan, R. (1982). *The evolving self: Problem and process in human development*. Cambridge, MA: Harvard University Press.

Kegan, R. (1994). *In over our heads: The mental demands of modern life*. Cambridge, MA: Harvard University Press.

Kegan, R., & Lahey, L. L. (2001). *How the way we talk can change the way we work*. San Francisco: Jossey-Bass.

Kohlberg, L. (1981). *The philosophy of moral development*. San Francisco: Harper & Row.

Kram, K. (1985). *Mentoring at work: Developmental relationships in organizational life*. Glenview, IL: Scott, Foresman.

Lahey, L., Souvaine, E. A., Kegan, R., & Felix, S. (1988). *A guide to the Subject-Object Interview: Its administration and interpretation*. Cambridge, MA: Harvard University Graduate School of Education, Laboratory of Human Development.

Levinson, D. J. (with Darrow, C., Klein, E., Levinson, M. H., & McKee, B.). (1978). *The seasons of a man's life*. New York: Ballantine Books.

Linley, P. A., & Stephen, J. (Eds.). (2004). *Positive psychology in practice.* Hoboken, NJ: Wiley.

Mazure, C. M. (Ed.). (1995). *Does stress cause psychiatric illness?* Washington, DC: American Psychiatric Press.

Mullen, E. (1994). Framing the mentoring relationship as an information exchange. *Human Resource Management Review, 4,* 257–281.

Perry, W. G. J. (1970). *Forms of intellectual and ethical development in the college years.* New York: Holt, Rinehart & Winston.

Piaget, J. (1948). *The moral judgment of children.* Glencoe, IL: Free Press.

Piaget, J. (1952). *The origins of intelligence in children.* New York: International Universities Press. (Original work published 1936)

Piaget, J. (1954). *The construction of reality in the child.* New York: Basic Books. (Original work published 1937)

Piaget, J. (1969). *The psychology of the child.* New York: HarperTorch.

Schein, E. H. (1990). *Career anchors.* San Diego, CA: Jossey-Bass/Pfeiffer.

Seligman, M. E. P. (1990). *Learned optimism.* New York: Knopf.

Selman, R. L. (1980). *The growth of interpersonal understanding: Developmental and clinical analyses.* New York: Academic Press.

Vaillant, G. E. (2002). *Aging well: Surprising guideposts to a happier life from the Landmark Harvard Study of adult development.* Boston: Little, Brown.

Winnicott, D. W. (1965). *The maturational process and the facilitating environment.* New York: International Universities Press.

17

The Role of Emotional Intelligence in the Mentoring Process

Cary Cherniss

J im was a rising young star at Telcom Corporation. Everyone thought he was destined for great things—including Jim himself. That is why it was a real blow to him when he made a presentation at a meeting of senior executives and rather than shower him with praise when he finished, they raised a number of critical concerns about the project.

Fortunately, Jim's mentor, Sid, was one of the senior executives who had been at the meeting. After the meeting, Jim and Sid met to discuss what had happened, and Jim bitterly complained about the criticisms. Sid heard him out, saying little. However, a few days later, Sid called Jim and asked to meet with him again. When they met, Sid gently but clearly told Jim that his reactions, while understandable, were way off base. Most of the criticisms were valid; and rather than respond defensively, it would be better for Jim if he could accept the criticisms and learn from them.

Jim was stunned. Even though Sid had been gentle in the way he framed his comments, Jim took them as a rebuke. However, he trusted and admired Sid; he believed that Sid cared about him and wanted to help him. As a result, Jim seriously considered what Sid said and began to look more critically at himself. He realized that Sid was right: Too often, Jim rejected criticism and regarded it as a symptom of dysfunctional resistance from others rather than as an opportunity for him to learn and improve. Jim vowed that he would change, and he did. He went on to

AUTHOR'S NOTE: "Telcom" is a fictitious name.

have the distinguished career that everyone had expected of him, and 30 years later, he still vividly remembered that afternoon when Sid helped set him straight.

The above example illustrates mentoring at its best. An older, experienced mentor helps his protege to learn and grow in ways that foster positive career development. The example also illustrates some of the ways in which emotional intelligence influences the mentoring relationship. Sid's emotional intelligence helped him to develop a trusting relationship with Jim, and Sid also displayed considerable emotional intelligence in the way he handled Jim's response to criticism. Finally, Sid's mentoring helped Jim to develop aspects of emotional intelligence that enabled him to go on and achieve his potential. Stories like this one suggest that emotional intelligence often plays a large role in the mentoring process.

The Concept of Emotional Intelligence

Emotional intelligence refers to the way in which people perceive, express, understand, and manage emotion in themselves and others (Cherniss, 2004; Mayer & Salovey, 1997). People who score high in emotional intelligence are better able to understand why they feel the way they do in different situations, and they are able to manage their emotional reactions in ways that help them to adapt to the demands of living. Emotional intelligence also enables people to better read how others are feeling or might feel in different situations and to use that knowledge to relate to others in ways that promote positive outcomes (Goleman, 1998).

A growing body of research suggests that emotional intelligence is particularly important for success in life and effectiveness at work. For over 100 years, psychologists have assumed that cognitive intelligence—the kind of mental ability measured by IQ tests, SATs, GREs, and so on—is the key for success. However, despite numerous attempts to refine our measures of cognitive ability, its observed relationship to personal effectiveness has been limited. For instance, a recent meta-analysis, which examined dozens of studies, found that "the relationship between intelligence and leadership is considerably lower than previously thought," with a corrected correlation coefficient of only .27 (Judge, Colbert, & Ilies, 2004, p. 542). This finding suggests that IQ accounts for only about 8% of the variability in leadership effectiveness, which leaves much of the variability in performance unexplained.

Emotional intelligence, and the competencies associated with it, seems to play a more significant role than cognitive intelligence, particularly in determining who will be among the top performers in any organization. For instance, a study conducted by the Hay Group (2002), a large multinational consulting firm, compared executives who eventually advanced to become president of a company with those who were passed over. The biggest differences involved the competencies associated with emotional intelligence. Most important was *self-control,* the ability to regulate one's own emotional responses. Those who became president were 7 times more likely to score high on this quality than those who were passed over. The next most important differentiator was *empathy,* or the ability to accurately read how others feel and to understand why they feel as they do. Those who became president were 3 times more likely to score high on empathy (Hay Group, 2002).

Cognitive ability also differentiated the presidents from others, but it was less significant than the emotional competencies. Those who rose to the top were 1.5 times more likely to score high in conceptual thinking and 1.2 times more likely to score high in analytical thinking (Hay Group, 2002). Thus, emotional competence was a more important factor than cognitive ability in who reached the top.

A similar finding emerged from a study by Egon Zehnder, a large international executive search firm. A group of 515 executives who had been placed in various companies as a result of the search process were rated on three dimensions: the relevance of their previous experience, their intellectual ability, and their emotional and social competence. Then, the researchers determined whether the search had led to a successful placement. They found that emotional and social competence was a better predictor of success than either relevant experience or intellectual ability. More specifically, they found that the executive was strongest in emotional and social competence in 74% of the successes and only 24% of the failures. The original study took place in South America, but identical results emerged when the study was replicated in Germany and Japan (Fernandez-Araoz, 2001).

One other study involved over 400 principals and vice principals in the province of Ontario, Canada. Stone, Parker, and Wood (2005) asked each administrator's superior and up to three subordinates to evaluate their performance with a leadership questionnaire designed for the study. Then, they tested the administrators' emotional intelligence. They found that the top performers scored significantly higher than the poorest performers on every dimension of emotional intelligence.

Like many new areas of research, the study of emotional intelligence has been marked by a certain amount of controversy concerning both conceptualization and measurement. At least three distinct models have emerged, each with its own measure and more than a few advocates.

First, there is Bar-On's model, which covers five main dimensions (Bar-On, Handley, & Fund, 2005). The first he calls "Intrapersonal," and it covers personal attributes such as self-regard, emotional self-awareness, and assertiveness. The second dimension, "Interpersonal," includes empathy, social responsibility, and interpersonal relationship. Third is "Adaptability," which includes problem solving, reality testing, and flexibility. "Stress Management" is the fourth dimension in Bar-On's model, covering stress tolerance and impulse control. The last dimension is "General Mood," which includes optimism and happiness. Bar-On has developed a self-report measure of each of these attributes, which he calls the "EQ-i." A clinical psychologist by training, Bar-On's model is the result of research on those personal qualities that are most important for positive mental health. Several studies have demonstrated that those who score higher on the EQ-i also are more successful at work (Bar-On et al., 2005; Ruderman, Hannum, Leslie, & Steed, 2001; Stone et al., 2005).

In the early 1990s, Salovey and Mayer (1990) put forth a somewhat different model of emotional intelligence. Their model covers four dimensions, or "branches," which they call "Perceiving Emotion," "Using Emotion," "Understanding Emotion," and "Managing Emotion." As academic psychologists interested in human intelligence and the psychology of emotion, they were primarily interested in identifying aspects of intelligence that involved the processing of information related to emotion and that are not well captured in traditional tests of cognitive ability. They have developed a test to measure these emotional abilities. The test, called the "Mayer-Salovey-Caruso Emotional Intelligence Test" (MSCEIT), requires the test taker to complete various tasks designed to tap different aspects of their emotional intelligence. For instance, in one subtest, there is a series of faces expressing emotional reactions, and the test taker must indicate how much sadness, gladness, anger, fear, and so on is expressed in each face. There is some research suggesting that those who score higher on the MSCEIT perform better in certain work situations (Lopes, Cote, & Salovey, 2005).

A third model of emotional intelligence has been put forth by Goleman (2001). His work began with an interest in identifying the competencies that best predict effectiveness in the workplace. Building on the earlier work of David McClelland (1973, 1998) and his students, Goleman identified about 20 social and emotional competencies that most strongly differentiate between superior and average performers. He and his colleague Richard Boyatzis found that these competencies could be grouped into four basic dimensions of emotional intelligence: Self-Awareness, Self-Management, Social Awareness, and Relationship Management. Self-Awareness includes competencies such as emotional self-awareness and self-confidence. Self-Management includes emotional self-control and adaptability. Social Awareness covers empathy, organizational awareness, and service orientation. Relationship Management encompasses competencies such as influence and conflict management. Boyatzis and Goleman have developed a multirater ("360-degree") assessment instrument called the "Emotional Competence Inventory" (ECI) to measure these aspects of emotional intelligence. A number of studies have found that those who score higher on the ECI tend to be among the top performers in a variety of jobs (Boyatzis & Sala, 2004; Cavallo & Brienza, 2004).

Although there is much overlap between the three models, there also are important differences. On a conceptual level, the Mayer, Salovey and Caruso model focuses on the basic, underlying skills involving the perception, understanding, and management of emotion. The Bar-On and Goleman/Boyatzis models include some of these foundational skills, but they also include a host of competencies that mediate between these skills and effective performance or adaptation.

There also are important differences in the measures associated with each model. The MSCEIT is designed to directly test the abilities associated with its underlying conception of emotional intelligence. The EQ-i asks individuals to indicate the extent to which they believe they display the competencies associated with Bar-On's conception of social and emotional intelligence. The ECI expands this rating approach by asking several people who know the individual well to rate him or her on the Goleman and Boyatzis competencies. Each measure has its advocates who make eloquent and impassioned appeals on its behalf, and each also has data supporting its psychometric soundness. All of the major players also agree that more research is needed to resolve the remaining disputes about the tests and what they measure.

On a theoretical level, however, Goleman (2001) has made a major contribution toward clarifying and resolving some of the major differences between the models. He has proposed that there is a difference between the underlying abilities of emotional intelligence and the *competencies* based on those abilities. Goleman further suggests that the specific competencies make the greatest difference for performance. For instance, a precocious child can have a high level of mathematical intelligence yet not know how to balance an algebraic equation until someone teaches her how to do so. To do competent work in many areas of mathematics, it is more important that one be able to balance algebraic equations. However, one's ability to learn how to balance equations and how adept one ultimately will be at doing so are related to one's underlying mathematical intelligence. Similarly, how well one mentors another will depend in part on how well one listens. But how quickly and easily one can learn the skill of "active listening" and how adept one ultimately will be in using this skill will depend on one's emotional intelligence. This "theory of performance," as Goleman refers to it, does not resolve all of the controversies in the field, but it does go a long way toward clarifying how the different models fit together and complement each other.

There also is some question about whether adults can become more emotionally intelligent through systematic training and development efforts. Differences in one's ability to perceive, understand, and manage one's emotions emerge very early in life. For example, the "marshmallow study" demonstrated that children as young as four differed in emotional self-control. In this experiment, an adult researcher brought a child into a room in which there was a marshmallow on a plate. The adult told the child that he or she could eat the marshmallow immediately, but if the child could wait a few minutes until the adult returned from an errand, the child could have two marshmallows. The researchers found that about one third of the children succumbed to temptation almost immediately. However, about 20% were able to resist eating the marshmallow until the adult returned, a period of 10 minutes or longer. And when the researchers tracked down the children 10 years later, they found that the children who were best able to control their impulses were significantly more popular, less likely to get into trouble, did better in school, and scored an average of 210 points higher on the combined verbal and math sections of the Scholastic Aptitude Test (Shoda, Mischel, & Peake, 1990). This study suggests that at least some aspects of emotional intelligence emerge very early in childhood and persist over time despite the multitude of social learning experiences that children encounter.

Nevertheless, there also is research suggesting that many of the most critical social and emotional competencies can be improved later in life through formal training experiences. For instance, a group of 19 managers from the U.S. government's Defense Finance Accounting Service improved an average of 24% on the competencies measured by the ECI as a result of a yearlong development effort (McClelland Development Center, n.d.). In another study, 29 managers from the Swedish firm Skanska improved their total EQ-i scores from an average of 97 to 106 after participating in a group training program (Bar-On, 2004). And in yet another study, 60 managers from a retail chain in the United Kingdom participated in a training program involving 1 day per week for 4 weeks. Their emotional intelligence was tested with the EQ-i prior to training and again 6 months after training. Their scores increased on average from 95 to 100, while a control group that did not go through the training showed no change (Slaski & Cartwright, 2003).

There also is evidence that certain kinds of life experiences can promote the development of emotional competencies. Dulewicz and Higgs (2004) found that the experience of having to manage a complex project led to an increase in emotional intelligence competencies. A group of individuals who captained a yacht for several months in competition also showed an increase in emotional and social competence.

Thus, while it is not easy to increase one's emotional intelligence past childhood, it is possible to improve one's emotional competence, given the right conditions. Effective mentoring seems to be one of those conditions that helps promote social and emotional competence. And emotionally intelligent mentors and protégés seem to get more out of the mentoring experience.

Mentoring and Emotional Intelligence

Emotional intelligence and mentoring seem to be related in two basic ways. First, the emotional intelligence of both the mentor and the protégé appears to influence the quality of mentoring. Second, the best mentoring relationships often help people become more socially and emotionally competent. Figure 17.1 illustrates these different ways in which emotional intelligence is related to mentoring.

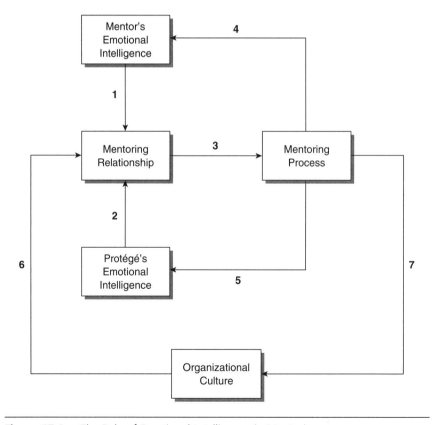

Figure 17.1   The Role of Emotional Intelligence in Mentoring

The Impact of Emotional Intelligence on the Mentoring Relationship

The incident with which this chapter began illustrates how important the quality of the relationship is for the mentoring process (arrow 3 in Figure 17.1). The situation involved two individuals who had formed a close relationship characterized by mutual trust and respect. The quality of that relationship was critical for the mentor's ability to gently confront his protégé and for the protégé's ability to receive the feedback and learn from it. If they had not had a close, trusting relationship, Sid would have felt less comfortable about giving Jim the feedback. As a result, he might have chosen not to meet with Jim in order to avoid the unpleasantness it might cause and the threat of damaging their relationship further. Or he might have given the feedback in a brusque, clumsy way that would have made Jim more defensive and less able to hear it. On the other hand, even if Sid had been able to meet with Jim and give him the feedback skillfully, Jim might have dismissed it as just more resistance from the senior executive leadership if he and Sid had not had a good relationship.

Several studies have confirmed that there is a link between emotional intelligence and the quality of relationships among people. For instance, one study found that those who scored high in the "Managing Emotions" section of the MSCEIT were rated by friends as more caring and emotionally supportive (Grewal & Salovey, 2005). Furthermore, the qualities that make for a strong, positive mentoring relationship are similar to those found in any good helping relationship. As Bennetts (2002) noted, "The mentor alliance . . . is sustained by Rogers's (1957) core conditions for learning, i.e., empathy, genuineness, unconditional positive regard, and the ability to communicate these conditions" (p. 156). All of these qualities are related to emotional intelligence (Goleman, 1998).

A study by Brechtel (2004) underscored the importance of the quality of the relationship in mentoring, particularly the role of emotion. He asked mentors and protégés to indicate what qualities were most important in a good mentoring relationship. There was considerable agreement that good mentoring relationships involved feelings of respect, of being valued, and of belonging. Protégés and mentors also felt safe in good mentoring relationships. People's capacities to form positive, safe relationships seem to be strongly influenced by emotional intelligence (arrows 1 and 2 in Figure 17.1). As Kram and Cherniss (2001) noted, both mentors and protégés "must rely on their willingness to invest in the relationship and their capacities to initiate contact, actively listen, invite and give feedback, and foster ongoing communication" (p. 263). Also, the best mentoring relationships require the mentor and protégé to "manage the continuous tension between autonomy and connection" (p. 272).

Emotional intelligence is especially important in more intense, ongoing relationships, such as a mentoring relationship. Mentoring has been described as "an intense, emotional relationship, in which the protégé is not only interested in learning about work but [is] also willing to become a new person" (Baum, 1992, p. 225). Thus, how well mentors and their protégés are able to perceive, understand, use, and manage emotions in themselves and others should have a significant impact on how much a protégé gets out of the relationship.

Emotional intelligence is especially important in the way it helps mentors and protégés to manage the anxiety associated with the intimacy of the mentor relationship. As Kram and Cherniss (2001) pointed out, the "willingness to be vulnerable" is a "necessary" condition for the development of more rewarding mentoring relationships (p. 270). Bennetts (2002) struck a similar note when she wrote, "There has to be a willingness to become intimate for a mentoring relationship to work well" (p. 157). She found in her research that "the essence and meaning of the [mentor relationship] was somehow present at such moments when all defences were dropped and neither party was in a role" (p. 156).

Kalbfleisch and Davies (1993) conducted a study that showed how the anxiety associated with intimacy can interfere with the development of mentoring relationships if it is not managed adequately. They found that those who perceived a higher risk of intimacy in interpersonal relationships were less likely to become involved in a mentoring relationship, and this was true for both mentors and protégés. And for mentors, the perceived risk of intimacy was an even stronger predictor than communication competence or self-esteem. (See also Kalbfleisch, Chapter 20, this volume.)

People who lack the ability to manage the anxieties associated with the vulnerability of intimacy thus will be less willing to engage in close mentoring relationships. And managing this kind of anxiety requires a considerable amount of emotional intelligence.

Emotional intelligence also helps people assess whether the risk of intimacy is great enough that embarking on a relationship would be unwise. In some situations, there may in fact be risks associated with developing more intimate relationships with coworkers or superiors, and the more prudent course of action is to avoid becoming too close. Emotionally intelligent individuals are not only able to accurately perceive the anxiety that is associated with engaging in a more intimate relationship; they also are better able to understand whether such anxiety is realistic. If it proves to be unfounded and the mentoring relationship offers unique opportunities for learning and growth, then emotional intelligence can enable the person to prevent the anxiety from interfering with the development of the relationship. (For more on the issues of vulnerability and intimacy in mentoring relationships, see Fletcher & Ragins, Chapter 15, this volume.)

Emotional intelligence is especially important in cross-gender and cross-race mentoring relationships. Although such relationships can be valuable for both the mentor and the protégé, there also can be a greater degree of ambiguity and tension when mentoring relationships involve male-female or Black-White group differences. Prior socialization, gender and racial stereotyping, and intergroup dynamics pose special challenges to people who want to form relationships with individuals who come from backgrounds different from their own (Ibarra, 1993; Kram, 1996; Thomas & Alderfer, 1989; Thomas & Gabarro, 1999; see also Blake-Beard, Murrell, & Thomas, Chapter 9, this volume). Thus, it is not surprising that there appears to be greater interpersonal comfort in same-gender and same-race relationships than in cross-gender and cross-race relationships, and this affects the quality of mentoring (Allen, Day, & Lentz, 2005; Chao, Walz, & Gardner, 1992; Fagenson-Eland, Marks, & Amendola, 1997; Ragins & Cotton, 1993).

Dealing effectively with the challenges posed by cross-race and cross-gender relationships requires a high level of emotional intelligence on the part of both mentor and protégé. Imagine, for example, that in the incident that began this chapter, Sid was not only older but also White, while Jim was younger and African American. As Alderfer (1986) noted, any interpersonal relationship will be influenced by the parties' most salient group memberships and by the history of relationships between those groups. In this case, the history of relationships between Whites and Blacks in our society, marked by slavery, oppression, and, more recently, concerns of Whites about "affirmative action," have made contemporary relationships between White and Black Americans particularly charged. Thus, it is likely that these intergroup dynamics would be acting on Sid and Jim and that both of them would need an especially high degree of emotional intelligence in order to manage the strong feelings associated with these dynamics and to develop a close, trusting mentoring relationship. And their emotional competence would be tested particularly in the situation where Sid believed that it would be helpful for him to give negative feedback to Jim. The intergroup dynamics might well lead to a heightened level of anxiety and guilt in Sid, which would make it especially difficult for him to initiate a conversation with Jim about Jim's reaction to the meeting; and the same dynamics might lead to a heightened level of anger and resentment in Jim, which would make it especially difficult for him to receive negative feedback from Sid.

In a recent review of the research on cross-race and cross-gender mentoring, McGlowan-Fellows and Thomas (2005) began by noting that "Black women and people of color generally are excluded from access to influential people and organizational networks that are key to achieving long-term success" and they have "fewer intimate informal relationships with influential people" (p. 8). These authors went on to argue that although mentoring is essential for addressing this problem, it must be done in a way that deals with the negative self-images and stereotypes that continue to afflict African American women in the corporate world. Mentors need to be skilled in dealing with the anger, depression, and performance anxiety that are generated by these negative images. And emotional intelligence provides the foundation for such skill.

Aspects of emotional intelligence such as self-awareness and empathy help mentors and protégés to "recognize how long-standing stereotypes limit their own and others' behavior and learning" (Kram & Cherniss, 2001, p. 275). Only by being acutely aware of one's own emotional reactions and those of the other can one successfully navigate the emotionally turbulent waters of cross-race and cross-gender relationships. Similarly, for these relationships to work, both parties need to be able to manage their own emotional reactions as well as those of the other person.

Emotional Intelligence and the Mentor Role

The model in Figure 17.1 suggests that the mentoring relationship is influenced by both the mentor's emotional intelligence (arrow 1) and the protégé's emotional intelligence (arrow 2). The importance of emotional intelligence for the mentor seems apparent. The mentor presumably takes the lead in the relationship and therefore sets the emotional tone. If the mentor is not able to tolerate the intimacy and other kinds of emotional risks inherent in mentoring relationships, it seems unlikely that a satisfactory mentoring relationship will develop.

Once a close mentoring relationship forms, effective mentors continue to draw on their emotional intelligence. As Bennetts (2002) found in her research, mentors utilize emotional processes to help protégés become more adept at utilizing emotion in their own work and careers. In her study of highly significant mentoring relationships, "emotion was utilized rather than denied" (Bennetts, 2002, p. 162).

The mentor's emotional intelligence also seems to be important, because the mentor often becomes an emotional model for the protégé. Protégés develop the competencies they need for advancement in part by observing their mentors and emulating them. In the above example, Sid was modeling for Jim how to deal with difficult feedback and also how to constructively give feedback to another person.

Emotional intelligence also seems to play a role when the mentor serves as sponsor and advocate for the protégé. For instance, to provide "protection" to a protégé, a mentor must effectively cope with the anxiety that might be associated with standing up for someone who lacks status in a corporate environment. And providing the protection in a skillful manner that minimizes negative fallout requires a high degree of sensitivity to emotional nuances in the organization. Similarly, while "coaching" often involves imparting information about the organization and the work, doing it in a skillful way so that the protégé truly understands and incorporates the message seems to require a high degree of emotional intelligence.

The developmental work that mentors must do for themselves also draws on their emotional intelligence. After focusing on one's own development and advancement for many years, it can be difficult for many senior leaders to change their focus in order to become sponsors for younger protégés. They may be conflicted about promoting the advancement of others rather than themselves. Those who are aware of these feelings and who are able to manage them constructively will be the best mentors.

Most research on mentor characteristics has focused on demographic factors rather than social and emotional competencies or emotional intelligence, but there have been a few studies that point to the importance of emotional skills. In a qualitative study of the role of mentor relationships in the lives of creative people, participants described mentors as "displaying the personality characteristics of what has come to be known as emotional intelligence" (Bennetts, 2002, p. 162). Smith, Howard, and Harrington (2005), in summarizing the results of several quantitative studies, reported that effective mentors tend to score high on social and emotional competencies, such as flexibility, authenticity, nurturance, approachability, inspiration, and conscientiousness. Caring and empathy also seem to be important.

In their own research, Smith et al. (2005) used a Delphi technique to identify a list of 38 characteristics associated with effective mentoring. Then, they built these into a survey completed by over 300 formal mentors. When they factor analyzed the results, three factors emerged: respectability (e.g., honesty, integrity), wisdom (e.g., organizational savvy), and sensitivity (empathy, compassion, genuineness). These results provide further support for the notion that emotional intelligence plays a significant role. The ability to manage one's own emotions is the foundation for qualities such as honesty and integrity, while the ability to perceive and understand others' emotions provides the foundation for empathy and compassion (Goleman, 1998). It also is worth noting that wisdom, which was viewed as least important of the three factors, is probably the one most strongly linked to cognitive as opposed to emotional intelligence.

Research also suggests that a person's emotional intelligence is important in determining whether other people will seek out that person to become a mentor. Olian, Carroll, Giannantonio, and Feren (1988) found in a series of experiments that people sought out as mentors those who scored higher in interpersonal competence. Being connected to crucial decision-making networks in the organization also made one more attractive as a mentor, but only if interpersonal competence was low. And interpersonal competence was a more important factor than either the mentor's age or gender.

A recent study found that "personality," defined as the "Big Five" global factors (openness, conscientiousness, extraversion, agreeableness, and neuroticism), played a relatively minor role in whether or not an administrator provided mentoring to others (Bozionelos, 2004). This study, however, says little about the significance of the mentor's emotional intelligence in the mentoring process, because there is, at best, a weak association between emotional intelligence and most facets of personality (Mayer, Salovey, & Caruso, 2000). For example, how well one perceives, understands, uses, and manages emotion in oneself and others has little to do with whether one is an introvert or extravert, how open one is to new experience, or even how conscientious one is.

Thus, research on the link between personality traits and mentoring is suggestive, but it does not directly assess the role of emotional intelligence. In fact, it often is emotional intelligence that enables mentors or protégés to develop positive mentoring relationships even when they possess personality traits that might be inhibiting. Emotional intelligence encompasses those abilities that enable one to be aware of one's underlying personality traits and to assess the degree to which they might impede desirable action. It also is emotional intelligence that enables one to use this knowledge to modify one's behavior and to act in ways that run counter to those underlying personality traits, such as when an introvert pushes himself to seek out younger colleagues and initiate interactions that might lead to productive mentoring relationships.

Emotional Intelligence and the Protégé Role

The protégé's emotional intelligence also plays a significant role in the mentoring process (arrow 2 in Figure 17.1). This point was emphasized by Turban and Dougherty (1994), who wrote that "mentoring relationships often occur at the initiative of the protégé" (p. 698). Unfortunately, many potential protégés never find satisfying mentoring relationships because they lack the social and emotional competencies that are so crucial.

A good example of how important the protégé's emotional intelligence can be in the initiation of mentoring relationships was provided by Cherniss (1995) in his study of professional burnout. One of the participants in the study was a special education teacher who had taught in a "resource room" program for several years. (In this type of program, a few children who spend most of the day in a regular class come in for an hour or so of special help from the resource room teacher.) Then, at the end of 1 academic year, the teacher learned that she was being reassigned to a self-contained classroom for the following year and that she would be working with a more challenged group of students. The school district offered her no additional training or other supports. The teacher was dismayed by this unexpected and unwanted change. She felt totally unprepared, and she almost quit. However, she decided instead to find a mentor. She reached out to a more experienced colleague who had taught in self-contained classes for many years. The colleague responded positively to the request for help, and the two teachers developed a close bond. During the next year, they met at least once a week for an hour or more, and they also spent considerable time in each other's classrooms. As a result, the teacher who was transferred not only enjoyed the new assignment, but had one of her best years of teaching.

This example suggests that several aspects of emotional intelligence can be important in determining whether potential protégés initiate mentoring relationships. For instance, when initially faced with the challenge of being transferred, the teacher managed to move beyond her initial upset and to seek out a good mentor, which required a high degree of emotional self-control. She then used considerable social skills to engage a colleague whom she barely knew and convince her to become an informal mentor for her.

Other researchers have confirmed that a protégé's emotional and social competence can be important in the initiation of fulfilling mentoring relationships. In their study of how protégés initiate mentoring relationships, Turban and Dougherty (1994) found that individuals with "low emotional stability" were "less likely to initiate mentoring relationships because such individuals, who lack confidence, do not . . . want to increase their level of nervousness and tension by establishing relationships with upper-level managers" (p. 690) (see also Dougherty & Dreher, Chapter 3, this volume).

Turban and Dougherty's (1994) research indicated that another aspect of a potential protégé's emotional intelligence—the ability to accurately read social cues—was also related to the initiation of mentoring relationships. They measured a personal quality called *self-monitoring*, which they defined as follows:

> The extent to which individuals vary in their sensitivity to social cues and in their ability to adapt their behavior to the requirements of a situation (Snyder, 1987). Individuals high on self-monitoring are sensitive to social cues, can modify their behavior using those cues, are concerned with behaving in a situationally appropriate manner, and change their behaviors on the basis of what they believe is appropriate for a situation. Those low on self-monitoring lack either the ability or the motivation to change their behavior to fit situations, rely less on social cues to regulate their behavior, and therefore behave more consistently across situations. (Turban & Dougherty, 1994, p. 689)

Consistent with their prediction, the authors found that high self-monitors were more likely than low self-monitors to initiate and sustain mentoring relationships. Self-monitoring appears to be closely linked to two fundamental aspects of emotional intelligence: emotion perception and emotion management (Grewal & Salovey, 2005).

One can imagine other ways in which the protégé's emotional intelligence could be an important factor. For instance, the emotional expressiveness of a protégé can facilitate the development of positive mentoring relationship, because mentors are more likely to provide good mentoring to protégés who respond with gratitude, appreciation, and enthusiasm (Young & Perrewe, 2004). Protégés who are able to convey these feelings in a clear and authentic way thus will be more likely to develop positive mentoring relationships. And emotional intelligence enables some individuals to do this better than others.

Other research also has pointed to the importance of the protégé's emotional intelligence in effective mentoring relationships. For example, Kalbfleisch and Davies (1993) found that communication competence, self-esteem, and perceived risks of intimacy were as important in determining whether one would become a protégé as they were in predicting who would become a mentor.

Finally, a protégé's emotional and social competencies seem to have more influence on the mentoring relationship than other factors, such as gender. For example, Turban and Dougherty (1994) found that while a protégé's emotional stability and ability to accurately read social cues were strong predictors of the initiation of mentoring relationships, protégé gender was not (for more on the importance of research on protégé behavior, see Higgins, Chandler, & Kram, Chapter 14, this volume).

The Impact of Mentoring on Emotional Intelligence

At the same time that emotional intelligence contributes to effective mentoring, effective mentoring can enhance emotional intelligence (see arrows 4 and 5 in the model depicted in Figure 17.1). Some of the earliest empirical work on mentoring showed that "psychosocial development" is an important function (Kram, 1985). Such development is often associated with increases in social and emotional competence. For instance, Kram and Cherniss (2001) described a midlevel manager in a large corporation who was experiencing high levels of ambiguity and overload. He was worried about how he was going to manage all of his commitments and responsibilities. He confided his concerns to his mentor. The mentor not only reassured him but also helped him to cope by figuring out what commitments were most critical, setting priorities, and taking time away from work to reflect and restore himself. In the process, the protégé became more competent in managing time and work demands and also in managing stress more generally.

There are several ways that people in the work setting can try to improve their emotional intelligence, such as coaching and formal training programs. However, mentoring seems to be particularly effective. The development of emotional and social abilities in adults usually requires a long-term process, with alternating periods of action and reflection (Cherniss & Adler, 2000; Kram & Cherniss, 2001). It often is difficult to provide for such a process in formal training programs. Mentoring provides a natural context for such learning.

For instance, in the example that opened this chapter, Jim could have become more aware of his defensive reactions to criticism through a formal training program in leadership. Such a program also might have helped Jim develop the self-management competencies that would help him to curb those reactions so that he could learn from criticism. However, most conventional corporate training programs do not provide the kinds of sustained conditions necessary for such emotional learning to occur (Cherniss & Adler, 2000). They tend to be too brief, and the participants do not open themselves up in a way that is conducive to such learning. The close, ongoing mentoring relationship that Jim had with Sid provided a more effective context for such learning to occur.

A number of studies suggest that good mentoring relationships can enhance social and emotional competence. For example, McGlowan-Fellows and Thomas (2005) found that "mentoring of black women is generally correlated with improved psychosocial development, increased motivation, increased optimism about achieving career goals, and an abatement of hopelessness and despair associated with their career outlooks" (p. 12). Brem (2001) also found that good mentors foster a number of emotional and social competencies that are vital for career success, including resiliency, intuition, nurturing, creativity, passion, self-value, and sensitivity.

Although the protégé is usually the primary beneficiary in mentoring relationships, mentoring relationships can help mentors develop emotional and social competencies as well. Empathy is one that is particularly likely to increase. For instance, one large corporation developed a formal mentoring program in which White male senior executives were chosen to be mentors for younger female managers. To help the mentors to be effective in this role, the company arranged for each of them first to interview a female manager in order to become more familiar with the trials and tribulations associated with being a member of a marginal group in their corporate environment. The mentors then spent some time discussing among themselves what they learned, with the help of two outside consultants. These experiences not only made them more helpful mentors, but they also likely became more sensitive and understanding toward all individuals who were more marginal.

This example also suggests that cross-gender and cross-race mentoring relationships can be especially valuable in promoting empathy on the part of the mentor. As Kram and Cherniss (2001) noted, "The empathy a mentor develops during the experience of getting to know an assigned protégé of a different race or gender can be helpful in strengthening relationships with other colleagues in his immediate work setting" (p. 262). Thus, while such relationships can be particularly challenging, they also can be especially powerful vehicles for enhancing the emotional intelligence of both mentor and protégé. (For another perspective on how mentoring can contribute to the enhancement of emotional and social competence, see Lankau & Scandura, Chapter 4, this volume.)

The Impact of Organizational Culture

Although a mentor's or protégé's emotional intelligence can facilitate the development of mentoring relationships, the influence of the organizational environment should not be underestimated. Research on mentoring suggests that it flourishes in organizational settings where the expression of emotion is more tolerated and there is a greater appreciation for the role of emotion and emotional expression in organizational life (Kram & Cherniss, 2001). If the organization's culture and reward structures devalue mentoring relationships (arrow 6 in Figure 17.1), high levels of emotional intelligence in individual members will not likely have much impact.

For instance, consider the case of Marie, a new faculty member in a doctoral program in clinical psychology, situated in a prestigious, research-oriented university. The faculty in the program, as well as the program director, were all well-trained clinicians who displayed a high degree of emotional and social competence in their work with patients. However, the highly individualistic and achievement-oriented norms of the academic culture discouraged them from paying much attention to their own emotional reactions (outside of therapy relationships) or those of new faculty like Marie. As a result, no one reached out to Marie to provide her with the kind of mentoring that new faculty need. And Marie quickly got the message that she was supposed to "figure things out" on her own. In this example, a high degree of emotional intelligence on the part of individuals in the setting was mitigated by a paucity of what might be considered "organizational emotional intelligence."

In addition to having supportive norms and values, emotionally intelligent organizations tend to use a number of processes and structures that help promote and sustain positive mentoring relationships. For instance, if they establish formal mentoring programs, the programs are likely to be more comprehensive, involving not only interpersonal skills training but also 360-degree feedback practices, rewards for those who take on the mentoring role and do it effectively, and development plans that recognize and utilize the mentoring relationship. Also important are human resource systems, such as the extent to which mentoring relationships are encouraged in performance management and succession planning processes (Kram & Cherniss, 2001).

Emotionally intelligent organizations also support mentoring in less direct ways. An example would be the institutionalization of structures and processes that encourage organizational learning, such as setting aside time periodically for individuals and groups to reflect on their own social and emotional dynamics.

However, emotionally intelligent leadership can play a crucial role in making the organizational culture more conducive to mentoring. Emotions play an important role in organizational life. If organizational leaders fail to acknowledge this or seek to deal with this reality by suppressing any expression of emotion or discussion of it, they will tend to create a culture in which mentoring is likely to suffer. Organizational culture will be more supportive of mentoring in organizations where there is a critical mass of individuals in leadership positions who are high in emotional intelligence.

Mentoring, as we have seen, can help to make leaders more emotionally intelligent. Thus, effective mentoring that is sustained over time and occurs at all levels of an organization can eventually contribute to a more emotionally intelligent organizational culture, which, in turn, promotes even better mentoring in the future (see arrow 7 in Figure 17.1). However, there needs to be a minimal amount of support within the organization from the beginning for such mentoring to occur frequently enough. Although a few individuals who excel in emotional intelligence might be able to initiate and sustain good mentoring relationships in organizational environments that are not particularly supportive, mentoring is more likely to flourish in emotionally intelligent organizations.

Recommendations for Mentoring Theory and Research

The model presented in this chapter and illustrated in Figure 17.1 not only provides a way of organizing existing research but also points to recommendations for future research and theory on the link between emotional intelligence and the mentoring process (see Box 17.1). A basic premise underlying this chapter has been that emotional intelligence—and the social and emotional competencies that are based on it—is vital for the initiation of effective mentoring relationships. Furthermore, I have suggested that through effective mentoring relationships, both mentors and protégés can increase their abilities to perceive, use, understand, and manage their own emotions and those of others and that this can promote positive career development. Finally, I have suggested that organizational contexts differ in the extent to which they support emotionally intelligent mentoring.

BOX 17.1   Propositions for Future Research

1. Those levels of emotional intelligence will be more likely to become natural mentors to others.

2. Those with higher levels of emotional intelligence will be more likely to seek out mentoring from others.

3. Mentors with higher levels of emotional intelligence will form stronger, more positive mentoring relationships with their protégés.

4. Protégés with higher levels of emotional intelligence will form stronger, more positive mentoring relationships with their mentors.

5. Mentors and protégés with higher levels of emotional intelligence will be more likely to successfully navigate the stages of a mentoring relationship.

6. Mentors and protégés with higher levels of emotional intelligence will be more likely to benefit from mentoring relationships.

7. Those with higher levels of emotional intelligence will be more likely to avoid negative mentoring relationships.

8. The impact of emotional intelligence will be even greater in cross-race and cross-gender mentoring relationships.

9. The emotional intelligence of the mentor and protégé will be a better predictor of mentoring effectiveness than either demographic or personality factors.

10. Effective mentoring relationships will contribute to the development of greater emotional and social competence in both mentors and protégés.

11. Mentoring will be more prevalent and effective in organizational settings where social norms support the expression of emotion and there is a greater appreciation for the role of emotion in organizational life.

12. Mentoring will be more prevalent and effective in organizational settings where a critical mass of individuals in leadership positions are high in emotional intelligence.

13. A potential mentor's empathy, or awareness of how others are feeling, will be particularly predictive of good mentoring.

14. A potential protégé's self-management and relationship management competencies will be particularly predictive of good mentoring.

15. Managers who become more emotionally competent as a result of emotional intelligence training will become more active and effective mentors and protégés.

16. Those with higher levels of emotional intelligence will be more likely to establish effective developmental networks among peers.

17. Peer-based developmental networks and traditional dyadic mentoring relationships will tend to differ in their effectiveness at developing different emotional intelligence competencies.

We have seen that there is already some research supporting all of these basic points, but we need more. Some aspects of the model have less research support than others. For instance, there is considerable research suggesting that the emotional and social competencies of mentors are correlated with the inclination to become mentors and the quality of the mentoring relationship. There is less research on the role of the protégé's emotional intelligence. There also is relatively little research on the impact of mentoring on emotional intelligence—particularly the impact on the mentor.

The organizational culture's impact on mentoring is even less well studied, and it is here that the concept of emotional intelligence can make a particularly useful contribution. The model presented in this chapter suggests that the organizational culture will impact mentoring particularly through the way in which it influences people's *thinking about feeling*. Good mentoring is most likely to flourish in organizations where people are encouraged to express, talk about, think about, and use emotion. Exploring this basic premise and all its vicissitudes is a relatively uncharted area of research.

The concept of emotional intelligence is also useful in the way it systematically differentiates between various social and emotional abilities that could be more or less important for the mentoring process. For instance, there is a distinction made between awareness of one's own emotional life and awareness of how others are feeling. Similarly, there is a distinction made between awareness of emotion and the ability to manage it. At the same time, the theoretical work on emotional intelligence points to how these different facets are interrelated. For instance, Mayer, Salovey, and Caruso (2004) and Goleman (1998) suggested that awareness of emotion, especially in oneself, provides a foundation for management of emotion.

These theoretical advances point to a new set of questions concerning the relationship between emotional intelligence and the mentoring process. For instance, we now can ask whether certain facets of emotional intelligence or certain social and emotional competencies are more important than others for the mentoring process. One hypothesis is that a potential mentor's empathy, or awareness of how others are feeling, is particularly predictive of good mentoring, while self-management and relationship management competencies are more important for the would-be protégé.

In testing these and other hypotheses, we need to rely more on action research methodology that utilizes experimental designs. Much of the previous quantitative research in this area relies on correlational designs. Theoretical progress increasingly will require that we conduct good field experiments. An example of such research would be to take a group of managers who participate in a training program designed to enhance their social and emotional competence and then compare their mentoring relationships to those of a control group 1 to 2 years later. One hypothesis would be that the managers who become more emotionally competent as a result of the training would become more active and effective mentors and protégés.

Progress in research and theory also depends on the development of better measures of emotional intelligence. There currently are several different competing measures, and all show promise. However, each test has weaknesses as well as strengths. Collectively, they represent only the beginning of what will likely be a long process of methodological refinement. Until we have developed better measures of emotional intelligence, our ability to understand the role of emotional intelligence in the mentoring process will be limited.

Nevertheless, there is already enough good research and theory to suggest that emotional intelligence plays a significant role in the mentoring process. Furthermore, the concept of emotional intelligence provides a new and potentially powerful lens for studying, understanding, and promoting mentoring in organizations. Future research and theory in this area promises to be both fruitful and fulfilling.

References

Alderfer, C. P. (1986). An intergroup perspective on group dynamics. In J. W. Lorsch (Ed.), *Handbook of organizational behavior* (pp. 190–222). Englewood Cliffs, NJ: Prentice Hall.

Allen, T. D., Day, R., & Lentz, E. (2005). The role of interpersonal comfort in mentoring relationships. *Journal of Career Development, 31,* 155–169.

Bar-On, R. (2004, October 28–30). *Applying the power of emotional intelligence.* Paper presented at the EQ Symposium, Golden, CO.

Bar-On, R., Handley, R., & Fund, S. (2005). The impact of emotional intelligence on performance. In V. Druskat, F. Sala, & G. Mount (Eds.), *Linking emotional intelligence and performance at work: Current research evidence* (pp. 3–20). Mahwah, NJ: Lawrence Erlbaum.

Baum, S. (1992). Mentoring: Narcissistic fantasies and oedipal realities. *Human Relations, 45,* 223–245.

Bennetts, C. (2002). Traditional mentor relationships, intimacy, and emotional intelligence. *International Journal of Qualitative Studies in Education, 15,* 155–170.

Boyatzis, R. E., & Sala, F. (2004). Assessing emotional intelligence competencies. In G. Geher (Ed.), *Measuring emotional intelligence: Common ground and controversy* (pp. 147–180). Hauppage, NY: Nova Science.

Bozionelos, N. (2004). Mentoring provided: Relation to mentor's career success, personality, and mentoring received. *Journal of Vocational Behavior, 64,* 24–46.

Brechtel, M. F. (2004). The affective correlates of a good mentoring relationship. *Dissertation Abstracts International: Section B: The Sciences & Engineering, 64*(9-B), 4604.

Brem, M. L. (2001). *The seven greatest truths about successful women.* San Francisco: Jossey-Bass.

Cavallo, K., & Brienza, D. (2004). *Emotional competence and leadership excellence at Johnson & Johnson: The emotional intelligence and leadership study.* New Brunswick, NJ: Rutgers University, Consortium for Research on Emotional Intelligence in Organizations.

Chao, G. T., Walz, P. M., & Gardner, P. D. (1992). Formal and informal mentorships: A comparison on mentoring functions and contrast with nonmentored counterparts. *Personnel Psychology, 45,* 619–636.

Cherniss, C. (1995). *Beyond burnout: Helping teachers, nurses, therapists, and lawyers overcome stress and disillusionment.* New York: Routledge.

Cherniss, C. (2004). Intelligence, emotional. In C. Spielberger (Ed.), *Encyclopedia of applied psychology* (Vol. 2, pp. 315–321). Oxford, UK: Elsevier.

Cherniss, C., & Adler, M. (2000). *Promoting emotional intelligence in organizations.* Alexandria, VA: American Society for Training & Development.

Dulewicz, V., & Higgs, M. (2004). Can emotional intelligence be developed? *International Journal of Human Resource Management, 15,* 95–111.

Fagenson-Eland, E. A., Marks, M. A., & Amendola, K. L. (1997). Perceptions of mentoring relationships. *Journal of Vocational Behavior, 51,* 29–42.

Fernandez-Araoz, C. (2001). The challenge of hiring senior executives. In C. Cherniss & D. Goleman (Eds.), *The emotionally intelligent workplace* (pp. 182–206). San Francisco: Jossey-Bass.

Goleman, D. (1998). *Working with emotional intelligence.* New York: Bantam.

Goleman, D. (2001). An EI-based theory of performance. In C. Cherniss & D. Goleman (Eds.), *The emotionally intelligent workplace: How to select for, measure, and improve emotional intelligence in individuals, groups, and organizations* (pp. 27–44). San Francisco: Jossey-Bass.

Grewal, D., & Salovey, P. (2005). Feeling smart: The science of emotional intelligence. *American Scientist, 93,* 330–339.

Hay Group. (2002). Unpublished study. Boston, MA.

Ibarra, H. (1993). Personal networks of women and minorities in management: A conceptual framework. *Academy of Management Review, 18,* 56–97.

Judge, T. A., Colbert, A. E., & Ilies, R. (2004). Intelligence and leadership: A quantitative review and test of theoretical propositions. *Journal of Applied Psychology, 89,* 542–552.

Kalbfleisch, P. J., & Davies, A. B. (1993). An interpersonal model for participation in mentoring relationships. *Western Journal of Communication, 57,* 399–415.

Kram, K., & Cherniss, C. (2001). Developing emotional competence through relationships at work. In C. Cherniss & D. Goleman (Eds.), *The emotionally intelligent workplace* (pp. 254–285). San Francisco: Jossey-Bass.

Kram, K. E. (1985). Improving the mentoring process. *Training and Development Journal, 39,* 40–43.

Kram, K. E. (1996). A relational approach to career development. In D. T. Hall & Associates (Eds.), *The career is dead—Long live the career: A relational approach to careers* (pp. 132–157). San Francisco: Jossey-Bass.

Lopes, P. N., Cote, S., & Salovey, P. (2005). An ability model of emotional intelligence: Implications for assessment and training. In V. Druskat, F. Sala, & G. Mount (Eds.), *Emotional intelligence and workplace performance* (pp. 53–80). Mahwah, NJ: Lawrence Erlbaum.

Mayer, J. D., & Salovey, P. (1997). What is emotional intelligence? In P. Salovey & D. J. Sluyter (Eds.), *Emotional development and emotional intelligence* (pp. 3–34). New York: Basic Books.

Mayer, J. D., Salovey, P., & Caruso, D. R. (2000). Emotional intelligence meets traditional standards for an intelligence. *Intelligence, 27,* 267–298.

Mayer, J. D., Salovey, P., & Caruso, D. R. (2004). Emotional intelligence: Theory, findings, and implications. *Psychological Inquiry, 15,* 197–215.

McClelland, D. C. (1973). Testing for competence rather than intelligence. *American Psychologist, 28,* 1–14.

McClelland, D. C. (1998). Identifying competencies with behavioral-event interviews. *Psychological Science, 9,* 331–339.

McClelland Development Center. (n.d.). *Developing emotional intelligence.* Retrieved July 4, 2005, from http://www.haygroup.com/ww/research/index.asp?Country=26&Topic= 3&filterGo=Go&pn26=2&pgs=26,9&pn9=8

McGlowan-Fellows, B., & Thomas, C. S. (2005). Changing roles: Corporate mentoring of black women—A review with implications for practitioners of mental health. *International Journal of Mental Health, 33*(4), 3–18.

Olian, J. D., Carroll, S. J., Giannantonio, C. M., & Feren, D. B. (1988). What do protégés look for in a mentor? Results of three experimental studies. *Journal of Vocational Behavior, 33,* 15–37.

Ragins, B. R., & Cotton, J. L. (1993). Gender and willingness to mentor in organizations. *Journal of Management, 19,* 97–111.

Rogers, C. R. (1957). The necessary and sufficient conditions for therapeutic personality change. *Journal of Consulting Psychology, 21,* 95–103.

Ruderman, M. N., Hannum, K., Leslie, J. B., & Steed, J. L. (2001). Making the connection: Leadership skills and emotional intelligence. *Leadership in Action, 21*(5), 3–7.

Salovey, P., & Mayer, J. (1990). Emotional intelligence. *Imagination, Cognition, and Personality, 9,* 185–211.

Shoda, Y., Mischel, W., & Peake, P. K. (1990). Predicting adolescent cognitive and self-regulatory competencies from preschool delay of gratification: Identifying diagnostic conditions. *Developmental Psychology, 26,* 978–986.

Slaski, M., & Cartwright, S. (2003). Emotional intelligence training and its implications for health, stress, and performance. *Stress and Health, 19,* 233–239.

Smith, W. J., Howard, J. T., & Harrington, K. V. (2005). Essential formal mentor characteristics and functions in governmental and non-governmental organizations from the program administrator's and the mentor's perspective. *Public Personnel Management, 34,* 31–58.

Snyder, M. (1987). *Public appearance/private realities.* New York: Freeman.

Stone, H., Parker, J. D. A., & Wood, L. M. (2005). *Report on the Ontario principal's council leadership study.* Toronto, Canada: Ontario Principals' Council.

Thomas, D., & Gabarro, J. J. (1999). *Breaking through: The making of minority executives in corporate America.* Boston: Harvard Business School Press.

Thomas, D. A., & Alderfer, C. P. (1989). The influence of race on career dynamics: Theory and research on minority career experiences. In M. B. Arthur, D. T. Hall, & B. S. Lawrence (Eds.), *Handbook of career theory* (pp. 133–180). New York: Cambridge University Press.

Turban, D. B., & Dougherty, T. W. (1994). Role of protégé personality in receipt of mentoring and career success. *Academy of Management Journal, 37,* 688–702.

Young, A., & Perrewe, P. L. (2004). The role of expectations in the mentoring exchange: An analysis of mentor and protégé expectations in relation to perceived support. *Journal of Managerial Issues, 16,* 103–126.

18

Mentoring for Intentional Behavioral Change

Richard E. Boyatzis

For all of the time, effort, and money invested in attempts to help individuals develop through education, training, mentoring, and coaching, there are few theories that help us to understand the change process. Research into the change process seems to always document the importance of others in the process, whether those others are various forms of support or reference groups (Ballou, Bowers, Boyatzis, & Kolb, 1999) or mentors, coaches, counselors, or trusted advisors (Allen, Eby, Poteet, Lentz, & Lima, 2004; Hall, 1996; Kolb & Boyatzis, 1970a, 1970b; Kram, 1985; McCall, Lombardo, & Morrison, 1988; Noe, Greenberger, & Wang, 2002; Wanberg, Welsh, & Hezlett, 2003). Other than Prochaska, DiClemente, and Norcross (1992) and McClelland (1965), the actual process of change and the role of the mentor or others are often left like a mysterious black box. The emerging literature on relational theories (Hall, 1996; Kram & Cherniss, 2001) and the contribution of leader-member exchange theory (Graen & Uhl-Bien, 1995) and attachment theory (Popper, Mayseless, & Castelnovo, 2000) offer hope of more insight.

Theories or models of how teams, organizations, communities, countries, or even global change occur are more frequent, but, again, the role of the change agent or charismatic leader are often a post hoc description of how the consultants or change agents went about the process. Each new framework has the potential of being a new "change fad," but seldom are they put to the empirical test of demonstrating sustainable results.

One reason is that most of the literature has focused on career advancement as the beneficial consequences of effective mentoring (Wanberg et al., 2003). It is not surprising that the dependent variable of such studies is promotion or salary increases or performance appraisal ratings. These have been called "indicators of success" but not necessarily "indicators of effectiveness" (Luthans, Hodgetts, &

Rosenkrantz, 1988). But what of the deeper, more sustained changes of individuals' behavior, their dreams and aspirations, their self-awareness or adaptability? These have often been called the "psychosocial effects of mentoring" (Higgins & Kram, 2001). They can easily be confused with other psychosocial variables, like satisfaction with the mentor, or protégé, or the mentoring relationship.

A second reason for this paucity of good theory is that the underlying paradigm on which they are conceptualized is lacking in credibility. The idea of smooth, continuous change does not fit with the reality most of us experience.

In this chapter, a theory of change is proposed that has produced demonstrable results at the individual level. The focus of the chapter will be the specific role of mentors and the process of mentoring in helping achieve desired change, in addition to the psychophysiological benefit to the mentor of being in this process. The requirement that complexity theory is used to understand the process of change will be explained. Once concepts from complexity theory are applied, it then becomes a distinct possibility that this theory of change and the role of mentors in the process will also help to explain sustainable change at many other levels of social organization.

Intentional Change and the Role of Mentors

At the individual level, *intentional change theory* (ICT) describes the essential components and process of desirable, sustainable change in one's behavior, thoughts, feelings, and perceptions (Boyatzis, 2006). The "change" may be in a person's actions, habits, or competencies. It may be in their dreams or aspirations. It may be in the way they feel in certain situations or around certain people. It may be a change in how they look at events at work or in life. It is "desired" in that the person wishes it so or would like it to occur. It is "sustainable" in that it endures—lasts a relatively long time. In this sense, ICT may be said to describe and explain learning as a form of this desired adaptation. Indeed, the name of the theory was *self-directed learning* for many years (Boyatzis, 1999, 2001; Goleman, Boyatzis, & McKee, 2002). The theory and supporting research focus on adults. Although it may apply to younger people, the work cited here and the focus of its development over the past 38 years has been on adults. Although the person must drive the change, it is clear from the research that a person cannot engage in the process alone. It is primarily through the help of mentors that a person can realize the discoveries and continue to change.

A "desirable, sustainable change" may also include the desire to maintain a current desirable state, relationship, or habit. But knowing that things can atrophy or drift into a less desired state, the desire to maintain the current state requires investment of energy in this maintenance, while external (or internal) forces may naturally provoke a change.

Desired sustainable changes in an individual's behavior, thoughts, feelings, or perceptions are, on the whole, discontinuous. That is, they appear as emergent or catastrophic changes over time and effort. The experience is one of an epiphany or discovery. Self-awareness or mindfulness (of self and context, both social and natural) (Boyatzis & McKee, 2005) is inversely proportionate to the degree of surprise or discovery. When one is highly self-aware, he or she will experience the change process as more of a set of smooth transitions. Mentors help a person with such necessarily conscious realizations. They may do it by asking questions, being supportive, or offering an insight. The more self-aware a person is, the easier the role of mentor is in provoking these conscious epiphanies.

For example, individuals not mindfully aware of their bodies may not notice an additional pound or two added to their weight. But when they realize they cannot easily get into a favorite and formerly comfortable pair of jeans, they realize they may have gained weight (or claim the jeans shrunk). Another example involves individuals who become more involved in their work than previously. It starts with slightly longer days—starting work at 8:30 a.m., not 9, then 8 a.m., and then doing e-mail at home from 6:30 a.m. to 7:30, to save time at work. They stay at work a little longer, first until 6 p.m., then 6:30, then 7. They start to take one thing home to work on over the weekend—and it grows to 2 to 3 hours of work on Saturday and Sunday. A person low in self-awareness will not see these changes, for example, until his or her child asks for an appointment for them to be together. Both of these examples illustrate the discontinuous or, in complexity theory terms, the catastrophic change in awareness of change. Contrast this with a smooth, emerging awareness in a mindful, aware person who would see these small changes along the way—although whether they change their behavior is another issue.

The same forces result in the changes often being nonlinear. So, this brings us to the first feature of ICT as a complex system: The change process is often nonlinear and discontinuous, appearing or being experienced as a set of discoveries or epiphanies. They are emergent phenomenon that used to be described as "catastrophic occurrences" in the language of complexity theory (Casti, 1994). This chapter will explore the critical roles played by others, helpers whom we can call mentors, coaches, guides, gurus, or friends. Without them, intentional, desired change would appear chaotic and unpredictable to us. Without the guiding observations or support of a mentor, or mentors, the result might be fear or avoidance of that which appears chaotic—and therefore render us unable to pursue or foster such change.

For example, in trying to predict performance from individual characteristics, studies have overlooked the concept of the "tipping point." Gladwell (2000) popularized the idea and showed how it can often explain the sudden outbreak of a riot, a run on a bank, or surprising stock market drops. This idea, taken from complexity theory, is that up to a certain point, the relationship between a person's abilities and his or her performance may not appear to exist. But once a specific point is reached, a discontinuity occurs, and the effect of a small, incremental increase in the person's behavior produces a dramatic increase in effectiveness (Boyatzis, 2006; McClelland, 1998). This relationship has also been referred to as "the butterfly effect" or "trigger point." We believe a similar dynamic affects the process of change. This adds to why its documentation may not have appeared in research using continuous statistical methods or sufficiently frequent measurement of effects to note a point of discontinuity or tipping point. Here again, the mentor may have sufficient emotional distance from the actual changes that he or she can help a person understand the tipping point or see whether or not they are close to it.

The studies reviewed in the next section and endnotes of this chapter show that adults learn what they want to learn. Other things, even if acquired temporarily (e.g., for a test), are soon forgotten (Specht & Sandlin, 1991). Students, children, patients, clients, and subordinates may act as if they care about learning something, going through the motions, but they proceed to disregard it or forget it—unless it is something they want to learn. This does not include changes induced, willingly or not, by chemical or hormonal changes in one's body. But even in such situations, the interpretation of the changes and behavioral comportment following it will be affected by the person's will, values, and motivations. In this way, it appears that most, if not all, sustainable behavioral change is intentional.

The process of intentional change is graphically shown in Figure 18.1 (Boyatzis, 1999, 2001; Goleman et al., 2002). This is an enhancement of the earlier models developed by Kolb, Winter, and Berlew (1968) and Kolb and Boyatzis (1970a, 1970b).

It is important to note that often, an intentional change process must begin with a person wanting to change. This desire may not be in the person's consciousness or even within the scope of his or her self-awareness. Wake-up calls, or moments and events that awaken the person to the need for consideration of a change, may be required to bring the person to the process of desired, intentional change (Boyatzis, McKee, & Goleman, 2002).

RESEARCH QUESTIONS

Because a major objective of this chapter (and the handbook) is to inspire future research into mentoring and its effectiveness, research questions that remain at this point unanswered will be raised at the end of each section of this chapter:

1. *Is intentional, desired change more sustained than unintentional desired change?*

2. *How much self-awareness or consciousness of the desired change is necessary and sufficient for sustained change?*

3. *What are the ways in which a mentor can help a person move through the process?*

The Role of Mentors

As portrayed, the presence of trusting relationships is placed in the model as the "fifth discovery." But this is merely a labeling convention. Without the presence of these relationships, a person seldom experiences more than one discovery in the process of intentional change. For example, identification of one's "Ideal Self" almost always requires deep, personal discussions with another person. Sometimes, these moments occur in mentoring sessions involving parents, grandparents, teachers, or coaches (Boyatzis, Howard, Rapisarda, & Taylor, 2004). But sometimes, they come from friends, spouses, or a manager. These people and these relationships play crucial roles in all of the discoveries in the intentional change process and predict sustainable behavior change on learning goals 5 to 7 years after the goals were identified (Wheeler, 1999).

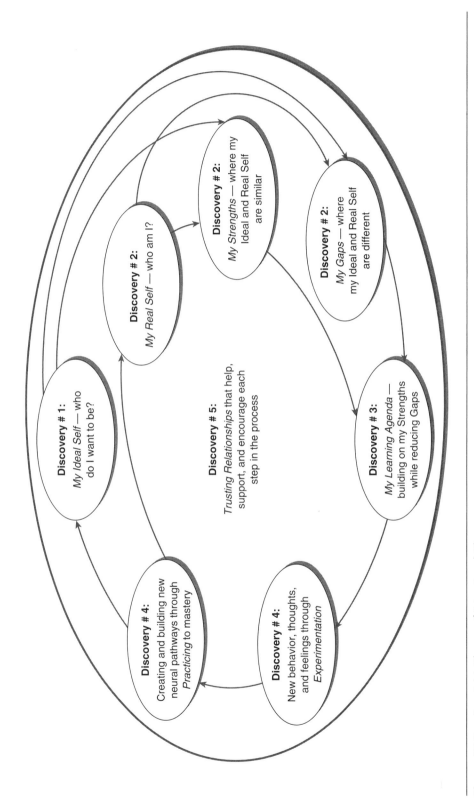

Figure 18.1 Boyatzis's Theory of Intentional Change

SOURCE: Used with permission from Richard Boyatzis.

If we think of mentoring as a process, we can see that people in many roles in our lives help us through mentoring. The critical issue in these relationships does not appear to be the role of the other person or persons, but the experience within which the help is offered. These are relationships in which the helper, or mentor, is experiencing compassion, defined below.

Compassion

Compassion is defined as having three components: (a) empathy or understanding the feelings of others, (b) caring for the other person (e.g., affiliative arousal), and (c) willingness to act in response to the person's feelings (Boyatzis, Smith, & Blaize, 2006). In their conceptualization, Boyatzis et al. claimed each of the components is a necessary but not sufficient condition of compassion. That is, compassion requires the presence of all three components.

A key distinguishing factor of our conceptualization of the construct is that it incorporates the desire to reach out and help others, whether or not their conditions are based on suffering and pain. It is closer to compassion as the emotional expression of the virtue of benevolence evident in Confucian philosophy (Van Norden, 1998), specifically the concept of *ren* (Cua, 1998). Alternative reasons to help others may include others' relative distress from not moving toward desired goals or wanting to help others extend and reach for their dreams or new aspirations. Therefore, the experience of pain or suffering on the part of others, which is typically an element in definitions of compassion, is not a necessary condition for the demonstration of compassion as defined here and by Boyatzis et al. (2006).

Mentoring With Compassion

Mentoring with compassion requires a caring relationship between the mentor and the other person. A caring relationship is one in which the parties of the relationship are on the same "emotional wavelength" (i.e., are attuned to and in touch with one another's feelings) and have a commitment to the other person (Boyatzis & McKee, 2005; Goleman et al., 2002). Through this process, a person's emotional intelligence enables them to establish and promote such caring relationships (Goleman et al., 2002). However, not all relationships between leaders and subordinates (or between those who mentor others and those who receive that mentoring) will necessarily be characterized as caring (Boyatzis et al., 2006). As we know from leader-member exchange (LMX) theory (Graen, Novak, & Sommerkamp, 1982), leaders actually differentiate between their subordinates and form different types of exchange relationships with each of them, rather than demonstrating a single leadership style across all subordinates. A similar process is probably involved in how people approach others and determines whether there is compassion involved or mere instrumental objectives. This is consistent with the distinction between the instrumental and psychosocial support aspects of relationships originally explained by Kram (1985) and later discussed by Ibarra (1995). It has been well accepted in the mentoring literature (Allen et al., 2004; Noe, 1988; Noe et al., 2002; Ragins & McFarlin, 1990; Wanberg et al., 2003). Although it is probably critical to both psychosocial and instrumental mentoring, this mutual trust and arousal seems to be a particularly essential requirement for effective psychosocial mentoring.

For example, in a study of peer counseling of alcoholics, Boyatzis (2005) reported three competencies to significantly predict the work performance ratings of those counseled, 1 year after counseling was completed. The three critical competencies were (a) self-awareness, (b) empathy, and (c) pattern recognition. In both regression and discriminant function analyses, the degree of counselors' use of these three competencies predicted the effectiveness of their helping. Carkhuff (1969) summarized years of studies in psychotherapy showing the positive impact of therapists using empathy, genuineness, and unconditional positive regard. Although it may be a conceptual leap, this same set of competencies may distinguish the most effective psychosocial mentoring. Past research examines characteristics of the mentor that result in protégé satisfaction (Wanberg et al., 2003), but that is hardly an empirical test of effectiveness.

[handwritten margin note: process observations]

Mentoring others for their development is different than mentoring others strictly for the organization's benefit (Noe, 1988). The latter is an instrumental perspective in approaching others. Kram (1985) discusses the distinction between instrumental and psychosocial functions of a relationship, offering that psychosocial functions enhance an individual's sense of competence, identity, and effectiveness in a professional role. Ibarra (2003) adds that these psychosocial functions stem more from the nature of the relationship than from instrumental functions, such as providing management exposure or advocacy for promotion. Such instrumental mentoring relationships are described as "weak ties" by Higgins and Kram (2001). They contend that weak ties result in less effective psychosocial mentoring relationships. Therefore, to engage in mentoring where the primary concern is the achievement of organizational goals and getting the person being mentored to fit into this scheme, it is likely that instrumentality will be aroused, which may or may not contribute to increased stress arousal.

Compassion Goes Both Ways

Mentoring with compassion elicits a dramatically different neural circuitry and hormonal process (Boyatzis et al., 2006). By focusing the mentoring on the person, and not on trying to make the individual fit into the organization, mentoring with compassion invokes physiological benefits to the mentor. It involves a focus on the person being mentored for his or her development that may or may not include a direct benefit to the organization. These physiological processes invoke compassion by helping people open their minds and hearts to or others—and they are also invoked by compassion!

Emotions are contagious (Hatfield, Cacioppo, & Rapson, 1994). Recent research suggests that beyond the open-loop nature of human emotions (i.e., we need others' emotions to experience our own), the excitation of mirror neurons causes us to mimic and resonate with others' emotions—positive or negative. This seems to occur in relationships with high or low emotional intensity. So, we would expect this physiological, psychological, and behavioral interaction to occur in both psychosocial (i.e., high-emotional-intensity relationships) and instrumental mentoring (i.e., low-emotional-intensity relationships, or at least lower than in psychosocial mentoring).

Mentoring does not always involve compassion, as noted earlier. Work by Kram (1985); Ibarra (2003); Eby, Butts, Lockwood, and Simon (2004); and Scandura (1998) document dysfunctional and negative outcomes. At the minimum, this suggests that many experiences and practices of mentoring involve human experiences other than compassion and goals other than improvement in the person's behavior or moving closer to their dreams. Individuals often help another at work in an instrumental way and never experience compassion toward the other person. Furthermore, mentoring may be an attempt to influence behavior, such as trying to get a person to improve in a specified way or to "fit into" the organization's culture.

Finally, mandated mentoring programs may merely lead to compliance, which is an administrative response that adds to job responsibility and possibly more stress (or at the minimum, indifference and apathy on the job). The mentoring literature (Kram, 1985; Higgins & Kram, 2001) suggests that such mandated programs invoke an instrumental mind-set.

RESEARCH QUESTIONS

1. *Is compassion more important in psychosocial than instrumental mentoring?*

2. *Does the mentor experience the same psychophysiological benefits as the protégé of mentoring with compassion?*

How Do We Know It Works?

To claim effectiveness of mentoring with compassion, we have to examine work from a number of fields. Decades of research on the effects of psychotherapy (Hubble, Duncan, & Miller, 1999), self-help programs (Kanfer & Goldstein, 1991), cognitive behavior therapy (Barlow, 1988), training programs (Morrow, Jarrett, & Rupinski, 1997), and education (Pascarella & Terenzini, 1991; Winter, McClelland, & Stewart, 1981) have shown that people can change their behavior, moods, and self-image. However, most of the studies have focused on a single characteristic, like maintenance of sobriety, reduction in a specific anxiety, or a set of characteristics often determined by an assessment instrument, such as the scales of the Minnesota Multiphasic Personality Inventory (MMPI).

In organizations, the impact of mentoring is often associated with training programs. The "honeymoon effect" of typical training programs might start with improvement immediately following the program, but within months it drops precipitously (Campbell, Dunnette, Lawler, & Weick, 1970). The few published studies examining improvement of more than one of these competencies show an overall improvement of about 10% in emotional intelligence abilities 3 to 18 months following training (Cherniss & Adler, 2000; Hand, Richards, & Slocum, 1973; Latham & Saari, 1979; Noe & Schmitt, 1986; Wexley & Memeroff, 1975; Young & Dixon, 1996). More recent meta-analytic studies and utility analyses confirm that significant changes can and do occur, but they do not have the impact that the level of investment would lead us to expect with many types of training (Baldwin & Ford, 1988; Burke & Day, 1986; Morrow et al., 1997).

The results appear no better from standard MBA programs, where there is no attempt to enhance emotional intelligence abilities. The best data here come from a research project by the American Assembly of Collegiate Schools of Business. They found that graduating students from two highly ranked business schools behavior, compared with their levels when they began their MBA training, showed improvement of only 2% in the skills of emotional intelligence (Development Dimensions International, 1985). In fact, when students from four other high-ranking MBA programs were assessed on a range of tests and direct behavioral measures, they showed a gain of 4% in self-awareness and self-management abilities but a decrease of 3% in social awareness and relationship management (Boyatzis, Renio-McKee, & Thompson, 1995; Boyatzis & Sokol, 1982).

The honeymoon effect is often the cause for practitioners and scholars overlooking the "sleeper effect." The sleeper effect is that a sustainable change in a person's behavior, thoughts patterns, or emotional reactions to events does not appear until 6 to 12 months following completion of the change effort (McClelland, 1965). Since it appears to be disconnected from the timing of the intervention, it is a discontinuous effect and is easily overlooked or wrongly attributed to other factors.

Effects of Mentoring

The literature on the effects of mentoring are similar. Most of it documents antecedents or consequences of protégé satisfaction with the mentor (Wanberg et al., 2003). The rest examines career outcomes. However, the literature says little about the impact on behavioral change, the sustainability of such changes, and the longer-term impact on the person's aspirations.

A series of longitudinal studies under way at the Weatherhead School of Management of Case Western Reserve University has shown that people can change on this complex set of competencies that we call emotional intelligence, which distinguish outstanding performers in management and professions. Moreover, the improvement lasted for years. The course that produced these changes was designed on the basis of ICT and involved developing compassionate relationships both with specific mentors (i.e., faculty or trained coaches) and the development of peer mentoring through development of reference groups. A visual comparison of the percentage improvement in behavioral measures of emotional intelligence from different samples is shown in Figure 18.2 (Ballou et al., 1999; Boyatzis, Stubbs, & Taylor, 2002).

═══════════════ **RESEARCH QUESTIONS** ═══════════════

1. *What is the evidence that mentoring leads to improvements in a person's behavior and effectiveness that is sustained years later?*

2. *Does mentoring positively affect changes in a person's dreams and aspirations, as well as their behavior?*

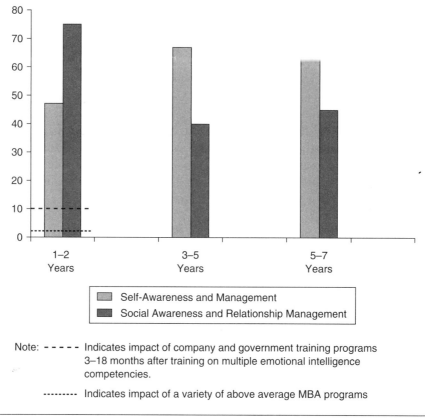

Note: - - - - - Indicates impact of company and government training programs 3–18 months after training on multiple emotional intelligence competencies.

.... Indicates impact of a variety of above average MBA programs

Figure 18.2   Percentage Improvement of Emotional Intelligence Competencies of Different Groups of MBA Graduates Taking the Intentional Change Course

SOURCE: Used with permission from Richard Boyatzis.

The Five Discoveries of Intentional Change Theory and the Role of Mentoring

The First Discovery: Catching Your Dreams

Our Ideal Self is an image of the person we want to be. There appear to be major components that drive the development of this image: (a) an image of a desired future, (b) hope that one can attain it, and (c) aspects of one's core identity, which include enduring strengths on which one builds for this desired future. This is explained in detail in Boyatzis and Akrivou (2006). It emerges from our ego ideal, dreams, and aspirations. The past 20 years have revealed literature supporting the power of positive imaging or visioning in sports psychology, meditation and biofeedback research, and other psychophysiological research. It is believed that the potency of focusing one's thoughts on the desired end state or condition is driven by the emotional components of the brain (Goleman, 1995).

This research indicates that we can access and engage deep emotional commitment and psychic energy if we engage our passions and conceptually catch our dreams in the image of our Ideal Self. It is an anomaly that we know the importance of consideration of the Ideal Self, and yet often, when engaged in a change or learning process, we skip over the clear formulation or articulation of the image our Ideal Self. If a parents, spouses, bosses, or teachers tell us something that should be different, they are telling us about the person they want us to be. As adults, we often allow ourselves to be anesthetized to our dreams and lose sight of our deeply felt Ideal Self.

It is also clear from this framework that "strengths-based" approaches to development will probably work better than current methods but will fall short of what the person can achieve. In focusing on the person's established strengths, such approaches develop the *core identity* component of the Ideal Self as a driver of change. Because strengths-based approaches are based on what the person has done in the past, they do not adequately engage the energy inherent in a person's dreams of the future or new possibilities.

The role of a mentor can be in two forms: (a) helping a person to see an aspiration or dream that had not been considered or (b) role-modeling a way of acting. The latter is to illustrate to the person a new model of how to act as a mature adult, contributing citizen, or functional employee. Mentors can often, because of the trusting relationship, help a person "wake up" to the need for change. This wake-up call precedes possible discovery of a new Ideal Self or creation of a personal vision.

"Wake-up calls" are moments when we pause, reflect, and consider big questions about life, work, and our purpose. Too often, major external events are wake-up calls, like the terrorist attacks on the United States on September 11, 2001, the tsunami in Banda Aceh, or the bombs in the London Tube on July 7th, 2005. Medical emergencies may be wake-up calls—a heart attack, cancer, or diagnosis with HIV-positive or type II diabetes. Social trauma, like a divorce or getting fired, as well as joyous events, like the birth of a child or being awarded tenure, may be wake-up calls.

The possible role of a mentor in helping a person use wake-up calls constructively may be crucial to their effectiveness. While not all sustained desired change needs a wake-up call, people who are less mindful, self-aware, or more distracted often need several wake-calls before they are moved into action (Boyatzis & McKee, 2005). A mentor can highlight a wake-up call for a protégé and can help a person see an experience with a larger, more reflective purpose or context. The timing of the mentor's observations are crucial here. An event, whether negative or positive or traumatic, can be an opportunity for a mentor to ask about the protégé's Ideal Self, purpose, and values. Converting the experience into the initiation of or recommitment to an ICT process could be the most important contribution of a mentor. Of course, this leans toward psychosocial mentoring but could also be useful in instrumental mentoring.

RESEARCH QUESTIONS

1. What are the necessary and sufficient components of a person's Ideal Self or "personal vision" that drive desired change?

2. Can wake-up calls be a sufficient motivator of change, or must they be converted, first, into a positive image of a desired future to be effective?

3. How can a mentor help a person realize or develop his or her Ideal Self?

The Second Discovery: Am I a Boiling Frog?

The awareness of the current self, the person that others see and with whom they interact, is elusive. To maintain "normal" or healthy functioning, the human psyche protects itself from the automatic "intake" and conscious realization of all information about ourselves. These ego defense mechanisms serve to protect us. They can also conspire to delude us into seeing an image of who we are that feeds on itself, becomes self-perpetuating, and eventually may become dysfunctional (Goleman, 1985).

The greatest challenge to an accurate current self-image (i.e., seeing yourself as others see you and consistent with other internal states, beliefs, emotions, and so forth) is the "boiling frog syndrome." It is said that dropping a frog into a pot of boiling water will result in it immediately jumping out. But place a frog in a pot of cool water and gradually raise the temperature to boiling, and the frog will remain in the water until it is cooked.

Several factors contribute to us becoming boiling frogs. First, people around you may not let you see a change. They may not give you feedback or information about how they see it. Also, they may be victims of the boiling-frog syndrome themselves, as they adjust their perceptions on a daily basis. Second, enablers, those forgiving the change, frightened of it, or who do not care, may allow it to pass unnoticed.

For individuals to truly consider changing a part of themselves, they must have a sense of what they value and want to keep. These areas in which one's Real Self and Ideal Self are consistent or congruent can be considered "strengths." Likewise, for people to consider what they want to preserve about themselves involves admitting aspects of themselves that they wish to change or adapt in some manner. Areas where one's Real Self and Ideal Self are not consistent can be considered "gaps."

All too often, people explore growth or development by focusing on the "gaps" or deficiencies. Organizational training programs and managers conducting annual reviews often make the same mistake. There is an assumption that we can "leave well enough alone" and get to the areas that need work. It is no wonder that many of these programs or procedures intended to help a person develop result in the individual feeling battered, beleaguered, and bruised—not helped, encouraged, motivated, or guided.

So, it can be seen that others around us can either help us with this discovery or the opposite—help us remain deluded or mislabeling our current behavior and its effect on others. Mentors in the context of a trusting relationship can extend a person's reality and give that individual a "check" against what he or she is currently seeing and hearing. In other words, mentors can provide feedback; they can interpret it when received from other sources; and they can investigate and discover unspoken feedback. They can also help people to explore and examine vague feelings or senses that something is not or may not be right.

This "reality-testing" function can come as a gentle observation or a harsh confrontation, but when delivered in the context of compassion, it is experienced as caring feedback.

In addition, the mentor can frame feedback in a way that is more digestible to the person. The mentor can use his or her pattern recognition competency to perceive themes of strengths as well as themes of weaknesses in the composite of feedback to a person. This is clearest when the feedback is from multitrait, multimethod sources, like an assessment center, or even multisource and multitrait, as from a 360 assessment. Beyond the perspective that allows for such thematic analysis, the mentor can also see which weaknesses are closer to the tipping point and therefore should be worked on, as opposed to resolutely accepted as unmovable.

RESEARCH QUESTIONS

1. *What is the relative proportion of strengths to weaknesses that helps produce the most sustainable desired change?*

2. *Does working on improving a behavior close to the tipping point lead to more improved effectiveness than working on a large gap?*

3. *How does a mentor help a person see and articulate their "personal balance sheet" (i.e., strengths and weaknesses)?*

4. *How does a mentor help a person choose those behaviors close to the tipping point to work on?*

The Third Discovery: Mindfulness Through a Learning Agenda

The third discontinuity in intentional change is development of an agenda and focusing on the desired future. While performance at work or happiness in life may be the eventual consequence of one's efforts, a learning agenda focuses on development. A learning orientation arouses a positive belief in one's capability and the hope of improvement. This results in people setting personal standards of performance, rather than "normative" standards that merely mimic what others have done (Beaubien & Payne, 1999). Meanwhile, a performance orientation evokes anxiety and doubts about whether or not we can change (Chen, Gully, Whiteman, & Kilcullen, 2000).

As part of one of the longitudinal studies at the Weatherhead School of Management, Leonard (1996) showed that MBAs who set goals desiring to change on certain competencies improved significantly on those competencies as compared with other MBAs. Their faculty mentors and peer mentoring from classmates were a crucial part of the process of developing and refining these goals. Previous goal-setting literature had shown how goals affected certain changes on specific competencies (Locke & Latham, 1990) but had not established evidence of behavioral change on a comprehensive set of competencies that constitute emotional intelligence.

1. *How many "learning goals" is optimum for increasing effectiveness?*

2. *Do differences in planning, cognitive, and/or learning styles mean that the form and format of goal setting should be varied for those with the different styles to result in sustained change?*

3. *How does a mentor guide a person in developing a meaningful learning plan?*

Self-Organizing and the Pull of Two Attractors

Intentional change produces sustainable, desirable changes as an iterative, cyclical process. As a complex system, sustainable change engages the cycle again through the self-organizing properties of the human organism. Two attractors, the positive and negative emotional attractors, determine the context of the self-organizing process and whether it is an adaptation to existing conditions or adaptation to new, emergent conditions. A self-organizing system is inherently homeostatic, with the possibility of some form of deterioration if it is not perfectly efficient (which human organisms do not appear to be) (Casti, 1994; Holland, 1995). Just like the properties in a closed system moving toward maximum entropy over time, as predicted from the Second Law of Thermodynamics, dissonance occurs in the human and our social organizations unless there is intentional investment. Another way to say this is that adaptations and adjustments based on Argyris's (1985) concept of "single-loop learning" will result in a self-sustaining system of a person, his or her life, and performance. But over time, even with these properties of self-organization deterioration will occur.

This happens because the human organism is not a fully closed system. Among other things, we need social interaction to allow our "open-loop" emotional system to function (Goleman et al., 2002). Even more dramatic in its destabilizing effect is the advent of one's life and career cycles. Whether these are the traditional "7-year itch" cycles or those of varying periodicity described by Erikson (1982), Sheehy (1995), and Levinson (1978), a person occasionally looks for a change. These are moments of invitation for what Argyris (1985) called "double-loop learning." This helps to explain why double-loop learning is so difficult and so relatively infrequent. It is inherently destabilizing and must fight against the self-organizing property inherent in a person.

ICT offers an explanation as to how the disequilibrium occurs, and then the force that drives a new self-organizing system. An attractor becomes the destabilizing force. We call this the *positive emotional attractor* (PEA). It pulls a person toward his or her Ideal Self. The process of the person focusing on future possibilities and filling them with hope arouses the parasympathetic nervous system (PSNS) (Boyatzis et al., 2006). Once the PSNS is aroused, individuals have access to more of their neural circuits and find themselves in a calmer, if not elated state, in which their immune systems are functioning well and their bodies are sustained. They are able, in this state, to experience *neurogenesis* (i.e., the conversion of hippocampal stem cells into new neurons) and the new degrees and extent of learning that become possible. It is even suggested that formation of learning goals or learning-oriented goals works because it engages the positive emotional attractor and results in more successful change.

Another attractor is also at play in the system, however: the *negative emotional attractor* (NEA). In an analogous manner, it arouses the SNS, which helps human beings to deal with stress and threat and protect themselves. Within the threatened environment and state, the NEA pulls a person toward defensive protection. In this arousal, the body shunts blood to the large-muscle groups, closes down nonessential neural circuits, suspends the immune system, and produces cortisol—important for protection under threat (Sapolsky, 2004). Cortisol inhibits or even stops neurogenesis and overexcites older neurons, rendering them useless (Boyatzis et al., 2006). Because of the self-perpetuating nature of emotional attractors, it is easy to get stuck in the NEA and not change. Many mentors inadvertently provoke this by trying to diagnose the protégé's problem and tell him or her how to fix it.

If a person's adaptation is self-organizing, then desired change not already part of this system is possible only when it is intentional. We would add that because of the difficulty in sustaining the effort, it also must be driven by a powerful force. This is where the Ideal Self activates the energy of the PEA, and the two attractors can become cyclical and sustain individuals in their change efforts (Casti, 1994).

The process of desired, sustainable change requires behavioral freedom and permission to try something new and see what happens. This "permission" comes from interaction with others as, we will see in the fourth and fifth discoveries in the process.

Here, again, the mentor becomes the critical catalyst to the person's not getting stuck in the pull of one attractor, but instead being able to somewhat smoothly move back and forth. The mentor, through observations, support, and timing of interventions (not to mention dosage level) helps a person manage his or her way between the two attractors. When the mentor feels the person is too full of the NEA, the mentor creates a positive, supportive climate and emphasizes (and may only discuss) the PEA. This helps the person restore his or her balance. Mentors can also help in the reverse: If individuals believe too many of their reviews or sycophants praising them, the mentor can provide a dosage of reality and bring them into the NEA. Managing the balance to keep the person alert and eager and sustaining the momentum for change calls for a great deal of sensitivity and talent on the part of the effective mentor in these compassionate relationships.

RESEARCH QUESTIONS

1. *What is the optimum percentage of time spent in mentoring interactions in the PEA versus the NEA?*

2. *Are their other ways a mentor can arouse the PEA for a person?*

3. *Are there personality dispositions, like optimism, that would affect this balance?*

The Fourth Discovery: Metamorphosis

The fourth discovery is to experiment and practice desired changes. Acting on the plan and toward the goals involves numerous activities. These are often made in the context of experimenting with new behavior. Typically, following a period of experimentation, the person practices the new behaviors in actual settings within which he or she wishes to use them, such as at work or at home. During this part of the process, intentional change looks like a "continuous-improvement" process.

To develop or learn new behavior, the person must find ways to learn more from current or ongoing experiences. That is, the experimentation and practice does not always require attending "courses" or a new activity. It may involve trying something different in a current setting, reflecting on what occurs, and experimenting further in this setting. Sometimes, this part of the process requires finding and using opportunities to learn and change. People may not even think they have changed until they have tried new behavior in a work or "real-world" setting. Mentors become the vehicle for translating many of these "experiences" into "learning." As Kotter (1982) showed, a great deal of important feedback that is experienced as helpful occurs in the halls of buildings; for example, managers offer insights to subordinates or peers on the way to or from meetings. Mentors, when most effective, help a person reflect, to collect insight from experiences when they are current, and to interpret these insights into usable feedback or new frameworks.

Experimentation and practice are most effective when they occur in conditions in which the person feels safe (Kolb & Boyatzis, 1970a), another aspect where the presence of a trusted mentor makes a difference. This sense of psychological safety creates an atmosphere in which the person can try new behavior, perceptions, and thoughts with relatively less risk of shame, embarrassment, or serious consequences of failure.

RESEARCH QUESTIONS

1. *How long should a person practice new behavior in a relatively safe environment before trying it at work?*

2. *What can mentors do to facilitate experimentation and learning at work and in other settings?*

The Fifth Discovery—Or Really the First One: Relationships That Enable Us to Learn

Our relationships are an essential part of our environment. The most crucial relationships are often a part of groups that have particular importance to us. These relationships and groups give us a sense of identity, guide us as to what is appropriate and "good" behavior, and provide feedback on our behavior. In sociology, they are called *reference groups*. These relationships create a "context" within which we interpret our progress on desired changes, the utility of new learning, and even contribute significant input to formulation of the Ideal (Kram, 1996; Kram & Cherniss, 2001).

In this sense, our relationships are mediators, moderators, interpreters, sources of feedback, and sources of support and permission for change and learning. They may also be the most important source of protection from relapses or returning to our earlier forms of behavior. Wheeler (1999) analyzed the extent to which the MBA graduates worked on their goals in multiple "life spheres" (e.g., work, family, recreational groups, etc.). In a 2-year follow-up study of two of the graduating classes of part-time MBA students, she found those who worked on their goals and plans in multiple sets of relationships improved the most, and more than those working on goals in only one setting, such as at work or within one relationship. This is similar to the finding of Higgins and Kram (2001) that developmental networks have far more impact than one mentor.

In a study of the impact of the yearlong executive development program for doctors, lawyers, professors, engineers, and other professionals mentioned earlier, Ballou et al. (1999) found that participants gained self-confidence during the program. Even at the beginning of the program, anyone meeting them would say these participants were very high in self-confidence. It was a curious finding. The best explanation came from follow-up questions to the graduates of the program. They explained that the increase in self-confidence was due to an increase in the confidence to change. Their existing reference groups (e.g., family, groups at work, professional groups, community groups) all had an investment in them staying the same; meanwhile, the person wanted to change. The Professional Fellows Program allowed them to develop a new reference group that encouraged change.

Based on social identity, reference group, and now relational theories, our relationships both meditate and moderate our sense of who we are and who we want to be. We develop or elaborate our Ideal Self from these contexts. We label and interpret our Real Self from these contexts. We interpret and value strengths (i.e., aspects considered part of our core that we wish to preserve) from these contexts. We interpret and value gaps (i.e., aspects considered weaknesses or things we wish to change) from these contexts.

═══ RESEARCH QUESTIONS ═══

1. *What competencies of the mentor have the most impact on effectiveness of psychosocial and instrumental mentoring?*

2. *How many mentors should a person have at any point in their lives? Does one's life stage or career stage affect this number?*

Fractals and Interaction Among the Levels

Mentors can help dyads, teams, organizations, and larger social systems change. While we might relabel the role as that of *consultant* or *change agent,* individuals acting as mentors can have profound impact on sustained, desired change at many levels. Now, we come to the aspect of ICT in which the mentor becomes a key vehicle in it operating as a truly complex system: its multileveledness. According to the theory, sustainable change occurs at any level of human and social organization through the same ICT. In this sense, these other levels are fractals of ICT at the individual level (Boyatzis, 2006). In other words, desired, sustainable change within a family, team, or small group occurs through the cyclical iteration of the group through what can be called the "group-level definition" of the five discoveries (Akrivou, Boyatzis, & McLeod, 2006). In this case, the Ideal Self becomes a shared vision of the future of the group. What does the group want to be, and what can they be in the future? Similarly, desired, sustainable organizational change occurs through ICT's five discoveries at the organizational level, as well as at the other levels. These other levels are listed in order of increasing social size: (a) individual; (b) team, group, family, coalition; (c) organization; (d) community; (e) country/culture; and (e) global.

A primary feature of a complex system is that there is an interaction among the levels and that interaction produces adaptive or emergent behavior. The first degree of interaction between and among the individual, small-group, and organization levels of ICT is mentorship or leadership. The second degree of interaction, which in addition to mentorship or leadership allows interaction among all levels of ICT, is through the formation and use of reference groups. The latter may also be supportive of identity groups (which could be the developmental networks referred to by Higgins & Kram, 2001). Full discussion of this feature is beyond the scope of this chapter. The reader is referred to Boyatzis (2006) for more on the subject.

RESEARCH QUESTIONS

1. *What role can mentors play in intentional change in teams, organizations, communities, countries, and the world?*

2. *Can mentors facilitate constructive interface among fractals of ICT?*

Research Challenges

Theories of mentoring and desired change can become more holistic and comprehensive if they incorporate psychophysiological interactions. Without such development, we will continue to create models that may not be sustainable. A balanced physiological and psychological state for the mentor as well as the protégé should enable the sustainability of their energy, focus, talent, and the change process. If enough people adopted such an approach, this could also become a new component of the organization's culture. The culture would be one in which everyone was trained and socialized in the need for mentoring others with compassion. This would result in more emotional intelligence being demonstrated within the organization and more sustainable, effective organizations.

The challenges for universities or corporate universities would be to encourage compassion in the development methods. This may require more relational approaches to development. Mentoring, beyond the traditional notion of advising, would become a crucial pedagogical method. This may put pressure on faculty and training staff to update and retool their skills, role perspective, and attitudes.

We believe the implications for research on mentoring and change are many. First and foremost, careful longitudinal studies must be conducted to support or refute the theoretical propositions and research questions in this chapter and other chapters in this book.

Second, greater use of physiological measures should be considered when conducting these studies. Any one of the following would help build a holistic image of the effective mentor and effective mentoring processes: pulse rate, blood pressure, right versus left prefrontal cortex activity, testing for levels of secreted epinephrine and norepinephrine (urine catecholamines), saliva tests for immunoglobulin A and cortisol, or serum tests for other hormones, like oxytocin.

Third, a holistic theory of mentoring needs holistic methods. This calls for interdisciplinary research. It encourages new forms of collaboration between schools of management and other schools and/or departments, such as psychology, medicine, nursing, and social work.

Fourth, experiments could be designed to discover the degree to which a person feels better, experiences compassion, and activates their PSNS when mentoring—or being mentored. The effects of caring versus instrumental mentoring could be examined this way.

Fifth, epidemiological studies of mentors and protégés could be conducted with historical records and interviews. For such research to go beyond current insights, longitudinal designs would be required rather than merely retrospective studies.

Because of the likely discontinuous and nonlinear relationships among many of the variables mentioned above, the research would have to be conducted in such a way as to examine and document such effects. The multidisciplinary methods would require caution in design, as well as sampling, but most of all in the analysis and presentation of the data.

Concluding Thought

Adults can develop new behavioral patterns throughout their lives, but without the help of a mentor in a compassionate relationship, the change either will not occur or will not be sustainable. The actual process of change and the role of the mentor can be seen through intentional change theory and the five "discoveries" experienced in the process.

As leaders, helpers, or mentors, we can create environments in which others want to use their capabilities and emotional intelligence only if we are authentic and consistent in our own demonstration of these behaviors. Through the intentional change process, we have the opportunity to truly make a difference. Whether applied in universities or companies, government agencies, or nonprofits, this process can help us mentor each other to create the social environments we want and find so conducive to making a difference.

References

Akrivou, K., Boyatzis, R. E., & McLeod, P. L. (2006). The evolving group: Towards a prescriptive theory of intentional group development. *Journal of Management Development, 25,* 689–709.

Allen, T. D., Eby, L. T., Poteet, M. L., Lentz, E., & Lima, L. (2004). Career benefits associated with mentoring for protégés: A meta analysis. *Journal of Applied Psychology, 89,* 127–136.

Argyris, C. (1985). *Strategy, change, and defensive routines.* Boston: Pitman.

Baldwin, T., & Ford, J. K. (1988). Transfer of training: A review and directions for future research. *Personnel Psychology, 41,* 63–105.

Ballou, R., Bowers, D., Boyatzis, R. E., & Kolb, D. A. (1999). Fellowship in lifelong learning: An executive development program for advanced professionals. *Journal of Management Education, 23,* 338–354.

Barlow, D. H. (1988). *Anxiety and disorders: The nature and treatment of anxiety and panic.* New York: Guilford Press.

Beaubien, J. M., & Payne, S. C. (1999, April). *Individual goal orientation as a predictor of job and academic performance: A meta-analytic review and integration.* Paper presented at the meeting of the Society for Industrial and Organizational Psychology, Atlanta, GA.

Boyatzis, R. E. (1999). Self-directed change and learning as a necessary meta-competency for success and effectiveness in the 21st century. In R. Sims & J. G. Veres (Eds.), *Keys to employee success in the coming decades* (pp. 15–32). Westport, CT: Greenwood.

Boyatzis, R. E. (2001). How and why individuals are able to develop emotional intelligence. In C. Cherniss & D. Goleman (Eds.), *The emotionally intelligent workplace: How to select for, measure, and improve emotional intelligence in individuals, groups, and organizations* (pp. 234–253). San Francisco: Jossey-Bass.

Boyatzis, R. E. (2005). Core competencies in coaching others to overcome dysfunctional behavior. In V. Druskat, G. Mount, & F. Sala (Eds.), *Emotional intelligence and work performance* (pp. 81–95). Mahwah, NJ: Lawrence Erlbaum.

Boyatzis, R. E. (2006). Intentional change theory from a complexity perspective. *Journal of Management Development. 25,* 607–623.

Boyatzis, R. E., & Akrivou, K. (2006). The ideal self as a driver of change. *Journal of Management Development, 25,* 624–642.

Boyatzis, R. E., Howard, A., Rapisarda, B., & Taylor, S. (2004, March 11). Coaching can work, but doesn't always. *People Management,* pp. 26–32.

Boyatzis, R., & McKee, A. (2005). *Resonant leadership: Renewing yourself and connecting with others through mindfulness, hope, and compassion.* Boston: Harvard Business School Press.

Boyatzis, R. E., Renio-McKee, A., & Thompson, L. (1995). Past accomplishments: Establishing the impact and baseline of earlier programs. In R. E. Boyatzis, S. S. Cowen, & D. A. Kolb (Eds.), *Innovation in professional education: Steps on a journey from teaching to learning* (pp. 95–119). San Francisco: Jossey-Bass.

Boyatzis, R. E., Smith, M., & Blaize, N. (2006). Sustaining leadership effectiveness through coaching and compassion: It's not what you think, *Academy of Management Journal on Learning and Education, 5*(1), 8–24.

Boyatzis, R. E., & Sokol, M. (1982). *A pilot project to assess the feasibility of assessing skills and personal characteristics of students in collegiate business programs.* Report to the AACSB, St. Louis, MO.

Boyatzis, R. E., Stubbs, E. C., & Taylor, S. N. (2002). Learning cognitive and emotional intelligence competencies through graduate management education. *Academy of Management Journal on Learning and Education, 1,* 150–162.

Burke, M. J., & Day, R. R. (1986). A cumulative study of the effectiveness of managerial training. *Journal of Applied Psychology, 71,* 232–245.

Campbell, J. P., Dunnette, M. D., Lawler, E. E., III, & Weick, K. E. (1970). *Managerial behavior, performance, and effectiveness.* New York: McGraw-Hill.

Carkhuff, R. R. (1969). *Helping and humans relations: Volumes I and II.* New York: Holt, Rinehart & Winston.

Casti, J. L. (1994). *Complexification: Explaining a paradoxical world through the science of surprise.* New York: HarperCollins.

Chen, G., Gully, S. M., Whiteman, J. A., & Kilcullen, R. N. (2000). Examination of relationships among trait-like individual differences, state-like individual differences, and learning performance. *Journal of Applied Psychology, 85,* 835–847.

Cherniss, C., & Adler, M. (2000). *Promoting emotional intelligence in organizations: Make training in emotional intelligence effective.* Washington, DC: American Society of Training and Development.

Cua, A. S. (1998). Confucian philosophy: Chinese. In E. Carig (Ed.), *Routledge encyclopedia of philosophy* (Vol. 2, pp. 536–549). London: Routledge.

Development Dimensions International. (1985). *Final report: Phase III.* Report to the AACSB, St. Louis, MO.

Eby, L. T., Butts, M., Lockwood, A., & Simon, S. A. (2004). Protégés' negative mentoring experiences: Construct development and nomological validation. *Personnel Psychology, 57,* 411–447.

Erikson, E. H. (1982). *The life cycle completed: A review.* New York: Norton.

Gladwell, M. (2000). *The tipping point: How little things can make a big difference.* New York: Little, Brown.

Goleman, D. (1985). *Vital lies, simple truths: The psychology of self-deception.* New York: Simon & Schuster.

Goleman, D. (1995). *Emotional intelligence.* New York: Bantam Books.

Goleman, D., Boyatzis, R. E., & McKee, A. (2002). *Primal leadership: Realizing the power of emotional intelligence.* Boston: Harvard Business School Press.

Graen, G., Novak, M., & Sommerkamp, P. (1982). The effects of leader-member exchange and job design on productivity and job satisfaction: Testing a dual attachment model. *Organizational Behavior and Human Performance, 30,* 109–131.

Graen, G. B., & Uhl-Bien, M. (1995). Relationship-based approach to leadership: Development of leader-member exchange (LMX) theory of leadership over 25 years: Applying a multi-level multi-domain perspective. *Leadership Quarterly, 6,* 219–247.

Hall, D. T., & Associates. (Eds.). (1996). *The career is dead—Long live the career: A relational approach to careers.* San Francisco: Jossey-Bass.

Hand, H. H., Richards, M. D., & Slocum, J. W., Jr. (1973). Organizational climate and the effectiveness of a human relations training program. *Academy of Management Journal, 16,* 185–246.

Hatfield, E., Cacioppo, J. T., & Rapson, R. L. (1994). *Emotional contagion.* New York: Cambridge University Press.

Higgins, M. C., & Kram, K. E. (2001). Reconceptualizing mentoring at work: A developmental network perspective. *Academy of Management Review, 26,* 264–288.

Holland, J. (1995). *Hidden order: How adaptation builds complexity.* Reading, MA: Helix Books.

Hubble, M. A., Duncan, B. L., & Miller, S. D. (Eds.). (1999). *The heart and soul of change: What works in therapy.* Washington, DC: American Psychological Association.

Ibarra, H. (1995). Race, opportunity, and diversity of social circles in managerial networks. *Academy of Management Journal, 38,* 673–703.

Ibarra, H. (2003). *Working identity: Unconventional strategies for reinventing your career.* Boston: Harvard Business School Press.

Kanfer, F. H., & Goldstein, A. P. (Eds.). (1991). *Helping people change: A textbook of methods* (4th ed.). Boston: Allyn & Bacon.

Kolb, D. A., & Boyatzis, R. E. (1970a). Goal-setting and self-directed behavior change. *Human Relations, 23,* 439–457.

Kolb, D. A., & Boyatzis, R. E. (1970b). On the dynamics of the helping relationship. *Journal of Applied Behavioral Science, 6,* 267–289.

Kolb, D. A., Winter, S. K., & Berlew, D. E. (1968). Self-directed change: Two studies. *Journal of Applied Behavioral Science, 6,* 453–471.

Kotter, J. P. (1982). *The general managers.* New York: Free Press.

Kram, K. E. (1985). *Mentoring at work.* Glenview, IL: Scott, Foresman.

Kram, K. E. (1996). A relational approach to careers. In D. T. Hall (Ed.), *The career is dead—Long live the career: A relational approach to careers* (pp. 132–157). San Francisco: Jossey-Bass.

Kram, K. E., & Cherniss, C. (2001). Developing emotional competence through relationships. In C. Cherniss & D. Goleman (Eds.), *The emotionally intelligent workplace: How to select for, measure, and improve emotional intelligence in individuals, groups, and organizations* (pp. 254–285). San Francisco: Jossey-Bass.

Latham, G. P., & Saari, L. M. (1979). Application of social-learning theory to training supervisors through behavioral modeling. *Journal of Applied Psychology, 64,* 239–246.

Leonard, D. (1996). *The impact of learning goals on self-directed change in management development and education.* Doctoral dissertation, Case Western Reserve University.

Levinson, D. J. (with Darrow, C. N., Klein, E. B., Levinson, M. H., & McKee, B.). (1978). *The seasons of a man's life.* New York: Knopf.

Locke, E. A., & Latham, G. P. (1990). *A theory of goal setting and task performance.* Englewood Cliffs, NJ: Prentice Hall.

Luthans, F., Hodgetts, R. M., & Rosenkrantz, S. A. (1988). *Real managers.* Cambridge, MA: Ballinger Press.

McCall, M. W., Jr., Lombardo, M. M., & Morrison, A.M. (1988). *The lessons of experience: How successful executives develop on the job.* Lexington, MA: Lexington Books.

McClelland, D. C. (1965). Toward a theory of motive acquisition. *American Psychologist, 20,* 321–333.

McClelland, D.C. (1998). Identifying competencies with behavioral event interviews. *Psychological Science, 9,* 331–339.

Morrow, C. C., Jarrett, M. Q., & Rupinski, M. T. (1997). An investigation of the effect and economic utility of corporate-wide training. *Personnel Psychology, 50,* 91–119.

Noe, R. A. (1988). An investigation of the determinants of successful assigned mentoring relationships. *Personnel Psychology, 41,* 457–479.

Noe, R. A., Greenberger, D. B., & Wang, S. (2002). Mentoring: What we know and where we might go. *Research in Personnel and Human Resources Management, 21,* 129–173.

Noe, R. A., & Schmitt, N. (1986). The influence of trainee attitudes on training effectiveness: Test of a model. *Personnel Psychology, 39,* 497–523.

Pascarella, E. T., & Terenzini, P. T. (1991). *How college affects students: Findings and insights from twenty years of research.* San Francisco: Jossey-Bass.

Popper, M., Mayseless, M., & Castelnovo, O. (2000). Transformational leadership and attachment. *Leadership Quarterly, 11,* 267–289.

Prochaska, J. O., DiClemente, C. C., & Norcross, J. C. (1992). In search of how people change: Applications to addictive behaviors. *American Psychologist, 47,* 1102–1114.

Ragins, B. R., & McFarlin, D. (1990). Perception of mentor roles in cross-gender mentoring relationships. *Journal of Vocational Behavior, 37,* 321–339.

447

Sapolsky, R. M. (2004). *Why zebra's don't get ulcers* (3rd ed.). New York: HarperCollins.

Scandura, T. A. (1998). Dysfunctional mentoring relationships and outcomes. *Journal of Management, 24,* 449–467.

Sheehy, G. (1995). *New passages: Mapping your life across time.* New York: Random House.

Specht, L., & Sandlin, P. (1991). The differential effects of experiential learning activities and traditional lecture classes in accounting. *Simulations and Gaming, 22,* 196–210.

Van Norden, B. W. (1998). Menius. In E. Craig (Ed.), *Routledge encyclopedia of philosophy* (Vol. 6, pp. 302–304). London: Routledge.

Wanberg, C. R., Welsh, E. T., & Hezlett, S. A. (2003). Mentoring research: A review and dynamic process model. *Research in Personnel and Human Resources Management, 22,* 39–124.

Wexley, K. N., & Memeroff, W. F. (1975). Effectiveness of positive reinforcement and goal setting as methods of management development. *Journal of Applied Psychology, 60,* 446–450.

Wheeler, J. V. (1999). *The impact of social environments on self-directed change and learning.* Unpublished doctoral dissertation, Case Western Reserve University.

Winter, D. G., McClelland, D. C., & Stewart, A. J. (1981). *A new case for the liberal arts: Assessing institutional goals and student development.* San Francisco: Jossey-Bass.

Young, D. P., & Dixon, N. M. (1996). *Helping leaders take effective action: A program evaluation.* Greensboro, NC: Center for Creative Leadership.

23

19

Career Cycles and Mentoring

Douglas T. Hall

Dawn E. Chandler

I n this era of global business turbulence, we know that careers change at an astonishing rate, but we do not know a lot about what causes and influences these changes. If we think of a career as a series of learning cycles, in which a learner's[1] career unfolds through a sequence of exploration, trial, establishment, and mastery, followed by a period of new exploration (Hall & Associates, 1996, 2002), what is it that triggers a new learning cycle? What role might relationships, particularly mentoring and a person's developmental network, have on career change and a broader learning cycle? To be more specific, how do developmental networks facilitate career learning and transitions? Are there circumstances in which developmental networks might hinder career learning and transitions? These are the questions this chapter addresses. We hope that the ideas in this chapter will establish the foundation of a model of relationally driven career learning, which explains the role that mentoring and other developmental relationships play throughout the various stages of a career learning cycle.

More specifically, we assert the importance of a learner's developmental network—the set of people a protégé (learner) names as taking an active interest in and action to advance the protégé's career by providing developmental assistance (Higgins & Kram, 2001)—as a trigger, facilitator, and even hindrance of career learning cycles. The recent reconceptualization of mentoring as a developmental network of people highlights the reality that learners in today's turbulent environment draw upon a few to numerous relationships as vehicles of personal learning and career change (Higgins & Kram, 2001; Lankau & Scandura, 2002).

As we elaborate on later, little theoretical and empirical research exists that explicitly links mentoring and other developmental relationships to career change and the broader learning cycle. Given the shifting career context, which is characterized by more frequent career transitions, we believe that theoretical guidance in this area is timely. We introduce a model of developmental networks and career learning cycles that describes the role of the relationships that make up the network as triggers for career exploration (the first step in a learning cycle) and as facilitators, moderators, and possible obstacles to learning. Propositions are developed throughout the chapter in order to guide future research. We begin by describing the notion of career learning cycles, followed by an overview of research on the role of relationships in career change.

Careers as Learning Cycles

In prior decades, research suggested one's career unfolded as a single cycle of stages as a learner moved from novice to expert between his or her early and late career (e.g., Hall, 1976; Super, 1957). This career conceptualization was supported by the fact that learners often remained with a single organization—experiencing hierarchical advancement—for a long period of time, possibly the learner's entire career (Hall, 1976; Super, 1957).

As learners in today's turbulent career environment change jobs and industries and enact multiple career roles simultaneously (as would be the case if, for example, a learner took on a part-time role in addition to his or her full-time role), a new conceptualization is gradually replacing the traditional one from prior years. Consistent with this shifting career environment, Hall (2002) has proposed that the adult years of a person's career, rather than consisting of one long cycle consisting of by one set of stages (such as exploration, trial, establishment, mastery) (Hall, 1976; Super, 1957), may in fact be made up of multiple, short *learning cycles*. A learning cycle might last 3 to 5 years and consist of ministages of exploration of new areas of work, trial activity, becoming established, mastery and high performance, followed by renewed exploration of some new area of work to move into next.

Such a series of learning stages might look like that shown in Figure 19.1. A major question that we are addressing here is this: What triggers the transition from one learning cycle to the next? This is the area represented by the circle in Figure 19.1. Furthermore, what role might relationships play in triggering and then facilitating successful movement through a cycle?

As we elaborate in the next section, while some research on careers and mentoring has shown the role played by relationships (developmental or otherwise) during career change, our understanding is still limited, both in terms of theoretical and empirical guidance.

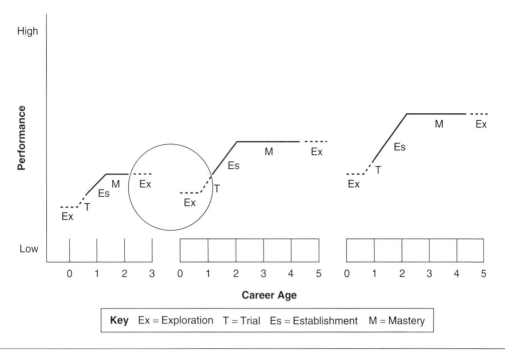

Figure 19.1 Career Learning Cycles and Career Transitions (Exploration, Trial, Establishment, Mastery, Exploration)

SOURCE: Hall (1993, p. 15).

Research on Career Learning Cycles and Relationships

Research on both careers and mentoring provides some insight as to the role played by relationships during a career transition (which represents the beginning of a learning cycle, as shown in Figure 19.1) and the broader learning cycle. We assert that while both literature streams are informative, neither provides sufficient theoretical guidance. The later discussion attempts to address this literature gap.

Careers Research

In the career research sphere, although there has been little research on career change among older employees (Hall & Mirvis, 1995), some of the studies that have been conducted are considered to be classics. Two longitudinal studies dating from the 1960s at the old AT&T organization (Bray, Campbell, & Grant, 1974; Howard & Bray, 1988) followed managers over the years of their careers, from entry-level jobs to late career, and documented many different types of change in their work activities, attitudes, and performance. They found that the centrality of work tended to decrease later in a manager's career and that supportive relationships and personal flexibility were important factors in a person's success at navigating these changes.

An even earlier study was conducted by Vaillant (1977) on a panel of World War II era Harvard students, now tracked into retirement. Vaillant found that good work and good relationships were important in generating work fulfillment and a long, healthy life. Levinson, in *Seasons of a Man's Life* (1978) and *Seasons of a Woman's Life* (1996), which studied life change in adult men and women, found that transitions were important and predictable parts of a person's life, marking the passage between one era of life and the next, and that relationships both in personal life and at work were found to be important facilitators of successful passages.

Ibarra (2004) conducted a study of 39 people who had made career changes. One of her most important findings was that participants tended to change through taking action (taking small steps, experimenting with new behaviors) rather than engaging in a lot of self-analysis first. A second significant factor in the change involved new connections, relationships with new people who could help the person move into new roles.

Mintz (2003) studied a group of highly successful men at midlife who had made major transformations of their careers and identities. He found that key relationships and a number of personality factors (most of the "Big Five") facilitated the change. In all of these studies of major career change, then, there is a theme of relationships playing an important role in triggering and facilitating the change process. Although not all of these studies focused specifically on mentoring or developmental networks, some of the qualities that we now associate with good developmental relationships, such as personal support, coaching, caring, and challenge, were found to be present in the career-enhancing relationships that were examined in these studies.

Mentoring/Developmental Relationships Research

As suggested by the foregoing discussion on career change, one factor that may trigger, facilitate, and even hinder career learning cycles is a learner's developmental network, defined as "the set of people a protégé (learner) names as taking an active interest in and action to advance the protégé's career by providing developmental assistance" (Higgins & Kram, 2001, p. 268). Developmental networks were borne out of the mentoring research, which has demonstrated the benefits that accrue to learners (protégés) who receive career and psychosocial support from a "portfolio" of advisors (Higgins, 2000), to whom we will frequently refer as "developers" (e.g., Higgins & Kram, 2001; Kram, 1985; for more recent research on developmental networks, see Chandler & Kram, in press; Dobrow & Higgins, 2005; Molloy, 2005).

To our knowledge, no comprehensive framework has specifically linked mentoring and developmental networks with the career transition or career learning cycle literatures. Despite the relative absence of a link between career learning, transitions, and mentoring, several studies have suggested relationships between developmental networks and career transition outcomes. In fact, these studies, to be elaborated upon next, suggest that developmental relationships can be beneficial to learners as they engage in transitions and learning.

Thomas (1990), for example, introduced the notion of dual support for managers of diverse backgrounds as they seek to establish and then advance their careers. Major, Kozloski, Chao, and Gardner (1995) examined how relationships between newcomers and their supervisors or workgroups ameliorate the negative effects of unmet expectations during career transitions. Ragins's (1997) work on diversified mentoring relationships suggested that learners with powerful mentors will better adjust during socialization throughout a transition. Brett and Werbel (1980) found that pretransition discussions with past and present supervisors concerning job duties and coworkers can assist transferees in preparing for new positions. Recent theoretical research has identified types of developmental relationships and functional support relevant during an international assignment (Crocitto, Sullivan, & Carraher, 2005; Mezias & Scandura, 2005). Crocitto et al. (2005) likened the three phases of an international assignment—predeparture, on assignment, and repatriation—to a "mini-learning" cycle (Hall, 2002; Hall & Chandler, 2005).[2]

A few studies have suggested that the greater the diversity and strength of ties within a learner's network of advisors (Higgins, 2000; Higgins & Kram, 2001), the greater the likelihood that a learner will change careers. For example, entrepreneurial networks—diverse networks made up of strong affective ties with developers—lead to more frequent career change. These findings suggest that career decisions are based in part on the advice and counsel of the learner's developmental network and that the greater the range of information and resources provided by the network, the greater the number of opportunities that exist.

While some of the foregoing studies can be more easily considered applicable to learning cycles than most studies on mentoring, when one conceives of learning cycles as a foundation for one's entire career (see Figure 19.1), it becomes clear that many, if not most, mentoring studies are relevant. Given that mentoring scholars have suggested a shift toward understanding how mentoring influences personal learning (Chandler & Kram, in press; Kram, 1996; Lankau & Scandura, 2002; Lankau & Scandura, Chapter 4, this volume), an emphasis on mentoring studies within the context of broader learning cycles will aid a better understanding of the impact of mentoring on a learner's career over time.

The relative scarcity of research and theory directly linking mentoring and developmental networks to transitions highlights the need for a more in-depth understanding of or more comprehensive framework describing *when, who,* and *how* developers can influence, and in some cases hinder, career learning cycle outcomes. A model of developmental networks and learning cycles is the necessary foundation to show the interconnectedness of mentoring and career transitions and cycles. Throughout the remainder of the chapter, we will describe a model of relationally driven career learning and change. We describe how developmental networks can *trigger, facilitate,* and even *hinder* career learning cycles.

Developmental Networks and Career Learning Cycles

Figure 19.2 presents a model of developmental networks and career learning cycles. Learning cycles can be triggered by myriad factors, which include organization or society-level (macro) changes and events (e.g., economic recessions, wars, or catastrophes), work role factors such as stretch jobs, and learner factors such as adaptability, identity awareness, and career self-efficacy.

Developmental relationships exist at multiple levels, in the immediate work role, in the organization, and outside the organization in the larger society. For example, important extraorganizational developmental networks can include relationships with spouses, parents, family friends, former bosses, colleagues, and subordinates, former teachers, neighbors, longtime friends, and schoolmates. These developmental relationships and networks can be a source of new career opportunities, new resources, new ideas, and so on and can thus have a direct impact upon learning cycles.

As is further elaborated upon in the next section, triggers "bust" existing career routines, leading a focal learner to engage in either self-exploration or external exploration. In addition to acting as triggers (direct causes), developmental networks also are facilitators of, and occasionally hindrances to, successful movement through career learning cycles. Put another way, a learner's network has both a direct and moderating influence between a trigger and the learning cycle. For example, if a learner experiences a layoff (a macrochange trigger), whether he or she successfully secures a position and moves toward mastery will be in part determined by the support provided by, and sought from, his or her network.

Throughout a learning cycle, a learner will experience varying degrees of stress, career and job satisfaction, success (both objective and subjective), and adjustment, all of which will be impacted by the network's influence. Further, the learner's employability (adaptability, human and social capital, and career identity) (Fugate, Kinicki, & Ashforth, 2004) will be influenced by how he or she experiences the learning cycle. Finally, during the learning cycle, a learner's network will shift in terms of both strength of tie (Granovetter, 1973, 1985) of the network's relationships and degree of diversity (measured as the extent to which the relationships stem from varying social spheres, or as the degree of diversity of age, gender, nationality, race, etc.).

Figure 19.2 shows a "bird's-eye view" of career triggers, career learning cycles, and learner outcomes. The purpose of this chapter is to closely examine how developmental relationships trigger and facilitate learning cycles. In the next section, we elaborate on how the three levels of cycle triggers—societal/organizational, work role (including developmental relationships), and learner—"bust" career routines, thus triggering career exploration. We then delve into how developmental relationships facilitate the stages of a career cycle.

What Triggers Career Exploration?

Figure 19.1 shows career exploration as the beginning phase of a learning cycle. Career exploration may be defined as activities directed toward enhancing knowledge of the self (self-exploration) and the external environment (external exploration), in which a learner engages to foster progress in career development (Zikic & Hall, 2006).

Hall (1986) discussed how a person can become bogged down in a career routine once he or she has become established in a field or organization. This occurs as a person achieves a high level of mastery performance in his or her work and begins to feel self-efficacy and satisfaction as a result. What can trigger a change in this

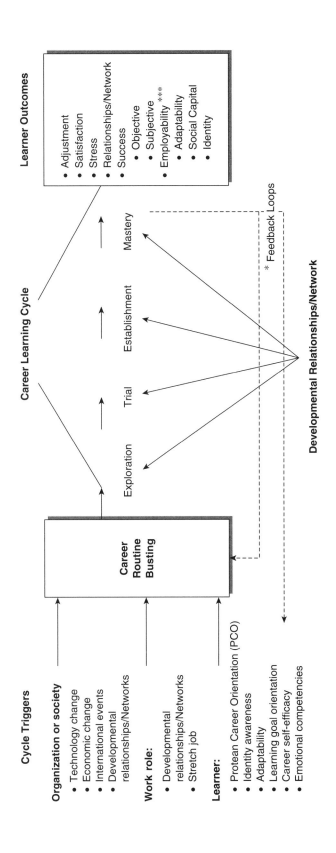

Figure 19.2 Developmental Networks and Career Learning Cycles

career routine and get the person into a process of exploring internally (self-reflection) and externally (exploring new work options)? Zikic and Hall (2006) have identified a cyclical model describing the process of career exploration. They suggest that triggers to exploration can include factors at three levels of analysis: societal or organizational, work role, and learner levels.

Societal/Organizational-Level Triggers

The external environment or organization includes shifts in the form of technological change, changes in the economy and business cycle, and the occurrence major international events (war, global competition, terrorism, etc.). Perhaps one of the most common examples of a trigger at this level is being laid off as a result of a recession. These macrochanges are not things that the average learner can control, but one can be aware of them, attempt to anticipate and monitor them, and learn to adapt to them.

Work-Role-Level Triggers

At a more immediate level, in the work role, triggers could come from the supervisor, from a new job assignment (e.g., a "stretch" assignment), and from developmental networks. A highly challenging assignment, by virtue of "stretching" the capabilities of a focal learner, creates a situation in which learning is a necessary byproduct of interacting within that particular work role.

Developmental networks influence both external exploration and self-exploration (Zikic & Hall, 2006). With respect to the former, developers, depending on their networks of strong and weak ties (*strength of tie* refers to the level of affect, reciprocity, and mutuality between a learner and his or her developers) (Granovetter, 1973; Higgins & Kram, 2001), are able to offer sponsorship and capture the attention of a wider range of potential employers who can offer different career possibilities (Higgins, 2001). Well-entrenched developers can open doors to new opportunities, making connections that support the protégé's role change. For example, friends, current supervisors, mentors, and work peers can all leverage their own networks to extend the reach of career opportunities for the protégé.

Zikic and Hall (2006) asserted that strong-tie relationships lead to more self-exploration, an examination "of one's identity, values, strengths, weaknesses, and developmental needs" (p. 14), that can trigger career exploration. Moreover, Zikic and Hall suggested that developers can influence a protégé's self-efficacy (Bandura, 1986, 1997) by acting as a role model who the protégé can emulate or through persuading the protégé of his or her capabilities. Both types of support can enhance the possibility of career exploration as the learner becomes increasingly confident in taking on greater challenges, responsibilities, and opportunities for personal learning. In the following section, we go into more detail on specific links between relational influences and new career learning cycles.

Learner-Level Triggers

At the learner level, several key factors can help trigger a learning cycle. One factor is a predisposition of the person that Briscoe, Hall, and Frautschy DeMuth (2006) call a "protean career attitude." This is a proactive stance toward the career characterized by self-direction and a strong concern for acting on one's values. Such a self-directed person would be more likely than an externally oriented person to recognize when a career path is not true to his or her deeply held values and would thus be likely to initiate a new round of career exploration.

In a similar manner, people with a clear awareness of their own identities and a high level of adaptability, as well as a strong sense of values, would be more likely to initiate career changes if their current work was not a good personal fit for them. Such people may have high standards for what they are seeking in their careers and may not always experience high levels of career satisfaction if the current job does not measure up to their ideals.

Three other personal qualities that we would expect to trigger a new learning cycle include a learning goal orientation, high career self-efficacy, and emotional competencies. Betz (1992) has found that people with high career self-efficacy tend to have a better person-job fit than learners with lower career self-efficacy. Other research has found that such a learning goal orientation is linked to high levels of exploratory activity and mastery (Briscoe et al., 2006). Also, emotional competencies, such as a learner's self-awareness to assess career goals and interests, can facilitate a new learning cycle, as well (Goleman, 1995).[3]

How Do Developmental Networks Facilitate Learning Cycles?

In the prior section, we discussed how developmental networks trigger career exploration, marking the beginning of a new learning cycle. In this section, we explain how networks can facilitate learning cycles, regardless of what factor triggers the initial exploration (see Figure 19.2; facilitation begins after a routine has "busted"). Another way to explain the relationship between networks and a learning cycle is that networks moderate (indirectly) how triggers influence learning cycle outcomes. For example, if a person experiences a layoff and hence begins exploring career options, the role that his or her network may play in finding an appropriate position moderates how the layoff ultimately influences outcomes such as career satisfaction and success.

Throughout the discussion, we suggest that in order for a learner to move with maximum success[4] from one stage to the next, he or she must meet specific goals associated with that stage; developmental support helps to meet those goals. Given our prior assertion of one's career as a string of learning cycles, it is noteworthy to consider that all types of psychosocial and career support will aid during one's career; however, certain types of support will be particularly helpful given the goals of each stage. Furthermore, while some support is valuable across cycle stages (e.g., personal counseling), the content of the support may vary differentially based on the goals of the stages. Table 19.1 illustrates how developmental support aids the primary goals associated with each stage of a career learning cycle.

Table 19.1 Career Cycle Learning Stages and Developmental Network Support

Stage & Types of Support	Developmental Challenges & Goals	Indications of Progress
Exploration	**"Getting Started & Letting Go"**	
Career:	Collaborating with developers to locate and learn about viable growth opportunities	Choose role consistent with global identity
Career counseling		Develop realistic expectations
Sponsorship/opening door	Psychologically shifting from existing role to newly chosen role	Successful role exit
New role information		Positive motivation toward change
Psychosocial:		
Personal counseling (aimed at role exit difficulties)		
Trial	**"Finding the Fit"**	
Career:	Selection	Confidence in coping
Sponsorship/exposure	Sense making	Enjoyment in sense making (dealing with surprise, unmet expectations)
Coaching (e.g., role information, political, cultural knowledge)	Person/organization fit	
Psychosocial:		
Role-modeling		
Friendship		
Personal counseling		
Establishment	**"Settling In"**	
Career:	Achieving high performance	Achieve a consonant relationship between oneself and one's environment (personal learning and role innovation)
Counseling (e.g., role, cultural)	Mastery of tasks and development of required competencies	
Feedback		Evaluations that reflect continual growth and high performance
Coaching		
Protection		

Stage & Types of Support	Developmental Challenges & Goals	Indications of Progress
Psychosocial:		
Role modeling		
Acceptance and confirmation		
Friendship		
Mastery	**"Sharpening the Saw"**	
Career:	Maintaining high performance	Social (capital):
Peer coaching	Participating in collaborative relationships	Sustaining trust, commitment with developers and other important role holders
Counseling	Maintenance of a developmental network that allows one to move to the next cycle	Task (human capital):
Feedback	Contemplation of one's values, strengths, weaknesses, and interests	Sustaining high performance
Psychosocial	Continued development of requisite skills and competencies	
Friendship		
Acceptance and confirmation		

Our discussion centers on the roles that developers play in facilitating successful transition through various cycle stages. It is noteworthy to consider that what types of and amount of support will vary based on the extent to which a focal learner seeks out assistance and the adeptness with which he or she cultivates and nurtures developmental relationships.[5] Learner factors such as one's emotional intelligence (Goleman, 1995), relational skills (Fletcher, 1996), developmental stage (Chandler & Kram, 2005), relational savvy (Chandler, 2006), and attitude toward authority (Kram, 1996) will influence whether, with what frequency, and how adeptly a learner reaches out to others.

Exploration

The exploration stage is characterized by contemplation of new areas of career work (Hall & Kahn, 2001). We first discuss an exploration stage that occurs as an inter-role (between work roles) transition, followed by one that is intra-role in nature. In either an inter-role or intra-role change, exploration can be either *planned* or *emergent;* the former occurs as a learner has the foresight to consciously design a transition, whereas with the latter, a learner gathers information prior to "crafting experiments" (Ibarra, 1999, 2004) without necessary intent to make an inter-role transition.

Inter-Role Planned Exploration

The exploration stage begins either when a learner starts thinking about changing roles and begins weighing alternative roles or when he or she is involuntarily forced into a situation of looking for a new role (e.g., layoffs). During the exploration stage of learning cycle stage, a learner must achieve a state of readiness for the change (Nicholson, 1987). The degree to which the exploration stage is successful depends on whether several important goals are met; more specifically, it is important for the learner to (a) choose a role consistent with his or her global identity, (b) develop realistic expectations, and (c) have positive motivation toward change (Ashforth, 2001[6]; Nicholson, 1984, 1987). Table 19.1 provides an overview of the goals that are salient at each stage and the types of support that developers can offer a learner to meet those goals.

To successfully transition through the exploration phase, a learner must choose a role that reinforces, complements, or extends his or her sense of self in personally and socially desirable ways (Ashforth, 2001). A learner's *global identity,* or core sense of self, will influence his or her selection of roles (Ashforth, 2001). Developers—for example, a learner's mentor or supervisor, friend, or spouse—can offer career counseling and coaching that may enhance a learner's ability to choose the role that best "fits" with that individual's global identity. Career coaching is more directive than counseling and specifically involves advising the protégé on issues such as whether certain roles are consistent with his or her global identity, as well as how to attain those roles. Career counseling should be more nondirective, including posing questions that promote self-reflection, helping the person obtain feedback to enhance self-awareness and explore potential positions that might offer a good fit with values, interests, and skills.[7]

Family members, spouses, and special friends, who know the focal learner intimately, are particularly helpful with respect to career advice. Current supervisors who have knowledge of the learner's knowledge, skills, and aspirations also can guide the protégé to a new role that is consistent with his or her sense of self. In general, developers can offer a learner counseling that enables effective preparation for a new role.

Another type of developmental support that is closely related to, but distinct from, career counseling, is informational support. Often, learners do not have enough or accurate information to make a clear decision about whether a potential role fits with their aspirations and identities. Developers can aid the learner by enhancing his or her knowledge base about a role. In the absence of perfect information, a learner may develop unrealistic—especially unrealistically high—expectations about a role (Wanous, 1992). On one hand, these expectations may fuel an initial "honeymoon effect" (Fichman & Levinthal, 1991), whereby the desire to think well of the role and organization buffers one from less positive discoveries. On the other hand, the more unrealistic the expectations, the more difficult it is to minimize the discrepancy, provoking reality shock (Hughes, 1958). Therefore, the more information a learner receives during the exploration phase, the more likely he or she will be to have the realistic expectations necessary to transition effectively.

Developers can also help the learner to be positively motivated toward the change and have positive feelings toward it by offering both informational and career counseling support. The more information the learner has, the more likely the individual is to feel comfortable with the role and his or her decision. Furthermore, psychosocial support can enhance the learner's motivation toward a change. By providing ongoing support, listening, acceptance, and affirmation of the protégé, the individual is more likely to feel confident with his or decisions (Kram, 1985). For example, a recent college graduate who is considering entering into an investment banking or a consulting career can gain insight from a family member or former schoolmate who has experience in either or both professions.

Throughout the exploration stage of an inter-role planned transition, developers can provide support that allows a learner to meet the goals necessary to successfully transition to the trial stage. Career counseling, sponsorship, and informational support help the protégé choose a new role consistent with his or her global identity, develop realistic expectations, and have a positive motivation toward a change. Psychosocial support helps the protégé develop realistic expectations and effectively exit the current role.

Intra-Role Emergent Exploration

Ibarra (2004) asserted that learners often experience change not through consciously preplanned and executed career transitions, but rather through an emerging process whereby the focal learner "crafts experiments"—small probes and projects that allow individuals to try out new professional roles on a minor scale. Ultimately, the learner may build a new working identity slowly, as experiments lead to new choices and routines (Zikic & Hall, 2006). Thus, rather than immediately transitioning between organizations or positions—an inter-role transition—an intra-role transition involves maintaining one's current role while experimenting with additional career possibilities. In this case, the exploration stage includes a process of ascertaining relevant information related to new activities and behaviors. A learner engaging in an emergent intra-role transition will also need to meet the goals of a planned inter-role transition, but it is also important for the learner to gain information relevant to the change and to receive psychosocial support from developers.

As an example of an intra-role transition, consider a stockbroker who wants to pursue a career in theater. Rather than quit his "day job," he contemplates taking theater classes at night and volunteering to perform in local performances. Developers can provide informational or role-modeling support in the event that they have experienced a transition from one career to a dissimilar other.

What may be most important at the exploration stage is psychosocial support from developers. Support of commitment to a career change from one's spouse may quell feelings of uncertainty and fear to leap into the unknown. Parry (2002), in the *Essene Book of Days,* metaphorically explained fear of a transition and life as a series of trapeze swings. The "transition zone" is the "dark void" between the comfort of swinging on an existing bar and a new bar swinging toward the learner. Parry wrote that although "it can be terrifying . . . it can also be a chance to learn how to fly" (p. 34). Given fear of the unknown, psychosocial support is critical in the exploration stage.

Intra-Role Exploration Stage

Intra-role change may be experienced as either emergent or planned as a learner reorients himself or herself toward an existing role. Two examples of intra-role exploration include a learner seeking to shift her work hours to reflect work-life balance (Zikic & Hall, 2006) or a learner deciding to pursue a challenging assignment within his existing role. Developers can be supportive by offering counseling that helps the learner to define what he or she wants the new definition of the role to look like, as well as coaching on how to negotiate such external changes in the work setting. Also, this kind of intra-role exploration change may involve no visible changes at all, but rather only internal cognitive shifts in how the focal person responds to the same demands of the role. Here, role-modeling and counseling can be particularly useful.[8]

The following proposition summarizes the relationship between the types of support offered by developmental networks and the exploration stage goals:

Proposition 1: Successful passage through the exploration stage of a learning cycle will be associated with developer career counseling, sponsorship, new role information, coaching, and/or and personal counseling.

Trial

The trial stage of a career learning cycle begins once a learner has ascertained what he or she perceives as relevant information related to new career avenues or activities and then starts trial activities to test for fit. During the trial stage, a learner must meet three primary goals: (a) to exit successfully from the existing role, (b) to develop confidence in coping, and (c) to take enjoyment in sense making (see Nicholson, 1987, for a discussion of the engagement phase of a transition cycle). Even when a learner has met all of the goals in the exploration stage, learners entering the trial stage may feel fearful, unready, and reluctant to change (Nicholson, 1987). And, of course, all of these cycles can happen in fits and starts. This is the nature of exploration, and there can be false starts.[9]

Planned and emergent transitions are similar during the trial stage of a learning cycle, in that they both involve new activities or behaviors aimed at career growth. The difference between the two is that trials in the planned transition occur within a new role (e.g., a sudden transition when a person has lost a job and has to find a new one), whereas trials in an emergent transition may occur as the learner holds roles simultaneously. In the example of the stockbroker who seeks a career in theater, he will engage in new activities (e.g., taking acting classes, volunteering for a local theater) while continuing to work as a stockbroker, until such time that he can financially support himself (or family) within the new career.

Successful Role Exit

First, a learner embarking upon a career transition and thus entering a new learning cycle will need to exit his or her current role effectively. Successful role exit, whether the result of a planned or emergent transition, is most salient during the trial phase. The process of role exit is intimately connected to the process of role entry (Ashforth, 2001). The learner's psychological exit from a role often begins long before the physical exit of the role. The more attractive an alternative new role, the more likely it is that the learner will be able to disengage from the current role (Ashforth, 2001). However, the more attractive the prior role (e.g., after a layoff situation), the more likely it is that the learner will identify with that role and will therefore have difficulty exiting the current role.

For example, a learner who is downsized from a role with which he highly identifies may experience feelings of loss and grief (Ashforth, 2001). Developers can offer personal counseling to a learner who is having difficulty exiting a role. Friends and family members who are most intimate with a learner and with whom he or she feels psychologically safe are good candidates for personal counseling (Fisher, Nadler, & Whitcher-Alagna, 1982). The stockbroker, rather than experiencing grief over the loss of his prior role, may feel joy from the new career. His role exit may occur slowly or quickly, depending upon the duration of simultaneously held roles as well as the degree to which his identity shifts from perceiving himself as a stockbroker to perceiving himself as having a career in theatrical arts.

Confidence in Coping and Enjoyment of Sense Making

The newness of the entry experience—including the objective difference between the latter and the former situation and the salience of contrasting features of the new setting—can trigger confusion for the learner (Louis, 1980; Nicholson,

1987[10]). Further, the learner can experience surprise when his or her anticipations are unfulfilled (Louis, 1980). Often, the learner has unmet expectations when he or she experiences less of something desirable than was expected (Dunnette, Arvey, & Banas, 1973; Nicholson, 1987). The environment can overwhelm the newcomer with unfamiliar cues that cannot be accommodated by his or her cognitive schema (Nicholson, 1987; Van Maanen & Schein, 1979).

Three types of career support—sponsorship/exposure, feedback, and informational support—are critical in helping learners meet the goals of the stage. Usually, intraorganizational developers or developers who worked with the organization at one point in time are most likely to offer these types of support. By introducing learners to their internal networks and signaling their legitimacy as employees, they are more likely to feel psychological safety and comfort in the new environment. Further, by exposing newcomers in the first few days or weeks to insider networks, they can more effectively gain a solid reputation when they demonstrate competence. Most important, sponsorship allows the learner to begin developing relationships and building trust with fellow employees.

As the career changer experiments with new activities and behaviors, developers' feedback can be critical to the individual's self-confidence and enjoyment. Informational support facilitates sense making, which is a particular thinking process through which a learner produces retrospective explanations (Louis, 1980; Nicholson, 1987). When learners experience surprise, contrast, and unmet expectations, developers can help a career changer make sense by providing explanations.

Developers who work, or worked for the organization during a prior period, have context-specific dictionaries of meaning (Berger & Luckmann, 1966) that "structure routine interpretations and conduct within an institutional area" (p. 138). These developers are capable of imparting knowledge that can help protégés cope with current situations (Louis, 1980; Nicholson, 1987). For example, suppose a protégé has had an early negative experience with his manager, thus leaving him with a sense of anxiety. The intraorganizational developer could explain that the manager has been irritable lately because he has a newborn at home that is keeping him up all night. In the absence of such an explanation, the protégé might engage in sense making and conclude that the situation is due to his own incompetence.

Developers can offer two types of psychosocial support during the trial stage: role-modeling, which reduces uncertainty and guides appropriate behaviors, and personal counseling, which is particularly valuable given the psychological strain a learner may face in an unfamiliar environment. Intraorganizational insiders can model valued behaviors, attitudes, and or skills that aid the protégé in achieving competence in the role, confidence, and a clear identity in that role (Kram, 1985). Role-modeling is present through both the encounter and adjustment phases. During the encounter phase, role-modeling helps the protégé in meeting both goals—confidence in coping and enjoyment in sense making—because by watching and potentially imitating developers (Ibarra, 1999), protégés can be more confident that their behavior and attitudes mirror those that are acceptable at the organization.

Personal counseling helps mitigate potentially destructive coping mechanisms brought on by stress and uncertainty. Developers—both inside and outside the organization—who are attuned to the learner's emotional needs and can demonstrate excellent listening, warmth, encouragement, trust, and rapport are capable of helping the learner to confidently cope with situations. For example, developers may choose to share the "human side" of their own career histories and transitions as well as challenges and difficulties they have faced.

The trial stage can be characterized by a great deal of uncertainty for the protégé. Developers can provide five types of support—sponsorship/exposure, feedback, information, role-modeling, and personal counseling—that allow protégés to meet the goals necessary to successfully transition to the establishment stage.

The trial stage can be likened to the "encounter" phase of Nicholson's (1987) transition cycle, which typically lasts for the first few days to weeks of a learner's immersion in a new role. The trial period ends when the learner considers the new activities or position to be a reasonable fit, at which time he or she works to become established in that area.

The following proposition summarizes the relationship between the types of support offered by developmental networks and the trial goals:

Proposition 2: Successful passage through the trial stage of a learning cycle will be associated with developer sponsorship, informational support, role-modeling, friendship, and personal counseling.

Establishment

During this stage, an individual (learner) is focused on role-learning, which is necessary for establishment in the chosen career role. The establishment and mastery stages can be considered representative of where most mentoring studies would be "placed" within a larger learning cycle. The mentoring literature has a strong body of studies that describe the functional support—career and psychosocial—that developmental relationships provide to protégés as they seek to become established in and master a role.

Role-learning is essential to effective transitioning (Ashforth, 2001). E. W. Morrison (1993) described the seven areas that constitute role-learning: (a) technical information about how to perform tasks, (b) referent information about role expectations, (c) social information about other people and one's relationships with them, (d) appraisal information about how one is evaluated, (e) normative information about the organization's culture, (f) organizational information about structure, products/services, and procedures, and (g) political information about the distribution of power. In short, any newcomer must learn about the nature of the role and the context within which it is embedded.

As the learners adjust to their new roles, they will make necessary adaptations to either the roles or themselves in order to function effectively. Developmental network assistance during this stage will harmonize assimilation and accommodation (Nicholson, 1987). Of utmost importance is that the person's relationship with the job seems to be heading toward an appropriate "fit" rather than a dysfunctional adaptation (Nicholson, 1987). Learners who are unable to fully use their skills or grieve for the lost past or foregone opportunities are not likely to adjust satisfactorily (Bridges, 1980).

Developers offer six primary types of support during the establishment stage. Career-related support is given through informational support necessary for role-learning and through timely feedback. Psychosocial support includes role-modeling, signaling social acceptance, acceptance and confirmation, and friendship. Peers at work and intraorganizational mentors and supervisors are the primary sources of informational support and feedback and successful adjustment outcomes. Intraorganizational developers can explain situations, people, and the organizational culture, validate the protégé's emergent perceptions, describe various ways of performing tasks, and generally facilitate the acquisition of knowledge either through their own understanding or by referring the protégé to another source of information.

Swift, reliable feedback from intraorganizational peers, subordinates, supervisors, and mentors is a necessary element in personal and organizational development (Kram, 1985; Nicholson, 1987). Role-modeling through the adjustment phase guides protégés' behavior and attitudes by providing accepted ways of interacting with others and enacting roles in the organizational context.

As learners interact within a relatively new environment, they will have begun to cultivate relationships and demonstrate their competence and skillfulness within the role. Often, they will not be fully aware of how others perceive their abilities and knowledge. Developers, who may have received open or confidential feedback about the learner's performance, can signal social acceptance that boosts the learner's self-esteem and self-image within that role (Kram, 1985). Further, as others personally confirm and accept the individual as a learner and offer their friendship, the learner will feel an emotional connection that enables him or her work on salient developmental tasks and goals (Kram & Isabella, 1985).

Although primary support during this stage comes from intraorganizational developers, extraorganizational developers can be important sources of support as well. Friends who work in the same industry or position with another organization can provide informational insight to the learner's role. Extraorganizational mentors, family members/spouses, and friends can provide a confidential forum for exploring professional dilemmas, acting as a sounding board and demonstrating positive listening, trust, and rapport, which enable learners to address their concerns and thoughts (Hall, 2002).

The establishment stage can last between a few months to a few years as the learner gains a foothold on the role. The following proposition highlights the relationship between developmental networks and the establishment stage:

Proposition 3: Successful passage through the establishment stage of a learning cycle will be associated with developer functional support in the form of challenging work, coaching, feedback, role-modeling, acceptance and confirmation, and protection.

Mastery

The goals of the mastery stage are effectiveness with tasks and people. This stage is similar to Nicholson's (1987) stabilization phase of the transition cycle.[11] At this point in the learning cycle, developers can offer several types of career and psychosocial support that aid the attainment of the goals. In essence, developers should watch and help steer the balance between control and discretion to ensure that the protégé's needs are met.

First, developers can career counsel in order to help protégés focus on their needs and goals. Intraorganizational and extraorganizational developers can engage learners in conversations about their career and life goals. Over time, learners will most likely aspire to obtain other roles that either represent more challenging work or involvement in line with their life stages. The extensive literatures on goal setting and management by objectives provide clear evidence of the motivational and performance outcome benefits (Locke, Shaw, Saari, & Latham, 1981). Informational support is critical during this stage so that the protégé feels control over his or her environment and is properly able to make sense of organizational changes.

Also, consistent feedback to learners will help them to enact their current roles properly and balance accommodation and assimilation as internal and external changes in the environment occur. Ideally, the mastery stage represents the time at which developers can bring learners smoothly toward the next role transition. Developers can encourage protégés to develop the skills necessary to enact the pursued role. Given that it takes time for learners to "master" tasks and become effective with people in their role sets (Katz & Kahn, 1966), the mastery stage will typically last a few years.

Finally, as a learner has successfully mastered tasks associated with a particular role, developers can encourage him or her to take an active role in developing others who are at earlier stages of a learning cycle. A learner who does so will aid knowledge dissemination and generally add value to an organization. Personally, the learner may feel a sense of enhanced confidence and enjoyment as he or she helps others.

During the mastery phase, developers ensure that protégés' needs are met, their skills evolve over time, and they participate in developing others. Developers can offer career counseling, goal-setting advice, informational support, and feedback. The following proposition highlights the relationship between developmental networks and the mastery stage:

Proposition 4: Successful passage through the mastery stage of a learning cycle will be associated with peer coaching, counseling, feedback, friendship, and acceptance and confirmation from one's developers.

Furthermore, as Belle Ragins and Kathy Kram have pointed out to us in their comments on this chapter, it is important to remember that we need to consider the effects of unsuccessful passage through this mastery stage. Failures can produce powerful learning, which could lead the person to "recycle" and perhaps start a new learning cycle. Also, another powerful source of assistance in moving through the mastery stage is being a developer for others. This deepens the person's own learning, as well as self-esteem, leadership capacity, and value to the organization.

Learning Cycle Outcomes

Throughout our discussion of the exploration, trial, establishment, and mastery stage sections of the career learning cycle, we have described goals that lead to successful transition through that particular stage. Successful completion of a career learning cycle can lead to an improved fit between the person and the work role (i.e., adjustment). Cable and Judge (1996) have found a positive relationship between successful learning and good positive person-job fit. And if the person's fit were improved, we would conversely expect that job-related stress might decrease (Barnett, 1999).

In a similar vein, as a result of the success of mastering a new role, the person would be likely to experience greater satisfaction and psychological (or subjective) success (Hall & Foster, 1977). And since the person has mastered the new role, one would logically expect that objective performance would increase along with subjective success (Nicholson & De Waal Andrews, 2005). In the process of learning how to master the new work role, the person probably would have reached out to a new network of people associated with this role. Thus, over time, this network would have expanded.

As a result of mastering and settling into the new role and acquiring a new developmental network, the person will likely have arrived at a revised awareness of his or her identity. In addition, since the best way to increase one's adaptability is through experience in adapting (Morrison & Hall, 2002), successfully transition through this learning cycle would have provided this experience. Thus, the person's adaptability will have increased. And since the person's developmental network has increased, this means that the person's social capital has increased. And the sum of this improved adaptability, social capital, and identity represents an increased level of employability (Fugate et al., 2004).

> *Proposition 5:* Successful passage through the learning cycle stages will be associated with positive outcomes, such as adjustment, job satisfaction, objective and subjective success, and employability.

As Figure 19.2 shows, a feedback loop occurs as routines are busted by triggers—and hence, a new cycle begins. Also, a learner's interaction with developers may lead to greater emotional intelligence, adaptability, a learning goal orientation, and other individual-level outcomes (see feedback loop between mastery- and individual-level triggers).

Developmental Networks as Hindrances to Career Learning Cycles

Our discussion thus far has considered how the mentoring and developmental relationships that comprise a network trigger and facilitate learning cycles. Given research on dysfunctional mentoring relationships (e.g., Eby, Chapter 13, this volume; Eby, Butts, Lockwood, & Simon, 2004; Scandura, 1998), it is important to consider how networks might at times hinder learning cycles. One way a network can have negative effects on learning is if the person's developmental network is very dense (density is measured as the degree to which developers in a focal person's network know one another). Dobrow and Higgins (2005) found that a dense network, which does not encourage the person to seek views outside that network, can hinder the exploration and growth of a clearer sense of identity. When the developmental network is less dense, the person is less tightly bound to that network and may receive more diverse views from that network and also may be more motivated to look outside it for developmental assistance. In a related way, if the developmental network is very homogeneous, this could have deleterious effects on learning. In this situation, the person would not be exposed to new and different ideas and possibilities, and thus the network would not push or encourage the person to explore different possibilities. Ibarra (2004) found a similar phenomenon in her study of career changers. The people who were initially central in the person's network were usually not the key people in their change process.

A third way that a developmental network could have negative effects on learning would be if members of the network collectively tended toward a performance goal orientation, as opposed to a learning goal orientation. That is, if they valued high achievement and successful performance, as opposed to exploration and learning, then the focal person might be disinclined to engage in new behaviors that might threaten his or her high performance. Some ways that such a performance goal orientation might manifest itself could be through stressing high-status positions (in elite organizations) and outstanding levels of achievement. If the focal person felt pressure to maintain these high levels of distinction as measured by objective indicators of success, then that individual would not be inclined to explore and experiment with novel career behaviors. A fourth way a learner's network can hinder a learning cycle is when developers offer advice or support that is contrary to the learner's career interests or goals. This can occur, for example, when a developer who fears loss of the friendship with the learner advises that person not to change careers.

Proposition 6a: A dense network will be likely to hinder an individual's successful passage through a learning cycle.

Proposition 6b: A homogenous network will be likely to hinder an individual's successful passage through a learning cycle.

Proposition 6c: A performance goal orientation will be likely to hinder an individual's successful passage through a learning cycle.

Proposition 6d: Developers who challenge a focal learner's decision to engage in a career transition will be likely to hinder successful passage through a learning cycle.

Conclusion, Practical Implications, and Future Research

This chapter has emphasized the impact of developmental networks on career cycles. We have described how networks not only trigger career transitions but are also influenced by transitions that are catalyzed by a macrolevel force, such as an organizational downsizing, or by a learner-level factor, such as one's protean orientation. Furthermore, we have asserted that while networks often bring about positive outcomes during career transitions (as suggested by much of the extant mentoring literature), they may also have detrimental effects.

The shifting career context, coupled with the simultaneous shift in the conceptualization of mentoring, illuminates the importance of understanding how networks influence, and are also altered by, career transitions. Learners today are more likely to transverse organizational boundaries than they were in previous decades. Moreover, trends such as globalization and technological sophistication imply the need for continuous learning in order to possess the competencies necessary to succeed in a fast-paced career environment.

A future research agenda should include empirical examination of developmental networks as triggers facilitators and hindrances of career learning cycles. The propositions offered here, summarized in Box 19.1, are empirically testable and can serve as the basis of initial research.

BOX 19.1   Propositions for Future Research

Proposition 1: Successful passage through the exploration stage of a learning cycle will be associated with developer career counseling, sponsorship, new role information, coaching, and personal counseling.

Proposition 2: Successful passage through the trial stage of a learning cycle will be associated with developer sponsorship, informational support, role-modeling, friendship, and personal counseling.

Proposition 3: Successful passage through the establishment stage of a learning cycle will be associated with developer functional support in the form of challenging work, coaching, feedback, role-modeling, acceptance and confirmation, and protection.

Proposition 4: Successful passage through the mastery stage of a learning cycle will be associated with peer coaching, counseling, feedback, friendship, and acceptance and confirmation from one's developers.

Proposition 5: Successful passage through the learning cycle stages will be associated with positive outcomes, such as adjustment, job satisfaction, objective and subjective success, and employability.

Proposition 6a: A dense network will be likely to hinder successful passage through a learning cycle.

Proposition 6b: A homogenous network will be likely to hinder successful passage through a learning cycle.

Proposition 6c: A performance goal orientation will be likely to hinder successful passage through a learning cycle.

Proposition 6d: Developers who disagree with a focal learner's decision to engage in a career transition will be likely to hinder successful passage through a learning cycle.

Given the complex nature of developmental relationships and career cycles and due to a lack of prior research, qualitative methods should initially be employed. For example, a group of learners at various points in career transitions could be interviewed with respect to the composition of their existing developmental networks, transition triggers, and the roles played by the network through the transition. Alternatively, longitudinal analysis of a group of learners as they move through a transition would capture the nuances of learner travails through stages, as well as be more suggestive of causality than cross-sectional designs. A specific focus on how learners differentially experience career transitions as a result of varying degrees of proactive behavior—for example, seeking out help, assistance, and job leads from their developers—would aid an understanding of what factors affect varying degrees of adjustment, satisfaction, and stress. The application of a learning cycle lens to examine mentoring illuminates that the well-established career and psychosocial functions (Kram, 1985) may be enacted differentially at various learning stages. For example, while personal counseling is important during all of the stages, the content of counseling will vary, based on the learner's needs during each stage.

Future research should be attentive to evidence showing developers or the network as a whole as hindrances to transition. An examination of the network as an outcome is also clearly relevant, in that new connections (Ibarra, 2004) as well as altered relationships will result from a transition. For example, research on changing network compositions (e.g., Dobrow & Higgins, 2005) suggests that learners may be more likely to seek out certain relationships or support from developers at various points of time during a cycle. Therefore, throughout a cycle, certain relationships may be altered as a learner interacts with greater or lesser frequency with them. Another fruitful area for research would be an in-depth examination of when and how recursive and other feedback loops occur. For example, a software engineer in the trial stage of a learning cycle whose position is eliminated will recursively experience the exploration stage as a result.[12]

From a practical standpoint, learners should become keenly aware of their networks at various points in their career cycles. Since developmental relationships can vary in the functions they provide, it is important to assess both the support offered as well as that which is needed on the basis of the learner's goals, life stage, and career needs. Learners should be aware of the possibility that their networks are not rich enough to provide the types of support to aid a particular point in the career cycle. For example, a learner who possesses a protean career orientation and is considering career opportunities in a few industries will possibly need an entrepreneurial network (Higgins & Kram, 2001)—a network with a high range of developers from various social spheres—in order to be aware of available positions.

An understanding of networks and career cycles helps place developmental support within a broader frame than is currently considered within the mentoring literature. Most of the extant literature considers the functional support, outcomes, and antecedents of developmental relationships without reference to where the learner is in a career cycle. Given that each stage in the cycle presents particular challenges and goals that must be met for the learner to move to the next stage (see Table 19.1), an understanding of developmental support within the context of the cycle brings clarity to how developmental networks enhance a learner's career.

Notes

1. We use the term *learner* in lieu of *focal individual* or *protégé* in order to highlight that developmental support aids personal learning and aligns with the notion of learning cycles.

2. Crocitto et al.'s discussion is underpinned by the three international stages—predeparture, on assignment, and repatriation—rather than by the stages of a career learning cycle.

3. More detail on learner factors that trigger career exploration can be found in Zikic and Hall (2006).

4. Regardless of the extent of support a learner receives, he or she will still likely pass through each learning cycle phase. However, the learner will likely experience varying levels of satisfaction, adjustment, and stress, among other outcomes, depending upon the type and amount of support received.

5. We would like to thank Kathy Kram for noting the importance of a career-changer's agency and adeptness in gaining developmental support in determining the amount and types of support provided.

6. Ashforth's (2001) work was particularly informative in that it defined the crucial goals necessary to advance through role transitions.

7. Thanks to Kathy Kram for these thoughts on career counseling.

8. Thanks to Kathy Kram for this observation.

9. Thanks to Belle Ragins for this observation.

10. Nicholson's (1987) discussion on career transitions was particularly helpful in guiding our discussion. In particular, Nicholson outlined challenges a learner may face at various transition stages. We build upon his discussion by describing how relationships can meet stage challenges.

11. However, we would argue that the term *stabilization* probably no longer applies in today's dynamic organizations. Rather, the "stability" that a person achieves is more akin to a state of ongoing turbulence and change. Yet this would be experienced as less disruptive than the discontinuous change the person experienced upon entering the new work role.

12. We would like to thank Kathy Kram for her insight on this point.

References

Ashforth, B. E. (2001). *Role transitions in organizational life: An identity-based perspective.* Mahwah, NJ: Lawrence Erlbaum.

Bandura, A. (1986). *Social foundations of thought and action.* Englewood Cliffs, NJ: Prentice Hall.

Bandura, A. (1997). *Self-efficacy: The exercise of control.* New York: Freeman.

Barnett, R. C. (1999). Fit as a mediator of the relationship between work hours and burnout. *Journal of Occupational Health Psychology, 4,* 307–317.

Berger, P. L., & Luckmann, T. (1966). *The social construction of reality.* New York: Anchor Books.

Betz, N. E. (1992). Counseling uses of self-efficacy theory. *Career Development Quarterly, 41,* 22–26.

Bray, D. W., Campbell, R. J., & Grant, D. L. (1974). *Formative years in business: A long-term AT&T study of managerial lives.* New York: John Wiley & Sons.

Brett, J. M., & Werbel, J. D. (1980). *The effect of job transfer on employees and their families: Final report.* Washington, DC: Employee Relocation Council.

Bridges, W. (1980). *Transitions: Making sense of life's changes.* Reading, MA: Addison-Wesley.

Briscoe, J. P., Hall, D. T., & Frautschy DeMuth, R. L. (2006). Protean and boundaryless career attitudes: An empirical exploration. *Journal of Vocational Behavior, 69,* 30–47.

Cable, D. M., & Judge, T. A. (1996). Person organization fit, job choice, and organizational entry. *Organizational Behavior and Human Decision Processes, 67,* 294–311.

Chao, G. T., Walz, P. M., Gardner, P. D. (1992). Formal and informal mentorships: A comparison on mentoring functions and contrast with nonmentored counterparts. *Personnel Psychology, 45,* 619.

Chandler, D. E. (2006). *Relational savvy: Why some protégés are more adept than others at cultivating and nurturing developmental relationships.* Unpublished doctoral dissertation, Boston University School of Management.

Chandler, D. E., & Kram, K. E. (2005). Applying an adult development perspective to developmental networks [Special Issue on Mentoring]. *Career Developmental International, 10,* 548–566.

Chandler, D. E., & Kram, K. E. (2007). Mentoring and developmental networks in the new career context. In H. Gunz & M. Peiperl (Eds.), *Handbook of career studies* (pp. 241–267). Thousand Oaks, CA: Sage.

Crocitto, M. M., Sullivan, S. E., & Carraher, S. M. (2005). Global mentoring as a means of career development and knowledge creation: A learning-based framework and agenda for future research [Special Issue on Mentoring]. *Career Development International, 10,* 548–566.

Dobrow, S. R., & Higgins, M. C. (2005). Developmental networks and professional identity: A longitudinal study [Special Issue on Mentoring]. *Career Development International, 10,* 548–566.

Dunnette, M. D., Arvey, R. D., & Banas, P. A. (1973). Why do they leave? *Personnel, 50,* 25–39.

Eby, L., Butts, M., Lockwood, A., & Simon, S. A. (2004). Protégés' negative experiences: Construct development and nomological validation. *Personnel Psychology,* 57, 411–447.

Fichman, M., & Levinthal, D. A. (1991). Honeymoons and the liability of adolescence: A new perspective on duration dependence in social and organizational relationships. *Academy of Management Review, 16,* 442–468.

Fisher, J. D., Nadler, A., & Whitcher-Alagna, S. J. (1982). Recipient reactions of aid. *Psychological Bulletin, 91,* 27–54.

Fletcher, J. K. (1996). A relational approach to the protean worker. In D. T. Hall & Associates (Eds.), *The career is dead—Long live the career: A relational approach to careers* (pp. 101–131). San Francisco: Jossey-Bass.

Fugate, M., Kinicki, A. J., & Ashforth, B. E. (2004). Employability: A psycho-social construct, its dimensions, and applications. *Journal of Vocational Behavior, 65,* 14–38.

Goleman, D. (1995). *Emotional intelligence.* New York: Bantam Books.

Granovetter, M. (1985). Economic action and social structure: The problem of embeddedness. *American Journal of Sociology, 91,* 481–510.

Granovetter, M. S. (1973). The strength of weak ties. *American Journal of Sociology, 6,* 1360–1380.

Hall, D. T. (1976). *Careers in organizations.* Glenview, IL: Scott, Foresman.

Hall, D. T. (1986). Breaking career routines: Midcareer choice and identity development. In D. T. Hall & Associates (Eds.), *Career development in organizations* (pp. 120–159). San Francisco: Jossey-Bass.

Hall, D. T. (1993). *Executive development roundtable. The new career contract: Wrong on both counts.* Unpublished technical report, Boston University.

Hall, D. T. (2002). *Careers in and out of organizations.* Thousand Oaks, CA: Sage.

Hall, D. T., & Associates. (Eds.). (1996). *The career is dead—Long live the career: A relational approach to careers.* San Francisco: Jossey-Bass.

Hall, D. T., & Chandler, D. E. (2005). Psychological success: When the career is a calling. *Journal of Organizational Behavior, 26,* 155–176.

Hall, D. T., & Foster, L. W. (1977). A psychological success cycle and goal setting: Goals, performance, and attitudes. *Academy of Management Journal, 20,* 282–290.

Hall, D. T., & Kahn, W. (2001). Developmental relationships at work: a learning perspective. In C. Cooper & R. J. Burke (Eds.), *The new world of work* (pp. 49–74). London: Blackwell.

Hall, D. T., & Mirvis, P. H. (1995). The new career contract: Developing the whole person at midlife and beyond. *Journal of Vocational Behavior, 47,* 269–289.

Higgins, M. C. (2000). The more, the merrier? Multiple developmental relationships and work satisfaction. *Journal of Management Development, 19,* 277.

Higgins, M. C. (2001). Career change: A social influence perspective. *Journal of Organizational Behavior, 22,* 595–618.

Higgins, M. C., & Kram, K. E. (2001). Reconceptualizing mentoring at work: A developmental network perspective. *Academy of Management Review, 26,* 264–288.

Howard, A., & Bray, D. W. (1988). *Managerial lives in transition: Advancing age and changing times.* New York: Guilford Press.

Hughes, E. C. (1958). *Men and their work.* Glencoe, IL: Free Press.

Ibarra, H. (1999). Provisional selves: Experimenting with image and identity in professional adaptation. *Administrative Science Quarterly, 44,* 764–791.

Ibarra, H. (2004). *Working identity: Unconventional strategies for reinventing your career.* Cambridge, MA: Harvard Business School Press.

Katz, D., & Kahn, R. L. (1966). *The social psychology of organizations.* New York: John Wiley & Sons.

Kram, K. E. (1985). *Mentoring at work: Developmental relationships in organizational life.* Glenview, IL: Scott, Foresman.

Kram, K. E. (1996). A relational approach to career development. In D. Hall & Associates (Eds.), *The career is dead—Long live the career: A relational approach to careers* (pp. 132–157). San Francisco: Jossey-Bass.

Kram, K. E., & Isabella, L. A. (1985). Mentoring alternatives: The role of peer relationships in career development. *Academy of Management Journal, 28,* 110–132.

Lankau, M. J., & Scandura, T. A. (2002). An investigation of personal learning in mentoring relationships: Content, antecedents, and consequences. *Academy of Management Journal, 45,* 779–790.

Levinson, D. J. (with Darrow, D., Klein, E. B., Levinson, M., & McKee., B.) (1978). *Seasons of a man's life.* New York: Knopf.

Levinson, D. J. (with Levinson, J.). (1996). *Seasons of a woman's life.* New York: Knopf.

Locke, E. A., Shaw, K. M., Saari, L. M., & Latham, G. P. (1981). Goal setting and task performance: 1969–1980. *Psychological Bulletin, 90,* 125–152.

Louis, M. R. (1980). Surprise and sense making: What newcomers experience in entering unfamiliar organizational settings. *Administrative Science Quarterly, 25,* 226–251.

Major, D. A, Kozloski, S. W. J, Chao, G. T., & Gardner, P. D. (1995). A longitudinal investigation of newcomer expectations, early socialization outcomes, and the moderating effects of role development factors. *Journal of Applied Psychology, 80,* 418–431.

Mezias, J. M., & Scandura, T. A. (2005). A needs-driven approach to expatriate adjustment and career development: A multiple mentoring perspective. *Journal of International Business Studies, 36,* 519–538.

Mintz, R. J. (2003). *The scripts we live by: How individuation, proteanism, and narrative disruption relate to personal transformation and renewal.* Unpublished doctoral dissertation, Fielding Graduate Institute, Santa Barbara, CA.

Molloy, J. C. (2005). Developmental networks: Literature review and future research [Special Issue on Mentoring]. *Career Development International, 10,* 536–547.

Morrison, E. W. (1993). Newcomer information seeking: Exploring types, modes, sources, and outcomes. *Academy of Management Journal, 36,* 557–589.

Morrison, R. F., & Hall, D. T. (2002). Career adaptability. In D. T. Hall (Ed.), *Careers in and out of organizations* (pp. 205–233). Thousand Oaks, CA: Sage.

Nicholson, N. (1984). A theory of work role transitions. *Administrative Science Quarterly, 29,* 172–191.

Nicholson, N. (1987). The transition cycle: A conceptual framework for the analysis of change and human resource management. In J. Ferris & K. M. Rowland (Eds.), *Personal and human resources management* (Vol. 5, pp. 167–222). Greenwich, CT: JAI Press.

Nicholson, N., & De Waal Andrews, W. (2005). Playing to win: Biological imperatives, self-regulation and trade-offs in the game of career success. *Journal of Organizational Behavior, 26,* 137–154.

Parry, D. (2002). *Essene book of days.* Bainbridge Island, WA: Earthstewards Networks.

Ragins, B. R. (1997). Diversified mentoring relationships in organizations: A power perspective. *Academy of Management Review, 22,* 482–521.

Scandura, T. A. (1998). Dysfunctional mentoring relationships and outcomes. *Journal of Management, 24,* 449–467.

Super, D. (1957). *The psychology of careers.* New York: Harper & Row.

Thomas, D. A. (1990). The impact of race on managers' experiences of developmental relationships (mentoring and sponsorship): An intra-organizational study. *Journal of Organizational Behavior, 2,* 479–492.

Vaillant, G. E. (1977). *Adaptation to life.* Cambridge, MA: Harvard University Press.

Van Maanen, J., & Schein, E. H. (1979). Toward a theory of organizational socialization. In B. M. Staw (Ed.), *Research in organizational behavior* (Vol. 1, pp. 209–264). Greenwich, CT: JAI Press.

Wanous, J. P. (1992). *Organizational entry: Recruitment, selection, orientation, and socialization of newcomers* (2nd ed.). Reading, MA: Addison-Wesley.

Zikic, J., & Hall, D. T. (2006). *Triggers of career exploration.* Unpublished working paper, University of Toronto.

20

Mentoring Enactment Theory

Describing, Explaining, and Predicting Communication in Mentoring Relationships

Pamela J. Kalbfleisch

Mentoring enactment theory (Kalbfleisch, 2002) emerges from the study of communication and personal relationships. The theory proposes proactive communicative strategies that can be used by mentors and by protégés to initiate, develop, maintain, and repair mentoring relationships. The theory is axiomatically composed of a series of base propositions regarding predictions of when communication strategies will be used and by whom. The theory is informed by mentoring research and by personal relationship research. It is proactive in that it proposes communicative strategies to facilitate the development, maintenance, and repair of high-quality mentoring relationships.

At the center of this theory is the postulation that mentoring relationships are close personal relationships. *Personal relationships* are those in which neither partner can be substituted from the relationship without significantly altering the nature of the relationship (Duck, Lock, McCall, Fitzpatrick, & Cayne, 1984). In other words, in this framework, mentoring relationships are considered unique, close relationships. In the mentoring literature, these would be classified as *high-quality relationships* (see Fletcher & Ragins, Chapter 15, this volume) and would be likely to be informal mentoring relationships rather than formally assigned pairings. However, explanation and prediction of behavior in high-quality formal mentoring relationships is not precluded by this theory. The important discriminator for a mentoring relationship as a personal relationship is that one could not have a different mentor or protégé and have the relationship be the same. Each member is not replaceable without altering the relationship.

Because mentoring relationships are unique and are personal in nature, they have many of the strengths and weaknesses of other personal relationships, such as love relationships, friendships, and family relationships. They also have unique challenges in that the partners are generally not considered to be equals with equal power. One partner, the mentor, generally has more resources, knowledge, and power, than the other partner, the protégé. Mentoring enactment theory defines a *mentor* as "more sophisticated" and having "achieved personal or professional success and is willing and able to share covert and overt practices that have assisted him or her in becoming successful" (Kalbfleisch, 2002, p. 63). The protégé is defined as "less advanced" and with "the potential or desire to learn the methods used by the mentor in becoming personally or professionally successful" (Kalbfleisch, 2002, p. 63). Furthermore, "Protégés receive guidance from their mentors and may in turn support them as their knowledge grows and the mentoring relationship develops" (Kalbfleisch & Davies, 1993, p. 63). And, "Together, the mentor and protégé form a relationship of care and assistance," a mentoring relationship (Kalbfleisch, 2002, p. 63). As with other personal relationships, these partners initiate their relationships, build trust, work on tasks, provide social support, and engage in relational maintenance and repair. These relational characteristics are all carried out by strategic and routine communication between the partners.

Predictions regarding who will enter mentoring relationships and how these relationships will develop are tempered by the perspective that mentoring relationships are being enacted by two participants. These participants may have predilections to assist others or to be assisted (cf. Allen, Chapter 5, this volume; Kalbfleisch & Davies, 1993) and have personality or demographic characteristics that will increase their likelihood of mentoring or being mentored (cf. Dreher & Cox, 1996; Kalbfleisch, 2000; Kalbfleisch & Davies, 1991; Ragins, 1989, 1997; Ragins & Cotton, 1999; Turban & Lee, Chapter 2, this volume) and the emotional intelligence to successfully engage in a mentoring relationship (see Cherniss, Chapter 17, this volume). However, a central notion in mentoring enactment theory is that the participants in a mentoring relationship are active participants in developing, maintaining, and repairing their relationships. This participation is done through strategic and routine communication. Relationship variables affect and interact with these communication strategies, and routines are used to actively forge these relationships.

Early development of this theoretical perspective is expressed in Kalbfleisch and Davies's (1993) interpersonal model of mentoring relationships and in Kalbfleisch and Keyton's (1995) model of the characteristics of mentoring relationships. These models used the relational, interpersonal, and communication literature to add new relational and communicative perspective to the mentoring literature as developed by Kram (1985), Ragins (1989), and other researchers breaking ground in the study of mentoring. The model is further developed through examination of verbal communication strategies Kalbfleisch (1997, 2004) and Kalbfleisch and Eckley (2003).

Mentoring enactment theory does not use a stage model of mentoring relationships (Kram, 1985) or a stage model of interpersonal relationships (Knapp, 1978), but rather an enactment perspective on relationships in which these relationships are continually evolving through communication. From this perspective, the relational maintenance and repair messages keep these relationships viable. The relational partners move forward, backward, fall apart, or come together, or the partners move on. This would be more similar to a less linear perspective of personal relationship development as expressed by Duck (1994).

Mentoring enactment theory is most concerned with initiating, maintaining, and repairing relationships and the use of routine and strategic communication to accomplish these tasks. These relational tasks would be considered among the conversational goals of the mentor and protégé, in addition to other goals of the mentoring relationship, such as building competence, assisting with tasks, and social support. From this theoretical lens, mentoring relationships, as with other personal relationships, may develop quickly or may develop over time, with many bumps in the road. They may last for a lifetime or only a short period of time. Optimally, these relationships bring quality to both the mentors' and the protégés' lives, and both benefit from this connection with another human being (Kalbfleisch & Davies, 1993).

This model expressed in Figure 20.1 gives an overview of mentoring relationships from the perspective of mentoring enactment theory.

While most readers of this volume are aware of the seminal work of Kram (1985) as well as the work of Ragins (1989) and others working toward understanding mentoring, readers may not be as aware of the communication and relational literature. The initial propositions of mentoring enactment theory, which predict the communicative strategies and conversational goals that can influence the development of mentoring relationships, provide a communication perspective on the mentoring research that has been published and read by many readers of this

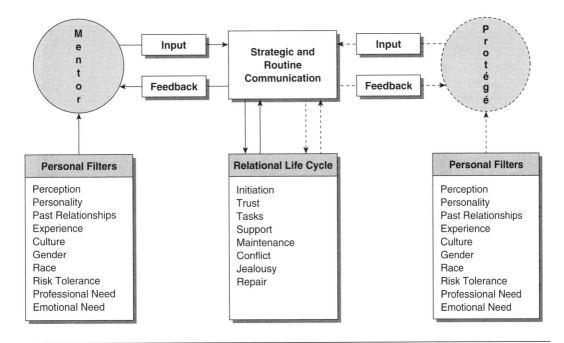

Figure 20.1   Illustration of Mentoring Enactment Theory From the Perspective of Mentor and Protégé

volume. The later propositions of mentoring enactment theory concerning relational maintenance and repair may provide an even more unique perspective that readers may appreciate and be able to use in their research. The contribution of communication and relationship scholars to the study of mentoring relationships and mentoring enactment theory should provide a heuristic tool and model for future development in mentoring theory and research. Other chapters in this volume also add perspective to mentoring enactment theory in terms of studying mentoring as a relationship (see Eby, Chapter 13, this volume; Fletcher & Ragins, Chapter 15, this volume; also see Ragins & Verbos, 2007) and the messages in mentoring relationships (see Ensher & Murphy, Chapter 12, this volume).

Now that an overview of mentoring enactment theory has been addressed, this chapter will articulate in greater depth the nature of a communication perspective, which is central to the theory as well as the nature of personal relationships, and a relational perspective, which is also central to mentoring enactment theory. The propositions of the theory will be presented, as well as descriptions of some of the research that led to these propositions. Additional suggestions are made regarding further applications of this theoretical perspective and the study of mentoring from this perspective.

Communication Perspective

Communication is used to strategically achieve desired outcomes in life. Using symbols such as verbal language and nonverbal cues, a communicator attempts to influence others to achieve desired ends. When two communicators interact, several strategies can come into play as verbal and nonverbal language is used to achieve desired ends. Neither receiver is passive; rather, each one is receiving and interpreting the messages sent by the communicative partner. Add additional communicators, and it becomes exponentially more complex.

Communicators use messages to strategically accomplish multiple goals, such as influencing others (Wilson, 2002) and achieving clarity in conversation (Kim, 1994). A multitude of messages and intentions of senders and receivers make up communication in private discourse as well as in the public sphere. It is precisely this message exchange that is of interest to communication scholars, be it individuals communicating with strangers or friends, in families or work groups, face-to-face, on the phone, via the Internet, or in public broadcast, blogs, speeches, or interviews. Verbal, nonverbal, written, and spoken, the interaction of human beings is central to the study of communication behavior.

Scholars studying communication may consider how people exchange messages via new technology, such as text messages and cell phones, or more traditional technology, such as television and radio. They could study a particular context for communication, for example, among health care professionals or in other work environments. Communication scholars could also examine messages exchanged between members of differing cultures, ethnic, and social groups or those occupying differing life perspectives and ages.

Communication between mentors and protégés is a particularly intriguing context for scholars working from a communication perspective. For example, in a communication study of hospital nurses, Kalbfleisch and Bach (1998) found that nurse protégés noted that their nurse mentors were supportive by encouraging them to do their best, providing support and encouragement when others criticized, and helping them deal with jealousy from other nurses. These protégés admired their mentors when they stood up to people who were treating them unfairly, such as doctors, patients, and administration. In some cases, protégés described their mentors as heroes. Heroes!

One gains perspective on the notion of a mentor who could be described as a "hero" when considering the context of a relationship between two human beings who care about each other. Placed in the context of personal relationships, the communication between mentors and protégés gains further depth and clarity. The progressive development of communication research such as Kalbfleisch (1997, 2000, 2004), Kalbfleisch and Anderson (1997), Kalbfleisch and Davies (1991, 1993), Kalbfleisch and Eckley (2003), and Kalbfleisch & Keyton (1995) as well as the development of mentoring enactment theory (Kalbfleisch, 2002) derives from the perspective of mentoring as a close personal relationship. This relational perspective combines with a communication focus to give character to this research and theoretical development.

The relational perspective is considered in the following section, particularly as it relates to the relationship between mentors and protégés.

Relationship Perspective

Interdisciplinary scholars studying personal relationships may study concepts such as attraction, attachment, trust, jealousy, envy, conflict, and play behavior, as well as relational development, maintenance, repair, and dissolution. Concepts such as these are studied in friendships, love relationships, and family relationships. The theoretical central concept is that these relationships must be unique to the participants and not replaceable (Duck et al., 1984).

Communication scholars are particularly interested in studying these close relationships through communication that accompanies these relational concepts or additional relationship concepts as they relate to these close relationships. From this work, we come to know how friendships are developed, the characteristics of love relationships, conflict-producing events, and how we communicate with those we care about and with whom we wish to maintain relationships.

In their state-of-the art review of the mentoring research, Wanberg, Welsh, and Hezlett (2003) stated that "despite differences between models and typologies of developmental relationships, it is generally agreed that mentoring is the most intense and powerful one-on-one developmental relationship, entailing the most influence, identification, and emotional involvement" (p. 41). The mentoring relationships encompassed by the theory of mentoring enactment are indeed powerful relationships. Through focusing most closely on those irreplaceable, unique personal relationships between mentors and protégés, numerous relational variables are considered, such as attraction, trust, conflict jealousy, and support. With theoretical input from the study of routine and strategic communication (e.g., Canary & Stafford, 1992; 1993; Duck, 1988, 1994; Kim, 1994; Stafford, 2005; Wilson, 2002), scholars examining message strategies, conversational goals, and plans can study how communicators initiate, maintain, and repair mentoring relationships.

This opens a rich perspective for the study of mentors and protégés engaged in these unique human relationships. The communication perspective adds the vehicle for these relational members to interact and to enact their mentoring relationships and play out relational challenges and opportunities through communication with one another.

Relationship Initiation and Development

There are two aspects to mentoring enactment theory. The first aspect concerns initiation of mentoring relationships. The propositions in this part of the theory are concerned with the types of communicative requests made to potential mentors and protégés that will be met with acceptance by the proposed relational partner.

The second aspect of mentoring enactment theory concerns communication in ongoing mentoring relationships. The propositions concerning this aspect of the theory focus on relational maintenance and repair and the communicative and relational events and outcomes that occur in these ongoing relationships.

The initiation of mentoring relationships has been considered in detail in the mentoring literature, especially in terms of the factors that lead mentors and protégés into mentoring relationships and the likelihood of becoming a mentor or protégé. The first aspect of this theory lends a theoretical lens that considers these elements from a communication perspective that may lead to successful initiation of mentoring relationships.

The publication of hundreds of popular press articles and scholarly research articles on the topic of mentoring has saturated the market in terms of a common understanding that a mentor can help a protégé succeed with professional and personal goals. Many people new to organizations and other professional and personal endeavors look to mentors to help them achieve success.

The challenge comes in finding a mentor to help—there are many more protégés than mentors, and attracting a mentor may not be easy. Protégés have encountered rejection when trying to follow the advice to directly ask others to be their mentors. While mentoring relationships can form through direct requests to mentor and mentors also select protégés for mentoring, the issue of protégés encountering rejection to their mentoring requests remains. The first proposition of the mentoring enactment theory addresses this communicative problem:

Proposition 1: Generally, requests to a more advanced other to be a mentor to the requestor are likely to be rejected in initial interactions between the advanced other and the requestor (Kalbfleisch, 2002, p. 66).

When examined from a relational perspective, this proposition can be clarified. In their work with people who perceive risk in being close to others in relationships such as friendships and love relationships, Pilkington and Richardson (1988) found that a person's perceived risk in intimacy is directly related to avoiding personal relationships with others. If a mentoring relationship is a personal relationship, then it would hold that as a relationship, it will have risks associated with becoming close to another person. In addition to general risks in close relationships, such as issues of trust, there are also professional risks that the mentor must consider when deciding to help a potential protégé. In examining the characteristics of who was likely or unlikely to mentor, Kalbfleisch and Davies (1993) found that potential mentors who perceive risk in being close to others will be less likely to mentor than those who perceive less risk.

Verbal requests to be a mentor may also symbolize a much deeper relational commitment than a potential mentor is willing to commit to early in a relationship. It would be analogous to a first-date marriage proposal that negates any chance of a second date. Generally, people enter into personal relationships gradually, with initial acquaintance, getting to know each other, engaging in activities together, and so on. Typically, people do not approach each other with offers of friendship or love. Asking someone to be a mentor in an initial interaction or early in a relationships may be relationally equivalent to saying "Will you be my best friend?" in a friendship or saying "I love you" too soon in a budding romance (Kalbfleisch, 2002, 2004). While sometimes, these approaches may be met with positive responses (instant friendships and whirlwind romances do exist), the likelihood of the development of a best friendship or a love relationship is more likely to occur over time (Bullis, Clark, & Sline, 1993; Kalbfleisch, 1993).

The second proposition in this theory provides some hope for a communicative strategy that may be more helpful than a direct request for mentoring. This proposition is based on the idea that a request for mentoring may be too much, too soon in a relationship. A less abrupt beginning to a mentoring relationship may be a simple request for help on a task. This provides a tangible form of assistance for the person making the request and is a way for the potential mentor to at least offer some form of help to the requestor. It is less likely that a potential mentor would say "no" to a simple form of request that has minimal relational overtones. Such a request may allow a relationship to begin more slowly, without the relational risk associated with a direct request to mentor.

Proposition 2: Generally, requests to a more advanced other to be a mentor to the requestor are more likely to be rejected than are requests for help on a specific task made by the same requestor (Kalbfleisch, 2002, p. 66).

Obviously, there is a next step that must be taken once a request for help has been granted. This could be a series of requests by the protégé or offers to help the mentor. A subproposition that can also be advanced is that the protégé could offer to help the mentor:

Proposition 2a: Generally, requests to a more advanced other to be a mentor to the requestor are more likely to be rejected than are offers to help with a specific task made by the same requestor.

A potential protégé's offer to help a more advanced other or request for help on some specific task is a rhetorical strategy for initiating a relationship that may be less threatening than a direct request for relationship commitment. In addition, an important aspect of the request to help is that the process of helping allows the potential mentor and potential protégé to have a context for relational development and conversation.

The potential rejection and relationship consequences of a direct mentoring request should not be overlooked when considering conversational development and relationship initiation in mentoring relationships. It may be that a third party can help facilitate relational initiation between mentors and protégés. In a 2004 study of Asian and Pacific Islander groups in Hawaii, Kalbfleisch found that some protégés reported that their parents had arranged for others to mentor them. This is a very personalized version of a third party arranging for a mentoring relationship. It may be that using other personal relationships to assist in finding a mentor for a protégé may facilitate mentoring relationships in new ways. Being a part of a personal network, such as a friend of a family, will enhance the opportunity for these relationships to become high-quality mentoring relationships. This would be a good use of a constellation of existing mentors and social support networks to develop additional relationships.

Proposition 3: Requests made to a more advanced other to be a mentor to the requestor will be more likely to be accepted when the advanced other previously has agreed with a third party to serve as a mentor in a relationship. (Kalbfleisch, 2002, p. 66)

An example of encouraging protégés to use requests for help with contacts made through a third party can be seen in Kalbfleisch and Eckley's (2003) electronic pairing of students interested in being mentors and protégés and monitoring their communication exchanges and conversational responses to communication directives prompted at differing intervals in their electronic conversations. Japanese referents of *Onshi* (mentor) and *Kogai* (protégé) were used in an effort to lessen the onus of being a mentor or a protégé and also in an effort to protect the anonymity of the electronic research participants. Requests for help and suggested conversational questions were built into the study design to assist these Onshi and Kogai pairs in relational development and conversational exchanges. Through monitoring message exchange, the researchers determined that these relationships were all able to at least begin initial relational development.

The next two propositions of mentoring enactment theory address relationship initiation by the mentor. There are potential mentors who look for promising protégés with whom to form mentoring relationships (see Allen, Chapter 5, this volume). Because there are fewer mentors inviting protégés to begin relationships than there are protégés asking for mentors, it is likely that the mentors' invitations will be successful. While there will always be potential protégés who want to go it on their own, want to work with other mentors, or are simply not interested in forming a relationship with the potential mentor, it is likely that there will be protégés who are interested in these offers of mentorship.

Proposition 4: Offers made to a less advanced other to be a protégé are likely to be accepted (Kalbfleisch, 2002, p. 66).

As with requests to help the mentor versus requests for mentoring on the part of the protégé, offers by the mentor to help will be likely to be accepted by the potential protégé. It may be that a potential protégé concerned with relational involvement with a particular potential mentor would be more willing to begin a relationship by being helped by the mentor, rather than beginning a relationship as an identified protégé and the relational characteristics that this label may imply.

Proposition 5: Offers of help made to a less advanced other are likely to be accepted (Kalbfleisch, 2002, p. 66).

These last two propositions are probabilistic statements and not deterministic statements, because with all the factors in a potential protégé's life, it is possible that help may not be needed, wanted, or desired. The likelihood, however, is that potential mentors will be successful in finding protégés who want or need their assistance.

The first five propositions of mentoring enactment theory are concerned with the initiation of mentoring relationships, because as a source of social support and career advancement, having a mentor can be so helpful. It is also the case that finding mentors can be a challenge, particularly if the protégé is not someone who would stand out and naturally attract a mentor's attention.

Kalbfleisch and Davies (1993) found that respondents who were communicatively competent and had high self-esteem were more likely to have mentors. Communicatively competent individuals are able to accomplish their goals using different and appropriate communicative abilities. The first propositions in mentoring enactment theory focus on using communication skills and third-party facilitators to successfully to get involved in a mentoring relationship.

Those with higher self-esteem may be more likely to be selected by mentors to be protégés, or they may have the confidence to seek out mentors, a process that may take several attempts to be successful. The propositions in this theory put forward a path that may be successful to this population and to others in finding mentors. Respondents in Kalbfleisch (2004) confirmed that they had asked for help as one way they developed relationships with their mentors. Clearly, these communicative strategies and others can be examined as potential paths to the development of mentoring relationships.

Renger, Kalbfleisch, Smolak, and Crago (1999) recommended targeting youth with low self-esteem for mentoring programs because they may have particular problems finding mentors. However, not everyone desiring a mentor can be part of a formal mentoring program, and membership in such a program does not guarantee that a mentoring relationship will grow and develop. Using mentoring enactment theory to guide hypothesis development may assist in developing knowledge regarding how protégés and mentors can use their own self-efficacy, communication skills, and personal networks to establish mentoring relationships.

When considering the initiation and development of a mentoring relationship, the personal filters of each mentor and protégé must be considered as influencing the communication strategies that are used by each relational partner to initiate and develop the relationship. Risk tolerance and emotional needs should be considered with professional needs and may alter the communication strategies employed. Past relationships, personality, perception, experience, culture, gender, and race may also influence communication strategies selected for enacting a mentoring relationship.

Relationship Maintenance and Repair

The second aspect of mentoring enactment theory is the description, explanation, and prediction of the communication used for relational maintenance and repair. For high-quality mentoring relationships to stay together, the mentor and protégé must direct communication toward one another just as in other personal relationships. This can be intentional communication directed toward maintaining and repairing the relationship. It can also be routine communication that is a part of general discourse that continues contact between the mentor and protégé.

There is more involved in the care and feeding of a mentoring relationship than simply finding a partner and initiating a relationship. Just as in other human relationships, things do not always go so smoothly. Living happily ever after is not a reasonable expectation in mentoring relationships any more than it is an expectation in any relationship.

Mentors and protégés are human beings engaged in human relationships. As humans in relationships, they will laugh and have fun and fight and cry. "Human beings engaged in a personal relationship become jealous, compete, cooperate, learn, become bored, have conflict, and forgive" (Kalbfleisch, 2002, p. 67). Given this, we can expect that all will not go smoothly without some effort and effective use of communication focused toward relational maintenance and repair.

Mentoring enactment theory provides a framework for examining these relational challenges and rewards, as well as considering the communicative messages between mentors and protégés that enact these challenges and rewards and the communication designed to maintain and repair these relationships. This approach considers quality mentoring relationships to be personal relationships in which both partners are engaged and are communicatively enacting in a relationship with characteristics, challenges, and joys, as in other relationships.

This enactment framework considers both mentors and protégés as valuing the relationship as a personal relationship and investing time, energy, and commitment to it. Relational challenges can be met with communicative strategies to maintain and repair a relationship. Relationship maintenance can be composed of routine communication strategies or strategies focused on repair or response to challenge. Duck (1988) described relationships as staying together unless something pulls them apart and as deteriorating unless efforts are made to keep them viable. In other words, challenges will occur that could ruin relationships, and relationships will not continue unless efforts are made by the participants. Examples of message strategies that can be used to overcome relationship challenges or maintain and repair relationships are discussed in the next three sections.

Challenges in Mentoring Relationships

Relational challenges in mentoring relationships and the communicative messages used in navigating these challenges and engaging in relational repair are illustrated in a series of three studies examining conflict events in mentoring relationships, as reported in Kalbfleisch (1997). This example also articulates some of the research methods that can be used to study the communicative enactment of a mentoring relationship. In the first study, participants identifying themselves as protégés in mentoring relationships were asked to keep their mentors in mind when answering three open-ended questions. They were asked "if (1) their mentor ever said anything that they felt was hurtful in nature, (2) their mentor was ever angry with them, and (3) they ever had a conflict with their mentor" (p. 393). In their responses, protégés described conflict events and their responses to these events. These open-ended responses from the first group of research participants where then placed into a questionnaire, with Likert responses gauging the likelihood of experiencing these messages from a mentor and using these messages in response to a conflict event in a mentoring relationship. A second set of protégés responded to these questionnaires. These responses became the stimuli for a third study, which included research participants identifying themselves as mentors in mentoring relationships. The mentors were asked to review the conflict events identified by the protégés and the protégés' responses to these events. They were asked to consider these responses as coming from their own protégés. On a questionnaire with Likert measures, mentors were then asked "the degree to which they would forgive their protégé, gain respect for their protégé, have increased esteem for their protégé, be less angry with their protégé, and the degree to which they thought conflict would be reduced" (Kalbfleisch, 1997, p. 394).

The conflict events identified by the protégés were reduced to four factors, labeled (1) *Disagreements,* with messages such as "My mentor has told me he/she does not like my ideas," and "My mentor has told me that I am not being realistic"; (2) *Embarrassment,* such as "My mentor has told me I am a disappointment"; (3) *Negativity,* such as "My mentor has told me I was not honest"; and (4) *Request,* "My mentor has asked me to help him or her with projects." This last category, that the mentor requests that the protégé help with projects, is the most frequently cited conflict-producing event by protégés.

Responses from the protégés to these events formed three factors, labeled (1) *Provocative/Distancing,* with messages indicating protégés had argued with their mentors, yelled at their mentors, and were avoidant of their mentors; (2) *Affable Appeasement,* with messages indicating protégés had complimented and praised their mentors and tried to become closer to them through gifts and favors; and (3) *Pragmatic Appeasement,* with messages of trying to do a better job, working harder, admitting wrongdoing, and vowing to not to make the same mistakes again.

From the mentors' perspectives, the protégé responses to the conflict events with the greatest likelihood of promoting reconciliation were the Pragmatic Appeasement repair strategies. For these protégé repair strategies, mentors had the highest ratings for forgiveness, respect, esteem, anger reduction, and conflict reduction. Lowest reconciliation from the mentors' perspectives was in response to the Provocative/Distancing protégé response strategies.

Face-threatening conflict events such as embarrassment and negativity were the most likely to engender provocative/distancing responses. Male protégés were more likely to see more mentor messages as conflict producing and respond by arguing with their mentors. Males were also more likely to report making sacrifices for their mentors and complying with their mentors' wishes.

Eby (Chapter 13, this volume) describes additional problems and challenges in mentoring relationships. Message strategies could also be used to overcome these challenges if the relational partners wish to keep their relationship viable in light of the problems faced.

Maintaining Relationships

Relational maintenance can be facilitated through a variety of communication strategies. Several communication researchers' work can provide guidance for theoretical testing of these propositions. For example, Canary and Stafford (1993; Stafford, 2005; Stafford & Canary, 1991) and their associates have tested and developed a robust set of communication strategies focused on relational maintenance. The communication strategies tested by Canary and Stafford and associates have been found as characteristic of communication patterns in friendships and love relationships that also have strong relational quality. These strategies include message strategies designed to maintain relational cohesion, such as messages of assurances stressing commitment and future relationships, and sending positive messages to relational partners and trying to make interactions enjoyable. Other strategies for maintaining relationships include sharing tasks, including the relationship partner in networks, and openness in communication.

Other researchers have also developed strategies for maintaining and repairing relationships, such as talking with a partner about the relationship, participating in ceremonies, and using verbal messages conveying positive messages to relationship partners (Dindia & Baxter, 1987). Additional messages strategies, such as those enacting psychosocial functions as described by Kram (1985), can be used to maintain mentoring relationships.

While some mentors and protégés may have studied or successfully practiced strategic communication and relational maintenance, many relational partners are simply using the routine strategic communication they have used to communicate in other life relationships, such as friendships, love relationships, family relationships, and work relationships. The strategies used may depend on the mentors' or protégés' personal filters, such as perceptions of the situation, past relationship experiences, culture, gender, and professional and emotional needs, among other characteristics.

Relationship Repair

The communicative strategies reviewed as examples of strategic and routine communication used during challenges in relationships and to enact relationship maintenance can also be used as communication strategies to repair relationships. Additional examples of message strategies used in repairing relationships include acknowledging and apologizing for harm (Metts, 1994), as well as offering explanations and accounts and pledging compliance with relationship conditions and rule-related communication relating to these pledges (Kelly & Waldron, 2005).

Propositions

The last four propositions of mentoring enactment theory focus on the participants in mentoring relationships using conversational goals and communication strategies to build strong relationships. The theoretical assumption behind these propositions is that without the participants focusing at least some communication on the relationship itself, it is unlikely that these relationships will thrive and ultimately be effective in helping the protégé succeed.

One important defining characteristics of mentoring relationships is that power is not shared equally, as the mentor is by definition more advanced than the protégé and there are generally fewer relational partners available and willing to mentor than to be protégés. The degree to which the mentor is tied to the professional and personal goals of the protégé and the relative scarcity of mentors will affect the communication the mentor and protégé use to enact their relationship in distinctive ways. Also acknowledged is that both partners bring personality, demographic, and other characteristics to the relationship, as well as experience with past relationships and the differential abilities to enact their relationships, such as communicative competence and emotional intelligence.

Because there are more protégés than mentors and mentors may be directly linked to protégés' professional and personal goals, these propositions place more of the communicative effort toward keeping the relationships going on the protégé than on the mentor.

Proposition 6: Protégés will be more likely than mentors to direct their conversational goals and communication strategies toward initiating, maintaining, and repairing their mentoring relationships.

Proposition 7: The closer a mentor is linked to a protégé's career success, the greater the protégé's communicative attempts to initiate, maintain, and repair a mentoring relationship (Kalbfleisch, 2002, p. 67).

Relational initiation is mentioned again in these two propositions in the theory because without becoming a part of a mentoring relationship, everything else is moot. It makes sense to consider additional conversational goals and strategies for developing mentoring relationships, as well as those in the initial propositions.

The next proposition focuses on the sex of the protégé. Just as the earlier propositions have placed more of the onus and strategy of relational development on the protégé because mentors are in greater demand than protégés, this proposition focuses on the sex of the protégé. While some mentoring research has found that more males than females have mentors, other research has not shown these findings (Kalbfleisch, 2000; Ragins, 1989, 1997; Ragins & Cotton, 1999). When considering personal characteristics or filters and the use of strategic communication to maintain relationships, studies such as Dainton and Stafford (1993) have found females to be more likely than males to use maintenance strategies in personal relationships. While these communicative differences may also be due to sex role orientation (Stafford, 2003), sex differences in mentoring and in strategic communication provide some indication that biological sex may differentially influence strategies used.

Proposition 8: Female protégés will be more likely than male protégés to direct their conversational goals and communication strategies toward initiating, maintaining, and repairing their relationship with their mentor (Kalbfleisch, 2002, p. 68).

The final proposition of mentoring enactment theory focuses on the mentors and the investment they may have in the success of their protégés and in keeping the mentoring relationship intact and well functioning from a communication and relational perspective.

Undoubtedly, mentors can be strongly vested in the success of their protégés and in their relationships with them. Human relationships take time and investment. The more invested one becomes in the success of a relational partner and a relationship, the more likely one will be to expend efforts toward maintaining the relationship and repairing it should problems arise. Less investment would suggest lower effort at maintaining such a relationship, particularly if a partner has less to gain from the relationship. It follows that the same would hold for mentoring relationships.

Proposition 9: Mentors will be more likely to direct their conversational goals and communication strategies toward maintaining and repairing their relationship when invested in the mentoring relationship (Kalbfleisch, 2002, p. 68).

Given that mentors and protégés can become like members of a family and that mentoring relationships develop over time and perhaps evolve into long-standing friendships or other life relationships, it makes sense that the efforts expended in these relationships will not all be expended by the protégé. Mentors can be proud of their protégés and feel that their protégés' success reflects well on them as well as the protégés. In a relationship, mentors would be expected to work to enhance the relationship if they were invested in seeing the relationship and protégé succeed and develop for the future.

Mentoring enactment theory focuses on how protégés and mentors can facilitate the initiation, maintenance, and repair of mentoring relationships. Such relations are not viewed as static entities or relationships that occur without at least some strategic development on the part of someone in the relationship or a third party to the relationship.

The theory does not conjecture about the trajectory or length of mentoring relationships or the ultimate success of these relationships in helping the protégé to accomplish personal and professional goals. However, what mentoring enactment theory does bring to the development of mentoring theory, research, and practice is a set of propositions for observing, understanding, and predicating the successful enactment of a mentoring relationship through the strategic use of communication to accomplish the goals and objectives of the mentor and protégé in having a successful relationship.

Without a relationship, there is no basis from which a mentor can help a protégé or a protégé can seek help from a mentor. The relationship is essential to the success of the protégé and mentor. It is one part of achieving personal and professional success that the mentor and protégé can use their communication and relational skills to accomplish.

Next Steps in Research

Mentoring enactment theory does not discount the other work of a mentoring relationship, such as building skills, learning finesse, and becoming successful personally and professionally. However, the context of having an ongoing relationship is necessary in order for a mentor to impart knowledge to a protégé and for this knowledge to have an opportunity to be developed. The premise of the theory is that the members of mentoring relationships can take an active part in their development. Part of relational development is keeping a relationship strong through attending to the relationship itself and not just the tasks and accomplishments of those within the relationship.

Propositions are presented in mentoring enactment theory that focus on using strategic and routine communication to initiate, maintain, and develop mentoring relationships. The model of the theory presented in Figure 20.1 suggests additional propositions that could be developed and areas for research.

Additional research is needed for examining personal filters as they influence strategic and routine communication used to enact relationship initiation, responses to relational events and issues, relational maintenance attempts, and relational repair. Biological sex differences as compared to the perceptions involved in gender role orientation would be a particularly informative area of study. There are numerous studies of sex differences in mentoring and communication strategy use, but researchers have yet to consider gender role orientation of the mentor and protégé and message strategy selection for relational outcomes.

The actual communication messages exchanged by mentors and protégés should also receive greater study. The robustness of some message strategies across personal relationship types, such as family, marriage, and friendship, suggests that mentors and protégés will also use these strategies to enact their relationships. Kalbfleisch has provided some study of these message strategies between mentors and protégées, and mentoring enactment theory provides the structure for greater exploration of these messages.

Nonverbal communication that is part of strategic and routine communication should also be considered in future research. This communication can amplify, modify, or negate the verbal strategies that are used by mentors and protégés communicating to develop or save relationships.

Series of message strategies and responses to message strategies should receive greater consideration, particularly as they impact the relational life cycle of a mentor's and protégés relationship. Because these relationships do not occur in a vacuum, consideration should be made of the effects of messages from others on how the mentor and protégé communicatively enact their relationship with each other in response to these messages.

Mentoring enactment theory does not preclude the development of mentoring relationships between larger groups of mentors and protégés. Personal relationships are defined by their uniqueness and that members of the relationship cannot be substituted without changing the relationship. Family relationships and friendship groups are examples of relationships that may be close personal relationships: unique and irreplaceable. In other words, personal relationships are defined by the characteristics of these relationships, not the size. More mentors and protégés could be a part of a close personal relationship, but at some point as size increases, it would not be possible for the group of mentors and protégés to maintain relationship closeness. Communication and energy go into these relationships. At the point when relationship partners can no longer sustain the mentoring relationship as a high-quality relationship, they become part of a larger support network more than a mentoring relationship. This larger-model adaptation would also be interesting research to develop, as researchers could study peer mentoring and larger constellations of mentors and protégés.

The context in which the mentoring relationship develops could be a fruitful area for study, as could the effects of the availability of other developmental and personal relationships that are not part of the mentoring relationship under consideration. These external elements are a part of the social milieu that future research can examine as far as how these elements may affect the communication between mentors and protégés and how they enact their relationships.

Communication in personal relationships and mentoring relationships has often been studied through self-report measures. This research provides us with a body of knowledge regarding what the mentors and protégés perceive their communication patterns and relationships to be like. This perceptual knowledge is valuable and can be helpful for future study. In studying mentoring relationships as well as studying other relationships, it is important that the researcher specify that the respondents consider a specific mentor, protégé, or relationship and consistently think about this person or relationship in answering research questions or reporting message strategies and reactions to the relationship partner and the context of the relationship.

Alternatives to studying mentors and protégés separately is reported in research such as Kalbfleisch and Keyton (1995), in their focuses on mentoring pairs and how the mentor and protégé responded about each other and the intimacy of the relationship. Measuring reactions of intact mentoring pairs to conflict events and reconciliation would be more informative, and researchers may be able to learn more about both mentor and protégé perspectives on the communication in the mentoring relationship and how the partners are actively enacting this relationship.

Mentors and their protégés could also be given diary logs to note the ongoing communication they are having with their partners. These logs record in a structured manner specified events, messages, and strategies, or they record perceptions in an open-ended fashion. These responses could be content analyzed for frequency and communication and events precipitating message production occurrence and outcomes.

These are several options for gathering data in addition to or instead of self-report information. To study actual message strategies exchanged between mentors and protégés, a Web-based study capturing ongoing interactions, such as Kalbfleisch and Eckley (2003), would allow researchers an opportunity to study what is actually being said, as opposed to what respondents reported saying.

Another setting for studying communication in intact mentoring relationships would be in an interaction laboratory, where messages and responses could be captured visually and through audio and analyzed for relational maintenance, repair, and routine communication occurring in the ongoing relationships. This could be accomplished using a structured coding system for messages and analyzing their sequences and responses. This would be a study design similar to those used by Fitzpatrick (1988) and Gottman (1979) in their studies of couples' communication. Coding schemes could be developed specifically for the study of interactions in mentoring relationships. Of interest would be the communication indicating relational maintenance and repair and how the partners work toward the communication goals of task accomplishment and success building in addition to communication goals of relational maintenance and repair.

In these laboratory studies, measures can also be taken prior to interactions for personality, demographics, and factors affecting the relational partners' abilities to communicate effectively in these relationships, such as communicative competence and emotional intelligence (Cherniss, Chapter 17, this volume), and these measures can be compared with actual communicative response of the mentoring pairs. Other individual difference variables, such as those identified by Turban and Lee (Chapter 2, this volume), can also be examined in greater depth using a laboratory environment and the opportunity for mentors and protégés to interact.

There are a large number of personal relationship issues that have not been explored in mentoring relationships, such as how relational partners communicatively respond to discovered deceit, jealousy, envy, and competition. How do mentors and protégés communicate play and joy? How do mentors respond to protégés who move on to a more powerful and influential mentor? How do protégés respond to mentors who have given up on them ever being successful or mentors who discourage them from becoming independent? All of these are questions that can be examined from the perspective of mentoring enactment theory. All are worthy questions for researchers to pursue and for future theorists to consider in structuring the development of mentoring theory.

The possibilities for study of mentoring relationships from the perspective of mentoring enactment theory are challenging and exciting. The challenges are similar in many ways to those of studying communication in other types of close relationships, and some experience with those other types can transfer to the study of mentoring relationships.

Mentoring enactment theory is a theory of how mentors and protégés interact in and enact the nature of their mentoring relationships. The theory is unique in that it gives both the mentor and the protégé the self-efficacy to become members of a mentoring relationship and to communicatively influence their relationship's development and growth. Communication can be empowering, and this empowerment can allow us to build a community of mentoring relationships for our future.

References

Bullis, C., Clark, C., & Sline, R. (1993). From passion to commitment: Turning points in romantic relationships. In P. J. Kalbfleisch (Ed.), *Interpersonal communication: Evolving interpersonal relationships* (pp. 213–236). Mahwah, NJ: Lawrence Erlbaum.

Canary, D. J., & Stafford, L. (1992). Relational maintenance strategies and equity in marriage. *Communication Monographs, 59,* 243–267.

Canary, D. J., & Stafford, L. (1993). Preservation of relational characteristics: Maintenance strategies, equity, and locus of control. In P. J. Kalbfleisch (Ed.), *Interpersonal communication: Evolving interpersonal relationships* (pp. 237–260). Mahwah, NJ: Lawrence Erlbaum.

Dainton, M., & Stafford, L. (1993). Routine maintenance behaviors: A comparison of relationship type, partner similarity, and sex differences. *Journal of Social and Personal Relationships, 10,* 255–272.

Dindia, K., & Baxter, L. (1987). Strategies for maintaining and repairing marital relationships. *Journal of Personal and Social Relationships, 4,* 143–158.

Dreher, G. F., & Cox, T. H, Jr. (1996). Race, gender, and opportunity: A study of compensation attainment and the establishment of mentoring relationships. *Journal of Applied Psychology, 81,* 297–308.

Duck, S. W. (1988). *Relating to others.* Chicago: Dorsey.

Duck, S. W. (1994). *Meaningful relationships: Talking, sense, and relating.* Thousand Oaks, CA: Sage.

Duck, S. W., Lock, A., McCall, G., Fitzpatrick, M. A., & Cayne, J. C. (1984). Social and personal relationships: A joint editorial. *Journal of Social and Personal Relationships, 1,* 1–10.

Fitzpatrick, M. A. (1988). *Between husband and wives: Communication in marriage.* Newbury Park, CA: Sage.

Gottman, J. M. (1979). *Marital interaction: Investigations.* New York: Academic Press.

Kalbfleisch, P. J. (1993). Public portrayals of enduring friendships. In P. J. Kalbfleisch (Ed.), *Interpersonal communication: Evolving interpersonal relationships* (pp. 189–212). Mahwah, NJ: Lawrence Erlbaum.

Kalbfleisch, P. J. (1997). Appeasing the mentor. *Aggressive Behavior, 23,* 289–403.

Kalbfleisch, P. J. (2000). Similarity and attraction in business and academic environments: Same and cross-sex mentoring relationships. *Review of Business, 21*(1), 58–61.

Kalbfleisch, P. J. (2002). Communication in mentoring relationships: A theory for enactment. *Communication Theory, 12,* 63–69.

Kalbfleisch, P. J. (2004). Will you be my mentor? In S. H. Ng, C. N. Candlin, & C.Y. Chiu (Eds.), *Language matters: Communication, culture, and identity* (pp. 375–382). Hong Kong: City University of Hong Kong Press.

Kalbfleisch, P. J., & Anderson, A. (1997). Mentoring across generations: Culture, family, and mentoring relationships. In H. Noor al-Deen (Ed.), *Cross-cultural communication and aging in America* (pp. 97–120). Mahwah, NJ: Lawrence Erlbaum.

Kalbfleisch, P. J., & Bach, B. W. (1998). The language of mentoring in a health care environment. *Health Communication, 10,* 373–392.

Kalbfleisch, P. J., & Davies, A. B. (1991). Minorities and mentoring: Managing the multicultural institution. *Communication Education, 40,* 266–271.

Kalbfleisch, P. J., & Davies, A. B. (1993). An interpersonal model for participation in mentoring relationships. *Western Journal of Communication, 57,* 399–415.

Kalbfleisch, P. J., & Eckley, V. K. (2003). Facilitating mentoring relationships: The case for new technology. *Informing Science,* 1581–1590.

Kalbfleisch, P. J., & Keyton, J. (1995). Power and equality in mentoring relationships. In P. J. Kalbfleisch & M. J. Cody (Eds.), *Gender, power, and communication in human relationships* (pp. 189–212). Mahwah, NJ: Lawrence Erlbaum.

Kelly, D. L., & Waldron, V. R. (2005). An investigation of forgiveness-seeking communication and relational outcomes. *Communication Quarterly, 53,* 339–358.

Kim, M. S. (1994). Cross-cultural comparisons of the perceived importance of conversational constraints. *Human Communication Research, 21,* 128–151.

Knapp, M. (1978). *Social intercourse: From greeting to good-bye.* Boston: Allyn & Bacon.

Kram, K. E. (1985). *Mentoring at work: Developmental relationships in organizational life.* Glenview, IL: Scott, Foresman.

Metts, S. (1994). Relational transgressions. In W. R. Cupach & B. H. Spitzberg (Eds.), *The dark side of interpersonal communication* (pp. 17–34). Mahwah, NJ: Lawrence Erlbaum.

Pilkington, C. J., & Richardson, D. R. (1988). Perceptions of risk in intimacy. *Journal of Social and Personal Relationships, 5,* 503–308.

Ragins, B. R. (1989). Barriers to mentoring: The female manager's dilemma. *Human Relations, 42,* 1–22.

Ragins, B. R. (1997). Diversified mentoring relationships in organizations: A power perspective. *Academy of Management Review, 22,* 482–521.

Ragins B. R., & Cotton, J. L. (1999). Mentor functions and outcomes: A comparison of men and women in formal and informal mentoring relationships. *Journal of Applied Psychology, 84,* 529–550.

Ragins, B. R., & Verbos, A. K. (2007). Positive relationships in action: Relational mentoring and mentoring schemas in the workplace. In J. E. Dutton & B. R. Ragins (Eds.), *Exploring positive relationships at work: Building a theoretical and research foundation* (pp. 91–116). Mahwah, NJ: Lawrence Erlbaum.

Renger, R., Kalbfleisch, P. J., Smolak, L., & Crago, M. (1999). A self-esteem approach to effective resiliency building: The process of mentoring. *Resiliency in Action, 4*(1), 1–3.

Stafford, L. (2003). Maintaining romantic relationships: Summary and analysis of one research program. In D. J. Canary & M. Dainton (Eds.), *Maintaining relationships through communication: Relational, contextual, and cultural variables* (pp. 51–77). Mahwah, NJ: Lawrence Erlbaum.

Stafford, L. (2005). *Maintaining long-distance and cross-residential relationships.* Mahwah, NJ: Lawrence Erlbaum.

Stafford, L., & Canary, D. J. (1991). Maintenance strategies and romantic relationship type, gender, and relational characteristics. *Journal of Social and Personal Relationships, 8,* 217–242.

Wanberg, C. R., Welsh, E. T., & Hezlett, S. A. (2003). Mentoring research: A review and dynamic process model. *Research in Personal and Human Resources Management, 22,* 39–124.

Wilson, S. R. (2002). *Seeking and resisting compliance: Why people say what they do when trying to influence others.* Thousand Oaks, CA: Sage.

21

Mentoring and the Work-Family Interface

Jeffrey H. Greenhaus

Romila Singh

R esearch on the mentoring process has grown steadily over the past 20 years (Allen, Eby, Poteet, Lentz, & Lima, 2004; Noe, Greenberger, & Wang, 2002; Ragins, 1999; Wanberg, Welsh, & Hezlett, 2003). However, despite Kram's (1985) critical observation that developmental relationships revolve around career, self, and family concerns, research has focused almost exclusively on the effects of mentoring on protégés' career outcomes (Noe et al., 2002; Wanberg et al., 2003). The mentoring literature has been relatively silent on whether mentors can affect protégés' success in balancing their work and family lives. Although several scholars have alluded to the importance of mentoring relationships in enabling protégés to manage the work-family interface effectively (Kram, 1985; Ragins, 1999; Sosik, Godshalk, & Yammarino, 2004; Wanberg et al., 2003), empirical research is limited (Nielson, Carlson, & Lankau, 2001; Wallace, 2001) and theory is virtually nonexistent.

This gap in our understanding is significant because the escalating representation of dual-earner couples and single parents in the workforce has made juggling work and family roles increasingly challenging for a growing number of employees (Greenhaus, Allen, & Spector, 2006). Addressing the gap can reveal when the mentoring process promotes balance in a protégé's life and when the process undermines it. Moreover, examining linkages between mentoring and work-family outcomes is consistent with an emerging relational mentoring perspective that emphasizes learning, growth, and development in career, professional, *and* personal domains (Fletcher & Ragins, Chapter 15, this volume; Ragins & Verbos, 2007).

The aim of this chapter is to stimulate thinking and research regarding the impact of mentoring on the intersection of a protégé's work and family lives. First, we briefly discuss the work-family interface and highlight two important work-family linking mechanisms, work-family conflict and work-family enrichment. Next, we present a theoretical model that proposes a series of paths through which mentoring affects protégés' work-family conflict and work-family enrichment. We conclude the chapter by identifying directions for future research on the relationship between mentoring and the work-family interface.

It is important to identify two significant perspectives that are not incorporated into the model presented in this chapter. First, our model focuses exclusively on the impact of the mentor on the protégé's work-family interface. More than 20 years ago, Kram (1985) asserted that a mentor-protégé relationship is characterized by complementarity, in which each partner is responsive to the needs and concerns of the other partner. The impact of the mentoring relationship on the protégé as well as the mentor has been increasingly recognized in recent years (Allen, Chapter 5, this volume), and mutuality of learning, growth, and development is a cornerstone of the relational mentoring perspective (Fletcher & Ragins, Chapter 15, this volume; Ragins & Verbos, 2007). Nevertheless, including both directions of influence in our model would have made it excessively unwieldy. Instead, we discuss the mutuality of the mentor-protégé relationship in the context of an agenda for future research.

Second, we acknowledge that employees can profit from a wide array of developmental relationships with individuals of different status levels, both inside and outside the employee's organization (Higgins, Chandler, & Kram, Chapter 14, this volume; Higgins & Kram, 2001). Our model examines the impact of mentoring on protégés' work-family interface through the lens of a primary organizational mentor. The focus of our model on the primary organizational mentor was intended to avoid further complicating an already complex process. As with the mutuality issue described above, we discuss the possible impact of multiple developmental relationships in the section of this chapter devoted to future research.

The Work-Family Interface

Extensive research on the work-family interface over the past several decades has focused primarily on understanding the ways in which work and family lives are interdependent (Barling & Sorensen, 1997; Barnett, 1998, 1999; Barnett & Hyde, 2001; Eby, Casper, Lockwood, Bordeaux, & Brinley, 2005; Edwards & Rothbard, 2000; Lambert, 1990; Repetti, 1987). The interdependencies have been represented by a series of linking mechanisms (Edwards & Rothbard, 2000) by which work and family roles affect one another. This chapter focuses on two of the most widely researched linking mechanisms, work-family conflict and work-family enrichment.

Work-family conflict, which represents the negative side of the work-family interface, is produced by simultaneous and incompatible pressures from work and family roles (Greenhaus & Beutell, 1985; Kahn, Wolfe, Quinn, Snoek, & Rosenthal, 1964). Because of the incompatibility of role pressures, work-family conflict occurs when experiences in one role interfere with meeting the requirements and achieving effectiveness in the other role (Edwards & Rothbard, 2000; Greenhaus & Beutell, 1985). Researchers agree that work-family conflict is bidirectional: Work can interfere with family life (work interference with family, or WIF), and family can interfere with work life (family interference with work, or FIW) (Frone, 2003). The importance of understanding the effect of mentoring on protégés' work-family conflict is underscored by the substantial harmful effects of extensive conflict on employees' psychological and physical well-being (Allen, Herst, Bruck, & Sutton, 2000; Bellavia & Frone, 2005; Eby et al., 2005; Frone, 2003; Greenhaus et al., 2006; Kossek & Ozeki, 1998).

Work-family enrichment (sometimes referred to as *work-family facilitation*) embodies the positive effects that work and family roles have on one another. Greenhaus and Powell (2006) defined work-family enrichment as the extent to which experiences in one role improve the quality of life (performance and positive affect) in the other role. Like work-family conflict, enrichment is bidirectional: Work can enrich family (WEF), and family can enrich work (FEW). Work-family enrichment occurs when resources acquired in one role (such as new skills, different perspectives on life, and self-confidence) are successfully applied to the other role, such that performance and positive affect are enhanced in the receiving role. Recent research has shown that work-family enrichment can have beneficial effects on employee well-being (Brockwood, Hammer, & Neal, 2003; Grzywacz, 2000; Grzywacz & Bass, 2003; Hanson, Colton, & Hammer, 2003; Hill, 2005).

Work-family conflict and work-family enrichment can affect feelings of work-family balance. Greenhaus and Allen (2006) have defined *work-family balance* as the extent to which an individual's effectiveness and satisfaction in work and family roles are compatible with the individual's priorities in life. They suggest that extensive work-family conflict, whereby one role interferes with performance and satisfaction in the other role, detracts from an employee's work-family balance. In contrast, work-family enrichment, whereby one role enhances performance and satisfaction in the other role, promotes work-family balance. Therefore, understanding the impact of mentoring on protégés' conflict and enrichment can provide insight into the role that mentoring plays in promoting a balanced lifestyle.

The Effect of Mentoring on the Work-Family Interface

Overview of Model

Our model, shown in Figure 21.1, introduces the concept of a *work-family lens*, the extent to which a mentor is sensitive to—and supportive of—a protégé's values and goals regarding the attainment of work-family balance. We propose that a mentor's enactment of a work-family lens in a particular mentoring relationship shapes the nature of the career development and psychosocial functions that the mentor provides to a protégé. The model further proposes that the career development and psychosocial functions provided through a work-family lens affect the work-related demands that a protégé experiences, as well as the resources that a protégé acquires from work.

The model also shows that contextual factors moderate the relationship between the adoption of a work-family lens and the enactment of the lens with a particular protégé, as well as the relationship between the enactment of a work-family lens and protégés' demands and resources. Consistent with a differential salience perspective (Voydanoff, 2004a, 2004b), extensive work-related demands can interfere with family life (WIF), whereas extensive resources acquired at work can enrich family life (WEF).

This brief overview reveals the complexity of the effects of mentoring on a protégé's work-family interface. This complexity may explain why prior research has not revealed a significant impact of being mentored or receiving mentoring functions on a protégé's work-family interface (Nielson et al., 2001; Wallace, 2001). In subsequent sections of the chapter, we provide a conceptual rationale for each of the linkages in the model and specify moderators of several of these linkages. Because a mentor's work-family lens drives our proposed model, we next discuss the meaning of a work-family lens.

The Meaning of a Work-Family Lens

As noted earlier, a mentor who holds a work-family lens is sensitive to, and supportive of, a protégé's values and goals regarding the attainment of work-family balance. We view the work-family lens as a facet of a mentoring schema. Ragins and Verbos (2007) defined a *mentoring schema* as a cognitive map or a mental knowledge structure that guides perceptions, expectations, and behaviors in a mentoring relationship. A mentoring schema includes three components (Ragins & Verbos, 2007). A *self-schema* signifies a mental representation of oneself in a relationship (who I am as a mentor in a relationship). An *other-schema* is a mental representation of the other person in the relationship (who a protégé is in a relationship). Self-schemas and other-schemas collectively produce interpersonal scripts (how I and the other person act) that guide sequences of interactions in the mentor-protégé relationship.

The self-schema of mentors who adopt a work-family lens might include the following elements: "I respect a protégé's life outside of work"; "I try to understand a protégé's values and feelings regarding work-family balance"; and "I support a protégé's desire to achieve balance between work and family roles." Mentors who view the mentoring relationship through a work-family lens might perceive the following elements of an other-schema: "A protégé is willing to share concerns about work and other parts of life"; and "A protégé experiments with different strategies to address work-family challenges." Mentors' self-schemas and other-schemas might produce the following interpersonal scripts: "I encourage a protégé to understand his or her priorities regarding work, family, and other personal life roles"; "I initiate discussions of work-family balance when I believe they are central to a protégé's work situation"; and "I try to provide tangible support to relieve a protégé's stress."

In sum, a mentor who views developmental relationships through a work-family lens holds specific perceptions about his or her role in the relationship, as well as the protégé's own role, and as a result develops a conception of how each acts in the relationship. Although our discussion might imply that a mentor either holds or doesn't hold a work-family lens, it is more likely that a mentor's adoption of such a lens represents a continuum from low (or weak) to high (or strong).

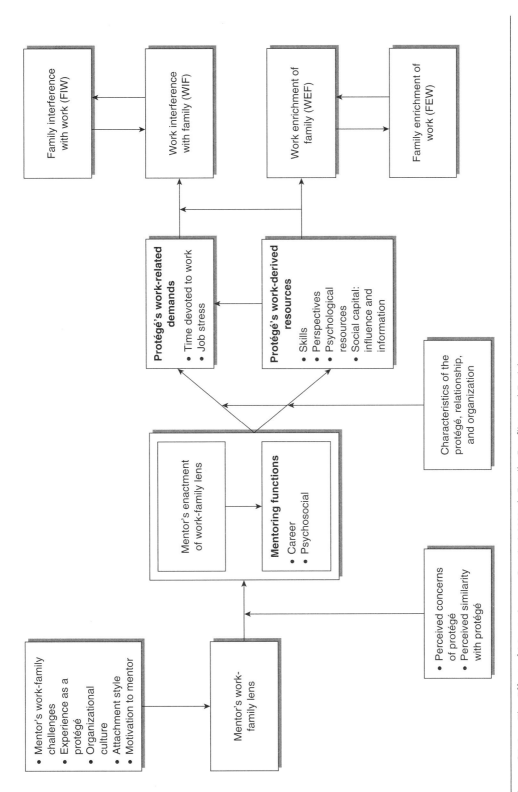

Figure 21.1 The Effect of Mentoring on Protégés' Work-Family Conflict and Enrichment

As Ragins and Verbos (2007) noted, mentors and protégés ultimately engage in behaviors that are consistent with their respective schemas and scripts. Figure 21.1 indicates that a mentor's enactment of a work-family lens affects the provision of the career development and psychosocial mentoring functions. The enactment of the lens provides support to a protégé in balancing his or her work and family responsibilities (Nielson et al., 2001). We do not suggest that a mentor with a strong work-family lens provides more or less of a particular mentoring function than a mentor with a weak lens. Rather, we believe that a mentor with a strong work-family lens provides a mentoring function in a somewhat different manner than a mentor whose work-family lens is not as strong. Table 21.1 illustrates how a work-family lens might influence the provision of each of the mentoring functions.

The behaviors associated with the adoption of a work-family lens cluster into five areas. First, the mentor is willing and able to discuss with a protégé the work-family implications of a particular job, career path, or career strategy. Second, the mentor is willing to share his or her own experiences with the protégé and provide advice when requested. Third, the mentor encourages a protégé to achieve greater self-awareness and to live in accordance with his or her values. Fourth, the mentor attempts to act nonjudgmentally in all interactions, pointing out the possible implications of a protégé's decision, while accepting the protégé's values and aspirations as legitimate. Finally, the mentor engages in specific actions on behalf of the protégé by advocating, protecting, and providing resources where feasible.

The Origin and Enactment of a Work-Family Lens

Mentors who incorporate a work-family lens into their schemas (a) understand the relevance of work-family issues to employees, their families, and organizations; (b) feel comfortable interacting with other people about personal and sensitive issues, such as the relationship between work and family lives; and (c) believe that engaging a protégé around work-family issues is consistent with their motivation for becoming a mentor. The first factor represents accumulated knowledge based on the mentor's prior and current experiences, and the second factor reflects a mentor's approach to interacting with other people. The first two factors are consistent with the two classes of antecedents to a mentoring schema identified by Ragins and Verbos (2007), relational knowledge and relational differences.

Mentors' understanding of the relevance of work-family issues is partially based on their own prior experiences. For example, it is reasonable to expect that mentors who have experienced significant work-family challenges in their own lives will realize the importance of these issues to one's quality of life and appreciate the importance of attending to these issues in a purposeful manner. These beliefs should sensitize mentors to the significance of protégés' work-family issues in their lives and should promote the adoption of a work-family lens in their mentoring relationships.

Proposition 1a: Mentors who have experienced work-family challenges in their lives will be more likely to adopt a strong work-family lens in their mentoring relationships than mentors who have not experienced work-family challenges in their lives.

Table 21.1   Mentor Behaviors Enacted Through a Work-Family Lens

Mentoring Function	Definition	Examples of Mentor Behaviors
Career Functions		
Sponsorship	Speaks on behalf of protégé regarding promotions and other new assignments both formally and informally.	Discusses with protégé the work-family implications of promotion or other assignment before sponsoring protégé; advocates on behalf of a protégé's attempt to pursue an alternative work arrangement.
Coaching	Suggests specific strategies for meeting work objectives, achieving recognition, and achieving career aspirations.	Discusses with protégé the work-family implications of different career strategies; encourages protégé to understand the work-family implications of the protégé's career aspirations; discusses with protégé the family supportiveness of the organization's culture.
Exposure and visibility	Gives protégé responsibilities that require contact with senior managers.	Considers, and discusses with the protégé, the time expectations and stressors associated with potentially new responsibilities.
Protection	Shields protégé from potentially damaging contact with senior managers.	Protects protégé from the negative stigmas associated with pursuing an alternative work arrangement.
Challenging assignments	Assigns challenging work with necessary training and feedback.	Considers, and discusses with the protégé, the time expectations and stressors associated with alternative challenging assignments; explores assignments that meet protégé's developmental needs without unduly intruding into family and personal time; tries to provide the necessary resources to prevent the protégé from becoming overwhelmed.

(Continued)

Table 21.1 (Continued)

Mentoring Function	Definition	Examples of Mentor Behaviors
Psychosocial Functions		
Counseling	Conveys acceptance, support, and empathy and becomes a confidant.	Encourages the protégé to examine the relative priority of work family, and other personal commitments in the protégé's life; shares with the protégé his or her own life role priorities and strategies; explores with the protégé the ways in which work and family lives interfere with each other and strengthen each other; responds nonjudgmentally to the protégé's expression of concerns and anxieties regarding balancing work and family lives; helps the protégé with strategies to balance work and family commitments.
Acceptance/confirmation	Provides support and encouragement.	Accepts protégé's values and role priorities as legitimate; encourages protégé to be true to his or her values.
Friendship	Engages in informal social exchanges with the protégé.	Does not permit differences in life role priorities between mentor and protégé to interfere with mutual liking, understanding, and enjoyable informal exchanges.
Role-modeling	Expresses attitudes and values through behavior.	Role-models self-awareness, understanding others, experimentation, and living true to one's own values.

Moreover, mentors base their conceptions of the mentoring process in part on their own prior experience as a protégé (Allen, Poteet, Russell, & Dobbins, 1997; Kram, 1985; Ragins & Cotton, 1993) and tend to interact with their protégés in a manner consistent with how their mentors treated them (Kram, 1985). A mentor whose own prior mentor adopted a work-family lens is not only likely to recognize that it is legitimate to focus on work-family issues, but may associate the mentor's work-family lens with the successful resolution of his or her own work-family challenges.

Proposition 1b: Mentors who have been protégés of mentors with a work-family lens will be more likely to adopt a strong work-family lens in their mentoring relationships than mentors who have been protégés of mentors without a work-family lens.

Mentors may also take their cues regarding mentorship relationships from the culture of the organization in which they work (Allen, Poteet, & Burroughs, 1997; Aryee, Chay, & Chew, 1996; Kram, 1985; Ragins & Verbos, 2007). Through their norms, practices, and policies, organizations with family-supportive cultures convey a respect for an employee's life outside of work and encourage managers and other employees to help their colleagues achieve an appropriate balance in their lives (Thompson, Beauvais, & Lyness, 1999). Consistent with this notion, Foley, Linnehan, Greenhaus, and Weer (2006) found that supervisors who work in family-supportive organizations provide more work-family support to their subordinates than supervisors who work in less family-supportive cultures.

Proposition 1c: Mentors who work in organizations with family-supportive cultures will be more likely to adopt a strong work-family lens in their mentoring relationships than mentors who work in organizations with less supportive cultures.

Ragins and Verbos (2007) also posited that relational differences—that is, broad psychological reactions to interpersonal relationships—shape individuals' mentoring schemas. One variable identified in the literature (Noe et al., 2003; Ragins & Verbos; 2007; Wanberg et al., 2003) that seems particularly relevant to the development of a work-family lens is an individual's relationship attachment style. Based on an individual's self-image and image of other people, Bartholomew (1990) proposed a four-category model of attachment style: *secure* (positive image of self and others), *preoccupied* (negative self-image and positive other-image), *dismissing* (positive self-image and negative other-image), and *fearful* (negative image of self and others).

We suggest that the incorporation of a strong work-family lens into a mentoring schema is more likely for individuals who hold positive images of themselves and other people. A positive self-image may enable a mentor to comfortably reveal his or her own work-family difficulties and vulnerabilities to a protégé and to encourage the protégé to engage in similar disclosure. A perception of other people as good, trustworthy, and accepting should also empower a mentor to broach intimate and sensitive subjects regarding work, family, and personal life with a protégé without fear of resistance or rejection.

Proposition 1d: Mentors with a secure attachment style will be more likely to adopt a strong work-family lens in their mentoring relationships than mentors with a preoccupied, dismissing, or fearful attachment style.

We also believe that an individual's motivation for becoming a mentor is associated with the adoption of a work-family lens. Allen (2003) identified three motives for individuals to become mentors: self-enhancement, intrinsic satisfaction, and benefiting others. We propose that mentors whose dominant motive is self-enhancement are unlikely to incorporate a work-family lens into their mentoring schemas. These individuals view the benefits of a mentoring relationship primarily in terms of enhancing their own visibility, reputation, and power base in the organization (Allen, 2003). Such mentors might believe that injecting work-family issues into mentoring relationships could discourage protégés from pursuing a high-involvement, fast-track career, thereby failing to enhance the mentor's own power and prestige in the organization. On the other hand, mentors motivated by intrinsic satisfaction and benefiting others are more likely to encourage protégés to identify and solve work-family difficulties because the successful resolution of these issues can bring mentors feelings of fulfillment and the knowledge that they helped other individuals achieve harmony between their work and family lives.

Proposition 1e: Mentors who are motivated by intrinsic satisfaction or benefiting others will be more likely to adopt a strong work-family lens in their mentoring relationships than mentors who are motivated by self-enhancement.

Our model distinguishes a mentor's adoption of a work-family lens from the mentor's enactment of the lens in a relationship with a particular protégé. This distinction is consistent with the differentiation between *generic schemas* and *particularistic schemas* (Ogilvie & Ashmore, 1991; Ragins & Verbos, 2007), respectively. A mentor's work-family lens reflects his or her general tendency to incorporate work-family issues into mentoring relationships. Figure 21.1 proposes that the particularistic enactment or application of the generic lens in a specific mentoring relationship is contingent upon two factors.

First, we suggest that a mentor who holds a work-family lens makes a judgment regarding a particular protégé's needs in determining whether the enactment of the lens will benefit the protégé. Ragins and Verbos (2007) suggested that relational mentoring is characterized by a need-based fit between mentor and protégé that is derived from communal norms emphasizing responsiveness to the other party's needs.

We believe that mentors who hold a generic work-family lens are more likely to enact the lens when they believe that a protégé's concerns warrant it. For example, a mentor may observe a protégé's demeanor or behavior ("She seems upset with her child's day care arrangement") or may use a protégé's disclosure of a concern ("I can't decide whether to accept a new work assignment until my children enter school") as a basis to assess a protégé's needs. The assessment of a protégé's concerns may trigger the enactment of a strong work-family lens.

Proposition 2a: A mentor who holds a strong work-family lens will be more likely to enact the lens with a protégé who has extensive work-family concerns than with a protégé who has less extensive work-family concerns.

Second, we propose that a mentor's enactment of a work-family lens depends on the perceived similarity of the mentor and the protégé. The enactment of a work-family lens can involve discussions of personal details of a protégé's values, goals, and experiences that go beyond work-related topics. Moreover, a mentor enacting a work-family lens is likely to disclose personal aspects of his or her own life to a protégé as they relate to the intersection of work and family roles. It is possible that mentors feel more comfortable revealing and discussing such personal topics with protégés they perceive to be similar to themselves in significant ways.

Mentors have been found to provide more extensive mentoring functions to protégés they perceive to be similar to themselves than to protégés they see as dissimilar (Burke, McKeen, & McKenna, 1993; Ensher & Murphy, 1997). More relevant to our model, perceived similarity in interpersonal relationships has been associated with feelings of personal attraction, psychological closeness, and trust (Byrne, 1971; Huston & Levinger, 1978), all of which should facilitate the discussion of personal, sensitive topics. Moreover, dyadic similarity in gender and race has been associated with mentors' provision of greater psychosocial support to protégés (Burke, McKeen, & McKenna, 1990; Koberg, Boss, & Goodman, 1998; Ragins, 1997; Thomas, 1990) and supervisors' provision of work-family support to subordinates (Foley et al., 2006).

Proposition 2b: Mentors who hold a strong work-family lens will be more likely to enact the lens with protégés they perceive to be similar to themselves than to protégés they see as dissimilar.

Relationship of Work-Family Lens With Protégé Demands and Resources

Researchers have generally ignored the processes that mediate the effects of mentoring on distal outcomes (Wanberg et al., 2003). Our model posits that protégé's work demands (time and stress) and resources mediate the effects of mentoring on work-family conflict and work-family enrichment. Time and stress are not only prominent demands in the workplace but also produce time-based and strain-based work-family conflict, respectively (Greenhaus & Beutell, 1985). The specific resources included in Figure 21.1 are based on Greenhaus and Powell's (2006) model of work-family enrichment. Our basic premise is that the enactment of a strong work-family lens in the mentoring process can help align protégés' work demands with their preferences and can facilitate the acquisition of more extensive resources.

Time Devoted to Work Mentoring can either increase or decrease the amount of time a protégé devotes to work. For example, a mentor's provision of challenging assignments and exposure/visibility can increase a protégé's work hours if the assignments or interactions with key organizational members are beyond the protégé's normal job duties and are time-consuming. Coaching can also increase a protégé's work hours if the strategies suggested by the mentor emphasize extended work involvement and/or face time (Greenhaus, Callanan, & Godshalk, 2000). Moreover, counseling, acceptance/confirmation, and role-modeling can all lead to long work hours if the protégé's emerging sense of self includes a level of career ambition that requires an extensive time commitment to work.

Conversely, mentoring functions could result in a protégé's decision to work fewer hours. For example, coaching can reduce a protégé's work hours if the mentor's strategies enable the protégé to accomplish work more efficiently or otherwise allow the protégé to work "smarter not harder." Counseling and acceptance/confirmation could result in a protégé's decision to work fewer hours if the protégé's emerging self places a strong emphasis on spending more time fulfilling other life roles.

A mentor who enacts a work-family lens is sensitive to a protégé's values and role priorities and, through observation and discussion, understands whether the amount of time devoted to work is an issue for the protégé. A mentor enacting a work-family lens who senses that a protégé is struggling with meeting the time demands of work and family roles might take the following approaches:

- Discuss time-related implications of a promotion or other assignment before sponsoring a protégé
- Advise the protégé to take advantage of the organization's family-supportive practices, support the protégé's attempt to do so, and protect the protégé from the negative stigma that might result
- Discuss the work-family implications of various career strategies
- Explore the use of challenging assignments that meet the protégé's developmental needs without unduly intruding into family and personal time

All of these actions can have the effect of enabling a protégé to adjust his or her work hours to a level that is commensurate with the protégé's values and priorities. If excessive work hours become an issue to the protégé, these actions can have the effect of reducing the protégé's time commitment to work. Even if work hours are not a significant issue to the protégé, a mentor enacting a work-family lens might still engage in a number of these behaviors to help ensure that the protégé's work hours are kept within an acceptable range and do not increase in the process of pursuing career success.

Proposition 3a: Protégés whose mentors enact a strong work-family lens will be likely to work fewer hours than protégés whose mentors do not enact a strong work-family lens.

Work Stress

The limited research in this area (Sosik & Godshalk, 2000) supports what is probably a widely held belief that mentoring can reduce the amount of work-related stress experienced by a protégé. Indeed, the provision of a number of mentoring functions is likely to reduce protégé stress regardless of whether the mentor enacts a work-family lens. For example, sponsorship and exposure/visibility might reduce the amount of stress experienced by career-oriented protégés, because they view the additional attention as instrumental to their career success. Similarly, coaching may be associated with reduced levels of protégé stress, because the information and advice the mentor provides is capable of reducing the uncertainty about how to succeed in the organization. Moreover, all of the psychosocial functions are capable of reducing a protégé's work-related stress. Counseling, friendship, and acceptance and confirmation enhance a protégé's sense of competence and self-esteem and clarify the protégé's self-identity (Kram, 1985). Self-esteem and feelings of competence can reduce stress, because they enable an individual to have confidence in his or her ability to cope with potentially harmful situations (Ashford, 1988; Callan, Terry, & Schweitzer, 1994). Role-modeling may also reduce a protégé's stress, because identification with someone more experienced and successful should make the protégé feel more secure, which, in turn, can enable the protégé to be more self-confident in potentially stressful situations.

However, we believe that mentoring through the vantage point of a work-family lens provides additional opportunities to reduce protégé stress because of the mentor's insights into the protégé's values, priorities, and work-family concerns. For example, a work-family sensitive mentor might take the following approaches:

- Guide a protégé toward less stressful assignments and career paths
- Discuss career strategies that do not violate a protégé's ethical values or interfere with a protégé's family's needs
- Validate the legitimacy of a protégé's role priorities and values, even if they are different from the mentor's priorities and values
- Provide the necessary emotional and tangible support that prevents the protégé from becoming overwhelmed with a new, challenging assignment

These types of actions have the capacity to reduce (or at least not increase) the stressfulness of the work environment, which leads to the following proposition:

Proposition 3b: Protégés whose mentors enact a strong work-family lens will be likely to experience less job stress than protégés whose mentors do not enact a strong work-family lens.

Work-Derived Resources

We focus on a subset of resources identified by Greenhaus and Powell (2006)—skills, perspectives, psychological resources, and social capital—because we believe that they are most likely to be enhanced by a mentor's behavior. Wanberg et al.'s (2003) model includes four proximal outcomes of mentoring (cognitive learning, skill-based learning, affective learning, and social networks), which represent changes in the protégé and are consistent with the kinds of resources that are included in our model.

Effective mentoring can facilitate a protégé's acquisition of resources regardless of whether a mentor enacts a work-family lens. For example, coaching (Olivero, Bane, & Kopelman, 1997), challenging assignments (McCauley, Ruderman, Ohlott, & Morrow, 1994), and other forms of career development support (Lankau & Scandura, 2002; Lankau & Scandura, Chapter 4, this volume) provide opportunities for protégés to enhance their skills and promote learning. Psychosocial functions can also promote skill development, because they enhance self-esteem and self-confidence, which encourage experimentation and skill acquisition (Kram, 1985; Waters, McCabe, Kiellerup, & Kiellerup, 2002).

Mentoring functions also enable a protégé to adopt new perspectives or views about themselves and the world. For example, a coaching session with a mentor might persuade a protégé that a vigilant focus on customer service will enable the protégé's unit to become more effective, and working on a challenging assignment could convince a protégé about the virtues of group decision making. The psychosocial functions also enable a protégé to adopt different views or perspectives because the growth of self-esteem opens individuals' eyes to new ways of looking at themselves and the world (Judge, Thoresen, Pucik, & Welbourne, 1999) and because identification through role-modeling may encourage a protégé to adopt some of the mentor's perspectives on self and life (Kram, 1985; Nielsen et al., 2001).

Psychological resources include positive self-evaluations, such as self-efficacy (Bandura, 1997; Gist & Mitchell, 1992), self-esteem (Brockner, 1988), and personal hardiness (Blaney & Ganellen, 1990; Kobasa, 1979). Mentoring has been found to enhance a protégé's self-efficacy and sense of power in the organization (Day & Allen, 2004; Fagenson, 1988). It is likely that the career development functions enhance positive self-evaluations, to the extent that they promote autonomy (Holman & Wall, 2002; McAllister & Bigley, 2002), high performance (Gist & Mitchell, 1992), social support (Koberg et al., 1998), and feelings of psychological success (Hall, 1976). Counseling, friendship, and acceptance/confirmation are not only capable of increasing self-esteem, self-efficacy expectations, and self-awareness (Kram, 1985; Seibert, 1999) but also provide a supportive environment, which has been shown to nurture personal hardiness (Blaney & Ganellen, 1990).

The two social capital resources included in the model are the information and influence that protégés acquire through their network of social relationships. Mentoring has been shown to enable protégés to receive information and advice (Ragins & Cotton, 1999) and to gain access to influential people (Fagenson, 1988; Seibert, Kraimer, & Liden, 2001). In a sense, all of the mentoring functions provide some type of information, advice, or potential influence that the protégé can draw upon in the future.

Although many resources acquired at work can enrich family life (Greenhaus & Powell, 2006), some resources seem especially relevant to the work-family interface because they can help an individual clarify the relative priority of work and family roles, interact effectively with role senders in the work and family domains, and make effective decisions regarding the work-family interface. These "balance-supporting" resources include self-appraisal skills, interpersonal skills, multitasking skills, positive self-evaluations, strategies for coping with stress, new perspectives on work and family roles, and information (e.g., advice on day care) and influence (advocating for a protégé to enter a nonpartner track) relevant to the work-family interface.

We suggest that a mentor who enacts a work-family lens is likely to facilitate a protégé's acquisition of balance-supporting resources. Because the mentor is particularly sensitive to work-family issues, he or she sees the relevance of a protégé developing the self-awareness, confidence, and the necessary skills and perspectives to achieve a desired balance between work and family commitments.

Proposition 3c: Protégés whose mentors enact a strong work-family lens will be more likely to acquire balance-supporting resources than protégés whose mentors do not enact a strong work-family lens.

The effects of mentoring on demands and resources are contextually based. Figure 21.1 indicates that the effects are moderated by characteristics of the protégé, the relationship, and the organization. The effectiveness of a mentor's actions depends in part on the responsiveness of the protégé. If the protégé resists new perspectives, ignores advice, or rejects tangible assistance, work-family focused mentoring is unlikely to reduce a protégé's work demands or increase resources. Like mentors, protégés develop mentoring schemas (Ragins & Verbos, 2007), and some schemas may produce resistance to a mentor's best efforts. Other protégé attributes, such as a limited aptitude to acquire a particular skill, closed-mindedness, or neuroticism, may also restrict the impact of mentoring on demands and resources.

Moreover, the quality of the mentor-protégé relationship and characteristics of the organization are also potential moderators. Ragins and Verbos (2007) posited that characteristics of relational mentoring (e.g., empathy, trust, disclosure, sensitivity) are essential to promote growth, learning, and flourishing. Mentoring relationships that do not possess these relational attributes may be less likely to reduce protégé demands and increase protégé resources because the successful enactment of a work-family lens depends upon openness, respect, trust, and effective communication. Similarly, organizations that do not reinforce learning and development may discourage a protégé from acquiring new skills, and highly autocratic and inflexible organizations can limit a protégé's autonomy and control regardless of a mentor's best effort.

The number of protégé, relationship, and organizational characteristics that can moderate the effect of mentoring on demands and resources are too numerous to specify. Instead, we offer the following general proposition to guide future research efforts:

Proposition 3d: The relationships between a mentor's enactment of a work-family lens and a protégé's demands and resources will be moderated by characteristics of the protégé, the mentoring relationship, and the organization.

The Impact of Demands and Resources on Work-Family Conflict

Figure 21.1 indicates that work-related demands have a direct effect on WIF. This relationship, well-established in the work-family literature (Frone, 2003), captures the processes underlying time-based conflict and strain-based conflict. That is, the time demands associated with work make it difficult to participate fully in the family role, thereby inhibiting performance in the family domain. Similarly, extensive work-related stress can produce strain symptoms that, if transferred to the family domain, may interfere with effective functioning in the family role.

Proposition 4: Work-related demands will be positively related to WIF.

The model also includes a reciprocal relationship between WIF and FIW (family interference with work) (Bellavia & Frone, 2005). For example, an individual whose work demands interfere with family life may experience dissatisfaction and stress in the family domain that subsequently interfere with fulfilling his or her work role requirements. This reciprocal relationship indicates that a mentor's influence is not limited to work's impact on family, but can extend to the effect of a protégé's family life on his or her work.

Figure 21.1 also depicts a negative relationship between resources and demands. Although the work-family literature has not examined this relationship, it is reasonable to expect that resources acquired in the work domain are capable of reducing demands in that role. For example, work-related skills and information derived from a social network should enable an employee to perform job duties more quickly, more efficiently, and less stressfully. Moreover, psychological resources, such as self-esteem and resilience, can reduce the protégé's work-related stress, because they enable the individuals to make an optimistic assessment of his or her ability to handle potentially stressful situations (Ashford, 1988). As a result of the connections among resources, demands, and WIF, we suggest the following proposition:

Proposition 5: Work-derived resources will have an indirect negative effect on WIF through their negative effect on work-related demands.

We also suggest that resources can attenuate the impact of work-related demands on WIF. For example, interpersonal skills can enable an employee to solve problems in collaboration with work and family role senders to minimize the extent to which long work hours intrude on family life, as when the employee attempts to reschedule a role activity that conflicts with an obligation in the other role (Powell & Greenhaus, 2005). Or an employee who has developed a new perspective on the importance of managing role boundaries (Friedman & Greenhaus, 2000) may learn how to prevent work-related stress from spilling over into the home environment.

Proposition 6: The relationship between work-related demands and WIF will be weaker for employees with extensive resources than for employees with limited resources.

The Impact of Work-Derived Resources on Work-Family Enrichment

The direct link in Figure 21.1 between resources and WEF is based on Greenhaus and Powell's (2006) assertion that resources acquired in a role can be used to enhance the quality of life (performance and positive affect) in another role. For example, listening skills acquired at work can improve one's parenting behavior; self-confidence derived from a challenging assignment may spur creative problem-solving at home; advice from a colleague can help an employee with a difficult family situation; and an influential mentor may help an employee get favored attention in placing his or her child in a high-quality day care center.

Proposition 7: Work-derived resources will be positively related to WEF.

We should note that the acquisition of a resource from the work domain does not inevitably enrich family life. As Greenhaus and Powell (2006) have proposed, the resource must be applied to the family role, and the applied resource must enhance performance and positive affect in that role. They have suggested that the acquisition of a resource is most likely to promote work-family enrichment when the receiving role is highly salient (which should increase the motivation to apply the resource) and when the resource is compatible with the norms and requirements of the role (which should increase the likelihood that the resource will enhance performance and positive affect in the receiving role).

Conclusion and Directions for Future Research

It is tempting to conclude that mentoring enables a protégé to minimize work-family conflict, increase work-family enrichment, and achieve a sense of balance between the two roles. However, it is not so simple. For mentoring to produce these benefits, our model indicates that the following must occur:

- The mentor incorporates a work-family lens into the mentoring relationship.
- The protégé is responsive to the mentor's efforts and is capable of benefiting from the mentor's behavior.
- The mentoring relationship is characterized by trust, empathy, and mutual concern.
- The organization supports learning and development and respects employees' lives outside of work.
- The protégé's work demands are decreased, and resources are strengthened.

These multiple conditions produce a complex relationship between mentoring and a protégé's work-family interface. However, the complexity of this relationship also provides a fertile opportunity for future research. In light of the paucity of research, perhaps the most pressing need is for scholars to initiate systematic research programs on this topic. Although the historical focus in the mentoring literature on career success outcomes is understandable, the incorporation of work-family variables in future research should provide a more comprehensive understanding of the impact of mentoring on protégés' lives. With that goal in mind, we offer a number of suggestions for researchers to integrate work-family issues into the examination of the mentoring process.

We encourage researchers to test the propositions embedded in our proposed model as well as to extend the model in new directions. As a new concept, it is necessary to develop a measure of a mentor's generic adoption of a work-family lens. Moreover, because the mentor's enactment of a work-family lens in a particular relationship is reflected in the nature of the mentoring functions the mentor provides, it is essential to determine the ways in which the career and psychosocial functions differ for mentors who enact a strong work-family lens and those who do not. In essence, the mentor behaviors identified in Table 21.1 need to be empirically verified.

In testing the antecedents of a work-family lens, researchers need not be limited to the variables identified in Propositions 1a-1e. The overarching rationale is that mentors adopt a work-family lens because they (a) understand the importance of addressing work-family issues; (b) are comfortable in close interpersonal relationships where personal, sensitive issues are discussed; and (c) believe that addressing work-family issues is consistent with their motivation to mentor. Therefore, any variable that influences one or more of these three factors is worthy of investigation as an antecedent to the adoption of a work-family lens.

We proposed that the relationship between the adoption of a generic work-family lens and the enactment of a particularistic lens is stronger when the mentor perceives the protégé to have work-family concerns (Proposition 2a) and when the mentor perceives himself or herself to be similar to the protégé (Proposition 2b). These propositions raise interesting questions about the effect of gender stereotypes and diversified relationships on mentoring and the work-family interface. For example, do mentors perceive that women protégés have (or should have) more intense work-family concerns than men protégés? Are they more likely to enact a work-family lens with a mother than a father? Moreover, there is some evidence that mentors provide more psychosocial support to protégés of the same sex than to protégés of the other sex (Burke et al., 1990; Ragins & McFarlin, 1990) and that women mentored by women experience less WIF than women mentored by men (Wallace, 2001). Are mentors more likely to enact a work-family lens with a same-sex protégé because they believe they understand the protégés' work-family needs or because they feel comfortable raising work-family issues with someone of the same sex?

We also suggested that the enactment of a work-family lens leads to reduced work demands (Propositions 3a and 3b) and more extensive resources (Proposition 3c) for the protégé. As noted earlier, this predicted effect is due to the manner in which a mentor with a work-family lens provides the career and psychosocial functions. In testing these propositions, it would be useful to examine whether some mentoring functions are more likely than others to reduce specific demands or increase specific resources. For example, are psychosocial functions provided through the vantage point of a work-family lens more likely to enhance the development of self-appraisal skills and self-confidence in decision making than the career functions? Or does the enhancement of these resources require both psychosocial and career support?

Testing these notions requires the development of new measures of the provision of mentoring functions. For example, it is not enough to ask a protégé whether his or her mentor provides challenging assignments. Instead, it is necessary to assess whether the challenging assignments (or any other mentoring function) are provided in the context of discussions or actions regarding the protégé's work and family lives. To illustrate, do the mentor and the protégé discuss the implications of a challenging assignment for the protégé's family and personal lives? Does the mentor select assignments with the protégé's work and family role priorities in mind?

Moreover, future research should examine the contextual factors that moderate the relationship between a mentor's enactment of a work-family lens and a protégé's demands and resources. Proposition 3d was necessarily broad, suggesting the relevance of characteristics of the protégé, the mentoring relationship, and the organization as potential moderators. One concept that might be useful in testing the implications of this proposition is the degree of congruence between the mentoring schemas of the mentor and the protégé (Ragins & Verbos, 2007). The career and psychosocial mentoring functions might be more likely to reduce work demands and increase resources when the mentor and the protégé hold similar mentoring schemas, because both parties agree on appropriate behaviors in the relationship. For example, a protégé who believes that only a protégé should initiate a discussion regarding personal life issues may be resistant to feedback or advice provided by a mentor who believes that he or she should be directive in initiating such discussions.

One mentoring function that seems especially relevant to a protégé's work-family interface is role-modeling, which enables a protégé to identify with an experienced and highly respected mentor (Kram, 1985). This raises interesting questions regarding the attitudes, values, and behaviors that an effective mentor should model. In their provocative discussion of the "happy workaholic," Friedman and Lobel (2003) suggested that a leader's ability to promote their employees' work-family balance does not require the leader to value a balanced lifestyle. Instead, they posited that leaders who have undergone extensive self-appraisal and act consistently with their values (that is, act authentically) understand that others may hold different values and encourage employees to act authentically with regard to those values, hence Friedman and Lobel's observation that an authentic workaholic leader can be a strong advocate for employees' choice of a different lifestyle. It would be interesting to test some of Friedman and Lobel's notions within mentor-protégé relationships.

In addition to testing the propositions in the model, we encourage researchers to extend the model in creative ways. We noted at the outset that our model focuses on a primary organizational mentor despite the widespread recognition that employees may enter an array of useful developmental relationships (Higgins et al., Chapter 14, this volume; Higgins & Kram, 2001). This constellation of relationships includes mentors who are inside or outside the organization, at the same level or a different level than the protégé, and who interact via face-to-face or electronic means. Even within more traditional organizational relationships, the mentor may be a formally assigned mentor or an informal mentor and may or may not be the protégé's supervisor.

This wide range of developmental relationships raises interesting questions regarding the effect of mentoring on protégés' work-family interface. For example, are peer mentors more likely than a more senior or more experienced mentor to place importance on work-family issues because peers may currently be experiencing similar work-family challenges? Are informal mentors more likely than formally assigned mentors to feel comfortable broaching sensitive, personal issues? Are mentors inside the organization more capable than outside mentors of helping a protégé reduce his or her work demands? Can supervisors advocate more effectively for a protégé's adoption of a flexible work schedule than mentors who are not the protégé's supervisor? Does having multiple developmental relationships enhance a protégé's ability to manage work and family roles effectively because of the diversity of supportive behaviors, or does it leave the protégé more confused because of conflicting advice (Baugh & Scandura, 1999)? These are just a sampling of the questions that can be addressed in future research.

Another perspective not represented in our model is the mutual learning, growth, and development that take place in highly effective relational mentoring (Fletcher & Ragins, Chapter 15, this volume; Ragins & Verbos, 2007). For example, mentor-protégé discussions of work-family issues might help mentors to gain clarity regarding their own life priorities, and assertive and insightful protégés might share their successful strategies with their mentors, enabling the mentors to experience a more harmonious balance between their work and family lives. It is reasonable to expect that mentors are more likely to benefit in these ways when their relationships with protégés are characterized by mutuality and responsiveness to each party's needs, that is, when the mentoring is relational in nature (Ragins & Verbos, 2007).

It would also be useful to explore the possibility of feedback loops that were not specified in the model. We can envision that a protégé's level of success in managing the work-family interface (that is, level of conflict and enrichment) might affect a number of prior variables in the model over time. For example, protégés' success might affect their expression of concern regarding their work and family lives, the type of support they request of their mentor, and their openness to their mentors' actions in the future. Moreover, a mentoring relationship that is characterized by such positive qualities as reciprocity, mutual learning, empathy, and sensitivity (Ragins & Verbos, 2007) might affect the mentor's motivation to mentor (away from self-enhancement) and strengthen or reinforce a mentor's secure-attachment style.

One of the factors that stimulated our interest in examining the relationship between mentoring and the work-family interface is the possibility that a traditional mentoring relationship may facilitate a protégé's objective career success (advancement and compensation) at the expense of the protégé's family and personal lives. A mentor's narrow focus on enhancing a protégé's career advancement might place the protégé in such a demanding work situation, in terms of work hours and stress, that family and personal commitments are ignored and ultimately victimized. A mentor who enacts a work-family lens, we suggest, avoids a myopic preoccupation with work that can produce a "career success-personal failure" syndrome (Korman & Korman, 1980) and instead focuses on the holistic well-being of the protégé.

However, this raises an interesting question regarding the possibility that the enactment of a work-family lens can be taken too far, such that the mentor is so concerned about a protégé's personal life that he or she jeopardizes the protégé's career advancement. This question warrants empirical attention, although we do not believe that the enactment of a work-family lens necessarily poses a risk to the protégé's career. Recall that we defined a work-family lens as the extent to which a mentor is sensitive to—and supportive of—a protégé's values and goals regarding the attainment of work-family balance. Employees differ in the priority they place on work and family commitments; some are career focused; others are family focused; and still others are both career- and family focused (Friedman & Greenhaus, 2000). Because individuals experience balance when their performance and satisfaction in the work and family domains are consistent with their life priorities (Greenhaus & Allen, 2006), *balance* means different things to different people.

Therefore, a mentor enacting a work-family lens helps the protégé clarify his or her life priorities, discusses the work and family implications of those priorities, and explicitly affirms the legitimacy of the protégé's priorities; the mentor's role is not to change the protégé's priorities. For example, a mentor of a career-focused protégé is most concerned with helping the protégé to understand the implications of a career focus on the protégé's life and to make effective decisions based on those implications. The mentor may encourage the protégé to pay somewhat more attention to his or her family and personal life, so that the protégé feels relatively competent and satisfied away from work, and may discuss how this can be accomplished while being deeply involved in work. The mentor is also likely to provide the necessary sponsorship, protection, challenge, and exposure/visibility to maintain or enhance the protégé's career prospects.

A protégé who holds a strong family focus places home and family at the center of his or her life and is willing to trade some amount of money and other external trappings of success for involvement and deep fulfillment within the family domain. Again, the mentor's role is not to change the protégé's life priorities, but to help the protégé understand them and their implications for career and life outcomes. A mentor enacting a work-family lens is likely to help a family-focused protégé maintain or improve job performance and be a valued contributor to the organization while still devoting substantial time and emotion to life outside of work. If a family-focused protégé does not advance rapidly in an organization, it is more likely to be due to the protégé's limited aspirations for advancement than to mentoring through a work-family lens. In fact, as noted above, the mentor might focus on helping the protégé become more valuable at work so that his or her employment is relatively secure and can provide for a fulfilling life outside of work.

A career- and family-focused employee places extensive importance on both roles. Such protégés are probably most challenging to mentor because they want to be highly effective and fulfilled in both domains. A mentor enacting a work-family lens may try to help the protégé define success in each domain, effectively manage role boundaries (Friedman & Greenhaus, 2000), and leverage resources in each role to enhance performance and satisfaction in the other role (Greenhaus & Powell, 2006). The mentor is also likely to help the protégé distinguish the work-family trade-offs that are acceptable from those that are not. The mentor does not ignore the protégé's job performance, but rather helps the protégé determine ways to maintain or improve effectiveness at work, while achieving substantial effectiveness and fulfillment at home. For these reasons, it seems unlikely that the enactment of a work-family lens will dampen the protégé's career prospects, at least as defined by performance on the job.

These speculations need to be examined in future research. Moreover, our discussion implies that future research should take a protégé's life values and priorities into account in assessing the effectiveness of a mentoring relationship. Simply examining relationships of mentoring or mentoring functions with compensation, organizational level, or rate of advancement does not do justice to the wide range of protégés' motives and values. Effective job performance is (or should be) valued by virtually all protégés as well as the organization and therefore is a valuable dependent variable in studies of effective mentoring. However, because substantial salary increases, frequent promotions, and increased power are not highly important to all protégés, routinely including them as dependent variables will not provide an accurate picture of the effectiveness of a mentoring relationship.

Instead, we suggest that future research will predict multiple criteria that are consistent with the values and priorities of the protégé and are relevant to the needs of the organization. Some criteria, such as job performance, the effective management of the work-family interface, and psychological well-being, are probably relevant to all protégés. However, other criteria, in particular compensation and advancement, should be used to assess the effectiveness of mentoring only for protégés whose priorities value these outcomes. This strategy, although admittedly complex, should provide a more realistic picture of the factors that contribute to effective mentoring.

References

Allen, T. D. (2003). Mentoring others: A dispositional and motivational approach. *Journal of Vocational Behavior, 62,* 134–154.

Allen, T. D., Eby, L. T., Poteet, M. L., Lentz, E., & Lima, L. (2004). Career benefits associated with mentoring for protégés: A meta-analysis. *Journal of Applied Psychology, 89,* 127–136.

Allen, T. D., Herst, D. E. L., Bruck, C. S., & Sutton, M. (2000). Consequences associated with work-to-family conflict: A review and agenda for future research. *Journal of Occupational Health Psychology, 5,* 278–308.

Allen, T. D., Poteet, M. L., & Burroughs, S. M. (1997). The mentor's perspective: A qualitative inquiry and future research agenda. *Journal of Vocational Behavior, 51,* 70–89.

Allan, T. D., Poteet, M. L., Russell, J. E. A., & Dobbins, G. H. (1997). A field study of factors related to supervisors willingness to mentor others. *Journal of Vocational Behavior, 50,* 1–22.

Aryee, S., Chay, Y. W., & Chew, J. (1996). The motivation to mentor among managerial employees. *Group & Organization Management, 21,* 261–277.

Ashford, S. J. (1988). Individual strategies for coping with stress during organizational transitions. *Journal of Applied Behavioral Science, 24,* 19–36.

Bandura, A. (1997). *Self-efficacy: The exercise of control.* New York: Freeman.

Barling, J., & Sorensen, D. (1997). Work and family: In search of a relevant research agenda. In C. L. Cooper & S. E. Jackson (Eds.), *Creating tomorrow's organizations: A handbook for future research in organizational behavior* (pp. 157–169). New York: John Wiley & Sons.

Barnett, R. C. (1998). Toward a review and reconceptualization of the work/family literature. *Genetic, Social, and General Psychology Monographs, 124,* 125–182.

Barnett, R. C. (1999). A new work-life model for the twenty-first century. *ANNALS, AAPSS, 562,* 143–158.

Barnett, R. C., & Hyde, J. S. (2001). Women, men, work, and family. *American Psychologist, 56,* 781–796.

Bartholomew, K. (1990). Avoidance of intimacy: An attachment perspective. *Journal of Social and Personal Relationships, 7,* 147–178.

Baugh, S. G., & Scandura, T. A. (1999). The effects of multiple mentors on protégé attitudes toward the work setting. *Journal of Social Behavior and Personality, 14,* 503–521.

Bellavia, G., & Frone, M. R. (2005). Work-family conflict. In J. Barling, E. K. Kelloway, & M. R. Frone (Eds.), *Handbook of work stress* (pp. 143–162). Thousand Oaks, CA: Sage.

Blaney, P. H., & Ganellen, R. J. (1990). Hardiness and social support. In B. R. Sarason, I. G. Sarason, & G. R. Pierce (Eds.), *Social support: An interactional view* (pp. 297–318). New York: John Wiley & Sons.

Brockner, J. (1988). *Self-esteem at work.* Lexington, MA: Lexington.

Brockwood, K. J., Hammer, L. B., & Neal, M. B. (2003, April). *An examination of positive work-family spillover among dual-earner couples in the sandwiched generation.* Paper presented at the Annual Conference of the Society for Industrial and Organizational Psychology, Orlando, FL.

Burke, R. J., McKeen, C. A., & McKenna, C. S. (1990). Sex differences and cross-sex effects on mentoring: Some preliminary data. *Psychological Reports, 67,* 1011–1024.

Burke, R. J., McKeen, C. A., & McKenna, C. (1993). Correlates of mentoring in organizations: The mentor's perspective. *Psychological Reports, 72,* 883–896.

Byrne, D. (1971). *The attraction paradigm.* New York: Academic Press.

Callan, V. J., Terry, D. J., & Schweitzer, R. (1994). Coping resources, coping strategies, and adjustment to organizational change: Direct or buffering effects. *Work and Stress, 8,* 372–383.

Day, R., & Allen, T. D. (2004). The relationship between career motivation and self-efficacy with protégé career success. *Journal of Vocational Behavior, 64,* 72–91.

Eby, L. T., Casper, W. J., Lockwood, A., Bordeaux, C., & Brinley, A. (2005). Work and family research in IO/OB: Content analysis and review of the literature (1980–2002). *Journal of Vocational Behavior, 66,* 124–197.

Edwards, J. R., & Rothbard, N. P. (2000). Mechanisms linking work and family: Clarifying the relationship between work and family constructs. *Academy of Management Review, 25,* 178–199.

Ensher, E. A., & Murphy, S. E. (1997). Effects of race, gender, perceived similarity, and contact on mentor relationships. *Journal of Vocational Behavior, 50,* 460–481.

Fagenson, E. A. (1988). The power of a mentor: Protégés and non-protégés perceptions of their own power in organizations. *Group and Organization Studies, 13,* 182–194.

Foley, S., Linnehan, F., Greenhaus, J. H., & Weer, C. (2006). The impact of gender similarity, racial similarity, and work culture on family-supportive supervision. *Group & Organization Management, 31,* 420–441.

Friedman, S. D., & Greenhaus, J. H. (2000). *Allies or enemies? What happens when business professionals confront life choices.* New York: Oxford University Press.

Friedman, S. D., & Lobel, S. (2003). The happy workaholic: A role model for employees. *Academy of Management Executive, 17*(3), 87–98.

Frone, M. R. (2003). Work-family balance. In J. C. Quick & L. E. Tetrick (Eds.), *Handbook of occupational health psychology* (pp. 143–162). Washington, DC: American Psychological Association.

Gist, M. E., & Mitchell, T. R. (1992). Self-efficacy: A theoretical analysis of its determinants and malleability. *Academy of Management Review, 17,* 183–211.

Greenhaus, J. H., & Allen, T. D. (2006). Work-family balance: Exploration of a concept. In E. J. Hill (Ed.), *Handbook of family and work.* Manuscript submitted for publication.

Greenhaus, J. H., Allen, T. D., & Spector, P. E. (2006). Health consequences of work-family conflict: The dark side of the work-family interface. In P. L. Perrewe & D. C. Ganster (Eds.), *Research in occupational stress and well-being* (Vol. 5, pp. 61–98). Amsterdam: JAI Press/Elsevier.

Greenhaus, J. H., & Beutell, N. J. (1985). Sources of conflict between work and family roles. *Academy of Management Review, 10,* 76–88.

Greenhaus, J. H., Callanan, G. A., & Godshalk, V. M. (2000). *Career management* (3rd ed.). Fort Worth, TX: Dryden Press.

Greenhaus, J. H., & Powell, G. N. (2006). When work and family are allies: A theory of work-family enrichment. *Academy of Management Review, 31,* 72–92.

Grzywacz, J. G. (2000). Work-family spillover and health during midlife: Is managing conflict everything? *American Journal of Health Promotion, 14,* 236–243.

Grzywacz, J. G., & Bass, B. L. (2003). Work, family, and mental health: Testing different models of work-family fit. *Journal of Marriage and Family, 65,* 248–262.

Hall, D. T. (1976). *Careers in organizations.* Glenview, IL: Scott, Foresman.

Hanson, G. C., Colton, C. L., & Hammer, L. B. (2003, April). *Development and validation of a multidimensional scale of work-family positive spillover.* Paper presented at the 18th Annual Meeting of SIOP, Orlando, FL.

Higgins, M. C., & Kram, K. E. (2001). Reconceptualizing mentoring at work: A developmental network perspective. *Academy of Management Review, 26,* 264–288.

Hill, E. J. (2005). Work-family facilitation and conflict, working fathers and mothers, work-family stressors and support. *Journal of Family Issues, 26,* 793–819.

Holman, D. J., & Wall, T. D. (2002). Work characteristics, learning-related outcomes, and strain: A test of competing direct effects, mediated, and moderated models. *Journal of Occupational Health Psychology, 7,* 283–301.

Huston, T. L., & Levinger, G. (1978). Interpersonal attraction and relationships. *Annual Review of Psychology, 29,* 115–156.

Judge, T. A., Thoresen, C. J., Pucik, V., & Welbourne, T. M. (1999). Managerial coping with organizational change. A dispositional perspective. *Journal of Applied Psychology, 84,* 107–122.

Kahn, R. L., Wolfe, D. M., Quinn, R. P., Snoek, J. D., & Rosenthal, R. A. (1964). *Organizational stress: Studies in role conflict and ambiguity.* New York: John Wiley & Sons.

Kobasa, S. C. (1979). Stressful life events, personality, and health: An inquiry into hardiness. *Journal of Personality and Social Psychology, 37,* 1–11.

Koberg, C. S., Boss, R. W., & Goodman, E. (1998). Factors and outcomes associated with mentoring among health-care professionals. *Journal of Vocational Behavior, 53,* 58–72.

Korman, A. K., & Korman, R. W. (1980). *Career success/personal failure.* Englewood Cliffs, NJ: Prentice Hall.

Kossek, E., E., & Ozeki, C. (1998). Work-family conflict, policies, and the job-life satisfaction relationship: A review and directions for organizational behavior-human resources research. *Journal of Applied Psychology, 83,* 139–149.

Kram, K. E. (1985). *Mentoring at work: Developmental relationships in organizational life.* Glenview, IL: Scott, Foresman.

Lambert, S. J. (1990). Processes linking work and family: A critical review and research agenda. *Human Relations, 43,* 239–257.

Lankau, M. J., & Scandura, T. A. (2002). An investigation of personal learning in mentoring relationships: Content, antecedents, and consequences. *Academy of Management Journal, 45,* 779–790.

McAllister, D. J., & Bigley, G. A. (2002). Work context and the definition of self: How organizational care influences organization-based self-esteem. *Academy of Management Journal, 45,* 894–904.

McCauley, C. D., Ruderman, M. N., Ohlott, P. J., & Morrow, J. E. (1994). Assessing the developmental components of managerial jobs. *Journal of Applied Psychology, 79,* 544–560.

Nielsen, T. R., Carlson, D. S., & Lankau, M. J. (2001). The supportive mentor as a means of reducing work-family conflict. *Journal of Vocational Behavior, 59,* 364–381.

Noe, R., Greenberger, D. B., & Wang, S. (2002). Mentoring: What we know and where we might go. *Research in Personnel and Human Resource Management, 21,* 129–174.

Ogilvie, D. M., & Ashmore, R. D. (1991). Self-with-other representation as a unit of analysis in self-concept research. In R. C. Curtis (Ed.), *The relational self: Theoretical convergences in psychoanalysis and social psychology* (pp. 282–314). New York: Guilford Press.

Olivero, G., Bane, K. D., Kopelman, R. E. (1997). Executive coaching as a transfer of training tool: Effects on productivity in a public agency. *Public Personnel Management, 26,* 461–469.

Powell, G. N., & Greenhaus, J. H. (2005, August). *Managing incidents of time-based work-family conflict: A three-stage process.* Paper presented at the annual meeting of the Academy of Management, Honolulu, HI.

Ragins, B. R. (1997). Diversified mentoring relationships in organizations: A power perspective. *Academy of Management Review, 22,* 482–521.

Ragins, B. R. (1999). Gender and mentoring relationships: A review and research agenda. In G. N. Powell (Ed.), *Handbook of gender and work* (pp. 347–370). Thousand Oaks, CA: Sage.

Ragins, B. R., & Cotton, J. (1993). Gender and willingness to mentor in organizations. *Journal of Management 19,* 97–111.

Ragins, B. R., & Cotton, J. L. (1999). Mentor functions and outcomes: A comparison of men and women in formal and informal mentoring relationships. *Journal of Applied Psychology, 84,* 529–550.

Ragins, B. R., & McFarlin, D. B. (1990). Perceptions of mentor roles in cross-gender mentoring relationships. *Journal of Vocational Behavior, 37,* 321–339.

Ragins, B. R., & Verbos, A. K. (2007). Positive relationships in action: Relational mentoring and mentoring schemas in the workplace. In J. E. Dutton & B. R. Ragins (Eds.), *Exploring positive relationships at work: Building a theoretical and research foundation* (pp. 91–116). Mahwah, NJ: Lawrence Erlbaum.

Repetti, R. L. (1987). Linkages between work and family roles. In S. Oskamp (Ed.), *Family processes and problems: Social psychological aspects* (pp. 98–127). Newbury Park, CA: Sage.

Seibert, S. E. (1999). The effectiveness of facilitated mentoring: A longitudinal quasi-experiment. *Journal of Vocational Behavior, 54,* 483–502.

Seibert, S. E., Kraimer, M. L., & Liden, R. C. (2001). A social capital theory of career success. *Academy of Management Journal, 44,* 219–237.

Sosik, J. J., & Godshalk, V. M. (2000). Leadership styles, mentoring functions received, and job-related stress: A conceptual model and preliminary study. *Journal of Organizational Behavior, 21,* 365–390.

Sosik, J. J., Godshalk, V. M., & Yammarino, F. J. (2004). Transformational leadership, learning goal orientation, and expectations for career success in mentor-protégé relationships: A multiple levels of analysis perspective. *Leadership Quarterly, 15,* 241–261.

Thomas, D. A. (1990). The impact of race on managers' experiences of developmental relationships (mentoring and sponsorships): An intraorganizational study. *Journal of Organizational Behavior, 11,* 479–492.

Thompson, C. A., Beauvais, L. L., & Lyness, K. S. (1999). When work-family benefits are not enough: The influence of work-family culture on benefit utilization, organizational attachment and work-family conflict. *Journal of Vocational Behavior, 54,* 392–415.

Voydanoff, P. (2004a). The effects of work demands and resources on work-to-family conflict and facilitation. *Journal of Marriage and Family, 66,* 398–412.

Voydanoff, P. (2004b). Implications of work and community demands and resources for work-to-family conflict and facilitation. *Journal of Occupational Health Psychology, 9,* 275–285.

Wallace, J. E. (2001). The benefits of mentoring for female lawyers. *Journal of Vocational Behavior, 58,* 366–391.

Wanberg, C. R., Welsh, E. T., & Hezlett, S. A. (2003). Mentoring research: A review and dynamic process model. *Research in Personnel and Human Resource Management, 22,* 39–124.

Waters, L., McCabe, M., Kiellerup, D., & Kiellerup, S. (2002). The role of formal mentoring on business success and self-esteem in participants of a new business start-up program. *Journal of Business and Psychology, 17,* 107–121.

PART IV

Mentoring in Practice

Programs and Innovations

Section Purpose and Structure

This section builds a bridge between the practice and study of mentoring by bringing together an internationally acclaimed group of practitioners to discuss current issues, challenges, and needs in the practice of mentoring. To accomplish this goal, we asked our contributors to address three major topics. First, they were asked to describe their mentoring practice, programs, or applications. Second, they were asked to share the challenges they have encountered in their practice, as well as the solutions, opportunities, and lessons they learned in meeting these challenges. Last, they were asked to specify the types of research and theory that have been useful to their practice and to give specific suggestions for research that would enhance their efforts to improve the practice of mentoring in a variety of organizational and cultural contexts.

Overview of Chapters

This section begins with Katherine Giscombe's chapter on formal mentoring programs that help women break through the glass ceiling. Based on her work with Catalyst, a nonprofit organization that works to advance women in the workplace, she reviews practices and characteristics of formal mentoring programs in 11 private sector companies headquartered in the United States. The author describes the format, goals, design, and practices of these programs and develops an important typology of the characteristics of formal programs that help women break through the glass ceiling. She then presents four programs as case examples that illustrate effective program features, strategies, and practices. The chapter closes with a detailed research agenda that offers mentoring scholars rich insight into the types of research that can be used to develop programs that successfully move women through the glass ceiling.

Cynthia McCauley and Victoria Guthrie leverage their extensive experience at the Center for Creative Leadership (CCL) to build a critical bridge between the leadership and mentoring arenas. Their chapter frames developmental relationships within the context of learning and offers specific examples of how developmental relationships can be used in leadership development programs. The authors apply the CCL Assessment, Challenge, and Support framework to examine how learning coaches, peer learning partners, and learning resources can maximize learning in developmental relationships for individuals in leadership roles. The chapter discusses the unique challenges involved with designing relationships for learning and the ways practitioners can meet these challenges. The authors integrate existing research and theory on leadership, mentoring, and learning relationships to offer a practice-based, but theory-inspired, agenda for future research.

The next chapter partners Lynn P-Sontag and Kimberly Vappie, practitioners from the MENTTIUM consulting firm, with mentoring scholar Connie Wanberg. Their chapter first offers a detailed description of MENTTIUM's nationally recognized mentoring programs, which involve one-on-one and group mentoring, as well as programs aimed at advancing the careers of high-potential women. They examine how formal mentoring programs can create synergy with other organizational programs and give a step-by-step description of the implementation process using a case study. The authors then explore the challenges and obstacles to instituting formal programs, from both an organizational and participant perspective, and offer insights and examples on how to successfully navigate these challenges. The chapter concludes with an in-depth discussion of research issues in studying formal mentoring relationships and cutting-edge recommendations for research that would help practitioners develop effective formal mentoring programs.

Stacy Blake-Beard, Regina O'Neill, and Eileen McGowan draw on their collective experiences as consultants and scholars to craft a practical chapter that explores the crevasses, caveats, and complexities of the matching process in formal mentoring programs. They start with an informative review of some of the key differences between formal and informal relationships and integrate research into practice by exploring how these relationships vary in terms of the initiation and subsequent relationship phases. The authors then offer a comprehensive overview of matching strategies that incorporate consideration of individual differences, program goals, and organizational context. They examine the advantages and disadvantages of these strategies, common challenges faced in matching participants, and best practices for overcoming these challenges. The authors present an assessment tool that can assist in the creation of effective matches and offer guidelines for future research that can assess the relative effectiveness of different matching strategies.

The last chapter, by David Clutterbuck, offers an insightful international perspective on the practice of mentoring. Drawing on his extensive experience as an international consultant, he first describes his mentoring practice and highlights some of the key distinctions between European and American models of mentoring. He offers a comparative analysis of mentoring and coaching relationships and traces how these relationships have evolved in the United States and Europe. He then explores how culture shapes mentoring relationships and offers specific examples of how culture affects mentoring programs across international settings. The author analyzes the complexities involved with cross-cultural mentoring and offers strategies and solutions for creating effective mentoring across cultures. The chapter concludes by offering insight into challenges for studying mentoring across cultures and a detailed agenda for future research on cross-cultural mentoring.

The chapters in this section offer the reader a practical perspective on the garden of mentoring. Combined, these authors provide rich insight into effective practices, as well as the challenges and solutions involved in developing effective mentoring programs and high-quality developmental relationships in organizations. These chapters plant seeds for new research that will make a difference in the practice of mentoring.

22

Advancing Women Through the Glass Ceiling With Formal Mentoring

Katherine Giscombe

Despite women's progress at moving into managerial positions, women continue to be underrepresented in senior management, particularly in critical line positions in private sector organizations (Catalyst, 2002). Mentoring is often cited as an essential strategy for career advancement, and recent meta-analytic research has provided evidence that mentored individuals have better career outcomes than nonmentored individuals, as indicated by both objective measures, such as compensation and promotions, and subjective measures, such as career satisfaction and commitment (Allen, Eby, Poteet, Lentz, & Lima, 2004). Whereas mentoring theory originally focused on experienced men serving as mentors to less experienced men (Levinson, 1978), mentoring theorists, such as Ragins (1997, 1999, 2002), have expanded the concept of mentoring to focus on members of other demographic groups and have suggested that mentors might be particularly important for helping nontraditional managers, such as women, to overcome glass-ceiling barriers that can impede their organizational advancement in male-dominated organizations.

Despite these apparent benefits of mentoring for women, earlier research indicated that women might encounter gender-related barriers to finding mentors or receive fewer benefits than men from mentoring relationships. For example, Ragins and Cotton (1991) found that women were more likely than men to report limited access to potential mentors, that potential mentors were unwilling to develop

AUTHOR'S NOTE: The author gratefully acknowledges the contributions of Karen S. Lyness and Rachel G. Levy to this chapter.

relationships with them, and that they had concerns that approaching men as potential mentors might be misinterpreted as sexual advances. Also, Dreher and Cox's (1996) study of MBA graduates found that women were less likely than men to have White male mentors and that participants with White male mentors were more successful, as measured by compensation, than participants whose mentors were women, or men of color. A number of studies of women in corporate management by Catalyst (1996, 1999, 2000, 2004) found that women cited lack of access to mentors as a barrier to further advancement. Furthermore, Lyness and Thompson's (2000) study of matched samples of female and male executives found that mentoring was more strongly associated with career advancement for men than for women.

In an effort to broaden access to the benefits of mentoring relationships, a number of companies have introduced formal mentoring programs, many of which are targeted at groups, such as women, who are underrepresented in leadership positions. Research suggests that while formal relationships are beneficial, they are not on par with informal relationships regarding individual outcomes (Baugh & Fagenson-Eland, Chapter 10, this volume). Specific results have differed across studies, but in each case, mentees in formal mentoring programs reported receiving less of one or more types of mentoring functions, including career development, psychosocial functions, and role-modeling (Chao, Walz, & Gardner, 1992; Fagenson-Eland, Marks, & Amendola, 1997; Ragins & Cotton, 1999; Scandura & Williams, 2001). A particularly troublesome finding from the Ragins and Cotton (1999) study was a pronounced gap in several mentoring functions for female protégés, such that women in formal mentoring programs reported receiving fewer benefits than women in informal mentoring relationships, whereas male protégés reported similar mentoring functions regardless of whether they were in formal or informal mentoring relationships.

The prior research findings suggest that it is important to learn more about how these formal mentoring programs operate and why they may not always be delivering benefits that are comparable to those of informal mentoring. To address these issues, I review 11 formal mentoring programs that had the goal of developing women leaders, identify what seems to be working and what might be improved on, and discuss areas where additional research and theory are needed to help inform practice.

Special Mentoring Needs of Women in Organizations

Women face a number of challenges that impede their advancement. As mentioned above, lack of mentoring is a critical factor, but there are other barriers that build on this challenge. Common barriers include work/family conflict, lack of significant general management/line experience, exclusion from informal networks, and gender-based stereotyping (Catalyst, 2004).

Gender stereotyping ascribes attributes to men that are consistent with those of successful managers and "nonleader" attributes to women, such as passivity. One outcome of gender stereotyping is that women are assigned to senior management roles less frequently than men (Heilman, 2001). Recent research suggests that senior executives, who are positioned to promote women into powerful roles, themselves hold gender stereotypes (Catalyst, 2005).

The gender-stereotyping literature suggests that compared with men, who often have access to inner circles and experience congruity between how they are perceived and senior leadership attributes, women need mentoring that helps them successfully navigate systems that do not embrace their presence. Mentoring can give women access to the "old-boys' network" (Ragins & Sundstrom, 1989) and offers them the protection needed to deal with workplaces that may range from nonsupportive to hostile. Further, many women who succeed in corporate environments cite the importance of developing a style with which male managers are comfortable (Catalyst, 1996). Senior male mentors can offer women protégés coaching in this area.

Finally, mentoring may be helpful in addressing work-life conflict as experienced by women. A model integrating work/family perspectives with mentoring suggests that mentors who support a protégé's work-family balance may help ease work-life conflict and enhance work-life enrichment for the protégé (Greenhaus & Singh, Chapter 21, this volume).

Characteristics of Formal Mentoring Programs That Target Development of Women Leaders

Catalyst, the organization that the author is affiliated with, is a nonprofit organization that works to advance women in the workplace. The organization compiles knowledge on mentoring practices, sometimes documenting these practices in its research reports or other venues to offer examples of effective programs. These practices use as source material interviews with program administrators and designers and information on program substance, including objectives, guidelines, program structure, and, in some cases, effectiveness.

I reviewed company practices of formal mentoring programs targeted to developing women leaders in 11 private sector companies headquartered in the United States. While they represent diverse industries, such as consumer packaged goods and retail, they are not necessarily representative of all U.S. organizations that offer mentoring programs and do not include some of the more difficult industries for women, such as manufacturing. Nevertheless, this review is intended to offer insight into characteristics of typical organizational mentoring programs as well as important variations across programs that may be related to overall effectiveness. This complements the work of Ragins, Cotton, and Miller (2000), one of the few studies to examine the effectiveness of formal mentoring programs. Whereas that study examined reactions of individual program participants, this work draws more on the perspectives of program developers.

The programs reviewed here all meet commonly used definitions of formal mentoring programs (e.g., Ragins & Cotton, 1999). Formal mentoring programs are designed to meet objectives developed by the organization, which may differ from objectives of informal mentoring relationships, though in the case of developing women leaders, there is significant overlap between protégés' goals and organizational goals (e.g., higher representation of women in senior positions). Mentors and protégés select each other in informal mentoring relationships, whereas in formal mentoring programs, organizations determine participant eligibility criteria and either match mentors and *mentees* (the term preferred by formal programs over the more intimate expression *protégé*) or structure a process whereby matching will occur. Organizations often provide guidelines and some level of program support.

The emphasis in the programs reviewed was usually on both women and people of color. In some cases, the program served the professional employee population at large while still retaining a focus on women and people of color.

Mentoring in these programs was defined as consisting of elements of psychosocial aspects of the mentor's role, including role-modeling and career development (Kram, 1985). Most programs defined the mentor role as distinct from other roles in the company, such as supervisor (and all companies excluded immediate managers as mentors). While sponsorship is one subcategory of career development, most programs, with a few exceptions that will be noted, excluded sponsorship from their definitions of mentoring.

Many of the characteristics chosen for typology of these formal mentoring programs are suggested in a review by Wanberg, Welsh, and Hezlett (2003), which hypothesized several requirements for successful programs. These include the types of mentoring received, participant/relationship antecedents, and program characteristics. The Wanberg et al. model looked at formal mentoring programs in general, not those for women's leadership development. Based on this chapter's focus on women's leadership, other criteria specific to the programmatic goal of developing women leaders have been added.

Table 22.1 summarizes characteristics of mentoring programs, and in some cases denotes whether the program received a positive evaluation. In most cases, the evaluations were reported by program administrators, with no distinction about relative effectiveness among target subpopulations (e.g., the women, people of color, or the men that the programs expanded to include). The inferences drawn about effectiveness of program characteristics are therefore open to consideration.

Location of Program

Table 22.1 indicates the functional location of the mentoring program. These include talent management (typically within human resources and overseeing career advancement programs and other training and resources for employee development), diversity and inclusion (or "D&I," often but not always located within human resources and not necessarily tied to talent management programs), or a combination. Alternatively, the programs could be stand-alone or administered cross-functionally outside of the human resources function.

Location of Program Summary/Effectiveness

Most women's leadership mentoring programs included some connection with talent management (including four of the six programs that received positive

Table 22.1   Characteristics of Mentoring Programs That Develop Women's Leadership

Company	Location of Program	Format	Selection of Participants	Matching	Program Support	Gender Addressed	Evaluation
A	Talent Management	Pairs	Mentee performance requirement	Complementarity Mentee Choice	Training Manager involvement	No	**Positive** Mentee assessment (360) Programmatic
B	Talent management	Pairs Group	Performance requirement Mentor selection-gender-addressed-sponsorship criterion	Complementarity	Orientation Training (Mentor training-encourages self-disclosure) Manager involvement	Yes, in participant selection (*mentor sensitivity to gender issues*)	**Positive** Programmatic
C	Talent management	Reverse Mentoring	Mentee level requirement	Subjective	Orientation Guidelines	No	**Positive** Organizational metrics
D	Diversity and Inclusion	Pairs	Open Mandatory (mentors)	Complementarity Mentee choice	Training Guidelines Ongoing support	Yes, in program support	**Positive** Programmatic
E	Diversity and Inclusion	Group External	Mentee performance requirement	External	Orientation Training Manager involvement	Yes, in participant selection	**Positive** Anecdotal Mentee assessment
F	D and I and talent mgt	Group (1 mentor and small group of mentees)	Open	Similarity Mentee choice	Orientation Training (Mentor training in sponsorship) Guidelines Ongoing support	Yes, in program support	**Positive** Programmatic

(Continued)

Table 22.1 (Continued)

Company	Location of Program	Format	Selection of Participants	Matching	Program Support	Gender Addressed	Evaluation
G	Talent management	Pairs	Open	Subjective	Guidelines (limited)	No	None yet
H	Talent management and D & I	Pairs	Mentee performance requirement/ development need Mandatory (mentors)	Subjective	Training Guidelines Accountability	No	Programmatic
I	Talent management	Reverse Pairs	Mentee tenure requirement	Complementarity/ similarity	Orientation Training Guidelines Manager involvement Ongoing support	Yes, in program support	Programmatic Mentee assessment
J	D and I	Pairs	Open	Subjective	Training Guidelines Accountability (mentor reward)	No	Programmatic
K	Talent management	Pairs	Mentee performance/level requirement	Complementarity/ similarity	Training Guidelines	No	Organizational metrics Programmatic

evaluations). An assumption is that support from talent management functions in organizations is essential for mentoring programs intended to facilitate the development of women leaders. This is in accord with the Wanberg et al. (2003) assumption that protégé change, one measure of effectiveness, will be enhanced by the existence of related development opportunities (typically accessed through organizational talent management functions).

Format and Summary/Effectiveness

The majority of these programs attempted to emulate typical informal mentoring relationships by pairing senior, experienced mentors with more-junior mentees. Three companies had group mentoring programs. Another two companies had reverse or "upward" mentoring programs, with hierarchical superiors in the role of mentees. The more well-resourced programs offered a variety of mentoring options (e.g., one-on-one programs for certain business units or populations and group mentoring for others). Each type of format had at least one positively evaluated program associated with it.

Selection Characteristics

Selection characteristics denote whether there were performance or hierarchical rank requirements for mentees or whether the process was "open." For mentors, I note only where there is some type of performance requirement (with the exception of the reverse mentoring programs, all programs required mentors to have achieved a particular hierarchical rank).

I also noted programs that were mandatory. Wanberg et al. (2003) hypothesized that voluntary participation on the part of mentors and mentees would be related to higher frequency of meeting. Finally, given this chapter's emphasis on mentoring women through the glass ceiling, I considered whether gender was explicitly addressed as part of the mentor selection criteria and whether mentor selection criteria facilitated enactment of sponsorship.

Selection Summary/Effectiveness

These programs tended to be exclusive in their selection of mentees, using some combination of performance rating data, subjective ratings by managers and executives, and, to a lesser extent, level in the management hierarchy. Two programs explicitly sought participants who had a combination of high achievement and development needs.

Most programs judged as effective were stringent in their selection of mentees. Evidence of mentees' achievements may make them more attractive to potential mentors; research has shown that informally mentoring successful protégés increased potential rewards for mentors (Allen, Poteet, & Russell, 2000; Olian, Carroll, & Giannantonio, 1993). Mentoring programs designed to develop leaders improve their chances for success by selecting those with some proven capacity to develop into leaders.

Two programs judged as successful were open. The lack of mentee performance requirements appeared to reflect the junior level of mentee sought and the organization-wide basis of the program. While no hard performance criteria were required for those open programs, self-ratings by the potential mentees and other tools were used to assess potential mentees' motivation.

In contrast with mentee selection, mentor criteria tended to be more general: that potential mentors understood the mentoring program, were committed to people development, and were available. One positively evaluated program used more stringent criteria, including demonstration of mentor behaviors that indicated sensitivity to gender issues. This company also ensured that mentors were able, at least potentially, to act as sponsors for mentees by requiring that mentors have well-established networks within the organization.

An effective upward mentoring program specified that all mentors be women, consistent with its goal of educating senior executives on issues facing women in the company. With this exception, no other company examined in this chapter explicitly addressed mentor's gender.

Two companies required participation in mentoring programs by executives at certain organizational levels. One of these programs was judged as effective, against Wanberg et al.'s (2003) prediction that voluntary programs would be more successful; this might have been because the company incorporated mentor performance into the formal performance evaluation process.

Matching

Wanberg et al. (2003) asserted that organizations that match protégés and mentors on the basis of similarity (e.g., an interest in common) and also some complement of each other's needs would produce pairs with strong interpersonal relationships. I note in Table 22.1 which programs use complementarity and similarity as matching criteria.

Other criteria include participant (particularly mentee) choice in the match versus no input. Wanberg et al. (2003) hypothesized that formal mentoring programs that solicit participant input in matching would produce pairs with strong interpersonal relationships.

I also examined whether gender was a factor in matching—whether the organization assumed that male mentors would be more effective or, alternatively, that women mentors would be better at addressing women protégés' issues.

Matching Summary/Effectiveness

Many matches were made using some combination of (a) complementarity of skills between the mentor and mentee (b) and similarity of interests. These were based on tools such as questionnaires, interviews, and biographical statements. Three out of the 11 programs allowed some choice by the participant (in all cases the mentee); all 3 of these programs that allowed some degree of mentee choice in the match were positively evaluated (out of a total of 6 programs receiving positive evaluations). Sometimes program administrators used their own personal knowledge of the mentor and mentee pool to match. These subjective matches were not based on any well-articulated criteria such as complementarity or similarity, but rather the "gut feeling" of the program administrators on compatibility of pairings. In general, the more positively evaluated programs tended to use some combination of complementarity of skill and similarity of interests, while the less positively evaluated programs were more likely to use subjective means.

With the exception of one reverse mentoring program that specified junior women as mentors, none of the programs took explicit account of mentor gender when matching. At most, programs took implicit account of gender when they identified "top executives" as the mentor pool, and very few women appeared in that pool.

Finally, most programs required that mentors and mentees come from different departments or units, in some cases to facilitate cross-functional information sharing but usually to ensure that the mentoring process did not interfere with the performance management functions performed by the mentee's manager.

Program Support

Program support was evaluated on the basis of whether any of the following features was included:

- Orientations, typically encompassing information on the program's philosophy, its support, and the parameters of the mentoring relationship
- Provision of guidelines, which include schedules of regular meetings
- Manager involvement, or the extent to which managers support participants' involvement in the mentoring program
- Training for skill development, or whether mentors are trained in sponsorship and whether gender is addressed in training of the mentor or mentee
- Ongoing support for development of the mentor/mentee relationship
- Accountability, or whether mentor performance was part of performance assessment

Program Support Summary/Effectiveness

Although resources varied, all mentoring programs had the stated support of senior management, and in some cases, mentoring task forces or steering committees administered the programs.

Wanberg et al. (2003) predicted that the presence of guidelines for a mentoring pair would impact positively on frequency of meeting. In support of this idea, most of the programs evaluated in this chapter had some level of guidelines. They typically included a schedule of regular meetings for the mentor/mentee pairs (monthly or bimonthly). Other guidelines included tips on enacting the roles of mentor and mentee (often emphasizing communication and commitment to goals); training materials; and guides to meeting agendas, which tended to emphasize task-oriented skill development and career planning. Additional tools to facilitate these meetings included discussion guides, progress logs to track meeting dates and discussion topics, and individualized monthly action assignments to ensure progress in goal attainment.

Guidelines often included the assignment of ownership for the mentoring process to the mentee. When mentees were given this responsibility, there was no indication that organizational power inequities between mentor and mentees were taken into account, so holding mentees responsible for the success of the mentoring relationships may not have been ideal. On the other hand, many programs selected fairly senior mentees, so it is reasonable to expect that they would be skilled in upward management. In one program with very junior mentees (described in the next section), responsibility for the relationship went to the mentor.

Programs that were judged positively tended to have a great deal of support, from skill development for participants and ongoing help with the relationship to mechanisms for detailed assessment of mentee growth in key areas. By contrast, one of the programs that were not judged as positive provided only limited guidelines on numbers of meetings. This program also did not describe mentor and mentee roles, following the lead of senior managers who judged these role prescriptions unnecessary. A few programs were most closely managed in the pilot or early phases in providing support and guidance to the pairs, and as the programs expanded, they lost some oversight and some measure of participant satisfaction.

Wanberg and colleagues (2003) hypothesized that support for the pair to develop the relationship would positively impact the intimacy of the relationship. However, only a few of the programs provided resources for helping mentors and mentees to manage their relationships. In one of the positively evaluated programs, described in the next section, experts were available to coach or answer questions about relationship issues from participants. Wanberg et al. also predicted that manager support would impact mentee goal achievement. In three of the six positively evaluated programs, the managers of the mentees were involved (compared with one of the other five programs).

When programs offered training to mentors, it was typically to address communication and feedback skills. Mentees in some of the better-resourced programs had access to skill-building sessions that taught core competencies required for their businesses.

Only two of the programs offered accountability for mentor performance (i.e., assessed mentor performance as part of the larger organizational performance evaluation system). However, other programs provided so much oversight and help to the mentor/mentee relationship, in keeping them on track with their meetings and goal attainment, that the administrators felt that the mentoring program infrastructure provided a level of accountability for participant performance.

Programs typically communicated to mentors the benefits of mentoring (e.g., learning the perspectives of a junior-level employee and being a good organizational citizen) but did not formally reward mentors. One of the programs that offered formal accountability for mentor performance also included events honoring mentors for their contributions.

In only a few cases did training explicitly address any issues related to cross-gender mentoring relationships (see Ragins, 1997, 2002, for more information about these issues). In two positively evaluated programs, one provided training on cross-gender issues in mentoring relationships, and another included training on tips for setting up contacts for mentees (i.e., training in how the mentor could enact the sponsor role).

Program Evaluation and Summary/Effectiveness

Mentoring program evaluation could consist of programmatic evaluation (the most popular choice among the programs discussed in this chapter), assessment of participant behaviors (especially perceived change in the mentee's behavior), and/or organizational metrics. Programmatic evaluation largely focused on measuring satisfaction with the program itself among participants, collected at various points during the mentoring program. This approach is consistent with research on organizational training programs, in which participant reactions are more commonly measured than other types of criteria that may be more meaningful but also more difficult to collect or accurately analyze, such as learning, behavioral changes, or organizational outcomes (Alliger, Tannenbaum, Bennett, Traver, & Shotland, 1997).

Two of the positively evaluated programs used changes in mentee leadership behavior to evaluate the success of the program, which were well linked to the goal of developing women leaders. The one program that used organizational metrics (the reverse mentoring program), which is described in the next section, had a good match between programmatic goals and assessment method, since the larger goal was to support creation of a culture that facilitated advancement of women.

Summary of Effective Programmatic Characteristics

In summary, the following characteristics specified by the Wanberg et al. (2003) model appeared to be effective in programs designed to advance women.

Related Development Opportunities. All positively evaluated mentoring programs either provided extensive training to participants or were located in the talent management area of the organization so that participants had access to training.

Matching: Complementarity of Skills and Similarity of Interests, and Mentee Choice. Consistent with Wanberg et al.'s (2003) model, the positively evaluated programs were more likely than the other programs to allow some degree of mentee choice in the match, making the matches more akin to informal relationships. Also consistent with Wanberg et al.'s prediction, the more positively evaluated programs tended to use some combination of complementarity of skills and/or similarity of interests, while the other programs usually employed subjective means. Matches created subjectively by administrators, while sometimes effective, were not replicable—the success of the procedure depended on the level of knowledge and insight of program administrators.

High Levels of Programmatic and Manager Support. Consistent with Wanberg et al.'s (2003) model, programs that were judged positively tended to have a great deal of support, including training in how to enact the mentor or mentee role or ongoing help with the mentor/mentee relationship itself.

Wanberg et al. (2003) also predicted that manager support would impact mentee goal achievement. The managers of the mentees were much more likely to be involved in the positively evaluated programs, either through initially selecting the mentees or supporting their work with the mentors.

In addition, other criteria specified by this author, as follows, appeared to be effective in programs designed to advance women.

Stringent Selection of Mentees. Mentee selection criteria of the effective programs typically included performance and/or hierarchy requirements (so that those selected had demonstrated the potential to become leaders and were also probably attractive to potential mentors). However, there were some exceptions noted, in particular those programs devoted to developing leadership pipelines at lower levels in the organization.

Mentor Sensitivity to Gender Issues. While few programs took gender-related issues into account in program design, a few positively evaluated programs either selected mentors with demonstrated sensitivity to gender issues or provided training to mentors to enhance gender sensitivity. It should be noted again, however, that because the evaluations usually made no distinction about relative effectiveness among women mentees versus others in the program, these findings are suggestive rather than firm.

Sponsorship Facilitation. While few companies encouraged mentors to sponsor their mentees, two of the positively evaluated programs either selected mentors on the basis of sponsorship capability (i.e., only those with well-established networks in the company were eligible) or provided training in enacting the sponsorship role.

Program Evaluation Closely Tied to Programmatic Goals. Rather than simply measuring participant satisfaction, the more positively evaluated programs tended to link assessment metrics with program objectives. Most meaningfully, two programs devoted to developing leaders included sophisticated assessment of change in leader behavior over the course of the mentoring programs.

Cases

The following four cases provide a holistic look at successful mentoring programs. They illustrate how good design features were made more powerful by meaningfully linking them with other programmatic elements.

Leveraging Mentee Participation in Mentor Selection

This formal mentoring program combines several features from the Wanberg et al. (2003) model hypothesized for program success: some level of complementarity between mentee needs and mentor strengths, a degree of participation in matching by participants (in this case selection of the mentor by the mentee), involvement of participants' managers in the program (in this case mentees' managers), and inclusion of the mentoring program within talent management, as well as access to developmental programs as part of the mentoring experience (see Table 22.2). This program is also quite well supported, with experts playing key roles in supporting mentee development. Selection is very limited to ensure adequate resources for participants.

Table 22.2   Leveraging Mentee Participation in Mentor Selection

Company	Location of Program	Format	Selection of Participants	Matching	Program Support	Gender Addressed	Evaluation
A	Talent Management	Pairs	Mentee performance requirement	Complementarity Mentee choice	Training Manager involvement	No	Positive Mentee assessment (360) Programmatic

All mentees are high potential in this leadership program targeting women and minorities. Immediate managers nominate all mentees, and then human resources selects senior-level mentors who have established reputations as effective mentors and/or have participated in the program before. Mentors are restricted to only one formal mentee at a time, to allow them to devote adequate time to the relationship.

As part of the matching process, mentees receive 360-degree feedback on their leadership skills. Coaches use the feedback to help mentees clarify their focus, and they write an action plan. Mentor leadership competency self-assessments are available in a database application. Mentees enter into the database mentor criteria and skills they want to work on, based on the developmental plan designed with the external coach, and the database application identifies three potential mentors. The mentees follow up to assess the chemistry, interest levels, and opportunities for the relationship.

As part of the mentoring program, mentees are taught key leadership competencies, specifically those required to transition from individual contributor to cross-operational roles. Mentees are assessed at the end of the program in a modified 360-degree feedback session that allows raters to identify areas for improvement; they then have a final session with their coaches to identify next steps.

Development of Mentors as Sponsors

This second case, in a *Fortune* 500 company, focuses on high-performing women and people of color. More than one mentoring format is offered: one-on-one and group mentoring (two mentors to a group of mentees) in various business sites. The discussion in this section is focused on the one-on-one program, which illustrates gender sensitivity in its program design. (See Table 22.3.)

This program has several of the features identified in the Wanberg et al. (2003) model, such as manager support of the mentoring relationship; complementarity between mentee needs and mentor strengths; and extensive program support, which includes an expectation-setting orientation session and training (in this case directed at the mentor). The manager nominates high-performing mentees in conjunction with a cross-functional task force. After mentors and mentees fill out a form on strengths and needs, human resources matches for complementarity of skills. Successful, long-tenured senior managers who are judged by top executives to understand organizational culture and practices are selected as mentors.

Table 22.3   Development of Mentors as Sponsors

Company	Location of Program	Format	Selection of Participants	Matching	Program Support	Gender Addressed	Evaluation
B	Talent Management	Pairs Group	Performance requirement Mentor selection-gender addressed-sponsorship criterion	Complementarity	Orientation Training (Mentor training—encourages self-disclosure) Manager involvement	Yes, in participant selection *(mentor sensitivity to gender issues)*	Positive Programmatic

This is the only program examined that includes the mentor criterion of demonstrated behaviors indicating sensitivity to gender and culture. Also unique to this program is a criterion suggesting sponsorship potential: Potential mentors are required to have well-established networks in the company.

Training and support in this program focuses on the mentor and includes an orientation workshop, coaching from the program staff in the unique perspectives of women and people of color, and training on self-revelation—how mentors can use their life experiences to create teachable stories for mentees—which is important to developing closeness and related to the level of trust and comfort in the relationship (Wanberg et al., 2003).

Making Organizational Change Through an Innovative Format

The explicit goal of this program, the third illustration in this chapter of an effective mentoring program, was to educate senior leaders on gender issues. The program was part of the organization's talent management program and provided discussion topics and meeting-frequency guidelines. The program paired junior women in the mentor role with predominantly male top executives in the mentee role. The pair shared perspectives, and the junior-woman mentor helped build the executive's understanding of new ways of looking at policy, business strategy, and work-life issues. While one purpose of the program was to create opportunities for midlevel women to develop quality relationships with senior managers, the larger purpose of the program was to help create a climate so that women could more easily advance by raising senior men's awareness of gender issues in the organization. (See Table 22.4.)

The program was a success according to organizational metrics, including representation of women in senior roles. The number of women in key leadership positions increased over 20% in a 2-year period, with the strongest results in the line organization (positions with profit-and-loss responsibility). It should be noted that other programs for women were part of this organization's talent management programs, including high-potential identification, succession planning, and resources for work-life support, and it is difficult to isolate the effect of the reverse

Table 22.4   Making Organizational Change through an Innovative Format

Company	Location of Program	Format	Selection of Participants	Matching	Program Support	Gender Addressed	Evaluation
C	Talent Management	Reverse Mentoring	Mentee level requirement	Subjective	Orientation Guidelines	No	Positive Organizational metrics

mentoring program on promotion rates. In addition, the highly visible support that senior managers lent the program probably reflects an existing positive climate for women in the organization. There might have been a circular effect, such that the program reinforced the culture of the organization, while the culture reinforced the program. It appears, however, that at the least, reverse mentoring was one element of a successful women's leadership development effort within this company.

Facilitating Formation of a Strong Mentor-Mentee Bond

In this final case, a *Fortune* 1000 company mentoring program focused on developing the leadership pipeline of women and people of color and targeted relatively junior professionals. It combines two features from the Wanberg et al. (2003) model hypothesized for program success: some level of complementarity between mentee needs and mentor strengths and a degree of mentee choice in selection of mentors. Unlike many of the other programs examined with the goal of developing women as leaders, this program did not require mentees to have reached a certain level of performance as a prerequisite for entering the program. This design feature reflects the fact that relatively junior levels of mentees were being developed for future leadership roles, rather than those just below the glass ceiling. However, mentees still had to demonstrate motivation to participate in the mentoring relationship and commitment to the company. Mentors, who were chosen by the human resources department, needed to demonstrate commitment to development, strong people skills, and commitment to the company. (See Table 22.5.)

This program assigned more than one mentee per mentor and was also fairly unique in mandating participation for mentors—both design features to handle the logistic constraints imposed by large numbers of mentees. The mandatory

Table 22.5   Facilitating Formation of a Strong Mentor-Mentee Bond

Company	Location of Program	Format	Selection of Participants	Matching	Program Support	Gender Addressed	Evaluation
D	Diversity and Inclusion	Pairs	Open Mandatory (mentors)	Complementarity Mentee choice	Training Guidelines Ongoing support	Yes, in program support	Positive Programmatic

nature of mentor participation appears to have been softened by the extensive training offered to participants. The program provided different types of support at different phases of the relationship, including preparation, development, and closing. It provided very detailed agendas for meetings and charged the mentors with creating an appropriate environment to build and maintain the relationship (reflecting the fact that relatively junior mentees were part of this program).

This program was unique in offering both process and content guidelines for conducting meetings, with a focus on communication, including conflict resolution, problem solving, and strategic perspectives. Training was offered on gender issues in the context of *cross-cultural mentoring* (defined as mentoring someone who is different from the mentor in one of several characteristics, including gender). This training addressed differences in male and female communication styles that might be relevant to mentoring relationships.

The program administrators analyzed program feedback from mentors to conclude that the mentors were satisfied with commitment to specified parameters of the working relationship and that the program helped them develop and maintain respectful, positive relationships.

Suggestions for Advancing Women Through the Glass Ceiling With Formal Mentoring

In this section, I prescribe several strategies and tactics that are particularly important for organizations and salient for mentoring programs intended to help women advance to senior management levels: (a) Integrate leadership development with leadership competency models; (b) provide sponsorship; and (c) focus more strongly on gender. It is also worth noting that any mentoring program, regardless of target audience, needs adequate support and resources. All programs that were positively evaluated provided support to encourage regular meetings between mentors and mentees. What makes such support crucial for women mentees, especially those in cross-gender pairings, is the relative ease such a structure lends to initiating and maintaining the relationship.

Integrate Leadership Development and Assessment With Leadership Competency Models

As noted in the earlier discussion of mentoring program evaluation, most organizations rely on attitudinal measures, such as participant satisfaction, or metrics, such as the number of employees who participated in their programs. However, these types of measures may have limited value because they are not always related to critical organizational outcomes (Alliger et al., 1997). On the other hand, some of the more positively rated mentoring programs include assessment of mentee leadership behavior. This was very appropriate, as it was linked to the goal of the mentoring programs. For mentoring women through the glass ceiling, criteria that measure improvement in mentees' leadership ability may be crucial.

However, for such criteria to be meaningful, there needs to be a link between what is developed during the mentoring program and how it links back to the organization. The Wanberg et al. (2003) model suggests that organizational contextual factors are relevant to the outcomes observed as a consequence of a formal mentoring program, including an organization's size, structure, and compensation and promotional systems. Integration with promotional systems is crucial, which is why these programs' location in talent management is important; I extend this point to identify the critical role of the organization/mentoring program interface. If the objectives of the mentoring program are to increase women's capacities to become leaders, then mentoring should fit in with leader development. Having a clear leadership competency model in the organization to work from is an important first step. Company A (shown in Table 22.2) integrated elements of its leadership competency model in the training of its high-potential mentees, and that appeared to be important in transitioning them from individual contributor roles to positions as senior managers with well-integrated understanding of a complex business.

Provide Sponsorship

While development of leadership competencies is important, sponsorship, as one facet of career development, is the most direct link between a candidate and a position. Rather than solely developing competencies through being coached by a mentor and eventually becoming a well-skilled candidate for a senior job, the beneficiary of sponsorship is often directly placed in a position. When stereotyping occurs, there is evidence that objective ability is discounted (Catalyst, 2005). Sponsorship is one facet of mentoring that women, as a marginalized and stereotyped group, need to break through the glass ceiling. This is complicated by the selection of mentors who would be willing to provide such a potentially risky service (e.g., sponsors may put their reputations on the line); the further research that is needed regarding selection of mentors is discussed in the next section. A beginning, however, is to apply some of the techniques that the positively evaluated companies used in selecting mentors, for example, selecting only those mentors who were well connected in the company and providing some support for the relationship so that greater trust and intimacy may develop (and the mentor may eventually consider becoming a sponsor).

Focus More Strongly on Gender

Formal mentoring is advantageous for women in that programs provide access to mentors and legitimate cross-gender relationships, which protect members from damaging gossip about romantic involvement. Yet many organizations are reluctant to limit programs to only women or other marginalized groups. The only company evaluated in this chapter that restricted its program to women mentees was one that used an external program. As one program administrator reported, senior management must buy in to an initiative. Buy-in is more easily achieved with a "business case" that the program will benefit all employees. Further, some programs that began as exclusively targeted to women and minorities have been rolled out to the larger employee population. There are therefore fewer initiatives that exclusively target women and marginalized groups.

An administrator of one mentoring program for high-potential employees that does not target women (and is not included in the analysis in this chapter) reported that gender was not an issue. The administrator's rationale was that because the high-potential program is based on the same measures that apply to all employees, women have equal opportunity to gain entry to the high-potential program and thus also the mentoring program. However, this perspective discounts the possibility that women may face barriers (such as gender stereotyping) that keep them from initially accessing the high-potential program. A suggestion for practitioners is to assess their work environments to identify any areas in which women are being underutilized and, if so, present a business case to management calling for mentoring programs that target women.

Most programs examined here did not consider gender as a criterion for selection of mentors and did not train mentors or mentees in cross-gender mentoring. However, given the mentor pools in several programs (senior executives), many such relationships resulted; at the least, program designers should be aware of potential issues and be prepared to address them. For example, male mentors should be alerted to the possibility that gender stereotyping may influence behavior in cross-gender relationships, for example, a male mentor overemphasizing the protector aspects of the mentor role (Clawson & Kram, 1984; Kanter, 1977), and that gender differences in organizational power might affect relationship dynamics (Ragins & Sundstrom, 1989). Suggested research on cross-gender mentoring is discussed further in the next section.

Ideas for Additional Research and Theory in Mentoring Women Through the Glass Ceiling

There is relatively little empirical research to guide the development of formal mentoring programs (e.g., Ragins & Cotton, 1999) and little research integrating gender and formal mentoring. The next section identifies questions and areas where new research or theory would be useful or, in some instances, areas where organizational practices are inconsistent with existing scholarly literature. Key issues include the mentor selection process and cross-gender mentoring, the mentoring relationship, and programmatic elements, including resource allocation and time span.

Mentor Selection Process and Cross-Gender Mentoring

Perhaps because mentors and mentees in informal mentoring relationships self-select, there is limited academic literature about how best to select mentors for formal mentoring programs. Selection criteria for mentors ideally should address motivational issues in addition to skills and organizational stature, to ensure that mentors will invest the necessary time and effort in mentees whom they may not have chosen.

While formal programs have emphasized general benefits to mentors, such as fulfilling organizational citizenship roles and broadening their perspectives, it is unclear how motivating these benefits are to potential mentors or, for that matter, whether there might be other benefits that could be emphasized (such as contributing to organizational change through participation in a mentoring program). Empirical research could provide direction in this area.

For formal programs targeting women, the mentor selection process is further complicated by gender. Ragins's (1997, 2002) theoretical work on diversified mentoring relationships has highlighted the pros and cons of women versus men as mentors of women. Cross-gender formal mentoring relationships may break down barriers to developing informal relationships by providing the means for informal and non-threatening feedback on understanding issues specific to, or disproportionately affecting, women in the organization. A woman mentee could provide perspectives on issues such as work-life conflict, rigid career paths that do not allow time off for family, or the embedded nature of stereotyping in organizational systems.

Because male mentors tend to have greater organizational power than female mentors, they may be better positioned to provide career development for their protégées, but male mentors may provide more limited psychosocial and role-modeling functions for female protégées than would female mentors. Further, in an organization in which the informal norms stress adherence to hierarchy and in which very few women are present at the upper echelon, a female mentee could feel quite constrained in asserting herself or challenging the suggestions of her male mentor. In hierarchical business organizations, the senior member of a working pair typically sets the boundaries of the working relationship. If there are sensitive issues that a female mentee might wish to discuss, such as gender-related inequities that she perceives in the work environment, she might be reluctant to raise these issues unless the senior member creates an environment that allows for discussion of such topics.

Furthermore, because stereotypically masculine behaviors have been traditionally linked with being a successful leader and stereotypically feminine traits have not, there is the possibility that gender stereotyping will lead male mentors to believe that women have less power and ability than they actually do (O'Neill & Blake-Beard, 2002) and to be less committed when working with female mentees than with male mentees. Empirical research would be useful for determining how to best approach these issues with participants in cross-gender relationships.

Dynamics of Mentor/Mentee Relationships

What appears to bind the mentor and mentee together in formal programs is the mentees' goals, which are often very concrete and tend to focus on some aspect of career development rather than more personal aspects of the relationship. By contrast, the strength of the relationship itself is a binding agent in many informal relationships. This raises the question about whether formal mentoring programs should attempt to emulate this aspect of informal mentoring or whether different goals and shorter time frames are more appropriate in the formal context.

While the academic literature identifies a "redefinition" phase in mentor relationships (Kram, 1985), there is often no such stage in formal mentoring programs. An important opportunity might be lost in premature termination of formal mentoring relationships; a larger research issue is whether there are different stages of development in formal relationships. Kram's (1985) initial work with formal mentoring relationships could be replicated, and it could be determined whether formal mentoring stages are the same as in informal relationships, whether they are accelerated or slower, or whether they are simply different.

Another possibility is that more programs could build in facilitation for transitioning formal relationships into informal mentoring relationships if the participants are interested in continuing their relationships. A measure that can be added to programmatic evaluation is the extent to which formal mentors retain their relationships with their formally assigned mentees; this could also help with future selection of formal mentors.

There also needs to be greater attention given to potential outcomes and benefits for mentors, rather than focusing primarily on benefits for their mentees. For example, researchers could directly examine whether motivation to mentor or be mentored increases after being in a formal relationship—in other words, whether formal mentors and mentees go on to develop informal relationships. Another question is whether formal mentees are more likely to become informal mentors, which represents a long-term, but important, investment.

Programmatic Elements: Resource Allocation and Time Limitation

Three programs in this chapter that were positively evaluated used different models for which "unit" received the most programmatic support: the mentee, the mentor, or their relationship. For example, in Company A (shown in Table 22.2), the mentee received the most direct support (through training programs that taught leadership competencies), while for Company D (shown in Table 22.5), the most support went into guiding the relationship between the mentor and the mentee. Depending on the context, each type of resource decision could be preferred, and there may be different long-term implications for each one. For example, the program that focused on development of the mentees' skill base could be crucial to each class of mentees, but it may not work to inculcate a mentoring culture over time. Longitudinal analyses may surface elements of long-term program effectiveness.

Most formal mentoring relationships in the reviewed programs were restricted to 1 year or less. However, prior research suggests that this time restriction may undermine the effectiveness of the relationships. Research by Turban, Dougherty, and Lee (2002) has suggested that the longer the mentoring relationships, the greater the benefit to gender dissimilar dyads (who in the short term received fewer benefits than same-gender dyads). This raises the possibility that shorter recommended time frames interfered with relationship effectiveness. Alternatively, there might be important but as yet undocumented benefits associated with shorter mentoring relationships in business organizations. One benefit, for example, could be intensive learning and the gathering of narrow but deep knowledge on a crucial leadership competency, or another benefit could be increased adaptability and flexibility, measured by how successfully mentees adapt to their mentors. Empirical research could uncover such benefits.

Conclusion

Among the formal mentoring programs intended to develop women leaders examined in this chapter, most incorporated some aspects emulating informal relationships, such as pairing hierarchically senior managers with more-junior mentees, matching mentors and mentees on the basis of complementarity of needs and similarity of interests, or allowing some mentee choice in selection of mentor. These formal programs also tended to provide resources not available to those in informal mentoring relationships, such as integration of the program with performance management systems and provision of at least some level of participant training. A few programs, particularly those judged effective, provided meaningful programmatic assessment, such as improvement in mentees' leader behavior, and encouraged mentors either through selection criteria or training to become sponsors to their formal mentees.

A number of business organizations are devoting significant time and resources to developing and implementing mentoring programs intended to advance female talent. There clearly exists potential for better leveraging these programs. Depending on resource constraints and the larger organizational context (e.g., the extent to which the culture supports mentoring), business organizations might consider either improving on the depth of formal mentoring relationships or, alternatively, increasing the breadth of available mentoring relationships. On one hand, corporations could improve on mentor selection, matching processes, and participant support, so that pairs could develop deeper, more committed relationships to better approximate informal relationships and improve the chances that formal mentors will enact sponsorship roles. On the other hand, corporations could explore providing a range of mentoring options to women. One possible approach is to more aggressively use women's networks as a mentoring resource. While many companies encourage informal mentoring within employee networks, they tend not to tie such mentoring into performance evaluation systems. A mentoring program within a women's network, which was charged with identifying or supporting high potentials, would be one such approach. A variety of mentoring options would be practical, as well, such as senior male mentors who could provide career development functions or less-senior or peer mentors who could provide role-modeling and emotional support.

Formal mentoring relationships will probably never approximate informal relationships, and perhaps they do not need to. With better grounding in theory and research, formal mentoring programs can be leveraged to more successfully achieve organizational and individual objectives and support the development of the next generation of women business leaders.

References

Allen, T. D., Eby, L. T., Poteet, M. L., Lentz, E., & Lima, L. (2004). Career benefits associated with mentoring for protégés: A meta-analysis. *Journal of Applied Psychology, 89,* 127–136.

Allen, T. D., Poteet, M. L., & Russell, J. E. A. (2000). Protégé selection by mentors: What makes the difference? *Journal of Organizational Behavior, 21,* 271–282.

Alliger, G. M., Tannenbaum, S. I., Bennett, W., Jr., Traver, H., & Shotland, A. (1997). A meta-analysis of the relations among training criteria. *Personnel Psychology, 50,* 341–358.

Catalyst. (1996). *Women in corporate leadership.* New York: Author.

Catalyst. (1999). *Women of color in corporate management: Opportunities and barriers.* New York: Author.

Catalyst. (2000). *Women and the MBA: Gateway to opportunity.* New York: Author.

Catalyst. (2002). *2002 Catalyst census of women corporate officers and top earners of the Fortune 500.* New York: Author.

Catalyst. (2004). *Women and men in corporate leadership.* New York: Author.

Catalyst. (2005). *Women "take care," men "take charge": Stereotyping of U.S. business leaders exposed.* New York: Author.

Chao, G. T., Walz, P. M., & Gardner, P. D. (1992). Formal and informal mentorships: A comparison on mentoring functions and contrast with nonmentored counterparts. *Personnel Psychology, 45,* 619–636.

Clawson, J. G., & Kram, K. E. (1984). Managing cross-gender mentoring. *Business Horizons, 27*(3), 22–31.

Dreher, G. F., & Cox, T. H., Jr. (1996). Race, gender, and opportunity: A study of compensation attainment and the establishment of mentoring relationships. *Journal of Applied Psychology, 81,* 297–308.

Fagenson-Eland, E. A., Marks, M. A., & Amendola, K. L. (1997). Perceptions of mentoring relationships. *Journal of Vocational Behavior, 51,* 29–42.

Heilman, M. E. (2001). Description and prescription: How gender stereotypes prevent women's ascent up the organizational ladder. *Journal of Social Issues, 4,* 657–674.

Kanter, R. M. (1977). *Men and women of the corporation.* New York: Basic Books.

Kram, K. E. (1985). *Mentoring at work: Developmental relationships in organizational life.* Glenview, IL: Scott, Foresman.

Levinson, D. J. (with Darrow, C. N., Klein, E. B., Levinson, M. H., & McKee, B.). (1978). *The seasons of a man's life.* New York: Ballantine.

Lyness, K. S., & Thompson, D. E. (2000). Climbing the corporate ladder: Do female and male executives follow the same route? *Journal of Applied Psychology, 85,* 86–101.

Olian, J. D., Carroll, S. J., & Giannantonio, C. M. (1993). Mentor reactions to protégés: An experiment with managers. *Journal of Vocational Behavior, 43,* 266–278.

O'Neill, R., & Blake-Beard, S. D. (2002). Gender barriers to the female mentor–male protégé relationship. *Journal of Business Ethics, 37,* 51–63.

Ragins, B. R. (1997). Diversified mentoring relationships in organizations: A power perspective. *Academy of Management Review, 22,* 482–521.

Ragins, B. R. (1999). Gender and mentoring relationships: A review and research agenda for the next decade. In G. N. Powell (Ed.), *Handbook of gender and work* (pp. 347–370). Thousand Oaks, CA: Sage.

Ragins, B. R. (2002). Understanding diversified mentoring relationships: Definitions, challenges and strategies. In D. Clutterbuck & B. R. Ragins (Eds.), *Mentoring and diversity: An international perspective* (pp. 23–53). Oxford, UK: Butterworth-Heinemann.

Ragins, B. R., & Cotton, J. L. (1991). Easier said than done: Gender differences in perceived barriers to gaining a mentor. *Academy of Management Journal, 34,* 939–951.

Ragins, B. R., & Cotton, J. L. (1999). Mentor functions and outcomes: A comparison of men and women in formal and informal mentoring relationships. *Journal of Applied Psychology, 84,* 529–550.

Ragins, B. R., Cotton, J. L., & Miller, J. S. (2000). Marginal mentoring: The effects of type of mentor, quality of relationship, and program design on work and career attitudes. *Academy of Management Journal, 43,* 1177–1194.

Ragins, B. R., & Sundstrom, E. (1989). Gender and power in organizations. *Psychological Bulletin, 105,* 51–88.

Scandura, T. A., & Williams, E. A. (2001). An investigation of the moderating effects of gender on the relationships between mentorship initiation and protégé perceptions of mentoring functions. *Journal of Vocational Behavior, 59,* 342–363.

Turban, D. B., Dougherty, T. W., & Lee, F. K. (2002). Gender, race, and perceived similarity effects in developmental relationships: The moderating role of relationship duration. *Journal of Vocational Behavior, 61,* 240–262.

Wanberg, C. R., Welsh, E. T., & Hezlett, S. A. (2003). Mentoring research: A review and dynamic process model. *Research in Personnel and Human Resources Management, 22,* 39–124.

23

Designing Relationships for Learning Into Leader Development Programs

Cynthia D. McCauley

Victoria A. Guthrie

The important role that relationships can play in individual learning and development is well documented (Kegan, 1994; Kram, 1985; Levinson, 1978; Schön, 1990; Wenger, McDermott, & Snyder, 2002). Thus, in creating leader development programs, it is only natural to think about using relationships as part of the program design. For example, relationships provide a source of feedback and coaching for participants. They afford access to advice and new ideas. They can provide opportunities to watch and learn from a role model. And they are sources of acceptance and confirmation. Feedback, coaching, advice, models, and confirmation are all ingredients for an effective learning process (see Boyatzis, Chapter 18, this volume).

In this chapter, we will provide examples of how developmental relationships can be a central design element in leader development programs. By *leader development program*, we mean a formal initiative—with identified participants, specified objectives, an intentional learning design, and a finite time frame—that has the goal of expanding the participant's capacity to be effective in leadership roles and processes. Leadership roles and processes facilitate setting direction, creating alignment, and maintaining commitment in groups of people who share common work (Van Velsor & McCauley, 2004). Because the relationships in these programs are an intervention in which people are intentionally matched and work together for a specified period of time, they have many similarities to formal mentoring relationships (Ragins & Cotton, 1999). The primary differences between developmental relationships in leader development programs and formal mentoring programs are that the former often have a narrower, more targeted focus and they are part of a larger design that uses multiple learning methodologies.

In the following section, we briefly describe several frameworks we use in designing relationships for learning in leader development programs. We then more closely examine a variety of relationships in three kinds of leader development programs: feedback-intensive open-enrollment programs, organization-specific programs, and programs incorporating action learning projects. We then summarize the challenges encountered in implementing relationships for learning and how the challenges can be dealt with. We end with thoughts for future research.

Relationships for Learning

Designing relationships for learning starts with the objectives of the program. Leader development programs vary widely in their specific objectives. For example, a program might be aimed at preparing high-potential midlevel managers for the more strategic leadership roles they will be expected to fulfill at the general-manager level in the organization and specifically target the development of systemic thinking, network building, and a more integrated understanding of how the business works. Another program might focus more on developing leaders to operate more effectively in cross-cultural contexts. The design questions become "What roles might a developmental relationship play in accomplishing the program objectives?" and "What types of relationship might be best in providing these roles?"

To explore potential roles further, we use a framework based on three key elements important in leader development: assessment, challenge, and support (Van Velsor & McCauley, 2004). *Assessment* refers to the formal and informal processes for generating and delivering data to individuals about themselves: their strengths, their levels of performance or effectiveness, and their developmental needs. *Challenge* refers to the aspects of situations that push individuals beyond their current capabilities and comfort zones, forcing them to learn and develop in order to continue being effective. Support helps people handle the struggles and difficulties of learning and maintain a positive view of themselves as capable, valuable people who can learn and grow. Relationships can be a source of each of these elements in a leader development program. Some examples of the specific roles related to each element are described in Table 23.1.

We also characterize relationships for learning in leader development programs into three broad types:

- *Learning Coaches:* Learning coaches collaborate with participants to assess and understand them and their learning goals, to challenge current constraints while exploring new possibilities, and to ensure accountability and support for reaching goals and sustaining development (Ting & Hart, 2004). Learning coaches are professionals with expertise in individual learning and development, and they work primarily one on one with participants, although in some cases they may work with a team of participants.

Table 23.1   Roles Played by Others in Relationships for Learning

Element	Role	Function
Assessment	Feedback provider	Ongoing feedback as person works to learn and improve
	Sounding board	Evaluation of strategies before they are implemented
	Point of comparison	Standards for evaluating own level of skill or performance
	Feedback interpreter	Assistance in integrating or making sense of feedback from others
Challenge	Dialogue partner	Perspectives or points of view different from own
	Assignment broker	Access to challenging assignments (new jobs or changes in current job)
	Accountant	Pressure to fulfill commitment to development goals
	Role model	Examples of high competence in areas being developed
Support	Counselor	Examination of what is making learning and development difficult
	Cheerleader	Boost in own belief that success is possible
	Reinforcer	Formal rewards for progress toward goals
	Cohort	Sense that you are not alone in your struggles and that if others can achieve their goals, you can, too.

SOURCE: Adapted from McCauley, C. D., & Douglas, C. A. (2004). Developmental relationships. In C. D. McCauley & E. Van Velsor (Eds.), *The Center for Creative Leadership Handbook of Leadership Development* (pp. 85–115). San Francisco: Jossey-Bass.

• *Peer Learning Partners:* Peer learning partners are dyads or small groups of participants who help each other with their ongoing learning during the course of a program. These partnerships might be narrowly focused on one type of role (for example, observing and giving feedback) or might be shaped more by the participants to meet their individual learning needs. And the partnerships might extend beyond the program to build in accountability and support as participants work on their development goals.

• *Learning Resources:* Learning resources are people in leadership roles who have experience, expertise, and perspectives that are particularly valuable to participants as they are working on their development goals. These leaders might work within the participant's organization but are often outside the organization.

Each program typically makes use of multiple relationships, thus providing each participant with a developmental network during their time in the program. This approach is consistent with the evolution of mentoring theory and practice toward a network perspective (Higgins, Chandler, & Kram, Chapter 14, this volume; Higgins & Kram, 2001) and an increased use of peer mentors (Eby, 1997; McManus & Russell, Chapter 11, this volume). We further illustrate this approach in the next sections by examining relationships for learning in three kinds of leader development programs: feedback-intensive open-enrollment programs, organization-specific programs, and programs incorporating action learning projects.

We should note as we begin describing specific programs that there are a wide variety of terms used when labeling the developmental relationships in these programs (e.g., *coach, mentor, advisor, facilitator, sponsor, partner*). Similar roles are often labeled differently, and different roles sometimes have the same label! We have not worked to be consistent with these labels, but rather collaborate with client organizations and with participants to craft labels that are most meaningful to them. However, throughout the chapter as we describe a specific formal relationship, we make note of which type of relationship it represents using the category labels listed above: *learning coach, peer learning partner,* and *learning resource.*

Feedback-Intensive Open-Enrollment Programs

The purpose of feedback-intensive programs is to enable individuals to develop a deeper understanding of their leadership strengths and weaknesses and to implement action plans to leverage that knowledge for greater effectiveness in their organizations (Guthrie & King, 2004). These programs provide a comprehensive assessment of an individual's preferences and capabilities, using multiple sources of data (e.g., personality inventories; measures of style, values, or preferred patterns of behavior; 360-degree assessments of leader competencies; observations during experiential exercises or simulations; and self-reflection). These assessments are embedded in a classroom experience that includes direct teaching of practical content about leadership and facilitated dialogue among participants.

Feedback-intensive programs typically take place away from work so that participants are better able to focus on learning, and the program is structured to create a safe and supportive learning community. The program may take place in one concentrated period of time (for example, a weeklong program) or may be spread over time with multiple classroom portions interspersed with periods in which participants engage in individual development work (e.g., practice new skills, try out different behaviors in the workplace, carry out a project, or work toward a goal). *Open-enrollment programs* are open for anyone to attend (although programs may have enrollment criteria, such as organizational level); thus, participants are typically from multiple organizations.

Learning Coaches. At the Center for Creative Leadership (CCL), the most common relationship for learning built into our feedback-intensive open-enrollment programs is that of *feedback coach.* A feedback-intensive program is an information-rich experience. By the second or third day, people have been given multiple pieces of feedback from a variety of sources, and this onslaught of data can be overwhelming. Feedback coaches help participants focus on the key elements of their data and consolidate their feedback. In highly interactive, confidential sessions, the participant and the coach work one on one to learn as much as they can from all the accumulated feedback the participant has received throughout the program— from assessment instruments, classroom experiences, observations during exercises and simulations, and personal observations from staff and fellow participants. Together, the two explore the implications, settle on some possible areas for change, and discuss various action plans for change. Typically, these sessions last a half day.

Participants often evaluate this session as the most meaningful part of the program (Conger, 1992; Guthrie & King, 2004).

Feedback coaches typically have an advanced degree in the behavioral sciences or a closely related field, in-depth knowledge of learning theories and the dynamics of individual development and change, awareness of their own strengths and weaknesses, strong interpersonal skills and the ability to work with a broad range of leaders, an understanding of organizational dynamics, and specialized training in the assessment methodologies used in feedback-intensive programs. These experiences and capabilities equip the coach to help participants interpret and integrate feedback, empathize with participants as they share both the satisfaction and pain associated with receiving a great deal of feedback, explore potential paths for development and change, and encourage optimism and commitment to a plan of action.

These same coaches often continue working with the participants for several months after the program or between sessions of a multisession program. The coach helps the participant focus on the action plan created during the program and maintain the high energy and momentum of the classroom experience after returning to work. The coach and participant generally work together in three to six phone sessions. They review progress, discuss what is working and what isn't, acknowledge progress, identify reasons for any setbacks, and consider additional developmental tools and opportunities. This extended relationship provides motivation to keep participants' developmental plans on track and follow through on the goals they set.

In addition to challenging and supporting participants as they work on their development goals, some feedback-intensive programs have used learning coaches to advance more targeted objectives of the program. One such program was CCL's LeaderLab (Burnside & Guthrie, 1992; Guthrie, 1999; Vicere & Fulmer, 1997). Although it provided many of the same assessment experiences as other feedback-intensive programs, LeaderLab particularly emphasized the goal of taking more effective action in one's leadership situation. Thus, the program extended over a 6-month period, with two classroom sessions, each followed by practice back in the participant's work setting and accompanied by coaching. In this program, the learning coaches were called *process advisors* to emphasize that development is an ongoing process (rather than an event) and that the role combined the functions of a trusted advisor: support, expertise, loyalty, and advocacy.

The process advisor's major job was to continually focus participants on asking themselves important questions, the two primary ones being (a) What does the situation call for from me as an individual, as a team leader, and as a contributing member of an organization? and (b) What is the ideal or purpose I am striving for? These two questions led to what were called *anchors,* the baseline principles of the process advisor's role that guided his or her work with the participant. Table 23.2 describes the anchors that moored the process advisor in a developmental relationship with participants.

An evaluation of LeaderLab provided evidence that program participants were perceived by their coworkers as having made significant positive change that led to taking more effective action (Young & Dixon, 1996). Participants rated process advisors as the program feature that most helped them take more effective action (an average rating of 8.9 on a 10-point scale). They cited the process advisors' learning-process expertise,

Table 23.2   Anchors for Process Advisors

Six-month process goal	Encourage and enable participants to take more effective actions in leadership situations, actions that develop individuals and others in pursuit of goals that benefit all
Sense of purpose	Help participants clarify their visions for their specific leadership situations through review of their life biographies and exploration of what they are striving for and what their leadership situations call for
Learning from experience	Help participants become more effective learners by encouraging them to identify blocks to learning and supporting efforts to overcome these blocks
Leadership competencies	Help participants practice five leadership competencies:
	Deal effectively with interpersonal relationships
	Think and behave in terms of systems
	Approach decision making from the standpoint of trade-offs
	Think and act with flexibility
	Maintain emotional balance by coping with disequilibrium

SOURCE: Adapted from Guthrie, V. A. (1999). *Coaching for Action: A Report on Long-Term Advising in a Program Context.* Greensboro, NC: Center for Creative Leadership

objectivity, positive regard for the participant, ongoing support, and pressure to follow through as their most beneficial functions.

Creating effecting coaching relationships in the context of an open-enrollment program has its challenges. Coaches know little about the work context in which the individual participant operates. They have a very limited time to establish rapport with the participant. When coaching continues after a program, the relationship has to be maintained with minimum face-to-face interaction. We return to these challenges and strategies for dealing with them later in the chapter.

Peer Learning Partners. In addition to learning coaches, CCL's feedback-intensive programs also make use of peer learning partners. Most forms of peer learning partners are designed to operate during the face-to-face program; however, some are also designed to support learning back in the workplace.

A common role that participants play for one another in feedback-intensive open-enrollment programs is *peer observer* (Guthrie & King, 2004). In peer observations, each participant is assigned to observe two to three other participants throughout the program. Participants generally do not know which of their fellow participants are observing them, but they do have the opportunity to ask that the observers pay particular attention to certain kinds of behaviors or situations that they are particularly interested in receiving feedback about. Participants are taught how to watch for patterns of behavior that might help their fellow participants understand more about the impact of their behaviors on others. Near the end of the program, individuals who were observing the same participant meet to consolidate their observations and reach consensus about the feedback, to be delivered by one of the observers to the participant. This process is an effective way to generate accurate and behavior-based feedback (Conger, 1992). Peer observations provide fresh feedback from individuals who don't have the biases developed from a history of knowing the individual or the tendency to carefully filter feedback (a tendency people often have when providing feedback to others with whom they expect to continue working over time).

Peer coaching is also often part of feedback-intensive programs. A *peer coach* is also a fellow participant, but one who plays a broader role than peer observer. In addition to providing feedback, a peer coach shares his or her own experiences related to an issue the peer may be struggling with, serves as a sounding board for the peer's ideas and a dialogue partner to explore different options, and is an empathetic companion in the journey of personal learning and leadership development. Peer coaches are often set up as coaching triads at the beginning of a program, given the opportunity to meet for reflection and consultation during the program, and may continue to stay in touch as a coaching triad after the program. Peer coaching was utilized in the LeaderLab program described above and was rated by participants as most effective when the peer coach was perceived as trustworthy, discreet, committed, and available (Young & Dixon, 1996). Thus, similar to the challenge faced by professional coaches working with participants in an open-enrollment development program, peer coaches must quickly develop high-quality relationships and maintain them after the face-to-face program experience.

Another peer-focused strategy for designing relationships for learning into open-enrollment leader development programs involves *alumni groups.* Meetings of alumni groups bring past participants together to network and share lessons and insights. Usually, 1 or 2 days in length, alumni meetings afford participants the opportunity to learn from each other's efforts to implement action plans and increase their effectiveness as leaders (e.g., what worked well and what didn't, how tools and frameworks presented in the program were applied in specific work settings, new insights from intentional improvement efforts), get further advice and coaching from peers, renew their motivation and commitment for pursuing action plans, and maintain their connections with fellow participants (Guthrie & King, 2004; Palus & Horth, 2002).

Organization-Specific Programs

Organization-specific programs are developed for a single organization, and participants in the program are thus all associated with that organization. In addition to developing the capabilities of individual leaders, these programs are often also designed to address particular organizational issues and strengthen networks of relationships in the organization. CCL's organization-specific programs are typically feedback-intensive programs, using many of the same methods, processes, and relationships for learning as our open-enrollment programs. However, these programs often have focused developmental objectives (e.g., developing midlevel, high-potential managers; increasing leaders' abilities to manage change) and are more likely to utilize relationships that we referred to earlier as *learning resources*—internal and external leaders who play valuable roles for the participants. We share three examples of organization-specific programs that make use of developmental relationships. The first two programs are programs designed and facilitated by CCL staff. CCL was directly involved in only the first week of the third program but enjoyed a partnership with the sponsoring organization that allowed us to learn how relationships for learning were used more extensively throughout the program (McCauley & Douglas, 2004).

Chief Executive Officer Leadership Development Program (CEOLDP). CEOLDP was designed to provide a leader development experience for school superintendents in the state of Florida. Sponsored by the Florida Department of Education and the Florida Council of Educational Management, the program's broad goals were to expand superintendents' leadership capacities and to stimulate their continuing personal and career growth. The program consisted of a weeklong feedback-intensive classroom experience and a year focused on development back at the job. During this year, superintendents worked toward individual and organizational goals set at the end of the classroom experience; worked with an assigned *executive facilitator,* an experienced superintendent from another part of the country who was available as a guide, advisor, and supporter; and continued introspection and reflection through journal writing.

The executive facilitator established a relationship with the participant during the classroom portion of the program. Two to 6 weeks later, the facilitator visited the participant in his or her school district. Beyond this initial site visit, the amount of interaction was up to the participants. Some pairs had several additional site visits; some met at professional meetings or training events; and a few participants visited their facilitators' school districts. All matches continued contact through telephone conversations, correspondence, and the sharing of the participant's learning journal.

An evaluation of the program (McCauley & Hughes-James, 1994) found that the executive facilitators were accessed most frequently by the program participants for their experience and expertise as educational leaders. The facilitators provided direct suggestions and advice, shared with or taught the participants particular strategies or techniques, related their own experiences and insights, provided training for the participants' staffs, pointed out pertinent resources or networks, or sent reading material. Other benefits varied more across participants, including (a) helping participants think through issues by serving as a sounding board, dialogue partner, and provider of feedback; (b) holding participants accountable for working on their individual and organizational goals; (c) encouraging participants by pointing out the positives and building their self-confidence; and (d) becoming a friend—someone with whom they could share problems, vent frustrations, be candid, and call on when needed. This last benefit was particularly salient for school superintendents; as CEOs, they felt they did not have peers in their organizations with whom they could interact as friends.

The evaluation also found that the program enhanced participants' peer networks. The joint experience of attending the program together and working within the same state educational system allowed the superintendents to get to know each other better, share their experiences and problems, and develop some common bonds (McCauley

& Young, 1993). During their interaction in the program, they discovered who had particular expertise in various areas (e.g., school law or finance) or who had already worked on an issue they were currently facing (e.g., year-round schools or dropout prevention). They then called on each other during the year as they needed expertise in particular areas. In general, the more inexperienced superintendents asked for input from those with longer tenure in the roles. The peer network also provided support for one another. For example, one subset of participants, each of whom wanted to develop a healthier lifestyle, created their own support group.

Leader Development for Junior and Senior Managers. A major construction company wanted to engage their senior managers in the development of high-potential junior managers in the organization. Working with CCL, they designed a process that began with a 4-day feedback-intensive leader development program. The centerpiece of this experience was a daylong business simulation. Forty managers attended the program; half were experienced senior managers in the organization, and half were junior managers (25–35 years old, in supervisory to middle-management positions). Attending the program together, senior and junior managers were able to get to know one another better, see each other's strengths and weaknesses, and begin experiencing themselves as a learning community.

One of the goals of the program was to match junior-senior pairs for 6 months of formal mentoring postprogram. At the end of the third day of the classroom session, each participant listed three learning partners that he or she would like to be matched with. The program manager used this information to match junior and senior managers. The last day of the program was spent on the topic of mentoring, and pairs had time to work together to set goals and expectations for their learning partnerships.

Even though the organization began the leader development initiative with the idea that junior managers had a great deal to learn from senior managers, everyone involved in the program soon realized that senior managers could learn from the relationship, too (e.g., exposure to new ideas, opportunities to learn about new technology and business processes, improvement of coaching skills); and thus came a switch in their language from *mentors* to *learning partners*. In a follow-up survey, 75% of the pairs reported that the relationships met or exceeded their goals. Participants reported a wide range of functions provided by the relationships: sounding board, source of feedback, dialogue partner, expert on a business topic, counselor, and career advisor. Those who reported that the relationships did not meet their goals cited "not committing adequate time to the relationship" as their major obstacle.

Mandel Fellows Program. The Council of Jewish Federations (CJF) sponsored a 2-year leader development program for high-potential professionals who were projected to attain the most-senior positions in major Jewish federations throughout North America. CJF is an association of over 180 Jewish federations, local organizations that raise money to help local Jewish communities respond to people in need and populations at risk. The CJF helps strengthen the work of its member federations by developing programs to meet changing needs, providing an exchange of successful community experiences, and leading joint efforts to meet local, regional, and international needs. The leader development program was funded in large part by the Mandel Associated Foundations, and participants were called "Mandel Fellows."

Over the course of 2 years, Mandel Fellows engaged in a variety of developmental activities. They began the program with a weeklong feedback-intensive program. They also spent a 2-week period in Israel, working with emerging Israeli leaders to understand various issues in the Jewish community worldwide. Throughout the program, there were several 2-day meetings focused on particular managerial issues, as well as opportunities to engage in distance-learning events focused on Jewish history and philosophy.

Two relationships for learning were part of the overall design of the program. First, each fellow was matched with an *executive mentor,* a successful large-city federation president. The major purpose of this relationship was to help the fellows see the issues and challenges faced by senior leaders in major federations (the type of position the program was preparing them for) and the strategies used to lead such organizations. The relationship was built around a visit by the fellow to the mentor's organization. A typical visit consisted of shadowing the mentor during normal work activities, debriefing and discussion time with the mentor, meeting the mentor's staff members and getting their views of the mentor's leadership behaviors and style, and being included in the mentor's nonwork activities.

The second relationship was a *leadership coach,* a recognized leader in a corporate or government organization in each fellow's own local community. These relationships were intended to help the fellows understand the leadership complexities, dynamics, and strategies in a markedly different type of institution—thus exposing them to new perspectives of effective leadership in large-scale organizations. In addition, fellows often looked for leadership coaches who were particularly strong in areas in which they wanted to learn and improve. The pairs engaged in a wide variety of activities, depending on the needs and interest of the fellow. Coaches were shadowed, used as sounding boards, or served as consultants on participants' projects. They shared their experiences, philosophies, leadership models, and other knowledge. Coaches opened up their organizations to fellows for observation and discussions with staff members. And coaches were asked to observe activities in the fellows' organizations or to share their expertise with a particular group in an organization.

Programs With Action Learning Projects

Leader development programs have increasingly made use of action learning projects in their designs. Action learning was developed by Revans (1982) as an educational approach that encourages people to apply and generate knowledge from real-world situations. It has evolved into a widely used methodology for combining individual and team learning with focused work on an organizational problem (Dotlich & Noel, 1998; Marsick & O'Neil, 1999). When action learning is utilized as part of a leader development program, participants are divided into teams to work for 3 to 6 months on a project that focuses on a complex organizational issue and that often involves multiple stakeholders (e.g., moving into new markets, introducing new technology, reorganizing work, or improving business processes). As they are working on the project, teams also work with an action learning coach to reflect on the work, extract learning, and discover new ways of accomplishing their objectives. Through this process of action and reflection with mutual learners, participants gain more in-depth knowledge and effective actions to apply to their work. Action learning projects, however, serve goals beyond development: They provide opportunities to work across units and build internal networks, to bring various perspectives and expertise to bear on an organizational issue, and to institutionalize a particular approach to problem identification and analysis.

In addition to mutual learning among team members, there are two key relationships for learning in an action learning project: those with the *action learning coach* and those with the *project sponsor*. The action learning coach is an individual, typically external to the organization, who is skilled in team facilitation and trained in action learning methodologies. The project sponsor is generally a senior-level executive in the organization. The two play distinct but complementary developmental roles. Action learning coaches are experts in team learning processes. They provide tools and interventions that encourage the team members to reflect and learn as they are engaged in project work. They interact with the team frequently, monitoring progress on the action and the learning of the team.

On the other hand, project sponsors are experts in the workings of the organization. They are more removed from the ongoing work of the team but check in regularly and are available to the team as needed. Sponsors can play multiple roles for the team. They can serve as sounding board and advisor for the team's work, hold the team accountable for timely and effective accomplishment of the project's goals, encourage the team to take a fresh look at and apply creative solutions to the project, help the team be aware of organizational dynamics or internal politics that could have implications for the project work, assist the team in accessing key project stakeholders, and provide feedback to the team members on both their process and outcomes. We have found that sponsors do not have to be experts in the content area of the project to effectively carry out their sponsor roles with the team. In fact, being an expert might get in the way of allowing the team to be in charge of the project.

Action learning projects are not limited to these two key developmental roles. We have found that they can serve as the focal point for developing multiple relationships for learning. This is readily illustrated in the Xerox High-Potential Manager Program. Working with Xerox, CCL designed a leader development program that combined face-to-face sessions, Web-based learning platforms, action learning projects, and several relationships for learning (Pulley, Sessa, & Malloy, 2002). The program's broad goals were to improve leadership skills and teach leaders how to function more effectively in an online environment. The various components of the program are described in Table 23.3. As noted in the table, multiple relationships for learning were utilized:

- *Individual coaches:* These coaches played a role similar to the feedback coaches in feedback-intensive open-enrollment programs. They helped participants interpret and consolidate their assessment data and create action plans. They were then available for coaching as the participants worked to implement their plans.

- *Team facilitators:* This was the title given to the action learning coaches in this program. As in other programs, these facilitators provided tools and interventions that encouraged team reflection and learning. Unique to this program, they were virtual facilitators, with much of their facilitation occurring online.
- *Internal mentors:* Project teams also identified and accessed these internal learning resources. With their knowledge of the business and the organization, internal mentors acted as sounding boards for the teams as they worked on their projects.
- *VP coaches:* After presenting their projects, all teams received feedback and reactions from several vice presidents assigned to their projects. These VPs also helped the teams think through how to further implement their projects at Xerox. The VPs received training and practice on coaching prior to their work with the teams.

Participants in programs that have utilized action learning projects frequently rate the action learning coaches high as a factor that contributed to the success of their teams (with *success* being defined as completing their projects and learning from their work). Sponsors and other internal relationships for learning are also seen as useful (although not as critical as the action learning coach). However, participants see the connections made with internal sponsors and executives as a lasting benefit for future work and learning in the organization.

Challenges in Designing Relationships for Learning in Leader Development Programs

There are challenges associated with making each type of relationship—learning coaches, peer learning partners, and learning resources in the organization—an effective source of learning and development for participants in leader development programs. And across all types of relationships, there is the issue of organizational support.

Learning Coaches. Learning coaches are generally external to the participant's organization and frequently work with the participants over time, often by phone and e-mail. Two challenges for these coaches are (a) maintaining the relationship with minimal face-to-face interaction and (b) developing a useful understanding about the participant's organizational context. Effective use of the face-to-face time with participants in the classroom portion of the program will help minimize these challenges. A structured conversation that covers key aspects of the participant's organization (e.g., history, strategic goals, structure, and culture); his or her current job responsibilities and challenges; relationships with the boss, direct reports, and peers; and career history and goals is important for connecting the coach to the participant's context. When possible, it is also useful to match participants with learning coaches who have had experience in the industry or type of organization the participant is in. Participant and coach should also discuss and agree on the role the coach will play in the virtual phase of their coaching relationship, the best schedule for coaching sessions, and what information will be exchanged between sessions. The

Table 23.3   Components of Xerox Program

Online prework	Individual assessment instruments completed online.
	Personal bio, photo, and symbol of leadership posted in online workspace.
Virtual kickoff	Synchronous virtual event hosted by Xerox vice president.
	Program staff provided overview of program and answered participant questions.
Three-day classroom session	Participants divided into six 6-person teams.
	Participants reviewed assessment feedback in 2-hour session with individual coaches.
	Participants also engaged in team-based activities, received guidelines for working as geographically dispersed teams, and practiced using the online workspace.
Action learning project	During the classroom session, each team identified a business project addressing a strategic initiative.
	Teams worked on the project over the next 3 months; the work was completed virtually, and each team had a coach.
Three 1-month e-modules	During the 3-month project work, additional content was delivered to participants via the online workspace.
	Each module also asked participants to complete an individual assignment and a team assignment.
Individual coaching	During the 3-month project, participants also arranged two 1-hour telephone coaching sessions with the coaches they had worked with in the classroom session.
Internal mentoring	Teams identified and worked with one or two internal mentors (typically vice presidents), who acted as sounding boards as they worked on their action learning projects.
Two-day classroom session	Teams reported on their projects to a group of 26 vice presidents and several senior executives.
	Several vice presidents were assigned to meet with each team to provide coaching on the projects and presentations.

program might also assist the virtual connection between participant and coach by making available a Web-based platform for communicating and sharing documents online (see Ensher & Murphy, Chapter 12, this volume, for an in-depth review of maintaining developmental relationships through electronic media).

Occasionally, after the initial meeting with his or her coach, a participant will voice concerns that the coach is not a good "fit." This is usually due to a sensed difference in values or interpersonal style. It is important for program facilitators to discuss the concern with the participant, examining the advantages and disadvantages of working with a coach a person feels comfortable with and working with one who might represent a different perspective or style. The final decision about whether to continue the relationship rests with the participant. However, we have found that when a participant decides to continue with a coach that he or she initially felt some dissonance with, the experience of working successfully across differences creates a strong bond.

As CCL is asked to deliver leader development programs in multiple countries and cultures, the challenge of cross-cultural coaching also emerges. One obvious way to deal with this challenge is for the coach and participant to come from the same culture. This requires the program provider to develop a cadre of coaches who understand the content and underlying philosophy of the program and who have the skills needed in a coach, in each of the major cultures represented in the participant population. At CCL, we have learned that this approach requires major investment in the selection and development of coaches, particularly as we work in countries whose cultures are most different from that of the United States. Often, we have to make use of another approach: using coaches who are particularly adept at working across cultures. These are coaches who have extensive multicultural experiences, closely monitor their own cultural biases and stereotypes, know how to tap into the cultural assumptions operating in the participant's environment, are patient in working across distances and languages, and are keenly aware when cultural differences are contributing to a misunderstanding between coach and participant.

Peer Learning Partners. One of the major challenges in the effective application of peer learning partners is the fact that participants vary a great deal in their skill at and motivation for this role. To "even the playing field" a bit more so that everyone has a competent learning partner, the program design must build in opportunities for enhancing learning partner skills. For example, giving useful feedback is a needed competency in learning partners. Participants can be taught a structured model for giving useful feedback and given multiple opportunities to practice using the model during the program. This might start by having participants provide each other with feedback in dyads after a role play, guided by a set of questions that each responds to. After a group experiential exercise later in the program, triads could practice giving and receiving feedback, based on their observations in the exercise. One member is the receiver of feedback; another is the giver; and the third observes and provides input on how well the giver and receiver utilized the feedback model. Roles are then shifted for two more rounds of the activity. Having multiple opportunities throughout the program to practice aspects of being a learning partner not only builds skills but also develops confidence in participants' abilities to be effective in the role. There is also a bit of peer pressure: When one sees others performing the role well, there is motivation to do well oneself.

In organization-specific programs, there is always the issue of whether it is better to match people in peer learning partnerships who already know each other and have working relationships in the organization or to match people who don't know each other and work in distant parts of the organization. These factors can influence participants' sense of trust and confidentiality in the relationship, as well as impact desired program outcomes, such as developing more cross-functional relationships in the organization or enhancing exposure to diverse viewpoints. We have found that it is best to be straightforward with participants about these issues, engage them in examining the dynamics that might be in play in different matching scenarios, and allow them to have a voice in shaping how learning partnerships are formed. This is consistent with advice given for creating effective formal mentoring programs (Douglas, 1997).

A final design issue is whether to create one learning partnership for the life of the program or to have multiple learning partnerships that participants move in and out of. The former allows for the formation of more in-depth relationships; the latter facilitates access to multiple perspectives; and both can facilitate learning. If the program is short, it is often more effective to rely on one learning partnership to create a consistent "home base" for the participant. For longer, multiple-session programs, there is more time for building multiple partnerships. Also, a rotational approach to learning partnerships is often part of the design when network building is one of the program objectives.

Learning Resources. Designing relationships for learning beyond those involving program staff and participants is often worthwhile but adds complexity to the program design. Key challenges include ensuring that these relationships are aligned with the overall goals of the program, that those serving in the roles have the skills they need, and that positive relationships do develop.

Individuals in these developmental roles—like the executive facilitator in CEOLDP (a peer administrator in another school district), the executive mentor (a federation president) and the leadership coach (a leader of another organization in the fellow's local community) in the Mandel Fellows Program, and the internal mentor in the Xerox program—first need education about the intent of the role, its place in the larger program design, expectations that participants will likely have of them, and ideas about useful strategies for engaging with the participants. This education can be accomplished one on one but works best when individuals can come together for an orientation and education experience. For example, in CEOLDP, executive facilitators met for an orientation session at the same time that the superintendents were attending the classroom portion of their program. This allowed the two groups to meet together and jointly discuss the role as a large group. Pairs of facilitators and superintendents then had formal meeting time and informal social time to begin establishing their relationships.

Written materials that reinforce the educational experience and a main program administration point of contact are essential elements for individuals to use as they get into the role—when more questions inevitably come up. We have also found it useful for individuals in developmental roles to meet as a group as the program progresses to share experiences, learn from one another, and get advice on how to best handle different circumstances they encounter. For example, in a program that uses action learning projects, action learning coaches hold two teleconferences as a group, and sponsors meet together once during the action learning phase of the program. In both cases, the meetings are divided into two parts: (a) a structured update by each coach or sponsor on how his or her team's work and learning is progressing and (b) an open time for sharing best practices and seeking advice from one another.

Program managers also need to develop strategies for monitoring the relationships to make sure that they are meeting the needs of participants. This can include formal and informal check-ins with participants, regular conversations with program liaisons within the organization, and formal documented updates required from those in developmental roles. The group meetings described above are also a useful source of information from coaches and sponsors on how the relationships are progressing from their perspectives.

Organizational Support. A leader development program's potential to motivate and promote learning and growth in participants is limited by the organizational context in which participants are embedded (Van Velsor, Moxley, & Bunker, 2004). The more the organization's system and culture support the behavioral changes targeted by the program and the learning methodologies used in the program, the higher the potential for positive impact on participants. Thus, for any programs that plan to utilize relationships for learning, it is important to ascertain the level of organizational support for these relationships. Are external learning coaches viewed as valuable assets? Are time and resources available for peer coaching? Are there high levels of trust among peers? Will people in the organization who take on "learning resource" roles be rewarded for this additional responsibility? Are developmental relationships modeled by influential people in the organization? In organization-specific programs, questions about organizational support can be explored in the design phase of the initiative. If there are indications that support may be low, the designers can opt to minimize the use of developmental relationships (e.g., use them only during the classroom portion of the program) or work with the organization to build in additional support mechanisms (e.g., communication from top management that time for coaching is supported, participation by top management in learning resource roles, tracking of outcomes of coaching relationships).

Research and Theory to Support the Design of Relationships for Learning

CCL's use of developmental relationships in leader development programs has relied heavily on our framework of assessment-challenge-support as key elements of developmental experiences. These three elements reflect the key themes in research-based theories of adult learning and development (Argyris & Schön, 1974; Bandura, 1986; Hellervick, Hazucha, & Schneider, 1992; Knowles, 1984; Kolb, 1984), which emphasize the role of goals, feedback, self-efficacy, role models, experience, reflection, and motivation in learning. Relationships are potential sources of all of these ingredients for effective learning (see Boyatzis, Chapter 18, this volume).

Designing relationships for learning has also relied on knowledge gained from mentoring research that focuses on the functions or roles mentors play in the psychosocial and career development of individuals (Kram, 1985; Noe, 1988; Ragins & Cotton, 1999). As noted early in the chapter, the roles we have derived from this research and our own practice (see Table 23.1) are at the forefront of our thinking when designing formal developmental relationships, and they also make a useful organizing framework for evaluating the impact of relationships on participants.

More recently, systematic examinations of the role of executive coaches have influenced CCL's use of learning coaches in leader development programs (Hall,

Otazo, & Hollenbeck, 1999; Hudson, 1999; Peterson, 1996; Ting & Hart, 2004; Witherspoon & White, 1996). And CCL has recently codified and published more of its knowledge and expertise related to leadership coaching (Ting & Scisco, 2006).

As we work to design and implement relationships for learning, we particularly feel the need for additional research in several areas:

- *Evaluation research that examines the impact of various types of formal developmental relationships on participants' learning and behavioral change in the workplace.* We have learned from our own evaluation research that it is often difficult to tease apart the contributions of the various program components to the overall impact of the program, but evaluations should at least tap into the perceptions of program participants, program staff, and learning coaches/partners/resources about what characterizes the relationships that contribute most to the learning goals of the program.

- *Research on the competencies of effective coaches and learning partners.* Our knowledge of what it takes to be effective in a developmental relationship role is based heavily on applied experiences. This knowledge base should be tested and further expanded by systematic research. Of particular interest is how basic capabilities (e.g., emotional competencies, dialogue skills) are utilized in formal relationships to generate the assessment, challenge, and support needed for leader development.

- *Research on how individuals build a network of developmental relationships and on the optimal networks for various developmental goals.* We find models of developmental relationships that emphasize the individual's network of relationships rather than focus on a single type of relationship, such as traditional mentoring (Higgins & Kram, 2001; McCauley & Douglas, 2004), to be particularly attractive to practicing managers. In addition to designing formal relationships for learning into our leader development programs, we also need to equip managers with the knowledge and skills needed to build their own networks of relationships to support their individualized developmental needs.

- *Diversity research.* As we noted earlier, more and more of the participants in our leader development programs are from outside the United States. We need to know more about the meaning, forms, and dynamics of developmental relationships in other cultures, particularly in non-Western societies. In addition, individuals are increasingly expected to mentor and coach others of different genders, ethnicity, religions, generations, and geographic regions. The dynamics of developmental relationships involving diverse partners is also an area in need of further research.

- *Research on organizational context.* Finally, we need to know more about how organizational systems and cultures impact the acceptance of and effectiveness of relationships for learning. For example, we have experienced strongly performance-oriented cultures in which external coaches are viewed as a necessary aspect of fine-tuning an individual's performance, and we have experienced similar cultures in which using an external coach is viewed as a weakness—a sign that the individual is in a remedial class and needs extra tutoring. What was at work in these two contexts that created different perceptions of coaching? Also, are there ways we should tailor developmental relationships for different contexts, for example, for organizations in different stages of their life cycles or facing different external challenges?

The adult learning, mentoring, and coaching literatures have provided a firm foundation for designing various types of relationships for learning in leader development programs. CCL's practice has created opportunities to extend this knowledge base. We have learned about (a) designing relationships so that they support the goals of the program, (b) thoroughly preparing individuals for their roles in the process, (c) adjusting the design to the needs of individual participants and to organizational and cultural contexts, (d) monitoring the relationships, and (e) quickly building relationships during face-to-face interactions so that virtual connections are more productive. However, we look to the continued interplay between research and practice to provide additional insight, strategies, and tools for maximizing the effectiveness of developmental relationships for individuals in leadership roles.

References

Argyris, C., & Schön, D. A. (1974). *Theory in practice: Increasing professional effectiveness.* San Francisco: Jossey-Bass.

Bandura, A. (1986). *Social foundations of thought and action: A social cognitive theory.* Upper Saddle River, NJ: Prentice Hall.

Burnside, R. M., & Guthrie, V. A. (1992). *Training for action: A new approach to executive development.* Greensboro, NC: Center for Creative Leadership.

Conger, J. A. (1992). *Learning to lead: The art of transforming managers into leaders.* San Francisco: Jossey-Bass.

Dotlich, D. L., & Noel, J. L. (1998). *Action learning: How the world's top companies are re-creating their leaders and themselves.* San Francisco: Jossey-Bass.

Douglas, C. A. (1997). *Formal mentoring programs in organizations: An annotated bibliography.* Greensboro, NC: Center for Creative Leadership.

Eby, L. T. (1997). Alternative forms of mentoring in changing organizational environments: A conceptual extension of the mentoring literature. *Journal of Vocational Behavior, 51,* 125–144.

Guthrie, V. A. (1999). *Coaching for action: A report on long-term advising in a program context.* Greensboro, NC: Center for Creative Leadership

Guthrie, V. A., & King, S. N. (2004). Feedback-intensive programs. In C. D. McCauley & E. Van Velsor (Eds.), *The Center for Creative Leadership handbook of leadership development* (pp. 25–57). San Francisco: Jossey-Bass.

Hall, D. T., Otazo, K. L., & Hollenbeck, G. P. (1999). Behind closed doors: What really happens in executive coaching. *Organizational Dynamics, 27*(3), 39–53.

Hellervik, L. W., Hazucha, J. F., & Schneider, R. J. (1992). Behavior change: Models, methods, and a review of the evidence. In M. D. Dunnette & L. M. Hough (Eds.), *Handbook of industrial and organizational psychology* (2nd ed., Vol. 3, pp. 821–895). Palo Alto, CA: Consulting Psychologists Press.

Higgins, M. C., & Kram, K. E. (2001). Reconceptualizing mentoring at work: A developmental network perspective. *Academy of Management Review, 26,* 264–288.

Hudson, F. M. (1999). *The handbook of coaching.* San Francisco: Jossey-Bass.

Kegan, R. (1994). *In over our heads: The mental demands of modern life.* Cambridge, MA: Harvard University Press.

Knowles, M. S. (1984). *Andragogy in action.* San Francisco: Jossey-Bass.

Kolb, D. (1984). *Experiential learning: Experiences as the source of learning and development.* Englewood Cliffs, NJ: Prentice Hall.

Kram, K. E. (1985). *Mentoring at work: Developmental relationships in organizational life.* Glenview, IL: Scott, Foresman.

Levinson, D. J. (with Darrow, C. N., Klein, E. B., Levinson, M. H., & McKee, B.). (1978). *The seasons of a man's life.* New York: Knopf.

Marsick, V., & O'Neil, J. (1999). The many faces of action learning. *Management Learning, 30,* 159–176.

McCauley, C. D., & Douglas, C. A. (2004). Developmental relationships. In C. D. McCauley & E. Van Velsor (Eds.), *The Center for Creative Leadership handbook of leadership development* (pp. 85–115). San Francisco: Jossey-Bass.

McCauley, C. D., & Hughes-James, M. W. (1994). *An evaluation of the outcomes of a leadership development program.* Greensboro, NC: Center for Creative Leadership

McCauley, C. D., & Young, D. P. (1993). Creating developmental relationships: Roles and strategies. *Human Resource Management Review, 3,* 219–230.

Noe, R. A. (1988). An investigation of the determinants of successful assigned mentoring relationships. *Personnel Psychology, 41,* 457–479.

Palus, C. J., & Horth, D. M. (2002). *The leader's edge: Six creative competencies for navigating complex challenges.* San Francisco: Jossey-Bass.

Peterson, D. B. (1996). Executive coaching at work: The art of one-on-one change. *Consulting Psychology Journal: Practice and Research, 48,* 78–86.

Pulley, M. L., Sessa, V., & Malloy, M. (2002). E-leadership: A two-pronged idea. *Training & Development, 56*(3), 34–47.

Ragins, B. R., & Cotton, J. L. (1999). Mentor functions and outcomes: A comparison of men and women in formal and informal mentoring relationships. *Journal of Applied Psychology, 84,* 529–550.

Revans, R. (1982). *The origins and growth of action learning.* London: Chartwell-Bratt.

Schön, D. A. (1990). *Educating the reflective practitioner.* San Francisco: Jossey-Bass.

Ting, S., & Hart, E. W. (2004). Formal coaching. In C. D. McCauley & E. Van Velsor (Eds.), *The Center for Creative Leadership handbook of leadership development* (pp. 116–150). San Francisco: Jossey-Bass.

Ting, S., & Scisco, P. (2006). *The CCL handbook of coaching: A guide for the leader coach.* San Francisco: Jossey-Bass.

Van Velsor, E., & McCauley, C. D. (2004). Introduction: Our view of leadership development. In C. D. McCauley & E. Van Velsor (Eds.), *The Center for Creative Leadership handbook of leadership development* (pp. 1–22). San Francisco: Jossey-Bass.

Van Velsor, E., Moxley, R. S., & Bunker, K. A. (2004). The leader development process. In C. D. McCauley & E. Van Velsor (Eds.), *The Center for Creative Leadership handbook of leadership development* (pp. 204–233). San Francisco: Jossey-Bass.

Vicere, A. A., & Fulmer, R. M. (1997). *Leadership by design: How benchmark companies sustain success through investment in continuous learning.* Boston: Harvard Business School Press.

Wenger, E. C., McDermott, R., & Snyder, W. M. (2002). *Cultivating communities of practice.* Boston: Harvard Business School Press.

Witherspoon, R., & White, R. P. (1996). Executive coaching: A continuum of roles. *Consulting Psychology Journal: Practice and Research, 48,* 124–133.

Young, D. P., & Dixon, N. M. (1996). *Helping leaders take effective action: A program evaluation.* Greensboro, NC: Center for Creative Leadership.

24

The Practice of Mentoring

MENTTIUM Corporation

Lynn P-Sontag

Kimberly Vappie

Connie R. Wanberg

I n 1990, the founder of MENTTIUM, Gayle Holmes, conducted her own research to discover why women were not reaching senior-level positions in *Fortune*-ranked companies. As part of her research, she asked senior executives to identify the key to their success. Three critical factors were identified: (a) having a mentor or mentors to provide guidance, (b) ongoing business education, and (c) networking. This informal research became the foundation for the formal mentoring programs MENTTIUM, a niche consulting firm, offers today.

This chapter is meant to give readers a close look at the formal mentoring programs provided by MENTTIUM. We describe MENTTIUM's programs, implementation processes, and challenges associated with formal mentoring programs. Finally, we discuss questions we would like to see scholars address in their research in order to best help practice in the area of formal mentoring.

MENTTIUM Programs

MENTTIUM provides three primary mentoring programs: MENTTIUM 100®, MENTTOR™, and *circles*™. The flagship program, MENTTIUM 100®, stemmed from Holmes's initial goal of helping women reach senior-level positions in organizations.

This program pairs midlevel, high-potential women from client organizations with senior executives (both male and female) from other organizations. In 1994, senior executives who had experienced the MENTTIUM 100® program asked Holmes how they could capture the essence of this process within their own organizations. Holmes then asked five Minneapolis/St. Paul companies to be part of a design team to develop a one-to-one, within-company mentoring program called MENTTOR™. In return, MENTTIUM conducted the training and supported the implementation of that program in those five companies. In 1996, the business landscape began to shift. Mentor pools became more limited; gaps in knowledge management were more pronounced as retirements and turnover increased; and communication across organizational functions and business units became more challenging. This combination of factors prompted organizations to search for an alternative to the within-company, one-to-one approach. As a result, Holmes became interested in developing a group mentoring process and engaged a client to fund the design and development of *circles*™. While the group process can vary from as few as 4 mentees with 1 mentor to 25 mentees with 3 mentors, the norm is typically 12 mentees with 2 mentors. A brief overview of each program follows; later sections delve deeper into implementation processes and challenges.

MENTTIUM 100®

MENTTIUM 100® is launched annually in two markets (Minneapolis, Minnesota and Chicago, Illinois), involving a total of 800 to 1,000 partnerships. Paring high-potential women from client organizations with mentors from other organizations, this program has three core components that span one calendar year: (a) the mentoring relationship, (b) business education sessions, and (c) monthly networking activities. Across different organizations, the mentoring partnerships are expected to meet monthly (either face-to-face or via conference call) for approximately 90 minutes. In addition, the mentees regularly attend the business education sessions and networking activities throughout the year.

As noted by Blake-Beard, O'Neill, and McGowan (Chapter 25, this volume), the matching process is an important part of a formal mentoring program. We have carefully honed our matching process for MENTTIUM 100® over the past 15 years. Mentees and mentors fill out their profiles online and are then interviewed by MENTTIUM staff. A mentee interview takes approximately 45 minutes, with an additional 15-minute recap completed by the interviewer. Both mentees and mentors are asked about functional and industry preferences, as well as competitors they could not be matched with. Questions to mentees range from "What are you looking for in a mentor?" to "Name five adjectives that describe you best." The focus of the interview is to find out what the mentee is looking to develop or improve upon with the aid of a mentor. A mentor interview takes approximately 30 minutes, with an additional 15-minute recap completed by the interviewer. Interviewers typically interview both mentees and mentors to keep both perspectives in mind as they probe during the interviews. Questions to mentors range from "Based on your personal experience and professional strengths, how can you best help someone?" to completing the statement "I'm looking forward to working with someone who . . ." The focus of the interview is to find out what the mentor has to offer to a particular mentee.

Whenever possible, all interviewers participate in the matching process, which takes a team of four approximately 6 weeks to match 250 partnerships. The focus of matching is on the mentee's criteria; therefore, interviewers take on an advocacy role, facilitating the match process to ensure that the mentee's needs and requests are preeminent. In the match session, an interviewer will highlight what he or she believes is the most relevant match information for the team. Then, all interviewers will start searching the mentor pool for appropriate mentors. The process is computer assisted so that it will identify the top-25 mentor matches, based on defined search criteria (such as identified competencies, industries, gender, etc.). The team will then, in approximately 7 to 10 minutes, narrow these down to the best mentor fit. If a match is not completed in that initial time frame, it is set aside to revisit at a later time. On occasion, a mentee may need to be called for additional information or to address specific requests that may not be met (i.e., someone may ask for a mentor of a specific religious affiliation, and we do not collect that type of information). Matching is the most critical piece of the MENTTIUM 100® program; the program has less than a 5% rematch rate.

The MENTTIUM 100® program is facilitated primarily through MENTTIUM. Trained members of the MENTTIUM staff conduct all mentee and mentor interviews, matching, participant orientation, check-in calls (to monitor partnership progress), and surveys. Clients appoint a program manager, who assists with the engagement of senior leaders, selecting mentee and mentor participants, preparing their employees for the experience, and encouraging manager support. Program managers solicit and receive feedback regarding program participation and success at predefined checkpoints throughout the 1-year program cycle. If a partnership is struggling, the MENTTIUM staff will work with the mentee and mentor to resolve the partnership issue—keeping the company program manager informed or involved in the process, when appropriate.

MENTTIUM 100®, due to its cross-organizational format, provides several unique advantages to mentoring pairs, such as insight into other organizational processes and ways of doing things, and improved cross-organizational networks. This program also leverages access to high-level mentors via the use of multiple organizations. Notably, we have in recent years developed a virtual (Virtual 100™) offering of our MENTTIUM 100® program, pairing individuals across 32 countries.

MENTTOR™

MENTTOR™ is an internal solution, helping companies leverage the expertise, wisdom, and experience of their own senior leaders. Similar to MENTTIUM 100®, it is a one-to-one program. However, the cross-company feature utilized in the MENTTIUM 100® program is eliminated. MENTTOR™ matches a mentee with a more senior mentor from another business unit or function within the *same organization*. The MENTTOR™ program provides a systematic approach that can be customized, based on the organization's goals and/or culture. Approximately

75% of MENTTIUM's 200 clients engage in a mentoring process to support their diversity and inclusion strategies. In these situations, it is important to align key messages and/or mentee and mentor orientation with other diversity and inclusion initiatives already in place.

In contrast to MENTTIUM 100®, where the program is administered by MENTTIUM staff, MENTTOR™ requires more within-company involvement in the implementation of the program. Specifically, MENTTIUM trains a team of people within the client organization, called the "Implementation Team," on all steps of the MENTTOR™ program. The Implementation Team is a diverse group combining human resource managers and line-of-business managers (see Table 24.1). Ninety percent of the time, MENTTIUM will conduct all of the program steps (discussed later and shown in Table 24.2) during an initial pilot program. Over the duration of the pilot program, MENTTIUM trains and coaches the internal team to take on all steps of the process for future program rollouts. However, many times organizations do not have the time, resources, or expertise to take on all components of the MENTTOR™ process. If this is the case, they will continue to engage MENTTIUM to deliver segments of the program. The orientation, matching, and follow-up components of MENTTOR™ are similar to the MENTTIUM 100® program. We provide further detail about and illustrate the implementation of the MENTTOR™ program though a case study later in this chapter.

Circles™

circles™ is a group mentoring model that matches senior leaders with *multiple mentees* within a given organization. This model provides organizations with an opportunity to leverage knowledge exchange among participants through a group discussion format, while maximizing the time and talent of their senior executives. The typical group is made up of 12 mentees and two mentors. Organizations are most likely to utilize the *circles*™ program in one of four types of employee groups/areas: (a) executives with a focus on leadership development, (b) new supervisors or new managers with a focus on knowledge transfer and socialization, (c) new employees with a focus on accelerated learning, or (d) affinity groups with a focus on diversity and inclusion. As we note later, it is important to understand where the process aligns in a company's employee development strategy.

A group mentoring process works best when mentees have similar roles or responsibilities in the organization (e.g., new supervisors) or some other common learning agenda (e.g., new employees). To avoid hierarchical issues, mentees and mentors in a *circles*™ group come from across the organization and from various functions. On occasion, an organization will have identified a functional group (e.g., marketing communication managers) they would like to focus on, but participants would still be from across the lines of business.

A matching process also occurs for the *circles*™ program. Mentees fill out their profiles online. The profile process takes anywhere from 30 to 45 minutes. Questions to mentees range from "What organizational and personal challenges are you most concerned about in this organization?" to "What do you hope to gain from your mentors?" Mentors are interviewed by the client program manager or MENTTIUM.

It takes approximately 45 minutes, with an additional 15-minute recap completed by the interviewer. Questions to mentors range from "Please rank your experience and skills in the following 11 areas" (e.g., leadership skills, career planning skills, etc.) to "What are you most concerned about in working with the identified mentee pool?" The focus of the interview is to find out not only what the mentor has to offer, but areas in which they might need support mentoring in a group setting.

The matching process has been honed through our work with over 30 clients. The focus of matching is on the mentee group. The implementation team reviews all of the mentee profiles and based on predetermined criteria (e.g., job function, gender, ethnicity, development needs, etc.) creates the appropriate number of *circles*™ groups. The program manager then reviews all of the profiles for a defined group and creates a "Mentee Profile Summary." This summary provides a snapshot of the mentee group, which is then used to match to the appropriate mentors. In the match session, the program manager will highlight the Mentee Profile Summary information for the team. Then, all match team members will start searching the mentor pool for appropriate mentors. The process is completely manual and takes approximately 30 minutes per *circles*™ group

The *circles*™ mentees along with their mentors identify their learning agenda for the yearlong program. Learning agendas vary from group to group, but common themes include gaining a better understanding of the organization's culture, learning how to influence upward, and career development planning. The mentoring circles meet monthly for approximately 2 hours. During that 2-hour session, participants generally hear from a subject matter expert (from inside or outside the organization) regarding a topic of choice and then spend time discussing the challenges and applications of what they learned with their mentors. While the group process does not allow for one-to-one time with the mentor(s), most mentors are willing to meet with mentees individually if the need arises.

A supplemental benefit of the *circles*™ process is the opportunity for peer-to-peer mentoring. Most *circles*™ groups have a breadth of experience and knowledge within the mentee group. If a mentee needs perspective and guidance on a specific topic, such as managing a virtual team, one or more of the mentees are likely to be able to share their experiences. Knowledge transfer and enhanced cross-functional/cross-business communications are almost always an expected outcome of the *circles*™ group experience. While the steps of the design and implementation of the program mirror those in our one-to-one programs, with the exception of the interview and match process, the group process can be more complex.

Synergy With Other Means of Development

Formal mentoring programs can have excellent synergy with other employee development tools and programs, such as feedback, challenging experiences, workshops, coaching, and other developmental relationships, including both hierarchical and peer mentoring relationships. Formalized mentoring, for example, is not intended to replace informal mentoring, but to capitalize upon the developmental aspects of workplace relationships in a more structured manner (McCauley &

Douglas, 2004). Unlike informal relationships, in formal programs, mentees are asked to set specific developmental goals; orientation and training are provided to both members of the pair; and the partnership is asked to meet a specific number of times to ensure progress. Such structure provides a unique leverage to developmental efforts in a relational context. Recognizing the important role of informal mentoring, we encourage mentees to develop their own "developmental networks" (Higgins & Kram, 2001). One mentor will, in most cases, not meet all of an individual's mentoring needs, and a mentee might even outgrow a mentor over time. Therefore, mentees might be engaged in both formal and informal mentoring relationships throughout their career arcs. In fact, supporting research that has shown that previous experience as a mentor is related to intentions to mentor in the future (Allen, Poteet, Russell, & Dobbins, 1997). Our observations confirm that experience with formal mentoring fosters informal mentoring. A mentee (protégé) who has experienced a formal positive mentoring relationship is more likely to informally mentor others.

MENTTIUM Implementation Processes

Organizations may initiate formal mentoring to support a variety of important organizational goals, including initiatives pertaining to diversity, inclusion, recruitment, retention, mergers and acquisitions, succession planning, leadership development, knowledge management, and other people development initiatives. While the specific goals of a mentoring process will differ for each initiative, we have found it quite critical that each application be grounded in a "strategic framework." Specifically, each new program launch requires that organizations think about four critical questions: (a) How does mentoring link to our overall business strategies? (b) What are the expected outcomes with respect to these strategies? (c) How does mentoring align to our human capital goals? and (d) How will we evaluate success? More comprehensively, the strategic framework includes the following:

1. Formalizing the vision, goals, and expected outcomes of mentoring

2. Creating a common frame of reference for mentoring at relevant organizational levels

3. Identifying the links to key business strategies and talent management objectives

4. Understanding the models and program components of mentoring and designating which of those may be best suited to achieve the objectives

5. Learning the essential factors needed to organizationally support mentoring

6. Raising awareness of and developing solutions for the barriers and constraints to mentoring within the organization

7. Defining evaluation and measurement goals and discussing means of achieving them

8. Gaining input into programmatic design components

9. Crafting a communication plan regarding mentoring strategy

There are 10 important steps in our mentoring process that facilitate the establishment of this strategic framework and contribute to the success of our programs. Using our MENTTOR™ program as an example, these steps are outlined in Table 24.2. It is important to highlight the first step of the process. We then provide a case study that portrays the complete process in one example organization.

Sponsor Meeting

The sponsor meeting includes senior stakeholders (typically, the CEO and his or her direct operating committee) in the organization who define why mentoring will be utilized to support human capital and business goals and how this will be accomplished. It is our experience that successful mentoring programs must closely align with the organization's mission and vision. During the sponsor meeting, we also facilitate a discussion of the organizational constraints that could impact the program, and we brainstorm solutions and strategies to ensure successful deployment.

One common organizational constraint is the role of middle management. When development initiatives are driven from the top down, middle managers are often not supportive of participation in the process for themselves or their direct reports. A successful mentoring process needs the support of the mentees' managers. Managers must understand the goals of the program, the role of the mentee and the mentor, as well as their role in supporting the process. Mentees are encouraged to obtain feedback from their managers regarding their development areas and incorporate this into their discussions with their mentors. Therefore, an ongoing communication plan for managers would be an important outcome of the sponsor meeting.

Finally, the program drivers, such as leadership development, diversity and inclusion, and knowledge transfer, are identified to confirm the targeted mentee (e.g., high potentials, diverse employees, new employees, etc.) and mentor (senior executives, cross-functional leaders, experienced employees/all levels, etc.) populations and to identify high-level deployment strategies (one-to-one structured program, structured group program, cross-company mentoring, etc.). Once the program drivers and mentee/mentor pools have been identified, the senior leaders are also asked what measures of success they deem important.

At the completion of the sponsor meeting, the Implementation Team should have enough direction from the senior leaders to develop an implementation plan. If all stakeholders are not present at the meeting, there may be a need to conduct one-to-one meetings to capture additional information and create the appropriate buy-in.

Case Study

A case study of the steps involved in the launch of our MENTTOR™ program will be used to more fully describe the steps in Table 24.2. In 2000, a pharmaceutical company initiated our MENTTOR™ program for 20 emerging leaders under the sponsorship of the CEO. The CEO believed that leveraging workforce diversity would increase the company's competitiveness and innovation. Affinity groups and other diversity programs were in place before the mentoring program was initiated.

The CEO communicated his commitment to the mentoring program along with the expectation that all senior leaders on his team would engage as program mentors. The initial reception by leadership was lukewarm. The company had a history of beginning initiatives that had not been sustained over time. MENTTIUM's insistence of ensuring alignment between mentoring and corporate strategic goals on the front end of the process with leadership was critical to the success of this initiative.

Human resources business partners met with MENTTIUM to prepare for *Step 1: The Sponsor Meeting* with the senior leaders. MENTTIUM provided ideas on approaches for the leadership dialogue and requested input on what would be effective. The CEO communicated his support of the program and asked that the financial commitment for mentoring be presented to the group.

At the Sponsor Meeting, the Implementation Team set the expectation for the session and introduced MENTTIUM. Senior leaders were asked to provide their input on how mentoring could assist the organization in reaching its strategic goals. MENTTIUM facilitated the dialogue among senior leaders. The group discussed mentoring concepts, including mentee and mentor role expectations and successful partnership factors. Leaders dialogued in small groups to assess their views about the program's goals, organizational benefits, critical success factors, and barriers. The small-group discussion was debriefed with the larger leadership team and provided valuable insight on leadership's expectation for success. Organizational objectives were defined: (a) to increase the satisfaction and retention of people of color in midlevel management positions and (b) to engage senior leaders in meaningful conversation with a diverse group of employees regarding critical personal and professional issues and opportunities. The pilot program took an inclusive approach and included Caucasian males within the mentee pool. The anticipated financial investment was clearly outlined. Senior leadership commitment, thorough planning, and a strategic dialogue created positive momentum for the mentoring program.

Over the next 2 months, *Step 2: Implementation Team Planning* occurred. The four Implementation Team members all had experience in development and delivery of learning, training, and organizational development (OD) interventions internally and externally. Team members were spread across multiple locations, including Europe. The Implementation Team Planning Session was conducted at corporate headquarters. After the initial planning session, team meetings were virtual, and the team did not meet face to face again until the program launch. After the initial planning session, two new line of business representatives were added to the team to enhance the planning process. These new team members communicated their frustration with not being involved in the front-end design of the process, but their input was sought throughout the planning stages. Non-U.S. team members were encouraged to challenge the process regarding cultural concerns for Europe.

Step 3: Nominate and Recruit Mentees and Mentors. Mentee candidates were nominated and chosen on the basis of global diversity demographics and the strategic priority of their development needs. The selection of mentees occurred through a prioritization process of diverse employees by the business and functional divisions (marketing, manufacturing, research and development, etc.). These groups were encouraged to nominate candidates that represented the diversity within their organizations (see Table 24.3). The senior leadership team approved 30 mentee candidates for final review by the CEO. The match process requires 15% to 20% more mentors than mentees to ensure effective partnership matches driven by the mentees' development needs; thus, 35 mentor candidates were also recruited.

All mentee and mentor candidates were invited to participate in the program. The CEO sent a letter to each potential participant that explained the goals, process, and timing of the program. A similar communication was sent to managers of each participant, advising them that their employees had received the invitations.

Participants could opt out of the pilot, and a few participants chose not to participate due to personal issues or job transitions. Most participants accepted the invitation because the opportunity came from the CEO. Showing initiative to accept new challenges was a highly valued behavior in the organization. Turning down the invitation without strong rationale was perceived to have a negative consequence.

The primary goals of these mentoring partnerships were to (a) positively impact participants' career success and satisfaction, (b) develop a diverse pool of leaders with mentoring skills, and (c) foster a learning environment that embraced diversity.

Step 4: Interview Mentees and Mentors. Because the program was new, MENTTIUM interviewed all potential participants in this process. The Implementation Team reviewed the interview materials and provided insight to enhance effectiveness.

Given the global nature of the program, the organization believed it was important to conduct all interviews face to face, including participants located in Europe. Interview questions had to be crafted appropriately, as they captured personal interest and values information. These questions required the participants to be candid, without feeling compromised, about taking the risk that personal information would be shared in the organization.

During Steps 2 through 4 (Implementation Planning and completion of the interviews), the organization went through significant change. Prior to completing the matching exercise, a voluntary workforce reduction occurred, which created voluntary retirement in the senior leadership ranks. The organization restructuring downsized the mentor pool and delayed the planned program launch.

Step 5: Match Mentees and Mentors. MENTTIUM spent 1 day with the Implementation Team matching mentees and mentors. The goals of the program and the match criteria were posted on flipcharts. Each interviewer presented the mentees they had interviewed. European mentees were matched first. Some challenges arose due to the limited number of women and people of color in the mentor pool. We addressed this by recruiting two more mentors. And, in one case, we felt it prudent to call a mentee to clarify whether the criterion she requested in her mentor was "nice to have" or "need to have." The mentees were partnered with senior leaders, based on their stated personal and professional development needs. The demographic profile of the participants in the program is shown in Table 24.3.

Step 6: Mentee and Mentor Orientation and Launch. Initial program launches were held in the United States and London, England. The sessions were conducted by MENTTIUM. These 4-hour interactive launches provided participants with a framework to become familiar with formal mentoring, as well as tools to develop a successful mentoring partnership. Information regarding his or her partner was shared with each participant to assist them in becoming acquainted.

The CEO spoke during each session about the strategic importance of the program and shared his personal experience with mentoring. Due to cross-geographic matches, mentees not attending the same launch as their partners completed a letter to their partners describing their expectations. The letters were delivered to their partners at the ensuing launch. The launch sessions included social time (over lunch or dinner) for participants. A group photo was taken commemorating their participation in the pilot and was provided to participants.

Even with thorough planning and review, unexpected issues arose. More emphasis should have been placed on cultural and geographic challenges posed by global partnerships, especially for partners who did not attend the same launch session. One significant concern surfaced during the launch. A mentee felt he should be in the role of mentor. He was later rematched in the process as a mentor. One mentee resigned from the company shortly before the launch. Though they were not anticipated, these issues were addressed successfully.

Step 7: 2-Month Checkpoint. Participants were expected to meet monthly for approximately 90 minutes over the next 12 months. A series of evaluative measures was planned throughout the year to assess program results. The Implementation Team completed a check-in phone call 60 days after the launch. The goal of the check-in call was threefold: (a) to determine whether partners had met, (b) to assess the progress made by the partnerships, and (c) to address concerns and/or residual questions from the program launch. Overall, it appeared most partners had met at least once and ground rules had been established for managing meeting logistics.

For those who had not yet met, the 60-day check-in provided a catalyst for partnership initiation. Competing priorities for participants' time caused a few partnerships to start slowly. The implementation Team shared assessment results with senior leadership and established a mentoring Web site.

Step 8: 4-Month Checkpoint. Mentees and mentors were invited to the 4-Month Checkpoint peer meetings to assess their partnerships and share best practices. These 2-hour meetings were held in the United States and Europe, with mentees and mentors attending separate sessions. Several tools were shared with the mentees and mentors to help them self-assess their partnerships and to discuss how they might maximize the next 8 months of the program. The goal was to gauge the level of partnership trust established and to share learning with peers.

Step 9: 8-Month Checkpoint. Mentees and mentors were invited to the 8-Month Checkpoint meeting together. The format of this checkpoint was a 90-minute meeting conducted virtually. During this checkpoint, all participants attended the meeting. Mentees and mentors were not separated for this session. The purpose of the meeting was to encourage mentees and mentors to share their challenges and successes within the program, to encourage partnerships to leverage the last 4 months of their time together, and to give participants time to connect and network with one another. It also provided the Implementation Team with key information on what was working and what process improvements needed to occur.

Step 10: Program Close and Evaluation. Evaluation of program outcomes is an important component of MENTTIUM's process. We have collected extensive data about mentor and mentee reactions postprogram (e.g., satisfaction with program, satisfaction with mentor/mentee, and perceived learning outcomes), and although it is difficult to attribute changes to the program itself, we have also collected data pre- and postprogram (e.g., career goal clarity, organizational commitment, intention to turnover) to assess changes before through after the program. We supplement examinations such as these with interviews, written comments, and/or discussions about the program and lessons learned. In the current case study, for example, we used the program close session to provide participants with the opportunity to formally close their partnerships, reflect on their accomplishments, and celebrate their successes. Two mentoring partnerships shared their stories of success with the group. The CEO spoke at an evening reception. Both mentees and mentors were given framed certificates of completion. MENTTIUM uses a continuous-improvement philosophy: We are always eager to receive feedback and improve aspects of our program on the basis of input from our participants and client organizations. Also, MENTTIUM chose to participate in a yearlong research study (sponsored by the Society of Human Resource Management [SHRM], conducted by the University of Minnesota, Carlson School of Management) of the MENTTOR™ program. Each participant in the MENTTOR™ program completed three surveys at the following points in the program: (a) before Program Launch, (b) 4-Month Checkpoint, and (c) Program Close.

The surveys asked the participants about their expectations around or about the mentoring program, their work attitudes, and their satisfaction with their mentoring experiences. Each survey took approximately 15 minutes to complete. Participation was voluntary, and mentees and mentors were not under any obligation to complete the surveys. The responses to the three surveys were kept confidential. Strict procedures were taken to keep the individual survey responses anonymous. The results of this survey indicated that the program was a highly effective development tool for the participants.

Critical Challenges and Obstacles to Formal Mentoring Programs

All development initiatives bring with them their own set of challenges. In the mentoring process, our clients experience challenges that fall into two categories: *organizational issues* and *participant issues.*

Organizational Challenges

Formalized mentoring programs started appearing in U.S.-based organizations in the late 1980s and early 1990s and are relatively new in the field of training and development. Thus, senior executives and human resource managers are just now gaining expertise in leading effective mentoring processes. Organizational challenges typically surface when leaders fail to position mentoring as a key initiative of their employee development strategy, when they attempt to use it as a onetime fix (especially for diversity applications), or when they do not provide the resources needed for sustained effort.

Mentoring is not a stand-alone process. It is one option in an organization's employee development strategy. It is best utilized in conjunction with other strategies, such as assessment of current strengths and developmental needs, challenging experiences, and supportive environments (Van Velsor & McCauley, 2004). One client who was recruiting from the top MBA/engineering schools enticed these top recruits to come work for the company by promising an accelerated leadership development program that included mentoring. In fact, the company had no mentoring component and asked MENTTIUM at the last minute to pull something together. During the mentee and mentor interview process, MENTTIUM found that 4 of the 16 recruits (less than 3 months into their jobs) were already disillusioned with the company. While specific individuals were not identified, MENTTIUM was able to give critical feedback to the organization regarding gaps in the leadership development program and take this into consideration when customizing the mentoring process. At the 4-Month Checkpoint, 3 of the 4 mentees determined they would stay with the organization, and the fourth person was undecided.

If mentoring is not integrated with the larger business and employee development strategies, it quickly becomes the "program of the month." Mentoring is not a program; it is a change process. Formal and informal mentoring can result in behavior change for employees. Over time, these individual changes engender culture change at a macrolevel within organizations. One of our pharmaceutical clients started mentoring in the organization from a grassroots effort through its women's affinity group. Seven years later, mentoring had spread to every one of the company's site locations, including Europe. The company was launching 500+ partnerships annually. Two years ago, for the first time, the organization was restructured and downsized due to financial concerns driven by market conditions. Mentoring was an integral part of the culture at the time of the restructuring, and, as such, it was the only development initiative that remained intact. Directors of the organization also indicated that they believed that key talent did not exit to the competition during this time of change as a result of their mentoring relationships.

Mentoring is also not the "silver bullet" that is going to fix a specific problem. On one occasion, MENTTIUM received a panicked call to facilitate a mentee and mentor orientation and launch at the last minute. The chemical company requesting our services had developed a "mentoring" program that matched diverse candidates with members of the operating committee. The human resources director had personally interviewed and matched 20 partnerships. No one was given the choice to opt out, and the program goals were not clearly communicated. MENTTIUM typically does not provide orientation and launch if we have not supported the planning stages of the mentoring process or if an organization differs from our philosophy on mentoring. In this case, at the pleading of the organization, we agreed to do the session. Early on in the training, it was clear that the mentees did not trust the organization's reason for initiating such a program. It also became clear that this organization needed to do a lot more work in the area of diversity before implementing a mentoring program. This initiative lasted less than 4 months.

Other challenges can occur with global applications of mentoring programs, mainly because mentoring outside of the United States is just now establishing its credibility as a development tool. When several of our U.S.-based clients chose to extend mentoring to their international locations, it became clear that other countries, such as France and Germany, respectively, tended to view mentoring as either remedial or as sponsorship. In Spain, they would not accept cross-gender partnerships. In these global cases, it is important to have representatives from targeted regions on the Implementation Team to give input into needed customizations. Language and cultural issues can create challenges for mentoring initiatives as well. In some regions of Canada, all training and materials must be delivered in both English and French.

Participant Challenges

While there is only a small amount of research addressing the relationship between voluntary participation and program outcomes (see, for example, Ragins, Cotton, & Miller, 2000), MENTTIUM strongly encourages voluntary participation by all participants regardless of the chosen nomination process. It is our experience that participant commitment is critical and that the voluntary nature of this development opportunity should be clearly communicated early and often in the process. At the interview, if mentees or mentors show signs that they are not fully committed, they should be asked to reconsider whether or not this is the right timing for their participation. If either a mentee or mentor does not appear committed to the experience but for other reasons will be required to participate, the Implementation Team should flag that individual for further follow-up at the 2-Month Checkpoint calls.

As we noted previously, matching mentoring partners is a core and critical component of the process. MENTTIUM experiences a less than 7% rematch rate with 95% of our client base; however, there are times when matches do not work. A number of factors can contribute to a failed match. An inexperienced match team may have difficulty knowing when to probe for additional information during the interview. Several years ago, a client added an interviewer to its Implementation Team without having her go through interview training. The mentoring process was company-wide but regionally focused. During a mentee interview, the mentee stated that there was someone she would not want to be matched with, but she said it was personal. The interviewer did not probe to find out who she was referring to, even though it was possible that the person was in the mentor pool. At the orientation and launch session, the Implementation Team found out that they had matched her with that very person. While the interviewer did not need to know why she didn't want to be matched with this person, she did need to know the person's name. As another example, a mentee's inability to articulate his or her needs to the interviewer is usually a red flag that the individual is not ready for the mentoring experience. Unforeseen complications can also require a rematch. Once, MENTTIUM matched a mentee and a mentor only to find that the mentee's spouse reported to the mentor. Confidentiality could not be easily maintained. Under those circumstances, a rematch was conducted.

Assuming a solid match, our research indicates that the top-two reasons partnerships can fail are (a) lack of commitment on the part of the mentor or mentee and (b) misaligned expectations on the part of the mentee or mentor. In most cases, the lack of commitment is not intentional. Senior executives who demonstrate strong mentoring skills are usually overextended, and while they would like to fit one more meeting into their schedules, their availability is severely limited. Mentors must make themselves accessible, or the mentee will disengage within the first few months of the program. Mentees already come into the program feeling like they are taking up the time of this important senior person. Building trust in the relationship takes time and requires regular meetings. The Implementation Team can minimize the impact of this by selecting the most committed mentors, clearly communicating the time commitment early on, and intervening at the 2-Month Checkpoint if the partnership has not met.

Most of the time, however, it is a mentee who demonstrates an apparent lack of commitment to the process. Again, this lack of commitment may not be intentional. Mentees appear to have less control over their schedules and can be significantly impacted by lack of support from their managers. In certain circumstances, something may have changed since they committed to the program (e.g., a job change or a personal issue). Whether it is the mentee or the mentor that cannot commit, the Implementation Team should intercede quickly. It is best to identify the source of the issue to determine whether the partnership needs some additional support, if the mentee needs to be rematched, or if the partnership must be dissolved. It is not easy to dissolve a partnership; however, it is better to address the issues proactively. One toxic partnership can derail the entire effort.

Misaligned expectations can occur when the mentee expects something out of a mentor that the mentor is unaware of or unable to provide or when the mentor expects something out of the mentee that the mentee is unaware of or unable to provide. There are many opportunities in a structured mentoring process for partnerships to align their goals and expectations, but many times, misaligned expectations start forming early if the organization hasn't clearly communicated its own goals and expectations for the program (Eby & Lockwood, 2005, report similar conclusions). Several times, MENTTIUM has encountered mentees who expect their mentors to immediately introduce them to the mentor's network. This is an unrealistic expectation early in the partnership. Relationship building and trust building take time. More often than not, mentors expect their mentees to come prepared. They prefer having an agenda of topics that the mentee wishes to cover in their discussions, and they expect mentees to know what issues or areas they want to focus on. If a mentee has a more informal view of how the partnership meetings should be managed, this can be frustrating for the mentor.

Navigating the Challenges

In this section, we illustrate these and other challenges faced by partnerships through case examples. We note specifically how real partners have found ways to navigate partnership challenges.

First, mentoring partnerships meet monthly for an average of approximately 60 to 90 minutes, and it is challenging for both mentees and mentors to find time to meet. However, our research has found that those partnerships that meet more frequently in the early stages of the relationship are more likely to enjoy a deeper level of partnership success. They are also more likely to overcome any partnership challenges they encounter along the way. For example, Josef C. and Leo R. have found that one of the ways of overcoming the issue of geographic separation is to use a recurring meeting notice to arrange a phone meeting every other Friday. The discipline of talking every 2 weeks and the fact that it is already on their schedule keeps them current with their mentoring agenda. While Mark S. and Dan M. enjoy regularly scheduled phone meetings, they also look forward to meeting in person. They have identified organizational events that they will both attend to provide a convenient means of getting together. Both will be attending the Lincoln-Mercury Introduction Show, and they have been able to arrange their schedules to go during the same time frame. Mark and Dan also plan to attend the Marketing Plans & Brand Development's Product Day together this fall.

Second, it is not unusual for those inexperienced in mentoring relationships to believe that mentoring is common sense and should be easy to do. It doesn't take long to realize that it is not as easy as it seems. Setting realistic partnership goals is critical to getting off to a strong start. One of the most difficult philosophical issues for mentees, mentors, and program administrators is the idea that the development agenda should be driven by the mentee. Assessing one's skills, knowledge, and abilities is a learning process in and of itself. The mentee needs to collect the appropriate input from his or her manager, colleagues, direct reports, and others. This critical information can come from formal mechanisms (like performance reviews or 360-degree feedback instruments) or via informal discussions. Once the information is collected, the mentee should work with the mentor to determine which competencies he or she would like to work on within the construct of the mentoring partnership. For example, Lisa D. completed a 360-degree feedback instrument and brought the report to her meeting with her mentor. Lisa and Avery B. then worked on a plan that aligned Lisa's development objectives to her desire to find a position in a different part of the company. Another mentor wrote,

> Gayleen, like many of us, is very self-sufficient—partly because of her professional role and partly because (ironically), the lack of mentoring and a type A personality. The tendency to be independent and not want to or have to rely

on another is sometimes a barrier one has to break when getting into a mentoring partnership. Hopefully, she sees the importance of letting go of control. I have asked her to send me some information—specifically on the goals that she completed for MENTTIUM and also something from her organization in terms of career development. We are hoping to use these instruments to see how best we can improve her progress towards those goals.

Third, mentors are used to problem solving, giving direction, and taking action. It is difficult to sit back, listen, and ask questions. Frequently, mentees think they have to have big issues for their mentors to solve. Or they have not had much experience with developmental goal setting. In a mentoring partnership, it can be tempting to bypass the introductions and move on to problem solving. Our research has found that pairs who take time to get to know each other beyond the surface of their work lives typically describe their partnerships as very successful at the end of the formal program. Our research also indicates that making an intentional effort to get to know each other in the first 3 months of the partnership accelerates the trust-building process. Therefore, it is important to take time to understand each other's personal and professional history. This fosters and contributes to a mutual understanding of values.

For example, Dave R. and Jerry L. have found that starting their mentoring partnership with a discussion of company and employee standards has allowed them to get to know each other better and begin dialogue on their agenda. Nicole H. and Lisa P. chose to spend their first two meetings focused on getting to know each other better. They both came prepared to discuss a variety of questions on work and life experiences, choices, and values. They also decided to spend the first 15 minutes of each meeting exchanging memorable moments and/or life-changing experiences.

Kim O. and Doug E. decided that in order to get to know each other better and develop a trusting relationship, they needed to work on something together. Since they both enjoyed hands-on, outdoor activities, they volunteered to work together on a Habitat for Humanity project. Glen R. and Guillian G. chose to meet every other week for coffee first thing in the morning to accelerate getting to know each other. In addition, they felt that it was important to see each other in action. Therefore, early in the process, Guillian invited Glen to observe her present at an operating committee meeting, and Glen invited Guillian to observe him work with a vendor.

Finally, when managers aren't informed and included in the intial stages of program implementation, they tend to become unintentional roadblocks due to lack of buy-in or understanding of the process. It is important to consider managers when developing the communication strategy. They should be clear on the goals and objectives of the program, the expectations of mentees and mentors, as well as their expected roles in supporting the process. Erin B. decided early on that she would like to keep her manager informed. She and Peter G. agreed to meet with her manager to gather input on competency areas she might need to work on with her mentor. Reney D. found that his manager did not support the mentoring initiative, so he and Leslie C. chose to meet off-site, over breakfast or dinner.

Regardless of the challenges, the stronger the mentor pool, the more likely partnerships will weather the bumps in the development of their relationships. Research employing participants in our program indicated that the more proactive the mentors were in initiating early partnership conversations, sharing perspectives and giving "homework" assignments between meetings, the more satisfied the mentees were with their personal and professional development at the end of the formal program. Specifically, mentor proactivity was related to more career-related mentoring reported by the mentee and to more career and psychosocial mentoring reported by the mentor at program close. (Wanberg, Kammeyer-Mueller, & Marchese, 2004).

In summary, we have identified several factors that characterize our most successful mentoring launches. There are also several challenges related to formal mentoring processes that can be anticipated and mitigated so that they do not become a problem. In the next section, we provide some thought about how mentoring research and theory has been useful to our practice, and discuss what research might be helpful to formal mentoring practitioners.

Research Issues and Recommendations

The wealth of research reviewed in this handbook makes it apparent that research on mentoring has made great strides in the past several years. For example, research and discussion has improved the understanding of mentoring outcomes (Dougherty & Dreher, Chapter 3, this volume), personality traits associated with the receipt of mentoring (Turban & Lee, Chapter 2, this volume), the matching process (Blake-Beard, O'Neill, & McGowan Chapter 25, this volume), and the extent to which gender and race play a role in mentoring (McKeen & Bujaki, Chapter 8, this volume). In this chapter, we discuss what research or theory has been useful to our applied practice, our thoughts on what additional research might be most helpful, and how academics and practitioners might best mutually benefit from research efforts.

First, the very nature of our work and the competitive business world means that consultants at MENTTIUM move at a fast pace. While individual development and continuous learning of our own staff is important, revewing academic research literature is not part of our daily practice. Instead, we continually improve our practice based on our client needs and conduct literature searches around our business needs. We find summaries of academic research progress in the mentoring field useful (see, for example, Noe, Greenberger, & Wang, 2002; Wanberg, Welsh, & Hezlett, 2003). Quality synthesis is valuable, as it creates synergy from multiple projects' findings and ideas, whereas it is sometimes more difficult for us to draw practice implications from single research pieces.

Historically, there have been a number of discussions about increasing the synergy between academicians and practitioners. In a special issue of *Academy of Management Journal* devoted to knowledge transfer between academics and practitioners, Mohrman, Gibson, and Mohrman (2001) noted, "We believe the usefulness of research depends, in part, on the extent to which the perspectives of organization members are included in the research process" (p. 357). They note that one way this perspective sharing can occur is via joint interpretive forums, where academic/practitioner teams might craft a research project to ensure that there is a synergy between the academic and practitioner needs. The team would also jointly discuss and interpret the data and jointly reflect upon the implications of the findings. Such an approach sounds promising. To do their part, practitioners must be willing to take time away from their daily activities to reflect upon research findings and needs and then to ponder research results in terms of what they mean for their business and client base. Academics must be willing to do some fieldwork and engage in discussions with mentoring participants and professionals (the mentoring field has several good examples of work doing just this, including Allen, Poteet, & Burroughs, 1997; Eby & McManus, 2004), although more needs to be done specifically in formal mentoring contexts (e.g., Eby & Lockwood, 2005).

Most research to date on mentoring has been completed with informal mentoring pairs. There are few empirical studies in the literature, consequently, that have focused on formal mentoring outcomes. A small number of studies have compared formal mentoring outcomes with informal mentoring outcomes and have suggested that there may be aspects of informal mentoring that are superior to formal mentoring (for a review of this previous work, see Wanberg et al., 2003). For example, because formal mentors and mentees are paired together rather than coming together via a natural relationship process, the formal pairs may lack the same level of identification or bond as an informal mentoring pair might have (Ragins & Cotton, 1999).

Eby and Lockwood (2005) argued, however, that formal mentoring relationships serve a "different purpose than informal mentorships" (p. 455) and thus have unique benefits. Formal programs provide the opportunity to be exposed to a high-level leader outside of one's regular network. The formal program orientation, structure, and 1-year time frame, furthermore, provide an important mechanism for organizations to excite individuals about self-improvement and to facilitate leadership development and knowledge sharing. The structure of the formal mentoring environment may be a good fit for some types of individuals who are not naturally "networking" types or individuals who may not otherwise have had the opportunity to explore issues important to them with someone within (or outside) of their organizations. In our view, direct comparisons of formal and informal mentoring to examine which "wins the prize" for being best are not needed. However, it would be useful to have a deeper understanding of how the two types of mentoring are complementary and to more clearly understand the extent to which traditional, informal mentoring functions and research findings translate to the formal mentoring environment. Due to the many differences between formal and informal mentoring contexts (Ragins & Cotton, 1999), we do not feel comfortable assuming that the wealth of research in informal contexts completely translates to formal mentoring programs.

Initial propositions have been made about formal mentoring from a relational context (Wanberg et al., 2003), but we have a lot to learn about the role of mentee and mentor personality and diversity in formal environments. For example, how do mentee and mentor demographic and personality similarities and differences impact factors such as interpersonal disclosure and learning through the relationship? Can we take the matching process to an even higher, more effective level? Such questions are particularly salient in a formal environment. We would also benefit from learning more about the nature and trajectory of self-disclosure during formal mentoring relationships and how formal mentoring pairs navigate challenges in their relationships.

While studies of mentee benefits from formal mentoring would also be valuable, we suggest there is a particular need to take a closer look at the impact of the formal mentoring process on mentors. How do they benefit; how does the organization benefit from their participation; and how could the mentoring process better support leadership development and skill building for mentors? Similar to research by Allen, Poteet, and Burroughs (1997), our qualitative evidence suggests that mentoring can provide mentors with enhanced support networks, self-gratification, and improved job performance. The latter is perhaps hardest to document quantitatively. Although the benefits are important, they are sometimes intangible and difficult to quantify. For example, one mentor commented,

> Mentoring has helped me to understand some of the needs of people at lower levels. Through this realization, it has made me adjust how I work with those in my organization—mainly at the lower levels. It has helped me to focus on the need to develop my direct reports. In addition, it has given me some ideas of what their challenges are and what tools might be effective.

Another mentor replied, "The mentoring relationship has allowed me to see and think about issues that I might not typically encounter in my routine environment. This has helped me to consider alternatives and strategies outside of my arena." Continued work on measurement and documentation of mentor benefits would be valuable.

Finally, we note that global mentoring is on the rise. The increase in cross-cultural mentoring and mentoring within other cultures brings new challenges. In addition to language and cultural barriers, time zones and technology can also be challenging. Identifying a convenient time as well as a universal and stable technology platform can be complicated. At an organizational level, this complex coordination requires a spectacular effort as groups of mentoring participants are gathered together across the globe. One example of this is trying to host a Web meeting with multiple participants. While it may be early morning in New York, it is early evening in Beijing, China. Often, some or many of the participants will have to sacrifice and gather at odd meeting times. We concur with Ensher, Heun, and Blanchard (2003) and Ensher and Murphy (Chapter 12, this volume) that more research regarding online mentoring would be valuable. Research studying challenges and rewards associated with cross-cultural and global mentoring is important as well.

Summary

This chapter was meant to give readers of the handbook a glimpse into the organizational/practitioner world of formal mentoring programs. In this chapter, we described three central formal mentoring programs offered by MENTTIUM: MENTTIUM 100®, MENTTOR™, and *circles*™. Each program was developed in response to distinct business needs. We provided information on our 10-step process for implementation of our programs, highlighting a case study implementation of our MENTTOR™ program. Organizational and participant challenges stemming from the formal mentoring experience were discussed, along with case examples of how our participants have overcome partnership challenges. Finally, we made suggestions about research needs from our practitioner perspective.

Table 24.1   MENTTOR™ Implementation Team Roles, Organizational Position, and Program Responsibilities

Program Role	Position Within Organization	Program Responsibilities
Program senior sponsor	Business executive or HR executive	• Engage senior management. • Provide sponsorship, support, and visibility. • Offer strategic view and communicate the business rationale for mentoring.
Program manager	HR professional or line professional	• Lead and coordinate program implementation. • Provide a mentoring vision and framework. • Provide guidance, consultation, best practices, etc. • Help seize opportunities to leverage mentoring within the organization. • Identify and guide use of resources. • Monitor program effectiveness.
Human resources advisor(s)	HR generalist OE/OD consultant Diversity specialist	• Support the program manager. • Advise regarding HR/employee relations considerations. • Advocate for the process and program.
Line advisor(s)	Line professional	• Act as liaison to program manager. • Influence "up, across, and down" within the line of business. • Advocate for the process and program.
Implementation team member	HR and/or line professionals	• Assist program manager as needed. • Advocate the process and program.
Communication specialist	Corporate communications	• Support development and implementation of communication tools.
Administrative coordinator	Typically aligned with the program manager	• Provide administrative support for the MENTTOR™ process.

Table 24.2   Implementation Steps: MENTTOR™ program

Steps	Description
Step 1: The Sponsor Meeting	Facilitated by MENTTIUM, this session strategically defines the mentoring direction and plan for the organization. In addition, discussion of the organizational constraints that could impact the program will yield solutions and strategies to ensure successful deployment. Finally, the program strategy is delineated to confirm the targeted mentee and mentor populations and to identify high-level deployment strategies.
Step 2: Implementation Team Planning	MENTTIUM equips the organization with the structure, process, and tools needed to effectively implement a mentoring program. During this session, a tactical deployment plan, communication approach, and evaluation strategy will be developed. In addition, training on the mentoring process, mentee and mentor interview and match method, individual coaching and check-ins, and ongoing mentee and mentor support/guidance is conducted.
Step 3: Nominate and Recruit Mentees and Mentors	Based on feedback from the senior leaders, Implementation Teams determine the mentee and mentor criteria for participation. Once the mentee and mentor pools have been identified, an organization may then choose to have mentees and mentors nominated by management, self-nominated, or a combination of the two approaches.
Step 4: Interview Mentees and Mentors	The Interview Process provides an understanding of mentees' and mentors' individual requirements and expectations of the mentoring experience. Both mentees and mentors are interviewed, ideally, in a face-to-face meeting. If a face-to-face meeting is not feasible, interviews may be conducted by phone as well. Interview questions cover both professional development questions as well as "life outside of work" questions, such as interests and hobbies.
Step 5: Match Mentees and Mentors	Matching is conducted on the basis of personal knowledge of the mentees and mentors gained from the one-to-one interviews. A successful match is critical to maximizing the success of the mentoring experience for the individual and the organization. Interviewers are trained through a review of a five-level matching protocol as well as mock-interview practice. The match process maintains a focus on the mentee's development needs but also takes into consideration the skills, knowledge, and experience a mentee is looking for in a mentor.
Step 6: Mentee and Mentor Orientation and Launch Session	The Orientation and Launch Session is designed to set expectations for the process and provide participants with the tools to initiate and manage their partnerships. The entire orientation and launch process is approximately 4 hours and includes concurrent mentee and mentor training, as well as structured time for the mentoring partnerships. The objectives of the session are (1) to introduce the philosophy and structure of the mentoring program; (2) to clarify roles, responsibilities, and expectations; (3) to provide tools and techniques that will support the development of healthy partnerships; and (4) to begin relationship building within the partnerships.

(Continued)

Table 24.2 (Continued)

Steps	Description
Step 7. 2-Month Checkpoint	The 2-Month Checkpoint conference calls engage participants in a one-to-one discussion about the success of their partnerships. Typically, members of the internal implementation team do the check-in calls, but some organizations prefer to have MENTTIUM do the check-ins as an objective third party. The objectives of the phone check-ins are (1) to ensure the pairs are meeting and are satisfied with their match, (2) to ensure participant understanding of the program, and (3) to identify and troubleshoot partnerships that may be struggling.
Step 8: 4-Month Checkpoint Meeting	The 4-Month Checkpoint allows for mentees and mentors to come together as a group. The meetings range from 2-4 hours and focus on providing the mentoring partnerships with the tools to deepen their partnership discussions. The objectives of this meeting are to (1) obtain feedback, (2) share best practices, (3) identify any systemic issues, and (4) network with program participants. This is also the juncture at which mentoring pairs assess their progress toward the mentee's goals, adjusting current goals or defining new goals in the process. The feedback received during the session is used in future process adjustments.
Step 9: 8-Month Checkpoint Meeting	The 8-Month Checkpoint meeting focuses on the revitalization of partnerships and offers another opportunity for participants to network. This session typically lasts 2 hours. Mentees and mentors participate in multiple interactive exercises that focus on knowledge exchange. New partnership tools are introduced to support the last 4 months of the partnerships. Mentees and mentors also begin to prepare to transfer what they have learned into their day-to-day work, as well as plan for the formal end of their mentoring partnership. Not all clients include the face-to-face 8-Month Checkpoint session in their process. However, most clients conduct some form of check-in at this time (e.g., virtual session or survey).
Step 10: Program Close	The Program Close session focuses on validating the structured mentoring experience and quantifying the program benefits. It provides a formal close for the partnerships, supports participants on how to carry mentoring learnings forward in their work, and celebrates the partnership accomplishments. The session is typically a celebration of the yearlong process as well as an opportunity to hear, firsthand, the changes and growth the mentees and mentors have experienced through the process. Most clients choose to conduct this session in conjunction with a luncheon or reception.
Evaluation	MENTTIUM provides tools and expertise in measuring important aspects of the mentoring program, including participant satisfaction, partnership success, process effectiveness, key learning, and organizational impact. The results of these important measures inform program design and program value. Typically, an organization will conduct telephone interviews at 2 months to assess the initial progress of the partnerships. Group meetings

Steps	Description
	are held at the 4- and 8-month marks. During these sessions, participants have an opportunity to share successes and challenges, as well as network with each other. At 11 months, a written survey to evaluate the program is distributed and summarized for presentation at the Program Close. A Program Close meeting is conducted at 12 months. During this session, participants formally conclude their relationships, share best practices, and provide feedback for future programs.
	A self-administered instrument designed to measure competencies in key aspects of leadership development is also available for mentees. The assessment provides participants with an opportunity to identify and reflect on strengths and opportunities, a foundation for goal setting, and a measurement of progress over time.

Table 24.3   Demographic Profile of Participants in Case Study

Diversity Within Partner Matches	Percentage	
Cross-gender partners	20%	
Long-distance partners	35%	
Cross-cultural partners (cross-nationality or race)	20%	

Mentee and Mentor Participants by Race	Percentage	
Black	70%	
Hispanic	3%	
Asian	3%	
Caucasian	24%	

Percentage of Participants by Geography	Mentees	Mentors
Europe	37%	32%
U.S.	63%	68%

Percentage of Participants by Gender	Mentees	Mentors
Female participants	35%	10%
Participant locations	10 work locations in Belgium, Germany, United Kingdom, and United States	

References

Allen, T. D., Poteet, M. L., & Burroughs, S. M. (1997). The mentor's perspective: A qualitative inquiry and future research agenda. *Journal of Vocational Behavior, 51,* 70–89.

Allen, T. D., Poteet, M. L., Russell, J. E. A., & Dobbins, G. H. (1997). A field study of factors related to supervisors' willingness to mentor others. *Journal of Vocational Behavior, 50,* 1–22.

Eby, L. T., & Lockwood, A. (2005). Protégés' and mentors' reactions to participating in formal mentoring programs: A qualitative investigation. *Journal of Vocational Behavior, 67,* 441–458.

Eby, L. T., & McManus, S. E. (2004). The protégé's role in negative mentoring experiences. *Journal of Vocational Behavior, 65,* 255–275.

Ensher, E. A., Heun, C., & Blanchard, A. (2003). Online mentoring and computer mediated communication: New directions in research. *Journal of Vocational Behavior, 63,* 264–288.

Higgins, M. C., & Kram, K. E. (2001). Reconceptualizing mentoring at work: A developmental network perspective. *Academy of Management Review, 26,* 264–288.

McCauley, C. D., & Douglas, C. A. (2004). Developmental relationships. In C. D. McCauley & E. Van Velsor (Eds.), *Handbook of leadership development* (pp. 85–115). San Francisco: Jossey-Bass.

Mohrman, S. A., Gibson, C. B., & Mohrman, A. M. (2001). Doing research that is useful to practice: A model and empirical exploration. *Academy of Management Journal, 44,* 357–275.

Noe, R. A., Greenberger, D. B., & Wang, S. (2002). Mentoring: What we know and where we might go. In G. R. Ferris (Ed.), *Research in personnel and human resources management* (Vol. 21, pp. 129–174). Oxford, UK: Elsevier Science.

Ragins, B. R., & Cotton, J. L. (1999). Mentor functions and outcomes: A comparison of men and women in formal and informal mentoring relationships. *Journal of Applied Psychology, 84,* 529–550.

Ragins, B. R., Cotton, J. L., & Miller, J. S. (2000). Marginal mentoring: The effects of type of mentor, quality of relationship, and program design on work and career attitudes. *Academy of Management Journal, 43,* 1177–1194.

Van Velsor, E., & McCauley, C. D. (2004). Our view of leadership development. In C. D. McCauley & E. Van Velsor (Eds.), *Handbook of leadership development* (pp. 1–22). San Francisco: Jossey-Bass.

Wanberg, C. R., Kammeyer-Mueller, J. D., & Marchese, M. C. (2004, April). *Antecedents and outcomes of formal mentoring quality.* Paper presented at the 19th Annual Society for Industrial and Organizational Psychology Conference, Chicago.

Wanberg, C. R., Welsh, E. T., & Hezlett, S. A. (2003). Mentoring research: A review and dynamic process model. *Research in Personnel and Human Resources Management, 22,* 39–124.

25

Blind Dates?

The Importance of Matching in Successful Formal Mentoring Relationships

Stacy D. Blake-Beard

Regina M. O'Neill

Eileen M. McGowan

F ormal mentoring programs have become popular and powerful initiatives that are increasingly employed by organizations (Allen, Eby, & Lentz, 2006; Blake-Beard, 2001; Douglas, 1997; Lyons & Oppler, 2004; McGowan, 2004; O'Neill, 2005; O'Reilly, 2001). These programs are being used as a way to address a number of issues, including leadership development, succession planning, the amalgamation of cultures as a result of mergers and acquisitions, and connecting geographically dispersed parts of the workforce. Formal mentoring has also recently been adapted as a strategic human resource intervention to aid in the retention, recruitment, and advancement of an increasingly diverse workforce (Kilian, Hukai, & McCarty, 2005; Seibert, 1999; Sosik, Lee, & Bouquillon, 2005). In fact, according to a recent edition of *Business Finance,* 77% of companies indicated that mentoring improved both employee retention and performance (Reisz, 2004).[1]

Based on our experiences with designing and implementing formal mentoring programs in a number of different organizations, we have found that one of the most crucial moments in a formal mentoring program centers around *matching* (P-Sontag, Vappie, & Wanberg, Chapter 24, this volume). Matching can be viewed as one of the potential "pitfalls" in companies' mentoring schemes (Eby & Lockwood, 2005). Whether we are working with investment banks, nonprofit organizations, institutions of higher education, or urban school districts, we face the essential question: How do you most effectively partner participants in their formal mentoring relationships? As organizations are trying to determine who should be involved in formal mentoring initiatives and how they should be matched, we often face challenges around this critical step—because, unlike other organizational initiatives that involve creating "activities," mentoring involves setting up "relationships" (Bloch, 1993; Collin, 1988). As in the typically dreaded "blind date," an assumption is often made that any match between two available people will work. In fact, how mentoring partners are selected and placed together is critical (Douglas, 1997; Gunn, 1995), and creating matches with high likelihoods of success is difficult.

In this chapter, we explore why the matching process and the beginnings of mentoring relationships are so important. Building on existing research, we show how the initial stages associated with formal mentoring are very different from those typically seen in informal relationships. We specifically examine how matching in formal mentoring relationships differs from the getting-together process that happens in informal mentoring. We share and assess the common processes by which mentoring partners are matched in formal mentoring initiatives. We conclude by offering suggestions for future research that can inform practitioners when matching mentors and protégés in formal relationships.

The Beginnings of Formal Mentoring Relationships in Contrast to Informal Mentoring

Beginnings are critical. Whether "the beginning" involves forming the foundation for a Manhattan skyscraper, creating initial impressions in a dating relationship, or supporting a baby's first steps, how things start often forms the basis for how they develop. Experience with informal and formal mentoring relationships in business, educational, and nonprofit settings suggests that important distinctions between formal and informal mentoring relationships are present at this critical moment— the beginning of the relationship (Chao, Walz, & Gardner, 1992; Ragins & Cotton, 1999; Underhill, 2005).

Beginnings of Informal Mentoring Relationships

We draw our understanding of the beginning of informal mentoring relationships from Kram's (1983, 1985) research, in which she described the *initiation phase* (see Kram, 1983, for a description of the cultivation, separation, and redefinition phases). Initiation is the first phase of informal mentoring relationships, in which the pairs are getting to know one another (Kram, 1983). Informal mentoring pairs typically form relationships with partners to whom they are attracted and with whom they feel a sense of similarity (Kalbfleisch, 2000). By the time they conceive of themselves as a mentoring pair, they have already self-selected a partner with whom they feel some connection and potential for future relational development

(McGowan, 2004). The similarity-attraction paradigm has been a strong force in their union (Byrne, 1971; Tsui & O'Reilly, 1989).

The Initiation phase has specific defining characteristics. In many informal mentoring pairs, as in many dating couples, this beginning phase is characterized by attraction to the other person and excitement at the sense of possibility that the new relationship offers. Fantasizing emphasizes the wide range of positive possibilities that are spontaneously attached to the prospect of relational development by both the mentor and protégé at the beginning of informal mentoring relationships. The protégés are pleased that a more senior person is taking an interest in their development, energized by the expanding opportunities, and complimented by the attention. Protégés are eager to please their mentors and develop their relationships further. At the same time, the mentors are flattered by the implicit respect and admiration that the protégés display and can imagine the potential benefits that the development of these talented but less experienced people will reap. They can visualize the possibilities for betterment of the organization, development of the protégés' careers, and the contributions that the protégés can make in support of their own professional development. While the range of initial expectations and emotions during the initiation stage of informal mentoring relationships may differ, in high-quality informal mentoring relationships, both mentors and protégés develop a sense of initial infatuation with the other and the possibilities that the relationship offers both (Fletcher & Ragins, Chapter 15, this volume; Kram, 1985).

Another factor related to the beginning of informal mentoring relationships is agreement on the developmental focus of the relationship. Higgins and Kram (2001) suggested that individuals who seek out developmental relationships in order to further their careers will display help-seeking behaviors that can be described as either *instrumental* (career functions) or *expressive* (psychosocial functions). According to Higgins and Kram, "Examining whether the developer(s)' preferences for certain types of developmental networks complement the preferences of the protégé may lend insight into the extent to which developmental relationships grow into mutually beneficial and reciprocal relationships" (pp. 281–282). Because we know from the literature that informal pairs tend to develop on the basis of perceptions of similarity (Blake-Beard, 2001; Byrne, 1971; Kalbfleisch, 2000) and because their help-seeking behaviors fall into predictable patterns (Higgins & Kram, 2001), it is reasonable to suggest that informal mentoring pairs identify and locate partners who share the same primary approach to development. Thus, informal pairs have already joined in an implicit agreement by sharing a similar emphasis on relational function. These informal mentoring partners are more easily able to develop congruency, in that they both enter the relationship with aligned goals and expectations.

As valuable as Kram and her colleagues' work has been in the development of understanding of the origins of informal mentoring, careful consideration is required before we use it as the primary foundation for understanding the beginnings of formal mentoring relationships. In fact, because of the many differences between formal and informal relationships, we find that the beginnings of formal mentoring relationships are shaped by a number of different forces and processes (Allen et al., 2006; McGowan, 2004).

Differences Between Beginnings of Informal and Formal Mentoring Relationships

Although far less research has been done on the beginnings of formal mentoring than those of informal relationships, when reviewing the literature, some inherent differences become immediately apparent. Formal mentoring partnerships begin prior to the initiation phase so often associated with the beginning of informal mentoring relationships (Kram, 1985). Instead, formal mentoring pairs have a very different beginning experience, best characterized by the concept of *orientation,* or the setting of a course or direction (McGowan, 2004).

The *orientation phase* in formal mentoring relationships is the initial process of relational alignment that mentors and protégés undertake in trying to "orient" themselves in relationship to their new partners. Like partners starting informal mentoring relationships, they typically do this by negotiating the most basic of mentoring tasks: the balance between career and psychosocial functions. However, while informal pairs have already joined in an implicit agreement by sharing a similar emphasis on the relative importance of the various career and psychosocial functions, formal mentoring pairs have not had the opportunity to develop that shared orientation prior to being associated as a mentoring pair. Thus, they must undertake the work of orienting the relationship toward career and/or psychosocial functions, while at the same time navigating the challenging territory of developing a new relationship within the context of programmatic goals. While there is no right or wrong way to orient the relationship in reference to career and/or psychosocial functions, research suggests that the degree to which newly formed pairs can achieve congruency in approach toward these functions portends higher degrees of satisfaction with the relationship (McGowan, 2004).

As participants enter formal programs, they bring with them their entering intentions, assumptions of role, and understanding of the program's purpose, based on their own personal mentoring experiences and life history. Given the complexities of these interactions, it is not surprising that the beginning phase of formal mentoring relationships tends not to be described "with excitement and strong positive feelings" that Kram (1985) associated with informal pairs during initiation. Rather, many formal mentoring participants begin their relationships with some degree of anxiety, anticipation, and awkwardness (McGowan, 2004). Some of this difference between formal and informal relationships may be due to expectations, but timing also plays a critical role. While some awkwardness may be present as informal partners explore relational possibilities, ultimately, they have more time to let the relationship develop naturally. Conversely, formal mentoring pairs, who may enter relationships as virtual strangers, are immediately faced with the most basic relationship work, which is to establish whether or not they share the same basic orientation toward their developmental journey and also whether or not they can coconstruct a shared focus for the relationship and integrate into their functional relationship the goals for which the program has been established.

The identification of orientation as the initial phase in formal mentoring relationships helps to explain some of the persistent functional differences between the origins of formal and informal mentoring pairs relationships and to highlight the importance of the matching processes (see Table 25.1). First, understanding these differences clarifies why we see such a wide range of performance within formal mentoring pairs, which encompass many failed as well as successful relationships. As formal partnerships are established, pairs are immediately launched into the orientation phase, in which no assumptions can be made as to primary developmental approaches. A poorly matched pair of individuals may discover that they differ drastically in their developmental orientations, for example, if one person prefers career functions and the assigned partner's approach is dedicated to a psychosocial slant. Second, while informal mentoring pairs do this same relationship work in privacy as they sift through a whole range of possible future mentoring partners, formal mentoring pairs progress through this initial orientation phase in the public domain, making the possibility of failure far more costly. Third, although informal pairs may at any point in relational development simply choose not to exist, formal pairs often don't exercise the option to change partners or leave the program. The differences in how formal and informal mentoring relationships are started, via orientation rather than initiation, speak to the importance of matching formal mentoring partners well. In the following section, we provide some guidance on best practices in matching mentoring partners.

Table 25.1   Characteristics of the Beginnings of Informal Mentoring Relationships vs. Formal Mentoring Relationships

	Informal Relationships	*Formal Relationships*
Beginning phase	Initiation (Kram, 1985)	Orientation (McGowan, 2004)
Driving forces	Similarity and attraction	Organizational needs
Knowledge of mentoring Partner prior to relationship	Personal: Observation Interaction	Impersonal: Reputation Forms
Accompanying emotions	Excitement Infatuation Fantasies Positive anticipation	Awkwardness Anxiety Tentativeness Possibly skeptical
Level of commitment	High levels of commitment— reflected by mentors and protégés coming together voluntarily and without assistance	Variable levels of commitment— may be affected by forced participation or uncertainty about the purpose of the program
Level of visibility	Low: Initiation of relationship is private	High: Launching of the program (and the relationship) is public
Level of congruence	Congruent: Primary orientation toward developmental function is shared by both partners	Undetermined: Partners enter without any sense of partners' developmental orientation

Practical Approach to Matching in Formal Mentoring Programs: Matching Strategies

While informal mentoring relationships develop through the initiative and subsequent relational engagement of individual mentors and protégés (Higgins, Chandler, & Kram, Chapter 14, this volume), formal mentoring relationships are initiated through the direct intervention of a sponsoring organization. Well before the formal matching process even begins, program creators must first consider programmatic goals, functioning, and infrastructure. Why is the program being instituted? Who should participate? How long will it run? Where will it be implemented? What will it accomplish? As the program's essential components are being developed, the matching process, a pivotal factor contributing to the success of the initiative, is often overlooked in the planning stages.

In our work with mentoring programs, we have found that the matching processes organizations use to identify and create pairs vary widely. In some instances, great care is given to the matching process by making good use of questionnaires, personal knowledge, and careful reflection in pairing perspective mentors and protégés. Programmatic models currently exist that attempt to maximize prior knowledge and attraction by either exposing the protégés to a range of mentor profiles and ranking priorities or having the protégés self-identify up to three potential prospects prior to determining the final match.

Conversely, it also occurs that due to high participant numbers and busy administrators, some programs devote very little time to developing careful matches. Two strangers may be quickly and arbitrarily identified as a "mentoring pair" on the basis of sparse information, minimal participant input, and little or no particular matching strategies. Program participants are then thrust into the very uncomfortable position of being identified as a formal pair prior to meeting their espoused partners.

In addition to the inherent difficulty in matching strangers in a meaningful mentoring partnership, if we also insert a contextual dimension, we find that formal mentoring programs are often used to address challenging issues that organizations are facing. Formal mentoring initiatives are often developed in environments where either mentoring relationships are not developing spontaneously or the particular goals of the organization, often targeted toward diversity initiatives for women or people of color, are not being adequately addressed. These programs are therefore often constructed to remedy a less than ideal situation to compensate for what is not developing naturally.

Yet with all of the challenges associated with implementing formal mentoring programs, particularly with matching pairs, this initiative is still a powerful catalyst for organizational change. With careful attention and strategic planning, organizations can reap the benefits of formal mentoring. The following are some suggestions for effectively matching mentoring program participants on the basis of the three broad ways we have observed partners being matched: *administrator-assigned matching, choice-based matching,* and *assessment-based matching.* In the next section, we discuss these methods, as well as pros and cons associated with each (see Table 25.2).

Table 25.2   Matching Methods

Overarching Matching Schemas	Methods	Applications	Strengths of Method	Weaknesses of Method
Administrator-assigned	Goal-driven Hunch method	Organizations in which administrator has personal knowledge of players and program	Matches are tightly aligned with organizational goals	Mentors and protégés have little or no input in the process
Choice-based	Priority lists Mutual selection activities Mentor or protégé choice	Multiple possible pair combinations exist, and participants are invested in process	Increases psychological ownership and commitment, sense of intimacy, meeting frequency	Increased costs, greater facilitation needs to coordinate activities More likelihood of partners selecting one another based on similarity and comfort with one another, not diversity
Assessment-based	Myers-Briggs Type Indicator PeopleMatch	Goals of the mentoring program indicate desirability of more prescribed matches	Increases likelihood of complementarity	Impersonal Increased costs due to assessment administration and data usage

Administrator-Assigned Matching

As formal initiatives are launched, one common method that planners use is to match mentors and protégés on their own. Administrators may use a variety of different criteria to pair mentoring partners, including organizational need (supporting high potentials, retaining diverse talent, nurturing cultural integration in mergers and acquisitions), developmental goals, functional level, and geography. Which factors constitute the decisive ones will depend upon the style of the administrator and the particular goals of the program. Another method administrators use to match participants is to draw upon their personal assessments. We label this particular format the "hunch method." With the hunch method, program planners match mentoring partners on the basis of their personal assessments of likelihood of interpersonal connection between mentors and protégés. We see the hunch method used with smaller programs, where program planners may feel that they know the various participants well enough to use their judgment to match mentors and protégés.

The benefit of an administration-assigned matching process is that it allows the program to be tightly aligned with organizational goals and needs. Administrators can be proactive and strategic about matching mentoring pairs in ways that will support the program goals. The challenge with matching using this process is that if mentors and protégés have no say in the process of selecting their mentoring partners, they may not be as invested in their mentoring relationships. The "buy-in" factor may be missing. We also see this method being associated with mentoring participants conscripted into mentoring programs rather than volunteering, which is a success condition for effective formal mentoring relationships.

Choice-Based Matching

What many formal mentoring planners are learning is that allowing participants to have some choice in the selection of their mentoring partners increases the efficacy of the resulting mentoring relationships (Allen et al., 2006). Wanberg, Welsh, and Hezlett (2003) noted that expert opinion favors allowing protégés to have some choice in the matching process. Allowing the participants to have some measure of choice introduces, to a small degree, the forces of similarity and attraction that are naturally present at the formation of informal mentoring relationships. Wanberg et al. (2003) proposed that greater protégé participation in the matching process will increase psychological ownership and commitment to the mentoring process, mentor/protégé intimacy, meeting frequency, and strength of influence; interestingly, they don't talk about mentor input into matching.

In our work with organizations, we have seen programs in which mentors select the protégés, programs in which protégés select the mentors, and programs in which there is a mutual selection process. We have seen participants become more involved in the matching process in several different ways. The process of including mentor and protégé feedback in the mentoring processes ranges from holding face-to-face networking events, where mentors and protégés come to meet one another and scope out potential partners, to creating virtual meeting rooms for mentors and protégés to peruse databases of information in the search for mentoring partners.

We have seen a number of benefits to allowing a greater measure of choice in the matching process on the part of participants. In programs with which we have worked, when we compare mentoring relationships in which matches were done with some choice versus those that were driven by the program administrator, we see marked differences, including greater commitment to the relationship, more willingness to spend time together, greater ability to work through conflictual issues, greater access to mentoring partners, and increased interest in maintaining the relationship after the conclusion of the formal mentoring program. Challenges of choice-based methods of matching include greater costs for the mentoring program as well as greater facilitation needs to coordinate either virtual or face-to-face activities. Another potential challenge occurs when some mentors are selected by a number of potential protégés while other mentors are not selected at all. We have also seen mentors and protégés select partners with whom they are comfortable; so if there is a need to reach across dimensions of difference or diversity, we may not see this goal realized in a choice-based matching scheme unless there is some administrator intervention.

Assessment-Based Matching

A final way that we have seen organizations match mentors and protégés in formal mentoring initiatives is through the use of assessment tools that allow them to make informed decisions about partnering participants. *Complementarity* is a key issue that assessment-based matching allows administrators to address. The mentoring literature suggests that it is helpful for mentors and protégés to have both similarities and differences in their relationships (Hale, 2000; Wanberg et al., 2003). Mentors and protégés benefit from some measure of similarity because it provides a basis upon which to connect. Yet it is also helpful for mentors and protégés to be exposed to perspectives, skills sets, and experiences that differ from their own. Matching mentors in a structured manner, based on styles and developmental needs, can help meet program goals and achieve relationship success because participants are paired according to complementary styles, developmental needs, and organizational program goals.

Assessment tools are particularly helpful in matching in formal mentoring because the feedback participants receive from these self-assessments helps them understand their own styles, strengths, and developmental needs. Participants in formal mentoring efforts can work more effectively when they have a clear view of themselves and a good understanding of their environments. A number of assessment tools have been used to match mentoring partners such that the relationship is complementary in nature, including the Myers-Briggs Type Indicator, dimensions of emotional intelligence, and PeopleMatch. The Myers-Briggs Type Indicator measures four dimensions of personality: introversion-extroversion, intuitive-sensing, thinking-feeling, and perceiving-judging. Emotional intelligence assessments measure leadership skills of self-awareness, self-regulation, social skills, motivation, and empathy. PeopleMatch is a comprehensive assessment that gathers information on multiple aspects, including values work style; personality; skills sets such as networking, career support, decision making, teamwork, and leadership; and all facets of emotional intelligence. Each assessment tool provides a foundation upon which mentoring partners can build their mentoring relationships.

There are a number of benefits to using an assessment-based matching strategy. Using the tools to match mentoring partners for complementarity is the biggest benefit. The assessments also give mentoring partners an idea of the strengths that each is bringing to the relationship as well as potential vulnerabilities. This information is quite helpful as mentoring partners create a developmental plan of action—a road map—for their relationship. Challenges with this form of matching are similar to those that we see with the choice-based matching options. There are additional costs incurred to administer the assessments, and there are the human costs to manage the data generated from the assessments.

Optimal mentor-protégé matches increase the likelihood of program success and participant satisfaction. Allen et al. (2006) found that when formal mentoring partners were involved in the matching process, they perceived the program as more effective, believed that their mentoring partners were more committed, and had a better understanding of the program objectives and goals. When participants are thrown together on that dreaded "blind date" that may mark the beginning of a formal mentoring program, it is critical to provide them with a way to orient to one another and to get the relationship off to a good start. Even when program administrators are thoughtful and purposeful about their matching strategies, there are still challenges they may face as they set up matches for formal mentoring relationships. The following are several of the common challenges that administrators overseeing the matching process may face.

Common Matching Challenges and Best Practices to Overcome Them

Practitioners working with formal mentoring programs must be empathic to the difficulties inherent in the "blind date." Within any formal program, there will be a range of relational functioning; an effective program planner realizes that some difficulties are inevitable and anticipates them. However, program administrators should be particularly cognizant that the initial stages of formal mentoring relationships are especially demanding, with predictable feelings of awkwardness, anticipation, and anxiety that are not characteristic of the initiation phase of informal mentoring relationships, but rather are specifically associated with the orientation phase of formal relationships (McGowan, 2001). And while some mentoring pairs will move through orientation without much difficulty, others will struggle and some ultimately will not survive. Activities that help mentoring pairs build on the matching strategy used to bring them together include assisting pairs in identifying their expectations, supporting the development of similar learning goal orientations (Egan, 2005), analyzing their preferred developmental approaches (McGowan, 2001), and orienting them to align with these preferences. Pairs are then well positioned to utilize the complementary aspects of their relationships.

Another common challenge that we have seen in our practice of working with organizations implementing formal mentoring is the underutilization of data and participant choice in matching mentoring pairs. Rather than addressing critical questions about goals and thinking through the strategic reasons for the initiative and how matching should support those goals, administrators rely heavily on the hunch method we described earlier in the paper. Although this may be an effective strategy if administrative intuition is based on personal knowledge of the individuals involved, a "hunch" approach that relies on pure guesswork offers no more likelihood of success than does pure random assignment. As a rule, the more data that are gathered (on both the mentor and protégé) and the more care that is given to prepare for matching, the more successful the resulting formal mentoring relationships are. So, while the hunch method can work in some instances, it is less accurate and offers less support for effective matching than do choice-based and assessment-based matching.

We believe that not only do organizations and formal mentoring administrators underestimate the value of a good match, they also underestimate the costs of poor matches. For example, a poor match in which mentoring partners feel they cannot connect can mean that the relationship never gets started in a productive way and is therefore not an effective one for either person. Similarly, matches in which tension exists between a mentor and protégé can actually be counterproductive. For example, in one program we developed, one protégé was randomly matched with a mentor who was his boss's boss, making it impossible for the protégé to have the kinds of conversations he felt were necessary to accomplish the goals of the mentoring program. When matching is done poorly, the mentoring program can receive a bad reputation for having done a substandard job with that initiative, adding to organizational skepticism and even further psychological withdrawal from the organization by mentors and/or protégés.

Finally, during the matching process, we also take into consideration organizational program goals. As Hegsted and Wentling (2005) noted, organizations should not put formal mentoring in place without tying it to critical organizational goals. We extend that thinking by recommending that program administrators match mentors and protégés in a way that helps them meet their organizational goals. For example, in an organization interested in a mentoring initiative for knowledge transfer, the matching process should factor in participants' lines of business so that mentors and protégés are exposed to the most appropriate areas of the organization.

Future Research

While matching is a critical part of making a formal mentoring program successful, we are aware of no research to date that empirically addresses this particular aspect of mentoring relationships. As such, we consider relevant mentoring research and new directions for research that can inform practitioners when matching mentors and protégés in formal relationships. We identify future research directions we believe will enable both academics and practitioners to mutually benefit from these research efforts.

One important area for future research is to consider the criteria that are used to determine matches in formal mentoring relationships, as well as the effectiveness of these different criteria. Our experience has been that there is wide variation in the matching processes organizations use to identify and create mentoring pairs. For example, some programs use developmental focus of the protégé to determine matches, while other programs focus on race or gender in determining mentoring pairs. Future research that examines the effectiveness of different matching criteria can shed light on the most successful means of matching, especially if a combination of criteria and weighting is used to determine the most successful types of mentor-protégé relationships.

Future research can also examine the plethora of anecdotal information about linking the purpose of the program to the ways mentors and protégés are matched. As Hegsted and Wentling (2005) suggested, organizations should connect their critical organizational goals to a formal mentoring program. While we recommend that our clients match mentors and protégés in ways that help them meet their program goals, we know of no empirical research that examines the relationship between mentoring program goals and the matching process. Research of this nature can provide invaluable insight for practitioners into ways the mentoring program objectives can guide a successful matching process, ultimately helping to make mentoring relationships effective.

Another key area for future research is empirical work that compares different matching processes and their impact on the subsequent relationships and mentoring outcomes. Is it possible to systematize the process in an effective way, or is good matching dependent upon an individual, pair-by-pair decision-making process (Conway, 2005)? Clearly, both good and bad matching will impact the mentoring relationship in subsequent phases. Some relationships will be positive and productive because the matching works for the mentor and protégé, while other relationships might never get off the ground because of poor matching. Research that examines the differences in matching—whether random or with personal knowledge and careful reflection—will provide insight into both the most effective means of matching mentoring pairs as well as the implications of matching for the subsequent effectiveness and success of the relationship.

What do mentors gain from participating in formal mentoring programs? The benefits to the mentees are clearly evident: access to someone more powerful, visibility in their organizations, and exposure to different opportunities and other influential organizational members. But the mentoring literature has generally been skewed toward understanding the benefits and challenges of mentoring from the mentee's perspective. Eby, Durley, Evans, and Ragins (2006) noted that they found only two studies investigating the predictors of mentoring benefits for mentors. In their study of mentors' experiences of mentoring, Eby and her colleagues focused on the relationship between short-term proximal benefits reported by mentors (such as improved job performance, recognition by others, rewarding experience) and long-term distal outcomes (such as mentor career success, work attitudes, intention to mentor again in the future). They did find some connections between short-term and long-term benefits to mentors. Their work suggests that mentor benefits that are short-term and instrumental in nature are more important in predicting mentor work attitudes, while mentor benefits that are short-term and relational in nature are more influential in predicting intentions to mentor in the future. Eby and Lockwood's (2005) qualitative study of mentors participating in formal mentoring chronicled both the challenges and opportunities mentors gained from their participation. Mentors' benefits included learning, developing personal relationships, and enhanced managerial skills, while they also faced challenges of mismatches, scheduling difficulties, and feelings of personal inadequacy. Both studies point to the need to delve deeper (through qualitative studies) and in a more nuanced manner (through more sophisticated studies) to understand mentors' perspectives. And the stakes are fairly high: We need to answer these questions because as more and more organizations implement formal mentoring programs, it is going to become increasingly important for researchers to increase the depth of the empirical record on mentors' experiences in these relationships.

Mentoring scholars and practitioners alike stand to benefit from more research dedicated to exploring how diversity may impact the way matches are configured (O'Neill, 2002). What are the implications of placing program participants in same-race/same-gender mentoring matches compared with cross-race/cross-gender matches? Mentoring planners often ask, "Should I put a woman mentee with a female mentor or a male mentor? Should I match people of color only with mentors who are also people of color?" Future research that further sheds light on the questions raised here may offer critical information for effective planning during the matching phase. Research has consistently supported a differential impact in outcomes depending on whether the mentor is the same race/gender as the mentee. Burke, Burgess, and Fallon (2006) found that female respondents with female mentors reported higher levels of role-modeling and more psychosocial functions, which is consistent with what has generally been reported in the literature. But what happens as we start to examine dimensions of diversity beyond race and gender? Interest in learning as a source of competitive advantage is growing (Eddy, Tannenbaum, Lorenzet, & Smith-Jentsch, 2005). For example, Intel's mentoring program is based on knowledge transfer: Mentoring participants are placed together so that the mentor will pass on specific skill-related competencies to the mentee (which may lead to the mentor being at a lower hierarchical level than the mentee) (Neuborne, 2003). In their experimental study of 190 undergraduates, Allen and O'Brien (2006) found that individuals with greater learning orientation were more attracted to an organization when it was depicted as having a formal mentoring program than when it was not so depicted. In what other ways might learning orientation impact mentoring relationships? Do we see differences in learning in cross-gender versus same-gender relationships?

Finally, at an organizational level, it would be helpful to better understand the issue of potential backlash. Many mentoring initiatives are directed at recruiting and/or retaining diverse talent (de Vries, Webb, & Eveline, 2006). There may be unintended consequences as a result of the attention focused on these groups (Gunn, 1995; Friedman, Kane, & Cornfield, 1998). Gunn (1995) noted that mentoring programs dedicated exclusively to women and minorities may create backlash. He described *backlash* as the perception that a program exclusively for minorities and women constitutes a form of preferential treatment. White and male employees may resent the access and resources that they see accruing to participants in these exclusionary mentoring programs. So, formal mentoring programs that are offered to only one group within an organization have the potential to fragment delicate group interactions and work relationships; there may also be legal implications as well (Segal, 1995).

There is a particular sensitivity regarding backlash in relation to dimensions of demographic diversity. Interestingly, we do not hear the same concerns raised when examining formal mentoring programs dedicated to high-potential employees, another group receiving considerable attention. It would be interesting to study the factors that lead to backlash occurring. Research that allows practitioners to better understand the factors that evoke backlash will provide critical data to those planning and implementing formal mentoring programs. From a practical perspective, mentoring researchers suggest that organizations should consider moving beyond using mentoring as a tool to reach narrowly drawn affirmative action objectives. In Gunn's (1995) article, Kram suggested, "There's a shift in orientation from helping women and people of color to creating a culture that empowers all people of whatever background to succeed" (as cited on p. 66).

Conclusion

As organizations continue to turn to formal mentoring to address goals of retaining talent, building their bench strength and succession pipelines, integrating diverse perspectives and employees, and creating a learning environment, they will need to give careful consideration to matching mentors and protégés in a way that will enable these relationships to be successful and meet their program goals. Effective matching is a critical step in getting a program to launch correctly and also in building solid frameworks for mentoring pairs to have strong relationships that are supported by organizations. Yet unlike many other of the other challenges organizations face that involve locating a "formula" and implementing it, in matching, there is no one blueprint that can capture the multitude of factors, both tangible and intangible, that contribute to the dynamic quality of interpersonal relationships or that ensure the success of a "blind date." Instead, administrators will need to weigh the relative strengths and weakness of various approaches to matching and tailor them to the particular needs and cultures of their organizations.

Notes

1. The proliferation of formal programs began with the Equal Employment Opportunity Commission (EEOC) and organizations' need to find ways to create level playing fields for women and people of color (late 1970s and early 1980s). Then, as organizations grew, the need to develop "bench strength" led to the use of formal programs in accelerating development for high potentials. In recent years, formal mentoring has been seen as a human resources tool to attract, retain, and develop employees. Formal mentoring is also being suggested as a way to facilitate knowledge transfer.

References

Allen, T. D., Eby, L. T., & Lentz, E. (2006). The relationship between formal mentoring program characteristics and perceived program effectiveness. *Personnel Psychology, 59,* 125–153.

Allen, T. D., & O'Brien, K. E. (2006). Formal mentoring programs and organizational attraction. *Human Resource Development Quarterly, 17,* 43.

Blake-Beard, S. D. (2001). Taking a hard look at formal mentoring programs: A consideration of potential challenges facing women. *Journal of Management Development, 20,* 331–345.

Bloch, S. (1993, April). Business mentoring and coaching. *Training & Development,* pp. 26–29.

Burke, R. J., Burgess, Z., & Fallon, B. (2006). Benefits of mentoring to Australian early career women managers and professionals. *Equal Opportunities International, 25*(1), 71–79.

Byrne, D. (1971). *The attraction paradigm.* New York: Academic Press.

Chao, G. T., Walz, P. M., & Gardner, P. D. (1992). Formal and informal mentorships: A comparison of mentoring functions and contrast with nonmentored counterparts. *Personnel Psychology, 45,* 619–636.

Collin, A. (1988). Mentoring. *Industrial and Commercial Training, 20*(2), 23–27.

Conway, C. (2005). Mentoring: Back to basics. *Training, 42*(8), 42.

de Vries, J., Webb, C., & Eveline, J. (2006). Mentoring for gender equality and organizational change. *Employee Relations, 28,* 573–587.

Douglas, C. A. (1997). *Formal mentoring programs in organizations: An annotated bibliography.* Greensboro, NC: Center for Creative Leadership.

Eby, L. T., Durley, J. R., Evans, S. C., & Ragins, B. R. (2006). The relationship between short-term mentoring benefits and long-term mentor outcomes. *Journal of Vocational Behavior, 69,* 424–444.

Eby, L. T., & Lockwood, A. (2005). Protégés' and mentors' reactions to participating in formal mentoring programs: A qualitative investigation. *Journal of Vocational Behavior, 67,* 441–458.

Eddy, E. R., Tannenbaum, S. I., Lorenzet, S. J., & Smith-Jentsch, K. A. (2005). The influence of a continuous learning environment on peer mentoring behaviors. *Journal of Managerial Issues, 17,* 383–395.

Egan, T. M. (2005). The impact of learning goal orientation similarity on formal mentoring relationship outcomes. *Advances in Developing Human Resources, 7,* 489–504.

Friedman, R., Kane, M., & Cornfield, D. B. (1998). Social support and career optimism: Examining the effectiveness of network groups among Black managers. *Human Relations, 51,* 1155–1177.

Gunn, E. (1995). Mentoring: The democratic version. *Training, 32*(8), 64–67.

Hale, R. (2000). To match or mis-match? The dynamics of mentoring as a route to personal and organizational learning. *Career Development International, 5,* 223–234.

Hegsted, C. D., & Wentling, R. (2005). Organizational antecedents and moderators that impact on the effectiveness of exemplary formal mentoring programs in Fortune 500 companies in the United States. *Human Resource Development International, 8,* 467–487.

Higgins, M. C., & Kram, K. E. (2001). Reconceptualizing mentoring at work: A developmental network approach. *Academy of Management Review, 26,* 264–288.

Kalbfleisch, P. J. (2000, Summer). Similarity and attraction in business and academic environments: Same and cross-sex mentoring relationships. *Review of Business,* pp. 58–61.

Kilian, C. M., Hukai, D., & McCarty, C. E. (2005). Building diversity in the pipeline to corporate leadership. *Journal of Management Development, 24,* 155–168.

Kram, K. (1983). Phases of the mentoring relationship. *Academy of Management Journal, 26,* 608–625.

Kram, K. (1985). *Mentoring at work: Developmental relationships in organizational life.* Glenview, IL: Scott, Foresman.

Lyons, B. D., & Oppler, E. S. (2004). The effects of structural attributes and demographic characteristics on protégé satisfaction in mentoring programs. *Journal of Career Development, 30,* 215–229.

McGowan, E. M. (2001). *Texts and contexts of reciprocity: Five models of mentoring.* Unpublished manuscript.

McGowan, E. M. (2004). *Relationship work: A descriptive theory of a faculty-to-faculty formal mentoring program in higher education.* Unpublished dissertation, Harvard University, Cambridge, MA.

Neuborne, E. (March, 2003). Mentors as motivators. *Potentials, 36,* 16.

O'Neill, R. M. (2002). Gender and race in mentoring relationships: A review of the literature. In D. Clutterbuck & B. R. Ragins (Eds.), *Diversity and mentoring: An international perspective* (pp. 1–22). Oxford, UK: Butterworth-Heinemann.

O'Neill, R. M. (2005). An examination of organizational predictors of mentoring functions. *Journal of Managerial Issues, 17,* 439–460.

O'Reilly, D. (2001, July–September). The mentoring of employees: Is your organization taking advantage of this professional development tool? *Ohio CPA Journal,* pp. 51–54.

Ragins, B. R., & Cotton, J. L. (1999). Mentor functions and outcomes: A comparison of men and women in formal and informal mentoring relationships. *Journal of Applied Psychology, 84,* 529–550.

Reisz, S. (2004, May/June). Mentoring: A cost-effective retention tool. *Catalyst,* pp. 42–43.

Segal, J. A. (1995). Diversity danger zones. *HRMagazine, 40*(6), 31–41.

Seibert, S. (1999). The effectiveness of facilitated mentoring: A longitudinal quasi-experiment. *Journal of Vocational Behavior, 54,* 483–502.

Sosik, J. J., Lee, D. & Bouquillon, E. A. (2005). Context and mentoring: Examining formal and informal relationships in high tech firms and K–12 schools. *Journal of Leadership & Organizational Studies, 12,* 94–108.

Tsui, A. S., & O'Reilly, C. A. (1989). Beyond simple demographics effects: The importance of relational demography in superior-subordinate dyads. *Academy of Management Journal, 32,* 402–423.

Underhill, C. M. (2005). The effectiveness of mentoring programs in corporate settings: A meta-analytical review of the literature. *Journal of Vocational Behavior, 68,* 292–307.

Wanberg, C. R., Welsh, E. T., & Hezlett, S. A. (2003). Mentoring research: A review and dynamic process model. *Research in Personnel and Human Resource Management, 22,* 39–124.

26

An International Perspective on Mentoring

David Clutterbuck

This chapter takes two perspectives that are different from the others in the handbook. First, it explores the development of mentoring outside North America, where—in Europe at least—it has taken a very different route much closer to what Fletcher and Ragins (see Chapter 15, this volume) describe as "relational mentoring." Second, whereas almost all the evidence-based literature about mentoring emanating from the United States begins with an academic exploration of relationship phenomena and leads to drawing conclusions about practice, in Europe, the emphasis has been on identifying good practice (what works and doesn't work) and initiating subsequent quantitative or qualitative empirical investigation to elucidate underlying theory.

I begin by describing my personal practice and how it has led to specific research and the development of practical models to help mentors and mentees understand their roles. I next provide an overview of the development of mentoring in Europe and the implications of these developments—in particular, the establishment of a nondirective model of mentoring—for both my own practice and practice in general. I provide a short review of the development of mentoring in the rest of the non-U.S. world, leading to a discussion of perceived good practice in terms of managing cultural difference in mentoring programs and relationships. Finally, I describe an ongoing research program stimulated by practitioner needs and extrapolate an agenda for future practitioner-generated research.

The Development of a Mentoring Practice

My practice in mentoring has taken three directions. The first is as a mentor, working at one extreme with chief executives and, at the other, with a mixture of pro bono clients, ranging from young people at early stages of their careers to people in their midcareers. The second has been as the leader of an increasingly international practice, helping organizations design and implement mentoring programs. And the third is as a researcher and writer, seeking understanding of this powerful developmental phenomenon and sharing learning more widely. When asked what I do, I typically reply that I "ask difficult questions." Sometimes these are intended to stimulate the thinking of others, sometimes to open up new areas of research that will support one-to-one relationships or program practice, and sometimes to develop my own awareness and insight. Each element of my practice both supports and is supported by the others.

In all of my mentoring relationships, I have selected to work with people from whom I am able to identify significant opportunities for my own learning—for example, because they come from an age group, culture, and/or discipline that is different from my own. This is the same, whether I am mentor, mentee,[1] mutual or peer mentor, or peer supervisor of mentoring (in the counseling sense of supervision of professional practice). Only by engaging fully with all of these roles can I develop my own practice and, from that, clues to fruitful areas of research, which will have immediate practical application.

My practice in mentoring programs has covered Europe, North America, Africa, Asia-Pacific, and various other areas of the globe. My consultancy has franchises in Southern Africa, Australia, Turkey, and various European countries, and associates in many others. From an initial concentration on young graduate recruits, the range of applications has spread to programs for executives, for supporting diversity objectives, culture change, and managing retention. Some examples are as follows:

- Developing a program to link the management teams leading prisons with peer mentors in businesses
- Helping the World Bank develop an internal resource to support up to 20 ethnic groupings around the world establish programs that fit with their cultures and concerns.
- Helping a manufacturing multinational change its culture from a production orientation to a key account management orientation
- Preparing young professionals in the International Labour Office for first assignments in the field
- Helping international banks, both U.S. and European headquartered, adapt mentoring programs to local circumstances and cultures
- Developing a radical and massive program to elevate Black employees in U.K. National Health Hospitals into boardroom positions

The objective of our practice is to build the capacity of client companies to use mentoring effectively and sustainably. This has led us to develop an array of supporting services, from diagnostics that explore the organization's readiness to embark upon mentoring, to software tools to match and monitor relationship quality, to a portfolio of modularized training for mentors, mentees, and program coordinators. For many multinational clients, we also train and support internal trainers—an important element in adapting capacity to geocultural factors.

From Practice to Research

Both personal mentoring and programs provide a rich and constant stream of ideas for research and opportunities to design and carry out empirical studies, driven in most part by concerns expressed by client companies. Research in recent years—often with colleagues at the Mentoring and Coaching Research Group, Sheffield Hallam University—includes the following:

- A study of relationship endings, which found (a) a strong positive correlation between a structured review and "winding up" and perceived relationship effectiveness and (b) a strong correspondence between relationships that wound down (just drifted away) and negative perceptions (Clutterbuck & Megginson, 2001)
- An investigation of mentor and mentee competences (Clutterbuck & Lane, 2004)
- A qualitative study of practice and effectiveness in executive mentoring (Clutterbuck & Megginson, 1999)
- Collection and thematic analysis of case studies (Megginson & Clutterbuck, 1995; Megginson, Clutterbuck, Garvey, Stokes, & Garrett-Harris, 2005)
- A longitudinal and cross-sectional study of mentoring relationship dynamics (of which more will be described later in this chapter)

Areas of particular research interest, derived from both my personal and organizational program practice, have included the role of personal reflective space, the structure of the mentoring conversation, and mentoring behaviors. The following section takes these in turn.

Reflective Space

One of the reasons mentors and mentees say they value their meetings seems to be because they can take time out from doing to concentrate on thinking and being. It became clear several years ago that we needed to help participants on our programs create, manage, and make good use of this valuable resource of personal reflective space. Less than 2% of the thousands of people who attend our workshops every year say that they do any significant amount of deep, reflective thinking during the working day. Instead, they think in the car, the shower, walking the dog, in the gym, or anywhere where they can focus without interruption on one issue. One of my intended future research projects will be to carry out a structured analysis to examine frequency, process, and intensity of these journeys into reflective space.

I began to collect people's accounts of what happened to them when they did get into personal reflective space, both in general and in mentoring sessions, in the early 1990s. Gradually, a model emerged, described in Figure 26.1. This model has become a standard part of our explanation of how mentoring works, and in our workshop, feedback from participants is consistently rated one of the most valuable insights. The mentor's role is to help the mentee work through the various stages,

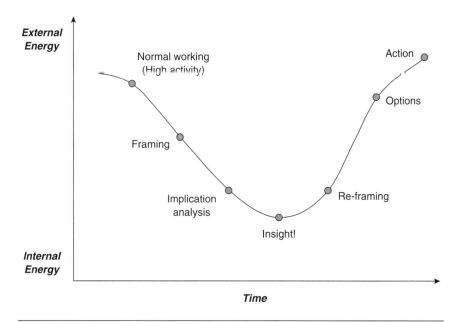

Figure 26.1   Phases of Reflective Space

SOURCE: Chutterbuck Associates © 2006.

over several sessions, if required. When both mentor and mentee both understand this model, it appears from feedback from program participants that they can collaborate more effectively in the process of inquiry.

The Nature of Personal Reflective Space

To be effective, people need time and an appropriate environment in which to think about what they are doing (or intend to do) and why. The typical cycle appears to begin with our normal state of affairs—having a number of issues that need thinking through but, for one reason or another, we have not yet addressed. It seems from our workshops that most professional workers have somewhere between 25 and 35 such significant issues at any one time. These may range, for example, from developing a strategy to deal with a difficult customer, to choosing between two alternative career moves, to how to manage competing work pressures.

When we allow ourselves reflective space, typically in an environment that allows conscious hand-eye movement to go on autopilot, one issue rises to the mental surface and dominates our thinking for a period. We ask ourselves questions about the issue, try to see it from different perspectives, examine the logic of our thinking and generally worry at it. Gradually, we see it sufficiently differently for an insight to occur. Once we have an insight, we are able to reframe the issue and develop alternative responses. When we come out of personal reflective space, which has many characteristics in common with hypnotic trance in terms of the level of mental focus (James, 2000), we have a need to release the energy that has been repressed. (People who do their deep thinking while taking exercise such as jogging, often report that they run faster when they come out of personal reflective space.)

What we do on our own can be far more thorough and effective when done with a skilled colleague who can offer different perspectives, will be more rigorous in following through logic, and will help us face up to uncomfortable concepts. This is the essence of the learning dialogue within mentoring.

The Mentoring Conversation

Another fundamental piece of research was to observe and chart mentoring conversations. Engineering and accounting clients in particular wanted a template of the mentoring dialogue, against which mentors could benchmark themselves. Over a period of 2 years, colleagues and I observed randomly selected mentoring pairs, both in real mentoring sessions and workshop practices. The effectiveness of the mentor was determined by a relatively crude measure of mentee satisfaction ("How useful was this discussion?") and an observer's rating of factors such as how much of the talking the mentor did and whether the mentee's issues were adequately identified and addressed. The effective mentors all acted as follows:

- Began by establishing or reestablishing rapport.
- Asked or allowed the mentees to explain what the issue was and what kind of help they wanted.
- Held back on drawing overtly on their own experience, or giving advice, until the issue had been explored in sufficient depth for both to understand it. (In doing so, they sought to establish the facts, as far as they were known, challenged statements and assumptions, drew attention to possible recurrent patterns, and explored the context of the issue. They also often helped mentees link the specific issue to broader or longer-term goals.)
- Summarized the dialogue so far.
- Reinforced the mentees' self-belief in their ability to manage the issue.
- Helped the mentees to think through options, actions, and time lines.
- Asked the mentees to summarize this part of the dialogue.
- Asked the mentees to consider how committed they were to the course of action proposed.

Ineffective mentors, by contrast, typically jumped into the presented issue, entirely missing the opportunity to develop a deeper, shared understanding and to contextualize. They summarized both times, taking responsibility—and therefore some of the ownership—away from the mentee. As a result, both mentors and mentees in these conversations reported less learning.

Behaviors of Mentors and Mentees

From the earliest days of our consulting work, it was clear that mentors performed a wide variety of roles and that in successful relationships, these were complemented by the roles and behaviors of mentees. Kathy Kram's (1985) concept of functions was useful from a theoretical perspective, but it didn't give participants a great deal of clarity about the range of behaviors they should and shouldn't use, or when.

Our interviews with effective and ineffective mentors led to a different, more flexible theoretical model, which participants and program managers could more readily apply. Two critical dimensions appeared. One of these relates to the degree of directiveness in the relationship: To what extent does the relationship depend upon the use of the mentor's authority or influence? Who decides the agenda for discussion and the goals? Who takes responsibility for managing the relationship? To what degree is relative power a factor in the dynamics of the relationship? The second dimension relates to mentee need. Is the purpose of the relationship and/or the specific conversation to stretch the horizons of the mentees' thinking and/or ambitions? To help them acquire and use new knowledge? Or is it to provide encouragement, support, and fellowship? The goddess Athena, the archetypical mentor, represents both ends of this spectrum of challenging and nurturing. Mentors' needs are also a factor. Are they, for example, seeking status confirmation, intellectual challenge, or mutual learning?

Surprisingly, although the concept of mentee need is recognized in the academic literature (e.g., Anderson & Enz, 1990; Bennetts, 1998; Cunningham & Eberle, 1990; Holloway & Whyte, 1994; Mullen, 1998), it has received little serious attention. Most studies of mentoring outcomes have focused on what mentees received, but not how this related to their specific and individual requirements from the relationship.

The implications of superimposing these two dimensions on each other include a range of behaviors, some or all of which may be shared with other helping styles, such as coaching or counseling. A directive, stretching style has much in common with traditional forms of coaching (set challenging task, observe, and give extrinsic feedback) but may also include demonstrating how to do something, tough questioning, and even Socratic argument. A directive, nurturing style may encompass the guardian or sponsor role, giving advice, steering through the organizational politics, and so on. It may also include being a role model, something effective mentors tend to undertake in a more proactive manner than ineffective mentors or managers in general.

A nondirective, nurturing style has much in common with counseling and may often involve career counseling, listening, and generally helping people to cope with the issues they face. A nondirective, stretching style involves activities such as helping mentees develop their own self-resourcefulness, for example, by building more extensive networks.

For participants in specific programs, this model of mentoring illustrates the breadth and complexity of the role and the importance of mentors being able to adapt their styles to the needs of mentees at particular times in their own development and the evolution of the relationship. It also provides the basis for a discussion on the behavioral boundaries of the relationship (for example, mentors would not normally set learning goals for mentees or provide therapy).

Thus, an effective mentor is able to adapt behaviors to react at different points on each spectrum, according to the needs of the mentee, the behavior of the mentee, and his or her assessment of the situational context. Equally, the mentor's experience may be influenced by his or her needs to be challenged (e.g., to enjoy the intellectual dialogue) and to feel valued. In one mentoring program aimed at young ex-offenders, many of the mentors had been unemployed, long term. They gained so much self-esteem helping the young offenders get their lives in order and find work that by the end of the program, most of the mentors were also in regular employment. (See Figure 26.2.)

Now commonly known as the *behavioral matrix* of mentoring, this model (as shown in Figure 26.2) has helped thousands of program participants position what is expected of them, both in general and in one-to-one discussions with their dyadic partners. Its validation was that it worked. However, in the late 1990s, I decided that a deeper validation, based on evidence from a formal academic study, was needed. The research project, described later in this chapter, compared expectations of behavior by both mentors and mentees with actual behaviors and linked these with outcomes for both parties. The initial results broadly support the model as an accurate depiction of the wide range of behavioral dynamics of different styles of mentoring.

One of the important lessons from practitioner experience, which informed the design of this research, was that success and failure of mentoring relationships were the responsibility (or at least influenced by) both mentor and mentee. With very few exceptions (e.g., Aryee, Wyatt, & Stone, 1996; Higgins, Chandler, & Kram, Chapter 14, this volume; Kalbfleisch, Chapter 20, this volume), the mentoring literature focuses almost entirely on the behaviors of the mentor (e.g., Allen, Chapter 5, this volume). Yet the mentee's behavior must have an influence on that of the mentor. For example, the phrasing of an issue for discussion (e.g., "I've got a problem with . . ."

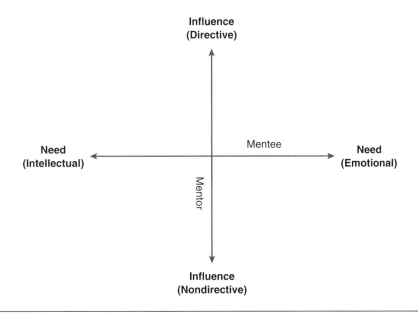

Figure 26.2   Dimensions of Mentoring

SOURCE: Chutterbuck Associates © 2006.

versus "I've been working through this issue and need a sounding board") is likely to affect the mentor's instinctive response. Even less attention has been paid to understanding the interaction dynamics between them. The following are among the many largely unanswered questions about this process of collaborative learning:

- What behaviors by each party elicit positive reactions from the other?
- To what extent does context influence these behavioral dynamics?
- What processes support effective behaviors in the relationship? (For example, it appears from fieldwork that occasional reviews of relationship quality and efficacy, conducted between mentor and mentee, stimulate positive behaviors and relationship commitment.)
- How do behaviors in both mentor and mentee need to change as the relationship evolves through its various stages? (Kram, 1985; Megginson & Clutterbuck, 1995)
- Are specific mentor and mentee behaviors more associated with particular outcomes than others?
- How does cultural identity affect both the type of mentoring sought and provided and the ability of people from different cultural backgrounds to learn together in the developmental dyad?

Questions such as these need to be answered, at least broadly, before we can claim a practical level of understanding of the mentoring phenomenon, whatever the style or culture.

The European Experience of Mentoring

In this section, I review both my personal journey of development and that of the field more generally. The two are closely intertwined.

My colleague David Megginson, at Sheffield Hallam University, and I cofounded the European Mentoring Centre (now the European Mentoring and Coaching Council, or EMCC) in the early 1990s as a forum for academics, providers, program coordinators, mentors, and mentees. Its primary activities were an annual conference and a small library. As interest in both coaching and mentoring blossomed, the trustees determined to enlarge the scope of interest to include coaching, and the EMCC was established in 2001. This body represents the interests of all parties in coaching and mentoring, at both a European and national level. Organizations representing executive coaches, such as the International Coach Federation, or representing companies buying coaching and mentoring services, such as the European Foundation for Management Development, are affiliated with the EMCC. The EMCC has conducted extensive research into coach and mentor competences, established standards for coach and mentor education, and is currently developing an extensive online bibliography of the field.

The Mentoring and Coaching Research Unit (MCRU) at Sheffield Hallam University has published a stream of books and papers on aspects of mentoring, from the use of storytelling to an investigation of the nature of relationship endings (relationships that plan the ending of the formal phases and undertake some form of review of what has been achieved tend to be regarded as positive by both parties; those that drift away tend to be seen negatively) (Clutterbuck & Megginson, 2001, 2004). The MCRU also publishes on behalf of the EMCC the *International Journal of Mentoring and Coaching*. There have also been active research agendas from EDHEC Business School in France, and other universities in Scandinavia and the United Kingdom.

With few exceptions, these research agendas have been driven by specific needs to improve the quality and/or effectiveness of structured mentoring programs. Evaluation, particularly of publicly funded initiatives, is strongly culturally ingrained in Europe. Program funders are concerned both to know what results their initiatives are achieving and to ensure that measures are robust and meaningful. In our own practice, for example, it has become the norm to apply a portfolio of measures at both program and relationship levels, using both hard and soft criteria and assessing both outcome and process factors. In 2003, a European-led initiative drew together program coordinators, academics, and consultants specializing in mentoring to agree on an international set of common standards for good practice in developmental mentoring.[2] The standards have six parts, covering clarity of purpose (program and relationship), selection and matching of participants, training, ethical issues, and administration. They have been used in the design and benchmarking of programs in a number of countries, but only a handful of organizations have taken the opportunity to be formally assessed against them and have their programs benchmarked. Gaining an international consensus in this way is potentially an important step forward for research purposes because it provides a basis for direct comparability between programs. However, although the standards are applicable across all styles of mentoring, they do not in themselves obviate the need to additionally ensure that relationships to be compared are based in the same style.

My personal journey of discovery in mentoring began in the early 1980s, when I interviewed Kathy Kram about her research and brought the concepts to Europe. Although Kathy's research focused on individual, informal relationships, a number of U.S. organizations had attempted to formalize what was happening informally, initially to support young graduate recruits starting out on their careers. My first book, published almost simultaneously with Kathy's, also reflected that perspective.

Mentoring in these early programs involved "overseeing the career" (Gray & Gray, 1990) of someone younger. The mentor was an influential figure, a sponsor who provided challenging assignments and opportunities.

Then, I was invited to help United Kingdom and European organizations design and implement structured mentoring programs. We quickly ran into cultural problems at both the national and organizational levels. At the national level, most of the countries in Northern Europe, including the United Kingdom, had very low power distance and a high intolerance of elitism. Northern European employers were trying to encourage people to take greater responsibility and accountability for their own career development and personal development. Sponsorship simply didn't fit well with this objective. (The exceptions are France and Germany, where deference to authority is relatively high, often based on expert status. Both countries have struggled to make mentoring work.)

This difference of emphasis is reflected in both the type of program initiated in Northern Europe and the expectations within it. Mentoring is widely used in the corporate environment. The following are typical workplace programs:

- A Norwegian project to develop women in middle management to become business leaders. The mentors are more-senior men from other companies. A significant outcome is increased confidence in their current job roles, for 83% of mentees and more than half of mentors.
- Programs to assist refugees to integrate into their new cultures.
- Programs for mothers returning to work and people heading into retirement.
- Peer mentoring between senior businesspeople and head teachers, prison governors, and executives of charities.
- Patients mentoring doctors.
- British Petroleum's reverse mentoring program, a global program to educate its executives about the real world through learning dyads with young people from different backgrounds.

In each case, participants are led to expect a significant amount of mutual learning in multiple contexts. Career outcomes are seen as outcomes of personal growth, rather than as the primary purpose of the relationship. Relationships are typically relatively short in duration (1 to 3 years), at least insofar as they are supported by the organization. Mentors have a responsibility to ensure that mentees achieve independence as rapidly as possible—hence, problems of dependency and counter-dependency are rare.

This divergence of perception, as to the nature and purpose of mentoring, can be seen in the wide variety of definitions of mentoring (see Dougherty & Dreher, Chapter 3, this volume). There is a broad, but not exclusively U.S. versus European division, which has come to be referred to as "sponsorship mentoring versus developmental mentoring" (Clutterbuck, 1985; Clutterbuck & Lane, 2004; Gardner, 1996, 1997; Garvey, 1988; Gibb & Megginson, 1992; Hay, 1995). The assumptions behind *sponsorship mentoring* include seniority of experience and position by the mentor, the use of the mentor's influence on the part of the protégé (e.g., Kram's, 1985, functions of a mentor include protecting and fostering visibility), a heavy emphasis on career progression for the protégé, and a largely one-way learning process (e.g., Fagenson, 1988; Phillips-Jones, 1982; Stone, 1999). The mentor may or may not be the protégé's line manager. The assumptions behind *developmental mentoring* include a significant difference in experience, but not necessarily in hierarchical level; the "parking" of the mentor's power and influence as largely irrelevant to the relationship; a heavy emphasis on personal growth and insight as the means to achieving career or other objectives; and a high level of mutual learning. Line managers cannot normally be mentors because they are unable to bring sufficient independence to the learning dialogue; however, they can use mentoring type behaviors in support of their role as coach (e.g., Cranwell-Ward, Bossons, & Gover, 2004; Hay 1995, Megginson, 1988; Mumford, 1993; Spero, 2000).

To a significant extent, these two models represent a difference of emphasis identified by Kram's (1985) original categorization of career and psychosocial functions. They also represent a difference of *purpose* and *assumptions*. Sponsorship mentoring places greater emphasis on career outcomes and may see personal development and learning as a secondary outcome of being exposed to opportunities inherent in more-senior or more-challenging assignments. Developmental mentoring assumes that the key outcome of the relationship is personal development and learning and that career development may be one of the second-order outcomes. Although there may be examples of developmental relationships evolving into sponsorship, or vice versa, this does not seem to be commonplace, and no studies have, to my knowledge, investigated this. The research we have carried out into mentee expectations (Clutterbuck, 2005) suggests that participants in European and international programs differentiate strongly between the two roles.

Depicting these two models as simply the result of cultural factors would be misleading, however. While culture undoubtedly played a strong part in the initial laying down of approaches to mentoring, there has also been a gradual evolution of what effective mentoring looks like in both Europe and North America, as well as on other continents. The following are among the components of this evolution:

- A shift from mentor experience as a source of knowledge transfer to mentor experience as a resource to help the mentee develop his or her own knowledge and wisdom. Potential influencing factors in this shift are the increased emphasis in the corporate world upon individual competencies, which tend to focus attention on more definable capabilities, and the expectation within diversity mentoring that the learner from a minority group may also be a teacher.
- For much the same reasons, a shift from individual, one-way learning to mutual learning (for example, see Lankau & Scandura, Chapter 4, and Higgins, Chandler, & Kram Chapter 14, this volume).
- A shift from an emphasis on doing to one on creating and using reflective space (focused thinking time). In our workshops with thousands of managers and other employees in Europe, North America, Africa and Asia-Pacific, a recurrent theme is that they find it increasingly difficult to achieve thinking space during working hours—except when they take time out for mentoring. Our analyses of when and how mentors and mentees use personal reflective space (Clutterbuck & Megginson, 1999) suggest that it is one of the main benefits perceived by program participants.
- A shift from an emphasis on good answers to one on good questions. To some extent, this has evolved because of increasing interchange between the world of mentoring and those of counseling (e.g. Egan, 1994) and developmental coaching (e.g., Whitmore, 1996).
- A shift from guidance to dialogue. A factor here may be the increasing complexity of the organizational environment, where specific experience may be less relevant to an individual's current issues than pulling learning from pooled experience.
- A shift from single, powerful, long-lasting relationships at an early part of a career to multiple learning relationships spread over a career. This last point has also been noted and explored by, among others, Kram (2004) and Higgins and Kram (2001). Anecdotal evidence suggests that good experiences with

mentoring at an early career stage encourage people to take advantage of later opportunities for mentoring, all the way through to their roles as top managers (Clutterbuck & Megginson, 1999). These later learning relationships may be simultaneous and of several different forms (for example, peer and upward mentoring).

What is driving this evolution is not clear. One possible explanation is that the factors that caused European organizations to take such a different perspective and emphasis on mentoring have become more widespread. Among these were the expectation that employees should take greater responsibility for their own development and career management. Anything suggesting "overseeing the career of another" (Gray & Gray, 1990) was not acceptable. Another partial explanation may be that alternative forms of mentoring, such as peer mentoring (Beattie & MacDougal, 1995) have encouraged a move away from directive, hierarchical modes and behaviors.

Coaching Versus Mentoring

A similar evolution appears to have taken place in the European context with regard to the role of coach, which is essentially concerned with helping an individual or group improve performance. Traditional coaching—still the majority of the coaching taking place in work and sporting environments—is seen as a process of feedback, observation, and review. The goal, or at least the standard (how achievement of the goal is assessed), is often set by an external agency (e.g., the company, the sports association). The coachee's decision about whether to buy into the goal and the standard has implications for how much progress he or she can make. The coach provides opportunities to tackle the task, observes, and engages the learner in a discussion of how to improve performance next time.

Really effective traditional coaches also help learners move beyond extrinsic feedback to intrinsic feedback. Here, learners experiment, observe their own actions, and bring their observations back to the coach for review and guidance on improving performance.

In more recent years, a definition of coaching has emerged from North America that is closer to counseling: working on goals set by the learner and using questioning to explore the drives and barriers to performance (Ellinger & Bostrum, 1999; Whitmore, 1996). This is sometimes confused with mentoring, especially when the focus of the relationship is primarily on personal growth and career self-management (for example, "life coaching").

A pragmatic method my international colleagues and I use to describe the differences between coaching and mentoring is illustrated in Figure 26.3. Both traditional and developmental coaching are concerned with performance and may be either directive or nondirective in the sense that the goals, agenda, conversation, and process may be driven either by the coach or the coachee. Directive relationships are sometimes described as "hands-on" and tend to be one-way learning relationships. The personal development that occurs tends to be relatively narrowly focused, often on specific tasks or competences (e.g., presentation skills or personal effectiveness).

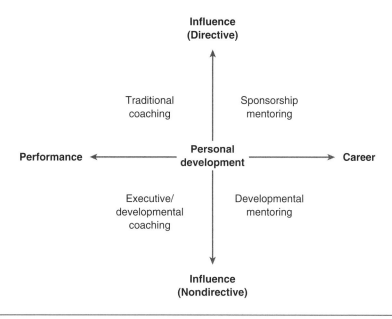

Figure 26.3   Styles of Coaching and Mentoring

SOURCE: Chutterbuck Associates © 2006.

Both sponsorship mentoring and developmental mentoring are concerned with helping people achieve longer-term career or other personal goals. As indicated earlier, the focus of sponsorship mentoring is much more heavily weighted on career outcomes as a route to personal development and is relatively directive; developmental mentoring focuses on personal development as a route to career achievement and is broadly nondirective.

In general, the more directive roles of both are more compatible with the direct reporting line than are the nondirective roles, where greater openness is required and the boss may be a significant part of the coachee's or mentee's problem. Both coaching and mentoring may involve an element of personal development. In coaching, this is typically more narrowly focused than in mentoring.

Explaining mentoring and coaching in this way gives participants a framework in which to position the roles they play and the roles the organization and their dyad partners expect of them. Many of the problems we observe in mentoring relationships and programs arise because of discrepancies between the role expectations of participants. However, in practice, there may be considerable overlap in roles. A mentor may be called upon to exercise some coaching behaviors, and vice versa. Among behaviors common to both coaching and mentoring are using challenging questions, collaboration (the mentor invites the mentee to observe or assist in a task, to understand how the mentor approaches it), and being a critical friend. Having a language for articulating expectations and indicating a shift in role allows participants to discuss mutual expectations of behavior and style.

Another way of looking at this issue is to consider what the question is. "How do you want to improve?" is generally regarded as a coaching question. "What do you want to achieve?" could be coaching or mentoring, depending on the nature of the goal. "What do you want to become?" is a mentoring question. In keeping with the greater duration of many mentoring relationships, it is a question that evolves with the individuals and with their relationships.

The Wider International Perspective

Structured mentoring programs around the rest of the world are less common, but examples can be found in many nations, including mainland China, Australia (e.g., McGregor, 1999), Hong Kong, Argentina, Malaysia, Zimbabwe, Nigeria, India, and South Africa (e.g., Geber, 2003). It is probably not accidental that most of these countries have had a strong influence from Anglo-Saxon cultures, through the British Commonwealth or general U.S. hegemony in South America. Very little comparative study has been carried out regarding cultural differences (Barham & Conway, 1998, is one exception), but the principal issues reported by multinational companies in our program design activities seem to be captured in the theories of Hofstede (1991) and Trompenaars (1993) concerning the primary components of cultural difference.

Two cultural dimensions seem particularly relevant. *Power distance* affects the willingness of mentees to challenge what they are told and makes it difficult for either mentor or mentee to admit weaknesses (lose face). Mentors, especially those from Western cultures, need to develop the skills of enabling mentees to voice concerns and criticisms in psychological safety. Similarly, mentors from cultures that emphasize individuality, rather than collectivity, may find it hard going if he or she focuses too much on the mentee's personal career progression as the core goal of the relationship. A broader dialogue about goals and outcomes for the team, for example, may achieve more.

Fatalism may be as a factor in some cultures, especially where failure may be seen as "God's will" rather than a personal responsibility. Key skills for mentors here are to help open up wider ranges of possibilities from which mentees can choose and to help mentees relate these options to both personal and societal (or religious) values.

High power distance cultures may tend to favor the sponsorship model, but this may clash with the cultural expectations of multinationals dominated by low power distance countries, such as Northern Europe. (See Figure 26.4.)

When Shell attempted to introduce a mentoring program in Brunei some years ago, one of the issues that had to be overcome was near-complete opposite expectations by the local young engineers (most of whom had been educated for at least a year in European or U.S. universities) about the learning relationship compared with those of the Dutch and British expatriate mentors. Broadly speaking, the mentees expected a sponsoring relationship, with a great deal of direct advice giving; they found it difficult to challenge what was said to them, even if they did not agree. The mentors, on the other hand, expected to help the mentees set and follow their own paths and to stimulate learning through mutual challenge and insightful questions. Only when this conflict of expectations was made overt could the two sides begin to develop a style of relationship that was comfortable to both of them.

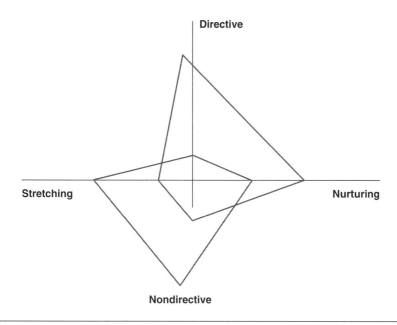

Figure 26.4   Contrasting Expectations

SOURCE: Chutterbuck Associates © 2006.

The metaphors or stories from each culture, which illustrate and shape participants' instinctive reactions to mentoring, appear to be deeply rooted in the cultural
psyche. When we asked people from a number of Black African ethnic groups to
describe the story that most closely represented the role of mentor, they provided
similar, but always subtly different legends. Sharing these stories helps mentor and
mentee understand to a greater extent each other's expectations of what the relation is about. An important area for future study, I suggest, is to map these cultural
metaphors against the styles of mentoring preferred by mentor and mentee in
different regions. It would also be revealing to explore what happens when the
metaphors of racial culture clash with those of the corporate culture.

Multinational companies introducing mentoring programs around the world
have attempted a variety of strategies (Mezias & Scandura, 2005). Imposing a mentoring style and structure relevant to the parent country on countries with a different sets of expectations can lead to apathy or resistance. (Expecting a high degree
of challenge in mentoring dialogue is unrealistic if the hierarchy gap is large and the
program takes place in a Chinese culture, for example!) The laissez-faire approach
also has a poor history of success because local units often lack the skills and confidence to initiate programs. Two strategies that have worked are the culturally
adaptable approach and the "thousand fires" approach.

The *culturally adaptable approach* starts with a generic and broad understanding
of what mentoring is and its purpose. A range of support materials, built around
a core of program management and mentor/mentee education resources, is
made available to each national or regional operation. The headquarters function

measures the extent of mentoring taking place but accepts that the styles of mentoring will vary considerably. Examples of multinationals operating in this manner include British American Tobacco and Standard Chartered Bank. The strength of this approach is that it encourages local buy-in. However, it is vulnerable to local changes in personnel—if the local champion and/or trainer moves on, there may be a rapid loss of momentum.

The *thousand fires approach,* used, for example, by the World Bank, encourages employees to link up and create their own mentoring networks, based on social groupings (i.e., division, discipline, regional culture). A support team from the headquarters in Washington ensures that the program organizers have the knowledge and resources to design a program that will suit their specific needs and cultural environment. The advantage of this approach is that mentoring occurs with a high degree of spontaneity. However, the penalty may be considerable variation in quality of support.

It all gets more complicated when the mentoring program matches people across cultures, especially if they are living in different countries. Mentoring relationships carried out by telephone and e-mail are becoming increasingly common (see Ensher & Murphy Chapter 12, this volume). The potential is high for different expectations between people from different cultures or who have previously been exposed to different styles of mentoring; and these expectations may affect the quality of the relationship. The solution adopted by companies such as airline SAS (Jelbring-Klang & Tamm-Buckle, 1996) or mobile telephone company Nokia is to educate participants about these issues at an early stage of the relationship. In addition, they help participants recognize the opportunity for additional learning from someone who has perspectives different from themselves.

There are many unanswered or partially answered questions relating to cross-cultural mentoring, the following among them:

- Do participants in cross-cultural mentoring relationships need specific skills or attitudes beyond those of participants in more homogeneous relationships? (For example, a common theme from our workshops is willingness to have assumptions challenged about one's own and other cultures.)
- Does culture difference make e-mentoring more difficult?
- How can we measure increases in "culture cognition" as an outcome of the cross-cultural mentoring relationship?
- How is the relationship dynamic affected by the position of cultural difference (central or peripheral to the learning dialogue)?

The following are some of the lessons from practical experience with these issues:

- Factors such as "learning maturity" (a construct that includes individuals' capabilities of managing their own learning, seeking out opportunities to learn, tolerance of ambiguity, and acceptance of the pain of learning), personal conservatism, breadth of previous experience, and exposure to diversity affect what constitutes an "ideal" pairing in each situation. Successful program coordinators tend to match people with an eye to both how much similarity is required to establish and maintain rapport and how much difference they can absorb. (Too much similarity and there is insufficient scope for learning; too much difference and the relationship may not gel.)

- Mutual learning across the barriers of difference needs to be an overt goal at both program and relationship levels.

- Many programs now include a steering committee, representative of the diverse audiences in the organization. Each member of the steering committee is a backup resource for several dyads, someone with whom they can discuss issues and concerns that may have roots in individual differences or stereotypes.

- In our own practice, we now typically include a module of training in "diversity dialogue": the skills of maintaining open, interested conversation to recognize, respond to, and capitalize upon difference.

- When delivering mentoring training in different cultures, it is helpful for materials to be localized, for example, using case studies that resonate with people from that culture.

It is important to recognize that most of these observations from practice have not been subject to empirical research. There is an opportunity to investigate the following:

- The components and dynamics of the similarity/difference equation in various contexts.

- How goal orientation and goal achievement are affected by intradyadic diversity makes a relationship more or less successful, both in absolute terms and in comparison with other goals.

- The roles and activities of a successful steering committee, for mentoring in general and for culturally diverse mentoring in particular.

- What level of dialogue skills do mentors and mentees need to make the diverse relationship really productive? Does the requirement for skills in diversity dialogue increase with the scale of difference?

These questions don't apply just to mentoring across cultures, of course. In one sense, all mentoring is diverse, and the differences between participants in the dyad are the foundation for learning.

Integrating Research and Practice

The feedback loop between research and practice in Europe and Australasia in particular has been relatively strong compared with that in the United States, for several reasons. The first is that the faculties of university research units specializing in mentoring and coaching studies often include a high proportion of practitioners, both as full-time and visiting staff. As a result, research is typically built around in-company mentoring programs, which faculty are guiding. Feedback from participants is therefore both part of continuing program adaptation and specific empirical enquiry. The downside of this approach is that large-volume quantitative studies are more difficult to initiate and hence are less common, as are multiorganization studies.

The second reason is that in seeking guidance as to good practice in program design and relationship management, practitioners have found that the extensive literature on sponsorship mentoring has only partial relevance, and it is not easy to determine where this literature is and isn't relevant to a developmental mentoring context, as no substantive empirical comparisons have been made.

Another issue reflecting the sometimes uneasy interaction between practitioner requirements and research quality concerns the depth to which empirical investigations can go. The researcher in me wants to construct detailed questionnaires to explore an aspect of mentoring effectiveness; the client has an interest only in immediate program and relationship troubleshooting and in demonstrating that the program is delivering value. So, promising avenues often remain unexplored. For example, in a global pharmaceutical company, we were able to compare retention rates of 100 participant pairs in a mentoring program with those of several hundred nonparticipants. Losses among the participants were a remarkable 2% compared with 27.5% for nonparticipants. A very limited amount of qualitative follow-up interview indicated that the explanation for some of this difference (that people who had signed up for the program were already more likely to stay) was inaccurate. In fact, some of those interviewed had joined because they saw the mentoring program as a route out of the organization! Unable to carry out more detailed investigation, a great many questions remain about the motivational factors that lead people to join mentoring programs, how these change as a result of the relationship, and how these relate to subsequent attitudes toward the organization and levels of organizational commitment.

Our Current Research

A Longitudinal and Cross-Sectional Study of Developmental Mentoring

Several years ago, it became clear in our attempts to help companies design robust mentoring systems that a great deal of the advice we were giving was based on general observation, inspired extrapolation, and limited benchmarking. While many companies were happy to accept that approaches that seemed to work for their peer organizations would be good enough for them and our surveys of relationship survival and utility for both parties showed positive relationships between the program designs and participant education, we understood little about how and why these results arose or what we could do to improve them further.

The following are some of the critical questions that remained unanswered:

- How does context affect relationship quality? (i.e., What can the organization do to create a climate in which the relationship will thrive?)
- What behaviors by mentor and mentee in a developmental mentoring relationship are associated with positive outcomes? (Ideas suggested in Fletcher & Ragins, Chapter 15, and Kalbfleisch, Chapter 20, this volume)

- How do expectations by mentor and mentee influence behaviors, relationship quality, and outcomes for each of them? (Addressed somewhat in Dougherty & Dreher, Chapter 3, this volume)
- How important are goal clarity and goal commitment in the relationship dynamic?

My current research involves both longitudinal and cross-sectional sampling of matched pairs in developmental mentoring at three points in the first year of the relationship. This has required the development of a range of instruments and scales to measure organizational supportiveness (toward mentoring), goal clarity, mentor and mentee behaviors, and mentor and mentee outcomes. All of these instruments were validated in a pilot study and are now available online.

The value of these scales in practice is severalfold. First, they enable the program coordinator to identify potential or actual problems relating to misaligned expectations. Second, they allow mentor and mentee to begin the relationship with a clear and detailed exposition of what each expects from the other. The administration of the scales again, after 4 to 6 months, stimulates mentor and mentee to review their relationship and identify behavior and skills issues, which can be addressed in follow-up training sessions and mentor supervision. It has also been helpful in evaluating program return on investment to identify more specific ways of describing and measuring outcomes for mentor and mentee. Four distinct types of outcome have emerged:

- Development outcomes, which may include knowledge, technical competence, and behavioral competence (e.g., Jacobi, 1991; Ostroff & Koslowski, 1998)
- Career outcomes, which may include the achievement (in part or whole) of career goals (Aryee et al., 1996; Burke, 1984; Fagenson, 1988; Scandura, 1992; Whitely, Dougherty, & Dreher, 1991)
- Enabling outcomes, such as having a career plan, a (self-) development plan, a wider network of influencers, or learning resources (Aryee & Chay, 1994)
- Emotional outcomes—less tangible, but often powerful changes in emotional state, including increased confidence, altruistic satisfaction, reflective space, status, and the pleasure of a different kind of intellectual challenge. (Kram, 1985; Noe, 1988)

Again, these scales play a practical role in relationship management, by providing a language and framework participants can use to review what has been achieved. Having this dialogue appears to be closely correlated with positive retrospective perceptions of the relationship by both parties.

From the initial data cut, it seems that many of our assumptions about mentoring need to be reexamined against the paradigm of developmental mentoring. What will probably emerge is a much wider spectrum of applications and approaches to mentoring, which take into account differences of culture and different emphases of relationship purpose, and a clearer understanding of what contributes to effectiveness both generically and in particular circumstances. Our view of mentoring will thus have evolved from a single, narrow type of helping relationship into a much broader panoply that more closely represents the reality of an international phenomenon.

The Next Decade in Mentoring

Given that mentoring involves learning dialogue, it is remarkable—and perhaps even reprehensible—that it has taken until now for real dialogue to take place across the globe between those practicing and researching different approaches to mentoring. The establishment of organizations parallel to the EMCC in Southern Africa and Australia will help, although even more could be achieved with similar organizations in Latin America and China. Genuinely international research conferences are now taking place, and we are seeing increasing international collaboration in the writing of books on mentoring (e.g., Clutterbuck & Lane, 2004; Clutterbuck & Ragins, 2002).

Underpinning this learning dialogue is a growing recognition that mentoring is a widely diversified phenomenon, influenced in its structure and dynamics by purpose, culture, and context. New models and explanations are needed to encompass this diversity and to enrich both practice and research.

Areas for Future Research

I have already identified a number of potential areas of research for cross-cultural mentoring, but there are also extensive areas of mentoring in general in which additional research would build upon and inform good practice at both the program and relationship levels. Some of these issues are as follows:

- Are sponsorship and developmental mentoring different models or part of a spectrum? Which works best against different participant and organizational goals and in which circumstances?
- What mentor and mentee behaviors are most efficacious at each phase of relationship evolution?
- Regarding transitions between mentoring phases, what is good practice in managing and supporting each transition?
- How and to what extent do mentoring support mechanisms (such as mentor and mentee training, relationship monitoring, mentor supervision) influence relationship quality?
- Are different relationship durations associated with different outcomes?
- How does the experience of being a mentee influence competence as a mentor, and vice versa?
- What is the role of an effective mentoring program coordinator? How do we define effectiveness in this context?

Common to these issues is that they answer the pragmatic needs of program coordinators and their organizational paymasters for guidance in helping both programs and relationships deliver greater value for participants and the organization. If there is one core lesson from our experience working with organizations around the world, it is that there is a very limited appetite for additional fundamental generic research and a high demand for research that focuses on specific aspects of mentoring in closely defined applications or contexts. It is my personal belief, however, that research derived from practitioner experience can provide the stimulus for new questions that address generic issues of learning dialogue. If such a virtuous cycle can be created, then that would be to the benefit of both the practitioner and the academic world.

Notes

1. The term *mentee* is commonly preferred over the term *protégé* in most of the world for several reasons. First, *protégé* is associated with a style of mentoring that is very directive and sponsoring—"someone who is protected." Second, the linguistic and syntactic origins of the word *mentor* derive from "mind," not in the context of "minding" (as in "child minding"), but as "one who makes another think." A *mentee* is "someone who is caused to think." (Of course, the actual wise counselor to Telemachus, in the *Odyssey*, was not the character Mentor, but the goddess Athena.) The term *mentoree*, sometimes found as an alternative, is grammatically incorrect and linguistically meaningless; the "or" and "ee" suffixes can be applied only to a verb, not a noun, and cannot be combined. (For comparison, consider *counselor* and *counselee*.)

2. See *International Standards for Mentoring Programs in Employment:* http://www.ismpe.com

References

Anderson, G. A., & Enz, R. (1990, April 18–20). *A two-year study of mentoring functions: Mentors' and residents' initial and changing perspectives.* Paper presented to American Educational Research Association Annual Meeting, Boston.

Aryee, S., & Chay, Y. W. (1994). An examination of the impact of career-oriented mentoring on work commitment, attitudes, and career satisfaction among professionals and managerial employees. *British Journal of Management, 5,* 241–249.

Aryee, S., Wyatt, T., & Stone, R. (1996). Early career outcomes of graduate employees: The effect of mentoring and ingratiation. *Journal of Management Studies, 33,* 95–118.

Barham, K., & Conway, C. (1998). *Developing business and people internationally: A mentoring approach.* Berkhampstead, UK: Ashridge Research.

Beattie, R. S., & McDougall, M. (1995, September). *Peer mentoring: The issues and outcomes of non-hierarchical developmental relationships.* Paper presented to British Academy of Management Annual Conference, Sheffield, UK.

Bennetts, C. (1998, November). *Interpersonal aspects of informal mentor/learner relationships: A research perspective.* Paper presented to proceedings of the European Mentoring Centre Conference, London.

Burke, R. J. (1984). Mentors in organizations. *Group & Organization Studies, 9,* 353–372.

Clutterbuck, D. (1985). *Everyone needs a mentor.* Wimbledon, UK: Chartered Institute of Personnel and Development.

Clutterbuck, D. (2005, November). *The dynamics of mentoring.* Paper presented to the European Mentoring & Coaching Council Annual Conference, Zurich, Switzerland.

Clutterbuck, D., & Lane, G. (Eds.). (2004). *The situational mentor.* Aldershot, UK: Gower.

Clutterbuck, D., & Megginson, D. (1999). *Mentoring executives and directors.* Oxford, UK: Butterworth-Heinemann.

Clutterbuck, D., & Megginson, D. (2001, November). *Winding up or winding down?* Paper presented at proceedings of the 8th European Mentoring Centre Conference, Cambridge, UK.

Clutterbuck D., & Megginson, D. (2004). All good things must come to an end: Winding up and winding down. In D. Clutterbuck & G. Lane, (Eds.) *The situational mentor* (pp. 178–193). Aldershot, UK: Gower.

Clutterbuck, D., & Ragins, B. R. (2002). *Mentoring and diversity: An international perspective.* Oxford, UK: Butterworth Heinemann.

Cranwell-Ward, J., Bossons, P., & Gover, S. (2004). *Mentoring: A Henley review of best practice.* Basingstoke, UK: Palgrave.

Cunningham, J. B., & Eberle, T. (1990). Characteristics of the mentoring experience: A qualitative study. *Personnel Review, 22*(4), 54–66.

Egan, G. (1994). *The skilled helper: A problem management approach to helping.* Pacific Grove, CA: Brooks & Cole.

Ellinger, A. D., & Bostrum, R. P. (1999). Managerial coaching behaviours in learning organizations. *Management Learning, 18,* 752–771.

Fagenson, E, A. (1988). The power of a mentor. *Group & Organization Studies, 13,* 182–194.

Gardner, C. (1997, November). *Mentoring: A professional friendship?* Paper presented at proceedings of the 4th European Conference on Mentoring, European Mentoring Centre, Sheffield Business School, Sheffield, UK.

Gardner, C. E. (1996). *Mentoring: A study of the concept, theory, and practice of mentoring in the educational field.* Unpublished master's thesis, University of Central England, Birmingham.

Garvey, B. (1988). *Mentoring in the marketplace: Studies of learning at work.* Unpublished doctoral dissertation, Durham University.

Geber, H. (2003). Fostering career development for Black academics in the new South Africa. In F. K. Kochan & J. T. Pascarelli (Eds.), *Global perspectives on mentoring* (pp. 107–128). Greenwich, CT: Information Age.

Gibb, S., & Megginson, D. (1992). Inside corporate mentoring schemes: A new agenda of concerns. *Personnel Review, 22*(1), 40–54.

Gray, M. M., & Gray, W. (1990). Planned mentoring: Aiding key transitions in career development. *Mentoring International, 4*(3), 27–32.

Hay, J. (1995). *Transformational mentoring.* Maidenhead, UK: McGraw-Hill.

Higgins, M., & Kram, K. (2001). Reconceptualizing mentoring at work: A developmental network perspective. *Academy of Management Review, 26,* 264–288.

Hofstede, G. (1991). *Cultures and organizations: Software of the mind.* Maidenhead, UK: McGraw-Hill.

Holloway, A., & Whyte, C. (1994). *Mentoring: The definitive workbook.* Manchester, UK: Development Processes.

Jacobi, M. (1991). Mentoring & undergraduate career success: A literature review. *Review of Educational Research, 61,* 505–532.

James, T. (2000). *Hypnosis: A comprehensive guide.* Carmarthen, UK: Crown House.

Jelbring-Klang, C., & Tamm-Buckle, R. (1996, November). *Mentoring in SAS.* Paper presented at proceedings of the 3rd European Mentoring Conference, European Mentoring Centre, London.

Kram, K. (1985). *Mentoring at work: Developmental relationships in organizational life.* Glenview IL: Scott, Foresman.

Kram, K. (2004, November). *Mentoring* and *developmental networks in the new career context.* Paper presented at proceedings of the 11th European Mentoring and Coaching Conference, Brussels, Belgium.

McGregor, L. (1999, November). *Mentoring: The Australian experience.* Paper presented at proceedings of the Sixth European Mentoring Conference, Cambridge, UK.

Megginson, D. (1988). Instructor, coach, mentor: Three ways of helping for managers *Development, 19*(1), 34–46.

Megginson, D., & Clutterbuck, D. (1995). *Mentoring in action.* London: Kogan Page.

Megginson, D., Clutterbuck D., Garvey, B., Stokes, P., & Garrett-Harris, R. (2005). *Mentoring in action* (2nd ed.). London: Kogan Page.

Mezias, J. M., & Scandura, T. A. (2005). A needs-driven approach to expatriate adjustment and career development: A multiple mentoring perspective. *Journal of International Business Studies, 36,* 519–538.

Mullen, E. J. (1998). Vocational and psychosocial mentoring functions: Identifying mentors who serve both. *Human Resource Development Quarterly, 9,* 319–331.

Mumford, A. (1993). *How managers can develop managers.* Aldershot, UK: Gower.

Noe, R. A. (1988). An investigation of the determinants of successfully assigned mentoring relationships. *Personnel Psychology, 41,* 457–479.

Ostroff, C., & Kozlowski, S. W. (1988). The role of mentoring in the information gathering processes of newcomers during early organizational socialization. *Journal of Vocational Behavior, 3,* 15–37.

Philips-Jones, L. (1982). *Mentors and protégés.* New York: Arbor House.

Scandura, T. A. (1992). Mentorship and career mobility: An empirical investigation. *Journal of Organizational Behavior, 13,* 169–174.

Spero, M. (2000, November). *Mentoring as double task.* Paper presented at proceedings of the 7th European Mentoring Centre Conference. Cambridge, UK.

Stone, F. M. (1999). *Coaching, counseling, and mentoring: How to choose and use the right technique to boost employee performance.* New York: Amacom.

Trompenaars, F. (1993). *Riding the waves of culture: Understanding cultural diversity in business.* London: Economist Books.

Whitely, W., Dougherty, T. W., Dreher, G. F. (1991). Relationship of career mentoring and socioeconomic origin to managers' and professionals' early career progress. *Academy of Management Journal, 34,* 331–351.

Whitmore, J. (1996). *Coaching for performance.* London: Nicholas Brealey.

PART V

Integration

27

The Landscape of Mentoring in the 21st Century

Kathy E. Kram

Belle Rose Ragins

A s the authors in this volume have consistently demonstrated, the garden of mentoring has evolved over the past 25 years, and the landscape of our discipline will be quite different in the 21st century. Through our research and practice, we have uncovered new explanations for why some relationships continue to grow and flourish, while others become stagnant or dysfunctional. Our vision of mentoring has expanded with the emergence of new forms and hybrids—such as peer mentoring, cross-gender mentoring, cross-cultural mentoring, mentoring circles, and e-mentoring. Our conception of mentoring has evolved from an acknowledgement of "constellations of relationships" to an emphasis on "developmental networks." Equally important, the work in this volume highlights how environmental conditions that surround mentoring—globalization, increasingly diverse workforces, flattened hierarchies, team-based organizations, new technologies, and a persistently rapid pace of change—influence the nature and potential of mentoring at work.

In this chapter, our aim is to highlight the most critical elements of the new landscape of mentoring so that scholars and practitioners can work together to create the conditions for mentoring to flourish in all of its forms. We begin with an examination of the new paradigms that have emerged in the mentoring arena. We offer several insights into these newly defined forms of mentoring and crystallize the subtle yet important factors that distinguish their quality and purpose. Then, we highlight several new approaches for illuminating the root causes and broadened outcomes of these new forms so that we can deepen our understanding of the nuances in quality, process, and outcomes of developmental relationships. We then examine the role of context in the development and maintenance of mentoring relationships. Finally, we highlight the practical implications for fostering growth-enhancing relationships in organizations and make suggestions for moving forward with the research agenda that emerges from the collective wisdom developed in this volume.

Paradigm Shifts: Understanding Variations In Relational Structures and Processes

In contrast to the early work on mentoring, we now have several new paradigms for describing mentoring relationships and processes that more fully account for variations in their purpose, structure, and quality. In this section, we discuss three primary paradigm shifts that have influenced the mentoring arena. First, and perhaps most dramatic, is the acknowledgment that mentoring occurs within the context of developmental networks (Higgins, 2007; Higgins & Kram, 2001; Higgins & Thomas, 2001; Molloy, 2005). Second, there is increasing recognition of the dyadic and reciprocal nature of mentoring relationships and the critical role that mutuality and reciprocity play in relationship structure, processes, learning, and outcomes (see Allen, Chapter 5; Fletcher & Ragins, Chapter 15, Lankau & Scandura, Chapter 4; McManus & Russell, Chapter 11). Third, we now recognize that mentoring relationships fall along a continuum of quality, and we have made important inroads into understanding when and why relationships are of high quality, marginal quality, or even dysfunctional (see Fletcher & Ragins, Chapter 15; Eby, Chapter 13; see also Ragins & Verbos, 2007). This has led to important new ways for viewing mentoring relationships at the level of single interactions or mentoring episodes that may combine to create relationships that reflect various levels of quality.

Developmental Networks

Although Kram (1985) observed early on that individuals actually have a constellation of developmental relationships, it was not until social network theory was brought to the study of mentoring that we had a language and method for describing and understanding these multiple sources of support (Higgins & Kram, 2001; Higgins & Thomas, 2001; Thomas & Higgins, 1996). This social network perspective provides an important framework for understanding the dimensions of developmental networks, such as the range of sources from which individuals receive developmental help and the emotional closeness and frequency of communication in these relationships. This paradigm shift allows us to more accurately describe multiple sources of developmental support and detail the cumulative impact of developmental networks on outcomes such as satisfaction, personal and task learning, and career advancement (Higgins & Kram, 2001).

This paradigm shift calls for further inquiry into how individuals' needs, group memberships, and relational skills shape the types of relationships they invite into their developmental networks at a given point in time. This topic is addressed in a number of chapters in this volume. For example, Eileen McGowan, Eric Stone, and Bob Kegan (Chapter 16) explore how individuals' developmental stages (i.e., cognitive and affective development) shape their experiences of developmental relationships. Other chapters examine the role of race (Blake-Beard, Murrell, & Thomas, Chapter 9) and gender (McKeen & Bujakee, Chapter 8) in shaping mentoring relationships. These chapters examine the role diversity plays in the experiences, needs and expectations of mentors and protégés, as well as the dynamics that unfold in relationships. Tim Hall and Dawn Chandler (Chapter 19) demonstrate how the career learning cycles of both members of a relationship shape what developmental assistance is sought and provided. Finally, Cary Cherniss (Chapter 17) illustrates how mentors' and protégés' emotional competence affects and is affected by the quality of connections in developmental networks.

Reciprocity and Mutuality

Many of our authors point out that developmental relationships benefit those who provide *and* receive mentoring and developmental support. Emerging literature from related disciplines clearly illustrates that reciprocity and mutuality are key attributes that characterize growth-producing developmental relationships (Dutton & Heaphy, 2003; Miller & Stiver, 1997). This theme was emphasized in many chapters. For example, Stacy McManus and Joyce Russell (Chapter 11) examine mutuality and reciprocity processes in peer relationships and observe that individuals give and receive in ways that both parties perceive as equally beneficial. Joyce Fletcher and Belle Ragins (Chapter 15) discuss how mutuality and reciprocity contribute to the development of high-quality mentoring relationships. In her chapter on the mentor's perspective, Tammy Allen (Chapter 5) identifies the benefits received by mentors (e.g., loyalty, recognition for developing talent for the organization, generativity) and suggests that it is because of these unique benefits that individuals are motivated to mentor and coach others. In her chapter on relational problems, Lillian Eby (Chapter 13) observes that there are both tangible and intangible costs and benefits for both mentors and protégés and these factors combine to affect the investment, commitment, and stability of the relationship.

Continuum of Relational Quality and Mentoring Episodes

One of the greatest strides in recent years has been the discovery of ways to distinguish high-quality mentoring relationships from marginal, or even dysfunctional, relationships (see Dutton & Heaphy, 2003; Dutton & Ragins, 2007; Eby, Chapter 13; Eby, Butts, Lockwood, & Simon, 2004; Fletcher & Ragins, Chapter 15; Ragins, Cotton, & Miller, 2000; Ragins & Verbos, 2007; Scandura, 1998). In particular, a focus on both the processes and outcomes of relationships has resulted in several new schemas and methodologies to help us understand why some relationships flourish, while others stagnate or self-destruct. Using the idea that relationships fall along a continuum of quality, Fletcher and Ragins Chapter 15) draw on the Stone Center's Relational Cultural Theory (Fletcher, 1996, 1998; Jordan, 1986; Jordan, Kaplan, Miller, Stiver, & Surrey, 1991; Miller, 1976; Miller & Stiver, 1997; Surrey, 1985), relational mentoring theory (Ragins, 2005; Ragins & Verbos, 2007), and research on high-quality connections (Dutton & Heaphy, 2003; Dutton & Ragins, 2007) to illuminate the conditions that are necessary for high-quality relationships. Similar to the emotional competencies identified by Cherniss (Chapter 17), Fletcher and Ragins observe that relational stances (i.e., interdependent self-in-relation, mutuality, vulnerability, fluidity, and coresponsibility) combine with relational skills to create relational behaviors and processes involving interdependence, reciprocity, fluidity, and mutual learning. These relational processes result in growth-fostering interactions, or *mentoring episodes,* that involve increased zest, empowered action, self-esteem, new knowledge, and a desire for more connection (see Miller & Stiver, 1997). Fletcher and Ragins (Chapter 15) define mentoring episodes as short-term developmental interactions that occur at a specific point in time. They propose that the cumulative experience of mentoring episodes yields a mentoring relationship and that a series of high-quality relational mentoring episodes results in the experience of a positive mentoring relationship that can, in turn, lead to positive outcomes in career, work, and nonwork domains.

By analyzing the relationship at the level of one interaction, the notion of mentoring episodes offers important insights into understanding the development of mentoring relationships. As Fletcher and Ragins (Chapter 15) point out, while all mentoring relationships involve mentoring episodes, individuals can engage in mentoring episodes without being in a mentoring relationship. The concept of mentoring episodes may therefore be very helpful in future research that clarifies "tipping points"—that is, the critical moment when members come to view their relationship as a mentoring relationship. A number of the contributors to this handbook converge on the idea of "tipping points" as a useful approach for understanding distinctions in how relationships evolve and the purposes they serve over time (Boyatzis, Chapter 18; Eby, Chapter 13; Fletcher & Ragins, Chapter 15).

The concept of a mentoring episode is also helpful in understanding variations in the quality of peer relationships (McManus & Russell, Chapter 11) and may be particularly helpful for explaining why relationships become dysfunctional (Eby, Chapter 13). For example, Eby observes that understanding problems in mentoring relationships requires an understanding of specific experiences and uses of the concept of mentoring episodes to examine how the culmination of negative mentoring episodes leads to a range of relational problems. She proposes a continuum of relational problems that is anchored by minor relational problems on one end (e.g., poor communication skills) and serious relational problems on the other (e.g., an episode involving sabotage). Her work offers the perspective that mentoring episodes differ in their "weight" and that a serious negative mentoring episode may essentially move a mentoring relationship from the positive to the negative side of a relational continuum.

The concept of mentoring episodes can also be applied to single communication interactions. Toward that end, Pamela Kalbfleisch (Chapter 20) offers a useful lens for understanding communication interactions that yield both problematic and effective mentoring relationships. She draws on communication theory to establish a model of mentoring relationships that invites scholars to observe the strategic and routine communications that transpire as relationships begin and unfold over time. In identifying a number of personal filters that both mentors and protégés bring to these developmental relationships and categories for describing various types of communication, Kalbfleisch predicts that these combine to produce dynamics that may require relational repair. Her methodological suggestions regarding how to study relationship processes combined with episodes as a unit of analysis will enable scholars to better describe and calibrate relationship quality. While much work remains to be done on understanding the antecedents, processes, and outcomes associated with the continuum of relational quality, we have made important inroads and have new conceptual perspectives and tools for approaching this area of research.

In sum, the chapters in this volume illustrate that we have moved forward from the study of a single mentoring relationship to the study of a range of relationships that offer developmental assistance at various points in individuals' lives and careers. The garden of mentoring has been enriched by paradigm shifts, and our field is now poised to illuminate and understand the structure, process, and quality of mentoring using the concepts of developmental networks, mentoring episodes, "tipping points," relationship continuums, mutuality, and reciprocity. Let us now turn to examining some of the key antecedents to effective mentoring that were revealed in this volume.

The Roots of Differences in Relational Quality and Processes

During the past two decades of research in the field of mentoring, we have made great strides in uncovering the root causes of differences in the quality and dynamics of developmental relationships. Many of the authors in this text have charted promising new paths for understanding antecedents to effective mentoring and the role these factors play in shaping the development and evolution of mentoring relationships. Some of the key factors identified here include personality, developmental needs and stages, and a range of skills and competencies relating to emotional intelligence, relational skills, compassion, and the ability to understand and grow from work-family and diversity challenges.

Personality

In many ways, personality represents the foundational bedrock of effective mentoring relationships. In their chapter on the role of personality in mentoring, Dan Turban and Felissa Lee (Chapter 2) examine which personality traits are most likely to impact mentoring and explore how the mentor's and the protégé's personality characteristics combine to influence effectiveness at various phases of the relationship. Turban and Lee examine the role of personality in partner selection and offer the idea that complementary personality profiles may be critical predictors of effective mentoring relationships.

A number of personality factors are presented as worthy of future research. Turban and Lee urge us to assess the five-factor model of personality (conscientiousness, extraversion, openness to experience, agreeableness, and neuroticism), as well as other individual difference variables, such as perspective taking, empathic concern, learning goal orientations, and emotional stability. They point out that these traits will have differential impact on the formation, cultivation, and dissolution of mentoring relationships. Consistent with Monica Higgins, Dawn Chandler, and Kathy Kram's (Chapter 14) idea of developmental initiation, Turban and Lee predict that extraversion, being open to new ideas, and a learning goal orientation are traits that may explain why some individuals will find mentoring relationships more readily than others.

Personality emerged as a theme in other chapters as well. Georgia Chao (Chapter 7) suggests that personality may interact with mentoring to influence experiences of organizational socialization. Ellen Ensher and Susan Murphy (Chapter 12) observe that personality characteristics may distinguish those who embrace electronic mentoring from those who do not. Finally, if researchers discover that complementarity of personality profiles among mentors and protégés predicts relationship quality, then this factor should be used when selecting and matching members of formal mentoring relationships (see Blake-Beard, O'Neill, & McGowan, Chapter 25).

Developmental Needs and Stages

Individual differences in stages of development may serve as an important antecedent to effective mentoring relationships. Using adult development theory (Kegan, 1982, 1991), McGowan, Stone, and Kegan (Chapter 16) propose that mentors at the "interpersonal stage" of development can serve protégés only in certain ways: providing direction, coaching, and advice. Due to their developmental stage, these mentors are not yet able to encourage autonomy or to nurture creative thinking if it departs from what they believe is the correct way to proceed. For protégés who have progressed beyond this interpersonal stage, this type of inflexible mentoring is likely to result in disillusionment and frustration. In contrast, mentors and protégés who are in complementary stages of development may experience heightened stages of growth and effectiveness in their relationships.

Mentoring relationships may also be influenced by members' career stages. Through systematically outlining the challenges that individuals face in the exploration, trial, establishment, and mastery stages of a career learning cycles, Hall and Chandler (Chapter 19) illustrate which mentoring functions are likely to be most effective when protégés are at particular stages in their career learning cycles. They suggest that some relationships may start to hinder future learning and growth if the protégé's needs at a particular point in the learning cycle are not met. Similarly, they point out that mentors at certain stages of development may be less able to provide needed mentoring. For example, a mentor entering a new learning cycle in his or her own career may be unable to assist a protégé who is striving to move into a new learning cycle at the same time. This offers a compelling reason to see developmental networks, made up of a diverse group of developers, as essential to individual learning and development. When individuals have diverse developmental networks, they can enlist help from others and will therefore be less vulnerable to a particular mentor's limited ability to provide the help needed at a critical juncture in a career learning cycle.

Skills and Competencies

Relational Competencies

A number of relational skills and competencies serve as antecedents and, as we will discover later, outcomes of effective mentoring relationships. In his chapter on emotional intelligence, Cherniss (Chapter 17) demonstrates that that an individual's capacity to form positive, safe relationships seems to be strongly influenced by his or her ability to manage the anxiety, uncertainty, and increasing intimacy of a mentoring relationship. In addition, mentors frequently utilize emotional processes to help their protégés become more adept at managing emotion in their work and careers. In this regard, mentors serve as emotional role models for their protégés. Finally, protégés' and mentors' self-awareness, empathy, and social skills will affect what actually transpires in their developmental relationships, thus having a direct impact on the quality of the relationships.

Relational skills also play a key role in the development of high-quality mentoring relationships. Fletcher and Ragins (Chapter 15) identify a range of relational skills, conditions, and stances that serve as "prerequisites" for relational mentoring, such as vulnerability, empathic and emotional competence, fluid expertise, authenticity, and holistic thinking. Applying this to practice, Cynthia McCauley and Victoria Guthrie (Chapter 23) point to the need for research that illuminates the specific relational competencies needed to become effective coaches, leaders, and learning partners. This has important practical implications not only for leadership development programs but also for the selection and training of participants in formal mentoring programs.

A final set of relational competencies involves the skill set necessary to initiate effective mentoring relationships. Higgins, Chandler, and Kram (Chapter 14) introduce the concept of developmental initiation—that set of skills and behaviors that enable protégés to build their development networks. Without these development-seeking behaviors, they argue, developmental networks are likely to be less helpful because they lack a range of relationships reflecting network diversity. These authors suggest a number of interesting potential antecedents to developmental initiation, such as protégé socioeconomic status, gender, nationality, and age. We note here that this construct may be very useful in distinguishing important differences in the patterns of mentoring relationships and networks. In fact, building on these ideas, Chandler recently developed the construct of "relational savvy," which is the set of attitudes, behaviors, and skills necessary to both initiate and sustain effective developmental relationships (Chandler, 2006).

Since there is considerable conceptual overlap among these relational skills and competencies, empirical research is needed to delineate the root causes of differences in relationship quality and outcomes attributed to various combinations of skills and competencies. In addition, we need to examine the "tipping point" in these competencies that moves mentoring relationships from adequate to exceptional.

Compassion

In looking at the role of relationships in fostering personal change, Richard Boyatzis (Chapter 18) crystallizes yet another competence that may be critical to significant personal learning and growth outcomes in mentoring relationships. He calls our attention to the mentor's capacity for compassion and how the ability to empathize, express caring, and act in response to another's feelings distinguishes relationships that serve individuals' personal development from those that serve instrumental outcomes related only to performance and promotion. As discussed later, compassion may also be an outcome of effective mentoring; individuals who bring compassion to their relationship may experience a deepening of that competence as the relationship evolves over time.

Work-Family Lens

Jeffrey Greenhaus and Romila Singh (Chapter 21) identify a new type of competence that reflects mentors' ability to help their protégés effectively manage work-family conflict. This competence involves the mentor's awareness of work-life issues, a willingness to share his or her own experiences with work-life conflict, and a nonjudgmental approach that facilitates protégés' self-awareness and ability to obtain congruence across life domains. By introducing a work-family lens to the mentoring arena, Greenhaus and Singh urge us to consider a new skill set that underlies a mentor's ability to help his or her protégé effectively manage role boundaries (Friedman & Greenhaus, 2000) and achieve states of work-life enrichment by leveraging resources in one domain to enhance performance and satisfaction in the other (Greenhaus & Powell, 2006; (Parasuraman & Greenhaus, 1997).

The chapter by Greenhaus and Singh offers a comprehensive model and a helpful list of propositions for future research on the effects of a work-family lens on protégé outcomes. Future research could also examine consequences from the mentor's side of the relationship. For example, it would be interesting to assess whether the process of helping protégés achieve work-life balance helps mentors reexamine and obtain more balance in their own lives; there may be a cyclical process in which the achievement of work-life balance in one partner changes norms and facilitates a spiraling process of reassessment that leads to more balance in the life of the other member of the relationship.

Gender and Race

Gender and race have long been acknowledged as important roots of differences in mentoring relationships (Collins, 1983; Kram, 1985; Ragins, 1989; Thomas, 1990). In this volume, Carol McKeen and Merridee Bujaki (Chapter 8) offer a comprehensive review of studies that have examined the influence of gender on protégés' access to mentors, mentor behaviors, and outcomes of the relationship. Drawing on

Wanberg, Welsh, and Hezlett's (2003) conceptual process model of mentoring, McKeen and Bujaki highlight the way gender and the gender composition of the relationship influence outcomes across phases of the relationship. A core point revealed in their review is that research on the effects of gender on mentoring has produced inconsistent results. This may be a function of differences in the degree to which studies control for or examine the effects of gender composition on the relationship, as well as differences in controlling for relationship duration, type, and position of mentor (see Ragins, 1999a, 1999b). However, McKeen and Bujaki point out an additional factor that may account for these inconsistent findings. Concurring with other authors in this volume (Fletcher & Ragins, Chapter 15), they attribute these mixed findings to contextual factors that can be accounted for only by considering gender as a systemic factor nested within social and organizational contexts. For example, organizational cultures can be more or less masculine or feminine, and definitions of mentoring effectiveness can be more or less rooted in male models of careers. As discussed below, these factors have a profound effect on our research questions, our research methods, and how we interpret the results of our research.

As with gender, research on the effects of race on mentoring relationships has been restricted by how race is viewed, or not viewed, in organizations. Blake-Beard, Murrell, and Thomas (Chapter 9) assert that while the challenges of cross-race mentoring have long been established, the role of mentoring in minority group members' careers has been viewed through the lens of assimilation. People of color are expected to assimilate to models of dominant-group behaviors, and when race differences are found, they are often framed as reflecting a deficit in the minority group. As a consequence, explanations of observed differences may be incorrect, or at best incomplete, as we fail to adequately understand the unique mentoring needs and experiences of protégés and mentors of color. It is clear that employees of color who have access to mentoring from both White and minority mentors generally experience more positive career outcomes than those who do not (Thomas, 1993; Dreher & Cox, 1996). What is less clear is how the interpersonal strategies employed in cross-race mentoring and the organizational context in which mentoring is embedded shape individual and organizational outcomes.

Given the research reviewed here on cross-gender and cross-race relationships, we can postulate that when these relationships are of high quality, they will not only have the potential to enhance the careers of individuals from nondominant groups but can also prompt the personal learning of both mentors and protégés. While same-gender and same-race relationships have been found to be a critical source of psychosocial support in individuals' developmental networks (Higgins & Kram, 2001; Ibarra, 1993) and mentoring relationships (Koberg, Boss, & Goodman, 1998; Kram & Hall, 1996; Ragins & McFarlin, 1990; Sosik & Godshalk, 2000; Tharenou, 2005; Thomas, 1990, 1993), cross-race and cross-gender relationships are opportunities for individuals from all backgrounds to acquire emotional competencies and relational skills essential to leading and thriving in a diverse workforce (see Cherniss, Chapter 17; Clutterbuck, Chapter 26; Fletcher & Ragins, Chapter 15; Ragins, 2002, 2007).

This discussion illustrates that an assessment of the effects of race and gender on mentoring relationships needs to incorporate an understanding of the impact of social and political context on the research questions we ask, the variables we study, and the conclusions we draw. For example, Ragins (2007) points out that research that examines whether women and people of color experience the same processes, benefits, and outcomes as their White male counterparts often uses the experience of White males as the "gold standard" for evaluating mentoring relationships. This ignores the possibility that diverse relationships may produce an entirely different array of processes, benefits, and outcomes that are related to the unique needs, capacities, and abilities of nondominant groups. So, for example, researchers comparing female and male mentors that use the protégé's career advancement as the metric for evaluating the effectiveness of the relationship may find that women provide less of the sponsorship function than men and, as a consequence, may conclude that women are less effective as mentors. However, this research may not measure or capture the unique and important functions female mentors may bring to the table, such as helping their protégés develop emotional competence, relational learning, self-knowledge, and other skills related to personal growth and connection.

In sum, the authors in this volume have identified a number of important antecedents that may affect the quality and processes in mentoring relationships. Variations in mentors' and protégés' personality may combine with their developmental needs and stages, their relational skills and competencies, and their gender, race, and ethnicity to influence the quality and dynamics of the relationship. Even as we pursue promising new paths to understanding the antecedents to effective mentoring, so must we also critique and consider the type of outcomes we employ in our research. This leads us to the next section, in which we synthesize and present the range of mentoring outcomes presented in this volume.

Extending the Range of Mentoring Outcomes

A consistent theme throughout this collection is the call for considering a wider range of outcomes in future mentoring research. Whereas the first two decades of research on mentoring emphasized instrumental career-related outcomes, such as increased performance, compensation, promotions, advancement, job attitudes, and career satisfaction (see Allen, Eby, Poteet, Lentz, & Lima, 2004; Noe, Greenberger, & Wang, 2002), there is now a collective view that outcomes related to personal learning, development, and growth are equally relevant and important. As we progress in our understanding of variations in the quality and processes of developmental relationships, we have also begun to acknowledge that these outcomes may be more difficult to measure yet are critical for understanding the full impact of mentoring on individuals, relationships, and organizations. These new outcomes include factors such as personal and task learning, organizational socialization, relational competencies, adult development, personal growth, physiological outcomes, and outcomes related to the nonwork domain. As our discussion will reveal, some of these outcomes iteratively function as processes as well as outcomes of mentoring relationships.

Learning Across Relationships and Career Cycles

Learning can be both a process and outcome of mentoring relationships. In their chapter, Melenie Lankau and Terri Scandura (Chapter 4) build on prior empirical (Lankau & Scandura, 2002) and theoretical work (Kram & Hall, 1996) to examine personal learning as a major category of mentoring outcomes. Personal learning involves the acquisition of knowledge, skills, or competencies that contribute to an individual's personal development (Kram, 1996). Drawing on Hall's (2002) dimensions of career effectiveness, Lankau and Scandura offer a typology that uses the dimensions of task/personal focus and short-term/long-term time orientations to present different types of learning outcomes from mentoring relationships. These include personal skill development, relational job learning, personal identity growth, personal adaptability, and professional and organizational socialization. Their chapter also illuminates the fact that learning processes and outcomes in mentoring relationships are driven by the needs of the members as well as the social and organizational contexts in which the relationships are embedded.

Organizational socialization is a key learning outcome that has received relatively little attention in the mentoring literature (see Chao, O'Leary-Kelly, Wolf, Klein, & Gardner, 1994). In Chapter 7, Chao addresses this gap by examining how mentoring and other developmental relationships combine to facilitate organizational socialization. She makes the key point that different mentors address different socialization needs of protégés and that it is important to examine organizational socialization, and perhaps other learning outcomes, within the context of multiple developmental relationships. Combined, these chapters point not only to the need to address different types of learning outcomes of mentoring relationships but also to the need to examine these outcomes within the context of multiple relationships that occur across career stages and organizational settings.

The learning that occurs in mentoring relationships may also influence career-related learning processes. In their model of relationally driven career learning, Hall and Chandler (Chapter 19) illustrate how developmental relationships influence stages of career learning cycles. They observe that turbulent career environments create situations in which individuals change jobs and industries more frequently than in the past. Rather than viewing careers as a long single cycle of stages (i.e., exploration, trial, establishment, and mastery), Hall and Chandler propose that individuals enact multiple career roles simultaneously and therefore experience multiple, short-career learning cycles. These cycles involve a range of potential outcomes that include the development of new skills as well as increased self-awareness, self-confidence, self-esteem, psychological success, identity growth, and adaptability. They explain how developmental networks and relationships can trigger, facilitate, or even hinder the task and personal learning that occurs within career learning cycles. While mentoring scholars have examined the relationship between the presence of a mentor and career outcomes, such as advancement and career satisfaction, we have not empirically examined the relationship between mentoring and career learning, planning, and development for both mentors and protégés. The need to understand the role of mentoring in career development processes is even more salient given the new career context of boundaryless and protean careers (see Arthur & Rousseau, 1996; Hall & Associates, 1996).

Taken together, these chapters illustrate that learning is both a process and an outcome of mentoring relationships, that there are multiple forms of learning in mentoring relationships, and that these forms of learning occur over the course of learning cycles that are spread across career spans. Moreover, different types and combinations of developmental relationships offer different learning processes and outcomes for both mentors and protégés. Finally, the organizational environment and the composition of the relationship represent key contextual factors that affect learning outcomes in mentoring relationships.

Relational Competencies, Cycles, and Caches

The contributors to this book broaden and deepen our perspective on the range of relational outcomes that may occur in mentoring interactions, relationships, and developmental networks. For example, Fletcher and Ragins (Chapter 15) apply Miller and Stiver's (1997) theory of growth-fostering interactions to the mentoring arena by identifying "five good things" that occur for both mentors and protégés in growth-fostering mentoring episodes. These include a zest for learning in the relationship, empowered action, increased sense of worth, new knowledge and the desire for more connection (Miller & Stiver, 1997). Fletcher and Ragins propose that repeated episodes in which these five good things are achieved will lead to increased levels of relational competence for both members of the relationship. *Relational competence* is defined as the ability to operate effectively in a context of interdependence (Fletcher, 1999). Fletcher and Ragins point out that relational competence is transferable across relationships and settings and is linked to more effective work relationships, work performance, developmental growth, and other positive career outcomes (Fletcher, 1999; Goleman, 1995). They observe that since individuals carry their relational competence with them, high-quality mentoring may lead to the development of skills that influence relationships both within and outside the workplace. They propose that by developing relational competence and the ability to build high-quality connections across life domains (see Dutton & Heaphy, 2003), high-quality mentoring may contribute to both mentors' and protégés' life satisfaction, health, well-being, and balance.

These chapters also reveal that relational competence may affect the outcomes of mentoring relationships in an iterative manner. As Cherniss points out in his chapter on emotional intelligence and mentoring (Chapter 17), the self-awareness, self-management, empathy, and social skills *required* for effective mentoring relationships are also frequently *acquired* in the context of developmental relationships. For example, effective mentors need relational competence, but the process of effective mentoring may also enhance a mentor's capacity for active listening and empathy. Similarly, protégés may build their relational savvy as they initiate and build mentoring relationships (Chandler, 2006), resulting in richer developmental networks in the future. Along similar lines, Higgins, Chandler, and Kram (Chapter 14) illustrate how developmental initiation leads to rich developmental networks that, in turn, result in enhanced career-related and personal learning outcomes.

Understanding these iterative effects may also help us find the "tipping point" in the process of developing skills across networks that lead to positive, productive developmental relationships.

These perspectives offer the idea that there may be a cyclical, self-generating process that occurs within and between relationships that leads to and builds on relational outcomes. We offer the idea that mentors and protégés in high-quality relationships may develop and build on each other's set of relational competencies, thus creating a positive cycle of relational caches. We define *relational caches* as a transportable sets of relational skills and competencies, which may include skills relating to effective communication, empathic listening, personal learning, knowledge transfer, adaptability, emotional intelligence, self-reflection, self-awareness, and other indicators of personal growth (see Fletcher, 1996; Kram, 1996; Fletcher & Ragins, Chapter 15; Miller & Stiver, 1997). Since these competencies transfer across time, relationships, and settings, the acquisition of relational caches in one relationship may affect the processes and outcomes of other relationships within and outside the workplace. High-quality mentoring episodes and relationships may therefore help both mentors and protégés create and sustain high-quality developmental networks. In addition, since relational caches are passed from one partner to another in high-quality relationships, relational caches can be passed from one relationship to another.

This web of connection and growth can help explain the development of high-quality mentoring cultures in organizations. This process may also explain how individuals become high-quality mentors; individuals who develop a cache of relational skills as a protégé may seek high-quality mentoring relationships in the future, and these relationships may, in turn, broaden and build the skills cache needed to provide effective mentoring. Ultimately, as high-quality mentoring proliferates within an organization, we are likely to witness the institution of a developmental culture and improved organizational performance. Combined, these perspectives not only point to new types of relational outcomes to study but also to the need to study the potentially iterative, spiraling effects of relational outcomes and processes in current and future developmental relationships and in the surrounding organizational context.

Personal Development, Growth, and Change

A wider lens on mentoring relationships and outcomes also leads us to think in new ways about the iterative process by which mentoring relationships affect adult development, personal growth, and change. For example, McGowan, Stone, and Kegan (Chapter 16) examine how stages of adult development both affect and are affected by mentoring relationships. They observe that some mentoring relationships lead to enhanced cognitive and affective capabilities, thus enabling mentors and protégés to transition through increasingly complex stages of adult development. Applying Kegan's (1982, 1991) earlier work, McGowan, Stone, and Kegan offer an in-depth analysis of how mentoring relationships facilitate advancement to higher stages of adult development. They point out, however, that this advancement is contingent on the developmental position of both the mentor and the protégé. In her early work on mentoring, Kram (1985) also speculated that complementarity of developmental stages was critical to realizing the potential value of mentoring and has since extended this perspective to developmental networks (see Chandler & Kram, 2005).

Combined, these perspectives suggest that mentoring can either enhance or smother individual growth, depending on the developmental position of each member of the relationship. Thus, once again, we see that a potential outcome of mentoring relationships (e.g., transition to a higher stage of development) can also shape the relationship in an iterative manner. This also points to the importance of assessing dyadic congruency effects when studying outcomes associated with mentoring relationships. Congruent dyads in which members share similar levels of development and relational skills are likely to be more readily established and effective than dyads that reflect incongruence in members' level of development. However, whether incongruence leads to negative outcomes will depend on the nature of the differences in developmental positions between the two parties. For example, a mentor at a higher developmental position may be better able than a protégé to help his or her partner advance to the next developmental stage.

Although the topic of personal growth and change is central to the very essence of mentoring, it has received relatively little attention in the mentoring literature. Boyatzis (Chapter 18) addresses this gap by using his intentional change theory (Boyatzis, 2006) to examine how mentoring relationships influence personal growth and change throughout the life course. His chapter points to two constructs, trust and compassion, that have been examined in the management literature (see Dutton, Worline, Frost, & Lilius, 2006; Kramer, 1999; Pratt & Dirks, 2007) but have been neglected in the garden of mentoring. Boyatzis proposes that developmental relationships characterized by trust and compassion are key to bringing about individuals' self-awareness, identity growth, and ability to reassess circumstances and adapt to these changes over time. For personal change outcomes to evolve, however, he identifies a number of preconditions, including the relational skills to pose questions, give feedback, and prompt self-inquiry within the context of a safe, compassionate relationship. Boyatzis's chapter illustrates that while mentoring scholars have focused on how mentoring affects career outcomes, advancement, and job attitudes, we know little about the effects of mentoring on the mentor's and protégé's personal growth, identity, and self-awareness.

Taken to a broader level, a key question that comes to mind when reviewing these chapters is how mentoring influences dreams, aspirations, and the ability to achieve one's "ideal" or "best self" (see Roberts, Dutton, Spreitzer, Heaphy, & Quinn, 2005). Underlying this question is the perspective of viewing employees holistically. For example, we know that the effects of relationships in the workplace extend to life domains outside work, and vice versa (see Ragins & Dutton, 2007). Applying a holistic perspective to the mentoring arena opens empirical doors for assessing a rich range of psychological outcomes of mentoring relationships that have not yet been examined in the literature.

Applying a personal growth lens to the mentoring literature also opens up new possibilities and alignments with related areas of scholarship. In particular, the personal growth outcomes identified in this volume complement emerging perspectives from the positive psychology (Lopez & Snyder, 2002) and positive organizational scholarship movements (see Cameron, Dutton, & Quinn, 2003; Dutton & Ragins, 2007; Luthans, Youssef, & Avolio, 2007; Ragins & Verbos, 2007; Roberts, 2006). These positive perspectives identify a rich new array of growth-related outcomes that can be studied by mentoring scholars (see Ragins & Verbos, 2007). For example, mentoring relationships may yield positive psychological capital outcomes involving increased self-efficacy, optimism, hope, and resilience (Luthans, 2002; Luthans & Youssef, 2004; Luthans et al., 2007). Mentoring scholars may also investigate outcomes associated with high-quality connections (Dutton & Heaphy, 2003), such as resilience, energy, zest, flourishment, flow, and vitality (Cameron et al., 2003). Mentoring may contribute to the psychological state of *thriving*, which is defined as the experience of both vitality and learning at work (Spreitzer, Sutcliffe, Dutton, Sonenshein, & Grant, 2005). Spreitzer and her colleagues propose that mentoring may be a relational resource that creates thriving and that individuals who achieve states of thriving may seek mentoring relationships to build and sustain that experience.

Future research could also assess whether mentoring affects mentors' and protégés' experiences of courage (Worline & Quinn, 2003), empowerment (Feldman & Khademian, 2003), and the ability to obtain states of meaningfulness and connection at work (Kahn, 2007; Pratt & Ashforth, 2003). Finally, mentoring may lead to the development of positive and authentic identities (Roberts, 2007) and may offer the opportunity for members of diverse relationships to leverage their experiences into increased knowledge about diversity in the workplace (Davidson & James, 2007). By broadening the study of mentoring to include this rich array of outcomes, we add needed dimensions of depth and texture to the garden of mentoring.

Physiological Outcomes

An emerging and exciting new area of inquiry is the effect of mentoring relationships on physiological and health-related outcomes. A related stream of research has found that the social support generated in relationships can have positive effects on cardiovascular and immune outcomes, such as blood pressure, cortisol (stress-related hormone), and other health-related indices (see review by Heaphy, 2007; see also Fredrickson & Losada, 2005; Seeman, 2001). Heaphy (2007) proposes that high-quality mentoring relationships may offer long-term health benefits for their members and notes that the decreased intrusiveness of physiological measures makes the time ripe for organizational scholars to team with scholars from the health sciences to study the physiological effects of positive relationships at work.

The connection between mentoring and physical outcomes is also highlighted in Boyatzis's Chapter 18, on intentional behavioral change. He urges mentoring researchers to include measures of physiological changes that occur as the personal change process unfolds in the relationship. After defining positive and negative emotional attractors, he offers the idea that the parasympathetic nervous system (PSNS) will be aroused when there are positive attractors at work, giving the individual access to more of their neural circuits. He explains that this process allows them to experience neurogenesis (i.e., the conversion of hippocampal stem cells into new neurons), which allows for new types of learning (Boyatzis, Smith, &

Blaize, 2006). He contends that as new behaviors are practiced and a new sense of identity is formed, new neural pathways can be developed and measured.

This line of thought offers mentoring scholars an impressive new array of outcome measures that offer strong practical utility for organizational scholars and practitioners. Stress scholars have long documented the harmful physiological effects of workplace stress (Cooper & Payne, 1988), but what are the physical outcomes associated with dysfunctional mentoring relationships? Can positive mentoring relationships not only support positive physiological outcomes but also serve as a psychological buffer to stress in both work and nonwork domains? What contextual factors optimize the physiological effects of positive relationships or minimize the effects of negative relationships? How do multiple developmental relationships interact in determining physiological outcomes? What is the influence of mentoring relationships on both mental and physical health? Given the rising cost of health care and the concomitant emphasis on workplace wellness, the effects of mentoring relationships on health is a very promising and important area for future research.

Nonwork Outcomes

Increasingly, organizational scholars are recognizing that we need to examine the interface between work and nonwork domains and the effects of work relationships on nonwork outcomes. Toward that end, Greenhaus and Singh (Chapter 21) urge us to cast a broader net by considering the work-family interface within the context of mentoring relationships. They offer a theoretical model that examines how mentoring affects protégés' work-family conflict, work-family enrichment, and the psychological well being gained as a consequence of work-life balance. They point out that traditionally, mentoring research has focused on a relatively narrow range of protégés' career outcomes (e.g., advancement, compensation) and has failed to recognize the potential impact of mentoring on protégés' family and personal lives. Greenhaus and Singh identify four different outcomes related to work-family balance that can be studied by mentoring scholars: (a) family interference with work, (b) work interference with family (c) work enrichment of family, and (d) family enrichment of work.

In addition to these outcomes, Greenhaus and Singh propose that the mentor's views and practices around work-family issues shape more immediate outcomes reflecting the mentor's behaviors in the relationship. These behaviors, in turn, influence both the protégés work-related demands and the resources they obtain from work. Greenhaus and Singh present the idea of a work-family lens, which is the extent to which mentors are sensitive to and supportive of their protégés' values and goals regarding the attainment of work-family balance. They explain that a work-family lens is a type of mentoring schema (Ragins & Verbos, 2007) that guides behaviors and ultimately enables the protégé's ability to achieve work-life balance. As with the additional outcomes noted earlier in this section, they observe that work-family balance outcomes are shaped not only by the mentor's inclinations but also by the surrounding organizational context.

In sum, our landscape architects have provided several blueprints for examining a range of developmental outcomes that extends far beyond the traditional instrumental outcomes that have historically served as the centerpiece of mentoring research. Our authors have outlined fruitful new areas for research on learning across relationships, organizations, and career cycles. They offer new perspectives on how mentoring builds and broadens relational and emotional competencies and, in so doing, creates iterative cycles of relational caches that can be transferred across time, relationships, and settings.

A wider lens on mentoring also allows for a deeper understanding of how mentoring affects the transition to new developmental positions, personal growth, and change. We can examine how mentoring affects the creation of new identities, dreams, and aspirations, as well as the creation and maintenance of work-life balance. Mentoring may be associated with a range of positive psychological outcomes, such as thriving, resilience, optimism, and self-efficacy, as well as positive physiological outcomes relating to physical and mental health and well-being. The idea that several of these outcomes (e.g. self-awareness, empathy) have the potential to launch a cycle of positive growth, both in the individual actors and in developmental relationships and networks, calls for study of the iterative processes inherent in relationships over time. We can infer that the potential for a negative cycle of dysfunctional relationships and outcomes is equally possible, as when the lack of self-awareness can lead to ineffective mentoring that can result in mistrust and despair. These new lines of inquiry may help to find the "tipping points" for relationship quality, positive and negative outcomes, and the conditions necessary for growth-enhancing connections. To complete our description of the new landscape of mentoring, we now examine how particular aspects of context influence mentoring relationships, processes, and outcomes.

Understanding the Role of Context

More than ever before, the field of mentoring now recognizes the critical nature of context and the role context plays in shaping the initiation, processes, and outcomes of mentoring relationships. Context involves not only the system within which mentoring relationships are embedded but also the structure and medium by which mentoring relationships are enacted within and outside organizations. Our contributors offer five new paths of inquiry that illuminate the role of context in the development, processes, and outcomes of mentoring relationships: (1) the organization's role in fostering mentoring relationships, (2) the effects of diversity climate and norms, (3) the role of leadership in mentoring, (4) the impact of technology on mentoring, and (5) the role of societal culture in shaping mentoring processes and outcomes. These contextual factors illuminate the embedded nature of mentoring and offer important new insights for future research and practice.

The Organization's Role in Fostering Mentoring

Formal and Informal Mentoring

As we consider the factors that distinguish relationships in terms of quality, processes, and structure, a key contextual factor is whether the relationship was initiated through informal or structured means (see Allen, Eby, & Lentz, 2006; Chao, Walz, & Gardner, 1992; Ragins & Cotton, 1999; Underhill, 2006). While the continuum of quality in formal and informal mentoring relationships clearly overlaps (Ragins et al., 2000), it can be quite helpful to consider differences in how this contextual factor influences the norms and expectations of mentoring relationships. In their chapter on formal mentoring relationships Gayle Baugh and Ellen Fagenson-Eland (Chapter 10) observe that differences between formal and informal mentoring may be a function of different expectations for the relationship, the time-bound nature of formal mentoring, and differences in the training, quality, and structure among formal programs. They observe that due to the requirements, expectations, and time constraints of formal programs, it is quite likely that some of the personal benefits experienced by protégés and mentors in informal mentoring relationships (e.g., long-term friendship, increasing intimacy) are less likely to occur in formal relationships.

A key consideration here is the matching process used in creating formal relationships. In Chapter 25, Blake-Beard, O'Neill, and McGowan discuss some of the differences in techniques used in the matching process and offer insights into some of the factors that contribute to successful matching in formal mentoring programs. In their discussion of criteria for matching mentors and protégés, they illustrate how decisions about matching can significantly shape both relationship dynamics and outcomes. When efforts are made to ensure that the criteria for matching are aligned with key objectives of the program, both career advancement objectives and personal learning objectives can be met.

Organizational contexts also influence the values and expectations associated with formal and informal mentoring relationships. Even though practitioners and scholars agree that focusing on the differences between formal and informal mentoring is not as useful as understanding how these relationships complement one another, it can be quite instructive to examine how expectations about these relationships differ across organizational contexts (see Baugh & Fagenson-Eland, Chapter 10; P-Sontag, Vappie, & Wanberg, Chapter 24). Toward that end, McCauley and Guthrie (Chapter 23) advocate for research on how organizational systems and cultures impact the acceptance and effectiveness of relationships for learning. They point out, for example, that in some performance-oriented cultures, executive coaches are viewed as necessary, while in other contexts, coaches are evidence of weakness. Similarly, in some organizations, individuals are responsible for finding their own mentors, while other organizations offer programs to help employees develop the skills and competencies necessary to develop effective informal mentoring relationships. For example, Cherniss (Chapter 17) observes that organizations can play a key role in promoting and sustaining effective mentoring relationships by encouraging training in emotional competence, as well as establishing support systems that reward this important work. We clearly need more systematic research to ferret out the ways in which organizational contexts influence the development of effective formal and informal mentoring relationships.

Our practitioner authors acknowledge the criticality of organizational contexts and offer insights into fostering effective mentoring relationships. For example, Lynn P-Sontag, Kim Vappie and Connie Wanberg (Chapter 24) explain how MENTTIUM considers the organization's strategic business and talent development goals, along with the current culture and practices, when implementing hierarchical or peer mentoring programs. Along similar lines, Catalyst's Kathy Giscombe (Chapter 22) observes that the organization's resources, sponsorship, and priorities play a key role in whether mentoring programs are effective in helping women advance through the glass ceiling. McCauley and Guthrie, at the Center for Creative Leadership (Chapter 23), offer insights into the interface between organizational support for leadership development and mentoring by describing how different types of relationships—learning coaches, peer learning partners, executive facilitators, and feedback coaches—are targeted to serve different roles in leadership development programs and practices.

Climate for Mentoring and Learning

Irrespective of whether formal mentoring programs are offered, the organization's culture and talent management practices will influence whether individuals invest energy and time in developmental relationships. When learning is explicitly valued (i.e., it is permissible to make a mistake), managers are rewarded for taking the time to coach and mentor others, work is designed to foster teamwork and collaboration, and leaders model their own commitment to developing others. In this organizational context, mentoring is far more likely to flourish than when these same actions and priorities are disvalued (Kram, 1985; Kram & Hall, 1996). The importance of culture is also reflected in Cherniss's Chapter 17, which illustrates how these factors shape individuals' willingness to develop the necessary emotional competence to be effective in mentoring relationships. Combined, these perspectives illustrate the key role organizational context plays in determining the nature, learning processes, and effectiveness of developmental relationships.

The Effects of Diversity Climate and Societal Norms

The contextual effect of diversity is a consistent theme threading throughout the volume (see Blake-Beard, Murrell, & Thomas, Chapter 9; Giscombe, Chapter 22; Fletcher & Ragins, Chapter 15; McKeen & Bujaki, Chapter 8). As our authors point out, societal norms, expectations, and stereotypes not only filter down through organizational culture to influence the definition of careers but also directly influence the form, functions, processes, and outcomes of mentoring relationships. For example, McKeen and Bujaki (Chapter 8) point out that mentoring has historically been defined as providing guidance for career success; however, career success has generally been defined in masculine terms. One of their key concerns is that both researchers and practitioners have accepted masculine definitions of success, which fails to examine mentoring processes and outcomes that may be more important to women. Similarly, Fletcher and Ragins (Chapter 15) observe that while relational practices in mentoring relationships are critical predictors of success, these practices become invisible and devalued when viewed as "women's work." This concern is echoed by Blake-Beard, Murrell, and Thomas (Chapter 9), who point out that models of mentoring have consistently been based on majority/White male paradigms and that these models fail to recognize aspects of the relationship that serve the unique needs of nondominant groups in organizations.

These authors point to the importance of considering how our society shapes the values used to view, develop, and evaluate mentoring relationships. For example, Fletcher and Ragins (Chapter 15) urge us to think beyond organizational context to the impact of societal-level systemic forces. Like our other authors, they emphasize how our views of gender and racial dynamics in mentoring relationships are shaped by the gendered nature of mainstream theories of human growth and development. They make the point that we must focus not only on whether race or gender differences exist but also, more important, on how our theories have been "gendered" to reflect traditionally male values. They point out that since mentoring occurs within the context of societal systems, power dynamics at the societal level (i.e., the legacies of patriarchal laws, slavery, and homophobic secrecy) need to be taken into account when studying the processes and outcomes of mentoring relationships, as well as the conditions under which they flourish. As Thomas (1993) asserted in his original work on cross-racial mentoring and racial taboos, the history of power relations between groups combines with social identities to shape relational interactions and the ability to achieve effective mentoring relationships. The impact of societal context on mentoring relationships is critical not only from a power and diversity perspective but also, as we will see later, from a cross-cultural international perspective.

Our authors also reveal an interesting paradox in the relationship between technology and diversity. Ensher and Murphy (Chapter 12) observe that electronic mentoring may be helpful for meeting the challenges of diverse mentoring relationships. They point out that electronic communication lacks the salient visual clues that can trigger stereotypes, biases, and discrimination. E-mentoring may enable mentors and protégés to focus on similar values, attitudes, and goals rather than surface-level similarities or differences. This may also allow nondominant group members to be viewed more in terms of their individual attributes than their group membership. However, this form of invisibility has a negative backside when we consider Blake-Beard, Murell, and Thomas's chapter on race and mentoring (Chapter 9). They point out that when race becomes invisible, the unique complexities, issues, and insights in cross-race relationships also become unacknowledged and unaddressed. They point to the need to make race more visible in organizations and mentoring relationships in order to acknowledge the role of race in organizational life. If e-mentoring puts race, gender, and ethnicity in the background, this dynamic could undermine efforts to promote the deep change in organizational cultures that are needed for a diverse workforce to flourish. E-mentoring may be good for the short term if it allows individuals to connect who otherwise would not do so, but it could also have the unintended consequence of restricting the development of diversity awareness and the competencies (i.e., self-awareness, empathy, social skills) necessary to build mutually enhancing diverse mentoring relationships.

Future research could examine the optimal use of e-mentoring in diverse mentoring relationships. For example, e-mentoring may be useful in the early stages of initiation and development, as it avoids triggering stereotypes that may curtail the development of the relationship (see Blake-Beard, 1999; Ragins & Cotton, 1991; Viator, 2001). However, once the relationship is established, it may be best for the relationship to transform to face to face in order for members to obtain optimal states of learning and growth from their relationship.

The chapters in this volume illustrate the evolution of our understanding of the role of diversity in mentoring relationships. Although early perspectives emphasized the importance of diversity (Kram, 1988; Ragins, 1997; Thomas, 1993), until now, broadened views of what constitutes mentoring for various identity group members has not been fully examined. Blake-Beard, Murrell, and Thomas (Chapter 9) warn that when we use narrow definitions to describe mentoring dynamics within a diverse organizational setting, we undermine our ability to accurately understand the situation or determine what might impede growth and development for diverse groups of employees. A broadened perspective is not limited to race or gender, but takes a kaleidoscope view in examining the full range and combination of differences that may occur in mentoring relationships (see Ragins, 2002). Emerging perspectives also acknowledge that mentoring involves the exchange of power, knowledge, and social capital and prompts researchers to examine how some developmental network structures enable success among members of nondominant groups, while other structures result in failure (see Ibarra, 1993). It is clear that we need to continue to explore how the cultural context of diversity reciprocally influences the development and effectiveness of diverse mentoring relationships and developmental networks.

The Interface of Mentoring and Leadership

Several chapters in this volume prompt us to examine how mentoring occurs within the context of leadership and how leadership can further our understanding of mentoring relationships. This interface can take two forms. First, leaders can model and create a developmental culture that promotes mentoring relationships, and, second, mentoring can build leadership capability within individuals and within the organizational context.

In their chapter on leadership and mentoring, Veronica Godshalk and John Sosik (Chapter 6) demonstrate how theories of transformational leadership and leader-member exchange can be used to illuminate mentoring processes and outcomes. For example, some of the behaviors that characterize transformational leaders are equally observable in high-quality mentoring relationships (Godshalk & Sosik, 2000). It appears, too, that the functions and outcomes of both leadership and mentoring vary depending on similar relationship dimensions—which include the form of the relationship (one-to-one or one-to-many), the relationship type (formal or informal), the relationship's primary goal focus (individual or organizational), and the context in which the relationship exists (within or outside an organization's boundaries). Furthermore, there is considerable overlap between mentoring and leadership on these dimensions, suggesting that in many circumstances, the same individual may enact both leadership and mentoring behaviors.

What is not yet clearly articulated are the distinctions between leaders and mentors. While we may see similar behaviors in those that lead and those that mentor, these are not always embodied in the same individual, nor do they always have the same objectives or outcomes. And though both have been defined as relational rather than individual phenomena, the practical and conceptual distinctions between leaders and mentors have not been precisely articulated. A recurring theme in this volume and elsewhere (Kouzes & Posner, 2003; McCauley & Guthrie, Chapter 23; Ting & Scisco, 2006) is that leadership focuses primarily on organizational change, while mentoring focuses primarily on individual change; leaders aim to inspire individuals, groups, and organizations to move in a particular direction, while mentors aim to inspire individuals to define and more forward on their own developmental paths. One implication of this is that mentors, particularly informal mentors, operate primarily for the best interest of their protégés, while leaders have a larger constituent group that includes other stakeholders. In some cases, mentors may advise their protégés to engage in behaviors and career paths that are in the best interest of the protégé but not the organization. For example, retaining a high-performing protégé may be in the best interest of the organization, but a mentor may advise the protégé to leave if the organization does not support or value the protégé's development. In contrast, leaders and formally assigned mentors have a different set of responsibilities, expectations, and role requirements that may lead to an entirely different set of behaviors, as described by Baugh and Fagenson-Eland (Chapter 10).

Applying a leadership lens to mentoring offers new insights and questions about the relationships between these constructs. For example, what is the role of mentoring in enabling individuals to develop their leadership capabilities? McCauley and Guthrie begin to address this question (Chapter 23), on the role of learning partnerships in leader development programs. Their chapter offers examples on how developmental relationships can be leveraged into leadership programs. This line of thought suggests that by maximizing relational processes underlying learning and development, mentoring others may increase one's leadership capability. The relationship qualities that characterize high-quality mentoring may be the same as those required for transformational leadership, making mentoring a training ground for critical leadership characteristics and skills. And in coaching and developing others, mentors can develop a good understanding of the values, interests, and capabilities of the workforce they aspire to lead. These questions offer provocative insights for a fertile new area of growth in the garden of mentoring.

The Impact of Technology

Technology plays an increasing contextual role in the development and maintenance of mentoring relationships within and outside organizations (Ensher, Heun, & Blanchard, 2003; Hamilton & Scandura, 2003). Ensher and Murphy (Chapter 12) offer key insights into the electronic future by examining electronic mentoring (e-mentoring), yet another new form of a developmental relationship that can foster both personal and organizational outcomes related to learning and development. They demonstrate how e-mentoring may supplement face-to-face mentoring or be construed as a separate resource for individuals striving to expand their developmental networks. Their chapter offers guidance for mentoring scholars by examining how the antecedents and consequences of e-mentoring may differ from face-to-face mentoring relationships.

The role of technology in mentoring relationships represents a bountiful area for future research. We need to better understand the conditions and practices that maximize positive outcomes in computer-mediated mentoring. At a minimum, we need to clarify how match quality, frequency of communication, and perceived similarity affect relationship quality in formal and informal electronic relationships. We also need to understand how these processes differ from the processes involved in face-to-face relationships. Organizational context may also play a role in these processes; it may be that e-mentoring works better as primary or supplemental developmental relationship in a particular organizational context. Diversity context may also affect these processes; as discussed earlier, diversity and status differences may shape computer-mediated relationships in unique and unexamined ways. Future research needs to explore the impact of e-mentoring within these contexts, as well as others. It is clear that with increases in globalization, telecommuting, and the permeable boundaries of work across location and time zones, e-mentoring is likely to have an increasing presence in the garden of mentoring for many years to come.

The Role of Societal Culture

The final contextual variable identified in this volume perhaps has the broadest impact on the development and functioning of mentoring relationships. Our practitioners identified the impact of culture on the practice of mentoring and offered important insight into the types of research that needs to be conducted in this area. For example, in his comparison of European and U.S. models of mentoring, David Clutterbuck (Chapter 26) uses a cross-cultural perspective to illuminate how the cultural context in which an organization is embedded influences the definition and enactment of mentoring. He illustrates how European mentoring programs are based on a different set of assumptions regarding the purpose and scope of mentoring. For example, he notes that European mentoring takes a more developmental tact—emphasizing personal learning and development—while U.S. mentoring tends to emphasize career outcomes and the idea of mentors sponsoring their protégés' advancement. It is interesting to note that the mutuality and reciprocal learning process of mentoring relationships has long been acknowledged in European settings but is just beginning to take hold in theory and practice in the United States.

Along similar lines, P-Sontag, Vappie, and Wanberg (Chapter 24) describe the challenges they faced when applying the MENTTIUM mentoring framework to international locations. They describe how language and cultural differences limit what is transferable from U.S.-based initiatives. For example, they discovered that managers in Spain would not accept cross-gender partnerships, while managers in France viewed formal mentoring as remedial in nature.

Clutterbuck (Chapter 26) urges both researchers and practitioners to make use of systematic research on cultural differences as the study of mentoring progresses. He notes that cross-cultural researchers offer clear dimensions on which to assess cultural differences (Adler, 1997; Hofstede, 2003; Trompenaars & Woolliams, 2004) and highlights two dimensions that may be particularly relevant for understanding mentoring within different cultural contexts: power distance (which may influence protégés' willingness to challenge what they are told) and individuality (which may lead to a focus on the protégé's individual career progression as the core goal of the relationship). In addition, the reliance on fatalism (where failure may be seen as "God's will" rather than a personal responsibility) may also influence mentoring relationships in some cultures. Clutterbuck notes that high power distance cultures may tend to favor a hierarchical sponsorship model but that this approach may clash with multinationals that are dominated by low power distance countries, such as in Northern Europe. Finally, with increased globalization, he observes that U.S. and European mentoring are becoming increasingly similar with respect to cultural effects on mentoring. Indeed, we may discover new "cultural hybrids" of mentoring (see Mezias & Scandura, 2005) that reflect cultural combinations of values, needs, and differences across cultural settings.

As described in this section, the landscape of mentoring is enriched by the consideration of a range of embedded contextual factors involving the organization and the societal culture in which it is nested. Mentoring relationships are also enacted within the context of technology, leadership, and diversity. The research and practice of mentoring do not exist in a vacuum, but are profoundly affected by these contextual factors.

In sum, the authors in this volume have offered us rich insight into a new array of antecedents, processes, outcomes, and contextual factors that can be examined in research and explored in practice. A summary of these new horizons is presented in Figure 27.1. These new horizons do not necessarily replace traditional perspectives, but instead may serve to complement and extend our knowledge of traditional variables that have been studied extensively in the past (i.e., mentor functions, phases of relationship, career and job attitudes, advancement, compensation and performance). In addition, these new horizons reflect themes that were raised in this volume, which do not reflect all new and emerging themes in mentoring, such as mentoring schema theory (Ragins & Verbos, 2007) or relational mentoring (Ragins, 2005).

The new horizon of mentoring certainly represents a challenging research agenda. Fortunately, our authors have equipped us with the tools needed to successfully navigate the practical and methodological challenges that we will inevitably face as we move our field into the 21st century.

Tools and Challenges in Tending the New Landscape

In presenting new frameworks and posing new questions, our authors have planted the seeds of growth for research and innovation in many undernourished areas in the garden of mentoring. Each chapter has offered unique elements and critical tools needed to nurture the growth of developmental relationships in organizations. Our intention is to encourage scholars and practitioners, both new and experienced, to make use of the theoretical frameworks, research propositions, research methods, and practical applications presented in this volume. As we continue to tend to the garden of mentoring, we can anticipate new theoretical advancements, revelations, and insights into how to create and encourage positive outcomes for individuals, groups, and organizations.

The volume reveals three key priorities in tending the landscape of mentoring. Our first priority is to further understand and delineate how various forms of

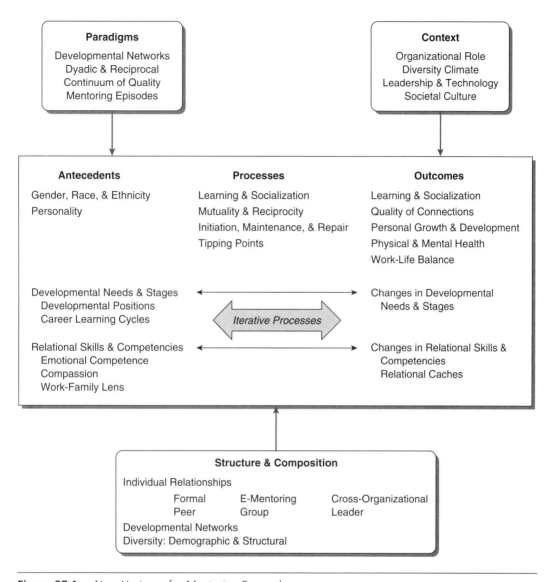

Figure 27.1   New Horizons for Mentoring Research

mentoring complement one another within the context of developmental networks. These hybrid forms of mentoring include peer mentoring, group mentoring, cross-organizational mentoring, diversified mentoring, cross-cultural mentoring, and e-mentoring. Second, in addition to acquiring a better understanding of dyadic and group mentoring relationships, there is much to learn about the structure, texture, and potential outcomes of developmental networks for individuals at successive life and career stages. Whether the focus is on a relationship or on a developmental network, we are now in a position to learn how individual and contextual factors combine to shape the dynamics, processes, and outcomes of developmental networks and relationships. Third, from a practical perspective, we need to understand how developmental networks and relational learning can enhance organizational performance and development, as well as capitalize on the inevitable impact of rapidly changing technology, diverse workforces, and globalization.

Recommendations for Next Steps

Our progress on each of these three fronts hinges on utilizing research approaches and methodologies that allow us to address some of the critical issues and questions that emerged in this volume. We offer four key recommendations here. First, in recognition of the dyadic nature of the relationship, many of our authors have called for a deeper examination of both parties' experiences, behaviors, and outcomes (see Allen, Chapter 5; Fletcher & Ragins, Chapter 15; Giscombe, Chapter 22; McManus & Russell, Chapter 11). Whereas protégés were considered the primary beneficiary of the relationship in the first two decades of mentoring research, we now understand that this is only one part of the story. From a methodological perspective, mentoring researchers need to expand their methods to include both mentors and protégés who are in dyadic, peer, group, or e-mentoring relationships. This approach would also allow us to assess the behaviors and functions provided by protégés, an area we know little about. In essence, a dyadic, multifaceted approach could offer a more complete picture of the landscape of mentoring.

Second, the new outcomes and processes revealed in this volume call for theoretically driven research that employs qualitative and observational research methods. As discussed earlier, we now recognize that traditional measures capture a limited snapshot of the true meaning of mentoring. It is clear that we need to extend our measures of processes and outcomes to include variables such as personal learning, relational competence, growth, and development. Some of these variables are very difficult to measure, and traditional quantitative measures (e.g., promotion rates, salary, performance ratings) will not suffice. Qualitative and observational methods are critical tools for uncovering the rich array of processes and outcomes of mentoring relationships.

Third, for both conceptual and methodological reasons, our field needs more longitudinal research. Many of our authors have called for an examination of how relationships and networks change over time. This call recognizes that individuals' needs change as their career cycles begin and end (Hall & Chandler, Chapter 19) and as they transition to new developmental stages and positions (McGowen, Stone, & Kegan, Chapter 16). Our authors also point out that relationships change as they evolve through various states of development and connection (Eby, Chapter 13; Fletcher & Ragins, Chapter 15; Kram, 1985). Relationships may also transition across states of quality (see Ragins & Verbos, 2007). Finally, changes in individuals and relationships occur within the context of constant changes in organizations, technology and work design (see Cherniss, Chapter 17; Clutterbuck, Chapter 26; Ensher & Murphy, Chapter 12; P-Sontag, Vappie, & Wanberg, Chapter 24).

In essence, longitudinal research helps capture the effects of these contextual changes on the unfolding and dynamic processes of mentoring relationships. These designs not only help us discover the true dynamics of mentoring relationships but also, as pointed out by Tom Dougherty and George Dreher (Chapter 3), help us address specific threats to internal validity that have historically plagued mentoring research. In particular, longitudinal designs can help clarify directionality and causal relationships. This is particularly important given the fact that many of the factors identified in this volume may serve as both antecedents and consequences of mentoring relationships (e.g., developmental position, emotional competence, compassion, career cycles). As pointed out by Dougherty and Dreher, rigorous longitudinal designs should include key control variables and incorporate control groups when assessing outcomes of formal mentoring relationships.

Finally, mentoring scholars need to systematically examine the range of developmental relationships that occur within and outside organizations. These relationships take various forms (supervisory, peer, group, network) and structures (formal, informal, electronic). The authors in this volume have identified a number of factors that may affect mentoring relationships. For example, we are urged to examine how gender (McKeen & Bujaki, Chapter 8; Giscombe, Chapter 22), race (Blake-Beard, Murrell, & Thomas, Chapter 9), personality (Turban & Lee, Chapter 2), developmental position (McGowen, Stone, & Kegan, Chapter 16), career stage (Hall & Chandler, Chapter 19), emotional intelligence (Cherniss, Chapter 17), cultural context (Clutterbuck, Chapter 26), and work-family lens (Greenhaus & Singh, Chapter 21) influence mentoring relationships. This is a mighty task, made even larger by the idea that these factors may lead to different outcomes depending on the form and structure of the mentoring relationship. This task will keep mentoring scholars busy for many years to come, as we explore how the type and structure of the relationship interact with antecedents and processes to influence an array of proximal and distal outcomes.

Methodological and Conceptual Tools for the Garden of Mentoring

Fortunately, the methodological advances of the past 25 years have given us tools that will help us systematically study the complexity of factors that shape relational processes and outcomes discussed in this volume. For example, Higgins, Chandler, and Kram (Chapter 14) remind us of the methodological advances in the study of social networks (see Granovetter, 1982; Higgins & Kram, 2001) and how these can be applied toward advancing our understanding of mentoring and developmental networks. Godshalk and Sosik (Chapter 6) draw on the leadership literature to help us untangle methodological issues in defining leaders and mentors, a dilemma that is clarified by McCauley and Guthrie Chapter 23, on leadership as a process nested within the context of learning and mentoring. Given the call for research that acknowledges the multiple forces that shape relational learning and the need to consider varied perspectives and voices, future studies will require researchers with deep expertise in theoretical perspectives and methodologies, as well as a firm grasp of the issues facing practitioners.

This volume also offers a number of conceptual tools that can be used to design the landscape of mentoring. For example, our authors have illuminated the relationship dynamics and processes that, up to very recently, have remained a "black box" in our field. We now have the tool of "mentoring episodes," which offers a snapshot into the types of relational processes and dynamics present in positive and negative mentoring interactions (Fletcher & Ragins, Chapter 15). Fletcher and Ragins point out that an increase in positive mentoring episodes may create a "tipping point" in which members come to view their work relationship as a high-quality mentoring relationship. Eby (Chapter 13) applied this tool in her discussion of problematic mentoring relationships and illustrated how mentoring episodes help distinguish high-quality from marginal or dysfunctional relationships.

Our authors offer a number of other conceptual tools that will help us capture the complex dynamics and processes in mentoring relationships. For example, Cherniss (Chapter 17) and Boyatzis (Chapter 18) encourage us to consider the "tipping points" in relationships—when sufficient compassion, empathy, self-awareness, and social skills are manifested to foster dynamics that enable personal learning and development. And, in her chapter on mentoring enactment theory, Kalbfleisch (Chapter 20) offers an examination of communication patterns that signal relationship initiation, maintenance, or repair. Higgins, Chandler and Kram (Chapter 14) offer the idea of "developmental initiation," which is defined as behaviors that set developmental relationships in motion. Their chapter suggests that the structure of developmental networks is in part determined by the focal person's use of development-seeking behaviors. Combined, these conceptual tools offer a behavioral focus that can be used to examine how episodes involving specific communication patterns and behaviors combine to create relationships reflecting various degrees of quality and effectiveness.

Moving Our Vision of the New Landscape Forward

Our vision of the landscape of mentoring in the 21st century includes a world of work in which mentoring is readily available to individuals who seek to learn new skills, gain new self-knowledge, build their performance and career capacities, and establish ongoing personal growth throughout their life courses. In addition, our vision is aimed at promoting high-quality mentoring—in all of its hybrid forms—so that individuals from all backgrounds can create developmental relationships and networks that serve their unique career and developmental needs. Finally, we anticipate that organizations that use mentoring to foster relational learning—at and across all levels and boundaries—will achieve enhanced performance and effectiveness, as well as the crucial ability to adapt to a persistently rapid pace of change.

The research and practice compiled in this volume identify the next steps toward achieving this vision. We now have the tools to better understand the causes of dysfunctional mentoring as well as the conditions that foster high-quality mentoring relationships. In addition, we now realize the importance of acknowledging that mentoring involves a range of developmental relationships—including hierarchical, peer dyadic, and group forms—and that these relationships combine to form an individual's developmental network. We now recognize that each developmental network is unique, given the surrounding context, the network's members, and the actions taken by its members. Each network may therefore offer different types of relational learning processes, behaviors, and outcomes. One of our next steps must be to further clarify the conditions that lead to relationships and networks that best serve the unique developmental needs of their members. This may include research and innovative practices that explore how emotional competence, relational skills, career stage, developmental position, work-family lens, gender, race, and cultural factors work individually and collectively to influence the quality, processes, and outcomes of developmental networks and relationships. Finally, as we implement and systematically assess the impact of innovative practices, we will be better positioned to accurately assess a wider range of outcomes for both individuals and organizations.

This new agenda is ambitious. In the end, we are suggesting that as scholars and practitioners, we must enact what we have highlighted in this book: the development of high-quality relationships that lead to personal learning, skill development, enhanced performance, and a rich array of other outcomes critical for the continued growth of individuals, groups, and organizations. By building high-quality partnerships between researchers and practitioners, we not only capitalize on our diverse expertise and experiences but also increase the possibility of realizing our collective aim of understanding and leveraging the potential of mentoring in many different contexts. Together, we can cultivate a garden rich with possibilities for future research and practice. The new landscape of mentoring is ready to be tended.

References

Adler, N. J. (1997). *International dimensions of organizational behavior* (3rd ed.). Cincinnati, OH: South-Western College.

Allen, T. D., Eby, L. T., & Lentz, E. (2006). Mentorship behaviors and mentorship quality associated with formal mentoring programs: Closing the gap between research and practice. *Journal of Applied Psychology, 91,* 567–578.

Allen, T. D., Eby, L. T., Poteet, M. L., Lentz, E., & Lima, L. (2004). Career benefits associated with mentoring for protégés: A meta analysis. *Journal of Applied Psychology, 89,* 127–136.

Arthur, M. B., & Rousseau, D. M. (1996). The *boundaryless career: A new employment principle for a new organizational era.* New York: Oxford University Press.

Blake-Beard, S. (1999). The costs of living as an outsider within: An analysis of the mentoring relationships and career success of Black and White women in the corporate sector. *Journal of Career Development, 26,* 21–36.

Boyatzis, R. (2006). An overview of intentional change from a complexity perspective. *Journal of Management Development, 25,* 607–623. Bradford: Emerald Group.

Boyatzis, R. E., Smith, M., & Blaize, N. (2006). Developing sustainable leadership through coaching and compassion. *Academy of Management Learning and Education, 5,* 8–24.

Cameron, K. S., Dutton, J. E., & Quinn, R. E. (2003). *Positive organizational scholarship: Foundations of a new discipline.* San Francisco: Berrett-Koehler.

Chandler, D. E. (2006). *Relational savvy: Why some protégés are more adept with developmental relationships.* Unpublished doctoral dissertation, Boston University.

Chandler, D. E., & Kram, K. E. (2005). Applying an adult development perspective to developmental networks. *Career Development International, 10,* 548–566.

Chao, G. T., O'Leary-Kelly, A.M., Wolf, S., Klein, H. J., & Gardner, P. D. (1994). Organizational socialization: Its content and consequences. *Journal of Applied Psychology, 79,* 730–743.

Chao, G. T., Walz, P. M., & Gardner, P. D. (1992). Formal and informal mentorships: A comparison on mentoring functions and contrast with nonmentored counterparts. *Personnel Psychology, 45,* 619–636.

Collins, N. W. (1983). *Professional women and their mentors: A practical guide to mentoring for the woman who wants to get ahead.* Englewood Cliffs, NJ: Prentice Hall.

Cooper, C. L., & Payne, R. (Eds.). (1988). *Causes, coping, and consequences of stress at work.* Chichester, NY: John Wiley & Sons.

Davidson, M. N., & James, E. H. (2007). The engines of positive relationships across difference: Conflict and learning. In J. E. Dutton & B. R. Ragins (Eds.), *Exploring positive relationships at work: Building a theoretical and research foundation* (pp. 137–158). Mahwah, NJ: Lawrence Erlbaum.

Dreher, G. F., & Cox, T. H. (1996). Race, gender, and opportunity: A study of compensation attainment and the establishment of mentoring relationships. *Journal of Applied Psychology, 8,* 297–308.

Dutton, J. E., & Heaphy, E. D. (2003). The power of high-quality connections. In K. S. Cameron, J. E. Dutton, & R. E. Quinn (Eds.), *Positive organizational scholarship: Foundations of a new discipline* (pp. 263–278). San Francisco: Berrett-Koehler.

Dutton, J. E., & Ragins, B. R. (Eds.). (2007). *Exploring positive relationships at work: Building a theoretical and research foundation.* Mahwah, NJ: Lawrence Erlbaum.

Dutton, J. E., Worline, M. C., Frost, P. J., & Lilius, J. (2006). Explaining compassion organizing. *Administrative Science Quarterly, 51,* 59–96.

Eby, L. T., Butts, M. M., Lockwood, A., & Simon, S. A. (2004). Protégés' negative mentoring experiences: Construct development and nomological validation. *Personnel Psychology, 57,* 411–447.

Ensher, E., Heun, C., & Blanchard, A. (2003). Online mentoring and computer-mediated communication: New directions in research. *Journal of Vocational Behavior, 63,* 264–288.

Feldman, M. S., & Khademian, A. M. (2003). Empowerment and cascading vitality. In K. S. Cameron, J. E. Dutton, & R. E. Quinn (Eds.), *Positive organizational scholarship: Foundations of a new discipline* (pp. 343–358). San Francisco: Berrett-Koehler.

Fletcher, J. K. (1996). A relational approach to the protean worker. In D. T. Hall & Associates (Eds.), *The career is dead—Long live the career: A relational approach to careers* (pp. 105–131). San Francisco: Jossey-Bass.

Fletcher, J. K. (1998). Relational practice: A feminist reconstruction of work. *Journal of Management Inquiry, 7*(2), 163–187.

Fletcher, J. K. (1999). *Disappearing acts: Gender, power, and relational practice at work.* Cambridge: MIT Press.

Fredrickson, B. L., & Losada, M. F. (2005). Positive affect and the complex dynamics of human flourishing. *American Psychologist, 60,* 678–686.

Friedman, S. D., & Greenhaus, J. H. (2000). *Work and family—Allies or enemies? What happens when business professionals confront life choices.* New York: Oxford University Press.

Godshalk, V. M., & Sosik, J. J. (2000). Does mentor-protégé agreement on mentor leadership behavior influence the quality of a mentoring relationship? *Group & Organization Management, 25,* 291–317.

Goleman, D. (1995). *Emotional intelligence: Why it can matter more than IQ.* New York: Bantam Books.

Granovetter, M. S. (1982). The strength of weak ties: A network theory revisited. In P. V. Marsden & N. Lin (Eds.), *Social structure and network analysis* (pp. 105–130). Beverly Hills, CA: Sage.

Greenhaus, J. H., & Powell, G. N. (2006). When work and family are allies: A theory of work-family enrichment. *Academy of Management Review, 31,* 72–92.

Hall, D. T. (2002). *Careers in and out of organizations.* Thousand Oaks, CA: Sage.

Hall, D. T., & Associates. (Eds.). (1996). *The career is dead—Long live the career: A relational approach to careers.* San Francisco: Jossey-Bass.

Hamilton, B., & Scandura, T. (2003). E-Mentoring: Implications for organizational learning and development in a wired world. *Organizational Dynamics, 31,* 388–402.

Heaphy, E. (2007). Bodily insights: Three lenses on positive organizational relationships. In J. E. Dutton & B. R. Ragins (Eds.), *Exploring positive relationships at work: Building a theoretical and research foundation* (pp. 47–71). Mahwah, NJ: Lawrence Erlbaum.

Higgins, M. (2007). A contingency perspective on developmental networks. In J. E. Dutton & B. R. Ragins (Eds.), *Exploring positive relationships at work: Building a theoretical and research foundation* (pp. 207–224). Mahwah: NJ: Lawrence Erlbaum.

Higgins, M. C., & Kram, K. E. (2001). Reconceptualizing mentoring at work: A developmental network perspective. *Academy of Management Review, 26,* 264–288.

Higgins, M. C., & Thomas, D. A. (2001). Constellations and careers: Toward understanding the effects of multiple developmental relationships. *Journal of Organizational Behavior, 22,* 223–247.

Hofstede, G. (2003). *Cultures and organizations: Software of the mind.* London: Profile.

Ibarra, H. (1993). Personal networks of women and minorities in management: A conceptual framework. *Academy of Management Review, 18,* 56–87.

Jordan, J. (1986). *The meaning of mutuality* (Working Paper #23). Wellesley, MA: Wellesley Centers for Women, Wellesley College.

Jordan, J. V., Kaplan, A. G., Miller, J. B., Stiver, I. P., & Surrey, J. L. (1991). *Women's growth in connection: Writings from the Stone Center.* New York: Guilford Press.

Kahn, W. A. (2007). Meaningful connections: Positive relationships and attachments at work. In J. E. Dutton & B. R. Ragins (Eds.), *Exploring positive relationships at work: Building a theoretical and research foundation* (pp. 189–206). Mahwah, NJ: Lawrence Erlbaum.

Kegan, R. (1991). *In over our heads: The mental demands of modern life.* Cambridge, MA: Harvard University Press.

Kegan, R. (1982). *The evolving self: Problem and process in human development.* Cambridge, MA: Harvard University Press.

Koberg, C. S., Boss, R. W., & Goodman, E. (1998). Factors and outcomes associated with mentoring among health-care professionals. *Journal of Vocational Behavior, 53,* 58–72.

Kouzes, J., & Posner, B. (2003). *The leadership challenge.* San Francisco: Jossey-Bass.

Kram, K. (1985). *Mentoring at work: Developmental relationships in organizational life.* Glenview, IL: Scott, Foresman.

Kram, K. (1988). *Mentoring at work: Developmental relationships in organizational life* (2nd ed.). Lanham, MD: University Press of America.

Kram, K. (1996). A relational approach to career development. In D. T. Hall & Associates (Eds.), *The career is dead—Long live the career: A relational approach to careers* (pp. 132–157). San Francisco: Jossey-Bass.

Kram, K. E., & Hall, D. T. (1996). Mentoring in a context of diversity and turbulence. In E. E. Kossek & S. A. Lobel (Eds.), *Managing diversity: Human resource strategies for transforming the workplace* (pp. 108–136). Oxford, UK: Blackwell.

Kramer, R. M. (1999). Trust and distrust in organizations: Emerging perspectives, enduring questions. *Annual Review of Psychology, 50,* 569–598.

Lankau, M. J., & Scandura, T. A. (2002). An investigation of personal learning in mentoring relationships: Content, antecedents, and consequences. *Academy of Management Journal, 45,* 779–790.

Lopez, S. J., & Snyder, C. R. (Eds.). (2002). *Handbook of positive psychology.* New York: Oxford University Press.

Luthans, F. (2002). The need for and meaning of positive organizational behavior. *Journal of Organizational Behavior, 23,* 695–706.

Luthans, F., & Youssef, C. M. (2004). Human, social, and now positive psychological capital management: Investing in people for competitive advantage. *Organizational Dynamics, 33*(2), 143–160.

Luthans, F., Youssef, C. M., & Avolio, B. J. (2007). *Psychological capital: Developing the human competitive edge.* New York: Oxford.

Mezias, J. M., & Scandura, T. A. (2005). A needs-driven approach to expatriate adjustment and career development: A multiple mentoring perspective. *Journal of International Business Studies, 36,* 519–538.

Miller, J. B. (1976). *Toward a new psychology of women.* Boston: Beacon Press.

Miller, J. B., & Stiver, I. P. (1997). *The healing connection: How women form relationships in therapy and in life.* Boston: Beacon Press.

Molloy, J. C. (2005). Development networks: Literature review and future research. *Career Development International, 10,* 536–547.

Noe, R. A., Greenberger, D. B., & Wang, S. (2002). Mentoring: What we know and where we might go. *Research in Personnel and Human Resources Management, 21,* 129–173.

Parasuraman, S., & Greenhaus, J. H. (1997). *Integrating work and family: Challenges and choices for a changing world.* Westport, CT: Quorum.

Pratt, M. G., & Ashforth, B. E. (2003). Fostering meaningfulness in working and at work. In K. S. Cameron, J. E. Dutton, & R. E. Quinn (Eds.), *Positive organizational scholarship: Foundations of a new discipline* (pp. 309–327). San Francisco: Berrett-Koehler.

Pratt, M. G., & Dirks, K. T. (2007). Rebuilding trust and restoring positive relationships: A commitment-based view of trust. In J. E. Dutton & B. R. Ragins (Eds.), *Exploring positive relationships at work: Building a theoretical and research foundation* (pp. 117–136). Mahwah, NJ: Lawrence Erlbaum.

Ragins, B. R. (1989). Barriers to mentoring: The female manager's dilemma. *Human Relations, 42,* 1–22.

Ragins, B. R. (1997). Diversified mentoring relationships in organizations: A power perspective. *Academy of Management Review, 22,* 482–521.

Ragins, B. R. (1999a). Gender and mentoring relationships: A review and research agenda for the next decade. In G. Powell (Ed.), *Handbook of gender and work* (pp. 347–370). Thousand Oaks, CA: Sage.

Ragins, B. R. (1999b). Where do we go from here and how do we get there? Methodological issues in conducting research on diversity and mentoring relationships. In A. Murrell, F. J. Crosby, & R. Ely (Eds.), *Mentoring dilemmas: Developmental relationships within multicultural organizations* (pp. 227–247). Mahwah, NJ: Lawrence Erlbaum.

Ragins, B. R. (2002). Understanding diversified mentoring relationships: Definitions, challenges and strategies. In D. Clutterbuck & B. R. Ragins, *Mentoring and diversity: An international perspective* (pp. 23–53). Oxford, UK: Butterworth-Heinemann.

Ragins, B. R. (2005). *Towards a theory of relational mentoring.* Unpublished manuscript.

Ragins, B. R. (2007). Diversity and workplace mentoring: A review and positive social capital approach. In T. D. Allen & L. T. Eby (Eds.), *Blackwell handbook of mentoring: A multiple perspectives approach* (pp. 281–300). Oxford, UK: Blackwell.

Ragins, B. R., & Cotton, J. L. (1991). Easier said than done: Gender differences in perceived barriers to gaining a mentor. *Academy of Management Journal, 34,* 939–951.

Ragins, B. R., & Cotton, J. L. (1999). Mentor functions and outcomes: A comparison of men and women in formal and informal mentoring relationships. *Journal of Applied Psychology, 84,* 529–550.

Ragins, B. R., Cotton, J. L., & Miller, J. S. (2000). Marginal mentoring: The effects of type of mentor, quality of relationship, and program design on work and career attitudes. *Academy of Management Journal, 43,* 1177–1194.

Ragins, B. R., & Dutton, J. E. (2007). Positive relationships at work: An introduction and invitation. In J. E. Dutton & B. R. Ragins (Eds.), *Exploring positive relationships at work: Building a theoretical and research foundation* (pp. 3–25). Mahwah, NJ: Lawrence Erlbaum.

Ragins, B. R., & McFarlin, D. (1990). Perception of mentor roles in cross-gender mentoring relationships. *Journal of Vocational Behavior, 37,* 321–339.

Ragins, B. R., & Verbos, A. K. (2007). Positive relationships in action: Relational mentoring and mentoring schemas in the workplace. In J. E. Dutton & B. R. Ragins (Eds.), *Exploring positive relationships at work: Building a theoretical and research foundation* (pp. 91–116). Mahwah, NJ: Lawrence Erlbaum.

Roberts, L. M. (2006). Shifting the lens on organizational life: The added value of positive scholarship. *Academy of Management Review, 31,* 292–305.

Roberts, L. M. (2007). From proving to becoming: How positive relationships create a context for self-discovery and self-actualization. In J. E. Dutton & B. R. Ragins (Eds.), *Exploring positive relationships at work: Building a theoretical and research foundation* (pp. 29–46). Mahwah, NJ: Lawrence Erlbaum.

Roberts, L. M., Dutton, J. E., Spreitzer, G. M., Heaphy, E. D., & Quinn, R. E. (2005). Composing the reflected best self-portrait: Building pathways for becoming extraordinary in work organizations. *Academy of Management Review, 30,* 712–736.

Scandura, T. A. (1998). Dysfunctional mentoring relationships and outcomes. *Journal of Management, 24,* 449–467.

Seeman, T. (2001). How do others get under our skin? Social relationships and health. In C. D. Ryff & B. Singer (Eds.), *Emotion, social relationships, and health* (pp. 189–210). New York: Oxford University.

Sosik, J. J., & Godshalk, V. M. (2000). The role of gender in mentoring: Implications for diversified and homogeneous mentoring relationships. *Journal of Vocational Behavior, 57,* 102–122.

Spreitzer, G., Sutcliffe, K., Dutton, J., Soneshein, S., & Grant, A. M. (2005). A socially embedded model of thriving at work. *Organization Science, 16,* 537–549.

Surrey, J. (1985). *The self in relation* (Working Paper #13). Wellesley Centers for Women, Wellesley College, Wellesley, MA.

Tharenou, P. (2005). Does mentor support increase women's career advancement more than men's? The differential effects of career and psychosocial support. *Australian Journal of Management, 30,* 77–110.

Thomas, D. A. (1990). The impact of race on managers' experiences of developmental relationships (mentoring and sponsorship): An intra-organizational study. *Journal of Organizational Behavior, 11,* 479–492.

Thomas, D. A. (1993). Racial dynamics in cross-race developmental relationships. *Administrative Science Quarterly, 38,* 169–194.

Thomas, D. A., & Higgins, M. C. (1996). Mentoring and the boundaryless career: Lessons from the minority experience. In M. B. Arthur & D. M. Rousseau (Eds.), *The boundaryless career: A new employment principle for a new organizational era* (pp. 268–281). New York: Oxford University Press.

Ting, S., & Scisco, P. (Eds.). (2006). *The CCL handbook of coaching: A guide for the leader coach.* San Francisco: Jossey-Bass.

Trompenaars, F., & Woolliams, P. (2004). *Business across cultures.* Chichester, UK: John Wiley & Sons.

Underhill, C. M. (2006). The effectiveness of mentoring programs in corporate settings: A meta-analytical review of the literature. *Journal of Vocational Behavior, 68,* 292–307.

Viator, R. E. (2001). An examination of African Americans' access to public accounting mentors: Perceived barriers and intentions to leave. *Accounting, Organizations, and Society, 26,* 541–561.

Wanberg, C. R., Welsh, E. T., & Hezlett, S. A. (2003). Mentoring research: A review and dynamic process model. *Research in Personnel and Human Resource Management, 22,* 39–124.

Worline, M. C., & Quinn, R. W. (2003). Courageous principled action. In K. S. Cameron, J. E. Dutton, & R. E. Quinn (Eds.), *Positive organizational scholarship: Foundations of a new discipline* (pp. 138–158). San Francisco: Berrett-Koehler.

Name Index

Subject Index

About the Editors

Belle Rose Ragins is a Professor of Management at the University of Wisconsin–Milwaukee. Her research focuses on mentoring and diversity in organizations and has been published in such journals as *Academy of Management Journal, Academy of Management Review, Academy of Management Executive, Journal of Applied Psychology, Journal of Management,* and *Psychological Bulletin.* She is coeditor of *Exploring Positive Relationships at Work: Building a Theoretical and Research Foundation* (with Jane Dutton) and coauthor of *Mentoring and Diversity: An International Perspective* (with David Clutterbuck). She has served on the editorial review boards of the *Academy of Management Journal, Personnel Psychology, Journal of Vocational Behavior, Group & Organizational Management,* and *Journal of Applied Psychology.* Dr. Ragins has received a number of national awards for her research, including the Academy of Management Mentoring Legacy Award, the Sage Life-time Achievement Award for Scholarly Contributions to Management, the American Society for Training and Development Research Award, and the American Psychological Association Placek Award. She was awarded the first visiting research fellowship at Catalyst and was research advisor for 9-to-5, the National Association of Working Women. She was also a founder and the research director of the UWM Institute for Diversity Education and Leadership (IDEAL). Dr. Ragins is a fellow of the Society for Industrial-Organizational Psychology, the Society for the Psychology of Women, the American Psychological Society, and the American Psychological Association. Her joys include morning runs along Lake Michigan with her adopted dogs, Wally and Greta, and exploring the American wilderness with her husband Erik.

Kathy E. Kram is Professor of Organizational Behavior at the Boston University School of Management and Everett W. Lord Distinguished Faculty Scholar. Her primary interests are in adult development, mentoring, developmental networks, leadership development, and relational learning in organizations. In addition to her book *Mentoring at Work,* she has published in such journals as *Academy of Management Journal, Academy of Management Review, Harvard Business Review, Leaders in Action, Qualitative Sociology, Journal of Management Inquiry,* and *Organizational Dynamics.* Her research, consulting, and writing are aimed at understanding the role of a variety of developmental relationships in enhancing leadership effectiveness and individual development throughout the life course. During 2000–2001, she served as the H. Smith Richardson Jr. Visiting Research Scholar at the Center for Creative Leadership (CCL). She is a founding member of the Center for Research on Emotional Intelligence in Organizations (CREIO) and received the first Academy of Management Mentoring Legacy Award. She is currently serving on the Board of Governors at the Center for Creative Leadership and on the editorial boards of *Journal of Applied Behavioral Science* and *Academy of Management Learning and Education*. Professor Kram teaches undergraduate, MBA, and executive MBA courses in global management, leadership, and team dynamics. She consults with private and public sector organizations on a variety of talent development concerns. She enjoys traveling, hiking, and listening to music with her husband, Peter, and her son, Jason.

About the Contributors

Tammy D. Allen is Professor of Psychology at the University of South Florida. She has published extensively and has presented internationally on the topic of mentoring. Her mentoring research has received national awards, such as the 2006 ASTD Research Award, and has been funded by agencies such as the Society for Human Resources Foundation. She is coeditor of *The Blackwell Handbook of Mentoring: A Multiple Perspectives Approach*. Dr. Allen's expertise includes consulting with organizations with regard to the design, delivery, and evaluation of formal mentoring programs. She is associate editor for *Journal of Occupational Health Psychology* and serves on the editorial boards of *Journal of Applied Psychology, Personnel Psychology,* and *Journal of Vocational Behavior.* She is an active member of several professional associations and was the 2007 conference program chair for the Society of Industrial and Organizational Psychology.

S. Gayle Baugh is Associate Professor of Management at the University of West Florida. Her primary areas of research are career development, especially mentoring, leadership, and gender and diversity in organizations. She has published over a dozen articles in journals such as *Career Development International, Group and Organization Management,* the *Journal of Applied Social Psychology,* and the *Journal of Vocational Behavior,* and has made presentations regularly at the Academy of Management, the Southern Management Association, and the Southwest Academy of Management. She is a past division chair of the Gender and Diversity in Organizations Division of the Academy of Management and a past president of the Southwest Academy of Management. She serves on the editorial board for *Career Development International, Journal of Business and Psychology, Journal of Management,* and *Journal of Managerial Psychology.*

Stacy D. Blake-Beard is Associate Professor of Management at the School of Management at Simmons College. She is also research faculty at the Center for Gender in Organizations. Her primary research areas are mentoring relationships at the intersection of gender and race and formalized mentoring programs. She has published in a number of journals, including *Academy of Management Executive, Journal of Management Development, Psychology of Women Quarterly,* and *Journal of Career Development.* She is on the Executive Committee of the Academy of Management and Gender and Diversity in Organizations Division and is past chair of the Academy of

Management's Mentoring Committee. She is on the editorial board of the *Business Journal of Hispanic Research*. Prior to joining Simmons, she was an assistant professor at the Harvard Graduate School of Education. She has also worked in sales and marketing at Procter & Gamble and in corporate human resources at Xerox.

Richard E. Boyatzis is Professor in the Departments of Organizational Behavior and Psychology at Case Western Reserve University and in Human Resources at ESADE. Before becoming a professor, he was CEO of McBer and Company for 11 years and COO of Yankelovich, Skelly, & White for 2 years. He is the author of more than 100 articles on behavior change, leadership, competencies, and emotional intelligence. His books include *The Competent Manager, Transforming Qualitative Information* (in 2 languages), and *Innovations in Professional Education* (with Scott Cowen and David Kolb), and he is coauthor of the international best seller *Primal Leadership*, with Daniel Goleman and Annie McKee, published in 28 languages and, most recently, *Resonant Leadership: Renewing Yourself and Connecting With Others Through Mindfulness, Hope, and Compassion* (with Annie McKee, published in 16 languages).

Merridee L. Bujaki is Chair of and an Associate Professor in the Accounting, Finance, and Management Information Systems section at the School of Management, University of Ottawa. Her primary research areas are women in management, voluntary disclosures in corporate annual reports, and accounting history. She has published articles in *Women in Management Review, Applied Psychology: An International Review, Journal of Accounting Literature,* and *Accounting Perspectives,* as well as several professional accounting magazines. Previously, she worked as a chartered accountant.

Dawn E. Chandler is an Assistant Professor of Management at California Polytechnic State University. Her research interests include mentoring, developmental networks, and, more generally, careers. Of particular interest is "relational savvy," protégé adeptness with developmental relationships, which she examined in her dissertation study. She has coauthored articles in *Journal of Organizational Behavior, Action Research Journal,* and *Career Development International*. Prior to joining academia, Dawn worked for 4 years as a financial recruiter in Boston and San Jose, California.

Georgia T. Chao is an Associate Professor of Management at the Eli Broad Graduate School of Management at Michigan State University. Her primary research interests lie in the areas of organizational socialization, career development, mentoring, and international organizational behavior. She was recently appointed to an American Psychological Association (APA) Presidential Task Force on mentoring. Her responsibilities included developing a resource guide on mentoring, running a mentoring workshop, and managing a formal mentoring program. She is a fellow of the APA and of the Society for Industrial and Organizational Psychology (SIOP). She serves on four editorial boards and recently served as chair of APA's Committee on International Relations in Psychology. In 1995, she won the Academy of Management's Outstanding Publication Award in Organizational Behavior. She was elected and served on executive committees to the Academy of Management's Career and Human Resources divisions as well as the executive committee of SIOP.

Cary Cherniss is Professor of Applied Psychology at Rutgers University and Director and Cochair of the Consortium for Research on Emotional Intelligence in Organizations. His primary research areas are emotional intelligence, leadership, and planned organizational change. His research has been funded by such resources as the National Institute of Mental Health and the U.S. Office of Population Affairs. He has written six books and more than 60 journal articles and book chapters, including *Promoting Emotional Intelligence in Organizations.* He is a member of the Academy of Management, a fellow of the American Psychological Association, and former president of its division of Community Psychology, and he has consulted for such public and private sector companies as AT&T, American Express, Johnson & Johnson, and Colgate-Palmolive.

David Clutterbuck is visiting professor at Sheffield Hallam University's Coaching and Mentoring Research Unit and at Oxford Brookes University's coaching and mentoring faculty. He cofounded the European Mentoring and Coaching Council, where he chairs the United Kingdom and pan-European research committees. He led the international team, which developed the International Standards for Mentoring Programmes in Employment. He is the author/coauthor of nearly 50 books, including 11 in the field of coaching and mentoring. He is senior partner of Clutterbuck Associates, an international consultancy providing practical support for organizations implementing programs of coaching and/or mentoring. He is currently completing the first longitudinal and cross-sectional study of developmental mentoring, at Kings College London. His research interests focus on the development of good practice in creating and sustaining a coaching and mentoring culture and on the development of corporate governance in the public sector. He is currently compiling an online encyclopedia of coaching and mentoring.

Thomas W. Dougherty is the Hibbs/Brown Chair of Business and Economics, Professor of Management, and doctoral coordinator for management at the University of Missouri–Columbia. His current primary research interests include mentoring, networking, and career success in organizations. He has also published work in other areas, including interviewer decision making, recruitment, role stress, job burnout, and employee turnover. He has taught human resource management to undergraduate and graduate students in several countries, including China, Romania, and Ireland. His book *Human Resource Strategy: A Behavioral Perspective for the General Manager* (with G. F. Dreher) was published by McGraw-Hill/Irwin in 2002.

George F. Dreher is Professor of Business Administration in the Kelley School of Business at Indiana University–Bloomington. He recently was a visiting scholar at Hong Kong University of Science and Technology. His current research addresses the role of race, ethnicity, age, and gender in accounting for selection, promotion, and retention decisions in organizational settings (with a focus on managerial and executive talent pool management). His research has been published in journals such as *Academy of Management Journal, Academy of Management Review, Journal of Applied Psychology, Journal of Organizational Behavior, Personnel Psychology, Human Relations,* and *Journal of Vocational Behavior.* He also has coauthored three books and numerous other papers and book chapters. Currently, he serves as vice president on the board of directors for Options for Better Living (an organization devoted to helping individuals with developmental disabilities live more independent lives).

Lillian T. Eby is Professor of Psychology and Fellow at the Institute for Behavioral Research at the University of Georgia. Her research program focuses on career-related issues, such as workplace mentoring, job-related relocation, career success, the work-family interface, and gender issues in organizations. She has published over 50 research articles and book chapters, and her work appears in such outlets as *Personnel Psychology, Journal of Applied Psychology,* and *Journal of Vocational Behavior.* She is on the editorial boards of *Personnel Psychology, Journal of Vocational Behavior,* and *Group and Organizational Management* and is the current associate editor for *Personnel Psychology* (2007–2010). Lillian is also the principal investigator on a project funded by the National Institute on Drug Abuse, which is examining the relationship between mentoring relationships and employee turnover in substance abuse treatment centers.

Ellen A. Ensher is an Associate Professor of Management at Loyola Marymount University. Dr. Ensher, with coauthor Susan Murphy, wrote *Power Mentoring: How Mentors and Protégés Get the Most Out of Their Relationships* (Jossey-Bass, 2005). Dr. Ensher has published over 40 articles and book chapters and has made over 100 professional presentations. She has published in many academic journals, including the *Academy of Management Executive, Human Resource Development Quarterly, Journal of Career Development, Journal of Vocational Behavior,* and *Organizational Dynamics.* She has also published in practitioner magazines, including *Training and Development, Training, Leadership Excellence,* and *Success Magazine.* She has been quoted on the topic of mentoring in the *New York Times,* in the *Wall Street Journal,* and by the Associated Press. She has appeared as a guest on several radio and TV shows in Chicago, New York, and San Diego.

Ellen A. Fagenson-Eland (deceased) was Professor of Management at George Mason University. She was an internationally recognized scholar in the field of diversity and mentoring. She authored over 50 publications in the leading journals of our field and edited the groundbreaking book *Women in Management: Trends, Issues, and Challenges in Managerial Diversity.* She served on many editorial boards, including *Academy of Management Journal* and *Academy of Management Executive,* where she also served as an associate editor. She was a past division chair for the Academy of Management Gender and Diversity in Organizations Division and served on the board of the Academy's Careers Division and Mentoring Committee. In recognition of her outstanding contributions to our profession, Dr Fagenson-Eland received numerous awards, including the Academy of Management Mentoring Best Practice Award, the GDO Janet Chusmir/Sage Award for Service, the *Academy of Management Journal* Outstanding Service Award, and the Careers Division Best Paper Award. The list of her many accomplishments is too long to chronicle, and we will miss her most for her passion for justice, her wisdom, and her outstanding sense of humor.

Joyce K. Fletcher is Distinguished Research Scholar, at the Center for Gender in Organizations at the Simmons School of Management and a Senior Research Scholar at the Jean Baker Miller Training Institute, Wellesley College. She uses feminist theory to study a wide range of workplace issues and is a frequent speaker at national and international conferences on the topic of women, power, and leadership. She is the coauthor of a widely read *Harvard Business Review* article, "A Modest Manifesto for Shattering the Glass Ceiling" and author of *Disappearing Acts: Gender, Power, and Relational Practice at Work* (MIT Press), a book that explores the subtle dynamics that often disappear women's leadership behavior at work.

Katherine Giscombe is Senior Director in Research and head of the Women of Color Practice Area at Catalyst. Previously, she supported marketing and new product development in a variety of *Fortune* 500 companies. She is a member of the Academy of Management and has published on career development, mentoring, the business case for diversity, and glass- and concrete-ceiling issues. Other research interests include economic mobility issues among middle-class African Americans. As a Catalyst media spokesperson, she has been interviewed by National Public Radio, CNN-FN, CBS Radio, *Boston Globe, San Francisco Chronicle,* and *Essence,* among others. Honors include selection in 2005 by the *Network Journal* as one of "25 Influential Black Women in Business." She is on advisory boards for Black Enterprise Women of Power Summit, Working Mother Media Best Companies for Women of Color, Women's Inter-Cultural Exchange, and Girl Scouts Girls and Leadership Study.

Veronica M. (Ronnie) Godshalk is an Associate Professor in the Department of Management and Organization at the Pennsylvania State University School of Graduate Professional Studies. Dr. Godshalk teaches courses in organizational behavior, corporate innovative strategies, career management, and communication skills. She received the 2000 Arthur L. Glenn Award for Faculty Teaching Innovation. Dr. Godshalk's research interests include issues surrounding career management, mentoring, stress, and the intersection of work and nonwork domains. In 2000, she published a book, *Career Management,* with coauthors Jeff Greenhaus and Gerry Callanan, and is currently working on a fourth edition. She is an active member and presenter in professional associations, such as the Academy of Management and the Society for Industrial and Organizational Psychology. Dr. Godshalk had worked in the computer industry in sales and sales management prior to entering academia and has been a consultant for several *Fortune 500* companies.

Jeffrey H. Greenhaus is Professor and William A. Mackie Chair in the Department of Management at Drexel University's LeBow College of Business. His research, which focuses on work-family relationships and career dynamics, has been published in many of the field's leading journals. In addition, Jeff is coauthor of *Career Management* (Thomson Learning), now in its third edition, and *Work and Family—Allies or Enemies* (Oxford); and he is coeditor of *Integrating Work and Family: Challenges and Choices for a Changing World* (Quorum) and the *Encyclopedia of Career Development* (Sage). He serves on the editorial review boards of *Human Relations, Journal of Managerial Issues, Journal of Organizational Behavior,* and *Journal of Vocational Behavior.*

Victoria A. Guthrie is Honorary Senior Fellow at the Center for Creative Leadership and continues to be connected to the center through global adjunct work. She has more than 30 years of international experience in executive development, coaching, and global leadership development and has designed and conducted programs for the center and an array of organizations and clients in North America, Europe, and Asia. She has authored a number of publications relating to her areas of expertise in coaching and feedback; organizational and individual purpose, strategy, and leadership; learning; and understanding trade-offs. She serves on the executive committee for the Rotary Youth Leadership Program at Guilford College as program designer and advisor and on the Morehead Foundation Scholarship Selection Central Committee at the University of North Carolina–Chapel Hill. Previously, she was with Xerox Corporation.

Douglas T. (Tim) Hall is the Morton H. and Charlotte Friedman Professor of Management in the School of Management at Boston University. He has held faculty positions at Yale, York, Michigan State, and Northwestern universities, as well as visiting positions at Columbia, Minnesota, Boston College, and the U.S. Military Academy at West Point. Tim the author of *Careers In and Out of Organizations* (Sage, 2002). He is the coauthor, with Brad Harrington, of *Career Management and Work-Life Integration* (Sage, 2007), *The Career Is Dead—Long Live the Career,* as well as other books and articles on careers and management. He is a recipient of the American Psychological Association's Ghiselli Award for research design, the ASTD's Walter Storey Professional Practice Award, and the Academy of Management's Everett C. Hughes Award for Career Research. He is currently the H. Smith Richardson Jr. Visiting Fellow at the Center for Creative Leadership.

Monica C. Higgins is Associate Professor of Leadership and Organizations at Harvard University's Graduate School of Education. Her primary areas of research are leadership and career development, with a particular focus on the relational context in which development occurs. Professor Higgins's book *Career Imprints: Creating Leaders Across an Industry* (2005) examines the leadership development of executives in the biotechnology industry. In addition, she has a longitudinal project under way on the career choices and developmental networks of the Harvard Business School class of 1996. Her research has appeared in journals such as *Academy of Management Review, Organization Science, Journal of Applied Behavioral Sciences, Strategic Management Journal,* and *Journal of Organizational Behavior.* Prior to her academic career, she worked as a consultant for Bain & Company and for Harbridge House, an international organizational change consulting firm.

Pamela J. Kalbfleisch is Professor and Director of the School of Communication at the University of North Dakota. Her research reflects an active interest in personal relationships and communication. She has published six books and more than 50 articles and book chapters. She serves as the founding editor of *Journal of Native Aging and Health,* a collaboration between the University of North Dakota School of Medicine and Health Sciences, Center for Rural Health, School of Communication, and National Resource Center on Native American Aging.

Robert Kegan is the William and Miriam Meehan Professor of Adult Learning and Professional Development at the Harvard University Graduate School of Education. At Harvard, he is also educational chair of the Institute for Management and Leadership in Education (for leaders in higher education), codirector of the Change Leadership Group (for leaders in K–12 education), and codirector of a joint program between the school of education and the school of medicine for those leading educational reform in the health professions. The recipient of numerous honorary degrees and awards, his 30 years of research and writing on adult development have contributed to the recognition that ongoing psychological development after adolescence is at once possible and necessary to meet the demands of modern life. His seminal books, *The Evolving Self* and *In Over Our Heads,* have been published in several languages throughout the world.

Melenie J. Lankau is Associate Professor of Management in the Terry College of Business at the University of Georgia. Her research interests include mentorship, diversity, and work/family issues in the workplace. She has presented over 30 conference papers at annual meetings for the National Academy of Management, Society for Industrial and Organizational Psychology, Eastern Academy of Management, and Southern Management Association. She has also published 18 articles in leading academic journals such as *Academy of Management Journal, Journal of Management, Leadership Quarterly, Journal of Organizational Behavior,* and *Journal of Vocational Behavior.* One of her articles was recently recognized by the Center for Families at Purdue University and the Center for Work and Family at Boston College for high-quality work-family research. She currently serves on the board of the Southern Management Association and the editorial boards of *Journal of Management* and *Group & Organization Management.*

Felissa K. Lee is Assistant Professor of Management in the College of Business at Marquette University. Her research interests and publications are in the areas of personality and motivation, mentoring relationships, and career self-management. She has published articles in various journals, including *Journal of Applied Psychology, Journal of Vocational Behavior,* and *Harvard Business Review.* She teaches or has taught courses in organizational behavior, human resource management, career planning, and behavioral change.

Cynthia D. McCauley is a senior fellow at the Center for Creative Leadership and its former vice president of leadership development. Her research has focused on how developmental experiences (job assignments, developmental relationships, 360-degree feedback, and formal development programs) contribute to leader development and effectiveness. She is currently exploring leadership as a collective organizational capacity. She has written numerous articles and book chapters for scholars, HR professionals, and practicing managers and has codeveloped several management feedback instruments. Along with Ellen Van Velsor, she is coeditor of *The Center for Creative Leadership Handbook of Leadership Development.* She is an associate editor for *Leadership Quarterly* and for *Human Resource Planning.*

Eileen M. McGowan is the Director of the Field Experience Program, Coordinator of the Spencer Training Grant, Director of Doctoral Student Professional Development, and lecturer on education at the Harvard Graduate School of Education. Her work focuses on the establishment, implementation, maintenance, and evaluation of mentoring programs; her research interests are also centered on formal mentoring relationships, specifically within the higher education and public education sectors. She is a principal at Mentoring Strategies, a private consulting firm that has done extensive work with the Boston public schools, Harvard's Urban Superintendent's Program, New Leaders for New Schools, and Harvard Principals Program. Internationally she has been affiliated with the HERS (Higher Education Resource Services) South Africa Program. Her interest in mentoring can be traced back to her early work in primary special education and mentor teacher training at Lesley University.

Carol McKeen is Professor of Organizational Behavior and Accounting and Director of the Queen's Advanced Accounting Program at the School of Business, Queen's University, Kingston, Ontario, Canada. Her consulting experience has included work with Price Waterhouse, Bank of Montreal, and Corrections Canada, relating to the retention of high-performing women. She has received extensive funding for her research from the Social Sciences and Humanities Research Council of Canada and has published extensively in the areas of women's careers and life satisfaction as well as mentoring. Recent research has focused on cross-cultural comparisons of women's careers in Canada and China. She serves on the editorial board of *Women in Management Review* and on the national board of the Canadian Women's Foundation.

Stacy E. McManus is a management consultant at Monitor Executive Development, a member of Monitor Group. Prior to joining Monitor, she was an assistant professor at the Molson School of Business at Concordia University in Montreal and a visiting fellow at Harvard University, where she also taught courses in management and coauthored several Harvard Business School cases, including the best-selling *Ritz-Carlton Hotel Co.* Her scholarly research includes work on research methods, performance appraisal, and mentoring relationships with publications in *Journal of Vocational Behavior* and *Academy of Management Review.* An active member of the Academy of Management, she is past chair of the academy's mentoring committee and has regularly chaired symposia and presented research on topics including mentoring, leadership, career development, and research methods.

Susan Elaine Murphy is Associate Professor of Psychology at Claremont McKenna College and the Associate Director of the Henry R. Kravis Leadership Institute in Claremont, California, and is also an Adjunct Professor at Claremont Graduate University. She has published over 30 articles and book chapters on leadership, leadership development, and mentoring. Her most recent publication with Dr. Ellen Ensher is the book *Power Mentoring: How Successful Mentors and Protégés Get the Most Out of Their Relationships* (Jossey-Bass, 2005). Her other recent works include two edited books, *The Future of Leadership Development* (with Ron Riggio; Lawrence Erlbaum, 2003) and *Work-Family Balance to Work-Family Interaction: Changing the Metaphor* (with Diane Halpern; Lawrence Erlbaum, 2005). She previously worked for Battelle as a research scientist consulting in the areas of leadership and management education, as well as organizational change for clients in the United States and Japan.

Audrey Murrell is Associate Professor of Business Administration, Psychology, Public, and International Affairs at the University of Pittsburgh's Katz School of Business. She conducts research on the individual and organizational strategies that advance the careers of women in organizations with a special emphasis on topics such as mentoring, breaking the "glass ceiling," workplace diversity, and ending workplace discrimination. This research has been published widely in journals such as the *Academy of Management Journal, Journal of Vocational Behavior, Journal of Personality and Social Psychology, Career Development International, Business & Society,* and *Sex Roles* and in popular media outlets such as the *Wall Street Journal, Atlanta Journal and Constitution, Pittsburgh Business Times, Cleveland Plain Dealer, Black Enterprise,* and *Vida Executive* (in Brazil). Dr. Murrell is the author (along with Crosby and Ely) of the book titled *Mentoring Dilemmas: Developmental Relationships Within Multicultural Organizations,* published by Lawrence Erlbaum.

Regina M. O'Neill is Associate Professor of Management at the Sawyer Business School at Suffolk University. Her primary research areas are mentoring, diversity, leadership, and career development. She has published in a number of journals, including *Academy of Management Journal, Strategic Management Journal, Journal of Management Inquiry, Career Development International, Educational and Psychological Measurement, Journal of Managerial Issues, Journal of Business Ethics,* and *Human Resource Management Journal.* Her consulting experience includes designing and delivering mentoring programs for career development, diversity, and leadership succession planning for a variety of organizations, including financial services companies, nonprofit organizations, educational institutions, and hospitals. Prior to her academic career, she worked as an auditor for a large international firm, and she is a licensed CPA in the Commonwealth of Massachusetts.

Lynn P-Sontag is the President and Chief Executive Officer of MENTTIUM Corporation. She was the lead developer of MENTTIUM's mentoring models and launched the first-ever global cross-company mentoring program. She has spent 15 years consulting with *Fortune* 500 companies on their mentoring and key talent initiatives. Lynn received the *Twin Cities Business Journal*'s prestigious Women Changemakers award in 2004. She currently sits on the Advisory Board of the Human Capital Institute. Prior to MENTTIUM, she spent 15 years at 3M Corporation leading their executive development initiatives.

Joyce E. A. Russell is a Distinguished Tyser Teaching Fellow and a Senior Executive Education Fellow in the Robert H. Smith School of Business at the University of Maryland. Prior to joining UM, she was a tenured full professor in the College of Business Administration at the University of Tennessee. At both institutions, she received numerous teaching and research awards from students and faculty. Dr. Russell has published over 50 articles, books, or book chapters and has presented her research at national and regional conferences. She served as the associate editor for *Journal of Vocational Behavior* and on the editorial boards of *Journal of Applied Psychology, Human Resource Management Review,* and *Performance Improvement Quarterly.* She is an active member of the Academy of Management, American Psychological Association, American Society for Training and Development, Society for Industrial and Organizational Psychology, and the Society for Human Resource Management.

Terri A. Scandura is Professor of Management at the University of Miami. Dr. Scandura's fields of interest include leadership, mentorship, and research methods. She has authored numerous articles, published in *Journal of Applied Psychology, Industrial Relations, Academy of Management Journal, Journal of Management, Journal of International Business Studies, Journal of Organizational Behavior, Leadership Quarterly, Educational and Psychological Measurement, Research in Organizational Behavior, Journal of Vocational Behavior,* and others. She is a member of the American Psychological Association (APA) and the Academy of Management. She is past president of the Southern Management Association and past division chair of the Research Methods Division of the Academy of Management. She is an associate editor of *Journal of Management, Group & Organization Management,* and *Journal of International Business Studies.*

Romila Singh is Assistant Professor of Management at the Sheldon B. Lubar School of Business at the University of Wisconsin–Milwaukee. Her research focuses on understanding the dynamics among different aspects of employees' career development such as work-life balance challenges, mentoring experiences, the effects of diversity on career experiences, and a variety of person-environment fit issues. Her research has or will appear in journals such as *Journal of Applied Psychology, Journal of Management,* and *Journal of Vocational Behavior.* She has also authored and coauthored several refereed book chapters, most notably for the *Encyclopedia of Applied Psychology* and the *Encyclopedia of Career Development.*

John J. Sosik is Professor of Management and Organization and Professor-in-Charge of the Master of Leadership Development program at the Pennsylvania State University, Great Valley School of Graduate Professional Studies, where he has received awards for excellence in research, faculty innovation, and teaching. He has published over 70 academic articles, book chapters, and proceedings and delivered about 60 academic conference presentations since 1995; and he has conducted training and organizational development programs for profit and nonprofit organizations. He is associate editor of *Group & Organization Management* and also serves on the editorial board of *Leadership Quarterly.*

Eric M. Stone is a 2007 MBA candidate in the Wharton School's Health Care Management Program at the University of Pennsylvania. A Joseph Wharton Fellowship recipient, he is actively involved in campus and community leadership, mentoring, and nonprofit initiatives. He previously held marketing and business development roles with Medtronic, Model N, and Trilogy and ran an independent marketing strategy and organizational change consultancy serving corporate and nonprofit organizations in the United States and abroad. While a master's student at Harvard Graduate School of Education, he cofounded two mentoring organizations, including Harvard's Student-Alumni Mentoring Initiative (SAMI). He serves in various nonprofit volunteer leadership capacities, including vice chair of Livnot U'Lehibanot's Alumni Board and director and committee chair of the Harvard Alumni Association (HAA) Board.

David Thomas is H. Naylor Fitzhugh Professor of Business Administration, Senior Associate Dean, Director of Faculty Recruiting and Unit Head of Organizational Behavior at Harvard Graduate School of Business Administration. He is a recognized thought leader in the area of strategic human resource management. His research addresses issues related to executive development, cultural diversity in organizations, leadership, and organizational change. Thomas is coauthor of the best-selling *Harvard Business Review* article "Making Differences Matter: A New Paradigm for Managing Diversity." His book *Breaking Through: The Making of Minority Executives in Corporate America* (with John Gabarro) has met with critical acclaim in reviews by academics and journalists and is the recipient of the Academy of Management's George R. Terry Book Award for outstanding contribution to the advancement of management knowledge and practice. Thomas is the 2006 recipient of the Academy of Management's Mentoring Legacy Award.

Daniel B. Turban is the holder of the Stephen Furbacher Professorship and currently serves as the Chair of the Department of Management in the College of Business at the University of Missouri-Columbia. His research interests include mentoring relationships, organizational recruitment, job search processes, and personality and motivation. He has published over 35 articles in various journals, including *Academy of Management Journal, Journal of Applied Psychology, Journal of Vocational Behavior,* and *Journal of Applied Social Psychology.* He is serving or has served on the editorial boards of *Academy of Management Journal, Journal of Applied Psychology,* and *Personnel Psychology.*

Kimberly Vappie, Esq., is the Chief Operating Officer of MENTTIUM Corporation and provides the strategic direction for the organization. She has extensive expertise helping *Fortune* 500 companies initiate and implement innovative mentoring solutions. Kim received the *Twin Cities Business Journal's* prestigious Women Changemakers award in 2004. Currently, she is an advisory board member of the Human Capital Institute. She co-chairs the Program Committee for Minnesota Women Lawyers and also serves as a committee member for the Minnesota Multicultural Forum. While receiving her law degree, she served as a labor and employment law fellow and served on the executive council of the American Bar Association Labor and Employment Law Section. Prior to MENTTIUM, Kim worked in human resources and employee relations for Target Corporation and Prudential.

Connie R. Wanberg is a Professor of Human Resources and Industrial Relations and the Director of the Industrial Relations Center at the Carlson School of Management at the University of Minnesota. Wanberg has been recognized as a leading scholar in management research in the areas of unemployment, job search behavior, employee socialization, and employee development. She is on the editorial review boards for *Personnel Psychology, Journal of Applied Psychology,* and *Human Performance.* Her research has been funded by a variety of agencies, including National Institute of Mental Health, Department of Labor, and the Society for Human Resource Management Foundation.